Financial Information Analysis

Financial Information Analysis

Philip O'Regan
University of Limerick

John Wiley & Sons, Ltd

Copyright © 2006   John Wiley & Sons Ltd, The Atrium, Southern Gate, Chichester,
                       West Sussex PO19 8SQ, England

                       Telephone (+44) 1243 779777

Email (for orders and customer service enquiries): cs-books@wiley.co.uk
Visit our Home Page on www.wiley.com

This publication is designed to provide accurate and authoritative information in regard to the subject
matter covered. It is sold on the understanding that the Publisher is not engaged in rendering
professional services. If professional advice or other expert assistance is required, the services of a
competent professional should be sought.

Other Wiley Editorial Offices

John Wiley & Sons Inc., 111 River Street, Hoboken, NJ 07030, USA

Jossey-Bass, 989 Market Street, San Francisco, CA 94103-1741, USA

Wiley-VCH Verlag GmbH, Boschstr. 12, D-69469 Weinheim, Germany

John Wiley & Sons Australia Ltd, 42 McDougall Street, Milton, Queensland 4064, Australia

John Wiley & Sons (Asia) Pte Ltd, 2 Clementi Loop #02-01, Jin Xing Distripark, Singapore 129809

John Wiley & Sons Canada Ltd, 6045 Freemont Blvd, Mississauga, ONT, L5R 4J3, Canada

Wiley also publishes its books in a variety of electronic formats. Some content that appears
in print may not be available in electronic books.

Library of Congress Cataloging-in-Publication Data

O'Regan, Philip.
  Financial information analysis / Philip O'Regan. – 2nd ed.
      p. cm.
  Includes bibliographical references and index.
  ISBN-13: 978-0-470-86572-9 (pbk. : alk. paper)
  ISBN-10: 0-470-86572-5 (pbk. : alk. paper)
1. Financial statements. 2. Accounting. I. Title.
  HF5681.B2O74 2006
  657'.3 – dc22

                                        2006006409

British Library Cataloguing in Publication Data

A catalogue record for this book is available from the British Library

ISBN-13: 978-0-470-86572-9
ISBN-10: 0-470-86572-5

Typeset in 10/12 Palatino by Laserwords Private Limited, Chennai, India
Printed and bound in Great Britain by Bell & Bain, Glasgow
This book is printed on acid-free paper responsibly manufactured from sustainable forestry
in which at least two trees are planted for each one used for paper production.

This book is dedicated to Therese Hallinan, whose encouragement and support were vital.

BRIEF CONTENTS

C ONTENTS

PREFACE

At first glance, it seems obvious that this bird is destined for the dinner table. Two apparently cruel and merciless humans are about to ensure their hunt ends successfully. If, however, you are given more information, for instance, that this photograph was taken during one of the coldest winters in Europe in recent years, then the event takes on an entirely different perspective. Far from intending to devour the bird, those in the boat are actually trying to free it from the surrounding ice!

Financial information is a little like a photograph – it is essentially information presented from a particular, and often self-interested, perspective. Only when additional contextual information is obtained can the true significance of the information be properly appreciated.

The manner in which this text is structured reflects this insight. At all points readers are reminded of the need to gather additional information in order to properly appreciate the significance of the financial information being interpreted. Just as the information about the cold winter is important in allowing a proper interpretation of what is happening in the photograph above, additional insights about companies, markets and information dynamics in general, will often be critical.

Accounting Information and Accountants

Accounting information plays a crucial role in modern commerce and society. As a consequence, so do accountants. However, as the following extract outlines, in the wake of a number of large frauds and financial scandals in recent years, accountants find their role being challenged:

Accountants More Despised Than Osama Bin Laden, by Rory Godson

It is surely only a matter of time before the great and good of British business are dragged before a Commons committee and asked the question everybody fears most: "Are you now, or have you ever been, a member of the accountancy profession?"

The poor old bean counters, long the butt of cruel office jokes, are now considered more dangerous than the world's most wanted man. How else should we interpret the fact that the stock-market collapse triggered by accounting irregularities exceeds the lows recorded in the aftermath of Osama Bin Laden's attack on the heartland of American capitalism.

American legislators have wasted no time in drafting and voting through a vast series of measures designed to prevent corporate malfeasance, steamrollering objections from accountants who have discovered that their credit on Capitol Hill, despite years of political donations, isn't even sufficient to buy a decent cup of coffee. Public companies and their auditors are on trial and, as one American trade union boss put it: "We want them to spill their creative accounting juices."

The accountancy debate on this side of the Atlantic is less frenzied but Patricia Hewitt, the trade and industry secretary, seems as determined as her US counterparts to rewrite the rule book. Reforms unveiled last week have been characterised by some as a knee-jerk reaction but we are behind the minister on this one... The capitalist system cannot operate fairly and efficiently in the absence of trustworthy accounts...

Source: *Sunday Times*, July 28, 2002.

The events surrounding the collapse of Enron, WorldCom, Parmalat and others have proven quite traumatic for accountants. They have also been the catalyst for significant changes in the way in which accounting information is viewed by users (such as shareholders and analysts) and regulated by governments and other interested parties. The extent and rapidity of these changes are testament to the enduring importance of accounting information in modern society; as the extract above points out, the capitalist system depends on a reliable and dependable flow of accounting information.

This is especially so in those environments where accounting is recognized as a primary means of communication and control. In a world in which more and more people can expect to have to deal with complex financial information, and an increasingly sizeable proportion of the population acquires shares, this importance can only increase.

This text reflects these developments by seeking to address the nature and role of accounting information in modern society. In particular, it focuses on one of the principal accounting documents, the Annual Report, which in the Anglo-American world is normally produced annually by every company. A primary aim is to equip readers with the skills needed to appreciate the information content of this and other accounting documents.

The most significant feature of this text is that it attempts to place the discussion and analysis of the information contained in the Annual Report in as broad a set of contexts as possible. At its most basic this means recognizing that the Annual Report itself only partly comprises what is traditionally understood to be accounting information, i.e. financial data in a recognizable financial statement. In fact, reflecting the limited capacity of accounting numbers to communicate the essence of any corporate entity, and responding to the information requirements of an increasingly large range of users, the Annual Report has become a substantial document containing a wealth of non-accounting information. For example, Directors' Reports, Chairman's Statements, commentaries on the environmental impact of corporate activity, as well as information presented in the form of graphs and tables now supplement the basic accounting statements.

At another level, this broader contextualization means that issues such as the role of governance cultures, the demand for and supply of accounting information, and the regulatory, legislative and conceptual frameworks within which accounting information emerges are also investigated.

In seeking to broaden our understanding of the information content of the Annual Report, the text makes liberal use of extracts, quotations and articles from a variety of sources. This is done not only to supplement the narrative with original and incisive comment, but also to introduce readers to insights that often contradict the author's own viewpoint. The result is that the reader is challenged to confront issues and assimilate varying perspectives, rather than simply adopt one writer's prejudices.

What is "Financial Information Analysis"?

Financial information is presented in various forms. Financial statements, such as the balance sheet, income statement and cashflow statement that are found in an Annual Report, are probably the most common means by which financial information is made available.

These are complex documents, constructed according to detailed rules and regulations that reflect the accumulated wisdom of generations of accounting practice. In other words, they can often be extremely difficult to understand. It becomes necessary, therefore, to learn how to "read" them.

As employed in this text, the term "Financial Information Analysis" describes the processes and techniques used to identify and extract the critical information contained within financial statements and any supporting documentation. Thus, insights and skills developed by users of accounting information over many decades form a critical part of this text and are covered in considerable detail.

Significantly, however, the application of these techniques and processes is not presented as an end in itself. On the contrary, financial information analysis is presented as a more holistic exercise that contributes to an informed and balanced decision-making process. This process includes the application of various analytical techniques and skills. Critically, however, these are considered with reference to the broader strategic, commercial and social contexts that impact every commercial entity. Thus, the needs of a variety of users are considered, while the notion that any one interest group should dictate the financial reporting agenda is challenged.

Fundamental Analysis

The perspective, techniques and skills adopted in this text can be broadly grouped under the heading "Fundamental Analysis". This is an approach that seeks to analyze and interpret a company by investigating its fundamental financial, strategic and human elements.

This distinguishes it from "Technical Analysis", an approach that focuses more on stock market measures and seeks to find indications of future share performance in historical patterns.

The text is divided into six sections as follows:

Context

The text begins with an identification and discussion of the various contexts within which corporate financial communication should be considered. The intention is to challenge readers to consider the various forces and influences that have conjoined to produce financial information in the forms in which it currently emerges.

Separate chapters are devoted to the following topics:

- Regulatory and legislative contexts
- Conceptual context
- Theoretical context
- Governance context

In discussing these, particular attention is paid to international issues and developments.

Content

The Annual Report is a substantial document containing a huge volume of information in various formats, only some of which are recognizably financial in nature. The second section of the text is devoted, therefore, to a detailed analysis of the reporting and disclosure requirements underpinning what should be included in an Annual Report.

These requirements are considered under two headings, reflecting the most obvious subdivision in the nature of the information contained in an Annual Report:

- Narrative Reports
- Financial Statements

Analysis

Since one of the primary functions of the text is to equip readers with the ability to identify and extract the key information from an Annual Report, a separate section is devoted to explaining one of the more popular and useful means by which this is traditionally achieved – Fundamental Analysis. Under headings that reflect the principal areas of concern for most large corporate entities, readers are introduced to the main techniques of Fundamental Analysis and encouraged to use these in analyzing financial information. They are also made aware of the limitations of this approach and, most importantly, of the fact that techniques such as these are merely a means to an end.

Reflecting the principal areas of corporate activity, this section includes chapters dealing with the following:

- Fundamental Analysis
- Activity and Liquidity
- Financing
- Profitability and Return on Investment

Issues

This section deals with some of the more complex elements of financial accounting practice as these will need to be understood in order to analyze the financial statements of larger entities. These issues are considered in an international context and accounting practice in the UK is compared with that in the US and several continental European countries.

In addition, readers are alerted to some of the more common creative accounting techniques, as well as developments such as those occurring in the area of Corporate Social Responsibility.

Chapters addressing the following issues are included in this section:

- Business Combinations
- Pensions, Share Options, Leases Taxation, and Foreign Currency
- Creative Accounting
- Corporate Social Responsibility
- International Accounting and Harmonization

Interpretation

In this section readers are encouraged to bring together the various skills and contextual understandings gained so far. The purpose is not only to allow readers to see how these techniques can be applied, but also to highlight the fact that the process of interpreting such information involves more than merely the application of these skills.

There is one chapter in this section and it demonstrates the approach outlined thus far by presenting an analysis and interpretation of the Tesco plc 2005 Annual Report. This is included as an appendix to the text.

Challenges and Opportunities

The changing economic, social and political contexts induced by globalization and technological revolution have created a new set of challenges and opportunities for accountants and for those using accounting information. This final section seeks to identify some of these and to contour the outlines of the financial reporting culture that is beginning to emerge in response to these new dynamics.

This section includes chapters on:

- Alternative Approaches
- Future Reporting

Unique features

This text employs several unique features in an attempt to communicate to readers the relevance and immediacy of the topic:

- The role of accounting information as an aid to the decision-making process is emphasized
- Readers are not immediately confronted with masses of technical information. Thus, Section I introduces readers to fundamental theoretical and conceptual issues that need to be considered when approaching accounting information

- Extracts from newspapers, journals and websites are employed liberally in order to elaborate on points made within the text, and also, on occasion, to illustrate alternative viewpoints
- Each chapter starts with learning objectives that set out clearly what is covered
- "In practice" inserts are used to demonstrate how various regulatory, legislative and other provisions translate into practice
- Throughout, readers are referred to an Annual Report included in an appendix at the end of the text
- "Review Questions" at the end of each chapter enable readers to review the principal elements of the chapter
- End-of-chapter "Case Studies", often incorporating detailed extracts from other sources, are intended to stimulate discussion as well as allow readers to investigate particular events and companies in more detail
- Readers are referred to websites for supplementary reading and information
- While UK accounting is placed firmly in the Anglo-American context to which it belongs, international comparisons constantly alert readers to the fact that alternative practices and perspectives exist
- Interpretation is identified as an intuitive process that is assisted by techniques, contextual grounding and experience where the whole is often greater than the sum of the individual parts
- The interests of stakeholders other than shareholders are considered
- The role of corporate governance in shaping and informing accounting practice is highlighted
- The possible orientation of future corporate reporting is outlined
- Non-financial measures of corporate performance and position, such as the Balanced Scorecard, are considered
- Supplementary materials such as additional computational questions, answers to various questions included in the text, and illustrative examples are available on the associated website for this text
- The text is based on International Financial Reporting Standards (IFRS) produced by the International Accounting Standards Board. Some IFRS continue to use the title International Accounting Standard (IAS).

> The Tesco plc 2005 Annual Report, together with the IFRS Restatement, are included as appendices. Readers are referred to these throughout. Access to the company's website, where additional supplementary information can be found, is encouraged.
>
> The website for this text also includes a Report containing an analysis and interpretation of the Tesco 2006 Annual Report similar to that produced in Chapter 16 for 2005.

INTRODUCTION

The Plague, by David Smith and John Waples

Rod Aldridge, chairman of Capita, was locked in a meeting with his City advisers last Wednesday to prepare the half-year statement due later this month. Aldridge was unusually upbeat. Two days earlier he had dined with a number of investors and there had been unbridled support for the FTSE 100 outsourcing group. But just as the meeting began, shares in Capita dropped like a stone. They collapsed 13% and Aldridge was stunned. The market had been spooked by fears that the company was losing a big government contract as well as by concerns about its accounting. Capita managed to calm the market but the damage had been done and the shares closed 4% down on the day. "It was unreal," says Aldridge. "There is a complete over-reaction to everything at the moment. Our accounts are as conservative as you can get."

Aldridge was not alone in having to fire-fight the rumours that swept the market that day and dragged the FTSE 100 down to its lowest level since before Tony Blair was elected. Both Invensys – whose share price dropped 17% on Thursday before recovering on Friday – and Vodafone – which hit a four-year low of 79p – were forced to issue stock exchange statements saying there was nothing wrong with their accounts. Reed Elsevier, the publisher, also had to move swiftly to calm nerves when its share price dropped 5% following a court summons by activists questioning its 2001 accounts. The share price closed marginally up on the day but only after reassuring words from Crispin Davis, the chief executive.

For a while last week it looked like the market was staring into the abyss. Still spooked by the revelation last month of WorldCom's $3.8 billion (£2.5 billion) accounting fraud, investors now appeared to be in full flight. Jean-Marie Messier's departure as chairman and chief executive of Vivendi Universal had underlined the fact that the corporate excesses of the 1990s were not confined to America. Vivendi shares plunged 40% at one stage last week, triggering six trading halts on the Paris bourse.

The new fear was contagion – worries over the reliability of company accounts spreading like wildfire around the globe, but having their roots in the mood of deep underlying pessimism on Wall Street. A plague of uncertainty appeared to be spreading. "The big swinging dicks have never been gloomier," said one financial-market regulator. "Their fear is that we are going to have at least six more months of this, with new accounting scandals appearing with monotonous regularity." . . . While tens of thousands of small investors grimaced as the market slid last week, Britain's financial institutions worriedly checked their books. When even the most solid of companies are seen as vulnerable, the virulence of this particular plague is put into sharp focus.

Source: *Sunday Times*, July 7, 2002.

Introduction

This opening vignette highlights a number of the themes that will be central to this text:

- Accounting information is a very potent information source – it has the capacity to cause share prices of companies to rise and fall based on how the market interprets it.

- One of the most important user groups is investors (shareholders) and tens of thousands of these individuals and institutions eagerly await and respond to accounting information as well as to rumours and misinformation.

- Notice, too, the references to "concerns about accounting" and "worries over the reliability of company accounts". Traditionally, accounting data has been thought of as "correct" and "accurate" with little scope for imagination on the part of the preparers. It was, after all, a numerate discipline – so it had to be correct! More recently, however, it has become obvious to the many users of accounting information that accounting rules allow considerable scope for subjective judgements to be employed by accountants and management. Indeed, it is now accepted that accounting practice owes more to a political process in which various interest groups lobby for their preferred treatment, than it does to the discovery and implementation of any scientifically objective set of accounting rules. This in turn has focused attention on the regulation of accounting and the need for a more mature understanding of the various factors that contribute to the formulation of accounting information and regulation. An appreciation of these factors will also be a central theme of this book.

- For all of its faults, accounting information remains one of the most insightful and potent measures of corporate performance. While this text will highlight the need to supplement it with insights from other sources and acknowledge that it is open to manipulation, it will also demonstrate that interested parties ignore it at their peril.

Impact of Accounting Information

Accounting information is, therefore, a vital component of the information flows that underpin much of modern commerce and society. It can influence, for example, the manner in which wealth is measured and, as a result, how it is distributed amongst various competing interest groups. This applies not only to domestic instances such as wage negotiations, but also to macro-economic concerns such as wealth allocation between developed and developing worlds.

In practice:

A philosophical investigation into Enron, by Donald MacKenzie

Accountancy, it is often thought, is boring. The limited attention given to it by social scientists seems to suggest that we share that prejudice. However, the numbers that accountancy generates are consequential. Profit is the signal that a free-market economy uses to allocate resources to some activities and not to others...

Enquire into almost any of the numbers that abound in the world of finance, and one discovers that it is the endpoint of an often complex chain of construction. Those chains often lead deep into people's lives: into what happens to their savings and their pensions, into whether or not they have jobs or homes...

Source: The Guardian, May 26, 2003.

The following are a few examples of how accounting information and choices can impact companies, investors, employees and society in general:

1. Modern commercial society depends on the efficient allocation of capital and good financial reporting assists this, as explained by Cynthia Glassman, one of the most senior accounting regulators in the US:

In practice:

Why do we care about Financial Reporting?

Put simply, we care because capital is the engine of our economy, and information is the oil that keeps the engine running smoothly. It is on this premise that the entire disclosure framework of our securities laws rests. The assumption – and I think it is a good one – is that providing information on which sound investment decisions can be made is the best way to allocate the scarce resource known as investment capital. In an efficient market, capital will seek its highest use. It is, therefore, not an overstatement to say that without good information our markets could not function effectively.

Source: http://www.sec.gov/news/speech/spch090303cag.htm

---

2. Not unrelated to this capital allocation issue is the fact that the quality of accounting information directly affects the cost of capital, i.e. the cost to an enterprise of funding its activities:

In practice:

Advance to accounting's holy grail, by Henry Tricks

For all companies, the Holy Grail is that clearer accounts contribute to a lower cost of capital. This would not only show that they are increasingly attractive to investors but also enhance their own investment opportunities... "Rationalists often like to make the case that accounting doesn't matter," he [Chris Higson, associate professor of accounting at the London Business School] says. "But this transition will remind us that it does. It's going to be nice to be reminded just how obsessed companies are about their earnings numbers."

Source: Financial Times, January 5, 2005.

Or, as Glassman has expressed it, "Bad choices by reporting companies result in more opaque disclosures, thereby increasing the cost of capital".

3. Accounting rules change over time. As this happens it is possible to identify specific effects. In fact, at the moment accounting is undergoing the most profound transformation in a generation as the accounting rules for large public companies move away from national standards to International Financial Reporting Standards (IFRS). This will have a significant and observable impact on a variety of accounting measures. For instance, it may now become less attractive for many firms to use stock options as a means of remunerating employees and executives:

In practice:

Accounting rules hit share option schemes, by Barney Jopson

International financial reporting standards [IFRS] have triggered a sharp drop in the popularity of share option schemes, realising the fears of critics who said the rules would kill off a vital recruitment tool. Under IFRS companies are required to deduct the cost of issuing options from earnings for the first time. This has led to sudden reductions in reported profit at some companies. As a result, stock options are falling out of favour in the remuneration of FTSE 100 chief executives. The proportion of incentive awards made up by options has dropped to 21 per cent this year from 36 per cent, according to PwC.

Source: Financial Times, August 11, 2005.

---

4. Accounting information is the primary source of information for many service providers. Rating agencies, for instance, are heavy users of the financial

information published by public companies. It is, according to Standard and Poor's – one of the leading credit analysts in the world – "the lifeblood of their business". These ratings will, in turn, directly impact the debt funding capacity and profile of many companies.

5. Analysts and fund managers are key consumers of accounting information. Working for investment firms, banks or brokers, they effectively mediate between companies and other users such as shareholders, investors or the market. One of their most important sources of intelligence is financial accounting information and their confidence in it is a critical component of a healthy financial market.

In practice:

Increased faith in audited accounts

Investor confidence in UK audited financial information remains high, while faith in US audited accounts is recovering in the aftermath of major corporate scandals such as Enron, research by the Institute of Chartered Accountants in England & Wales has found. The survey claims that 87 per cent of UK investment fund managers express a 'great deal' or a 'fair amount' of confidence in UK audited financial information. The majority (56 per cent) of their US counterparts share this view of UK audited accounts. US fund managers are particularly bullish about the quality of their domestically audited information, with 92 per cent expressing a 'great deal' or a 'fair amount' of confidence in US audited accounts compared to 75 per cent of UK fund managers.

Gerald Russell, vice chairman of the ICAEW's Audit and Assurance Faculty, said: 'It is good news for the markets to be ending the year with evidence of high and growing levels of investor confidence in UK audited accounts'... 'Confidence in US audited accounts has clearly bounced back from the damage inflicted by Enron and other high-profile corporate collapses.'

...Audited annual accounts are regarded by UK fund managers as one of the primary sources of financial information, along with specialised media information such as industry magazines and financial wires – which themselves rely on and may incorporate extracts from audited financial statements...

Source: Birmingham Post, December 24, 2004.

---

6. The impact that accounting information has is apparent from the manner in which it can materially and immediately impact the share price of a company. As the following extract highlights, accounting disclosures, such as profit forecasts and announcements, must be carefully managed and the potential for significant downside is considerable.

In practice:

Chief executives can't win at the numbers game

Announcing earnings forecasts is a perilous activity. Joan Warner examines the tactics used by company heads to appease the various interested parties in today's regulation-laden world.

"Damned if we do, and damned if we don't" fairly sums up the way chief executives and their financial officers feel these days when it comes to giving future earnings guidance. On the one hand, investors and analysts pressure executives for a regular profit estimate – and unless the company meets or beats that number, millions of dollars' worth of market capitalisation can vaporise in minutes. On the other hand, intense scrutiny of corporate auditing and accounting procedures has called into question some time-honoured methods of bolstering current earnings statements. As a result, chief executives are hunkering down with their boards and advisers to figure out the new rules to the earnings guidance game.

The issue of how best to share critical information with the public is such a hot potato that few corporate officers, auditors and investor relations professionals are prepared to go on the record with their views. "People are lying low on this issue because they're not sure what to do," says Louis Thompson, president of the US National Investor Relations Institute, who has attended long, tense conclaves with his association's beleaguered members. The fear and confusion surrounding earnings predictions speaks volumes about a corporate climate that is full of uncertainty.

Source: Financial Times, June 13, 2005.

7. Accounting calculations can significantly influence macro-level economic measurements and calculations. These, in turn, can have major and long-lasting consequences for wealth determination and, ultimately, wealth distribution, for instance, as between financial and human capital.

In practice:

Woody Allen once quipped "If my films don't show a profit, I know I'm doing something right." For most other people, in most other circumstances, profit is a mark of success, and in most countries corporate profits are currently booming. Last year, America's after-tax profits rose to their highest as a proportion of GDP for 75 years; the shares of profit in the euro area and Japan are also close to their highest for at least 25 years. UBS, a Swiss bank, estimates that in the G7 economies as a whole, the share of profits in national income has never been higher. The flip side is that labour's share of the cake has never been lower. So are current profit margins (and hence equity values) sustainable? Are they fair?

Corporate profits may be inflated in various ways. If firms made full provision for the future cost of pensions, their earnings would be smaller. And especially in America, the share of profits in national income has been bolstered by the surging profits of the financial sector which have benefited hugely from falling interest rates. Even so, the impressive efforts of American firms to boost productivity and cut costs are genuine. Firms elsewhere, notably in Japan and Germany, are also restructuring aggressively. The share of profit in GDP always rises sharply after a downturn, but in the United States a bigger slice of the increase in national income this time has gone to profits than in any previous post-war recovery. Over the past three years American corporate profits have risen by 60%, wage income by only 10%.

If the share of wages in GDP continues to slide, there could be a backlash from workers who feel short-changed. Yet the chances of this are lower than before. The old divide between "them" and "us" is becoming blurred: many workers also own shares directly or through pension funds, which sooner or later will give them a slice of profits. In any case, there are good reasons to believe that profits growth will soon slow sharply and that workers will make up some of their lost ground.

Source: *Economist, February 11, 2005.*

These examples testify to the importance of accounting information in a variety of contexts. This importance has been achieved over many centuries as accounting and accountants have gradually assumed a critical importance in the commercial world and the information flows that underpin it.

History and Development

Accounting has been described as the language of business. While this may sound a rather extravagant claim, it does express something of the importance of accounting in today's world. For example, without accounting data much that is taken for granted in our society, from simple calculations of profit to the operations of international stock markets, would be impossible.

The manner in which accounting is practised today is a consequence of mankind's attempts to control the environment. Indeed, since earliest times people have felt the need to record events, and the emergence of some form of written record coincided with the development of basic recording skills. About 5,000 years ago writing and numbers were developed and with the large increase in trade and the growth of centres of habitation in the Middle East came the need to record financial events. As the following extract illustrates, excavations in modern day Iran, Iraq and Egypt have uncovered evidence of the use of clay tablets as one means by which crude records were maintained around this time.

Earliest Known Writing Uncovered in Egypt

Suhag Province, Egypt – Clay tablets just unearthed from the tomb of Egyptian King Scorpion I represent what is claimed to be the oldest discovered evidence of writing. German archaeologists say carbon dating places the age of the tablets at 3,300–3,200 BC. More than two-thirds of the translated hieroglyphic writings, on small pieces of clay tablets and the sides of jars, are tax accounting records.

Source: *http://www.acaus.org/history/hsanc.html.*

By the first century BC the need to account for wealth had developed to such an extent that the term "auditor" (a term still used today) had been adopted by the Romans to describe an individual who carried out such a task.

Accounting, therefore, emerged very early in the human record. This suggests that accounting for events is a basic social need. When people begin to organize they discover that accounting information is necessary for social control. It also shows that accounting develops in response to human needs, that is, accountants adapt their systems to accommodate social developments. Today this principle still applies, with accounting constantly being adapted and modified in response to the changing needs of business and society. Accounting is not an immutable science that possesses some absolute truths just waiting to be discovered by diligent researchers. It is a social discipline that responds to the needs of the society in which it functions. This is an important insight and informs the text throughout.

Another important thing to note is that one of the consequences of recording financial events is that those who do so begin to play a key role in the allocation of wealth. For example, it is accountants who define and calculate profit, one of the parameters for the division of wealth in modern society. It is this that gives accounting as a discipline and accountants as a profession such importance and ensures that those involved in business and management must understand how the accounting system operates.

Early Modern Developments

The origins of modern accounting and bookkeeping can be traced to the late middle ages when increased trade led to the need to account for profit and wealth. Gradually the method of accounting began to be standardized. In Venice in 1494, a monk and friend of Leonardo da Vinci, Fra. Luca Pacioli, produced a text, *"Summa de Arithmetica, Geometrica, Proportioni et Proportionalita"*, ("Everything About Arithmetic, Geometry, and Proportions"), which contained a treatise on bookkeeping entitled *"Particularis de Computis et Scripturis"* ("Details of Accounting and Recording"). This was an outline of the mechanics of the double-entry bookkeeping system that had been used for several decades in and around Venice. Over five centuries later this system remains the basis of modern bookkeeping.

The Industrial Revolution

The Industrial Revolution, particularly as experienced in Britain, changed the scale of business enterprise. Up to this point most businesses had been small family concerns. However, in response to investors' needs new business entities called joint-stock (or 'limited') companies emerged. These enabled a large number of individuals (called shareholders) to invest in a way that allowed them to limit potential personal losses. However, because it was impossible for all shareholders to be involved in the management of these limited companies, they usually appointed directors to manage the company on their behalf.

This meant that shareholders often knew very little about what was happening in their own companies. As a consequence the financial statements summarizing the company's performance became very important since only by understanding them could shareholders discover how their own money was being used.

The Twentieth Century

The demand for accounting information increased dramatically throughout the 20th century, driven not just by the requirements of international trade and global capital markets, but also, ironically, by the information demands of two world wars. And as the need for financial information increased so did the influence of accounting and the accounting profession. The accounting function is now seen as a critical element of any developed, liberal, capitalist society, providing much of the information on which the financial and corporate worlds depend.

The advent of computers, the internet and the "Information Age" have merely accentuated the importance of accounting information since financial data is now so prevalent and easily accessible that it has become one of the most powerful means of communication in the modern world. The new millennium, therefore, brings both challenges and opportunities.

Forms of Accounting Information

Those not familiar with accounting information will usually have the view that it is not only based on numbers, but also, because of that fact, somehow "accurate". In fact, while it is true that numbers are the primary form of expression of accounting information, this bestows neither intrinsic accuracy nor "correctness".

In practice:

The push for greater transparency and reduced risk is increasing corporate dependence on performance measurement and management tools. But how meaningful is the information they provide? As Lesley Meall finds, the devil is in the detail

During a month-long doctors' strike in Israel in 1973 the death rate dropped 40%; 3.7 m Americans claim to have been abducted by aliens; 80% of the cars found on Albanian roads were stolen elsewhere in Europe; in India 30% of the population have not heard of the USA; in 1997, 39 people visited the accident and emergency departments of UK hospitals because of incidents involving tea-cosies; 65% of CFOs say their main focus is measuring and monitoring business performance; 43.3% of statistics are meaningless.

We are obsessed with counting and measuring anything and everything we consider of potential value. Businesses, investors, and politicians all argue their corner, and plan for their futures, armed with as many supportive statistics as they can muster. When this means counting the number of DVDs Amazon has sold in Australia, or calculating the annual revenue of Nissan Europe, it is all very well. But when you start trying to measure the popularity of George W Bush, the performance of the Blacklow Brow Primary School, or customer satisfaction at Starbucks, then just how meaningful can the results possibly be?

James Anyon, a UK accountant was one of the founding fathers of US accounting, stead-fastly warned the profession against such antics. 'Use figures as little as you can,' he told accountants at the turn of the (20th) century. 'Your client doesn't want them or like them, he wants brains.' A hundred years on Anyon is probably turning in his grave. 'Think and act upon facts, truths and principles,' he advised, 'and regard figures only as things to express these.'

Source: accounting&business, July, 2004.

Because of the inherent limitations of numbers, accounting information is being supplemented by and, indeed, expressed in the form of, narrative communications. These can range from supplementary commentary on specific accounting numbers to more complex and comprehensive presentations and discussions of accounting data.

Accounting information can also be presented in a variety of formats, usually depending on the particular users in mind. For example, managers will often be presented with large amounts of financial detail in the form of budgets that enable them to plan and evaluate performance. Other forms of presentation include internal reports, asset schedules and forecasts. Information such as this is usually termed "internal" accounting information because it is intended primarily for use by management to assist in the efficient running of an organization.

The other principal category of financial information can be termed "external". This is because it is intended primarily to satisfy the statutory and public account-ability responsibilities of a reporting entity whereby it releases information for more widespread consumption. The prime example of this type is the Annual Report. This is a statutorily required document which each UK company listed on the London Stock Exchange must issue, normally every year. And it is also the primary focus of this text – the skills and insights provided over the course of the following chapters are intended to enable the analysis and interpretation of this document with a view to gaining an understanding of the company in question.

Typically an Annual Report will include:

- Accounting information:

  - Balance Sheet
  - Income Statement (previously the "Profit and Loss Account")
  - Cashflow Statement
  - Notes to the accounts.

- Narrative reports:

  - Directors' Report
  - Chairman's Statement
  - Auditor's Report
  - Other reports, such as the Operating and Financial Review.

As a principal means by which a company communicates with the various constituencies to which it is accountable, the Annual Report comprises a unique source of information about the company. Not surprisingly, therefore, it is the subject of considerable and detailed analysis and comment:

Reporting for Duty, by Ben McLannahan

If you want to know what Ken Lever thinks about shareholder value, look no further than the annual report at Tomkins, the £3.4 billion (€4.7 billion) UK engineering conglomerate where he's CFO. Since joining Tomkins four years ago, he's been pumping more and more information into the firm's annual reports... "We've tried to be much more transparent about the business, providing information that actually helps an investor, or a potential investor, make the economic decisions whether to invest or not," says Lever of 2002's 89-page annual report... While Lever's convinced that nothing beats an annual report as a conduit for shareholder value, other CFOs beg to differ. Reports – at least, the paper-based ones – are often criticised as unwieldy, backward-looking documents, costing companies millions of euros to produce and post to shareholders. So it's not surprising, that with the rise of quarterly reporting and continuous disclosure, annual reports have slid further and further down the agenda of many CFOs.

But Lever's not on a lonely mission. Despite all the knocks, annual reports remain the primary source of corporate disclosure for the investor community. Along with face-to-face briefings, reports are an essential outlet of information, says Stefan Seip, director general of BVI, the federal investment management association in Germany, which represents around 10,000 domestic and non-domestic funds. As he sees it, the annual report is still "a vital source when it comes to evaluating how transparent a company is, and how it feels about the future of its own business model." With a copy of a report in their hands, he adds, investors "can weigh investment decisions with the benefit of the full picture, rather than racing through quarterly figures." That's certainly something to give CFOs pause for thought as they reflect on ways to help restore investor confidence. As the OECD notes in its corporate governance guidelines: "Investor confidence and market efficiency depend on the disclosure of accurate, timely information about corporate performance. To be of value in the global capital markets, disclosed information should be clear, consistent and comparable."

The annual report is "the core unit of comparison on a global basis," confirms Nick Bradley, managing director and European regional practice leader of governance services at Standard & Poor's. But, he says, for the most part, the information provided in Europe's annual reports isn't as clear, consistent or comparable as it could be – not just at an individual company level but also at sectoral and country-wide levels. Granted, progress has been made, says Bradley, who completed a global transparency and disclosure study in April. Slowly but surely, he says, European reports are starting to include vital information such as the percentage of cross-ownership, the ownership structures of affiliates, audit and non-audit fees, and a full breakdown of director remuneration packages.

Against this backdrop, many companies in Europe are responding to investors' calls for greater transparency by fattening up their reports. According to Guillaume of Enterprise.com, so far, around half of this year's crop are over 100 pages – the average last year was closer to 90...

Are shareholders getting the information they want in their annual reports? Last October, Shelley Taylor & Associates, a London-based financial reporting consultancy, asked a group of 40 US and European institutional investors to rank in order of importance what they need to read about in annual reports. Respondents were unanimous that reports must provide a clear snapshot of a company's strategy. Management experience came in second place at 92%, followed by product information (88%). In a tie for fourth place – at 84% – were market positioning and – interestingly – bad news.

Source: *CFO Europe*, June 1, 2003.

The Annual Report provides, then, a mixture of financial and other information. This can be either in narrative or numeric form. There are, of course, other types of financial information available such as analysts' reports, prospectuses and media comment. And since the object is to consider information which will allow a comprehensive and contextual understanding of companies and their performance, it will be useful to refer to these in order to inform and supplement the information disclosed by the Annual Report.

Two of these other sources deserve particular mention:

- Interim reports: Annual Reports, as the title implies, are normally produced every year. However, a year is a long time for users to have to wait for information. For this reason UK companies listed on the Stock Exchange are required to issue half-yearly interim reports to shareholders either directly or by means of inserts in two national newspapers.

- Preliminary announcements: once draft accounts have been prepared, but before the Annual Report is actually issued, companies will normally make preliminary announcements about financial performance.

Users of Accounting Information

The critical role that accounting plays in the liberal democratic market economies that predominate in today's developed world is reflected in the number and range of users of that information:

- **Shareholders and investors**: because of their large numbers, shareholders are not normally involved in the running of the business. For this reason it is particularly important that they receive prompt and accurate accounting information about their business so that they can assess how it has performed. As the following extract explains, the Annual Report has traditionally been intended to satisfy the information requirements of this group. Ironically, the need to address an ever-increasing range of users as well as the impact of financial scandals may have had a negative effect on the quality of some of the information disclosed:

In practice:

Rise to the Annual Challenge

The world of annual reports is rapidly changing. On the one hand, companies are under increasing pressure to report electronically, and use the internet to spread their financial information throughout the world. On the other hand, changes in reporting methods are afoot as a result of suggestions from accounting bodies and accountancy firms about the relevance of financial information contained within annual reports.

The nature of shareholders has changed. Long gone are the days when the annual report was produced for accountants, by accountants. Thanks partly to the growth in individual shareholders – estimated in the UK at more than 16 million people – it has a far higher profile. Consequently, companies, their accountants and design consultancies are re-examining traditional financial reporting methods, with some arguing that the current format of the annual report will slowly wither and die.

But while new forms of reporting corporate information are inevitable, companies are in danger of taking their eyes off the ball. An analysis of company reports from Europe's top 100 companies by communications consultancy Prowse & Co has found that this year – for the first time in 13 years – companies are actually doing a worse job of communicating their corporate performance to shareholders through the pages of their company reports. 'Lacking innovation, poorly structured and, at times, woefully designed, the majority of this year's reports give the impression of being simultaneously under-resourced and undervalued,' says the survey's author, Matthew Grenier. 'In attempting to placate the fears of their stakeholders, many companies appear to have forgotten the fundamental rules of effective communication.'

> *Where are they going wrong? The report, published last month, found that most companies, in an attempt to respond to the impact of accounting scandals and new legislation, have crammed as much information into their reports as possible, often to the detriment of readability.*
>
> Source: *Accountancy Age, March 4, 2004.*

- **Financial analysts**: accounting information is prepared and presented in accordance with various regulations, concepts and terminology. Like any other language it is often incomprehensible to those who have not learned how to read it. Analysts and fund managers play a key role in mediating between the preparers of accounts and those who need to understand them. They advise existing or potential shareholders such as insurance companies, pension funds, investment trusts and individuals, and are among the most sophisticated users of accounting information.

Twists and Turns in Store for Analysts, by Ken Wild

...New [IFRS] rules, different measurement and transition accommodations do not make for straightforward comparisons. Market reaction is clearly a concern for businesses. Crucially, it is analysts' perceptions, not real economics, that drive share prices. If analysts are confused, capital will be misallocated. In January we saw a drop in share price when a company announced IFRS would see the deferral of income recognition and increase the volatility of profits. Neither of these affected its cash flows, so either the announcement contained new information, or the market got it wrong. It is the latter that UK companies rightly fear...

Source: *Financial Times*, July 21, 2005.

- **Management**: management, who will have access to all accounting data within a business, will be one of the principal users of accounting information. They will use it to assist them in checking past performance and in making decisions about the future activities of the business.

- **Employees**: accounting information is relevant to employees since they will want to know whether or not the company can offer safe employment and promotion. In recent years, with the advent of share option schemes and substantial numbers of shareholding employees, the relevance of accounting information to employees has taken on a new dimension.

- **Lenders**: lenders' primary concern is the security of their loans, so they will analyze the financial statements to determine whether the business will be able to repay amounts due. They will be particularly interested in the availability of cash and the value of any assets given as security against loans.

- **Taxation authorities**: HM Revenue & Customs use accounting information as a basis upon which to determine tax liability.
- **Others**: increasingly members of the general public or pressure groups such as environmental protection organizations are using accounting information to pressure companies into changes in their operating practices.

Summary

If accounting is a language, indeed, a highly technical language, then financial analysis can be seen as a means of interpreting that language and of reducing it to more manageable concepts and expressions. It also acts as a mediating influence in disseminating information about commercial entities to a broader range of users.

In order to interpret it properly it is necessary to understand some of the influences that shape both its form and the role it plays in modern society. This is the focus of Section I.

SECTION I

Contexts

One of the primary emphases of this text is that it is necessary to inform any interpretation of accounting information with as broad and rich a contextualization as possible. To coin a phrase, the three most important factors in enabling an informed understanding of accounting information are "context, context and context".

For this reason Section I is devoted to a discussion of four contexts that must be considered before any analysis and interpretation of accounting information is possible.

Chapter 1 looks at the regulatory and legislative frameworks that underpin accounting practice. The notion of accounting as the product of a "political" process is introduced. This is understood to mean that accounting rules result from a dynamic in which various interest groups, such as professions, governments or others, compete to influence the decisions of regulators. If true, then this means that accounting regulations must be seen as deriving from political choices and preferences, rather than from laboratory-style research that somehow reveals "correct" and immutable schemes of accounting practice. This has major implications for any analysis of the information content of financial statements. This chapter also highlights the fact that public companies listed on EU regulated stock markets must transfer their accounting basis from national standards to International Financial Reporting Standards (IFRS) from 2005. This represents one of the most important accounting developments in recent decades.

Chapter 2 develops the notion of accounting as a critical means of communication, albeit one which is still struggling to develop a set of unified principles and thought which would act as a base from which a more coherent and integrated set of practices might emerge.

Accounting information is, in many senses, simply a commodity. Chapter 3 extends the discussion, therefore, to attempt to answer the question "What is the role of accounting information in modern society?" Focusing specifically on the role of accounting information in the stock market, it looks at various theoretical approaches that seek to answer this question.

Having explored the role of accounting in the market, Chapter 4 changes the focus to the impact of corporate structure on the role and form of accounting information. Tracing the historical and commercial considerations that have resulted in the unique form of corporate governance that predominates in the Anglo-American world, this chapter considers the impact this has had on the nature and accessibility of accounting information.

REGULATORY AND LEGISLATIVE CONTEXTS

[1]

When you have completed this chapter you will understand that:

- Accounting is closely regulated.
- Various entities such as governments, international organizations, capital markets and accountancy bodies have a role in the regulatory process.
- Regulation was previously country-specific, but is now becoming more international in orientation and ambition.
- The significance and role of accounting standard setters such as the International Accounting Standards Board have increased in recent years.
- The impact that the introduction of International Financial Reporting Standards (IFRS) will have will be extensive.
- One way in which the regulatory role of governments is expressed is through legislation and this impacts directly upon accounting information.
- Stock Exchange rules represent another source of regulation.
- There are detailed provisions relating to the formation of a company in the UK.

The Enforcers: Crackdown on Crony Capitalism, by Dominic Rushe and Paul Durman

As an end to a business career, it does not get much worse than this. At 6am in Manhattan last Wednesday, John Rigas, the 78-year-old former king of American cable television, was led in handcuffs from his Upper East Side apartment. His two sons, also cuffed, followed. After a 50-year career building Adelphia into one of America's largest cable-television operators, Rigas is accused of looting the company coffers to fund a lavish lifestyle. . . Treating the company as their personal piggy bank, they borrowed billions. Corporate jets carried their friends to safaris in Africa. Some $12.8m (£8m) in shareholder cash was used to start building a golf course. In 2001, Rigas Sr had racked up $66m in debts and was withdrawing so much money from the company that his son Timothy set him a monthly limit. Father was allowed $1m a month. Shareholders of the bankrupt Adelphia will be lucky to see much compensation.

Bad as it was, the Adelphia scandal was not the only new instalment last week in the saga of the decline and fall of corporate America. In Washington, two of Wall Street's top banks, Citigroup and JP Morgan Chase, were taken to task over their role in the collapse of Enron, the Texan energy company. And in New York, AOL Time Warner, the world's biggest media group, revealed it was the latest to have its books queried by the Securities and Exchange Commission (SEC).

But what struck many observers about the Rigas arrests was not the magnitude of the charges but the dramatic response. "I can't imagine that John Rigas really needed handcuffs," says James Cox, law professor at Duke University and a legal adviser to the New York Stock Exchange. "He doesn't look like he's going to take a swing at anyone. But I think the feeling is, it's time to subject these people to some humiliation." He says public anger needs to be assuaged, leniency is not an option and that the political stakes are getting higher. "Often people in white-collar cases don't even bother turning up in court to hear their sentences. With the Rigases and others, a clear signal is being sent that things have changed." As America moves toward November's mid-term elections, Cox argues that we can expect to see more high-profile stick-wielding. Business heads are going to get cracked.

Britain is also trying to strengthen standards of corporate governance and financial reporting. Patricia Hewitt, the trade and industry secretary, last week ordered the Office of Fair Trading to investigate the Big Four accountancy firms. And this week Sir Howard Davies, chairman of the Financial Services Authority, will set out plans for a crackdown on City analysts who ramp shares in which they have an interest. British investors have suffered the near-collapse of Marconi, Energis, Telewest and other heavily indebted high-flyers but – so far at least – the biggest failures have been due to bad management rather than fraud or false accounting.

The accounting controversies that have come to light have tended to hit smaller, lesser-known firms. The software companies Cedar and AIT Group both came to grief after using projected revenue figures to flatter profits. Half the revenue in Cedar's 2000 accounts had still not been invoiced by year-end. Bioglan, the drugs company, collapsed into administration after *The Sunday Times* exposed its practice of generating instant profits through joint-venture licence deals. The same tactic is at the heart of the dubious finances of Elan, the big Irish pharmaceuticals company fighting insolvency. Numerous other companies have been hit by suspicion and rumour. Capita, the outsourcing group that collects the television licence fee, was forced to make a robust defence of its accounts last week.

Yet all this is small beer compared with the scandals that rocked Enron, World-Com and Adelphia. So how has Britain managed to escape so lightly? In part,

> Britain is benefiting from the safeguards put in place in the wake of the scandals of the 1980s and early 1990s – Guinness, Blue Arrow, Maxwell, Polly Peck and the rest...
>
> Some business leaders are concerned that the backlash could be disproportionate, and that the new checks imposed by regulators could cramp entrepreneurship and make it more costly to do business. Most would agree that regulators have a difficult balance to strike. The concern is that politicians are thinking primarily of the ballot box.
>
> Source: *The Sunday Times*, July 28, 2002.

Introduction

Corporate collapses throughout the developed world have prompted a variety of responses. As this opening vignette indicates, these have involved a range of interventions by politicians, regulators and businesses. In the US, for instance, the collapse of Enron and WorldCom lead directly to the introduction of the Sarbanes-Oxley Act, a political initiative intended to enforce greater regulation on the governance and accounting cultures of business. Those responsible do, however, "have a difficult balance to strike", on the one hand ensuring a more coherent regulatory structure, while at the same time not overly impeding the commercial environment that underpins economic activity.

As a critical element in international business, accounting finds itself at the centre of this ongoing jostling between regulators and politicians; between business and social interests. Furthermore, dynamics such as globalization and technological advances have forged new contexts within which accounting regulation must be assessed. Traditionally considered in far-less ambitious terms, the realization that accounting is a critical means by which businesses communicate allows it to be viewed as one element in an ongoing struggle between proponents of *laissez-faire* ("unregulated") market economics and those more alert to the potential for volatility and inequality in an unregulated economy.

Accounting regulation must, therefore, be viewed first and foremost in such contexts. Only such an approach allows the reasons for, and the agents of, its regulation to be properly assessed.

For much of the twentieth century government intervention and professional regulation were viewed as generally benign and disinterested influences. The result was the development of a complex regulatory process for accounting that embraced the law, governments, the profession and various other interested parties.

The latter decades of the twentieth century, however, witnessed something of a reaction to this view. The Thatcherite Revolution in Britain and the Reaganite years in the US generally espoused a *laissez-faire* culture that sought to reassert the role of the market as the primary means by which information flows should be determined. In the process, champions of this approach sought to disengage the government and its regulatory tentacles from functions more properly considered the domain of the market.

The potential for this to transform the regulatory approach that had been constructed over the earlier decades of the century was substantial. However, while the market-based focus of recent decades has caused some reconsideration of the nature and extent of the regulatory process, it is still the case that the traditional parties such as government and the accounting profession heavily control the preparation and dissemination of accounting information. This reflects the importance and significance of accounting information in modern society.

There is, therefore, widespread contention between proponents and opponents of increased regulation as one means of dealing with many of the governance and accounting issues raised by recent scandals. Some of these issues are addressed in the following article:

Why Red Tape Should not be Dismissed as a Company Killer, by Morgan Witzel

The idea that "regulation strangles business" or "red tape kills companies" is a common complaint among business leaders in Europe and North America. In these regions it is now an article of faith that the free market in and of itself is a good thing and must be zealously protected. It follows that anything that restricts the free market is inherently bad, and this leads to the belief that all regulation, of whatever sort, is bad for business. In this view, regulation is simply a matter of bureaucracy imposing itself on business for no good reason. But sometimes regulations are well intentioned. Even Adam Smith, whose *Wealth of Nations* is regarded as the gospel of free markets, conceded that some regulation may be necessary...

Even the US Sarbanes-Oxley act [see later in this Chapter], which brought in wide-ranging accounting regulations after high-profile scandals at companies including Enron and WorldCom, has its good points. Hank Boerner, a US consultant, writes that companies that successfully comply with Sarbanes-Oxley will become "paragons of accountability, and tough competitors" in the future. He cites the example of Roderick Hills, chairman of the audit committee of Chiquita Brands, who has stated publicly that large companies see competitive advantages in the provisions of the act. "Companies can realise substantial value from the compliance effort if they use it as a management tool," says Mr Hills.

Regulation is a powerful force in business, and anyone trying to ignore it will have about as much success as King Canute in turning back the tide. Those who choose to fight against regulation may well be strangled by it. But by coming to terms with regulation, understanding its purpose and looking for positive aspects, it is possible to turn a threat into an opportunity.

Source: *Financial Times*, August 11, 2005.

In practice:

Regulation Won't Stop Another Enron, Says Survey

The increasing weight of regulation in public companies has not done enough to prevent an Enron-style corporate scandal in the UK, a survey by law firm Eversheds shows.

Although three-quarters of board directors said the increasing tide of regulation had improved the quality of information and transparency in company reports, only 36% of directors and 42% of equity analysts think the current regulatory environment has actually reduced the risk of a scandal along the lines of Enron.

Source: Accountancy, September 2005.

Regulatory Framework

In an accounting context, the regulatory framework describes that system of rules and principles that controls and shapes the nature and content of financial information. Because of its critical importance in modern society, financial information has always attracted the interest of regulators. This has been true particularly since the early years of the last century. At that time the need to streamline and harmonize the flow of accounting information became apparent, particularly in the US, as the potential for accounting information to influence decisions of great importance became apparent.

The first part of this chapter outlines the regulatory apparatus as it has emerged in the Anglo-American world. It begins with an examination of the system that applies in the US, a model that has influenced the regulatory process in much of the developed world. It then deals with the system applying in the UK. Finally, it looks at the emergence and increasing importance of the International Accounting Standards Board (IASB). The second part of the chapter deals with the legislative context.

US

One of the catalysts shaping the regulatory environment of the twentieth century was the crash of the Wall Street stock market in October 1929. In the reaction to the supposedly unregulated market that was identified as a significant factor in this crash, the Roosevelt administration embarked upon a National Recovery Programme, known as the New Deal. This had as one of its core principles, the need for a greater regulation of capital markets. This was in line with the general thrust of US government commitment to control via regulation, as distinct from the interventionist model that led to extensive nationalization in contemporary Europe.

As part of this process the US government set up the Securities and Exchange Commission (SEC) and charged it with the task of regulating both the stock market itself and its constituent parts, one of which was the financial reporting process.

As evidence of its seriousness the government appointed Joseph Kennedy, father of the future president, and soon to be ambassador to Great Britain, as the SEC's first chairman. When critics objected that Kennedy was a notorious speculator and, therefore, not acceptable, Roosevelt replied that these were the very credentials needed for the job.

Prior to the inauguration of the SEC there were little or no standards governing the content of corporate financial reports. The scope that this gave companies to produce financial reports to suit their own purposes was identified as a critical feature of the *laissez-faire* regime that had precipitated the crash. Under the Securities Act (1933) and the Securities Exchange Act (1934) all companies whose securities were traded publicly were required to file reports with the SEC. This had the effect of imposing a certain level of uniform disclosure on companies, intended to provide investors with the information necessary to make informed decisions about their investments.

In practice:

For more on the SEC see http://www.sec.gov/. From this site access the EDGAR facility to view the vast number and range of submissions that US public companies must make.

Directly answerable to Congress and, therefore, operating within the political system, the SEC has developed into one of the most effective and potent regulatory agencies in the US. It is comprised of five commissioners, one of whom acts as chairman, and has a team of lawyers, accountants, analysts and others who monitor the companies under its aegis. In all a staff of approximately 3,000 monitors the 13,000 public companies within its remit. (There are almost 4 million US corporations in all.) A system of heavy penalties ensures, however, that much of the onus for securing compliance is placed directly upon companies themselves and their financial advisors.

Although it has occasionally issued standards, the SEC has been content to delegate to the private sector the task of determining Generally Accepted Accounting Principles (GAAP). In this process the American Institute of Certified Public Accountants (AICPA), as the pre-eminent accounting body in the US, has played an important role. In 1939, having worked closely with the New York Stock Exchange on a number of mutually important issues, the AICPA established the Committee on Accounting Procedure and the Committee on Accounting Terminology. These were crucial in developing a culture that recognized the importance of a uniform set of accounting practices devised by the accounting profession. Between 1939 and 1959 these committees issued fifty-one Accounting Research Bulletins that, to a limited extent, represented a broadly acceptable code of accounting practice.

By the late 1950s, however, the flaws inherent in a system that merely issued pronouncements in response to problems as they arose, as distinct from promulgating a set of principles that might form the basis on which to generate a more coherent GAAP, had become apparent. In 1959, therefore, the AICPA set up the Accounting Principles Board (APB) and the Accounting Research Division. These were charged with fostering an approach that would seek to establish just such a set of coherent, unifying principles, or theoretical framework. With limited success the APB pursued this agenda until 1973, by which time it was felt necessary to establish a new standard-setting regime.

In practice:

In recent years, and particularly since the significant accounting frauds of recent years, the role and activities of the SEC have been the focus of very keen interest. In the post-Enron climate, it was subjected to considerable criticism. However, as the following indicates, under its new chairman, it has responded in a very proactive manner:

Payback Time for the Battered and Bruised Investor?

Four months into his tenure as chairman of the Securities and Exchange Commission, few are questioning that William Donaldson is the right man for the job. The former banker and chairman of the New York Stock Exchange slapped the highest fines ever demanded by the SEC on Wall Street banks following a stock research abuse investigation. Earlier this month, Donaldson came good on his promise to hold top brass to account. The SEC demanded that six of Xerox's former senior-most executives pay $22m in fines and penalties and compensation after it accused them of personally profiting from a scheme that falsely inflated revenues and profits at the copier giant.

It takes a lot to impress the battered and bruised US investor however; after all, what did $400m in penalties and fines for Citigroup mean to Sandy Weill? The rotund chief executive admitted to asking one of his analysts to take a fresh look at the rating on the stock AT&T, a Citibank client, but walked away with his wallet as substantial as his persona. The $400m bill probably wouldn't even put a dent in Citigroup's mammoth capacity for barraging Americans with junk mail. Four of the banks facing fines were even seeking insurance to cover the fines. And at Xerox, it quickly emerged that the company would be covering the bulk of penalties itself because of an indemnification policy which protected officers and executives from such fines.

At least Donaldson has the good PR sense to speak out at the appropriate times and say the right things unlike his predecessor, Harvey Pitt. "In my mind, this just isn't good public policy," he said in that way he has of making people think that, in his mind, only upright and trustworthy thoughts reside. In response to constant bleating from Philip Purcell, Chief Executive of Morgan Stanley, that the bank's role in the stock abuse scandal had been minimal, he sent him a furious letter telling him to zip it. Furthermore, the SEC has started to include clauses in its agreements that prevent defendants from using insurance or indemnification against civil fines. It is now mulling whether to extend that to include disgorgement – the process of handing back the swag to harmed investors. Donaldson has also won extra backing for the overburdened and under-funded institution. Congress has nearly doubled the SEC's budget for the fiscal rule year beginning October to $841.5m.

Congress recently approved a bill that would allow the SEC to hire accountants more rapidly by avoiding certain rules. President Bush is expected to sign the measure. The SEC certainly needs to move on the issue – it is in the midst of some 600 investigations. . . When he took office four months ago, Donaldson's pledge was to restore investor confidence. The flip side of which translates to scaring the living daylights out of the financial world. . .

Source: *Accounting & Business, July/August, 2003.*

Financial Accounting Standards Board (FASB)

The FASB, which took over many of the functions of the APB, is an independent body governed by the Financial Accounting Foundation (FAF) which is itself comprised of representatives of nine organizations, including the AICPA, the Financial Executives Institute, the Security Industry Association, the Financial Analysts Federation, various not-for-profit organizations and others. Apart from appointing the seven-member FASB and the members of the Financial Accounting Standards Advisory Council (FASAC), which advises FASB on its agenda, the FAF is responsible for generating funding for the FASB as well as championing its role and its independence.

The stated purpose of the FASB is "to establish and improve standards of financial accounting and reporting for the guidance and education of the public, including issuers, auditors, and users of financial information". Implicit in this is recognition of the fact that the number and range of users of accounting information has been increasing, and that accounting information needs to address the interests of this broader constituency.

The role of the FASB was reinforced when the SEC explicitly confirmed that "principles, standards and practices promulgated by the FASB will be considered by the Commission as having substantial authoritative support".

FASB differs from its predecessors in a number of ways:

- Its membership is smaller (seven), full-time, more independent and well-compensated

- It is more autonomous from the accounting profession

- There is no stipulation that it should consist only of members of the AICPA

- Passage of a standard requires only a super-majority, i.e., five out of seven in favour

The FASB issues two types of pronouncement: Statements of Financial Accounting Concepts (SFACs) which deal with fundamental accounting concepts and principles and provide a framework within which Statements of Financial Accounting Standards (SFAS) are formulated. While SFACs are critical in providing a coherent theoretical underpinning for accounting practice, only the provisions of SFASs are regarded as constituting GAAP.

One significant feature of the FASB has been its sensitivity to social and economic changes that have highlighted the responsibilities of standard-setting bodies to an increasingly large range of users. This has been reflected not only in the make-up of the Board, but also in the adoption of a more transparent due process through which issues are expected to pass before emerging as a SFAS. The stages in this process can be summarized as follows:

1. A topic is placed on the FASB agenda by FASAC.
2. A task force is set up to identify the relevant issues.
3. The FASB technical section then investigates the topic.
4. A Discussion Memorandum is released seeking responses from the public.
5. Public hearings are conducted.
6. An Exposure Draft (ED) is released.
7. The ED is re-evaluated in the light of responses.
8. The FASB membership vote on the ED and issue a SFAS if a sufficient majority is secured.

One particularly potent element of the new structure was the establishment of an Emerging Issues Task Force (EITF). This group is charged with identifying potentially contentious issues and alerting the FASB, as well as resolving technical issues. It has proved to be a very useful mechanism for dealing proactively with current issues before they have had an opportunity to generate too much confusion and disagreement.

In practice:

That standard-setting is essentially a political process in which different groups lobby for their preferred outcome, rather than a scientific one in which "correct" accounting practices are "discovered" has already been alluded to:

Asked if there was one thing he learned in 2000, FASB chairman Edmund L. Jenkins said: "I have learned that it is important to defend independent standard setting, that you can not take it for granted. You need to keep talking about the benefits of the capital market having sufficient information for investors to assess opportunities." With that lesson tucked in his syllabus, Jenkins expects to have FASB dedicate more time to political tactics in Washington. Unfortunately this will detract from efforts to fulfil the Board's real mission: to produce high-quality, non-partisan accounting standards.

Source: Accounting and Business, March 2001.

Sarbanes-Oxley (SOX)

One of the principal legacies of the accounting frauds that embroiled the US in the early years of the millennium will be the huge raft of regulatory responses.

These were undertaken by accounting bodies, professional institutes, government and others. Perhaps the most high-profile intervention was the Sarbanes-Oxley Act. Enacted by the US Congress as an immediate response to these frauds in 2002, and named after its two principal sponsors, it has significantly impacted the nature and content of accounting disclosures by companies in the US and elsewhere. As the following extract illustrates, its origins and focus also highlight the political nature of much of the regulation surrounding accounting information and disclosures:

Sarbanes-Oxley's Creeping Intrusion, by Leo Strine

The US federal government's role in regulating corporate conduct towards investors has centred on demanding that public corporations give investors certified financial statements and other materially accurate periodic disclosures about their condition. The articulation and enforcement of the substantive duties owed by corporate managers to stockholders has largely been the province of state corporation law. After the first corporate scandals involving, among others, Enron, the stock exchanges and Congress began to consider reforms at their level. The exchanges began considering new listing standards that had the effect of mandating numerous board committees and specific duties that had to be carried out by independent directors. Soon, the sour scent of hypocrisy wafted from some congressional chambers. Federal legislators who had helped to stymie efforts at increasing the integrity of public accounting standards during the late Clinton years began to support rapid action. Many others genuinely desired a stronger federal role in corporate governance and saw an opportunity to turn their sincere beliefs into law.

What resulted came to be known as Sarbanes-Oxley. That strange stew coupled sensible ideas – such as the idea of a strengthened independent body to enforce meaningful accounting standards – with narrow provisions of dubious value – such as an outright ban on the making of loans to managers by public corporations. When combined with the new stock exchange rules, Sarbanes-Oxley had the effect of requiring corporate boards – and particularly independent directors – to spend a huge portion of their time fulfilling regulatory mandates. Many of these were unrelated to the core problems that gave rise to a legitimately perceived need for reform.

Those problems primarily involved financial fraud, and the incentive systems that led gatekeepers such as independent directors, public accountants and corporate lawyers to fail to stop it and, on occasion, even actively to facilitate accounting chicanery. But, instead of a focused initiative addressing the financial integrity of listed companies – which in fairness parts of Sarbanes-Oxley do speak to in useful ways that deserve credit – Congress and the exchanges also generated additional mandates that have the perverse effect of impinging on the time that independent directors have to spend on monitoring their corporation's legal compliance.

> For today, the issue is what it might mean for the US system if this creeping intrusion continues. For all their costs, the new exchange rules and Sarbanes-Oxley are survivable and, indeed, modestly beneficial, so long as regulators are flexible about giving boards leeway to implement the new mandates in a cost-effective manner.
>
> Source: *Financial Times*, July 6, 2005.

The different views of the role of regulators and regulation that this alludes to are consistent with the essentially political nature of the entire process. In addition, cost/benefit analysis of the considerably increased workload experienced by many firms (research suggests that compliance now consumes on average 1.25% of revenue for large US corporations) has lead to resistance to the "creeping intrusion" that new regulatory requirements represent. These issues, as well as the culturally conditioned responses to the challenges posed, are likely to determine how the regulatory regimes in different countries develop.

No More Rules, Says Europe

The Disadvantages of a Plethora of New Regulations are Emerging, writes Robert Bruce

No one in business wants more regulation. But when you find regulators agreeing you know implementation of new rules has reached a peak. In a report* on views on regulation across Europe, published by KPMG, the accountancy firm, Klaus Pohle, chairman of the German accounting standards board, says: "Everyone is doing too much"; and Paul Boyle, chief executive of the UK Financial Reporting Council, says: "We are reaching a high point of regulation". The plethora of new rules is becoming a problem for companies, the accountancy profession and regulators. After Enron no one denies the need for tighter rules, and companies operating in a global market increasingly want the fruits of convergence of regulations, but all the participants in this complex system find frequently that the unintended consequences are beginning to outweigh the advantages.

... It is when the US Sarbanes-Oxley legislation is assessed from the point of view of benefits created that the practical arguments break down. Doubts are increasing that the intentions of the rules, which tighten internal controls and push more responsibility for disclosure on to directors, are going to be achieved. John Coombe, who retired this year as chief financial officer at GlaxoSmithKline, says: "There is some evidence that the Americans didn't know what they were letting loose." He does not think Sarbanes-Oxley is likely to be effective: "It is a classically legally-driven American nightmare which is expensive and is not going to stop people stealing money from companies."

The view in Europe tends to be that Sarbanes-Oxley leads to greater documentation but not much else that is beneficial. "I suspect a significant part of companies' energies will have gone into the documentation of controls rather than getting the benefits of managing risks," says Neil Lerner, global head of regulatory issues at KPMG.

Europeans tend to see regulation as being more effective if it allows flexibility to follow from basic principles. Jaap Winter, who chaired the EU High Level Group of Company Law Experts, which advised on proposed changes in company law, says: "Flexibility is good. It requires companies to explain and take responsibility. Whereas under Sarbanes-Oxley companies just follow the rules and if anything goes wrong then they can blame the regulators."

... But while there is widespread distrust of many of the regulatory changes the overall long-term trend is seen as more hopeful, particularly across continental Europe. Mr Winter says: "Compare the annual reports of today with those of five years ago and you can see an enormous change." It is seen as being as much of a change in attitude as a change in rules. "Corporate governance was originally seen as something academic," says Mr Winter, "but companies now see they have to get it right."

The Pressure of Regulation On Business: www.kpmg.co.uk

Source: *Financial Times*, September 8, 2005.

In practice:

The impact of the SOX on the audit and management of companies has been considerable, particularly the Section 404 provisions relating to internal controls. And the fact that non-US companies with US listings must also comply means that its tentacles have spread worldwide:

Europeans Spend More Time on Compliance

European companies listed in the US are having to devote more time to Sarbanes-Oxley compliance than their American counterparts, Ernst & Young has found. Fifty-five per cent of European companies with revenues of more than $20bn (£10.3bn) spend more than 100,000 man-hours on work related to the stringent corporate governance rules. Only half of US companies face a similar workload.

The figures illustrate why the 2002 legislation – introduced to prevent the kind of fraud that sank Enron and WorldCom – has triggered such a sustained outcry from European business. Companies complain they are being forced to introduce expensive and time-consuming measures, such as stricter record keeping, with no obvious benefit to their business. The extra time reflects the fact that many large European groups are more global and decentralised than their US peers and have a greater variety of systems, the accountancy firm said.

In the tier below blue chips, Ernst & Young found that 60 per cent of European groups with revenues of $5bn–$20bn were devoting more than 25,000 hours to compliance, compared with

53 per cent of US companies. The findings will add weight to criticism of Sarbanes-Oxley by the Confederation of British Industry, the employers' organisation. "Poorly implemented regulation destroys wealth, with no upside for the consumer or investor," the CBI said.

One UK company seeking to escape the workload is Premier Farnell, a components distributor in the FTSE 250. The group delisted in the US last month and is now seeking to reduce its number of American shareholders to below 300, which would allow it to deregister from the Securities and Exchange Commission. The group estimated that US listing and compliance costs would amount to £1.3m, yet only 3 per cent of the company's shares were held in the US.

However, William Donaldson, chairman of the Securities and Exchange Commission, has insisted that Sarbanes-Oxley brings real benefits for companies and investors. "The requirements of Sarbanes-Oxley cannot be evaluated in a vacuum," he said in a speech in London earlier this year. "They are important because they have produced, and will produce, improvements that help to restore and reinforce investor confidence in our markets, and lower the cost of capital issuers."

Source: Financial Times, March 18, 2005.

The regulatory regime in the US, therefore, is robust, extensive and relatively effective. Characterised by government involvement as well as considerable input by accounting regulators and professionals, it favours a rules-based approach epitomised by the SOX legislation.

UK

In many ways, developments in the UK in the first half of the twentieth century mirrored those in the US. Not surprisingly, therefore, as had happened in the US some years previously, by the late 1960s it had become apparent that the requirements governing the presentation and disclosure of financial statements in the UK were inadequate. While accountancy bodies such as the Institute of Chartered Accountants in England and Wales (ICAEW) made "recommendations" to members, accounting practice varied considerably.

At the initiative of the ICAEW, an Accounting Standards Steering Committee was formed with a view to developing a set of accounting standards. By 1971 the Institute of Chartered Accountants in Scotland (ICAS), the Institute of Chartered Accountants in Ireland (ICAI), the Association of Chartered Certified Accountants (ACCA) and the Chartered Institute of Management Accountants (CIMA) had joined the project. In 1976 this committee was reformed as the Accounting Standards Committee (ASC) under the sponsorship of the Consultative Committee of Accountancy Bodies (CCAB), a group comprising the five original sponsoring bodies plus the Chartered Institute of Public Finance Accountants (CIPFA).

Accounting Standards Committee (ASC)

The ASC was charged with:

- Defining accounting concepts
- Narrowing differences in accounting practice; and
- Formulating best practice

By a due process which involved a degree of consultation with representatives of other interested parties, and the circulation of consultative documents called Exposure Drafts, the ASC made recommendations to the CCAB, which, if it approved of them, issued these as Statements of Standard Accounting Practice (SSAPs). These were then binding on the members of the constituent bodies. Significantly, the ASC and the CCAB claimed to carry out these tasks "in the public interest", the presumption being that accountancy bodies were the ones most suited to fulfilling this role.

By the late 1980s, in the face of several high-profile corporate failures and the obvious incapacity of the part-time ASC to respond more quickly to pressing issues, the CCAB appointed a committee chaired by Sir Ronald Dearing to review the standard-setting process.

The Dearing Report, issued in November 1988, contained a series of far-reaching proposals and recommendations. Specifically, it highlighted the need for:

- A standard-setting process which promoted compliance, reduced options and assisted interpretation by an emphasis on the production of standards which were based on core principles as distinct from the ASC approach of individual standards for individual issues.

- The development, following the model developed by the FASB, of a coherent conceptual framework (see Chapter 2).

- A reduction in the requirements to be met by small companies.

- The gradual incorporation of public sector bodies within the framework.

In terms of structure, it recommended that overall responsibility for the standard-setting process be placed in the hands of a Financial Reporting Council (FRC) intended to guide the standard-setting process, ensure financing and act as a strong public champion of the standard-setting approach. It was to comprise of representatives from a number of interested parties under the chairmanship of a joint nominee of the Secretary of State for Trade and Industry and the Governor of the Bank of England. Accounting interests would be represented by members from practice, industry and the public sector, but there would also be an equal number of representatives from other interested bodies, such as the legal profession and bankers.

Mirroring the US scheme, it was envisaged that the FRC would devolve the task of devising accounting standards to a new Accounting Standards Board (ASB) under a full-time chairman and technical director, supplemented by a full-time secretariat. To address the lessons learned from the ASC's inability to deal promptly with the vast array of emerging issues it was proposed that an Urgent Issues Task Force (UITF) be set up with authority to issue non-mandatory, but authoritative, guidance on matters requiring to be addressed immediately.

Finally, to ensure prompt compliance, it was recommended that a Financial Reporting Review Panel (FRRP) be established to examine, with the support of the Stock Exchange, deviations from accepted accounting practice by large companies.

The Dearing Report received widespread support and the basic structure recommended was quickly put in place. The FRC, initially under the chairmanship of Sir Ronald Dearing, was established in 1990 as part of the stated determination of the government to ensure that corporate reporting and governance conformed to the highest international standards. In August 1990 the ASB, with David Tweedie as chairman, Allan Cook as technical director, and seven other members, came into being. This was followed shortly afterwards by the inauguration of the FRRP. The ASB, in turn, inaugurated the UITF.

Accounting Standards Board (ASB)

One of the priorities of the ASB was to emphasize that, unlike its predecessor, it issued standards – called Financial Reporting Standards (FRSs) – in its own right. However, it was also anxious to avoid confusion over the status of SSAPs issued by the ASC. As a result it formally adopted the twenty-two extant SSAPs. It then set about issuing new standards in line with its stated aim to "establish and improve standards of financial accounting and reporting, for the benefit of users, preparers and auditors of financial information".

In pursuing this agenda, the ASB decided to adopt policies designed to ensure that standards:

- Are the product of a research and consultative process which is sensitive to issues such as usefulness, timeliness and the relative costs and benefits of the proposed standard.

- Reflect national and international environments to the extent that they take cognizance of current UK law and EU directives.

- Support endeavours to harmonize international financial reporting.

- Are clearly expressed and supported by a coherent analysis and rationale.

- Result in information which *faithfully represents* the underlying commercial reality.

- Reflect the desire for an evolutionary, as distinct from revolutionary, approach.

The procedure leading to the issuing of a standard reflects this determination to ensure as wide and informed a consultative process as possible. The sequence usually is:

1. Identification of issues by FRC.

2. Circulation of Discussion Paper by ASB which sets out issues and invites comment and encourages involvement.

3. Research and consultation leading to formulation of Exposure Draft (ED).

4. Circulation of Financial Reporting ED (FRED), an advanced draft of the intended standard.

5. Adoption of FRS.

The emergence of the International Accounting Standards Board in recent years has impacted the role of the ASB. This is discussed in more detail later in this chapter.

Financial Reporting Review Panel (FRRP)

FRSs and SSAPs are authoritative statements detailing the manner in which specific types of events should be accounted for. It is assumed, therefore, that compliance with these standards is necessary in order to produce financial statements that present a "true and fair view". Only in very exceptional circumstances will a departure be either necessary or allowed.

The FRRP, with support from the Department of Trade and Industry (DTI), the Stock Exchange and others, provides a very effective disciplinary component of the regulatory structure. In fact, the bulk of cases that the FRRP has reviewed have been resolved by obtaining the agreement of the companies concerned to amend their accounts.

Powers of Persuasion

There is a story, perhaps apocryphal, but widely repeated in the City, which illustrates the powers and limitations of the FRRP, the investigative wing of the regulatory structure which oversees company accounts in the UK.

...Edwin Glasgow QC, the panel's chairman, is in a meeting with the board of a company whose clearly defective accounts had been drawn to the panel's attention. The conversation has degenerated, so the story goes, into an arcane discussion of a particular technical point.

Glasgow, a lawyer who prides himself on a no-nonsense style, eventually suspects he is being blinded by science. "Do I get the impression, gentlemen", he says, "that, on the whole, you would rather discuss this matter with an accountant?" There are sage nods from the other side of the table. "Fine", says Glasgow, rising from his seat. "On the whole, I'd rather talk to a lawyer. I'll see you in court."

The issue did not go to court – an illustration of the panel's power as a deterrent... The panel has its supporters and critics. The supporters believe it is a minor miracle of arm's length self-regulation. Its critics believe that it chooses easy targets, is afraid to test big issues it might lose in court, and works so slowly that by the time amended accounts are published investors have acted on misleading data.

Source: *Financial Times*, February 20, 1997.

At an extreme, however, for example in cases where companies refuse to comply with requests to revise accounts, the FRRP can apply to the courts for an order requiring the directors of the company to conform. These powers have been extended under the provisions of the Companies (Audit, Investigations and Community Enterprise) Act 2004 and further enhanced by a memorandum of understanding with the Financial Services Authority (FSA) which is the overarching financial regulatory body in the UK. The more proactive approach that this has facilitated is reflected in the FRRP's 2005 Report: in all, the panel reviewed 226 sets of accounts in that period and selected 184 for further review during the twelve months dealt with, representing a huge increase in workload.

In practice:

The FRRP's new powers will be fully tested after its decision to undertake a review of the affairs of MG Rover:

Rover Probe Faces Mountain of Accounts

Investigators from the Financial Reporting Review Panel (FRRP) face a mountain of more than 150 sets of financial statements as they conduct an enquiry into the collapse of MG Rover... Michael Lewington of the Financial Reporting Council, of which the FRRP is part, told Accountancy: 'The scope of the exercise is to determine if the financial statements are in compliance with the Companies Act. The panel will conclude an initial investigation looking at accounts going back several years. If the panel has further questions then the scope of the enquiry will be widened.' Currently the investigation is limited to the published financial statements. In any subsequent investigation, the directors of MG Rover and its auditor Deloitte would, almost certainly, be interviewed...

Source: Accountancy, May 2005.

International Accounting Standards Board (IASB)

Increased international trade, coupled with the growing impetus of globalization, resulted in pressure from various sources for a greater harmonization of international accounting practice. This led in 1973 to the formation of the International Accounting Standards Committee (IASC), which by 1999 had representatives from accounting bodies in almost 100 countries, as well as other organizations with an interest in the financial reporting process.

In 1995 the IASC signed an agreement with the International Organization of Securities Commissions (IOSCO) to develop a set of new standards that, with the agreement of IOSCO, would form an acceptable basis for reporting purposes for companies with cross-border listings. This was a significant catalyst and helped to position the IASC as a potential challenger to FASB as the possibilities of developing a set of standards with a global application began to open up.

Probably the most important boost to what is now called the International Accounting Standards Board (IASB) came in 2000 when the European Commission decided that companies listed on EU markets would have to issue accounts based on International Financial Reporting Standards (IFRS) for accounting periods beginning on or after January 1, 2005. While there have been some difficulties in negotiating the various political hurdles involved in such an ambitious project this has, nevertheless, catapulted the IASB into a position where it can reasonably challenge FASB claims to dominance.

The adoption of IFRS by the EU and the requirement that all public companies prepare IFRS compliant accounts from 2005, represents one of the most significant and radical innovations in accounting practice for several decades. It will impact the way in which companies report, introduce additional volatility and make considerable demands on analysts, traditionally the mediators between companies and their many stakeholders, particularly investors:

Twists and Turns in Store for Analysts

The Switch to New Financial Reporting Standards is Like Driving a New Car on an Unfamiliar Route, writes Ken Wild

The UK markets will very soon see the first interim reports based on International Financial Reporting Standards. The seismic change in financial reporting can be compared to the introduction of employment protection legislation in terms of its pervasive impact on day-to-day operations of UK companies. With such fundamental change in the way they prepare financial statements, companies are concerned about how the market, and analysts in particular, will react.

IFRS presents a double challenge. It is a new accounting language and while it is similar to that used previously in the UK, there are some significant differences, most notably in the treatment of financial instruments, especially derivatives. Second, IFRS will increase reported volatility. While some of this volatility will be real, as economic cycles are real and affect companies in dramatic ways that should be reported to shareholders, some will be "accounting volatility", caused by the standards. Companies will have to rely on analysts' ability to differentiate between the two when assessing their performance.

Imagine an analyst as an experienced driver, driving a familiar car on a known route. The analyst drives safely with little conscious effort and reacting to change without thinking, taking actions based on experience. Then imagine the same driver in a new car. The layout and controls are different. The displays are in kilometres and litres, not miles and gallons. The route is unfamiliar, with lots of twists and turns. This is the challenge facing analysts in the conversion to IFRS. While they have years of experience from which they forecast future cash flows,

all of it was based on UK GAAP. The whole lot needs to be re-examined, for every listed company in the UK...
  The author is Deloitte Global IFRS partner

Source: *Financial Times*, July 21, 2005.

The change to IFRS represents a major shift for large plcs. Some of the practical changes that the adoption of IFRS will cause include expensing of share options, changes in the treatment of intangibles and a greater level of disclosure and transparency. As the following 'In practice' excerpts indicate, the effects will be quite significant for both companies and users.

In practice:

New Rules to Shock the Stock Markets, by Iain Dey

In what will look like the most creative accountancy of the year, Vodafone boss Arun Sarin will reveal next month that its first-half loss of £3.2bn was actually a profit of roughly £4.1bn. But Sarin, the chief executive, has not suddenly discovered a lost wad of cash stuffed down the back of the sofa. This £7.3bn swing in the profitability of one of Britain's biggest companies is a restatement of its results due to the introduction of new accounting rules. A true wolf in sheep's clothing, the International Financial Reporting Standards may sound like a set of hum-drum accounting regulations but will be one of the most decisive factors in the financial markets in 2005, transforming the figures unveiled by listed companies.

Every listed company in Europe has to be compliant with the new rules by January 1. Although the switch has been years in the pipeline, the City is unsure what impact many of the changes will have except that it will cause uncertainty and that shocks are likely to be aplenty, including some volatility in share prices. Banks are heavily affected by some aspects of the new rules. Technology companies are expected to be hardest hit by others. But until the trading statements begin to trickle out in the New Year, the full extent will remain unknown.

"Imagine it's a few weeks away from football's cup final," said Merrill Lynch analyst Karl Debenham. "Your team's been training hard and are completely focused on their strategy and tactics. Just before the teams take to the field someone mentions the rule changes, but they can't be important, can they? Actually the offside rule has been abolished, you can now have two goalkeepers, and the match is won by the side that concedes the fewest corners... But there are political pressures to all this. Even those investors who are informed about the changes will see this big jump in profits in the accounts. The workforce will start asking for more money, the politicians will want to find a way to make them pay more tax and the shareholders will want a bigger dividend".

Analysts already know about the impact this particular change will have on Vodafone and they've been factoring it into their calculations for a while. But this is just one aspect of the biggest shake-up in UK finance in a generation. If changing the rules can have that big an impact on a monolithic business such as Vodafone, the potential impact on the market as a whole becomes terrifying.

The broad principle of IFRS is to move towards greater transparency. Until the new system beds down, it will achieve the exact opposite. Given the scale of impact on some companies, it will become difficult to discern between real changes in earnings and artificial differences generated by the new rules...

Source: *Scotland on Sunday, December 5, 2004.*

BA profits take off under IFRS, by James Bennett

Operating profits at British Airways have skyrocketed by £16m, thanks to the switch to international financial reporting standards, the airline has announced. Under IFRS for the year ended March 31 2005, BA's operating profit increased from £540m under UK GAAP to £556m, while profit before tax increased by almost £100m from £415m to £513m.

... BA's chief financial officer, John Rishton, however, dismissed the impacts of new accounting rules on the airline's income statement as 'minor', but said that there would be a 'significant impact' on its balance sheet. 'Net assets under IFRS are reduced by £1.3bn to £1.4bn, mainly due to moving the pension deficit on to the balance sheet. It was previously fully disclosed as a note to the report and accounts,' Rishton added.

A statement said that the adoption of IFRS represented an 'accounting change only' and did not affect the underlying operation of the business or the airline's cashflows for 2004/05. Chris Avery, airline analyst at JP Morgan, said he 'wasn't surprised' at BA's figures and praised the airline for its detailed statement. 'There aren't that many changes to the profit and loss account, but the airline market is facing increased volatility going forward. The next few months will be interesting.'

Source: *Financial Director, July 5, 2005.*

"Prescriptive" IFRS will Force Up Clubs' Wage Bills, Says Manchester United Finance Director, by Nicholas Neveling

Top football clubs will see their wage bills jump under IFRS when expenses are included in player remuneration for the first time. Manchester United FD Nick Humby, who reported his club's interim results last week, told Accountancy Age that the cost of player wages would rise. 'IFRS is far more detailed and prescriptive on how wages are accounted for,' he said. 'Housing and flights home for players have always been treated as costs, but will now be included in wages.'

Humby said that there would be a 'notable' increase to the key wage-to-turnover ratio that clubs use to control player wages. United, whose playing staff includes Rio Ferdinand, currently has a 46.6% ratio, compared with an average of 61%, according to Deloitte's annual football survey.

Source: *Accountancy Age, March 31, 2005.*

> **UBS Analyses Impact of IFRS So Far**
>
> *Average reported earnings have increased by 25% under International Financial Reporting Standards. This is the main finding of a survey of 27 European companies by UBS, which analysed information from 27 major groups that have so far provided a full reconciliation between local GAAP and IFRS for 2004 earnings and shareholders' equity as at 31 December 2004.*
>
> *UBS points out that although IFRS brings more comparability, this is limited by the many choices companies have on transition to IFRS and in its subsequent application... UBS says: 'The scale of the changes and the company-specific nature of many of those changes, together with the choices available to companies, has made it very difficult for analysts and investors to predict the impact [of IFRS], and will also make it a challenge to interpret the results once the changes become known.'*
>
> *Source: Accountancy, May 2005.*

The impact of IFRS has already been considerable, therefore. In particular, it is obvious that greater transparency and comparability are going to significantly impact the manner in which accounting information is analyzed and understood. This highlights the central theme of this text – the need to understand the various contexts within which accounting information must be placed in order to appreciate what is really being communicated.

The impact of specific IFRS will be dealt with throughout this text, and the political aspects of the IASB agenda will be addressed in more detail in Chapter 15.

UK Legislative Framework

One of the other regulatory influences that must be grasped is legislation, in particular that relating to one of the most dominant entities in the modern world, the company.

The regulation of company accounts by statute originated with the Joint Stock Companies Act, 1844. Modern company accounts are governed by more recent legislation, however. The Companies Act 1948 (CA48) laid down some of the basic principles relating to disclosure requirements that still apply today.

The Companies Act 1981 (CA81) was significant in a number of respects. Principal amongst these was the fact that it was a response to the EU Fourth Directive, which was an attempt by the EU to harmonize elements of company law throughout member states. It contained detailed specifications with regard to the format, content and publication of accounts.

In the wake of the consolidation of these various statutes into the Companies Act 1985 (CA85), this statute, as amended (somewhat confusingly) by the Companies

Act 1989 (CA89), now forms the principal legislative framework for companies in the UK. There have also been more recent enactments dealing with, for example, the introduction of IFRS.

Nature of Companies

Companies are one of the most common forms of business entity in the UK. A company is defined as "a corporation that has an existence, rights and duties separate from its members (shareholders)".

Companies, other than those formed by Royal Charter or by act of parliament, are formed by registration under CA85. This involves the promoters of the company filing the following documents with the Registrar of Companies in England and Wales (or the Registrar of Companies in Scotland):

Memorandum of Association: This document essentially lays down the rules governing the company in its dealings with those outside of itself. The disclosure of the following is required:

- Name of the company
- Country in which Registered Office will be situated
- Objects of the company, i.e., the activities which the company may undertake
- Whether the liability of the members is limited or not
- The authorized share capital level and the nominal value of shares
- Whether it is a public company
- A list of the initial shareholders.

Articles of Association: This contains the rules and regulations pertaining to the internal workings of the company, and should include details of the following:

- Share capital: the different classes of share, restrictions on transfer rights and the mechanism by which authorized share capital levels might be altered (see Chapter 9)
- Annual General Meetings: rules regarding the period of notice and procedures to be followed
- Directors: information as to their duties, powers and the manner of their election, removal and retirement
- Dividends
- Procedures to be followed on winding-up.

Companies that submit these details to the Registrar of Companies will receive a Certificate of Incorporation at which point the company assumes a legal identity separate from its members.

Limited Companies

Companies can be classified as either "Limited" or "Unlimited".[1] However, most companies are limited companies, that is, the liability of the shareholders is limited. The two most common means by which this is achieved are:

- Guarantee: each member guarantees to provide a specified amount in the event of the company going into liquidation. This form is most commonly used by charities.

- Shares: the shareholder's liability is limited to any amount payable in respect of shares purchased. If, therefore, the shareholder has paid fully for any shares purchased, there is no further liability. It is the method most commonly adopted by companies. The most common types of share are ordinary shares and preference shares (see Chapter 9).

Private Companies

The vast bulk of companies are private limited companies, using the abbreviation Ltd. All such companies must prepare full statutory accounts for their shareholders, although those private companies classified as either small or medium may file less detailed information with the Registrar of Companies. Under Section 13(1) of CA89 companies are designated as small or medium, respectively if they satisfy two of the following criteria:

	Small	Medium
Turnover not exceeding	£5.6 million	£22.8 million
Assets not exceeding	£2.8 million	£11.4 million
Number of employees not exceeding	50	250

These financial thresholds are updated regularly in the light of inflation.

Public Companies

A public company is one which:

- Is stated to be such in its Memorandum of Association

- Is limited by shares or guarantee

- Has a minimum issued share capital of £50,000, at least 25% of which has been fully paid up (with any share premium fully paid up).

---

[1] Another form of company is a close company. Such a company is one that is under the control of five or less persons, together with their associates, or is under the control of its directors. The UKLA requires listed companies to state whether or not the company is a close company. A listed company is deemed not to be a close company if more than 35% of its voting power is beneficially held by the public.

A public company cannot trade until it is registered as such and the Registrar of Companies issues a certificate indicating that the share capital requirements have been met. The name of such a company must always end with the title Public Limited Company, abbreviated as "plc".

Stock Exchange Requirements

It is a common misconception that every plc is listed on the Stock Exchange. This is not necessarily the case, although only a plc can achieve such a listing. (Technically it is its securities, such as shares, as distinct from the plc itself, which is "listed".) In fact, there are over 13,000 plcs, but only about 2,500 of these are quoted on the London Stock Exchange (LSE). Since 2000, responsibility for UK listing lies with the UK Listing Authority (UKLA), a division of the Financial Services Authority (FSA).

Obtaining a Listing

The minimum requirements to which a company must conform in order to achieve a listing, i.e., to have its securities, such as its shares, debentures, unsecured loan stocks and warrants, admitted to the market, are listed in Part 4 of the Financial Services Act 1986. This implemented various EU Directives relating to the admission and regulation of listed companies across the EU. UKLA's Listing Rules are detailed in 'The Purple Book' (so called after the colour of its cover).

Companies seeking to have their securities admitted to LSE must first of all seek admission to the Official List from the UKLA. The particulars to be supplied to secure this, and to be included in any prospectus inviting public subscription, are outlined in Chapter 6 of the Purple Book.

In the case of an Initial Public Offering (IPO) the Prospectus must be freely available at a UK address to any member of the public. It should contain information relating to the following:

- General information on the company, its history, details of its activities, management and future prospects, including profit and dividend forecasts
- The nature of the offer and the purposes to which the proceeds will be put
- The company's share capital and existing indebtedness
- The company's directors, secretary, auditor, advisers, solicitors, bankers and brokers
- Profit and loss account and balance sheet for the previous three years
- Subsidiary and associated companies

- Share capital and share options
- Directors' interests and service contracts
- Material contracts
- Pending litigation
- Articles of Association.

Designed to ensure that a company makes available sufficient details regarding its history, performance and prospects to enable the public to make an assessment as to the value of its securities, a Prospectus provides very useful additional detail for any analyst or potential shareholder. Where such a document is available it should be referred to when attempting an analysis of a company.

Before listing, the LSE must also be satisfied as to the marketability of the securities. In relation to this there are two minimum criteria that must be satisfied before a company can have its securities considered for listing:

- The expected total market value for the security must be at least £700,000 in the case of shares and £200,000 in the case of debt.
- At least 25% of the security must be in the hands of the general public.

If the plc satisfies the UKLA under these headings then it can seek a listing. The principal ways in which a company can obtain a listing are summarized in Chapter 4 of the Purple Book:

1. **Offer for sale**: this involves new and/or existing securities being issued to the public via a sponsoring bank or broker. The invitation can be either directly to the public, for example by newspaper advertisement in which case it is called an Offer for Subscription, or by means of a Tender Offer where interested parties are invited to tender at a price equal to or greater than a minimum issue price, with the shares then issued at one "striking price". It is the most common method of obtaining a listing.

2. **Placing**: there is no offer to the public as securities are placed with clients of the sponsor.

3. **Intermediaries offer**: securities are offered to intermediaries who then allocate them to clients.

4. **Introduction**: this is a relatively unusual mechanism and involves a company which already has securities traded outside of the Stock Exchange being granted permission to have them traded on the Exchange. Companies already listed on overseas exchanges most commonly employ this method.

Issuing securities on the stock market is, therefore, a closely controlled and monitored activity. Indeed, the FSA has recently indicated that it will be seeking to streamline these rules further.

In practice:

As the following makes clear IPOs must be carefully managed and have both merits and demerits:

IPO Numbers Head Up, Up and Away, by Kit Bingham

The market for initial public offerings in Europe is booming. Tom Troubridge, head of London capital markets at PwC, said: "It's the best IPO market for sellers that I've seen since the dotcom boom." Nearly 170 companies came to market in the second quarter of this year, compared with just 95 in the same quarter last year, as groups cashed in on improved market conditions.

But a public listing is not the right choice for every ambitious company and, even for the best candidates, the process is long, tortuous and expensive. Moreover, it can all go horribly and unpredictably wrong. Even the most experienced company executive needs to think long and hard about how to execute a successful public offering.

MOTIVATION: Neil Austin, head of new issues at KPMG Corporate Finance, said the first question he asks wannabe public company directors is: "What do you want to do it for? If it's to build the business, gain currency for acquisitions and take the company to the next stage, it is absolutely the right thing to do but if someone says, 'I've built up this business and now I want to cash in,' you steer them away." "If that's your motivation, you'll find yourself hanging on in an unloved company and be disillusioned by the whole process." Tom Troubridge, head of London capital markets at PwC, added: "When a company comes to us saying it wants to float, we usually ask why." Prospective shareholders, he said, would ask the same question. "Investors want to know what's going to happen to their money. They like it when it's going back into the business rather than just back to a vendor."

PREPARATION: Austin said: "Some people come to us and say, 'we want to do an IPO', but they haven't looked at the other options and have little idea of what the process involves." "When we talk to companies 12 months after a flotation they say they didn't appreciate how time-consuming the process would be and didn't really understand what life as a public company involves. It's important to go and talk to other companies that have done it." Bedford said: "Unless someone on the management team has been through the process before, it will undoubtedly come as a surprise. You just can't comprehend in advance the amount of time you will spend in meetings. The public market is an incredibly different world for a company to move into." Armor Group, a protective security company that listed last December, underwent a management buy-out just a year before its IPO so its due diligence was relatively up to date. Without that, finance director David Seaton said the task might have been impossible. "I certainly wouldn't have had any hair," he said. Alan Gow, finance director of Virgin Mobile, which floated 30% of its shares in July 2004, said: "It was one of the best and one of the worst experiences of my life. It was a great thing to do but it was hard work..."

Source: eFinancialNews, August 14, 2005.

Continuing Obligations

The Purple Book also provides details of the requirements imposed on companies once securities have been issued and trading has begun. For instance, companies are required to submit for approval to the UKLA all circulars intended for distribution to holders of securities, as well as notices of meetings, proxy forms and advertisements intended for holders of bearer securities.

Companies must also provide the UKLA with details of:

- Profit announcements
- Dividends
- Acquisitions
- Changes in directors; and
- Any other information necessary to allow the public to evaluate the position of the company.

These rules also require that where forecasts are made that differ by 10% or more from the eventual outcome, an explanation of the difference must be provided. Additional disclosures are also required in respect of borrowings and investments.

Furthermore, if any information exists which can no longer be kept secret and which could result in significant share movements, then the company must inform the Companies Announcements Office immediately and disclose the relevant information.

Disclosure Requirements

The UKLA plays a significant role in determining the nature and content of a plc's Annual Report. This is because it imposes considerable disclosure requirements that are often over and above those imposed by legislation or required under accounting standards. For instance, in relation to each of the following categories, UKLA rules require these disclosures:

- Shares and shareholders:
  - Any authority for the purchase of its own shares by the company and any purchases made other than through the market
  - Participation of a parent company in any placing of shares
  - Shares issued for cash other than pro-rata to existing shareholders
  - Any dividends waived by shareholders
  - Holdings, other than by directors, of more than 3% of any class of voting capital.
- Directors:
  - The beneficial and non-beneficial interests of each director in the company's shares and options
  - Biographical details of each non-executive director
  - Any emoluments waived by directors.

- Contracts:
  - Any significant contracts in which a director is materially interested
  - Any significant contract with a corporate shareholder having 30% or more of the voting power.

Taken together with the disclosure requirements imposed by statue and accounting standards, therefore, the level of information that must be disclosed by a plc in its Annual Report is quite extensive. This reflects a general tendency in modern reporting culture to insist on greater and more focused disclosure by corporate entities.

Alternative Investment Market (AIM)

The funding requirements and ambitions of smaller and medium public limited companies differ radically from those of larger entities. For this reason the London Stock Exchange has created the AIM which commenced trading in 1995.

This market is less demanding in its regulatory emphasis. Nevertheless, although the amount of documentation required is less onerous, companies seeking a listing must still supply a Prospectus that entails considerable disclosure and expense. They must also make price sensitive information available promptly as well as interim figures and details of directors' share dealings.

However, no minimum capitalization levels are imposed, and it is not necessary to employ a sponsoring merchant bank or broker. For this reason it is attractive to small or medium-sized family firms with the ambition and capacity to obtain a listing, but with no appetite for a listing on the larger official market.

Summary

Accountants in the US, UK and elsewhere have traditionally played a key role in the regulation of accounting information. In the Anglo-American world this has usually taken the form of accounting standard-setting bodies being delegated authority to produce GAAP within a broader legislative and regulatory environment. However, this has never diminished the political aspect of accounting regulation, particularly in the US where the government, through the SEC, remains centrally involved.

The large number and range of entities involved in the regulatory process attest to the significance of accounting information in modern society. These include:

- Standard-setting bodies: by means of accounting standards, which delineate accounting practice
- Parliament: by means of legislation
- European Commission: by means of Directives and initiatives designed to facilitate a more harmonized perspective
- Accounting bodies: by means of their direct involvement as preparers, auditors and disseminators of accounting information

- UKLA: by means of monitoring those companies whose securities are listed
- International accounting entities: such as the IASB
- Other interested parties: such as IOSCO.

The result, particularly in the case of large public companies, is that the Annual Report must include a vast amount of information intended to satisfy the information requirements of a wide range of users. And it is this that makes the Annual Report such a significant document when attempting to analyze the financial status, performance and prospects of any large corporate entity.

Review Questions

Question 1
"Accounting information, by its very nature, needs to be regulated". Discuss.

Question 2
"Accounting information emerges in the form that it does as a result of a process that is essentially political, i.e., it is determined by a process in which different interests lobby for their favoured practices. Those with the most influence, whether commercial, social or political, usually prevail. In no way, therefore, can accounting practice be considered 'scientific', in the sense that one can discover a 'correct' or 'immutable' set of principles and practices. Accountancy is an art not a science". Explain what this means.

Question 3
Identify the principal characteristics of the US regulatory framework. Explain the role of the SEC in this system.

Question 4
Outline the way in which the UK system of regulation has evolved over recent decades and identify similarities between the UK and US systems.

Question 5
The IASB has emerged as a significant "player" in the global regulatory environment. Explain how this has happened and the implications for the accounting standard setting process internationally.

Question 6
Explain the role that legislation plays in determining the way in which accounting information is presented. In particular, identify the principal emphases of UK legislation as they relate to accounting information.

Question 7
Distinguish between the following:
• Public and private companies
• Limited and unlimited companies
• Small, medium and large companies

Question 8
The London Stock Exchange and UKLA are playing an increasingly proactive role in the area of accounting disclosure. Identify some examples of this and assess their significance in determining disclosure requirements for companies.

Question 9
"In a free-market economy it is somewhat ironic that the form of accounting disclosures is so heavily regulated". Discuss.

Case Studies

Case 1

The three principal regulatory bodies dealt with in this chapter have excellent web sites. Access these at the following addresses and explore their contents.
FASB: www.fasb.org/
ASB: www.asb.org.uk/
IASB: www.iasb.org/

Case 2

Elliot Spitzer, New York Attorney General, has been one of the principal enforcers of the new regulatory regime in the US. Working closely with the SEC, he has demonstrated how effective this new regime can be. Consider how appropriate his actions are and the extent to which his short term 'successes' may impact corporate culture.

Spitzer Reveals Tip of AIG Iceberg

The Speed of Greenberg's Fall Leaves no Doubt That Something is Very Wrong at the Insurance Giant, Edward Helmore Reports from New York

When, last Friday, a lawyer acting for Maurice 'Hank' Greenberg, began carting boxes of documents from a branch office of American International Group Inc in Bermuda, he set in motion events that swiftly brought down the legendary chairman of the insurance giant. The next day lawyers acting for AIG found that computer records and tapes of business meetings had also disappeared.

New York Attorney General Eliot Spitzer wasted no time in telling AIG's lawyers that so long as Greenberg was chairman, AIG was accountable and he would indict the company if the 79-year-old chairman did not resign immediately. No financial firm has survived a corporate indictment, but nevertheless Greenberg, who built AIG into a firm with revenues of $ 98.61 billion last year, resisted.

However, by last Monday AIG's independent directors, including ex-US Secretary of Defence William Cohen and former US ambassador to the United Nations Richard Holbrooke, had effectively taken control of the firm. They refused to offer Greenberg the title of 'director emeritus' and insisted he retire in what Greenberg is said to regard as a palace coup. It was an ignominious end to four decades of imperious rule at AIG.

The speed of Greenberg's fall left no one in any doubt that accounting at the world's top insurance firm has been seriously amiss. Indeed, two days later AIG confirmed that 14 years of improper accounting could cut its net worth by as much as $1.77 billion. But analysts believe this is only the tip of the iceberg and an investigation that started with the practice of reinsuring business through off-shore firms it owns may run far deeper. Since it was made public in mid-February, the fallout from Spitzer's criminal investigation has cost AIG 20 per cent of its value. It is not the first insurance giant Spitzer has collared.

Last year, the world's largest insurance broker, Marsh & McLennan, was shown to have betrayed its clients by steering their insurance business to favoured underwriters in exchange for millions in backdoor payoffs. In exchange for the resignation of Jeffrey Greenberg, Hank's son, guilty pleas from several executives and an as yet-to-be determined fine of as much as $2 billion, plus reforms, Spitzer agreed not to criminally indict the company.

But his investigation into AIG may go further. The investigation has put legendary investor Warren Buffett, the so-called sage of Omaha, in the spotlight. Buffett is one of the world's most successful insurers through his firm, General Re, a unit of Berkshire Hathaway. Investigators are looking at a deal Greenberg struck in 2000 with Buffett that enabled AIG to add to its reserves but in a way that that did not assume any risk (improper, say regulators, because without risk the $500 million in question should have been treated as a loan by accounting standards).

According to people close to the investigation, General Re is 'at the centre of the storm'. Buffett, who is set to appear before investigators on 11 April, denies detailed knowledge of the reinsurance contract in question. How close the scandal will get to Buffett himself remains open to question, but it is uncomfortable for him to be in such close proximity.

The developing scandal at AIG has also put PricewaterhouseCoopers, the largest independent auditing firm in America, in the spotlight. For now SEC investigators, working with Spitzer's officials, are trying to find out what AIG told its auditors about the deals under scrutiny. At some moment, the auditor will inevitably be asked why it missed the improper accounting. Details of the complex deals AIG has already admitted were improper are still surfacing. In essence, AIG was reinsuring through companies registered in Bermuda and Barbados that are owned and run by AIG executives, questioning the whole notion of reinsurance – spreading risk to others. On Wednesday AIG admitted it made deals specifically for account- ing purposes – 'transactions ... structured for the sole or primary purpose of accomplishing a desired accounting result'.

But since the infractions detailed so far – $500m of inflated reserves and com- paratively small loss of shareholder equity – analysts are bracing themselves for more bad news at AIG. In particular the problems so far have stemmed from its US-based units. Since AIG operates in 91 countries, more irregularities are feared. It is up to investigators on three continents to determine how far AIG's financial picture was manipulated and for how long. Already, three senior AIG executives, including the company's chief financial officer, have been dismissed after refusing to answer investigators' questions.

What becomes of Greenberg is ultimately in the hands of Eliot Spitzer. At the very least, Greenberg did not help himself by making it known publicly that he considered Spitzer's investigation 'McCarthy-istic'. But Greenberg is not used to being troubled by mere functionaries. He is not a man used to being challenged. At a recent board meeting, according to the Wall Street Journal, Greenberg was asked if the company should consider loosening the conflicted ties between itself and the firms now under investigation and effectively controlled by Greenberg. 'That,' he said, 'would be stupid!' But in Spitzer, as has happened with other US tycoons, he seems to have met his match.

Source: *The Observer*, April 3, 2005.

CONCEPTUAL CONTEXT [2]

When you have completed this chapter you will understand:

- What is meant by the term "conceptual framework".
- The meaning and significance of a conceptual framework for any discipline.
- How the development of accounting has been hampered by the lack of such a framework.
- How specific issues such as "recognition" and "measurement" can only be addressed in the context of such a framework.
- That considerable strides have been made in recent decades in addressing this deficiency.

A Horse's Ass

The US Standard railroad gauge (distance between the rails) is 4 feet, 8.5 inches. That's an exceedingly odd number. Why was that gauge used? Well, because that's the way they built them in England, and US railroads were built by English engineers and expatriates.

Why did the English people build them like that? Well, because the first rail lines were built by the same people who built the pre-railroad tramways, and that's the gauge they used. Why did "they" use that gauge then? Well, because the people who built the tramways used the same specifications that they had used for building wagons, which used that wheel spacing.

And why did the wagons use that odd wheel spacing? Well, if they tried to use any other spacing the wagons would break on some of the old, long distance roads, because that's the spacing of the old wheel ruts formed by centuries of being rolled over by cart wheels. So who built these old rutted roads? The first long distance roads in Europe were built by Imperial Rome for the benefit of their legions. The roads have been used ever since.

And the ruts? The initial ruts, which everyone else had to match for fear of destroying their wagons, were first made by Roman war chariots. Since the chariots were made for or by Imperial Rome, they were all alike in the matter of wheel spacing. And thus, we have the answer to the original question. The United States standard railroad gauge of 4 feet, 8.5 inches derives from the original specification for an Imperial Roman army war chariot. Specifications and bureaucracies live forever!

So, the next time you are handed a specification and wonder what horse's ass came up with it, you may be exactly right. Because the Imperial Roman chariots were made to be just wide enough to accommodate the back ends of two war horses.

Now the twist to the story ... There's an interesting extension of the story about the railroad gauge and horses' behinds. When we see a Space Shuttle sitting on the launch pad, there are two big booster rockets attached to the sides of the main fuel tank. These are the solid rocket boosters, or SRBs. The SRBs are made by Thiokol at a factory in Utah.

The engineers who designed the SRBs might have preferred to make them a bit fatter, but the SRBs had to be shipped by train from the factory to the launch site. The railroad line to the factory runs through a tunnel in the mountains. And the SRBs had to fit through that tunnel. The tunnel is slightly wider than a railroad track, and the railroad track is about as wide as two horses' behinds.

So, a major design feature of what is arguably the world's most advanced transportation system was determined by the width of a horse's ass!

Source: *Anonymous.*

Introduction

The point of this story, of course, is to demonstrate how long-forgotten concepts and ways of thinking can persist – indeed, how difficult it can be to break away from them. In the same way, accounting practices that owe their origins to long forgotten commercial contexts, persist simply because "that is how things have always been done".

In other words, many modern accounting practices and concepts have evolved over a number of centuries in response to the demands of particular circumstances, not as the logical outflow of an integrated set of theories with a coherent "conceptual framework". Because of the centrality of accounting information in today's world, this represents a serious and growing problem for accountants, other users of accounting information and society in general.

A conceptual framework may be described as "a unified and generally accepted set of theories and principles that provide a foundation from which specific practices and methods can be deduced". In other words it is a fundamental set of principles, somewhat like a "constitution", or a coherent system of thought about a discipline.

In the case of accounting, it relates to that basic set of unifying principles, if any, that underlies accounting practice.

Although often misunderstood by practitioners and dismissed as an academic irrelevance, a conceptual framework would be expected to impact centrally upon the practice of accounting, the content and manner of its communication and, consequently, the social and economic impact of accounting information.

For instance, such a set of principles would be influential in determining how the discipline deals with issues such as:

- How transactions should be accounted for

- Which events should be accounted for

- What set of user-requirements financial accounting should aim to satisfy

- How financial information should be communicated to users.

In practice:

This account from a former participant in the standard-setting process provides useful insights into how the presence of a conceptual framework can positively impact the standard-setting process. Note in particular the comment on the potential of such a framework to reduce political pressures:

The framework provides a basic reasoning on which to consider the merits of alternatives. Although it does not provide all the answers, the framework narrows the range of alternatives to be considered by eliminating some that are inconsistent with it. It thereby contributes to greater efficiency in the standard-setting process by avoiding the necessity of having to redebate fundamental issues such as "what is an asset?" time and time again. In addition, the framework contributes to greater efficiency in communications, both internal and external. By providing a common terminology and frame of reference, it greatly facilitates the Board's debates about specific technical issues. It also greatly facilitates communications between the Board and its constituents, particularly communications between the FASB and its constituents who offer comments and suggestions about the Board's proposals. A framework should also reduce political pressures in making accounting judgments.

The framework is used to guide the development of accounting standards that are intended to facilitate the provision of evenhanded, or neutral, financial and related information. Neutral information enables users of that information to make informed investment and credit decisions. Consequently, neutral information serves the public interest by helping to promote the efficient allocation of scarce resources in the economy and society. The framework helps the capital markets and other markets to function more efficiently in the same way.

The use of an agreed-upon framework reduces the influence of personal biases on standard-setting decisions. Without the guidance provided by an agreed-upon conceptual framework, standard setting would be quite different, as it necessarily would have to be based on the personal frameworks of individual members of the Board. As Charles Horngren, former APB member,

> *former FASAC member and former FAF trustee, once noted, "As our professional careers unfold, each of us develops a technical conceptual framework. Some individual frameworks are sharply defined and firmly held; others are vague and weakly held; still others are vague and firmly held." He added that: "At one time or another, most of us have felt the discomfort of listening to somebody attempting to buttress a preconceived conclusion by building a convoluted chain of shaky reasoning. Indeed, perhaps on occasion we have voiced such thinking ourselves. . . ."*
>
> *Source: John M Foster, Why does the FASB have a Conceptual Framework? 2004*

Unlike disciplines such as economics, which can trace their origins to great theoretical works such as Adam Smith's *The Wealth of Nations*, and their subsequent impact to a series of theoretical models, such as those credited to Keynes, accounting cannot lay claim to such a prestigious pedigree.

Consigned during its formative years to the role of servant of business, it invariably responded to, rather than shaped, commercial demands. Thus, for example, rather than frame a set of principles which would allow them to determine what to include in a set of accounts, practitioners responded to capitalism's need for statements that measured wealth and changes in wealth by devising the balance sheet and profit and loss account respectively. It was, in many senses, a case of "the cart before the horse".

While such a system could cope with the limited demands placed on it for a period, the increasing complexity of the commercial world has exposed accounting as a discipline that lacks the necessary conceptual framework to cope. In short, accounting stands indicted for both its lack of such a framework and its failure to adequately address this deficiency; a deficiency that opens it to legitimate criticisms and which contains the potential to undermine the self-assumed 'right' of accountants to regulate and control the supply of financial information to society and the market.

In practice:

The following extract from FASB's website explains the perceived advantages to the standard-setter of adopting a coherent conceptual framework:

The FASB develops broad accounting concepts as well as standards for financial reporting. It also provides guidance on implementation of standards. Concepts are useful in guiding the Board in establishing standards and in providing a frame of reference, or conceptual framework, for resolving accounting issues. The framework will help to establish reasonable bounds for judgment in preparing financial information and to increase understanding of, and confidence in, financial information on the part of users of financial reports. It also will help the public to understand the nature and limitations of information supplied by financial reporting.

Source: http://www.fasb.org/facts/

US

As with most accounting initiatives of recent decades, most of the earliest attempts to identify a coherent framework occurred in the US, gaining much of their impetus, as was the case with the regulatory process, from the events surrounding the Wall Street crash.

One of the first attempts at such a synthesis was undertaken by W.A. Paton and A.C. Littleton in the 1930s and 1940s. They were followed by Maurice Moonitz, appointed by the AICPA as its first Director of Accounting Research, and Robert Sprouse, who together published a number of research studies on the subject. At best their efforts met with indifference. At worst they inspired outright hostility from a community which questioned not only their methodology, but also the need for such a project.

Nevertheless, financial scandals which could be traced to certain accounting practices as well as sustained criticism of accounting's deficiencies compelled those within the SEC and the profession to initiate a more comprehensive review. This led to the formation of two groups specifically charged with investigating the issue.

The *Study Group on Establishment of Accounting Principles*, chaired by Francis Wheat, was requested to focus on issues related to the organization and operations of the Accounting Principles Board (APB). Its report, issued in 1972, resulted in the disbanding of the APB and its replacement by the Financial Accounting Standards Board (FASB). This opened the way for a structure more sensitive to the need for a conceptual framework.

The *Study Group on Objectives of Financial Statements*, chaired by Robert Trueblood, was charged with initiating a process intended "to refine the objectives of financial statements". Specifically, the group was expected to address issues such as: Who are the primary users of financial accounting information?; What are their financial accounting information needs?; How could financial accounting information be best presented to satisfy the legitimate requirements of users?

In addressing these questions the Trueblood Committee identified a number of critical objectives and qualitative characteristics that should attach to financial reports intended to comply with the basic objective of financial statements, which, significantly, was identified as being "to provide information useful for making economic decisions". In nominating these characteristics Trueblood provided the basis upon which the FASB could proceed to publish a statement dealing more specifically with an underlying conceptual framework.

FASB Conceptual Framework Project

Following the criticisms that had accompanied the APBs efforts during its final years, and the loss of public confidence as a result of various financial reporting abuses, the FASB was seen by many within the profession as the final opportunity to retain the standard-setting regime in the private sector. As a result it set as one of its first goals the development of a set of accounting principles upon which a coherent set of accounting standards might be based.

Taking as its starting point the recommendations of the Trueblood committee, it issued a Discussion Memorandum, *Conceptual Framework for Accounting and Reporting*, which called for comment from interested parties. Two years later, in December 1976, it issued its *Tentative Conclusions on Objectives of Financial Statements* as well as a document which set out its aspirations for the whole conceptual framework project, *Scope and Implications of the Conceptual Project*. Six Statements of Financial Accounting Concepts (SFACs) dealing with central elements of the conceptual framework followed.[1]

SFAC No. 1: Objectives of Financial Reporting by Business Enterprises published in 1978 represents a seminal work in the development of a conceptual framework. Distinguishing between two classes of user, those with a direct interest such as investors, creditors, management and employees, and those with an indirect interest such as analysts, advisers and unions, it focuses primarily on the information needs of the first group, particularly investors and creditors.

Thus, while acknowledging that the traditional responsibilities of management persist, it identifies the principal objective of financial reporting as "the provision of information that is useful to present and potential investors and creditors and other users in making rational investment, credit and similar decisions". One critical feature to emerge at this early stage, therefore, was the centrality of the concept of decision-usefulness of accounting information.

This statement has had a profound impact upon the way in which accounting practice and regulation has developed over the course of recent decades. A closer analysis of its constituent parts indicates several significant elements:

- The focus is placed firmly on the information needs of users, as distinct from the requirement that management account for their stewardship.

- Within the broad category of "user" investors and creditors are identified as the primary target group, and within the category of investor, potential investors are specifically acknowledged.

- The usefulness of accounting information is related to its capacity to assist in the decision-making process.

SFAC No. 1 was also important in extending financial reporting responsibilities to incorporate cash flow information. For instance, it explicitly listed prospective cash flows as one of the criteria which investors and creditors would find most useful in assessing the quality of their investment. However, it stopped short of requiring companies to include cash flow statements or forecasts in their reports.

SFAC No. 2: Qualitative Characteristics of Accounting Information also owed a considerable debt to the work of the Trueblood Committee.

---

[1] For a more complete analysis of these SFACs and of other elements of this chapter see Davies, M. et al., UK GAAP. 5th Ed., 1997, pp. 39–127.

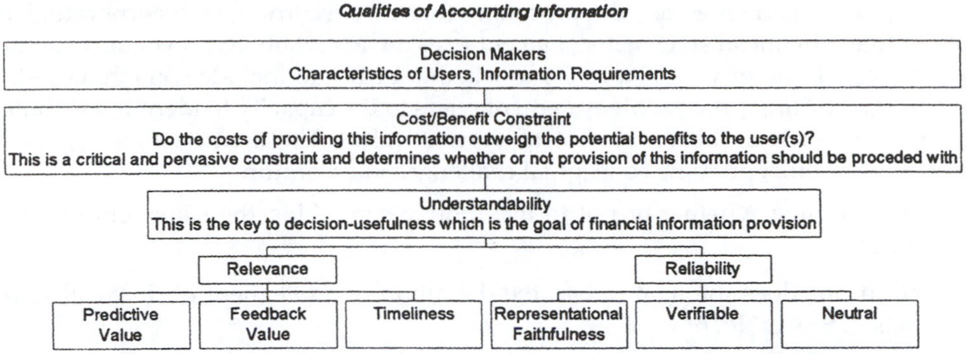

Qualities of Accounting Information

Figure 2.1   Qualities of accounting information. Adapted from Figure 1 of SFAC No. 2.

It examined, classified and prioritized the various characteristics that make financial statements useful. In the process it identified a hierarchy of qualities which can be used to determine whether or not financial statements achieve their stated purpose. The scheme can be represented diagrammatically in Figure 2.1.

A number of observations can be made on this scheme:

• **Users**: the user-centred approach to financial statements is reflected in the fact that the requirements of users are prioritized.

• **Cost/benefit issue**: before considering the financial information itself it is necessary to determine whether the potential benefits to the user outweigh the costs of providing the information in the first place.

• **Understandability**: this is identified as a key requirement if the information is to contribute to the decision-making process.

• **Reliability and relevance**: these are the primary qualities of useful information. The component parts of these elements all contribute to the capacity of the information to assist in enabling users to form opinions. As necessary, albeit secondary, qualities of financial information, SFAC 2 adds that it should be comparable with other financial information and consistent between and within accounting periods.

SFAC No. 3: Elements of Financial Statements of Business Enterprises, published in 1980, was replaced in 1985 by *SFAC No. 6: Elements of Financial Statements* (see below).

SFAC No. 4: Objectives of Financial Reporting by Non-Business Organizations, is not germane to this text.

SFAC No. 5: Recognition and Measurement in Financial Statements of Business Enterprises: Paralleling its work on the conceptual framework project, the FASB had also been engaged on a project relating to other fundamental issues. The work of this group was published in 1984 as SFAC No. 5. It dealt with two issues, "recognition" and "measurement", that had been identified as central concepts in accounting.

Recognition is defined as "the process of formally recording or incorporating an item into the financial statements of an entity as an asset, liability, revenue, expense, or the like". In other words, it refers to whether or not to include something in the financial recording process. Measurement refers to the capacity to identify attributes in an item, such as historical cost or current value. These two issues represent probably the most pressing conceptual challenges in accounting.

In determining whether or not to incorporate something the statement outlines four criteria:

1. **Definition**: does the item satisfy the definition of an element of financial statements in SFAC No. 6?
2. **Measurability**: does the item have attributes that can be measured with sufficient reliability?
3. **Relevance**: will the item make a difference in user evaluation and decision-making?
4. **Reliability**: is the information verifiable, representationally faithful and neutral?

In many senses this statement was a considerable disappointment. In particular, it tended towards a description of current practices rather than a discussion of their relative merits and demerits. For example, when discussing measurement it described a range of methods such as historical cost, current cost and net realizable value without discussing the circumstances in which each might be appropriate. It represented, in some respects, a return to the rather technocratic approach that had undermined the credibility of the APB in the first place.

SFAC No. 6: Elements of Financial Statements: as the title implies, the statement classified the various component parts of financial statements. Its principal contribution was that it provided definitions of a number of the more important elements of accounts, such as assets and liabilities, as well as various sub-categories within these:

- **Assets**: these are defined as "probable future economic benefits obtained or controlled by a particular entity as a result of past transactions or events".
- **Liabilities**: "probable future sacrifices of economic benefits arising from present obligations of a particular entity to transfer assets or provide services to other entities in the future as a result of past transactions or events".
- **Equity (net assets)**: "the residual interest in the assets of an entity after the deduction of its liabilities. Equity refers to the ownership interest in an enterprise".
- **Revenues**: "inflows or other enhancements of assets or settlements of its liabilities from delivering or producing goods, rendering services, or other activities that constitute the entity's ongoing major or central operations".
- **Expenses**: "outflows or other using up of assets or incurrences of liabilities from delivering or producing goods, rendering services, or other activities that constitute the entity's ongoing major or central operations".

All in all the FASB Conceptual Framework Project has had a significant impact. In stimulating discussion and identifying the need for a coherent conceptual basis upon which to construct accounting practice, it has served a useful purpose. It has also acted as a catalyst in motivating others such as the ASB and the International Accounting Standards Board to undertake similar projects.

However, fuelled by a sense of underachievement, doubts persist amongst those who have long championed the need for such a framework. To many it has seemed that the process has never quite engaged with the fundamental issues of recognition and measurement and has, thereby, surrendered much of the advantage to those who favour a more pragmatic approach. In the nature of all such ambitious endeavours, however, the historical perspective may show the project to have been an important stepping-stone on the road to a more intellectually coherent and satisfying discipline.

In practice:

One of the larger corporate collapses in the US in recent years was that of Kmart, a large merchandiser. Uncertainty about accounting practice in relation to vendor credit – a method of ongoing financing by suppliers – and certain old/new economy accounting issues, which could be directly traced to deficiencies in the conceptual framework, were identified as partly to blame.

. . .it is obvious that old Kmart's collapse resulted from a lack of vendor credit. The less apparent story is that the situation demonstrates a significant problem in vendor accounting that is only now gaining the attention it deserves. Starting in the late 1980s, a separation of commerce in goods from commerce in services occurred. The movement of goods through manufacturing, labour, physical delivery, and final consumption is understood in accounting theory. However, the way services are connected every step along the way is not as well understood in accounting theory. As a result, accounting guidance published during the 1990s lagged badly behind the changing nature of the service and goods economies. . .

In the EITF Minutes published by FASB, it is easy to see that an admirable amount of attention has been given to specific situations and how rules are applied or denied, depending upon the details of the situation. However, there was no discussion of the underlying broader conceptual framework for vendor-retailer commerce. . .

Source: *Richard D. Hastings, Credit & Collections World, August 2002.*

Although also the consequence of various political and cultural choices, one of the effects of the lack of a conceptual framework has been the adoption of a primarily 'rules-based' approach in the US. This has fostered a regulatory environment in which following the rules and adhering strictly to the legal form of transactions has predominated. Many see this as a fundamental weakness that enabled accounting scandals such as that at Enron to develop. More recently, however, the US has gradually begun to move away from its rules-based approach. Strongly influenced by the success of the ASB's principles-based approach and the adoption by the IASB of a similar approach, it has used the opportunity afforded by various high-profile corporate accounting frauds to gradually explore this approach.

Principles-Based Approach to Standard Setting, by Linda A McDonald

Recently, many have expressed concerns about the quality and transparency of financial reporting in the United States. In response, the FASB has issued for public comment a proposal for a principles-based approach to U.S. standard setting and plans to hold a public roundtable meeting with respondents to the proposal on December 16. In addition, the Sarbanes-Oxley Act of 2002 requires the Securities and Exchange Commission (SEC) to conduct a study on the adoption of a similar approach and to submit the results of that study to Congress by July 2003.

The idea of a principles-based approach to U.S. standard setting is not new. The Board's conceptual framework contains the body of principles that underlies U.S. accounting and reporting. The Board has used the conceptual framework in developing the principles in accounting standards for more than 20 years. However, many assert that the standards have become increasingly detailed and rules-based (with "bright-lines" and "on-off" switches that focus on the form rather than the substance of transactions), complex, and difficult and costly to apply. Many also assert that the standards allow financial and accounting engineering to structure transactions "around" the rules, referring to situations such as those in which complex structures or a series of transactions are created to achieve desired accounting results; for example, to remove assets from the balance sheet while retaining the overall economics of the assets or to re-characterize assets.

Under a principles-based approach, the principles in accounting standards would continue to be developed from the conceptual framework, but would apply more broadly than under existing standards, thereby providing few exceptions to the principles.

Source: *FASB Newsletter*, November 2002.

UK

Concern at the lack of a conceptual framework and the consequences that this had for the integrity of the standard-setting process were not unique to the US. A similar dynamic for change had developed in the UK. One of the more obvious consequences of this was the establishment of a new regulatory regime in the 1970s. Another was the formulation of SSAP 2, *Disclosure of Accounting Policies*, as one of the first acts of this new regime.

SSAP 2

To a limited extent, SSAP 2, *Disclosure of Accounting Policies*, issued in November 1971, represented at least an acknowledgement of the role which fundamental concepts could and should play in the regulatory process. SSAP 2 does not specifically aspire to present a coherent conceptual framework. In fact, as the title suggests, its primary objective was to improve the quality and consistency of financial information disclosed to users. However, in formulating a set of accounting concepts that it took to be fundamental to all accounting practice, it did articulate a set of principles that still underlie accounting practice in the UK.

SSAP 2 approached its task in three stages, dealing first with fundamental concepts, then with accounting bases and finally, accounting practices.

Fundamental Concepts

SSAP 2's main significance lay in the fact that it sought to identify those critical, unifying concepts that should underpin all accounting practice. In other words, it set out the basic principles which accountants should follow when preparing accounts. It identified four such concepts:

1. **Going concern**: assumes that a business (or enterprise) will continue in operational existence for the foreseeable future. This means that the financial statements are drawn up on the basis that there is no intention or necessity to liquidate the business or to curtail the scale of its operations.

2. **Accruals (matching)**: states that costs and revenues should be matched against one another and be dealt with in the accounting period to which they *relate*.

3. **Consistency**: requires that a business be consistent in its accounting treatment of similar items, both *within* a particular accounting period and *between* one accounting period and the next.

4. **Prudence**: requires that revenues and profits not be included in the accounts unless it is likely that they will yield cash eventually. It also requires that in situations where losses are anticipated they should be accounted for as soon as possible. An example of the prudence concept being applied would be where a business has an estimate of a future loss of between £1000 and £1500; in these circumstances the accountant should make provision for the highest estimate.

These concepts were accepted by CA85 as "accounting principles" and companies were required to explain any departure from them.[2]

---

[2] It is generally accepted that CA85 added a fifth fundamental concept of its own, "non-aggregation" or "separate determination" which requires that each individual item be evaluated individually before being incorporated into the total for its class. Furthermore, many accountants would argue that another fundamental concept, "substance over form", was introduced by FRS 5, *Reporting the Substance of Transactions*. This requires that the economic substance of a transaction should be reflected in the accounts, rather than simply its legal form. There are also a number of other accounting principles outlined in SSAP 2 besides those fundamental concepts listed above: entity concept: states that the business is a separate entity from its owners and that the accounts must be kept from the perspective of the business, not from the perspective of the owner; materiality convention: requires that the financial statements should separately disclose items that are significant enough to affect evaluation or decisions; historical cost convention: means that items are included in accounts at their historical cost, i.e. at the amount that they originally cost the business.

Accounting Bases

Accounting bases are defined as the "methods developed for applying fundamental concepts to financial transactions". They have particular application when determining the accounting period in which revenues and expenses should be recognized and the amounts at which they should be included in the balance sheet.

Bases are, therefore, techniques that have been developed over time for ensuring that the fundamental concepts can be applied to particular events. Depreciation is one such technique.

Accounting Policies

It will be necessary for management to choose from among the range of techniques available to it. An accounting policy, therefore, is "the specific accounting basis selected and consistently followed by a business enterprise as being, in the opinion of management, appropriate to its circumstances and best suited to present fairly its results and financial position". Where it has made choices such as this, management must then disclose details of those accounting policies adopted which it considers material to determining financial position in the accounting policies note which accompanies the financial statements.

For example, applying the fundamental concepts, most businesses will find it necessary to incorporate a charge for depreciation in the financial statements. Depreciation is an accounting basis since it is a method developed to ensure that the fundamental concepts are applied. There are, however, a number of depreciation techniques available. Management will, therefore, have to choose the one most appropriate to its circumstances. If, for example, it chooses the straight-line method for depreciation purposes, then this becomes its accounting policy.

In December 2000 the ASB issued FRS 18, *Accounting Policies*, which has replaced SSAP 2 with effect from June 2001. While acknowledging that SSAP 2 was still fundamentally sound, it does reconsider the relative importance of the four fundamental concepts and gives greater weight to the going concern and accruals concepts. It also provides useful direction in relation to disclosures to be made where estimates are employed.

Corporate Report

Commissioned by the Accounting Standards Steering Committee, the precursor of the ASC, this discussion paper took much of its inspiration from the Trueblood Committee in the US. Published in 1975, it sought to address three fundamental issues:

- *Types of organization* which should publish regular financial information: on this point, the Report concluded that economic entities of "significant size" (which it did not quantify) had a responsibility to report as part of their public accountability function.

- *Principal users* of such reports and their particular requirements: adopting the lead set in the US, the Corporate Report firmly established the necessity to address users and their respective needs as the primary focus of the corporate reporting function. It also categorized the various classes of user into seven sub-sections, each with specific but often overlapping needs, for example, evaluating performance, liquidity, funding requirements and future prospects.

- *Form of report* that best satisfies these requirements: the committee was of the opinion that the primary objective of a corporate report is to "communicate economic measurements of and information about the resources and performance of the reporting entity". To fulfil this objective it concluded that a report had to conform to various parameters which, echoing the Trueblood committee, included understandability, reliability, timeliness, comparability, objectivity and relevance.

The *Report* envisaged the publication of an annual report that not only provided financial information but was also sufficiently comprehensive that it completely described an organization's economic activity. While including basic financial statements such as the balance sheet, profit and loss account and funds-flow statement (the precursor to the cash flow statement), it proposed that such a report should also include narrative elements and other descriptive statements. With a view to satisfying the information needs of a broad range of users, it suggested that the following additional statements should be included in the Annual Report:

- Value-added statement
- Employment report
- Statement of foreign-currency transactions
- Statement of monetary exchanges with government
- Statement of future prospects
- Statement of corporate objectives.

Significantly, the committee also advocated an extension of the social reporting aspect of corporate accountability that would require companies to acknowledge and report upon their performance as "corporate citizens". For example, companies would be required to report on their impact on the local communities in which they operated.

In stimulating discussion as to the nature and role of accounting information, the *Corporate Report* confirmed that the profession in the UK was alert to the difficulties inherent in a regulatory process that could not point to a coherent conceptual framework from which to operate. It was also an acknowledgement that the emphasis in financial reporting had moved from basic stewardship, i.e., the responsibility of management to manage and account for resources, to a user-oriented, decision-making perspective.

However, in its failure to deal comprehensively with fundamental issues such as measurement and valuation bases it fell foul of the same dynamic which would see SFAC No. 5, *Recognition and Measurement in Financial Statements of Business Enterprises*, fail to deal fully with the issue in the US some years later.

Sandilands Report

On this valuation issue, however, the *Corporate Report* was to some extent overtaken by events, in particular the work of the Sandilands committee which had been commissioned by the Secretary of State for Trade and Industry in 1974 to consider whether company accounts should allow for price changes. This committee was expected to address the implications for accounting and the corporate reporting regime of the fact that the global economy was going through a period of seemingly intractable inflation.

Working from the now widely accepted paradigm of the primacy of user-oriented, decision-useful information, Sandilands proposed a gradual move towards a system of "current-cost-accounting". This was an approach based upon the notion of "value-to-the-business", where assets and liabilities were incorporated into the balance sheet at their value-to-the-business, and profit was to be calculated only after charging the value-to-the-business of any assets consumed in the process. The cumulative effect would have been to produce accounts that reflected a change in focus from crude measurements of profit based on historical costs to ones more concerned with the inclusion of assets and liabilities at values that reflected price changes.

Responding to this report the ASC embarked upon a frenzy of inflation accounting-related work that resulted eventually in the publication in 1980 of SSAP 16, *Current Cost Accounting*. This required companies to present current cost accounts either as their principal accounts or as supplements to the historic cost accounts. The standard encountered considerable opposition, however, both from within the profession and from industry. In 1985 it was withdrawn.

Making Corporate Reports Valuable (MCRV)

Other reports, such as the *Macve Report*, continued to be commissioned by the various regulatory bodies in the US and the UK. But the reaction from the public, profession and government was disappointing. Aware of this, the Institute of Chartered Accountants of Scotland commissioned its Research Committee to undertake a fresh investigation into the corporate reporting regime. Uniquely, the committee was allowed to consider the process without reference to existing laws, traditional practice or other constraints.

Starting from the assumption that users need the same information as management, although usually in lesser quantities, *MCRV* identified four principal user groups, all with legitimate, if varying, requirements. These were:

- Equity investors
- Loan creditors
- Employees
- Business contacts such as creditors.

The report then identified the following as issues on which a properly constituted financial report should be able to assist users:

- Understanding corporate objectives

- Explaining changes in corporate wealth

- Assessing future prospects

- Comprehending the economic environment within which the entity operates

- Providing information about ownership and control

- It was also suggested that management should be required to publish corporate financial plans as well as compare the entity's actual performance with previously published plans, explaining any variations in the process.

One of the most significant contributions of the *MCRV* was that it not only grappled with the challenges posed by problems of measurement, but actually made recommendations in the area. Dismissing the claims of historical cost and economic value as measures of economic reality, it proposed "net realizable value"[3] as the method that, albeit with important reservations, most comprehensively captured value.

Other significant conclusions of the report were:

- The substance of transactions, rather than merely their legal form, should be communicated.

- Increased disclosure should be considered as a way of satisfying user-requirements.

- There should be a greater focus on balance sheet valuations.

These aspirations caused the committee to completely reconsider the form in which information was communicated in the Annual Report. As a result *MCRV* proposed the following as the critical statements and elements of any report intended to achieve these purposes:

- **Statement of assets and liabilities**: this would include all assets and liabilities of the entity stated at net realizable value.

- **Operations statement**: this was intended to determine the change in corporate wealth resulting from the trading activity of the entity.

- **Statement of changes in financial wealth**: this would summarize changes in corporate wealth from all sources.

- **Distributions statement**: this would detail any changes in wealth resulting from distributions, such as dividends, and would address capital maintenance concerns by ensuring an inflation adjustment during periods of rising prices.

- **Cash flow statement**: this would include details of all inflows and outflows subdivided into various subsections.

---

[3] Net Realisable Value (NRV) can be defined as: "proceeds of sale less any additional unavoidable expenses of disposal."

MCRV represented one of the most radical, yet thoughtful, reappraisals of the accounting and reporting functions. It challenged fundamentally some of the preconceptions on which corporate reporting had been based for decades. But it not only recited problems and discussed alternatives. In championing a value-based approach, it created the possibility of major changes in the way in which the accounting function interacted with its various environments. In so doing it has had a considerable impact upon the standard-setting process in the UK and abroad.

Solomons Report

In 1987, responding to similar pressures to those that had resulted in the conceptual framework project in the US, the Research Committee of the ICAEW commissioned Prof. David Solomons, who had been an advisor to FASB, to undertake similar research in the UK.

Not surprisingly, his conclusions mirrored many of the findings of its US predecessor. In fact, its conclusions regarding the elements of financial statements reflected very closely SFAC No. 6, for example, in its definitions of assets and liabilities. Likewise, its summary of the qualitative characteristics of accounting information mirrored the thrust of SFAC No. 2 in emphasizing qualities such as decision-usefulness, timeliness, understandability, reliability and relevance.

One important aspect of the Solomons Report was a stated preference for a ''balance sheet approach'', i.e., one which favoured an asset and liability focus, as distinct from the traditional revenue-expense emphasis which it was felt allowed too much scope for profit manipulation.

Solomons concluded by devising a financial reporting model based upon the notion of ''maintenance of real financial capital''. This concept, which flowed from his balance sheet focus, considered income as the change in an entity's net worth. In other words, the primary focus was to be on determining the values at which to include assets and liabilities in the balance sheet. Income was then a by-product of this measure.

This model was useful in providing a definite rationale for a balance sheet approach. However, it was also helpful in pointing out potential difficulties with this emphasis. For instance, appropriate valuation bases and the ways in which intangible assets might be recognized and measured were highlighted as problematic, as were more specific issues such as the treatment of deferred taxation and pensions.

ASB's Statement of Principles

The Dearing Report, which had recommended the changes in the standard-setting regime that had led to the ASB, also made recommendations in relation to the development of a conceptual framework. In fact, conscious of the difficulties which the absence of a clearly articulated conceptual basis posed, it had identified work in this area as a priority:

> (the) lack of a conceptual framework is a handicap to those involved in setting standards as well as to those applying them. Work on its development should, therefore, be pursued at a higher rate than hitherto but consistent with the perceived scope for progress... We believe that work in this area will assist standard-setters in formulating their thinking on particular accounting issues, facilitate judgments on the sufficiency of the disclosures required to give a true and fair view, and assist preparers and auditors in interpreting accounting standards and in resolving accounting issues not dealt with by specific standards.

Consequently, the ASB set as one of its priorities the formulation of such a framework, which it called its Statement of Principles (SoP). This emerged over a number of years in the form of Exposure Drafts (EDs) or chapters, each dealing with a component part of such a framework.

The first draft version of the SoP encountered significant opposition, however, as much for the manner of its formulation as its contents. As a consequence the ASB decided that, rather than proceed directly to the development of a final Statement, a revised draft would be prepared. In the interim it issued a Progress Paper intended to clarify certain points.

A Revised SoP was published in December 1999. However, there were few changes from the first draft. In fact, other than the addition of an extra chapter dealing with "Accounting for interests in other entities", together with proposals regarding the presentation of "profit", there were almost no significant variations from what had been produced some years previously.

The thinking behind the Statement of Principles, and the role such a framework was envisaged as playing, are summarized in the introduction to this revised draft:

Purpose

1. This Statement of Principles for Financial Reporting sets out the principles that the Accounting Standards Board believes should underlie the preparation and presentation of general purpose financial statements.
2. The primary purpose of articulating such principles is to provide a coherent frame of reference to be used by the Board in the development and review of accounting standards and by others who interact with the Board during the standard-setting process.
3. Such a frame of reference should clarify the conceptual underpinnings of proposed accounting standards and should enable standards to be developed on a consistent basis by reducing the need to debate fundamental issues each time a standard is developed or revised. As such, it will play an important role in the development of accounting standards. It is

> expected that it will play a similar role in the development of Statements of Recommended Practice.
> 4. The Statement is being published because knowledge of the principles should assist preparers and users of financial statements, as well as auditors and others, to understand the Board's approach to formulating accounting standards and the nature and function of information reported in general purpose financial statements. The principles will also help preparers and auditors faced with new or emerging issues to carry out an initial analysis of the issues involved in the absence of applicable accounting standards.
>
> Source: Statement of Principles, ASB, December 1999.

The Statement of Principles does not, in itself, comprise an accounting standard. Instead, it is envisaged that it will provide a common reference point for the ASB in formulating standards, for preparers in determining appropriate accounting treatment where accounting standards are silent, and for users in interpreting the information contained in financial reports.

The SoP consists of eight chapters as follows:

1. The objective of financial statements.
2. The reporting entity.
3. The qualitative characteristics of financial information.
4. The elements of financial statements.
5. Recognition in financial statements.
6. Measurement in financial statements.
7. Presentation of financial information.
8. Accounting for interests in other entities.

Assessment of Statement of Principles

The Statement of Principles represents an attempt by the ASB to articulate a broadly acceptable conceptual framework that would provide the unifying theoretical base upon which a coherent system of accounting practice might be constructed. Its principal features are:

- The subordination of concepts such as matching and prudence to recognition tests.
- A greater emphasis on the balance sheet and its constituent parts.
- A gradual evolution from the historical cost approach to one in which assets and liabilities are stated at "value to the business".

- A corresponding downgrading of the profit and loss account where increases or decreases in wealth are viewed as net changes in the carrying values of assets and liabilities in the balance sheet.

- Useful advances in identifying criteria to be applied for recognition and measurement purposes.

IASC/IASB Framework

At the same time as the FASB was engaged on its conceptual framework project, and prior to the ASB undertaking its venture, the IASC had embarked on a conceptual framework project of its own. Its aspirations were complicated, however, by the fact that developing an international framework requires that the interests and biases of a variety of countries be negotiated. Thus, for instance, while Anglo-American regulators favour frameworks that emphasize the interests of the investor, continental European countries are less comfortable with this bias. In addition, the interests of developed and developing countries will often be diametrically opposed.

Nevertheless, in 1989 the IASC published its own ED, *Framework for the Presentation and Preparation of Financial Statements* that drew heavily on the US framework project. This document dealt with a variety of issues that Trueblood in particular had identified. Specifically it addressed:

- **Objectives of financial statements**: essentially its conclusions were that financial statements should provide decision-useful information to a variety of users to inform and assist them when making economic decisions.

- **Qualitative characteristics of financial statements**: the principal characteristics were identified as reliability and relevance. However, comparability was also strongly emphasized, particularly in the sense that it interacted with other key factors.

- **Elements of financial statements**: in identifying assets, liabilities and equity as critical elements, the IASC was closely following SFAC No. 6. Thus, when dealing with assets, it stated that "future economic benefit embodied in an asset is the potential to contribute, directly or indirectly, to the flow of cash and cash equivalents to the enterprise".

- **Recognition**: again this linked to the extent to which a transaction could be shown to have impacted upon the assets or liabilities of an entity.

- **Measurement**: the document was significant in recognizing that various measurement bases exist. However, like its US counterpart, it did not elaborate on circumstances in which one method might be preferable to another. In fact, it specifically stated that it did not see it as part of its function at that time to be prescriptive.

The dominant Anglo-American model, with its strong bias in favour of the interests of the private investor, has, therefore, been influential in shaping the thinking and approach of the IASB. One consequence of this is that the IASB Framework is vulnerable to the same criticisms to which the FASB and ASB equivalents have been exposed. And in the light of both ongoing accounting scandals and, more particularly, the political and conceptual difficulties that have surrounded the introduction of specific standards these have gathered momentum.

One response by regulators has been agreement between IASB and FASB on researching a joint conceptual framework. This joint conceptual framework project offers the prospect of a more harmonized approach to standard setting on a global basis. This will be discussed in more detail in Chapter 15.

FASB Returns Again to the Philosophy of Accounting, by Glenn Cheney

The Financial Accounting Standards Board is going back to that deep, dark place where accounting standards come from – the conceptual framework that underlies it all. FASB isn't going alone. Holding its hand in this cooperative, philosophical expedition is the International Accounting Standards Board. Ideally, the two boards will come to similar or identical conclusions about the fundamental principles on which accounting standards rest.

The conceptual framework is a coherent system of interrelated objectives and fundamentals that prescribe the nature, concept, function, objective and limitations of financial reporting. This is very abstract," said FASB senior project manager Halsey Bullen. "We are a couple of steps removed from standards. This concepts project won't lead directly to any changes in financial reporting. It may remove logjams and help us reach solutions more readily, but it doesn't create standards." Both FASB and the IASB have already established conceptual frameworks, but the frameworks don't always agree with each other. FASB issued its current framework in the form of "concepts statements," the first appearing in 1978, and all but one coming out by 1985. The most recent appeared in 2000.

Noting that "without a set of unified concepts, standard-setters are like a ship in a storm without an anchor," Bullen said that it's time for another look at the fundamental building blocks of accounting and reporting. "The framework wasn't really completed when we worked on it in the original effort," Bullen said. "It's been 20 years since then, and things have changed in the business world, and maybe things in the framework should change in response." Bullen pointed out that a solid conceptual framework is essential to the development of principles-based accounting standards. The board is making an effort to promulgate standards that are based more on principles, rather than on prescriptive rules.

FASB and the IASB have been working together to develop identical or similar standards and to converge existing standards to a common form. In doing so, they have noticed that they have been basing their decisions on frameworks that

> are similar, but not identical. Bullen said that the difference between the concepts of the two boards is mostly in the way that the concepts are expressed. But the differences in wording, he said, can result in differences in interpretation and subsequent differences – and conflicts – in standards.
>
> Source: *WebCPA*, August 29, 2005.

Fair Value

As has already been pointed out, many of the fundamental challenges facing accounting are often categorized (somewhat simplistically) as either recognition (*what* to include in accounts) or measurement (at what *value* to include items) issues. With the decision of the IASB to favour 'Fair Value' as a valuation basis, measurement has again become a topical and critical issue.

For centuries accountants have used historic cost as the most appropriate basis when considering at what 'value' to incorporate items into the accounting process. This ensured a conservative approach, while, at the same time, mirroring the directors' stewardship responsibilities.

As the following article highlights, the adoption of 'fair value' is both momentous and likely to lead to some radical changes in accounting information and its use:

Switch Over

Peter Williams Reports on the Implications of the New Accounting Standards

The introduction of international accounting standards across many countries from the start of this year represents a radical new approach to financial reporting. This is more than just a new set of accounting standards with detailed rules which have to be learnt and applied. The accounting standards being drawn up and implemented by the International Accounting Standards Board represent a dramatic shift from the traditional basis of preparing accounts – the historical cost based method – to the more complicated and uncertain model of fair value accounting.

The focus of financial reporting is now providing information for the capital markets and the accounting standards are designed primarily for use in consolidated accounts [i.e., the accounts of large groups]. The price of such a switch is that concepts that accountants across the globe were trained to see as fundamental to the whole basis of accounting – prudence, realization, accruals/matching – are being downgraded in importance. Accountants grew up believing that it was better to be "reliable" rather than relevant. This led to the criticism that accounts didn't help management or investors enough, so now relevance is seen as more important than pedantic reliability. As part of this, financial reporting is becoming less concerned with recording transactions and instead is looking more at the measurement of assets and liabilities.

The heart of this debate focuses on measurement in accounts. How should assets and liabilities be recognized and capitalized in the balance sheet? There are many potential bases but the one that has been used up to now is historical or actual cost. In its place, the IASB is increasingly using "fair value" – which in an IASB report is defined as "the amount at which an asset could be exchanged between knowledgeable and willing parties in an arms-length transaction".

The question is whether the move by the IASB towards fair value accounting has really been properly thought through and understood by both the preparers of accounts and the users, including capital market regulators. The European banking industry certainly understood what fair values meant for them in terms of the financial instrument standard and as a result forced the European Union to adopt a "carved out" standard. And certainly there is widespread opposition to the fair value concept which leads to significant charges in the income statement for providing share options.

Some accounting experts are angry with the IASB, believing that it is, in effect, conducting an academic experiment in accounting on a grand scale. Many say fair values for items such as financial instruments don't really exist and can only be found by companies producing complex theoretical models which are unintelligible to anyone other than skilled mathematicians. Much of this academic thinking emerged when the major economic preoccupation across the world was dealing with inflation. In the current low-inflation era that problem seems passé.

The IASB is convinced it is right to produce accounting standards which portray more accurately economic reality, even if that means wild swings in reported numbers which simply exposes the reality of the volatility that many businesses face, and the switch at first confuses investors.

It should be noted that for unquoted private companies which don't deal with complicated treasury operations, nor have large pensions funds, complex leasing arrangements and stock option schemes, the switch over would not actually produce radically different accounts than they are used to. But for the world's large global companies the switch over is potentially dramatic.

The trend away from historical cost to fair value is a gradual one and the standards have in-built transitional arrangements. Many people would agree that fair value up to a point is a good thing. Why not adjust the balance sheet to reflect a more accurate valuation of a company's fixed assets such as land and building? On the other hand, many have concerns over how far the IASB want to drive the concept. Whether the IASB is allowed to push fair value to the limits remains to be seen.

Peter Williams is a freelance journalist and a chartered accountant. He writes on accounting, financial reporting and auditing issues.

Source: *accounting & business*, February 2005.

As this article points out, the change confirms a fundamental paradigm shift amongst accountants and regulators: the focus is now on providing information for the capital markets, as distinct from the more traditional focus that was informed by considerations of conservatism and prudence. Accounts will now seek to capture economic reality, even at the expense of introducing more volatility.

The theoretical issues raised are brought out in the following extract, which highlights many similar points.

In Search of Needles in a Data Haystack

Jane Fuller Examines Some of the Knock-On Effects Emerging From The Spread of International Financial Reporting Standards

International financial reporting standards, spreading across Europe and elsewhere, may not be quite as detailed as US standards, but they have enough bulk to prompt the question of whether we will be able to see the wood for the trees. One way of looking at it is that the spread of IFRS marks a territorial gain for some clear trends in financial reporting.

The first is fair value accounting, which switches valuations from historic cost towards market values. Where inadequate markets prevent the application of fair value, its companion, "value in use", pops up, using methods that rely on discounted cashflow forecasts.

There are two crucial points about this trend. The first is the forward-looking nature of the information and the second is that management's view of value is being subjected to external tests. This supports the aim put forward in the framework – that accounts should help users make economic decisions. Notably, they should aid investors to allocate capital to companies with the best chance of securing good returns. Critics say this mars accounts as a record of the directors' stewardship of shareholders' assets. It is not hard, however, to regard changes in market values of those assets during the period as relevant to the assessment of that stewardship...

Source: *Financial Times*, February 24, 2005.

Summary

The need for a conceptual framework is now broadly accepted. What is in dispute is the form it should take and the fundamental principles it should embrace. While much of the debate has become mired in detail it is helpful to remember that most difficulty revolves around the twin issues of recognition and measurement. And the solutions devised differ. For instance, while in the US the FASB has been widely criticized for opting to retain the historic cost approach, in the UK the IASB has been widely criticized for trying to adopt a valuation scheme based on fair value.

Nevertheless, some common ground has been established:

- It is now generally accepted that whatever framework is devised it must be sensitive to user requirements in an environment in which financial statements are now but one source of information.

- Recognition and measurement have been identified as fundamental issues to be addressed.

- Increased disclosure may provide one means of satisfying user requirements without impinging on the accounting process.

While some progress has been made, further progress needs to be made, particularly under the Joint Conceptual Framework Project of FASB and IASB.

Review Questions

Question 1
Outline what is meant by the phrase "conceptual framework" and explain what the practical impact of having such a framework might be for accounting.

Question 2
Compare and contrast the experiences of accounting and economics in terms of the presence or absence of a conceptual framework.

Question 3
Outline the history of the "search" for a conceptual framework in the US. In particular discuss the role of the Trueblood Committee in setting the agenda for conceptual framework projects both in the US and elsewhere.

Question 4
Summarize the key elements of SFACs 1, 2, 5 and 6. Identify themes common to each as well as internal inconsistencies.

Question 5
"In providing definitions for such key elements as assets and liabilities, SFAC 6 represented a seminal document in the development of an accounting framework". Explain.

Question 6
Compare and contrast the IASB's *Framework for the Presentation and Preparation of Financial Statements*, with its US equivalent.

Question 7
To what extent could SSAP 2, *Disclosure of Accounting Policies*, be considered to have provided an adequate conceptual framework for the UK?

Question 8
Identify the role of the *Corporate Report*, the *Sandilands Report*, and various other contributions in identifying both a need for, and the likely elements of, a conceptual framework.

Question 9
Explain what is meant by 'Fair value' and why its acceptance as a valuation paradigm by IASB may prove controversial.

Case Studies

Case 1

The following article deals with the conceptual framework, particularly the challenges faced by FASB and IASB in devising a joint framework. However, it also specifically links issues surrounding valuation – fair value in particular – and attempts to show how these must integrate within the broader considerations of any framework. Consider the view of Paul McCrossan, one of the IASB's panel experts, that "the IASB and FASB could solve a lot of problems in existing and future standards if they could just get their framework right".

IASB – Model Solutions, by John House

McCrossan sent the IASB a wake-up call. His message was straightforward: the IASB's conceptual framework is 30 years out of date, and if it wants its revised framework to reflect the economic reality of today's financial markets it had better get in some expert help.

As part of their convergence efforts, the IASB and the US Financial Accounting Standards Board agreed last October to revise their conceptual frameworks. McCrossan told Tweedie that the IASB and FASB could solve a lot of problems in existing and future standards if they could just get their framework right. According to McCrossan, the fundamental issue that must be taken into account in any revised version of the framework is the way fair value is derived. Fair value is not difficult to ascertain in a deep and liquid market. But when there are no deep and liquid markets to observe, the preparer has to use statistical probabilities to calculate fair value. 'Both buyers and sellers will base the transaction prices on their probabilistic expectations of future events.' However, the IASB conceptual framework does not include clear guidance on how probabilities should be used to derive fair values.

Reflecting Economic Reality

'The purpose of accounting is to produce a true and fair reflection of the economic reality,' states McCrossan. 'If the purpose of accounting is to reflect economic reality, accountants have to do what the economists do.' According to McCrossan, the framework has not been adapted to the changes that have happened in the last 30 years. In manufacturing and other traditional industries this is not a problem. 'But in the financial sector, the product is money and the market is in tune with the latest economic theories. So they want reporting to reflect the economic reality.'

McCrossan says that a framework that takes into account modern economic theory will also be essential for the IASB's performance reporting project. 'Performance reporting must reflect operations and finance,' he explains. 'For material product companies it's easy to differentiate between operations and finance. But when the product is finance it's hard to distinguish between the two.' He says that no one would expect the standard-setters to have knowledge of the intricacies of economic theories employed in the financial sector. However, 'one would expect them to consult experts about these matters'. McCrossan's message to Tweedie is that 'the economists and actuaries are experts in the use of probabilities and we can bring that expertise to the IASB for them to use'.

Advanced Warning

The IASB has yet to start its joint re-write of the conceptual framework with its convergence partner, the US FASB, and it has said that it is open to suggestions. IASB board member Jim Leisenring told the SAC that both the IASB framework and the US FASB framework lack clarity on fundamental issues like definitions of assets and liabilities. Leisenring welcomed McCrossan's comments and said that he recognized that vague language is a problem and that there is a need to define assets and liabilities unequivocally.

Bob Herz, US FASB chairman, told Accountancy that he agrees that inconsistencies in the framework are an obstacle to coming up with standards on financial instruments, insurance and contingent assets and liabilities. 'That's why we're looking at this project to resolve some of the thorny issues that keep coming up.' Herz says the question of when and how probabilities should be used to arrive at a market value 'will be a point of debate'. He adds that there will be plenty of opportunity to influence the way the boards write their shared framework: 'People are going to be very involved and have lots and lots of advanced warning.'

Paul Cherry, chairman of the Canadian Accounting Standards Board, told Accountancy that he accepts that the IASB framework is grounded in outdated accounting practices. The conceptual frameworks of the IASB and the FASB, as well as his own board, 'reflect old economic models and traditional industry'. However, he is not convinced that the framework is 'the impediment to progress on fair value'.

Source: *Accountancy*, April 2005.

Case 2

The following article takes a more critical view of both the conceptual framework project and Fair Value, pointing out a number of potential difficulties. For instance, it highlights some of the inconsistencies between the valuation models discussed in the Framework and the adoption of Fair Value. It also points to a number of potential political problems revolving around the roles of national and international regulators. Discuss the proposition presented in the final paragraph that "international standards are being written without an effective conceptual framework".

Conceptual Framework – Which Way Forward?
By David Bence and Nadine Fry

When the International Accounting Standards Board (IASB) was instituted in 2001, it adopted many of its predecessor's regulations, most noticeably the 1989 Framework for the Preparation and Presentation of Financial Statements. The Framework is increasingly out-of-date given the complex and shifting nature of financial reporting.

For example, in relation to the valuation of assets and liabilities, the Framework lists the available options (historical cost, replacement cost, net realizable value, and present value), but fails to recommend the preferred measurement technique. The Framework was written in an era when there was a search for a single value-based model of income and thus there is no formal recognition of a 'mixed measurement' system.

Fair Value Concerns

A further illustration of how the Framework is out of date is the concept of fair value, which the IASB accepted as the 'relevant measurable attribute' in October 2003 as part of its revenue recognition project... Many existing (and proposed) International Financial Reporting Standards (IFRSs) are based on the concept of 'fair value', yet it is not referred to in the Framework.

If the IASB's movement towards the worldwide adoption of IFRSs is to be successful, the establishment of a more coherent international conceptual framework is necessary. This is particularly important given the IASB's principles-based, as opposed to rules-based, approach to standard-setting, and the political interest in accounting regulation.

However, the IASB has no plans to re-issue its 1989 Framework; although this would appear to be the most logical place to start if the IASB is to ensure that its output is theoretically sound. As a result of ignoring the need to harmonize conceptual frameworks, inconsistent standards are being developed.

So far, harmonization has only arisen at the standards level with the convergence of national and international standards. Discrepancies still arise between conceptual frameworks and standards at both the national and international level.

Although the IASB has stated that it will be guided by the Framework in its review of existing IFRSs and the development of future standards, there is much evidence to suggest that the reverse is true and that many conceptual issues are being inherently decided in the development of new standards. Although there may be some differences between national conceptual frameworks and standards, such differences are much more exaggerated at the international level as the IASB's framework is so archaic in nature.

Two Options

If the IASB were to re-write its Framework, it would have two options – to base it on either national frameworks or IFRSs. If it were to adopt the former option, any differences between the international conceptual framework and IFRSs would be the same as those identified at the national level. In any event, such an approach would be inappropriate, as other national standard- setters' frameworks are also out of date.

National frameworks will become even more outdated as the harmonization process proceeds at the standards level. The IASB will therefore have to base any new Framework on existing international standards, resulting in differences between national and international frameworks. However, IFRSs themselves are contradictory making the construction of a new Framework from existing standards highly problematic. Whichever way one looks at it, there will be inconsistencies because conceptual frameworks were not harmonized in the first instance.

To conclude, it appears that international standards are being written without an effective conceptual framework. The quality control over the production of international standards is therefore questionable and re-writing of the Framework should be placed on the IASB's agenda.

David Bence and Nadine Fry are senior lecturers at the Bristol Business School.

Source: *Accountancy*, November 2004.

THEORETICAL CONTEXT [3]

When you have completed this chapter you will understand that:

- Accounting information is a commodity that can be traded in a market.
- There are various theories that seek to explain the role of accounting information in these markets.
- The dominant paradigm over the course of recent decades has been the market-based perspective.
- The most important of these market-based theories has been the Efficient Market Hypothesis (EMH) or Theory (EMT).
- EMH poses a number of significant challenges to those who prepare and use accounting information.
- More recently the dominance of EMH has been challenged by other paradigms.

Ivan the Actuary has a Conspiracy Theory, by Terry Bond

My brain hurts. I've just spent two hours with Ivan the Actuary, a number-cruncher who makes up for his boring days at the investment bank genuflecting to his Bentley-driving bosses and ingratiating himself with the plutocratic customers, by turning belligerent when he enters the pub. He's not even an acquaintance so it is a surprise when he singles me out in the early evening crowd at the City Tup in Gresham Street.

"I read that piece of yours in the Indy," he says. "Load of rubbish. Absolute drivel. You're misleading people, telling them to identify undervalued growth shares. There's no such thing, mate. You're worse than Russell Grant and his stars. Haven't you ever heard of the Efficient Markets Hypothesis? The Random

Walk theory?'' Foolishly, I simply say: ''Sorry?'' It is all Ivan needs. A supplicant ear that will listen while he expounds his two great theories. Of course I have heard the phrases, efficient markets hypothesis and random walk theory, but I cannot define them precisely. Rather than admit the gap in my knowledge I let Ivan rabbit on.

Let's take efficient markets hypothesis. This says the price of a share at any given time incorporates all the relevant information available so it is the correct price and reflects the true value. So there is little point in investors re-analysing the facts or applying their sieves or theories hoping they will be able to spot winners. ''You see, mate, you've got your buyers and you've got your sellers,'' says Ivan patiently. ''The sellers sell their shares because they believe they are worth less than the selling price. The buyers buy their shares because they believe they are worth more than the selling price. The buyers and the sellers have the same information available so they create an efficient market. Trying to beat it is a gamble, not a skill.''

The random walk theory comes to a similar conclusion by a different route. It says share prices haven't got brains or memories so there is little point in using past performance to predict the future movements. ''Complete waste of time,'' says Ivan. ''The thing that moves prices is new information and the adjustment is so fast that there's no time to profit from it.'' He pauses to sip the top off the pint which I seem to have unaccountably paid for. It is my chance for a edgeways word. ''But if the investor does his analysis properly he can anticipate new information,'' I say. ''An exercise in futility,'' says Ivan. ''If you can predict it so can everybody else so it is already factored into the price. In any case, no one knows what is going to happen tomorrow. Forecasting is a waste of time. It's like forgetting your phone number then trying to guess it.''

Statistics, he says, are on his side. ''Look at the performance of the mutual funds,'' he says. ''Investment trusts and unit trusts. Most fail to beat the market and they employ what are laughingly supposed to be the best brains in the City.''

Ivan reckons that for decades there has been a conspiracy in the financial world to decry the efficient markets hypothesis and the random walk theory because if they were accepted as being correct thousands of City experts would be out of a job and we private investors would not know what to do with ourselves. His answer: buy and hold. ''Only one thing's certain, mate. Over time the market rises. Buy a tracker fund and sit tight.'' But surely that's taking what's happened in the past and using it to predict the future? I think it but I don't say it because it would prolong our one-sided conversation.

On the train home I have a chance for quiet contemplation. Ignoring Ivan's bombastic approach, he does have what seems to be a valid argument. I think it all through carefully and come to a personal conclusion: the efficient markets hypothesis and the random walk theory are bunkum. Equity markets are highly inefficient because they are not controlled only by facts. They are influenced by such ephemeral emotions as fear, greed, sentiment and fashion. There's nothing efficient or predictable about those. Share prices are not established solely by a set of predictable criteria. Dot.com mania and price-earnings figures in the hundreds graphically illustrate that. But any further thoughts on this matter can be discussed with Ivan in the City Tup. Unfortunately I will not be there.

Source: *The Independent*, July 7, 2001.

Introduction

The question being addressed in this chapter is "What is the relationship between accounting information and the market?" specifically the stock market, where, as the opening vignette explains, suppliers of information meet those seeking to acquire it. In other words, the intention is to seek to understand the significance and impact of accounting information by asking how it impacts upon market measures such as share price.

In order to consider this it is necessary first to explore some of the theoretical approaches, such as the Efficient Markets Hypothesis (EMH), that are more commonly employed to explain the role of such information. The significance of a theoretical model is that it can be employed to either explain something that has already happened or to predict what may happen. A theory's capacity in this regard will, however, be directly related to the degree to which it describes the "real" world. Herein lies one of the problems with theories: many incorporate such a range of assumptions that they no longer approximate to the reality they are trying to describe.

Nevertheless, simplifications such as these are often required in order to construct initial hypotheses. Subsequently, as empirical testing indicates, the model may be refined and should conform more to reality. Repeating this process then allows the model to be further refined.

As the following summary explains, these theoretical approaches not only help to explain and predict, but have themselves become catalysts for change:

Secrets of Success: Simple Lessons from a Wise Teacher, by Jonathan Davis

Most investors have little direct exposure to financial theory, and few seem to feel that they suffer very much as a result. The way it is presented in the standard textbooks is unexciting, to put it mildly. Even those "like MBA students" who feel they have to go through the process in order to advance their careers, rarely seem to come away with a profound understanding of the revolution in financial theory of the last 40 years.

Yet there has been a wave of theoretical advances in the way that we think about finance and investment since the late 1960s. In turn, this has completely transformed the way that financial markets operate. Way back then, to take one example, there was no financial futures market in which investors could hedge their risks. Now it is a multi-billion- dollar business that underpins the relentless growth of global capital markets and the consequent broadening of opportunities for millions of investors.

Way back then, there was no such thing, either, as an index fund, an innovation that has, whether they know it or not, materially improved the lot of millions of ordinary investors. Most importantly of all, there was only minimal understanding of what risk in financial markets was, and how it could be managed, not entirely surprising when we lacked basic reliable data on the behaviour of different asset classes over time. Now, however, we understand this issue a whole lot better, even if we cannot (and will never be able to) eliminate risk from our lives.

All three of these developments can be traced directly to some of the important advances in financial theory made since the late 1960s by groups of academics, mainly working in the United States. Allied to the widespread availability of computing power, their efforts mean, as successive Nobel Prize committees have acknowledged, that it is now possible for investors of all kinds to participate more safely in fair and liquid markets in a wide range of financial instruments that our forebears never had the chance to use.

Source: *The Independent*, July 30, 2005.

When considering accounting information and the role it plays in the modern capital-market economy it is necessary to speculate about the nature of accounting information and the way in which the market assimilates it. A number of different approaches have been adopted. However, they can basically be divided into three streams of thought, each reflecting different approaches to information at the macro-economic level as disseminated through more general theoretical developments in economics and finance. Each will be examined in turn.

The first of these is the Classical approach which predominated in accounting circles until the 1970s. Since that time market-based theories have been dominant and the bulk of this chapter is devoted to explaining the impact of this paradigm. Finally, Positive Accounting Theory and the impact it has had on accounting thought and practice is considered.

In order to make its point this chapter introduces various concepts from finance theory. These are merely means to an end, however, and should not be allowed to distract from the fundamental issue being addressed. Thus, mathematical constructs outlined here can be safely ignored by the fainthearted. The goal should simply be to appreciate that an understanding of accounting information is fundamentally impacted by the theoretical perspective from which it is viewed.[1]

Classical Theory

Finance theory in the decades following the Second World War inclined to the view that all financial instruments, for example shares, had a certain intrinsic value. This value, it was assumed, could be verified by financial analysis techniques which extracted the supporting data from the financial accounts of a business. The

[1] The structure of this chapter draws on White, G.I., et al. *The Analysis and Use of Financial Statements*, 2nd edn., pp. 215–256.

Classical (or Normative) approach, dominant in the academic accounting community particularly during the 1960s and early 1970s, reflected this perspective.

This approach assumes that it is possible to identify and measure the intrinsic value of a firm and evaluate the efficacy of the accounting function with that in mind. In other words, accounting practices are gauged in terms of how close they come to reporting the "true" economic reality about the firm.

Because there was a presumption that accounting can, in some sense, measure and report the "true" situation about a firm, the research emphasis was primarily on determining those accounting practices best suited to achieving this end. As a consequence a dynamic developed in which a preconceived notion of the intrinsic value of a firm was constructed which was in turn confirmed by techniques which it was assumed could measure this value. Academic energy was devoted therefore to developing and promulgating accounting practices that were presumed to be correct, rather than to testing these assumptions by means of empirical research.

Indeed, it is possible to argue that this perspective persists in the regulatory regimes in both the UK and the US which, in the main, have held to the Normative paradigm that a measurable economic reality exists which can best be captured by accounting methods as promulgated by accounting standards.

Market-Based Theory

It was partly as a reaction to this rather myopic approach, but also in response to developments in finance theory which moved the perspective to the decision needs of the user, that the Classical approach gradually gave way to the market-based paradigm.

While the Classical approach assumes that an underlying reality exists which accounting can best capture, market-based theory sees reality as something that the market determines, and in which process the accounting alternatives adopted make no difference. This approach posits that information can only be evaluated in the context of its effect upon users of that information, rather than in terms of any implicit reality that it purports to describe.

This perspective has had a number of fundamental implications for accounting and accounting research:

- One of the criticisms of the Classical approach was that it could not be tested. Market-based theory, by definition, was based on an empirical testing of the actual usefulness of the information content of accounting disclosures.

- The focus was on the needs of users – as distinct from preparers – of accounting information.

- Rather than presuming the existence of "correct" accounting practices, it was now possible to test how different practices impacted upon the usefulness of the accounting information and whether specific accounting practices existed which most suited user needs.

Portfolio Theory

This market-based approach was facilitated by developments in finance theory, such as the emergence of portfolio theory, particularly as mediated through the Capital Asset Pricing Model (CAPM).

A portfolio is simply a combination of various investments. Whether or not an investor chooses to invest in a security such as a share will depend upon a variety of factors, for example, price, expected capital growth, dividends and tax planning considerations. However, the principal requirement will be that the investment should yield a return proportionate to the risk involved. In finance theory risk is normally taken to refer to the chance that a cash flow or other return will not materialize as expected. For example, if an investor anticipates a return of 8%, but there is a probability that the return will be less, then the investor is assuming a risk.

Naturally, it would be of considerable advantage in constructing a portfolio if the associated risk could be quantified. Yet this would require an assessment of the probability of all possible future return profiles. Obviously this would involve an element of guesswork and could never be achieved with complete confidence. However, it is generally accepted that recent past performance can be taken as a reasonable guide to probable future returns.

But, if even this somewhat tenuous connection is accepted, difficulties remain in assessing the nature of the information contained in such probabilities. One option is to compare the projected distribution of returns with those for another security. Typically the approach adopted is to express the projected returns in terms of some statistical technique. One particularly suitable method is to assess the profile in terms of the mean and the standard deviation. These are appropriate for this exercise because, assuming a normal distribution, the standard deviation from the mean, since it is a measure of dispersion, can be used as a measure of risk: a low standard deviation indicates a low anticipated variability from the expected mean, that is, a relatively low risk, while a high standard deviation implies a high risk.

The following extract narrates how Harry Markowitz, one of the pioneers of portfolio theory, developed his ideas:

> On the other hand, investors *can* manage the risks that they take. Higher risk should in time produce more wealth, but only for investors who can stand the heat. As these simple truths grew increasingly obvious over the course of the 1970s Markowitz became a household name among professional investors and their clients.
>
> Markowitz's objective in 'Portfolio Selection' was to use the notion of risk to construct portfolios for investors who 'consider expected return a desirable thing *and* variance of return an undesirable thing,' The italicized 'and' that links return and variance is the fulcrum on which Markowitz builds his case.

> Markowitz makes no mention of the word 'risk' in describing his investment strategy. He simply identifies variance of return as the 'undesirable thing' that investors try to minimize. Risk and variance have become synonymous. Von Neumann and Morgenstern had put a number on utility; Markowitz put a number on investment risk.
>
> Variance is a statistical measurement of how widely the returns on an asset swing around their average. The concept is mathematically linked to the standard deviation; in fact, the two are essentially interchangeable. The greater the variance or the standard deviation around the average, the less the average return will signify about what the outcome is likely to be. A high-variance situation lands you back in the head-in-the-oven-feet-in-the-refrigerator syndrome.
>
> Source: Peter L. Bernstein, *Against the Gods*, Wiley 1996, p. 252.

This capacity to measure risk is important, since portfolio theory is concerned with identifying portfolios of securities that reduce risk through diversification on the assumption that investors are risk-averse, i.e., faced with a choice between two securities that offer the same return, the investor will choose the one with the lowest risk. In terms of the statistical techniques just described this can be restated as "faced with a choice between two securities that offer the same return, the investor will choose the one with the lowest standard deviation".

In terms of portfolio theory this has further significance in that, as the number of shares in the portfolio increases, the standard deviation for the portfolio as a whole decreases. For example, if an investor decides to put half of his or her funds into a software company and the other half into a retail chain then any misfortunes (resulting in negative variations) in one may be offset to some extent by the fortunes of the other. In other words, it is possible to reduce risk, although never eliminate it, by means of diversification.

In practice:

Eggs in the investment basket need to be of varied hues, by Edmond Warner

Overheard on the 6:41 from Bognor Regis to London Bridge:

Student One: "We did modern portfolio theory yesterday. It was hard but I really enjoyed it."

Student Two: "Yeah? What did it tell you?"

Student One: "Well, for starters, you should own shares in both sun lotion manufacturers and umbrella manufacturers."

Student Two: "Yeah, but what if the weather's just cloudy and dry?"

Student One: "Dunno."

One answer is that the canny marketing men at both Acme Sun Creams and Universal Umbrellas will persuade a gullible public to buy each of their products, just in case the weather takes a turn for either the better or the worse. So both will prosper. Another is that shares in both ASC and UU will broadly move up and down in tandem, their fluctuations dictated by the financial rather than the meteorological weather.

The rise of the large investment management houses was driven by modern portfolio theory, which (no longer so modern now) enjoyed its heyday in the 1980s. Investors were urged by its proponents to contemplate the benefits of diversification. Quantitative analysts drew up efficient frontier curves that purported to show how to achieve any given target rate of investment return at the lowest possible risk.

Investment was not just about picking stocks but about choosing the perfect combination of baskets among which to distribute one's nest eggs. Diversification takes two forms: owning a range of asset classes (bonds, shares, property, commodities and so on), and owning a range of investments within each class. . .

Source: The Guardian, August 1, 2005.

As the portfolio increases and the standard deviation of the portfolio as a whole accordingly decreases, the return attributable to this portfolio begins, more and more, to correspond to the return enjoyed by the market as a whole. Obviously, if the portfolio included all equities quoted on the market its return would correspond exactly to the market return. Interestingly, recent research suggests that the number of stocks necessary to gain effective diversification can be as low as eight or ten, provided there is a good mix of both size and sector.

In practice:

Take Buffet's advice and play to your assets: diversification is a good policy, but only in moderation, discovers Kathy Foley

Investment advisers have long beaten the diversification drum, stressing the importance of distributing money across different asset classes, sectors and markets. When capital is spread too thinly across too many assets, however, returns can be cancelled out by losses and acquisition costs can prove too high to be recouped.

Warren Buffett, the grandfather of investment gurus, once underscored the dangers of over-diversification, saying: "If you have a harem of 40 women, you never get to know any of them very well."

In other words, investors with large, unwieldy portfolios will find it very difficult to keep track of every asset and how it is performing. "If a fund holds a couple of hundred stocks, it is very hard to get excited about it because no matter how strong the fund manager is, it will be hard to keep an eye on them all," said Peter O'Reilly of the Finance Business, an authorised adviser. "And if one goes up in value, what difference does that really make to the fund? The same tenets apply to private investors.''

Of course, a certain amount of diversification is key to successful investing because it acts to eliminate risk. An investor who only owns one asset will be financially ruined if it fails. An investor with 10 assets should be able to take the pain if one bottoms out, as the returns from the others will neutralise the loss. Buying up all sorts of assets just to achieve diversification is an overly cautious and ultimately pointless strategy, however. The portfolio risk might fall to almost zero but the chances of earning an above-average return will also be smoothed out.

''There is definitely a risk-return trade-off so you have to be prudent and diversify,'' said O'Reilly, ''but I would err more on the side of trying to get bang for my buck while not jeopardising my risk profile.'' Those who follow a selective diversification path and concentrate on 10 or 20 assets also remain flexible. They can keep a close eye on their holdings and move quickly to take profits or minimise losses if prices move dramatically.

Source: Sunday Times, July 24, 2005.

CAPM

The Capital Asset Pricing Model (CAPM) builds on portfolio theory, but extends it to incorporate a measure of the relationship between risk and return. Essentially it is concerned with demonstrating how the minimum return required of a security is a function of its riskiness.

It makes a number of assumptions:

- All investors are rational, wealth maximizers

- Investors are risk averse

- Standard deviation is the most appropriate measure of risk

- There are no transaction costs, information has no cost and is available to all

- All investors can borrow and lend at the risk-free rate, i.e., the rate enjoyed on risk free investments such as government bonds

- All investors have similar expectations about future returns.

A portfolio of shares may commence with just one security, but the usual pattern will be for additional securities to be added over time. According to portfolio theory, as the number of securities in the portfolio increases the standard deviation (the measure of risk) decreases. In other words, the relevant risk to be considered when deciding whether or not to incorporate a security into a portfolio is not the total risk associated with it, *but the effect its incorporation would have on the riskiness of the portfolio as a whole.*

CAPM is a technique that allows this marginal effect to be measured by subdividing the risk element of a security into its component parts:

- The element that can be diversified away, i.e., unsystematic risk, for example, the risks particular to that firm such as its susceptibility to strikes. This will be diversified away by the fact that the portfolio will include other securities which will not be susceptible to such risk.

- The element that cannot be diversified away, i.e., the systematic (or market) risk. This is the element of risk deriving from considerations common to all firms in the market such as macro-economic issues, inflation, etc.

Since unsystematic risk will be diversified away in any balanced portfolio, CAPM posits that the only element of risk that needs to be assessed when deciding whether or not to include a security in a portfolio is its systematic risk. This is because it is the only element of risk which the portfolio will be rewarded for taking. A security with a high correlation to variations in the market, i.e., a high systematic risk, will do relatively little to reduce the risk element of a portfolio and, therefore, will be required to produce a high return. Correspondingly, a security with a low systematic risk is useful as a means of reducing the riskiness of a portfolio and, consequently, will only be required to yield a lower return.

The issue becomes, then, how to properly quantify the systematic risk element of a security, i.e., the degree of correlation to variations in the market.

The method used by CAPM to do this is an index, normally referred to as the beta (β) of a security. There are two bases to this index:

- **The risk-free security**: such a security, for example a government bond, carries no risk and, therefore, no systematic risk. It is assigned a beta of zero.

- **The market portfolio**: a market portfolio represents complete diversification and, as a result, only contains risks that can be specifically attributed to the market, i.e., it would be expected to replicate market movements exactly. This is assigned a beta of 1.

Every security will have a beta that can be expressed in terms of these bases. For example, a security with a β of 0.8 can be said to be less volatile than the market as a whole, one with a β of 1.1 is more volatile than the market as a whole, while one with a β of 0.05 shows very little volatility.

The importance of CAPM is that it provides a useful model of expected returns, relating them to a measure of risk, β, which quantifies the degree of relationship between that security and the market. Ideally, what should be determined for a security is its future β. In practice, however, past betas are usually taken as an appropriate basis upon which to appraise required returns.

Since, therefore, both the return and the risk on the market portfolio are known it is possible to express the relationship between them as follows:

$$E(R_p) = R_f + \beta(E(R_m) - R_f)$$

where $E(R_p)$ is the expected return on the security; R_f is the risk-free return; $E(R_m) - R_f$ is the risk premium on the market, i.e., the marginal return investors enjoy by taking market-related risk and in the UK it has traditionally been in the range of 6–9%; β is the riskiness of the security relative to the market.[2]

In reality many of the assumptions underlying the CAPM are transgressed. For example, a risk-free rate is difficult to identify because of inflation. It is also unrealistic to expect that all investors will have equal access and capacity to borrow and lend funds at this rate. Furthermore, there are obvious problems with calculating beta on the basis of past results. In addition, there are other difficulties with the model, since, for example, it only assesses the level of return, not its constituent parts, such as capital gains and dividends. For some investors these may be important considerations.

Notwithstanding this, analysts are concerned not so much with the underlying assumptions as with whether or not the model "works" in terms of explaining returns on the market. Empirical testing of CAPM yields somewhat ambiguous results. Nevertheless, until recently, the general consensus was that the model was relatively robust and does approximate to real world conditions, in that it demonstrates a strong relationship between systematic risk and rate of return.

Since it suggests that the expected return for a firm is not dependent upon risks that can be diversified away, with the obvious corollary that information regarding the prospects for a particular security is irrelevant, CAPM has had a major impact upon accounting theory and practice. Specifically, it questions the usefulness of company-specific accounting data to investors. In so doing it challenges the rationale for the production and analysis of such information. The real issue, CAPM suggests, is its systematic risk, expressed in terms of its beta.

How to Pick Better Shares

The Capital Asset Pricing Model (CAPM) was the work of William Sharpe. While Sharpe evolved his theory over a number of years, it is set out definitively in the book Portfolio Theory and Capital Markets, which was published in 1971. Sharpe's contribution to portfolio theory was the insight that an individual investment contained two types of risk: specific risk, unique to that investment; and market risk, sometimes called 'systemic risk'. Specific risk could be removed through diversification, but coping with systemic risk is what plagues investors.

The CAPM evolved as a way of isolating this risk. Sharpe found that the return on an individual investment, or portfolio of investments, should equate to the risk-free rate of return, plus the excess return that the market provided over that risk-free rate multiplied by a coefficient that Sharpe called a 'beta'. This term is the measure of the sensitivity of an individual investment or portfolio to the movement in the market.

Each individual investment has a beta, which varies over time and over the time period chosen to measure it. A stock with a beta of 1.5 would, for example, rise by

[2] For an excellent and more complete explanation of these models see Rees, *Financial Analysis*, 2nd edn., 1999.

15% if the market rose by 10%, and fall by 15% if the market fell by 10%. A beta is found by statistical analysis of individual, daily share-price returns, in comparison with the market's daily returns over precisely the same period. Betas of individual stocks can be combined together to generate portfolio betas.

The importance of Sharpe's model is also that it allows one to predict the expected return from a portfolio given its beta, the market rate of return and the risk-free rate. For example, if the portfolio beta is 2.0, the risk-free rate is 3% and the market rate of return is 7 per cent, then the market's excess return is 4% (7 − 3), the portfolio's excess return is 8% (2 × 4; multiplying market excess return by the beta), and the portfolio's total expected return is 11% (8 + 3; the portfolio's excess return plus the risk-free rate). What this means is that it is possible, by knowing these individual components of the CAPM, to establish whether or not the current price of an investment is consistent with its likely return – in other words, whether or not the investment is cheap or dear.

What it Means for You

Sharpe's derivation of a beta provides investors with a simple and convenient shorthand way of measuring how stocks have reacted in the past to overall movements in the market. While it is difficult to predict from the beta how individual stocks might react to particular market movements, one probably can deduce that a portfolio of high beta stocks will move significantly more than the market in either direction, and a low beta portfolio by less than the market. This is important for fund managers in particular, because they may be unwilling to, or prevented from, holding cash if they feel that the market is likely to fall. If so, they can hold low beta stocks instead.

Source: *Investors Chronicle*, August 5, 2005

Arbitrage Pricing Theory (APT)

The limitations inherent in a single-index model such as CAPM as a mechanism for understanding the relationship between risk and return have led to a search for models with greater explanatory power. One alternative developed by Ross is APT which expresses the relationship between expected returns and a wide range of factors to which a security may be sensitive. In contrast to the single-index (beta) CAPM, APT is a multi-index model. Thus, while CAPM can only incorporate sensitivity to market returns in the form of beta, APT can include a multitude of factors such as interest rate and industry specific indices.

Efficient Market Hypothesis (EMH)

CAPM and APT were important factors in the development of EMH, which has had a profound effect on the way in which the relationship between accounting information and the market is viewed. Specifically, by changing the perspective from that of the information provider to the information consumer, EMH claims to explain how the market for accounting information operates.

In practice:

The Efficient Market Theory (EMT) is conventional economic wisdom: "the market knows best" how to use capital resources to promote maximum growth. Since the 1970s EMT has provided the justification for dismantling the ubiquitous post-war financial market regulations, arguing "liberalization" would produce lower real costs of capital and higher output and productivity growth compared to the growth rates experienced between the Second World War and 1973, when international capital flow controls were widely practised.

Source: *The Guardian, March 15, 1999.*

An efficient market is defined as one where "stocks are valued fairly in the light of all available information". Such a market is assumed to immediately and rationally impound information relevant to the security. For example, as information that suggests increased profits becomes available the share price should increase to a level where the yield would be equivalent to that expected for shares with a similar risk profile. Likewise, information suggesting a decrease should lead to a drop in share price to a level that would yield an amount equivalent to that expected for shares with a similar risk profile.

EMH and Piranhas

Market efficiency is a description of how prices in competitive markets respond to new information. The arrival of new information to a competitive market can be likened to the arrival of a lamb chop to a school of flesh-eating piranha, where investors are – plausibly enough – the piranha. The instant the lamb chop hits the water, there is turmoil as the fish devour the meat. Very soon the meat is gone, leaving only the worthless bone behind, and the water returns to normal. Similarly, when new information reaches a competitive market there is much turmoil as investors buy and sell securities in response to the news, causing prices to change. Once prices adjust, all that is left of the information is the worthless bone. No amount of gnawing on the bone will yield any more meat, and no further study of old information will yield any more valuable intelligence.

Source: Robert C. Higgins, *Analysis for Financial Management*, 2nd edn.

EMH contends, therefore, that a market is efficient if share prices fully reflect all information available, i.e., it does not allow anyone to profit further from such information since it is assumed that the market has immediately and rationally impounded the implications of that information into the price of the share. In other words, any new or additional information is quickly absorbed by the market and used to determine the appropriate value of the shares. The agreed price for a security is seen to be set by the market, therefore, in a manner that represents some form of weighted consensus as to the value of a share on a given day, since the market, if it is efficient, will fully reflect all available and relevant information. Thus, there is an assumption that the market will only react in an extreme manner to surprise announcements. In short, EMH considers the stock market the most efficient mechanism for determining value.

Implications of EMH for Accounting Information and Users

These insights impact how accounting information, particularly as disseminated by means of the Annual Report, is perceived:

- EMH recognizes that accounting information is not the only information source used for decision making.

- EMH presumes, contrary to the Classical approach, that the market is a more efficient arbiter of value than accounting.

- EMH assumes that accounting information will be impounded in the share price when that information becomes available. By virtue of interim reports, preliminary announcements, profit warnings/forecasts, press briefings, leaks, insider information, insider trading and other means, such information will usually become available to the market prior to the publication of the Annual Report.

- This raises fundamental questions about the usefulness and timeliness of many accounting statements, such as the Annual Report – one of the most important (and lucrative) documents produced by the accounting process. Obviously, by extension, it questions the usefulness of any analysis of the information contained in an Annual Report.

Because the existence of an efficient market could have such significance, extensive empirical research has been carried out in the US and, to a lesser extent, in the UK. Among those identified as likely to be most impacted are:

- **Accounting regulators**: if the market can be shown to be capable of properly discerning attempts by management to mislead it by the use of "creative" accounting techniques, then the usefulness of regulations, intended, in part, to protect naïve investors, is open to question.

- **Accountants**: since EMH posits that by virtue of interim reports, preliminary announcements, insider trading, etc., the information contained in, for example, Annual Reports will already have been made available and impounded in the share price by the time it is actually published, there is little point in companies undertaking such expensive exercises.

- **Investors, fund managers and analysts**: if an efficient market exists then there is little point expending time and money on an analysis of financial information since possession of such information does not confer any advantage, as it will already have been impounded into the price of a security. Furthermore, it will not be possible to develop strategies that generate "abnormal returns" by identifying mis-priced shares. Eugene Fama, one of the developers and champions of EMH, has little time for analysts and those who purport to be able to beat the market: "I would compare stock-pickers to astrologers," he once observed, "but I don't want to bad-mouth astrologers".

In practice:

The following article highlights the nature of the challenge posed to preparers and analysts of accounting information by EMH. The conclusion that blindfolded chimpanzees stand as good a probability of success as informed analysts and advisors captures the extent of the challenge:

Random Advice: Author says using index funds, not advisers, is the best way to succeed in the stock market, by Bob Quick

Stock brokers and investment advisers make their livings by helping clients invest in the stock market and charging them for the advice that hopefully will make money for those investors. The idea behind that advice is that a rational investor can choose shares that are undervalued and are likely to rise in price over time.

Burton G. Malkiel's classic A Random Walk Down Wall Street came out in 1973, arguing it's impossible to predict how the stock market will behave. The only thing that can be said about the market is that it will fluctuate from day to day, following a "random walk." Malkiel, a professor of economics at Princeton University, believes in the "efficient market hypothesis," which states that the price of a company's stock already reflects everything known about that company's outlook. That means investors have no way of outperforming the market, no matter how much they study the stock pages. They could do just as well in making their investment choices by throwing darts at the stock pages. Malkiel's advice was to invest in a broad-based mutual fund on a regular basis and forget about trying to time the market. Since then index funds have proliferated, allowing investors to put their money in funds that track the S&P 500, the Nasdaq 100 and other indices...

By using index funds instead of other types of mutual funds or buying stocks, investors simplify their investing, avoid most sales and expense charges and also keep taxable gains to a minimum. These passive portfolios of index funds often do better than many actively managed portfolios. (It should be pointed out that Malkiel himself sits on the board of a Vanguard index fund, the Total Market Index Fund.)

Index funds also allow investors to fire their investment advisers, which is the very first "basic point" Malkiel makes in his book. "What are they good for?" Malkiel asks. "Their primary interest is not yours, but theirs; they are very good at making money for themselves." Advisers, Malkiel continues, are compensated by the commissions they earn on the products they sell clients. "Thus, they have a vested interest in making the investment process seem as complicated as possible so that you must turn to them for advice. And they are likely to push those products on which they make the largest commissions – not those that are likely to line your pockets."

The commissions might be worth it if the investment advice the brokers gave was accurate, but it often isn't, according to Malkiel: "The financial 'experts' know precious little more than you know. In fact, I will go out on a limb and tell you that the experts have no idea what stocks you should buy to provide superior future returns."

Malkiel added: "A blindfolded chimpanzee throwing darts at the stock pages can select individual stocks as well as the experts."

Source: New Mexican, October 19, 2003.

Is the Market Efficient?

The question is, therefore, "Is the market efficient?" Obviously, this is of particular significance to accountants since one of the matters at issue is the usefulness to users of incurring additional costs in acquiring and analyzing accounting information.

To answer this it is important to understand what is meant by the word "efficient". In the context of EMH, "efficiency" implies that share prices quickly adjust to "fully reflect" available information. In other words, possession of that information does not enable the possessor to profit from it. However, it does not mean that every user of this information will interpret it and/or use it in the same way.

The efficiency or otherwise of a market can be tested in a number of ways:

1. **Allocative efficiency** posits that a market is efficient if it directs savings towards the most productive enterprises. If this is so, then the most efficient firms should find it easier to raise funds than others. It is assumed that the amount of information required to obtain funds, for example on the Stock Exchange, is such that allocative efficiency is assured.

2. **Operational efficiency** relates to the cost of transacting business in a market. On the Stock Exchange, for example, the lower the brokerage costs the greater the operational efficiency. Operational efficiency can be shown to exist in the larger Stock Exchanges such as those in the US and London where transaction costs are low, and to have been secured by the huge increase in the range and type of trading activity facilitated by the Internet. Because of limited research, the position is less clear in relation to exchanges in continental Europe and Asia.

3. **Information processing efficiency** relates to the extent to which the current share price reflects the future prospects of the firm. Where all known information is reflected in the share price, then, because all investors have the same chance, as there is no advantage to be had from having information which has already been impounded, the investment process is termed "fair game". This does not imply that there is no risk to individual investors, but that returns will be "fair" since they will be commensurate with the risk taken. For example, suppose that a fund manager comes into possession of information that suggests the profits of a particular firm will far exceed even the most positive projections. In an

inefficient market this manager could capitalize on the fact that this information is not yet available to smaller investors and purchase shares from them at a price that has not impounded this information. In an efficient market, however, no such opportunity would exist as it is assumed that the market would immediately and correctly impound this information in the share price. Significantly, research is less conclusive about the existence of information processing efficiency.

Forms of EMH

Because research does not verify the existence of perfect information processing efficiency, it is necessary to test EMH in three forms, each reflecting the classification of information into categories, and positing the ability of the market to produce estimates of value corresponding to information availability:

- **Weak form**: In this form the information available is that relating to past share price movements only. The hypothesis is that past share price movements cannot be taken as a guide to future price movements. In other words, analysis of past share movements and trends is unlikely to yield better returns and as such is not a worthwhile activity. For example, if a company's share price has increased steadily over the previous few months, then this cannot be taken as an indication of future share movements, and the next change in price could, with equal probability, be either upwards or downwards. This randomness has given rise to the Random Walk Hypothesis, which says that share price movements over time approximate to a random, unpredictable walk. Empirical research has strongly supported the Random Walk Hypothesis, and so the EMH in its weak form is widely accepted, as the extract below illustrates:

Is financial acumen an oxymoron, like military intelligence? Or can the smartest money managers really fulfil their promise to beat average returns on the stock markets?

...Mr Malkiel's "A Random Walk Down Wall Street", first published nearly 30 years ago and now revised, is deservedly a perennial best-seller. It maintains that investors who buy and hold all the stocks in a broad stock market average – as index funds do – are likely to do better than investors who put their money into actively managed funds, not least because the higher charges and trading costs of professional money managers cut into investment returns.

Charts and tables are produced by Mr Malkiel to back his assertion. They show, for instance, that a person who invested $10,000 in 1969 in a Standard & Poor's 500-stock index fund would have seen its value increase to about $310,000 by mid-1998 – $140,000 more than $10,000 invested over the same period in the average actively managed fund. And in making these calculations, Mr Malkiel plays fair: he deducts the typical running expense (one-fifth of 1%) charged by an index fund. To the dismay of active equity managers, the ranks of the random-walk converts are swelling all the time, especially in the US where passive managers now handle most of the shares in public-sector pension funds.

> Even so, Mr Malkiel does not stick to the letter of his own fundamentalist text: "The market prices stocks so efficiently that a blindfolded chimpanzee throwing darts at the Wall Street Journal can select a portfolio that performs as well as those managed by the experts." He concedes that some money managers do succeed, at least for a time, in beating the stock market averages. The difficulty lies in identifying them before, rather than after, they do it.
>
> Source: *Economist*, 17 July 1999, review of B. Malkiel, *A Random Walk Down Wall Street*.

Semi-strong form: In this form the information set available is taken to be all publicly available data, including that contained in the Annual Report. Because the share price is assumed to fully reflect all such information, there is expected to be no advantage accruing to holders of this information. If verified, then this has major implications for both accountants, who provide such information, and financial analysts, who have traditionally applied various analytical techniques to accounting information in an attempt to identify mis-priced shares, which they could then exploit. This form has been widely tested by examining the way in which the market reacts to new information about a company and the evidence does suggest that it is fairly robust. Kaplan and Roll, [1] for instance, tested the impact on a company's share price of a change in depreciation methods which, while affecting earnings, had no effect on cash flows. Initially, the study showed, share prices rose but within three months share prices dropped once investors realized that these creative accounting practices were cosmetic. The significance of this was not only that the market was shown to respond rationally, but also that it appeared that it was the information they conveyed about future cash flows, not the accounting numbers as such, which was important to the investors. If the market is capable of extracting the significant information from accounts constructed according to complex accounting rules and standards then, supporters of EMH contend, the efficacy, necessity and costs to firms of such rules and standards are brought into question.

Strong form: In this form the information available is all data, including private (insider) information. This form can best be tested by examining the market's reaction to information about the company that has previously been confidential. If the EMH in this form is correct then the market should not react at all to the mere release of this information, as the assumption is that all information relevant to the company has already become available, whether by press release, interim reports or other means, and been impounded in the share price. As a result, it should not be possible to make profits by availing of inside information. (In any case "insider dealing" is illegal in both the UK and the US.) In fact, studies tend to demonstrate that markets do react to the publication of such information. In other words, illegal or not, it would be possible to make abnormal returns by exploiting insider information. It would appear, therefore, that in its strong form EMH is not sustainable.

In practice:

Why mid-caps offer a happy hunting ground, by Edmond Jackson

In principle, when market sentiment cools it is prudent to favour well-established companies with proven earnings power. That means companies in the FTSE Mid 250 index appear a sensible compromise – they are more dynamic than those in the FTSE100 index but less risky than small caps.

In practice, however, the City is usually well aware of changes, even at Mid 250 companies, so their share prices often discount what is known and may over-compensate in the short-term. Consequently a company may report excellent results, but see its share price fall. In the short-term at least expectations are in the price so profit-takers prevail.

This was the case on Tuesday when Icap (the world's largest interdealer broker, serving banks in a variety of financial instruments) reported a 38 per cent rise in normalised pre-tax profit to £170m and a 19 per cent rise in earnings to 18.4p. The shares opened the day down 2p at 270p.

According to Company Refs, these numbers for Icap's year to the end of March were precisely in line with several brokers' ''buy'' advice in April. There were also two ''buy'' notes issued in the New Year, after which the shares hit 331p. That suggests analysts doing their job well and managers communicating effectively, but in the short term at least it is hard for private investors to outwit everyone else.

This is what is meant by an ''efficient market'' – it discounts known information and insights about a share. It doesn't rule out buying but you need to be careful...

Source: Sunday Telegraph, May 30, 2004.

Throughout the 1970s and early 1980s EMH was the dominant paradigm in the literature and it was widely accepted that stock markets conformed, at least, to the semi-strong form of the thesis. Event studies, particularly those based on the US and UK stock markets, seemed to confirm that these markets were efficient to the extent that they priced information quickly and accurately and shares fully and fairly reflected all publicly available information as to the future net cash flows deriving from underlying assets. With the exception of a small number of individuals such as Warren Buffett, it was accepted that it was not possible to develop strategies that consistently outperformed the market.

Worryingly for supporters of EMH, however, studies began to identify an increasing number of anomalies that tended to challenge assertions that the market was efficient. For example, even the Kaplan and Roll study, which seemed to support the semi-strong form, was forced to confront the fact that, while the market eventually adjusted for creative accounting practices, this did not happen immediately but over a period of several months.

Gradually, evidence of a number of such ''anomalies'' began to accumulate. For instance, researchers claimed to have identified a *small-firm-in-January* effect whereby those investing in December in firms with relatively small market capitalization and selling in January generated abnormally high risk-adjusted returns. Others claimed to have identified a *mean-reversion* tendency, which asserted that while markets tended to overreact to new information, they gradually reverted to a mean value.

In practice:

Market Events make an irrational argument – received economic wisdom is that financial markets are efficient. But after looking at events of recent years, John Kay begs to differ

Doubts about efficient market theory have been growing for some time. Evidence has accumulated of market anomalies: systematic patterns of mispricing that ought not to happen in efficient markets. Prices show evidence of momentum effects (upward and downward shifts are often succeeded by further shifts in the same direction) and of mean reversion (moves away from long run share valuations, or the purchasing power values of currencies, are usually followed by a return to normal). These phenomena are evidence of herd behaviour: people base their opinions on those of other market participants rather than assessments of fundamental value.

There are too many extreme events in financial markets. The October 1987 crash, when stock markets fell 20% in a day, should, in ordinary statistical theory, happen only once in several billion years. We might accept one such event in our lifetime, but when you have seen several events that should only happen once in the history of the universe, you may question the way you see that universe. . .

Source: The Banker, December 1, 2003.

Supporters of EMH countered that anomalies such as the *small-firm-in-January* effect amounted to nothing more than a *neglected-firm-effect* that, as EMH hypothesized, tend to be traded away once larger institutions begin to invest in these previously "anonymous" companies. This, they argue, illustrates one of the great paradoxes of EMH: it is those analysts actively searching for market-beating strategies and disgruntled company executives complaining about inefficiencies, who actually contribute to market efficiency by making available additional information which the market can then assimilate. Ironically, they contended, it was actually efforts to prove market inefficiency that lead to the very efficiency that critics are working so hard to refute.

Slowly, however, in the face of a slowly accumulating body of evidence that the market did not always act efficiently, this scepticism extended to many economists who have begun to question some of the fundamental assumptions underpinning theories such as EMH.

Irrationality: Rethinking Thinking

"Are economists human?" is not a question that occurs to many practitioners of the dismal science, but it is one that springs to the minds of many non-economists exposed to conventional economic explanations. Economists have typically described the thought processes of Homo sapiens as more like that of Star Trek's Mr Spock – strictly logical, centred on a clearly defined goal and free from the unsteady influences of emotion or irrationality – than the uncertain, error-prone groping with which most of us are familiar. Of course, some human behaviour does fit the rational pattern so beloved of economists. But remember, Mr Spock is a Vulcan, not a human.

Even economists are finally waking up to this fact. A wind of change is now blowing some human spirit back into the ivory towers where economic theory is made. It is becoming increasingly fashionable for economists, especially the younger, more ambitious ones, to borrow insights from psychologists (and some-times even biologists) to try to explain drug addiction, the working habits of New York taxi-drivers, current sky-high American share prices and other types of behaviour which seem to defy rationality. Alan Greenspan, the chairman of the Federal Reserve, made a bow to this new trend when he wondered about the "irrational exuberance" of American stock markets way back in December 1996 (after an initial flutter of concern, investors ignored him).

Many economic rationalists still hold true to their faith, and some have fought back by devising rational explanations for the apparent irrationalities studied by the growing school of "behavioural economists". Ironically, orthodox economists have been forced to fight this rearguard action against heretics in their own ranks just as their own approach has begun to be more widely applied in other social sciences such as the study of law and politics.

The golden age of rational economic man began in the 1940s... By the late 1970s, economic rationality was not only the orthodoxy, it began to effect events in the real world. Macroeconomic policy, notably in America and Britain, fell into the hands of believers in the theory of "rational expectations". This said that, rather than forming expectations on the basis of limited information drawn from previous experience, people take into account all available information. This includes making an accurate assessment of government policy. Thus, when governments announced that they would do whatever was necessary to bring down inflation, people would adjust their expectations accordingly.

In the same way, Wall Street investment firms, too, increasingly fell under the spell of the "efficient markets hypothesis", an economic theory that assumes that the prices of financial assets such as shares and bonds are rationally based on all available information. Even if there are many stupid investors, went the theory, they would be driven out of the market by rational investors who could profit by trading against the investments of the foolish. As a result, economists scoffed at the notion that investors could consistently earn a higher return than the market average by picking shares. How times have changed. Some of those same economists have now become investment managers – although their performance has suggested that they should have paid heed to their earlier beliefs about the difficulty of beating the market.

   During the 1980s, macroeconomic policies based on rational expectations failed to live up to their promise (although this was probably because people rationally refused to believe government promises). And the stock market crash of October 1987 shattered the confidence of many economists in efficient markets. The crash seemed to have occurred without any new information or reason. Thus, the door of the ivory tower opened, at first only slightly, to theories that included irrational behaviour. Today there is a growing school of economists who are drawing on a vast range of behavioural traits identified by experimental psychologists which amount to a frontal assault on the whole idea that people, individually or as a group, mostly act rationally...

Source: *The Economist*, December 18, 1999.

In practice:

This scepticism is humorously illustrated in the following article, which identifies some of the fallacies inherent in many assumptions underlying economic theory:

A fortune built on defying the pull of theory, by John Kay

You have probably heard the joke about the economist who is walking along the street when his wife points out a $10 bill on the pavement. "Don't be silly," he replies, "if there was one, someone would already have picked it up."

The joke is more illuminating than funny. The economist is, of course, right. There are very few $10 bills on the pavement, for precisely the reasons he identifies. People rarely drop them and when they do the money is quickly picked up. If you see a $10 bill on the pavement, it is probably a piece of litter that looks like a $10 bill. You would not be well advised to try to make a living tramping the streets in search of discarded $10 bills.

The story is intended to mock the commitment of most economists to the efficient market hypothesis – the theory that it is hard to make money by trading because everything there is to know about the value of shares, currencies or bonds is already reflected in the price. A corollary is that share prices follow a random walk – past behaviour gives no guidance as to the direction of future changes, and the next market move is always as likely to be down as up.

Efficient market theory is central to modern financial economics, which has long been the jewel in the crown of the business school curriculum – it combines technical rigour with practical applicability and its successful practitioners command large salaries in financial institutions. In 1978 Michael Jensen, doyen of efficient market theory, famously wrote that "there is no other proposition in economics which has more solid empirical evidence supporting it than the Efficient Market Hypothesis."

So it comes as a shock when the latest rich list from Forbes reveals that Warren Buffett has collected $44bn (£24bn) by finding $10 bills among the trash on the pavements of Wall Street, *and now rivals Bill Gates for the title of the world's richest man. Mr Buffett's investment success has long troubled efficient market theorists. He himself noted that if 250m orang-utans kept flipping coins, one of them would produce a long string of heads. But if the lucky orang-utan keeps tossing heads even after you have picked him out from the crowd, that suggests he knows something you do not . . .*

Advocates of efficient market theory confuse a tendency with a law. As Mr Buffett himself has put it: adherents of the theory, "observing correctly that the market was frequently efficient, went on to conclude incorrectly that it was always efficient. The difference between these propositions is night and day". The joke demonstrates why this must be the case. There is a contradiction at the centre of the efficient market hypothesis. There is no point bending down to pick up a $10 bill because someone will have done it already. But if there is no point in bending down to pick it up, it will still be there. In an article published just after Mr Jensen's, Joe Stiglitz demonstrated that contradiction, in many lines of mathematics rather than the single line of the stand-up comic, and this was one of the contributions for which he received the Nobel Prize for economics. But for everyday purposes, it is quite enough to know the story of the $10 bill and its unexpectedly complex interpretation. The efficient market hypothesis is 90 per cent true, and you will lose money by ignoring it. The search for the elusive 10 per cent, like the search for discarded $10 bills, attracts effort greater than the rewards. But for the very few skilled searchers, the rewards can be large indeed.

Source: Financial Times, March 24, 2004.

Not only economists, but also others who approach matters from a behaviourist perspective, have begun to challenge some of the fundamental assumptions upon which EMH is built. For example, some cognitive psychologists argue that, because decision-makers have limited ability to interpret, assimilate and act on information, thus compromising their ability to make rational choices, one of the fundamental tenets of EMH, rational behaviour, is undermined. Thus, while a high probability of optimal pricing still exists, it is not assured. Furthermore, cognitive psychologists point out, the presence of anomalies points to some element of irrationality.

Arrow (1982) suggests that a heuristic (rule-of-thumb) approach replaces the rational process as decision-makers seek to assimilate information. [2] This in turn offers scope for management to massage information in such a way as to induce the desired effect on share price. Arrow has also argued that this both encourages and explains the short-termism of many investors. The short-term hypothesis suggests that there is a prejudice against long-term investment since the average investor expects abnormally high rates of return, which in turn increases the cost of capital to firms making such investments. Investors are inclined as a result to focus on information relevant to the immediate prospects of the firm. Therefore, management is encouraged to make accounting disclosures that intentionally exaggerate short-term profitability at the expense of long-term returns.

The large number of examples of management manipulation of accounting disclosures in Terry Smith's *Accounting for Growth* (1996) has been put forward by supporters of the cognitive psychology thesis as evidence of the rule-of-thumb approach in operation on a wide scale in the UK market. Smith argued that management in companies such as Coloroll, Polly Peck and Maxwell Communications Corporation had employed dubious and creative accounting practices intended to hide fundamental weaknesses in these businesses. Complicit in this was a market that employed a heuristic approach to make sense of the vast amount of complex financial information being presented to them.

Champions of EMH counter, however, that until the case-study approach of studies such as Smith's is complemented by rigorous statistical analysis these claims can be dismissed as merely anecdotal. Furthermore, supporters of the EMH model claim that much of what is identified as anomalous is merely the time-lag effect of private information becoming public. In other words, all that is being challenged is the strong-form EMH, and even that somewhat dubiously. More plausibly they point out that, while the cognitive psychology model does conceivably pose some challenges, until it is tested by more rigorous research its claims are somewhat compromised.

Nevertheless, because it highlights mental processes, in particular emphasizing the heuristic approach, the insights of cognitive psychology offer the possibility of re-asserting the need for regulatory processes. This may well prove decisive in defending the role of accounting regulation as a means of protecting users from those intent upon exploiting their inability to act rationally.

The insights from cognitive psychology have mirrored similar insights into the propensity of individuals to act irrationally from related fields such as behavioural finance. Accepting that markets are generally efficient, behavioural finance theorists recognize, nevertheless, that humans act in ways that are often contrary to the assumptions underlying theories such as EMH:

Human Nature Exposes 'Irrational Investors,' by Niall Brady

Fusing classical economic theory with studies about human psychology and the decision-making process, behavioural finance explores how investors systematically make mental mistakes or judgement errors. Behavioural finance proposes that, while markets are generally efficient, investors still behave irrationally. They follow the herd, trade excessively, get "anchored" to ideas and estimates, hold on to losing investments too long, sell winners too quickly and react too slowly to unexpected news. When they commit any of those sins, the financial pros are poised to strike...

The roots of behavioural finance trace back to the mid-1970s, when Daniel Kahneman, a Nobel Prize-winning economist at Princeton University, and psychology professor Amos Tversky published a paper arguing that people make decisions based on mental shortcuts that lead to "systematic and predictable errors". This challenged conventional thinking among economists and psychologists that people always make rational decisions, estimating the probability of positive and negative outcomes.

In the past two decades, Kahneman and other researchers began studying the behaviour of investors. They concluded that the main obstacle to sound investing is overconfidence: people think they know more than they know and act upon that belief. "During the stock market bubble, investors stayed heavily invested even when they knew it was a bubble," says Kahneman. "They thought they could get out in time. This is clearly an example of both exaggeration of skill and the illusion of control." Researchers into behavioural finance also contend that people take risks because they're deluded, not brave.

"Most people lose money by selling winners and hanging on to losers, and then buying stocks they're not certain of," says Kahneman. "Why do people frantically trade assets? Because people are overconfident. They are over-optimistic. They exaggerate their skills, and they do things not beneficial for them." This is borne out by separate research into the trading records of 88,000 US households in 1999. The data, which spanned two million stock trades over 10 years, showed that overconfident investors under-diversify; that men are more overconfident and trade more often than women; and that the more active investors are, the worse they perform.

The study also showed that having "ideas" – such as buying or selling a stock – costs investors money. The investor often wasn't selling to realise a deliberate tax loss or to raise money to pay off a debt. Rather, the investor believed the newly purchased stock would outperform the one that was sold. The study showed that, one year after investors had such an idea, the stocks sold were typically worth 2% more than the ones bought. When you take transaction fees, bid-offer spreads and taxes into account, "ideas" cost 4%.

Psychologists and economists also have learned that quantitative estimates are influenced by previous benchmarks. A car salesman, for example, starts negotiations with a high price. The goal is to "anchor" the customer to the high price, so that he will think he negotiated a good deal by lowering the amount. Behavioural finance adherents say this applies to the stock market. They offer as an example the $400 price target that legendary tech analyst Henry Blodget placed on Amazon.com in 1999. Investors held on to Amazon too long because they were "anchored" to that price.

These traits and behavioural characteristics cannot be overlooked, according to devotees of behavioural finance. "Many of them are embedded into human nature," says Arjen Pasma of ABN Amro Asset Management in Amsterdam. "People will always have the tendency to be overconfident. It's as ancient as the way to Rome."

Source: *Sunday Tribune*, October 5, 2003 – additional reporting by Bloomberg

The perspectives of disciplines such as behavioural finance have been significant in recent years in challenging the previously dominant market paradigms. Nevertheless, these paradigms, particularly as encapsulated in EMH, remain potent in both their practical and theoretical applications. From an accounting perspective, it is important to acknowledge the role of EMH – particularly in its semi-strong expression – as providing key insights and challenges.

Positive Accounting Theory

The third main stream of accounting theory to have a strong influence over the course of recent decades has been Positive Accounting Theory, sometimes called "contracting theory". As Ross Watts explains in the following extract, it arose partly as a reaction to what were perceived to be deficiencies in the methodologies of the classical and market-based approaches.

> "We have no theory of corporate financial statements, in the form of a group of internally consistent, interrelated hypotheses which have been subjected to formal tests and 'confirmed'. Prescriptions in the accounting literature are based on hypotheses about observed phenomena in capital markets, political process, and other areas. Rarely do any of the prescribers suggest that the hypotheses be tested formally, let alone perform such tests. Moreover, the hypotheses are often inconsistent with currently accepted theories in finance and economics.
>
> Even that part of the accounting literature which relies on the empirically-based efficient market hypothesis and the capital-asset-pricing models of finance does not include any tests of hypotheses which directly explain why financial statements take their current form. Instead the emphasis in that finance-based literature is on stock market reaction to the content of financial statements.
>
> The development of prescriptions and the development of theory are not incompatible. The development of prescriptions which are likely to achieve their objectives requires an underlying theory which explains observed phenomena: which predicts the effects of particular prescriptions. Thus, given the concentration on prescriptions, the lack of development of theory in financial accounting remains an enigma."
>
> Source: Watts, R. L. (1977), Corporate Financial Statements, A Product of the Market and Political Process, *Australian Journal of Management*, 2, pp. 53–75.
>
> Copyright: The Australian Graduate School of Management

The central hypothesis of Positive Accounting Theory is that accounting arose, not in response to market demands for information, but as a device by which the contracts which mediate relationships within a firm could be monitored.

In contrast to the Classical approach, which is predicated upon the notion of accounting as the best mechanism by which to capture the "correct" value of a firm, the Positive Approach assumes that there is no such "correct" value.

Consequently, it does not look on accounting as some external, neutral entity, but as a vibrant element of the firm which not so much describes that reality as helps to define and shape it. In other words, accounting data and systems are seen as a means of exerting control. Management, for example, can be employed on contracts that incorporate accounting measures such as profit as the basis for the bonus element of their remuneration packages. In this scenario, accounting methods and systems act as mechanisms by which resources are allocated within a firm.

From this understanding of the key role of accounting information within a firm it is postulated that managers have a vested interest in the effect of their actions on accounting information and disclosures. In other words, they will have incentives to change either their decisions or the firm's accounting policies in order to influence the accounting numbers. This will be most likely in circumstances where their remuneration is tied to performance. The effect of this insight has been to move the focus away from testing market reaction to accounting disclosures, and onto the study and observation of management behaviour in relation to the incentives underlying their choice of alternative accounting policies.

This paradigm found a natural ally in agency theory which is predicated on the belief that people are motivated primarily by self-interest. Management could, therefore, be assumed to act in ways that maximized the value of the firm only if this coincided with their own vested interests. Furthermore, unless owners were prepared to establish monitoring mechanisms, then management had incentives to minimize their input and increase their remuneration in ways that would be contrary to the interests of shareholders and creditors.

The significance of accounting measures and systems in this scenario is that they not only offer an obvious monitoring mechanism, but can also be employed as a "language" in which the contracts that are seen as integral to the operation of any set of relationships can be framed. The use of accounting information in this way allows it to be viewed as a medium through which relationships can be expressed and controlled, in other words as an efficient way in which to operate the firm.

One important aspect of the Positive Accounting paradigm is that it acknowledges that accounting information, and the actors who interact with it, play out their roles in a "political" context and are subject to a variety of political pressures. As a result the public and political perception of financial information is important. This is particularly the case for large firms, especially those in the utility sector. There will, for example, be pressures on management of entities such as water companies to show that they are not making exorbitant profits at a time of water shortage. As was the case several years ago in the UK, failure to respond to these pressures may result in political pressures to impose windfall taxes on such profits. Likewise there will be pressures on management of certain companies to ensure that the figures for management remuneration are not excessive.

In such circumstances management may be tempted to employ creative accounting practices to "massage" profits. For example, water companies responded to these pressures by incorporating provisions for "environmental costs" which had the double advantage of reducing profits without any immediate cash flow impact, while simultaneously allowing management to respond to criticisms from the green lobby about their environmental record.

By concentrating on the incentives for management to act selfishly and opportunistically, Positive Accounting Theory has provided a useful means by which the political aspects of accounting policy choice can be investigated. Furthermore, by focusing on issues such as why firms choose particular accounting methods, it has provided a significant counter-balance to the market-based approach. It remains to be seen whether its case-specific methodology can survive closer scrutiny.

Implications for Financial Information Analysis

The answer to the question "What is the relationship between accounting information and the market?" may not seem any clearer. However, the various theoretical frameworks that have sought to address this question have at least allowed some advances in our understanding.

By seeming to confirm that the market impounds all information immediately and fairly, the ascendancy for several decades of the market-based approach, particularly as manifested by EMH, posed great challenges for accountants and financial analysts. Essentially the usefulness of analyzing accounting data was being fundamentally questioned.

However, the validity of financial information analysis as a legitimate exercise has been reasserted in recent years as it has gradually dawned on those championing the market-based approach that various anomalies, coupled with the failure of empirical studies to confirm EMH in its strong form, as well as the insights of behavioural finance, demonstrate that it is not capable of capturing all of the various dynamics at work in a market.

Significantly, this has coincided with calls for a re-examination of the role of Fundamental Analysis by academics such as Ohlson who have re-established its academic credentials by virtue of longer-term studies. [3] In direct contrast to the fashion typical of the finance literature, where accounting figures are deconstructed to expose cash flows, Ohlson demonstrates the relationship between basic accounting measures and ratios, such as return on equity and book values.

The view of accountants, many academics and, of course, analysts, therefore, is that even if it is not possible to develop a strategy that secures superior returns to the market over the long-term, Fundamental Analysis is a legitimate and rewarding exercise. It offers one means of identifying firms that offer abnormal returns, since an ability to understand the implications of various accounting alternatives provides a competitive advantage to the user.

It is also worth remembering that financial information analysis is not carried out solely with a view to assessing the reaction of markets or the impact of financial information on share price. From the start of this text it has been emphasized that the analysis of financial information is an important element in the decision-making process of a variety of users, not just investors. Thus, financial information analysis is a valid exercise to the extent that it allows more informed, balanced and strategic decisions by those who see accounting information as an important element in the information resource of a firm.

Summary

One of the primary purposes of this text is to consider the information content of accounting disclosures, especially as incorporated in an Annual Report, and to do so in the context of the political, social and economic environments within which accounting operates.

In an attempt to understand one of these environments, this chapter has sought to answer the question "What is the relationship between accounting information and the market?" Until recently the effect of the dominant market-based paradigm has been to question the usefulness of accounting information and, consequently, its analysis, on the grounds that the market will have impounded into the share price the information contained in many of its statements prior to their publication.

More recently, however, a dawning realization that EMH, while robust, is not infallible, the insights of behavioural finance, coupled with research that has high-lighted the strong correlation between share returns and basic accounting measures when considered over a long period of time, have re-established the efficacy of Fundamental Analysis as a legitimate and potentially profitable exercise. So too have perspectives that challenge the notion that it is the needs of investors which should be the dominant concern of the preparers of accounting information. Indeed, it is to this theme that the following chapter turns.

Review Questions

Question 1
Explain why theory can be useful in aiding an understanding of the broader issues involved in any particular practice or series of events.

Question 2
Identify and distinguish between the three dominant paradigms that have been prevalent within accounting over the course of recent decades.

Question 3
Explain how changes in finance theory gradually impacted upon the way in which academics and practitioners began to think about the role of accounting information in the market.

Question 4
Explain what is meant by each of the following terms:
- Diversification
- Efficient market
- Portfolio
- Beta
- Riskiness

Question 5
CAPM builds upon portfolio theory and incorporates a measure of the relationship between risk and return. Explain how it achieves this.

Question 6
"The contribution of APT was to provide a complex model that approximated more closely to reality. This gave it a credibility that CAPM lacked". Explain what this means.

Question 7
Identify the challenges that EMH brings to the traditional understanding of the role of accounting information in the market. How does this affect the way in which accounting information is perceived by users?

Question 8
One of the implications of EMH is that there is no advantage to users in analysing the accounting information contained in an Annual Report with a view to identifying mis-priced securities. This represents a challenge to the role of the financial analyst. However, EMH assumes that relevant information will have reached the market by some means and, ironically, one of the conduits for this is the analyst, through regular briefings provided by companies. Consider the implications of this for financial accounting as a critical source of information.

Question 9
Identify the sources of recent challenges to the previously dominant EMH paradigm. In respect of each indicate whether these can be refuted by EMH or whether they represent fundamental challenges.

Question 10
Summarize the contribution of Positive Accounting Theory to accounting thought.

Case Studies

Case 1

This chapter has dealt with some of the informational and theoretical paradigms that should inform the construction of an investment portfolio. Using the following case as a starting point, discuss the issues that constructing a diversified portfolio raise.

Don't Dismiss 'Do as I say, not as I Do,' by Samuel Brittan

Around new year I look for a book to recommend to the proverbial nephew who does not intend to take an economics exam or become a practitioner but who wants the equivalent of a popular science book on the discipline. This time I recommend a recent book on the related subject of stock markets, namely *A Mathematician Plays the Market*, by John Allen Paulos (Allen Lane).

I stand to learn as much as the nephew when the author explains matters such as "beta values", which quantify past volatility. He also explains very well notions such as (the badly named) chaos theory that have entered the social sciences. Paulos covers the ground with simple arithmetic and very little algebra.

But I must warn that he does not explain how to pick winning stocks or even how to spot highs and lows in the equity market. Indeed it is only a slight oversimplification to say that his view on how to play the market is: "Don't." Near the end he lists four maxims: 1. Don't succumb to hype and vaporous enthusiasm. 2. Even if you do, don't put too many eggs into one basket. 3. If you violate even this last maxim, at least protect yourself against sudden drops with put options, which are options to sell at a given price. 4. Even if you neglect all the rest, at least don't buy on margin.

But now comes the irony. Paulos, who is professor of mathematics at Temple University in the US, has an enviable reputation for explaining elementary logic and mathematics to ordinary readers. Yet he himself used a small unexpected legacy to buy WorldCom shares on their way up at $47 a share. Even when the price plunged he continued to buy in the hope of recovery. He even tried to recoup his losses by buying on margin near the final debacle.

The only explanation he can give of why he disobeyed his own maxims is the word "addiction" – he is not inclined to be his own psychologist. This should also make me ponder my own dictum that what the public needs is not courses in economics but an introduction to the elementary arithmetic of risk and probability, which Paulos himself has provided in spades. We should not laugh at the saying "Do as I say, not as I do."

Paulos flirts with efficient market theory. The most realistic version of this is that it is almost impossible to outperform the market systematically. It accepts that markets overshoot and bubbles occur; but it denies that an expert or government official has the ability to spot these deviations consistently beforehand, however lucky on particular occasions.

In financial discussions you often hear about Ms X or Mr Y who has had a remarkably good record in beating the market indices. Paulos shows how such "successful" analysts can emerge purely by chance. Of 1,000 analysts, roughly 500 might be expected to outperform the market next year. Of these another 250 might be expected to do as well for a second year and 125 in a third. Continuing the series we might expect to find one analyst who does well for 10 consecutive years by chance alone. But will she do better in the 11th year? Who knows?

The efficient market hypothesis does not imply that financial market practitioners should retrain as market gardeners. Investors have varying requirements. A strategy based on the most likely average behaviour may not suit a fund with a lumpy liability due in 15 years' time; and individuals will have their own rates of future discount, depending on temperament and family circumstances.

Paulos points to a more subtle problem. If everyone believed that all publicly available information were already reflected in security prices, nobody would bother to do any fundamental research; and the market would not be fed the information it requires for "efficiency". Thus if the efficient market theory is true, it is false; and if it is false it is true, like the paradox of the Cretan who said all Cretans were liars.

Paulos exaggerates, however, how many people are required to make markets approximately efficient in his limited sense. Surely it requires only a few specialists who are not content to be free riders on the theory to set the ball rolling in the right direction...

Source: *Financial Times*: January 2, 2004.

Case 2

Behavioural finance was described in the course of this chapter as providing a perspective that recognized both the general efficiency of the market and the propensity of individuals to operate in what might be called an "irrational fashion". Using the following case, which describes a scenario in which the behavioural paradigm underpins investment strategy, identify the strengths and weaknesses of this perspective.

New Breed of Investors Profits From Blunders:

Behavioural Finance Adherents Exploit Errors in Judgment, by Adam Levy

On the morning of Jan. 28, Frederick Stanske sat in his San Mateo, Calif., office, staring at his computer screen as AirTran Holdings Inc.'s stock surged. The Orlando, Fla.-based airline had just reported fourth-quarter per-share earnings of US10 cents per share, and its stock was en route to a 9% gain that day. Mr. Stanske says he remembers thinking the rise wasn't enough – not after AirTran's profit had blown away Wall Street's average forecast of US3.6 cents a share by 178%.

Stanske, senior vice-president at Fuller & Thaler Asset Management Inc., pounced, buying blocks of AirTran stock. As of June 30, Fuller & Thaler was the carrier's 12th-biggest holder, with 1.26 million shares, or 2% of the company's total. And so far, Mr. Stanske's bet has paid off big: AirTran shares rose more than threefold to US$16.88 on Sept. 19, from US$5.53 on Jan. 28.

Mr. Stanske's trading that day was based on the theory that most investors react too slowly to information that will boost stocks over the long haul. It's one of many errors in judgment that investors make, according to Fuller & Thaler, and it's among the missteps that are being exploited by a growing number of adherents to an investment discipline called behavioural finance...

Confined to academia for more than a decade, behavioural finance is gaining prestige. Daniel Kahneman, an Israeli-born psychology professor at Princeton University, won the 2002 Nobel Prize in economics for work showing that, while markets are generally efficient, investors still behave irrationally. Behavioural finance theorists have become regular speakers on the investment conference circuit these days, and the "How Humans Behave" lecture was the headline event at the Federal Reserve Bank of Boston's summer gathering this past June.

Behavioural finance has attracted critics as well. Richard Michaud, president and chief investment officer at New Frontier Advisors LLC in Boston, dismisses the discipline as a marketing tool. "They've done well, taking a very old way of solving every valuation problem and calling it behavioural finance," says Mr. Michaud, who has a PhD in mathematics from Boston University and received a patent in 2000 for an asset allocation strategy he designed. His lectures boast sobering titles such as "The Behavioural Finance Hoax." "I'm extremely skeptical, bordering on total cynicism, that any of this stuff actually works," he says.

That's not what some big investors are saying. Margaret Stumpp, senior managing director and co-head of a 40-person team at Prudential Investment Management in Newark, N.J., invests US$35-billion in assets. More than US$6-billion of the total is earmarked for a computer-driven method that identifies stocks trading out of sync with their valuation because of what she calls "behavioural biases" of investors – in particular their slow reaction to companies' earnings improvements. "The trick has been to identify the mistakes that people make and exploit them to make money," says Ms. Stumpp, 51, who has a doctorate in economics from Brown University. "No one disputes the notion that people screw up – especially investors."

Mr. Kahneman drilled home that point last May in a speech to 1,000 money managers in Washington. When he asked how many considered themselves to be among the room's above-average drivers, hands shot up all over. "No," Mr. Kahneman told investors attending the Investment Company Institute's annual mutual fund industry conference. "About 95% of any group of people think they have above-average driving skills. That means 45% of you are wrong." His point: Overconfidence is an inherent human trait that can sabotage many of life's decisions, and stock picking is no exception.

Source: *National Post*, September 25, 2003.

References

1. Kaplan, R.S. and Roll, R., Investor evaluation of accounting information: some empirical evidence, *Journal of Business*, 45, pp. 225–257, 1972.
2. Arrow, K., Risk perception in psychology and economics, *Economic Enquiry*, 1982.
3. Ohlson, J.A., Earnings, book values and dividends in equity valuation, *Contemporary Accounting Research*, Spring, pp. 661–687, 1995.
4. Smith, T., *Accounting for Growth*, Random House, London, 1996.

GOVERNANCE CONTEXT

[4]

When you have completed this chapter you will understand:

- The meaning and importance of corporate governance.
- The role of corporate governance in determining the financial reporting culture.
- The interrelationship between governance and accountability.
- The dominant role which capital markets and the 'shareholder value' paradizm play in the Anglo-American corporate structure.
- That the corporate governance model in the UK is a product of unique economic, social, cultural and historical factors.
- That the UK governance model is undergoing a period of review and change.
- The more inclusive approach based on 'Stakeholder Theory'.

Are the City's Quiet Assassins Getting Too Trigger-Happy? by Claire Oldfield and Ruth Sunderland

Britain's bosses are living in fear of the bullets that come in the dark. Big institutional shareholders including Fidelity fund manager Anthony Bolton, nicknamed 'the quiet assassin' have recently claimed the heads of a number of directors. And it is not just board members who are under attack, but even senior employees. Piers Morgan, sacked as editor of the Mirror at the behest of big US shareholders, found that out to his cost.

New Labour has been an earnest advocate of shareholder power, urging fund managers to use their muscle to curb fat cat pay. But many now believe the corporate governance bandwagon is running out of kilter. Critics accuse shareholders of the twin sins of wading in where they have no place, yet backing off when they should intervene. Annabel Brodie-Smith at the Association of Investment Trust Companies, says it is a question of balance. 'Governance, it is not about ticking boxes, it is about performing. I think there is a very important role to be played by sensible intervention but at the same time one should not just get carried away,' she says.

The Mirror affair suggests shareholders do not always get the balance right. Piers Morgan may not be a man to inspire much sympathy. But the involvement of US shareholders, including Fidelity and Tweedy Browne, raises serious issues over who is in charge of Britain's boardrooms. Is it the directors, many of whom have years of service in a company, and have put their reputations on the line? Or is it the shareholders, who can pull their money in and out of companies at the touch of a computer keyboard? Shareholders, as part-owners, clearly should have a say. But critics say they are getting too big for their boots and trying to micromanage companies. While City or Wall Street investors may be good at picking shares, they are not qualified to run newspapers, or other businesses for that matter. And whatever the rights and wrongs at the Mirror, the prospect of a group of foreign investors compromising the freedom of the press is one that would rightly alarm many Britons.

Annabel Brodie-Smith points out that shareholders have come under increasing pressure to deliver good returns in the bear market. 'They feel they need to see a strong performance from the board and that they have the right to intervene,' she says. Recent corporate scandals, such as Enron in the US, have prompted shareholders to become more active. In the UK, there has also been a succession of reports, most recently the guidelines from investment banker Derek Higgs, aimed at promoting best boardroom practice. As Glyn Jones, chief executive of fund manager Gartmore, says: 'It is healthy that large institutional investors should make their voice heard.'

But sceptics now believe the pendulum has swung too far. A number of executives, including Luqman Arnold of Abbey National and Roger Holmes of Marks & Spencer, have big US shareholders breathing heavily down their necks. ITV at the weekend hit out at suggestions that Fidelity's Bolton, who earlier masterminded the ousting of Carlton chief Michael Green, now has his sights trained on chief executive Charles Allen. Fidelity has kept stum on the subject of Allen, who is being backed publicly by chairman Sir Peter Burt. But episodes like these breed distrust between shareholders and industry. City grandee Sir Bryan Nicholson, head of the Financial Reporting Council, recently accused major investors of sending out mixed messages to company chairmen on governance issues. Others, including CBI director general Digby Jones, attacked shareholders for conducting 'megaphone diplomacy,' and airing their grievances through the press.

Newly-militant investors have notched up several victories, including blocking Sir Ian Prosser's appointment as chairman of Sainsbury. Of course, it is a good thing for bosses to be held to account. Some industrialists, however, believe shareholders do not always play a straight bat. The problem is compounded by the fact that, even as fund managers are sticking their nose into boardroom business, they have on several occasions appeared weak over genuine governance concerns. At BSkyB, a revolt over the appointment of Rupert Murdoch's son James to succeed Tony Ball as chief executive was spurred by the National Association of Pension Funds, which then proceeded to do a U-turn. And though WPP shareholders objected to boss Martin Sorrell's pay package, a watered down version was voted through, which could net him £44m over nine years. At Glaxosmithkline, shareholders won an unprecedented victory last year, when they voted down the pay package of Jean-Pierre Garnier. This year, however, they nodded through an amended but still massively generous package.

Shareholders do have a legitimate role to play in corporate governance. They should concentrate on fulfilling that task. If relations between investors and industry are to improve, the moneymen should remember they are there to manage funds, not businesses.

Source: *Daily Mail*, May 25, 2004.

Introduction

This opening article manages to allude to many of the more significant issues relating to governance in modern companies: best boardroom practice; the roles and relative powers of directors and shareholders; executive remuneration; governance reports; guidelines, and, of course, accounting scandals. These are now central to the lives of all corporate entities and stakeholders. It also highlights the extent to which 'shareholder value', usually expressed in terms of share price, is such a critical driver in the Anglo-American world.

Ironically, a decade ago the term "corporate governance" would have been rarely heard, let alone understood, in many boardrooms. Apart from some academics and management gurus, few paid attention to a term that basically describes the way in which companies are structured or "governed".

However, a series of large and costly corporate scandals focused attention on the possibility that many of the problems could be traced to structural factors. In particular, collapses such as those that occurred at Maxwell Communications Corporation (MCC), Enron, Parmalat and others, suggested that the failure, or inability, of boards of directors to control and monitor business, laxity in accounting standards and an ethos of contented indifference on the part of many business leaders, had played important roles.

The term "governance" in this context is used to describe the way in which a company is structured and controlled, and, as the opening account illustrates, the manner in which this accommodates the relative rights of owners, managers, financiers and others. The resulting "balance of power" is regularly extended and tested by shareholders, managers, boards of directors, government, markets, employees and others with a stake in the company – with the result that the governance structure constantly mutates in response to political, social and economic pressures:

A Shift in the Balance of Power

Markets Hold the Key to the Direction of Reforms in the US, writes Dan Roberts

Beneath the dry jargon and esoteric debates corporate governance is about power. Nowhere is this more apparent than the US, home to the world's largest companies and some of the most sweeping governance changes in a generation.

One way of viewing the struggle to control corporate America is as a battle between the private and public sector; between regulators and the regulated. The collapse of a stock market bubble involving the savings of millions of ordinary Americans was followed by highly-publicised scandals at Enron and Worldcom that drew a predictably visible response from politicians. This took the form of reforming legislation named after its two Congressional sponsors: Senator Paul Sarbanes and Representative Michael Oxley.

More recently, corporate America has rebelled against some of the legislation's more onerous requirements such as the expensive internal control measures known as Section 404. Attempts by regulators to go beyond Sarbanes-Oxley by requiring stock options to be fully expensed – or through allowing investors more say in the replacement of directors – have been successfully delayed by powerful business lobbyists in Washington.

But this public backlash only captures one aspect of the power struggle. Another source of tension exists between companies and their investors; between managers and markets. Pressure from the investment community has followed a similar cycle of ebb and flow to that of the regulators. Fund managers angered by the abuses of the bubble were quick to punish companies caught making similar transgressions by selling their shares and driving down share prices still further. Companies anxious to secure a better stock market rating found they could actively promote a cleaner image by staying ahead of the demands of regulators and voluntarily giving up controversial perks such as stock options.

Here, too, the business community has complained of things going too far. So-called "activist" shareholders have themselves become a target, particularly because many companies suspect motives other than profit-maximisation lie behind some of their campaigns. Perhaps the clearest sign of this came this month with the forced departure of the head of the California Public Employees' Retirement System (Calpers) who was accused of acting in line with union interests when pursuing the management of Safeway, the US retailer.

Whatever the rights and wrongs of this particular case, it would, however, be wrong to assume the business backlash is now unstoppable. Attempts by the Financial Accounting Standards Board to force companies to treat stock options as an operating expense have merely been postponed, not derailed. Efforts by the Securities and Exchange Commission to reform the way directors are nominated look stalled rather than entirely dead in the water.

Preparations are even being made to open further fronts in the battle between regulators and companies. William Donaldson, SEC chairman, is pressing for new disclosure rules on executive pay that would give shareholders more meaningful information about compensation – one of the last untouched issues in corporate governance.

In spite of widespread irritation with the burden of compliance, corporate America is also far from unified about what to do about it. For every chief executive who says that parts of Sarbanes-Oxley were unnecessary, there are others who argue that all companies needed to take the medicine to cure a chronic lack of trust among investors.

All this points to a longer-lasting shift in the balance of power in corporate America. Increasingly, investors are demanding full transparency and compliance from managers on a remarkably detailed range of issues...

Source: *Financial Times*, December 14, 2004.

For historical, cultural, social and economic reasons corporate governance systems vary throughout the world. Thus, the structures in the UK, France and Germany are significantly different, in spite of efforts by the EU to sponsor some element of harmonization. And these differences profoundly impact both the role of financial reporting and the nature and content of financial disclosure in these countries.

Over the course of the last decade, as the implications of the governance structure for competitive advantage and added value have come to be appreciated, the issue has received greater attention. This is reflected in the recent launch of a number of indices – seeking, amongst other things, to identify a link between governance and performance – that will enable benchmarking and international comparison of governance structures:

As Indices Tracking the Best-Run Companies are Launched, Pauline Skypala Finds that the Jury is Still Out on Whether the Benefits of Good Governance Outweigh the Costs

Believers in the link between good corporate governance and greater shareholder value may finally get highly visible evidence to back their views. The new corporate governance indices from the FTSE Group, part owned by the Financial Times, and Institutional Shareholder Services (ISS) launched last week will track the performance of six indices from which the worst governed companies have been excluded. If they can demonstrate consistent outperformance of the benchmark FTSE indices, gainsayers will have a harder time denying any link.

William Crist, chairman of the FTSE ISS advisory committee and former chairman of Calpers, the $80bn pension fund for Californian public employees, suggests there is a consensus view that good corporate governance is not only relevant to managing risk but also to adding value. "There is really no evidence that it does not add value," he says. The evidence that it does is steadily accumulating, but is little known, says Craig Mackenzie, head of investor responsibility at Insight Investment, the asset management subsidiary of banking group HBOS. He cites a 2004 study by US academics, Gompers et al. This found that a fund that had bought companies with top ranked governance and sold short the bottom companies throughout the 1990s would have outperformed the market by 8.5 per cent a year.

Research by Deutsche Bank also showed a link between corporate governance and share price performance for FTSE 350 companies in the UK between 2000 and 2003. The top 10 per cent of companies by governance structure outperformed the bottom 10 per cent by 25 per cent over the period. The research also showed well governed companies were more profitable. But this does not convince everyone. This year's PwC Global CEO survey showed 70 per cent of UK chief executives regard spending on governance, risk management and compliance as a cost rather than an investment. Just under 50 per cent consider the costs to outweigh the benefits. In contrast, 60 per cent of CEOs globally consider governance expenditure to be an investment. This may reflect the UK's progress on corporate governance compared with other countries. It is the only country of the 24 included in the FTSE ISS ratings to appear in the top five for each of the five major themes that go towards the overall ranking. Canada makes four appearances, although it does get top place for board structure, the most important constituent of the overall ranking, and for audit process and ownership.

The US only makes two top five appearances, at number four for both ownership and audit process. France, Germany and Switzerland are the only European countries that make any top five appearances. UK companies also make up six of the top 10 global constituents, including BHP Billiton, Smith Nephew, Scottish Power and BT. Continental European companies make up the bottom 10, with Denmark and Sweden accounting for three companies apiece. Greater awareness of the international diversity in corporate governance, especially across continental Europe, is one of the positive outcomes Mr Mackenzie expects to see from the launch of the indices. "I think it will also broaden the public debate about and awareness of corporate governance, which is overly focused on directors' pay." Directors' compensation and stock ownership only account for 9 per cent each in the overall ratings for companies, compared with 44 per cent for board structure and independence. He discounts concerns that the new indices may encourage companies to treat corporate governance as a box ticking exercise. "If it was the only thing driving corporate governance – if there wasn't a shareholder activist community having a more subtle dialogue with companies – there would be such a danger."

Source: *Financial Times*, April 17, 2005.

In practice:

Big Government, by Lex

Board meetings were once delightfully idiosyncratic... Tyco's 2001 "executive board meeting" in Sardinia cost the company $1m and coincided with an exuberant toga party. Those days are *over. But one form of excess may be replacing another. The wave of governance initiatives that followed such corporate scandals has now turned into a rising tide of red tape.*

... All this virtue is expensive. The average cost of enforcing Sarbanes-Oxley is $5m, according to consultancy Korn/Ferry. But the real burden is on management time. One survey found that many US chief financial officers already spend more time on their company's pension fund than its operations. Governance burdens will add to this problem. Litigation risk and increased time commitment have also made it hard to recruit non-executive directors.

Is there any performance benefit in return? Surprisingly, the evidence suggests, "yes". A study by two Harvard academics, reviewing 1,500 US companies between 1990 and 1999, concluded that companies with the strongest rights for shareholders substantially outperformed those with the weakest. A Deutsche Bank study between 2000 and 2003 found that UK companies with independent chairmen, boards, and audit committees materially beat the market, although recent evidence for continental Europe is mixed. Unlike most red tape, corporate governance rules are designed to protect capital, not the state, labour, or the consumer. Investors should give them the benefit of the doubt. But like all bureaucracy, they tend to get out of hand.

Source: Financial Times, March 21, 2005.

Corporate Governance in the UK

The UK corporate governance regime is typical of the Anglo-American system of corporate structure. Indeed, the model of corporate structure characteristic of the English-speaking world originated in England and was disseminated throughout the British Empire.

The unique characteristics of the Anglo-American (or Anglo-Saxon) form of corporate governance can be traced to the growth in numbers and significance of Joint-Stock companies in the 18th century. These entities, whose emergence coincided with the advent of the Industrial Revolution, were designed to facilitate the raising of the huge sums of money necessary to finance the large-scale industrialization then beginning.

Prior to that, the dominant business entity had been the sole-tradership. Typically, however, these sole-traders did not have the finance needed to benefit fully from the opportunities offered by industrialization. The genius of the Joint-Stock company was that it allowed those with finance to team up with those who had skill and vision.

By investing in a company these investors were deemed to own a "share" in the company, hence the term shareholder. Typically, several of these individuals would invest, thus providing a number, often hundreds, of such shareholders. By allowing external holders of capital to invest in these entrepreneurial enterprises with limited risk, these Joint-Stock companies acted as catalysts to British industry and, in part, help to explain the extent to which Britain enjoyed such an early advantage in the industrialization process.

Over time the market in which these investors purchased and sold their shares evolved into the Stock Exchange. In contrast to many continental European countries where the principal form of business structure continued to be the sole-tradership or partnership, the Stock Exchange has, therefore, played a critical role in the financial and governance structure in the English-speaking world, particularly in the UK and the US.

This structure had other implications. Shareholders saw their role primarily as providers of capital, not entrepreneurial or managerial skill. For this reason, and because it would be simply impractical for all shareholders to involve themselves at management level, they delegated this task to others. A central feature of the British form of corporate governance, therefore, is this division between owners and those who manage the entity on their behalf. In this scheme of things the Board of Directors came to represent a crucial element in the governance structure as it was here that the often-diverging interests of investors and managers were mediated.

Because shareholders were divorced from the operation of their own business, it became necessary to devise a mechanism by which they might be kept informed of the performance of the company. It was in response to this that management began preparing accounts that were then made available to the owners. Consequently, the practice of distributing Annual Reports to owners needs to be considered first and foremost in this context: whatever about their usefulness or timeliness, Annual Reports are primarily intended as a means of bridging the gulf between owners and managers that results from the corporate governance model peculiar to the English-speaking world.

As the number of shareholders grew and the quantities of money raised on the market increased so too did the significance of these accounts. As a result parliament took a greater interest in the process to the extent that the accounting and auditing functions are now the subject of considerable statutory control.

In recent years, particularly as a number of scandals that could be traced, in part, to faulty governance cultures came to light, various stakeholders have eagerly sought to establish their rights. Shareholders, one of the groups most affected by governance malaise, have been to the fore. The result has been the emergence of a culture of "corporate activism", whether inspired by large pension funds or small groups of shareholders that champions 'shareholder value' – usually related to share price – as the principal consideration. Particularly in the Anglo-American world, which assigns such prominence to investors and the market, this has led to conflict between owners and executives.

Corporate Activism: Why More Shareholders are Showing Executives the Red Card, by Richard Brass

The concerns of shareholders have long been a low priority in many companies. Few shareholders are prepared to go public with their negative views about a company and then watch the share price slide, and many executives have been happy to listen politely and then do nothing. But shareholders now appear prepared to take things that crucial bit further, and both executives and non-execs are learning to sit up and pay attention, writes Richard Brass.

Shareholders used to be such a well-behaved bunch. Not many years ago, unless the share price went into sudden freefall, the only time most company executives expected to hear from their shareholders was at the AGM, when they would show up, dutifully approve everything, then shuffle off home to wait for their dividends. There might be the odd crank who liked to get up and make some noise, but the big investors, the pension funds and insurance companies that really mattered kept nice and quiet.

Those tranquil days became history last summer in the wave of shareholder rebellions that crashed through the AGMs of some of the biggest corporate names. At the first opportunity, after the Government gave shareholders the right to hold an advisory vote on companies' remuneration policies, such giants as GlaxoSmithKline, Reuters, HSBC and Corus found themselves staring down the wrong end of large disapproving votes from shareholders. It was the biggest rebellion in British corporate history, and the message from investors was that it wouldn't be the last.

But, away from the high drama of these big moments, day-to-day corporate activism, mostly conducted behind closed doors, is also becoming bolder. While spectacular shareholder rebellions in the very public environment of an AGM may be brand new, groups of powerful investors have been quietly expressing their concerns about the direction of companies in private for a long time. The difference now, however, is that they're prepared to go further and, if necessary, to go public.

Whether triggered by the new-found vigour of shareholder activism over remuneration, or by the shadow of such corporate disasters as Enron, WorldCom and now Parmalat, the cases of behind-the-scenes activism that have come to light in recent months are a sign that, if company executives were happy to overlook their big shareholders in the past, those days are over.

When rebel shareholders claimed the scalp of Carlton chairman, Michael Green, last October, they took corporate activism to a new level. Never before had the head of a big Plc been so publicly humiliated by investors, and the rebellion, which scuppered Green's plan to be executive chairman of the new ITV company formed by the merger of Carlton and Granada, was a clear case of what can happen when companies don't listen.

The rebel group, led by Anthony Bolton of Fidelity, included powerful names such as UBS Global Asset Management, Legal & General and Schroders, and together represented 36% of Carlton's equity and 33% of Granada's. They made it clear as soon as the merger plans were announced in 2001 that they would not accept being overlooked, but the companies' executives believed the fund managers wouldn't take it to the wire, knowing that to do so would expose their problems to the public gaze and put the value of their shareholdings at risk. They were wrong. The obliging fund manager had turned into something completely different.

In the US, high-profile corporate activism has long been a feature of the business environment, but a month after the Carlton dispute it too claimed one of its most spectacular scalps when the dogged persistence of the New York private investment company, Tweedy Browne, unveiled to shareholders and the world at large the real state of things at Conrad Black's Hollinger empire. The unseated Black is no doubt now ruing the fact that he didn't pay more attention to the investors.

Back in Britain, this year has already seen a shareholders' rebellion when the state of the finances of WH Smith burst into the open, despite the efforts of the retail group's non-executive directors to deal with the rising dissatisfaction through weeks of meetings with unhappy shareholders. Another case of too little listening, too late. At the same time, several large investors in Shell became involved in what was described as 'active engagement' with the oil giant over its management structure and its financial position, and once again the dispute went public, amid calls for the resignation of the chairman, Sir Philip Watts.

Such an outbreak of public disputes between investors and companies is unprecedented. . .

Source: *accounting & business*, April, 2004.

The shareholder value lobby has, therefore, been both proactive and successful in ensuring that the interests of shareholders, however defined, are kept to the forefront in the endless jostling for position in the governance area. Reflecting the fluid nature of the situation, however, this, in turn, has been challenged by those who point to the limitations of a model that mostly favours the shareholder value paradigm, with its concomitant emphasis on share price appreciation:

A Misleading Obsession With Share Prices

Can or must the obligations of directors to their company be translated into an obligation to achieve the highest possible price for the company's stock? That is the claim made by the shareholder value movement. The market, which represents the distilled wisdom of thousands of players in financial markets, knows best. The board of MCI, the telecoms group, has just rejected an offer from Qwest on the basis that the lower bid from Verizon would be better for the business. They have certainly deprived stockholders of the chance of a quick buck, but have they also frustrated the central purpose of financial markets: to direct assets to the managers who can deploy them most efficiently?

If you believe they have, you would do well to study the chaotic reign of "Chainsaw Al" Dunlap, arch-champion of shareholder value and one-time chief executive of Sunbeam, providers of toasters, mixers and blenders to generations of Americans. As I recounted in my last column (May 24), the agreement that took the business out of Chapter 11 bankruptcy left stockholders, whom Mr Dunlap described in his tract Mean Business as "the only constituency I am concerned about'', with nothing. The longest chapter of that book is entitled ''Impressing the Analysts''. It records Mr Dunlap telling a group of fund managers ''we will be successful because I say we will be''. The remark was greeted, he notes modestly, with ''enthusiastic shouting and applause''. Such exchanges are a powerful means of creating shareholder value. But not of building businesses.

The price of a company's stock depends not on the value of a company but on the market's perception of that value, which is often easier to change than value itself. Mr Dunlap's relentless self-promotion and his purported emphasis on the primacy of shareholder interests achieved this. The mere announcement that he was taking the helm at Sunbeam almost doubled the stock price. At its peak, barely three months before Mr Dunlap was fired as the company fell to pieces, Sunbeam's market value had increased fivefold since his appointment. Stock prices reflect underlying realities in the long run, but, even at Sunbeam, the five years from Mr Dunlap's appointment to corporate collapse were longer than the ''long run'' of most executive incentive schemes...

Some people still believe, against all evidence, that the market is generally successful in giving a clear view of a company's real performance through the rose-tinted lenses provided even by reputable finance directors. But judging the quality of a manager by his effect on the stock price is exactly equivalent to judging a weather forecaster on whether you like what they tell you.

Understandably, chief executives largely paid in stock options may check their company's share price several times a day, but it is extraordinary that some of them believe that by doing so they gain information about their business. Anyone tempted to think this should remember the fate of Chainsaw Al. Or that of Bernie Ebbers, WorldCom chairman, whose familiar routine was to point to a chart of the stock price and ask fawning analysts for questions. Where business judgment and market judgment differ, managers' responsibility is to implement their business judgment.

And since they are hired for their business judgment, it is for that, not for their ability to generate ''enthusiastic shouting and applause'', that executives should be rewarded. Managers who focus closely on the stock price, whether by inclination or because they have incentives to do so, will often fail to serve the best interests even of their stockholders.

Source: *Financial Times*, June 7, 2005.

Best Practice

The governance system operating in a country has profound implications for both accounting as a discipline and the accounting and auditing professions in general. Thus, in the UK, as the providers of a critical information component of the corporate edifice, accountants assumed a role and status significantly greater than their continental counterparts. So too did the information they provided. To a large extent the influence of accountants in the Anglo-American world derives from their key role in constructing and controlling the accounting information that has traditionally bridged the communications gap between owners and managers.

Many of the problems and challenges facing accounting, however, stem directly from this same gulf. Specifically they derive from the realization that the nature and form of information supplied by accountants is no longer adequate to bridge it. This is especially the case as the numbers of those with an interest in this information increase. Furthermore, spectacular failures of the accounting and auditing functions in recent years have exposed both the inadequacies of the Anglo-American governance model, and the inability of accounting information as currently presented to satisfy the interests of an increasing range of stakeholders.

This has led to a series of investigations and reports initiated by government and others. These have resulted in a more focused and formalized understanding of governance best practice.

Cadbury Report

Since the late 1980s, therefore, there has been considerable pressure on those responsible for the regulation of the accounting and governance functions to address these perceived inadequacies. One response was the commissioning by the FRC, the Stock Exchange and the accounting profession of an investigation into corporate governance practice in the UK. Under the chairmanship of Sir Adrian Cadbury, a committee on the Financial Aspects of Corporate Governance was formed and charged with reviewing governance practice with specific reference to the following:

- The responsibilities of executive and non-executive directors for reviewing and reporting on performance to shareholders and other financially interested parties.
- The frequency, clarity and form in which information should be provided.
- The case for audit committees, including their composition and role.
- The principal responsibilities of auditors and the extent and value of the audit.
- The link between shareholders, boards and auditors; and
- Any other relevant matters.

Cadbury's approach was to attempt to establish a framework within which good corporate governance and accountability might flourish. To this end the Committee's final report emphasized matters such as transparency, disclosure and accountability as critical unifying features of any mature governance system.

In its final form the Cadbury Report concentrated on four key areas:

1. **Board of directors**: the importance of an efficient board was emphasized. There were specific recommendations in relation to their composition and the respective roles of executive and non-executive directors. It was observed that under the board system that applies in the UK the Chairman plays a key role in ensuring that best practice is encouraged. One part of this is making sure that there is a healthy level of accountability and division of responsibilities. Although it stopped short of recommending that the roles be split, the Report strongly advised that proper

accountability would be facilitated by a system in which the same person did not hold the functions of Chairman and CEO.

2. **Executive directors**: with the accountability of executive directors in mind, the Report recommended that service contracts should not exceed 3 years without shareholders approval. Without pressing the point, it also argued for increased disclosure of directors' remuneration. Specifically, it recommended that a remuneration committee comprised mainly of non-executive directors should set directors' pay.

3. **Non-Executive directors**: one surprising element was an emphasis on the way in which non-executive directors could play a far more proactive and independent role in a healthy corporate governance regime. As the Report outlined, non-executive directors "should be independent of management and free from any business or other relationship that could materially interfere with the exercise of their independent judgement, apart from their fees and shareholding. Their fees should reflect the time which they commit to the company". It was also envisaged that they would dominate audit and remuneration committees.

4. **Reporting and controls**: finally, the Report addressed the respective responsibilities of directors and others in relation to the presentation of information about a company's performance and position. It specifically identified it as a responsibility of the board "to present a balanced and understandable assessment of the company's position". In achieving this the Report recognized that this can mean presenting not only audited accounting data but also additional narrative material covering the company's performance and future prospects. (In response to this, the Accounting Standards Board recommended that Annual Reports incorporate a new narrative statement, called the Operating and Financial Review, in which the directors provide more information on the principal issues underlying performance. This is considered in more detail in Chapter 5).

The Report also made some other specific recommendations:

- Every company should establish an audit committee comprised of "at least three non-executive directors with written terms of reference which deal clearly with its authority and duties". This committee would then liaise with the external auditor and ensure that the audit function was carried out "efficiently and objectively" without any undue pressure being exerted on the auditor. Since this recommendation was made, the audit committee has emerged as a critical element in the governance architecture of complying companies. In particular, it has come to be seen as a forum in which the competing interests of preparers and users can be addressed and the concerns of auditors can be expressed. The result has been the gradual acceptance of the audit committee as a key component in any developed corporate governance structure.

- On the question of responsibility for the preparation of accounts and the audit process, it recommended that "directors should explain their responsibility for preparing the accounts next to a statement by the auditors about their reporting responsibilities". This was intended to ensure that readers, particularly shareholders, understand the respective responsibilities of directors and auditors in relation to the production of accounts. In many eyes, however, it was seen as a sop to the Report's sponsoring bodies, intended to protect them from legal action.

• The effectiveness of the company's system of internal control and its risk management culture should be given prominence. This has since been dealt with by the Turnbull Committee and is discussed below.

The Cadbury Report represented a seminal development in UK – indeed, global – appreciation of the importance of corporate governance. In particular, by adopting a principles-based approach, it set the tone for future governance initiatives. And in highlighting specific issues such as the role of non-executive directors and audit committees, it pointed to potential solutions to some long-established problems.

Greenbury

The Cadbury Report represented only the first in a series of efforts by regulatory bodies to deal with corporate governance issues. Indeed, one consequence of the publicity surrounding its publication and adoption was that public pressure ensured that other, related issues would have to be dealt with.

For instance, while the general public is usually indifferent to the issues surrounding the corporate governance debate, one specific element of it, the level of executive remuneration, has the capacity to generate heated reaction. And this is stoked on a regular basis by media reports of excessive remuneration packages being awarded to CEOs and directors.

In practice:

The magazine Business Week last year found CEOs of quoted companies made 531 times the amount earned by the average worker, compared with 42 times in 1980. But what really rankled is so-called "payment for failure": an investigation into remuneration practices of the 25 biggest corporate failures since January 2001 by the FT found executives who brought about bankruptcies walked away with 3.3bn. As the following extract highlights, in spite of attempts by regulators to contain executive and boardroom pay, the remuneration packages of CEOs show little sign of being controlled:

Chief Executive pay rises 168% in five years, by Chris Evans

Chief executive remuneration pay rose by a staggering 168% from 1998 to 2003, despite campaigns by investor groups against fat cat pay, according to a survey by consultants, Independent Remuneration Solutions. Average remuneration, excluding pension, for leading chief executives last year was £2.6m, the survey showed. These findings are based on data contained in the 2003 annual reports of 800 quoted companies, and include the value of options and share schemes, not just the total cash paid. The growth of the non-salary parts of the remuneration package means that salaries now make up less than half of the total package for many companies and only one quarter for the average FTSE100 CEO, the survey reveals.

Chief executive pay compared to that of other executive directors also differs depending on the size of the company. In smaller companies the second highest paid director is paid at 75% of the rate of the CEO. But in the larger companies he or she is paid on average 60% of the rate of the CEO. Total remuneration awarded to chief executives of the UK's largest companies rose an average of 22% a year in the five years to 2003. Cliff Weight, the report's author and IRS director, blamed this rise on the government for not forcing companies to detail share options, long term incentive plans and pension awards alongside pay and bonuses in company reports. 'There is no incentive for companies to clearly disclose total remuneration awarded. Because of a lack of transparency and the complex pay plans pushed by some advisers, total remuneration awarded to chief executives has soared without many realising it,' Weight stressed.

Source: Accountancy, May 2004.

In 1995 the Confederation of British Industry instituted the "Study Group on Directors' Remuneration" and charged it with producing a statement of best practice in relation to directors' remuneration. The chairman, Richard Greenbury, chairman of Marks and Spencer, made it quite clear that he did not intend a radical overhaul of the current system. Nevertheless, responding to considerable public pressure and some injudicious awards to the directors of several newly privatized utilities, the Greenbury Report produces some useful proposals.

The Greenbury Code, as it came to be called, made recommendations under four principal headings:

- **Remuneration committee**: reflecting the tenor of the Cadbury Report, it proposed that the remuneration of executive directors be decided by a remuneration committee made up of non-executive directors, the names of whom should be disclosed in the Annual Report.

- **Disclosure and approval provisions**: this committee should report annually on the criteria adopted in arriving at the remuneration levels of individual directors. This report was to be included in the Annual Report and should disclose details of the full remuneration packages, including pension contributions, share options and other entitlements.

- **Remuneration policy**: as a general principle, remuneration packages should reflect generally accepted rates and be consistent with industry standards. Performance-related pay elements, in particular share-based schemes, would be expected to be long-term in focus.

- **Service contracts and compensation**: the period of notice required under service contracts should generally be 1 year or less.

> **In practice:**
>
> The impact of accounting policy on social and economic policy is neatly illustrated in the effect that the new IFRS accounting rules on share options are having on their use as a means of remunerating executives:
>
> *Executive pay moves away from options*
>
> *RIP the executive share option. Died 2005 after a long decline. Much-loved and mourned by those who cashed theirs in during the bull market. Scorned by those whose dreams of lucre vanished with the bear. Options as a form of executive reward may not be totally dead and pushing up the daisies but a report yesterday from consultants PwC is the latest in a line suggesting that they are rapidly on the way out. And they need little mourning. Among FTSE 100 chief executives, options as a proportion of delivered long-term incentives declined from 36 per cent to 20 per cent over the past year and a similar trend is clear among medium-sized companies.*
>
> *A significant catalyst is the new international accounting rule that requires options grants to be charged for the first time to the profit and loss account, thus removing the accounting advantage they had over the other main form of long-term pay – grants of shares that vest if certain performance conditions are met.*
>
> *Source: Financial Times, August 11, 2005.*

Hampel

In November 1995 Sir Ronald Hampel, chairman of ICI, was appointed to chair a successor body to Cadbury. Its remit was to continue the work of its predecessor by seeking to "promote high standards of corporate governance in the interests of investor protection". The chairman interpreted this to mean that his task was primarily to "fine-tune" Cadbury.

Published in 1998, its main provisions merely reiterated many of the points made by Cadbury and Greenbury, albeit in somewhat stronger terms. The main recommendations were:

- The positions of Chairman and CEO should be filled by different people.

- Directors should be on contracts of 1 year or less.

- The remuneration committee should consist of non-executive directors only.

- Non-executive directors may be paid in the form of shares although this is not recommended.

- One senior non-executive director should be nominated with responsibility for liaising with shareholders and addressing their concerns.

- Directors should be required to undertake some form of training for their role.

The Cadbury, Greenbury and Hampel Reports were brought together to form what came to be known as the Combined Code, a code of best practice which was incorporated by the Stock Exchange into its Yellow Book effective for accounting periods ending after December 31, 1998. This was subsequently endorsed by the UKLA. This Code, which is discussed later in more detail, would be first supplemented by the Turnbull Report.

Turnbull

The Cadbury Report had highlighted the role of internal controls and risk management as significant elements in the corporate governance debate. In response, the ICAEW set up a committee under the chairmanship of Nigel Turnbull, chairman of the leisure group Rank, to issue recommendations. In September 1999 this committee issued its final report, Internal Control: Guidance for Directors on the Combined Code.

As the title suggests this report is mainly concerned with indicating to directors how the various elements of the Combined Code relating to internal control and risk management are to be implemented.

To the surprise of many, it did make some significant contributions to the whole corporate governance debate, particularly in the importance which it attaches to the whole area of risk management. In terms of corporate strategies and perspective it effectively assigns to the whole area of risk management a strategic and operational importance which had not previously been articulated.

The Turnbull Report is predicated on the notion that "internal control is embedded in the business processes" and assumes that a company's board adopts a risk-based approach to establishing a sound system of internal control. Consequently, it emphasizes that the internal control system plays a critical function in efficiently managing risks that are central to a company achieving its business objectives. In all of this it places effective financial controls and the maintenance of proper accounting records firmly at the centre.

This emphasis on risk, transparency and internal controls has succeeded in establishing these as part of the corporate governance equation. Issues pertaining to corporate governance can now be demonstrated to have the potential to impact directly upon more that merely the reporting and accountability responsibilities of an organization.

In 2003, following the Sarbanes-Oxley Act in the US, the FRC initiated a review of Turnbull. The resulting report was submitted in 2005 and made a number of important recommendations:

- The Turnbull guidance should continue to cover all internal controls, and not be limited to controls over financial reporting.

- Boards should confirm that necessary action has been or is being taken to remedy any significant weaknesses.

- The guidance should not restrict a company's ability to apply it in a manner appropriate to its own circumstance.

- Boards should continue to review their application of the guidance.

- Boards should not be required to make an annual statement on the effectiveness of internal controls, but should include such information as they consider necessary to assist shareholders' understanding of the main features of the risk management and internal control systems.

- External auditors' responsibilities in relation to internal control statements should not be expanded.

Significantly, therefore, while some elements of Turnbull were tightened, the conclusion was that a radical revision was not necessary. This provides a striking contrast with the more prescriptive, box-ticking approach adopted by the US.

Review Group Favours Guidelines With a Light Touch

US-style legislation on corporate risk management has been rejected by a high-level review group of business-people and investors appointed by the regulator for corporate reporting. The group, which was set up last year by the Financial Reporting Council, the independent regulator for accounting and auditing, has given a vote of confidence to Britain's existing guidelines on internal controls used to manage corporate risk. Its report, published today, finds fault with some provisions of the US Sarbanes-Oxley Act, the detailed corporate governance legislation passed in the wake of the financial scandals of recent years, and says that the UK's principles-based approach has helped to strengthen internal controls and needs only "limited" adjustments to be brought up to date. Businesses have become increasingly alarmed at the prospect of that approach being superseded in coming years by new European Union legislation. Internal controls are the mechanisms that companies put in place to manage corporate risk by regulating business activities, the use of company assets and the compilation of accounts. They have been brought to prominence by the Sarbanes-Oxley Act, which requires US-listed companies to test and document the effectiveness of controls against financial reporting fraud.

The equivalent of the controversial US legislation is the five-year old Turnbull guidance, which supplements the UK's Combined Code on corporate governance. The guidance came from a working party led by Nigel Turnbull, a former executive director of Rank, that reported in September 1999, before the scandals that triggered Sarbanes-Oxley came to light. It is wider-ranging, covering operational as well as financial controls, and uses a lighter touch, based on principles rather than rules.

The FRC review group led by Douglas Flint, group finance director of HSBC, has concluded that the British approach – which lacks prescription and gives management considerable discretion – remains most appropriate. It rejected one of the most contentious provisions of Sarbanes-Oxley, which requires companies to make a public statement on the effectiveness of their internal controls. The concept of "effectiveness" would not be meaningful, the group said, "when considering many operational risks... where the company's response is determined by its risk appetite and cannot be mandated by reference to some objective standard". US-listed companies have undertaken expensive verification work to produce effectiveness statements, and some have seen their share prices drop after they disclosed control weaknesses. The original Turnbull guidance advises British companies to carry out effectiveness tests, but they are not obliged to disclose the results. The review group, however, recommends that boards confirm when action has been taken to remedy significant failings. Mr Flint said he expected "a very high proportion" of companies to fix faults. "In the context of the evolving environment in which businesses operate it would be extraordinary if companies reviewed controls and didn't find something they could improve," he said.

The group concluded that Turnbull's use of high-level principles, as opposed to the detailed checklists common to Sarbanes-Oxley, helped to explain why it had yielded benefits. "Boards have been required to think seriously about internal control and not simply delegate a piece of process to a project team lower down the organisation," the report says.

Source: *Financial Times*, June 16, 2005.

Higgs

One of the most unexpected, yet significant, conclusions reached by Cadbury was the potential for non-executive directors (NEDs) to play a key role in modern boards. This represented a dramatic shift in how they were perceived: one chairman of a plc had famously compared his company's NEDs to bidets – a good idea, but he wasn't sure how to use them. As the following extract illustrates, NEDs are now expected to bring a range of skills and perspectives to a board. These should be underpinned by an "independence" that enables them to make a unique contribution to board conduct, company strategy and governance functions.

Big Power Shift in the Boardroom: by Ross Tieman

Effective Non-Executive Directors Should Have Strong Ethical Principles – and Always be Ready to Ask the Tough Questions

There was a time when being a non-executive director was a handy source of pocket money and a badge of status at the golf club. Today, it is a demanding occupation fraught with responsibility and risk – so much so that four out of five candidates approached for non-executive directorships in the US are now said to decline. In the UK, too, headhunters say they struggle to fill non-executive vacancies, while the list of skills and obligations of non-executives grows ever-longer. In continental Europe, meanwhile, the non-exec is also acquiring new significance in the wake of corporate governance reviews in France and Germany.

Throughout the western world, the job of non-executive director is shifting from sinecure to hard graft. This is not just a response to corporate scandals in the US, although the exposure of corporate governance failures at Enron, Tyco and the rest has crystallised concerns that were mounting there and prompted action.

In numerical terms, US boards are already dominated by supposedly "independent" directors. But according to Bob Monks, US shareholder activist, the reality of the past decade has been the domination of the chief executive officer – who usually chairs the board and selects his non-executive colleagues. This has allowed, he says, the subordination of shareholder interests to those of executive remuneration, leading to an era in which executive pay differentials have outstripped any historic precedent.

The torrent of legislation and regulation in response to corporate scandals and rising shareholder activism is intended to rectify a host of shortcomings that are now widely acknowledged. By 2004, boards of companies listed on the Nasdaq and New York exchanges will be required to have a majority of truly independent directors, as well as audit, compensation and nominating committees made up entirely of non-execs. In many respects, US practice is moving closer to that in the UK, where the introduction of the voluntary Cadbury Code a decade ago as a benchmark has already triggered significant change in the way boards work.

According to Dr Steven Young, of Lancaster University Management School, who has been monitoring Cadbury implementation, about half of FTSE 100 companies now have a majority of non-execs on their boards, and the separation of the roles of chairman and chief executive is now the rule, rather than the exception. The evidence now shows, he says, that "companies that have a high proportion of non-execs on their board are much less likely to have doubtful accounting practices". Moreover, "both our research and broader academic research does provide some pretty strong evidence that non-execs can play a key role in some board decisions and in protecting shareholder wealth," he adds.

Source: *Financial Times*, February 24, 2003.

The emergence of NEDs as key players in the governance culture was reflected in the commissioning by the DTI in 2002 of a report specifically intended to review the role of NEDs. Undertaken by Sir Derek Higgs, the resulting report, *Review of the Role and Effectiveness of Non-Executive Directors,* sought to reinforce the role and responsibilities of NEDs in modern corporate governance. Among the principal recommendations that this led to in the revised Combined Code issued in 2003 were:

- At least half of all board members should be independent NEDs
- A CEO should not become Chairman of the same company
- A senior independent director should be appointed to act as conduit for shareholders to raise issues
- NEDs should meet by themselves at least once a year
- NEDs should normally serve two three-year terms. NEDs would not be considered after 10 years service
- No individual should chair more than one major company.

In practice:

The non-exec power players: a new breed of professional, independent directors is replacing the more deferential old school. Robert Watts finds out who they are.

A quiet revolution is taking place in Britain's boardrooms. Non-executive directors are being transformed from the passive, low-key pals of the management into well-paid, professional watchdogs who are expected to oust underperforming bosses. In the latest high profile boardroom coup 10 days ago, five non-executive directors at Rentokil Initial ousted Sir Clive Thompson, the chairman who had practically built the rat-catching-to-security group from scratch in 22 years as chief executive. The coup, after an apparent disagreement over strategy, underlines once again how non-executive directors are taking on a greater role in strategic and corporate governance issues.

The price of this extra responsibility has been a surge in pay for non-executives. Over the past 12 months the annual fee paid to the average FTSE100 non-executive director has risen by 36 per cent to around £40,000, according to Income Data Services, the employment research house. The average earnings for a FTSE100 non-executive chairman reached £218,000 while a quarter were paid £300,000 or more.

... A non-executive director should now expect lengthier board meetings, more strategy discussions, greater dialogue with shareholders and mountains of reading and research. "The pay has doubled, but so have the hours they're putting in," Viney says. The workload has particularly increased for non-executives who serve on the audit, nomination and the remuneration committees...

Source: Sunday Telegraph, May 30, 2004.

Significantly, Higgs was seen to have both properly gauged the corporate mood, and also represented an important political statement, particularly in the context of the more prescriptive regime represented by SOX.

Higgs Does the Business in Heading Off a Sarbanes-Oxley, by Jeremy Warner

It is impossible to think of any sensible proposal for improving the role and effectiveness of non-executive directors that hasn't been thought of before, so it shouldn't come as any surprise that the Derek Higgs review has so few surprises in it. On one level, his report is no more than a reworking of previous codes and ideas, updated and strengthened to take account of recent scandals. Those hoping for more will be disappointed.

Business and the City, on the other hand, will be counting their blessings, for what Mr Higgs has done is perform the vital public service of defusing the debate and heading off at the pass the army of do-gooders hell bent on root and branch reform or something worse. Post the scandals of Enron and WorldCom, the chances of what Mr Higgs refers to as the corporate equivalent of a Dangerous Dogs Act were high. In the US, they already have one, in the shape of Sarbanes Oxley Act, and jolly poor, divisive, badly thought out, prescriptive legislation it is too.

Previous standard bearers for the corporate governance reviews occasionally foisted on the City by hostile public opinion have generally come bitterly to regret ever taking the job, most notably Sir Richard Greenbury, who by the end thought it a poisoned chalice. The fact that his business, Marks & Spencer, was going to hell in a handcart while he was off undertaking the review is almost by the by. All he got for his trouble was criticism and mockery.

Mr Higgs is a different kettle of fish altogether. He's a former corporate finance adviser and head of investment at Prudential, and as such he's had as much experience as any in dealing with issues of poor corporate governance. As a consequence he's been criticised as a bit of a poacher turned gamekeeper, a perception to some extent supported by the fact that his own position as a non-executive director of British Land is compromised by his role as a former adviser to the company and a consultant to the company's existing investment bank adviser, UBS Warburg. Furthermore, corporate governance has been a big issue at British Land.

Mr Higgs neatly sidesteps the suggestion that his review puts him in breach of his own guidelines by making his recommendations "a counsel for best practice", and not an absolute obligation. It is "a comply or explain" regime that he wants to put in place and it is surely the right approach...

Source: *The Independent* January 21, 2003.

The phrase "comply or explain" captures well the essence of the UK approach to corporate governance, particularly when compared to the more prescriptive approach adopted by the US as epitomised by SOX. The UK principles-based approach encourages enterprises to comply and only requires explanations where the regime has not been complied with.

Smith

While Higgs had undertaken a broader brief in relation to non-executive directors, Sir Robert Smith was commissioned at the same time by the FRC to undertake a complementary review of the role of audit committees. This was a reflection of the fact that since Cadbury the audit committee had assumed such an important role. In January 2003, Smith produced his report – *Audit Committees: Combined Code Guidance* – which made a number of recommendations in relation to the audit committee, which had emerged in recent years as a significant element of a robust governance structure. The principal recommendations were:

- Audit committees should comprise of at least three members, all of whom should be independent non-executive directors

- At least one member should have significant, recent and relevant financial experience

- The audit committee should, amongst other tasks, monitor the integrity of the financial statements; review the company's internal control and internal audit systems; recommend the external auditor and also approve terms of engagement and remuneration; and, crucially, in light of the extent to which auditor's independence has been compromised in some cases (such as Enron), develop an acceptable policy on the external auditor supplying additional, non-audit services.

In practice:

While the Smith Report has been helpful in identifying ways in which the role of the audit committee can become more focused and bring greater value, as the following report highlights, there are likely to be problems in seeing it fully implemented:

Audit committees still lack 'financial experience': Survey finds that a quarter of FTSE100 companies still do not have audit committees containing someone with 'recent relevant financial experience'.

More than 25% of the UK's largest 100 quoted companies do not have audit committees that possess someone with 'recent relevant financial experience' as required by corporate governance guidance, according to a survey by KPMG. The KPMG survey of the first half of the FTSE100 to disclose their compliance to the new Combined Code found the UK's largest companies have 'been active in reshaping their boards to meet the enhanced corporate governance requirements laid down by the Higgs and Smith reviews'. KPMG warned that more than a quarter of companies chose to rely on the collective experience of the audit committee members rather than an individual, contrary to the guidance.

Timothy Copnell, director of Corporate Governance at KPMG, said: 'A fear at the time of the corporate governance reforms was that companies would struggle to find non-executives willing, or able, to be classified as having recent relevant financial experience – a problem that may be exacerbated by the introduction of IFRS. This appears to be bearing out.'

The survey showed audit committees averaged 5.5 meetings per year, half a meeting more than last year and one and a half more than the minimum recommended by Sir Robert Smith's Guidance on Audit Committees. The research also found that the average number of independent non-executive directors per board rose by an average of a quarter person in 12 months. And, women now constitute over 10% of FTSE100 board members, up by a percentage point in 12 months.

John Collier, a director at non-executive specialist headhunter Clive & Stokes International, believes the time commitment of audit committees is a far bigger issue for potential non executives than risk concerns. He said that some non-executives, especially at financial service companies, are devoting upwards of 40 days to their duties. He said of audit committee non-executives: 'the pre-meeting work is more severe than many other sub committees, and the sheer burden on them is tremendous.' Collier said the burden on non-executives is reflected in soaring remuneration. He said: 'Non-executive annual remuneration of £50,000 is common among FTSE100 companies now: a threefold increase in five years.'

Source: AccountancyAge, May 2005.

Combined Code

In 1998 the Cadbury, Greenbury, Hampel and Turnbull were amalgamated, effectively, into a Combined Code. The adoption of the Combined Code by the London Stock Exchange, and its incorporation into its Yellow Book with effect for accounting periods ending after December 31, 1998, meant that there were significant disclosures to be made by listed companies in relation to their corporate governance cultures and practices. In 2003 the FRC issued a revised Code, incorporating the recommendations of the Turnbull Review, Higgs and Smith Reports. These were incorporated by the UKLA into its listing rules. As a consequence, a UK company listed on the London Stock Exchange must now include a considerable amount of information pertaining to governance in the Annual Report. And the fact that a "comply or explain" culture – as distinct from one that insists omissions amount to breaches of a governance code – applies has, in the opinion of many commentators, contributed to a more enlightened approach by companies.

The past decade has been a period of intense activity in relation to corporate governance issues. Corporate failures as well as international, competitive and regulatory pressures have combined to inspire a flurry of activity as already outlined. The result is that the UK has been to the fore in initiating many innovative reforms.

UK Governance is the Best in Europe

Britain has Europe's best corporate governance with Germany, Spain and the Netherlands among the worst, although the continental standards as a whole are improving, according to Brussels research firm Deminor. The 2003 ratings, released on Monday, were based on 300 indicators ranging from shareholder rights to the proportion of independent directors, disclosure of remuneration and rules for capital increases.

'The UK is by far the best country in Europe in terms of shareholders rights. They also have very limited authorised capital,' Kristof Hotiu, one of the authors, told Reuters. 'Overall, one could say that the Netherlands is definitely the worst country. It is hardly possible to take over a Dutch company,' he said.

The report noted substantial improvements in France, which is now rated second after Britain among European countries, and in Switzerland, which showed the strongest improvements in board structure and shareholder rights in 2003. But it downgraded Germany, Europe's biggest economy, because of what it called a setback in shareholders' rights, faulting the absence of any obligatory remuneration report or approval of pay and benefits at company general meetings. 'German companies still fail to identify independent directors on the supervisory board, where half of the members are employee representatives,' the study said. Germany has a peculiar two-tier board structure. There is a management board and a supervisory board, which has an oversight function but is not always independent.

Source: *Accountancy*, March, 2004.

In practice:

Combined Code doing the job, says Higgs: SOX puts UK corporate governance in good light

The tide is running with the 'comply or explain' regime for corporate governance. So says Derek Higgs, UBS senior adviser and author of the Higgs Review of the Combined Code. Speaking at a roundtable on the subject at the ICAEW annual conference, accountancy2005, this morning, he told delegates he believes that the US Sarbanes-Oxley rules have shown the 'dark side' of rules-based governance.

The Combined Code, which has evolved since the Cadbury Report in 1992, is a 'great British product' he said, adding that there has no been no corporate fraud in the UK on the scale of that seen in Italy, Holland and Germany since Cadbury was published. 'We have a code that is effective, pragmatic and flexible. There is a greater recognition of the need for independence and greater realism in pay. It is understood in boardrooms and by investors,' he said.

Source: *Accountancy, June 2005.*

Companies are reaping rewards from governance reporting, by Kit Bingham

UK companies are beginning to use their corporate governance report to communicate information to investors, rather than merely comply with requirements, an analysis of reports has found. A survey of more than 80 recent annual reports of FTSE 100 companies by Independent Audit, which advises boards and audit committees, found that a few companies had dramatically improved their reporting.

Jonathan Hayward, chief executive of Independent Audit, said: "More companies are breaking away from boilerplate. Companies have discovered that by introducing a narrative, by telling a story, they can transform the impact of their reporting. "Last year, the only companies offering good reporting were corporate governance recovery stories like Marks & Spencer or Cable & Wireless. This year, you have got companies that don't need to build bridges."

Source: eFinancialNews.com, July 10, 2005.

The effect of almost a decade of investigation, analysis and reports has been, therefore, to provide the UK with arguably one of the most credible and mature corporate governance regimes in the world. And this is gradually being seen as a template for more widespread adoption.

Corporate Governance in Europe

The accounting and governance regimes applying in continental Europe, specifically in France and Germany, are outlined in Chapter 15.

Stakeholder Theory

While the cumulative effect of these various reports would seem to suggest that over the course of the 1990s corporate governance practice in the UK has undergone a radical overhaul, critics argue that all that has happened has been some "tinkering at the edges". In particular, they point to the persistence of shareholder value as the single most important paradigm and share price growth as the "holy grail".

One of the more coherent critiques comes from those who advocate a much broader understanding of the whole subject of how and for whom companies are run, an approach which extends the consideration of interested parties beyond the traditional one of investors to the more inclusive notion of "stakeholders".

Stakeholder theory is predicated on the notion that it is not the primary task of democracy to underpin the role of the market in society. In this scheme of things corporations are understood to be, first and foremost, corporate citizens with rights and corresponding obligations. These obligations extend beyond the obvious and oft-repeated duties to shareholders, to the less-frequently articulated duties to other interested parties.

One of the principal effects of stakeholder theory is to challenge business to recognize its responsibilities to a larger constituency. Typically this would include, in addition to shareholders and investors, the following:

- Employees
- Environmentalists
- Creditors
- Customers
- Local communities and interest groups.

Once the field of potential stakeholders is extended in this fashion it becomes possible to completely reconsider not only the way in which a company should relate to them but also, at a very fundamental level, the capacity of any company, as currently structured, to meaningfully engage on these terms.

In practice:

While the interests of shareholders, managers and other stakeholders are all legitimate, one interest group whose interests are often subordinated are employees. Recent corporate collapses in which workers and their pension funds have suffered disproportionate losses have highlighted this:

What about the workers? Rover is a classic case of shareholders coming first, writes Simon Caulkin

Why didn't the Rover workers revolt? They certainly have a right to be angry. They have lost pretty much everything: jobs and prospects, and their pension fund has a £67 million hole in it. To add insult to injury, the residual value of the cars they were persuaded to buy as a show of support is now in many cases less than what they owe. Meanwhile, their bosses and shareholders – the Phoenix Four – have walked away with pockets and pension pots brimming. They are unlikely to need to work again.

The legacies left by Rover on its deathbed to its shareholder and worker inheritors could hardly be more different. Yet, despite belated protest and token wringing of hands, the only remarkable thing about the indignation is the speed with which it has died down. The truth is that the Rover workers (and we) are resigned to the despoliation. We have so internalised the idea that this is the way the world is that while, as in this case, we can be indignant about individual abuses, that is precisely what we assume they are – aberrations rather than something inherent to the system that produced them.

But Rover demonstrates just how rotten the foundations of that system are. Consider how any company really works. Its unique potential resides in the ability to combine the resources of different constituencies to create value that neither could on their own. Without the human capital contributed by employees, the financial capital of investors is sterile. Employees need financial capital to amplify their efforts. Each is necessary to the other. Neither is the company actually 'owned' by the shareholders in any normal sense – the whole point of the 'limited-liability' trade-off is that shareholders shed final responsibility for the assets and liabilities on to the 'legal person' of the company itself, embracing all its constituents.

So how come that the Phoenix Four can make off with all the swag without being arrested? The answer is that we have bought the orthodoxy that the company exists to maximise returns to financial capital alone. From this principle a whole set of consequences flow and all the participants have acted out their roles in textbook manner. Behind it all lurks the argument that financial capital is entitled to the greatest returns (or, in some cases, all of them) because it shoulders the major risks. True to form, this has indeed been argued in the case of Rover...

Why then do we accept a model that so comprehensively fails the tests of justice and common sense, stacking up neither in theory nor practice? The underlying reason is that corporate purpose is a classic casualty of the well-documented and overdeveloped propensity of managers (and politicians) to reduce as many as possible of the variables with which they have to deal to numbers. Numbers are important – the choice of what and how to measure is one of the most crucial and least well understood tasks of management. Unfortunately, they are also treacherous. All too often the measure subverts the purpose. As Igor Ansoff, the father of strategic management, put it: 'Managers start off trying to manage what they want, and finish up wanting what they can measure.'

That is precisely the case with shareholder value. Common sense says that companies and societies prosper when interests are balanced – when companies look after customers, suppliers and employees in such a way that they can nurture the human capital to innovate and improve alongside the financial capital to invest in the future. But that's messy and difficult; unlike returns to shareholders, it is hard to express in numbers and impossible to reduce to a single figure. As a model, shareholder value is a travesty, as is what happened to Rover in the past five years. It may well be true, as a new report from the Cambridge-MIT Institute claims, that by 2000 Rover was already doomed and we have just been witnessing the longest corporate death scene in history. But that should not be allowed to disguise the fact that the episode truly represents in every respect 'the unacceptable face of capitalism'. Tellingly, it took a German company, previous owner BMW, with its different traditions of labour-capital relations, to point it out.

Source: The Observer, May 1, 2005.

Stakeholder theory provides a useful and important perspective in its own right, highlighting the rights and duties of a variety of interested parties, especially those commonly excluded from governance debates. It also provides a significant counter to the seemingly pervasive "shareholder value" paradigm that dominates much of what passes for "discussion" on governance and corporate culture. Its implications for both corporate governance and financial reporting will be discussed further in Chapter 14. So too will the notion of the company as a "corporate citizen" with social and ethical responsibilities to the communities within which it operates.

Summary

In an increasingly global, competitive and technology-driven environment, corporate governance is seen as a source of considerable competitive advantage. Consequently it has attracted the attentions of not only practitioners and company executives, but also of regulators. This has resulted in a raft of reports, recommendations and voluntary codes aimed at enforcing some element of accountability and uniformity.

Simultaneously, the fact that many European and Asian companies have been compelled to seek funds on the New York and London Stock Exchanges has highlighted the fact that it is the Anglo-American system of corporate governance that has proven most robust. This has resulted in a situation in which the Anglo-American corporate governance model, with all of its flaws, is being increasingly championed as the one that offers the most suitable basis upon which to proceed.

Those who see the entire edifice as fatally flawed champion the more inclusive stakeholder paradigm as an alternative to one dominated by shareholder value and share price.

Review Questions

Question 1
Explain what is meant by the term "corporate governance" and identify specific reasons for divergences in corporate governance cultures.

Question 2
Explain how corporate governance impacts upon notions of accountability and, consequently, upon the nature and form of accounting practice.

Question 3
Identify the role, if any, which the following may play in the future in the area of international corporate governance practice:
- UK government
- EU
- SEC
- IASB
- Stock Exchanges
- International accounting bodies
- Shareholders
- Other stakeholders

Question 4
Explain what "Best Practice" means in the context of UK corporate governance. Identify the reasons why this became an issue in the 1990s.

Question 5
Identify the principal contributions of the following reports to the corporate governance regime as it currently exists in the UK.
- Cadbury
- Greenbury
- Hampel
- Turnbull
- Higgs
- Smith

Question 6
"In focusing attention on risk management and in requiring management to integrate this into the governance and operational aspects of corporate life, Turnbull will be seen in a few years time as having had the most profound effect upon corporate governance, practice and accountability". Discuss.

Question 7
For a variety of reasons 'shareholder value' is the pervasive and dominant paradigm, especially in the Anglo-American world. Outline the significance of this and explain how it informs so much of the agenda for change.

Question 8
Explain what "Stakeholder Theory" means and identify specific ways in which pressure from stakeholders other than shareholders has influenced corporate governance and reporting practice.

Case Studies

Case 1

The article with which this chapter concludes, "What about the workers", makes some very interesting observations on the shareholder value paradigm that has informed the corporate governance regime in the Anglo-American world for so long. In the light of this, and the arguments made in the following article, consider the view that the shareholder value approach "fails the test of justice and common sense, stacking up neither in theory nor in practice".

The Futile Hunt for the Holy Grail: Investors Now See Shareholder Value for What it is: Something that Enriched Undeserving CEOs, by Robert Heller

The kings and knights of capitalism have lost their latest Holy Grail. The cult of 'shareholder value' has been shattered by slumps in share prices (which are supposed to enshrine that value) and by the accountancy and allied shenanigans that expose shareholder value for what it really was, and is: a screen for the naked pursuit of the unachievable (a steady, high rate of perpetual growth) by people whose behaviour was often unspeakable.

Even the more speakable value-chasers moved from good businesses into bad, grossly overpaid for acquisitions, grossly overpaid themselves, destroyed businesses by 'downsizing' and eventually decimated the very value they were supposed to be creating. If that sounds like a fair description of GEC, now Marconi, so be it. Shareholder value, which sounds like a creditable attempt to put the owners' interests first, ends up by putting them last.

The underlying problem is the constant lust for that Holy Grail – a clearly identifiable, all-embracing measure that tells corporate bosses what to do and when it's been well done. At times this guiding light has been return on capital employed; at others, growth in earnings per share. These have been found wanting, and for good reasons – the targets were nearly always missed. In booming stock markets, by contrast, shareholder value soared as shareholders (by buying overvalued shares) obligingly created their own added value.

The bosses were not slow to draw undeserved credit and excessive reward from the flood. The bad behaviour of ABB's former chairman, Percy Barnevik, makes the point in spades. He won his fame not only for creating a starry transnational engineering giant, but also for demanding high standards of boardroom rectitude. Notoriously, he waived those standards when it came to his own ultimate reward: a monstrous £60 million (tax-free), secretly negotiated, hidden from fellow directors, and now slashed (under pressure) by 60 per cent.

Like others in the greed mode, Barnevik could argue that £60m is a smidgen compared to the rich feast of value he created for shareholders. But the claim is tarnished by the poor performance of ABB since he passed over the reins to a handpicked (and overpensioned) CEO. Having doubled under Barnevik's lead, ABB is now a shrunken empire that lost $691m in 2001, with value down 70 per cent in two years. The wealth created in the 17 glory years (a 54-fold rise in market capitalisation) has been succeeded by lean pickings for employees (many dismissed) and everybody else – except Barnevik and his top-level colleagues.

Maybe 'CEO value' should be substituted for shareholder value. By the CEO criterion, companies prospered mightily even during the profit recession that bridged the 11 September savagery. The recipe is simple. CEOs and their cohorts regularly receive (really from their own hands) higher and higher salaries, plus larger and larger stock options and other capital goodies. While stock markets have lately cut into this wealth, sometimes savagely, most beneficiaries need only wait for the tide to turn.

The tide will float them off, rather than any brilliance of strategies or tactics. Two forces come into play here. First, companies go through purple patches (like ABB) when strategy and tactics drive them forward under effective leadership. Wonders always cease, though. At some point, new strategies, radical tactics and changed leaders are required to regenerate a business whose old formula is failed or failing. Insiders, especially the highest, are in general painfully slow to spot the turning point and lamentably lax in reacting to the necessity for radical renewal.

Outsiders are little more acute or perceptive, which is the second force at work. Outside praise reinforces inside failure. In 1998 Price Waterhouse published a book that sought the lessons of success straight from the CEO. Its six 'giants of value creation' included Sir Colin Marshall (BA), Eckhard Pfeiffer (Compaq) and Robert Shapiro (Monsanto) – all three, today might well be selected as titans of value loss, men who missed, or messed up, the moment of change with destructive results. PW's consultants, like analysts and journalists (and the managements themselves) were living in the past, when it's the future that feeds the true fortunes.

When downsizing's day was dying, many management gurus leapt into the pulpit to proclaim its defects. How could companies grow future value by destroying it – shutting plants, dismissing employees, slashing costs, dropping products and axing whole product lines?

You can, by such methods, mightily raise return on capital and earnings per share, possibly with wondrous short-term effect on the shares. But what can management do for an encore? Many gains were one time only. Many slashed and burned the prospects for the future.

The critical voices, however, were drowned out by the flood of unearned stock market riches. The most articulate growth proponent, Gary Hamel, even fell for the intellectual seductions of Enron. The difficulty is that the share price is the only thing that matters to shareholders. That same price, however, should never matter to managers – not directly, that is. Other things being equal, the shares will indirectly reflect what super-investor Warren Buffett calls the 'intrinsic value' of the business.

The basis of this number is the difference between the net cash return from a company and the interest on long-term government bonds. If there's no differ-ence (or still worse a negative one), Buffett won't buy. He asks simple financial questions – like what percentage is the company earning on the shareholders' equity? Chris Higson, of the London Business School, has demonstrated that, even on its heavily doctored published figures, Enron would have failed elementary Buffett-style tests. But as the cult of shareholder value raged, no one bothered to apply them.

Long ago, when the future Lord Weinstock was richly rewarding GEC shareholders, he observed that profit wasn't a target, but a residual: the end-result of doing the right things in the right way. Chasing phoney financial targets is the wrong thing. And that invariably, inevitably, is wrongly done.

Robert Heller's latest book is Roads to Success (Dorling Kindersley, £25)

Source: *The Observer*, March 17, 2002.

Case 2

While the general view is that recent governance developments have, on balance, proven beneficial, not everyone agrees. The following article presents an alternative view. In the light of the arguments the author makes, consider the claim of one of the contributors that "The likelihood of another long cycle that repeats the past 20 years and ends with another crisis of corporate governance is high".

Non-executive Misdirection: Slavish Adherence to the New Rules of Corporate Governance is Doing More Harm Than Good, by Simon Caulkin

A week in which Bernie Ebbers, the unlovable former chief executive of WorldCom, was convicted of an $11 billion fraud, and another prominent US CEO was forced to resign on suspicion of fiddling the figures, seems an uncomfortable one in which to query the direction of current corporate governance. Yet while the crooks deserve everything that the law flings at them, it's harder to see the greater good that was served by the sacking of Boeing's chief executive, Harry Stonecipher, for having a fling with an (unmarried) Boeing employee. Stonecipher's behaviour may not be admirable, but it does not seem a hanging offence. Yet such is the climate of corporate correctness that conformance to the letter of the law now takes precedence over all other considerations – with the very real danger that corporate governance 'improvements' are starting to have the opposite effect to the one intended, making senior recruitment more difficult and destroying the cohesion of the board.

Anecdotal evidence certainly points this way. US headhunters say prominent companies now have to settle for ninth or 10th choice when recruiting outside executives for the board. According to a survey by PricewaterhouseCoopers, for 70 per cent of UK chief executives governance and compliance activities represent pure cost, rather than investment, and less than half believe they could be a source of competitive advantage. Even in the US, where CEOs are more positive, a different survey a year ago showed that fewer than one-third of directors thought that new governance standards would improve board operations, ensure detection of unethical behaviour or better protect shareholders. Overwhelmingly, boards were spending more time monitoring accounting and governance practices and financial performance rather than on more positive issues.

Special pleading? Academic evidence gives little support to the official line. For example, a Henley Management College study found that companies with many executive directors on the board did better than those with a high proportion of non-execs. This finding – which echoes those of two Australian surveys – contradicts two of the tenets of the combined code on board structure and director tenure. Other studies say the same thing over and over: the forms that are currently accepted as a prerequisite for 'good governance' do nothing for company performance.

Do they have an effect on wrongdoing? Probably, says Professor Vic Dulewicz, co-author of the Henley paper, but he warns that no amount of rules will deter the real villains. Enron is notorious proof that the form of best practice is worth very little without the content.

But some go even further. Said Business School's Chris McKenna, author of a forthcoming book on the history of management consulting, believes that, the best intentions of the US Sarbanes-Oxley Act on corporate governance notwith-standing, the stage is unwittingly being set for more Enron and WorldCom type scandals. He argues that making directors personally and financially liable for mismanagement – in a January settlement Enron and WorldCom directors agreed to stump up $31m to shareholders – will not only have the effect of pushing up directors' salaries and liability insurance premiums to match the increased risks; it will also cause board members to offload ever more responsibility on to outside advisers, consultants and auditors. It was just this tactic of bringing the audit inside – acting as 'insurance policy' to management rather than independent regulator – that caused Enron's advisers to lose their objectivity.

'The likelihood of another long cycle that repeats the past 20 years and ends with another crisis of corporate governance is high,' McKenna concludes. He doesn't add it, but the equal likelihood is that the next crisis will trigger yet another round of regulatory corset-tightening, further increasing bureaucratic drag. Meanwhile, as Anthony Hilton in the Evening Standard has pointed out, a boardroom split between power centres – chairman, lead non-exec, heads of remuneration and audit – and where non-execs are forbidden to trust the execs, is a recipe for dysfunctionality, not teamwork. It is difficult, notes the Henley paper, 'to envisage how 50 per cent non-executive director representation is calculated to do other than encourage adversarial friction with executive colleagues.'

How have we got into this mess? The fuel of the governance arms race, whether Sarbanes-Oxley or the UK's combined codes, is an American doctrine known as 'agency theory'. Under this ideology, the function of the board is to ensure that managers (agents) act on behalf of the shareholders (principals) to maximise shareholder value; without this surveillance, the theory goes, managers will exploit their inside knowledge to advance themselves at the expense of the principals.

In governance terms, this requirement to police management is the basis for 'duality' (splitting chairman and chief executive roles), boosting the number of non-execs, incentivising managers and encouraging the market for corporate control. Unfortunately, as we have seen, these prescriptions don't work. As Dulewicz notes, agency theory, like all the other board theories in existence (13 at the last count), isn't particularly helpful for analysing what boards do, which is far more complex than the mechanistic and simplistic theory suggests.

The trouble is, though, that the theory is doubly bad: not just wrong, but self-fulfilling. Assuming that managers are self-interested opportunists who need sacks full of share options to do their jobs creates managers like that. Telling them that their job is exclusively to maximise shareholder value ensures that they leave no legal stone unturned in their effort to do so. Then new inhibitions have to be put in place to temper the abuses and the whole cycle starts again.

It's time to rethink the whole corporate governance issue – not on the basis of tightening or modifying existing codes but from an entirely different starting point. Companies don't thrive and prosper by concentrating only on shareholder value, and agents and principals, but by simultaneously looking after all the elements that go into success – customers, suppliers, employees – and even communities. Unless it acknowledges that, governance practice will remain part of the problem, not the solution.

Source: *The Observer*, 20 March 2005.

Case 3

The various themes covered in this chapter are also dealt with in some detail in a report by accountancy firm PricewaterhouseCoopers. This can be accessed and read at the following site: http://www2.pw.com/uk/conv&underscore;cult&under-score;exec&underscore;sum.htm.

Case 4

Shell, often presented as a paragon of governance virtue, encountered serious problems when the manner in which it sought to account for the quantity and value of its reserves was questioned. The following article tracks some of the governance issues raised and details how governance reform was identified as one way in which some of these issues could be addressed. Investigate this case further and consider the implications for both the company and the broader governance debate.

Why Shell Must Act Now to Calm Troubled Waters, by Robin Pagnamenta

But Restructure May Not be Enough After Scandal, Resignation and Fines

Jeroen Van de Veer smiled broadly in the cavernous interior of the New York Stock Exchange last week as he rang the opening bell for trading. The bespectacled Royal

Dutch/Shell chairman was celebrating the 50th anniversary of the firm's listing. For perhaps the first time since his emergency appointment five months ago – after Sir Phil Watts was sacked after a misreported oil reserves scandal – van de Veer must have felt he was being feted rather than assaulted from all sides. Nevertheless, after one of the ugliest episodes in the company's history, van de Veer has his work cut out if he is to restore Shell's tarnished reputation.

That effort edged forward last week when it emerged Shell had reached a preliminary agreement to combine the group's two management boards, possibly paving the way towards a single united company. Such a move would represent a tectonic shift for the Anglo-Dutch giant, one of the world's largest companies. The dual structure dates from 1907, when Royal Dutch Petroleum and Shell Transport & Trading embarked on a joint venture. They maintained separate management and head offices and are listed as different companies on the London and Amsterdam stock exchanges. The company is overseen by a committee of managing directors, though Royal Dutch retains an edge because it controls 60 per cent of the company, compared with Shell's 40 per cent.

There had been rumblings of dissent about the structure from investors before but Shell began its review in earnest only after it emerged the group had overstated "proven" oil and gas reserves by 23 per cent or 4.5 billion barrels. Much criticism focused on "confusing" corporate governance, particularly when it emerged senior bosses sought to hide the scandal from peers and investors.

The debacle bore a financial cost. In July, Shell agreed to pay £17 million to regulator the FSA and $120 million to America's SEC to settle official investigations.

Regarding structure, van der Veer said in New York: "We are looking at many different options. We rule nothing in and nothing out." But many independent observers and investors would welcome a change. Robeco, a Dutch asset management group based in Rotterdam, said: "In general we are in favour of transparent and straightforward company structures. . . But we are waiting for concrete proposals from Shell." Another oil industry insider said: "There is relief Shell is actually listening to the market – for too long there was a belief it was too arrogant to make changes."

A final recommendation is not expected before November and it will be April 2005 before any changes can be approved. Implementation would take several months more. However, Angus Mcphail, oil analyst at ING Financial Markets, Edinburgh, argues the governance debate obscures the underlying problem and the main reason for concealing misreported reserves. "The real problem is Shell needs more exploration successes and it should be revaluating that side of its business, " he says. "It doesn't necessarily follow that a unified structure equates to improvements in exploration and production."

Shell's record has been dismal in recent years, while rivals BP and ExxonMobil have had a string of fresh discoveries, hence managers felt pressured into concealing the true state of Shell's reserves. The "reserves replacement ratio" shows how much new oil and gas a firm is discovering as against the amount it pumps out. In 2003 Shell's was 98 per cent. BP's was 175 per cent.

To rub salt into the wounds, Shell executives learned this week Cairn Energy, a small Scottish exploration company, had made a fourth oil discovery on a field in India's Rajasthan region it bought from Shell two years ago for a paltry £4 million.

Cairn now believes the concession could be worth hundreds of millions of pounds. At least Shell can breathe a sigh of relief about one thing. High global oil prices have kept profits – and the group's share price – bubbling away. With $4 billion profits in the first quarter alone investors can't complain too much. Meanwhile, analysts say there is little sign oil prices will fall away any time soon.

Source: *Sunday Express*, August 17, 2004.

SECTION II

Content

The Annual Report is one of the most important means of communication between a company and its stakeholders, particularly its shareholders. As a result it is a highly regulated document containing a mass of data in the form of both financial statements and narrative reports. From humble beginnings in the 19th century it has grown to become a large, glossy production often reaching over 100 pages in length.

While the financial statements and notes still represent the core of the Annual Report, recent decades have witnessed a significant increase in the number and range of non-financial data. Chapter 5 looks at these qualitative reports and narrative commentaries, which range from the heavily regulated Directors' Report and Auditor's Report, to the Chairman's Statement and Operating and Financial Review.

Chapter 6 deals with the financial statements and attendant notes, which, despite the rising importance of the qualitative elements, still constitute the core of the Annual Report. Because these statements are heavily regulated by both statute and accounting standards this chapter, of necessity, sets out some technical information regarding formats, accounting principles and disclosure requirements. It is, therefore, somewhat out of kilter with the remainder of the text, which is more concerned with contextual rather than technical issues. Nevertheless, it is critical that the relevant provisions be understood as they underpin the way in which financial statements are constructed and the thinking behind their current configuration. Reflecting the change to IFRS, this chapter presents disclosure and accounting rules applicable to that regime particularly those deriving from IAS 1, *Presentation of Financial Statements*.

NARRATIVE REPORTS

When you have completed this chapter you will understand:

- The importance of the Annual Report as a primary means of communication between a company and its various stakeholders.

- The increasing importance of non-financial disclosures.

- The nature and purpose of the narrative elements of the Annual Report.

- That these narrative reports include some that are statutorily controlled and others that are not.

- The importance attaching to the Operating and Financial Review (OFR).

- That the structure of the Annual Report allows companies to employ various techniques intended to influence readers' impressions.

Other Ways to Inform Investors: Management Commentary is Playing an Increasingly Important Role, writes Robert Bruce

The increasing complexity of reported corporate figures has prompted much debate. At present, there is a growing realisation that one effect is going to be greater dependency on other ways of providing investors with useful information. Indeed, the International Accounting Standards Board recently published a discussion paper on what it calls "management commentary". This pulls together all the work that has been done in this area and acts as an early stage in the process of the IASB producing a standard on the topic.

It is not going to be easy. In the US, management commentary has existed for years in the form of management discussion and analysis (MD&A). In the UK, companies are only now gearing up to provide an Operating and Financial Review (OFR)... The complexities of providing global cohesion in this process are numerous. In the US it is governed by the main investor regulator, the Securities and Exchange Commission. In the UK the Accounting Standards Board, part of the Financial Reporting Council, provides the rules under the aegis of government legislation.

In the long term the question of whether management commentary is the responsibility of securities regulators or accounting standard bodies must be sorted out. "It is a global trend," says David Loweth, a member of the project team that produced the IASB paper, and secretary of the ASB. "There is a need for some sort of global structure for narrative and commentary." Many other questions must also be resolved. "This is the first step," says Mr Loweth. "People can comment on it, dispute it if they wish and provide reactions – for example, should it be put forward as best practice, or should it be mandatory, which is what we would prefer."

What is not disputed is the growing importance of management commentary in the process of providing investors with corporate information. The experience over the past year of implementing international financial reporting rules has shown that, at least in the short term, figures are becoming more opaque to the users of accounts. Mr Loweth says: "The danger is that financial reporting becomes more complicated and difficult to follow." The techniques of management commentary will have to fill the gap. Since intangible measures rather than the underlying figures are seen to provide greater understanding, the movement is towards documents such as the OFR. "The OFR gives an opportunity to tell the story in a balanced way which can set the financial statements in context," says Mr Loweth.

It also fits with other global trends of providing different types of reporting. The International Federation of Accountants (IFAC) has set up a narrative reporting project. The US accounting profession is attempting to create a process called enhanced business reporting. All these point to the reporting of more non-financial issues. Richard Mallet, director of technical development at the Chartered Institute of Management Accountants, says: "You need a way that management can explain a company's performance and prospects."

So far... the effort has been put into creating a loose structure within a legal framework in the hope that it will encourage companies to produce useful rather than legalistic information for users of reports and accounts. Mr Loweth says: "The big challenge is in the forward-looking element. The parameters of the big box have been set but within that there is plenty of scope for discretion and judgment."

One area developing fast is the use of key performance indicators, (KPIs). In its discussion paper the IASB quotes from a Deloitte survey last year that showed that "99 per cent of respondents agreed that financial indicators alone cannot adequately capture their companies' strengths and weaknesses". This is where KPIs come in but precisely which KPIs should be disclosed is up to each company. The choice has been left open so that each market sector can gradually work out what is required. Mr Loweth says: "This would have to come from the market. It is very difficult to impose commonality in KPIs now. The people who want to compare companies, the users of accounts, can get together and try to develop it so that companies can consider it on a comparable basis. This will have to come from the investment community."

... Companies in the UK should be well on their way to marshalling their information ahead of publication. It is a first step towards a revolution that could produce more intelligible and more relevant information for investors. The results will be watched closely. "At the moment we are on an evolutionary testbed," says Mr Loweth.

Source: *Financial Times*, November 10, 2005.

Introduction

While the information to be included in Annual Reports appears to be ever increasing, the statements and reports required can basically be classified into two types – financial and narrative. Historically, an Annual Report consisted almost entirely of financial statements supplemented by an Auditor's Report and a Directors' Report. However, as its importance as a primary means of communication between a company and its stakeholders has come to be appreciated, its form and content have changed.

As the opening article highlighted, although recent decades have seen increased financial disclosure, "financial indicators alone cannot adequately capture their companies' strengths and weaknesses". For this reason, there has been a greater emphasis on incorporating more narrative reports into Annual Reports. These, it is argued, would allow disclosures that supplement financial information, but also extend disclosure policy to include reference to future strategies and ambitions.

In practice:

The full report mentioned here, 'From Carrots to Sticks,' is available at www.deloitte. com/ and is worth accessing as it provides very useful insights into the nature and content of Annual Reports.

A 2004 review of the Annual Reports of 100 listed UK companies by Deloitte revealed the following:

- *the average length of annual reports was 65 pages, 16% more than in 2000;*
- *the longest annual report was 327 pages (173 in 2000; 160 in 1996);*
- *25% of companies identified and discussed the principal risks facing the business (29% in 2000, 17% in 1996);*
- *65% of the surveyed companies were not in full compliance with the existing Combined Code;*
- *53% of companies published their reports within 75 days, compared to 50% in 2000.*

Source: From Carrots to Sticks, Deloitte, 2004.

Financial disclosures, which still form the core of an Annual Report, will be covered in Chapter 6. This chapter will deal with those sections of an annual report that are narrative in form.

Narrative Reports

One of the principles of the Combined Code is that "the board should present a balanced and understandable assessment of the company's position and prospects". It is generally accepted that financial statements on their own do not achieve this. Consequently, various narrative sections that provide both additional information and a commentary on the company's position, performance and prospects have been added over time in order to supplement the financial information.

Typically these narratives would include:

- Chairman's Statement
- Directors' Report
- Auditor's Report
- Operating and Financial Review (OFR).

In practice:

A recent analysis of FTSE-100 annual reports has calculated that in a "typical" 80 page Annual Report, the financial data take up around 31 pages, while the narrative and visual elements comprise the remaining 49. Of these 49, the Operating and Financial Review (OFR) takes up around 16 pages and information regarding directors and their remuneration about 6.

Because the Directors' Report and the Auditor's Report are subject to considerable legislative control, they offer little scope to those responsible for running the company to communicate more openly with users. More recently, in response to the Combined Code and with the support of the Accounting Standards Board (ASB), the government decided that all public companies must also include an OFR. This, unfortunately, has recently been rescinded and will not now proceed. However, with a majority of large plcs already producing one voluntarily, "best practice" considerations, together with the guidelines issued by the ASB, will probably ensure that the OFR increases in importance.

As Chapter 18 will demonstrate, the likelihood is that under the twin impulses of new technology and a corporate governance culture that emphasizes the qualities of transparency and disclosure, the narrative sections of an Annual Report will continue to grow in terms of both quantity and scope.

The remainder of this chapter looks at each of the four principal narrative reports listed above in more detail.

Chairman's Statement

There is no legal requirement to include a Chairman's Statement in the Annual Report. However, as the profile of the company chairman has increased in recent years, so too has the demand, and, on many chairmen's part, the desire, to comment in fairly general terms on the company's performance and prospects. The Chairman's Statement, therefore, provides a useful forum in which the chairman can set forth his or her thoughts on the company and, increasingly, discuss various macro-economic and political issues that impinge upon the company.

The Chairman's Statement normally appears at the front of the Annual Report and research shows that it is the most widely read section. In many senses it is a public relations statement in which the chairman presents a personal perspective on how the company has performed and its future prospects. It is, as a result, often a rather bland document full of hyperbole and optimistic aspirations. Nevertheless, properly used, it can provide a useful conduit between the chairman, who in many instances plays a key role in shaping corporate ethos and objectives, and stakeholders.

Content

There is no standard format for the Chairman's Statement. However, in most cases some or all of the following would appear:

- A brief account of the company's financial and operating performance over the previous year
- Details of significant events that had a material effect on performance, for example, acquisitions or disposals
- A summary of activities within key categories of the company
- Reference to changes in board membership
- Outline of new strategies, corporate goals or changes in focus or emphasis
- An often over-optimistic assessment of future prospects.

The growing importance of the Chairman's Statement has meant that there are now calls for it too to be subject to some form of control with regard to its content, particularly in ensuring some element of consistency between its often self-congratulatory tone and the actual financial performance as disclosed in the remainder of the Annual Report.

In practice:

The following article takes a rather sceptical look at the content of many Chairmen's Statements:

A statement in obfuscation: Annual Reports seem to be growing more turgid and Less illuminating, reports Carlos Grande

Corporate copywriters sharpen your pencils! For if there is one thing worse than having to read a company annual report, it is having to read a bad company annual report. That is admittedly not the world's greatest intro. But if you are still reading this piece, it has a greater claim to posterity than the following soporifics: "The turmoil surrounding the operating, regulatory and stock market environment in which we operate has been unprecedented in recent times." "The decoupling of the real economy and the financial markets, a trend that began in 2000 and grew throughout 2001, became fully apparent in 2002." Or the clincher: "The industrial plan worked out at the beginning of last year to relaunch the group gave strategic priority to the development of the competitive capacity of the various business units, continuous innovation, cost-cuts and a stronger financial structure, with the aim of ensuring the creation of value for internal and external shareholders alike."

The examples above are the opening lines of the chairman's statements in the 2002 annual reports of, respectively, Lloyds TSB, AXA, the French insurance group, and TIM, the Italian telecommunications company. They come from The Company Report, an analysis of the latest annual reports filed by Europe's top 100 companies by October 2003, which is published by Prowse & Company. And despite much City talk about encouraging shareholder communications, they show that the tradition of statements that combine the portentous and the meaningless is alive and well.

But for the chairman or harassed PR officer faced with the thankless task of penning such forewords year in, year out, what are the stylistic options for that crucial opening gambit? One could try a modest statement: "This year marked the arrival of Tesco as an international group." Or reach for something a touch more statesmanlike: "We are living in a time of extraordinary uncertainty" (Siemens); "The economic and political decision-makers in Germany faced great challenges in 2002" (Volkswagen). There has also been a noticeable increase, the report says, in chairmen using the space to sound off about current political developments. Electrabel and Lloyds TSB are cited.

On a musical analogy, one could blow one's own trumpet ("This has been a really good year for BT") or sound the last post ("We all know these are difficult times in the telecommunications industry – probably the worst in history". Ericsson). If you are not sure whether praise or opprobrium is needed, throw in a reference to a past year of "challenges" or "opportunities", or if you are AstraZeneca both in the same sentence. The textbook example of "good cop, bad cop" style is surely France Telecom's Thierry Breton: "My assessment is positive with regards to our operating performance, but the year definitely merits a black mark given the net loss." C'est vrai, mon brave, particularly as the net loss was €20.7bn ($26bn).

Alternatively, one could avoid all this flummery and just cut to the chase: "One question you may be asking is whether the turnaround at Marks & Spencer has been completed." Or avoid a chairman's statement altogether, as was the case with Orange, Nokia, the French industrial group Suez and Generali, the Italian insurer...

Source: Financial Times, February 10, 2004.

In practice:

The Tesco plc 2005 Annual Report does not incorporate a Chairman's Statement. Instead, this is included as part of its Annual Review and Summary Financial Statements. The text is set out below:

Our team has excellent plans to continue to improve our offer for customers, which drives the sales and results for shareholders.

Tesco has a well-established, consistent strategy for growth, which is strengthening the core business and driving our expansion into new markets such as non-foods, new services and new countries. To succeed in the long term, a first class company needs seamless succession, good management and great leadership. In Terry and the Board, we have leaders that are hugely experienced, energetic and capable of directing and motivating all the team leaders throughout the business to do the right things for customers. Retailing is about relentless execution, day in – day out. Our management and staff are trained, developed and given authority to do their jobs well, but also to innovate. Every year, we strive to make the shopping experience that bit better for customers. At the same time we make major improvements in our own productivity through our approach of better for customers, simpler for staff and cheaper for Tesco. As a responsible company, we work hard to bring real benefits to the communities we serve, the environment and the economy. Our commitment is embedded in the way we run the business through programmes like Computers For Schools, Race For Life and our charity of the year – which this year was Help the Hospices. This commitment was also the driving force behind the fundraising efforts by the Red Cross for the Tsunami appeal, which raised over £2.8 million in our stores. All of this adds up to a company that is taking on the challenge of being a leader for Britain in retailing, both at home and abroad. It is something that you and we can feel proud of and it shows in our results. Tesco has again delivered an outstanding performance:

- *Exceptional like-for-like sales growth in the UK*
- *Strong international sales*
- *More than 20% growth in underlying pre-tax profit*
- *Further strong progress on increasing our return on capital employed.*

For shareholders it has also been a good year with dividends up 10.5%. Total Shareholder Return (TSR) over one year has increased by 25% compared to just over 15% growth for the FTSE 100. Our return on shareholders' funds has also increased to 24%. As always, this success is the result of the hard work and skill of the whole Tesco team in delivering for customers every day. I am delighted that our people are benefiting from £169 million from Shares in Success and Save As You Earn schemes. We have further strengthened our Board with two new Non-executives. Karen Cook, a Managing Director at Goldman Sachs, joined us on 1 October

> 2004 and Carolyn McCall, Chief Executive of Guardian Newspapers Ltd, joined us on 1 March 2005
>
> Source: David Reid Chairman

The Directors' Report

The Directors' Report is intended to provide a narrative supplement to the financial information contained in an Annual Report. It is a statutory report under CA85 (as amended). Consequently, certain information must be included. However, the directors are free to include additional information if they so wish. Furthermore, for companies listed on the Stock Exchange, the UKLA will require additional disclosure as already outlined in Chapter 1. Finally, the Combined Code has specified particular items, such as directors' remuneration, that should be commented on by the directors and it is usual to see these alluded to either in the Directors' Report or in a separate section of the report.

The Directors' Report is intended to provide the directors of the company with an opportunity to comment on various aspects of the company's activities during the period in question. There is no set format for such a report and they vary widely in both content and format. However, the following areas must be addressed:

Activities and Trading Results

By law the Directors' Report is required to contain details of:

- The principal activities of the company and its subsidiaries; and
- Any significant changes that occurred during the period.

Developments During the Period

One of the main functions envisaged for the Directors' Report is the provision of an opportunity for the directors to give a review of any significant developments that have occurred during the year and of the position of the company at the end of the period. This provides an important narrative supplement to the financial data. In addition, the directors are expected to provide their own assessment of possible future developments, together with an assessment of how these may affect the company. Any narrative would be expected to refer to, and be consistent with, the financial information.

This section should include comment on the following:

- Turnover and profits deriving from trading activities

- Taxation
- Foreign currency management
- Significant changes in activities
- Existing borrowings and proposals for funding future capital expenditure
- Details of "non-adjusting" post-balance sheet events
- Significant changes in fixed assets – in terms of both value and physical changes
- Research and development activities
- Likely future developments.

In recent years, it has become common for a number of the items listed here to be discussed, in varying detail, in other parts of the Annual Report, principally the OFR.

Directors

As indicated in Chapter 1, one of the most sensitive issues for companies and shareholders concerns the role, remuneration and interests of the directors of the company. Legislation and UKLA rules require the disclosure of significant amounts of information under this heading.

At a minimum the following must be disclosed:

- Names of any individuals who held office as directors at any time during the period.
- The interest of those directors, (including that of their spouses, children and wards of court), in the shares and debentures of the company and its subsidiaries at the beginning and end of the period. Alternatively this information can be given in the notes to the accounts.
- Details of any loans, quasi-loans or credit facilities extended to directors, while, in certain circumstances, details must also be given of a director's service contract.
- The emoluments and remuneration of all directors – (this will often run to several pages).

Listed companies must also distinguish between directors' beneficial and non-beneficial holdings.

In practice:

The combined effect of accounting standards, legislation, UKLA rules and the Combined Code has been to increase the level of disclosure in relation to directors. These disclosures may often run to several pages with considerable space devoted to detailing directors' remuneration in particular.

Refer to the Tesco plc 2005 Annual Report for an indication of the level of disclosure required.

Substantial Holdings

Where any person or other entity owns or acquires 3% or more of the nominal value of any class of voting capital of a public company then this fact must be disclosed.

Employees

One of the most interesting developments of recent decades has been the increasing focus upon the employees of a company as both stakeholders and users of accounts. As a result there is now a considerable amount of information in the Annual Report in relation to employees and employment conditions, much of it under CA85. For example, in the notes to the accounts the total average number of employees must be given, with a breakdown of this total into the various categories of company activity. In addition, the total for staff costs must be disclosed either on the face of the profit and loss account or as a note. The Directors' Report of a company that has more than an average total of 250 employees must also include a statement of its employment policy in relation to disabled persons. Significantly, companies are voluntarily disclosing information relating to health and safety.

Auditing

While the appointment of the auditor is the business of the shareholders at the AGM, it has become customary for the directors to indicate the willingness or otherwise of the existing auditors to continue. In the event of the existing auditors being unwilling to continue, then the Directors' Report provides the directors with an opportunity to comment on this situation.

Donations

Where political or charitable donations exceed £200 per annum then the directors must disclose this fact in the Directors' Report. Where the donations are for a political purpose then the name of the recipients and the individual amounts must be disclosed. Given the relative sensitivity over the issue of political donations in recent years, where companies do not make any such contributions they have taken to explicitly stating so.

Corporate Governance

The Combined Code has had a considerable influence on the content of the Directors' Report. For instance, in line with the overall 'comply or explain' approach, directors must now specifically state whether or not the provisions of the Code have been complied with. In addition, the number of issues that must be addressed has also increased, although with the advent of the OFR, many of these may be covered there rather than in the Directors' Report.

The Code also recommends that a statement of directors' responsibilities be included. This should specify in accordance with CA 85:

- That it is the director's responsibility to prepare financial statements for each year which give a true and fair view of the state of affairs of the company as at the end of the financial year and of the profit or loss for that period.

- The responsibility of directors in relation to maintaining adequate accounting records, safeguarding the assets of the company and preventing or detecting fraud.

- That suitable, consistent and prudent accounting policies have been employed.

- That applicable accounting standards have been followed, subject to any material departures being disclosed and explained in the notes to the accounts.

While these statements are useful in having directors acknowledge their legal responsibilities in relation to the preparation of accounts, they are seen by many as merely an attempt to insulate auditors from litigation. It remains to be seen how effective they would be in serving this purpose.

In practice:

Tesco is considered to be a very good example of a company that conforms to best practice in this area. Note the extent of the disclosures that company makes under this heading (pp. 11–16).

Other

The Directors' Report must also deal with a number of other items. An important example is the requirement that directors disclose the amount by which market value of land and buildings differs from book value. This provision is intended to allow shareholders to take a view on the extent of asset backing that the company enjoys.

Auditor's Report

An audit has been defined as "an independent review, and expression of opinion on, the financial statements of an enterprise". The purpose of an audit is to provide independent verification that "the financial statements have been properly prepared in accordance with the legislative and regulatory requirements, that they present the information in a true and fair manner and that they comply with best accounting practice". While the auditor is not expected to audit the Directors' Report, it is required that he or she draws the attention of the reader to any inconsistencies between it and the financial results.

In recent years, particularly in the wake of several large corporate collapses, the audit process has been the subject of intense criticism. To an extent, this derives from a misunderstanding on the part of many users who are under the misapprehension that the audit is primarily a fraud detection exercise. Auditors counter that, while they would expect to uncover incidences of material fraud, this is not the main focus of an audit. This difference between what users expect of an audit and what auditors are actually providing has been termed the "expectations gap".

One way in which the auditing profession has attempted to counter criticism has been to embark on a process of educating the users of financial statements as to the precise nature and function of an audit and to inform the various interested parties of their respective roles. For example, directors must now acknowledge in the Directors' Report that it is their responsibility, and not the auditor's, to prepare the financial statements. Other innovations have seen the emergence of the audit committee as a key element in the governance structure and a more explicit recognition of auditor's responsibilities in relation to the detection of fraud and error.

Horrified by a "deep pocket" syndrome, that saw various firms sued for massive amounts of money, auditors have also sought to limit their exposure to claims for negligence. Recent proposals in the White Paper *Company Law Reform* (2005) indicate that support exists for greater protection of auditors from such claims. This is also reflected in a greater onus being placed on directors to disclose relevant information to auditors:

In practice:

Penalty threat to company directors

Legislation coming into force today makes company directors liable to criminal penalties if they fail to disclose relevant accounting information to auditors. Companies Act amendments require directors to sign declarations that they have not concealed any material information from auditors. If they are subsequently found to have done so, they can face fines or imprisonment.

Auditors are also being given powers to demand information from a broader range of people at their client companies. Aside from directors, they can request figures from anyone who handles or is accountable for financial statements. The moves are part of legislative and regulatory changes made to reduce accounting fraud and restore investor trust after Enron and other high-profile fraud cases.

Source: Financial Times, April 5, 2005.

True and Fair

The principal requirement of an audit is that the auditor expresses his or her opinion in relation to whether the accounts present a "true and fair" view of the performance of the company over the period and of its position at the balance sheet date. This is done in the Auditor's Report.

This phrase "true and fair" has never been defined in any legislation. As a result, it is the subject of considerable uncertainty. Case law has established, however, that it does not imply mathematical accuracy, as it would be unrealistic to expect that the financial performance and status of any corporate entity could ever be reduced to a set of figures that could be termed "correct". This is not surprising given the subjective nature of many of the valuations and judgements required when preparing any set of accounts.

Significantly, the phrase was incorporated into the provisions of the EU Fourth Directive, an important catalyst in harmonizing financial reporting within the EU. The provisions of this Directive were enacted in CA81, and are now contained in Section 226 and 227 of CA85, which reiterates that financial statements should give a true and fair view. CA81 also stipulated that ensuring that a true and fair view was provided was now to be an "overriding consideration". This means that companies are required to disclose more than the basic legal minimum if this is necessary in order to give a true and fair view.

However, the question of "true and fair view" must now also be considered in the context of the IAS 1 *Presentation of Financial Statements (see Chapter 6)* threshold of "fair presentation", the emerging importance of International Standards of Auditing (ISAs) and the intentions of the EU in this area. As the following extract explains this will have a significant impact on both the nature and conduct of the audit:

'True and Fair' View of British Audits is in Jeopardy, by Keith Jones

The "true and fair view" assessment of a company's state of affairs has been a cornerstone of UK accounting. It is now in jeopardy. Britain and Europe are moving dangerously close to a weak, narrow and limited US-style audit based on technical compliance. While in recent weeks the debate on protecting auditors from negligence claims has re-emerged, for investors it is a sideshow to the main event. Our worry is about the nature and quality of the audit itself and the potential for reduced shareholder protection.

The audit is a key safeguard in the relationship between management and the owners of their company, the shareholders. Under the current regulatory framework, an auditor has to make qualitative judgments about whether a company's accounts present a true and fair view of a business's state of affairs – not simply an arithmetic compliance with the letter rather than the spirit of accounting standards. Technical benchmarks of compliance can never hope to be flexible enough to capture all the issues that arise in a company's affairs. The dangers can be seen in such cases as Enron. Before it collapsed, the energy trading group regularly received a clean bill of health under the more restricted focus of US audits.

The threat to the UK approach arises from two factors. The first is the unilateral imposition of the International Auditing Assurance Standards Board's US-derived international standards of auditing (ISAs). These process orientated standards create a significant shift in the emphasis and focus of the audit which could undermine the current overriding principle that audit opinions must encompass the "true and fair view" of a business's state of affairs as enshrined by the UK Companies Act of 1985. Under these ISAs, we would move to a much narrower US-style technical compliance-based audit, which gives priority to rules at the expense of robust judgment and common sense. Second, their impact will be compounded by proposals to give these standards a legislative footing. Under the European Union's proposed eighth company law directive, ISAs could change the application and interpretation of existing auditing principles. We believe this will significantly reduce the scope and rigour of UK audits.

As the Association of Certified Chartered Accountants said in its submission to the Department for Trade and Industry on directors' and auditors' liability: "US-influenced audit standards are heavily influenced by the 'tick box' approach which has the aim of demonstrating that the auditor has not been negligent. In our view, this reduces the essential quality of an audit."

Here it is worth recalling why we have audits. Their purpose is to act as a safeguard and check on "agency problems and costs" that arise from the separation of ownership and control in companies. The risk is that management may not always act in the best interests of the shareholders. There may also be an imbalance in the availability and control of information that can affect the quality of reporting. Auditors act for and in the interests of shareholders. To this end, they are given privileged rights of access to a company. The purpose is to protect the company itself from the consequences of undetected errors or, possibly, wrongdoing and, in particular, to provide shareholders with "reliable intelligence". Investors rely on the auditors' professional and independent judgment, based on the exercise of skill, care and caution. . .

The writer is chief executive officer of Morley Fund Management.

Source: *Financial Times*, July 6, 2005.

This threat from a US-style auditing ethos, as well as the advent of new International Auditing Standards, ISAs, has been compounded by the provisions of IAS 1, which specifies 'fair presentation' as the standard. Together, these had the potential to significantly undermine the traditional qualities of an audit. However, recent statements from the FRC have reassured users.

In practice:

Review Gives Judgement on Implications of IAS, by Paul Gosling

"The concept of the 'true and fair view' remains a cornerstone of financial reporting and auditing in the UK," says the Financial Reporting Council. Replacing the phrase "true and fair" with "fair presentation" as the over-arching test of financial statements has not substantively changed the objectives of audits, or the nature of auditors' responsibilities, explains the FRC.

The FRC made its judgement clear in its newly published analysis of the implications of the adoption of International Accounting Standards, responding to concerns by some investors about the implications of IAS – and new International Auditing Standards – on the quality and consistency of accounts. But the review should also assist investors and others to better understand how IAS affects financial reporting, believes the FRC.

FRC chairman, Sir Bryan Nicholson, said: "This analysis provides useful guidance to preparers, auditors and users of financial statements on the implications of recent changes to financial reporting in the UK. Our analysis provides reassurance that, notwithstanding the changes that have taken place, the framework for financial reporting and auditing remains robust. The FRC is committed to facilitating a clear channel for all stakeholders to participate in the debate on the future evolution of the framework."

The analysis rejects criticisms of IAS that it weakens safeguards against corporate scandals, or that new auditing standards involve a "tick box" approach. But FRC concedes that, given the lack of legal case precedent inevitably attached to new standards, "many years may elapse before the courts can provide legal certainty (if ever)" on the obligations of companies and accountants in discharging their amended duties...

Source: accounting & business, September 2005.

FRRP gains 'True and Fair' opinion

The Financial Reporting Review Panel has published a legal opinion on the effect of the International Accounting Standards Regulation on the requirement to give a 'true and fair' view. The IAS regulation requires companies listed on an EU regulated market to prepare accounts in accordance with IAS for financial periods beginning on or after 1 January 2005. Under IAS 1, companies are required to 'fairly present' their accounts. Under the Companies Act 1985, accounts are required to give a 'true and fair' view.

The opinion, from Freshfields Bruckhaus Deringer, says that although the application of IFRS is presumed to result in a fair presentation, it may be necessary, in extremely rare circumstances, to depart from strict compliance with IFRS in the interests of fair presentation. The IAS regulation provides that IASs can only be adopted if they are not contrary to the principle that accounts must give a true and fair view...

Source: Accountancy, July 2005.

Reports

At the conclusion of an audit, the auditor issues a report. SAS 600, *Auditors Reports on Financial Statements*, details the format, content and standards pertaining to the Auditor's Report. The auditor has a number of options as to how to report:

1. **An unqualified report**: this certifies that the financial statements do give a "true and fair view".

2. **An unqualified report with reference to fundamental uncertainty**: provided these fundamental uncertainties are properly accounted for, however, the auditor may still be in a position to issue an unqualified opinion.

3. **A qualified opinion** can be issued in a number of scenarios:

   - **Disagreement** – this occurs where the auditors disagree with the directors' treatment or disclosure of one or more items in the financial statements. In such circumstances the auditor's report will explain the issues involved and state that except for this the accounts give a true and fair view.
   - **Adverse opinion** – this occurs where the effect of the item or items of disagreement are such as to lead the auditor to believe that the financial statements are misleading. In such circumstances the auditor's report would state that the accounts do not give a true and fair view.
   - **"Except for" limitation or scope** – this occurs where the scope of the audit has been limited by an inability to obtain acceptable explanations or evidence or because proper accounting records have not been maintained such that this prevents the auditor giving an unqualified report. Where the limitation is perceived to be so material, then it may be necessary for the Report to contain a disclaimer, indicating that the auditor was unable to form an opinion on whether the accounts give a true and fair view.

ISA 700, *The Auditor's Report on Financial Statements*, explains these options in similar terms (paras 36–39).

In practice:

More companies are falling out with their auditors, study finds, by Paul Rogerson

Listed companies are increasingly likely to fall out with their auditors over critical accounting decisions, new research has found. The number of qualified audit reports arising from an accounting treatment or disclosure problem was almost an unknown phenomenon two years ago. So far this year, however, such conflicts have accounted for two-thirds of all qualifications, according to a survey by Edinburgh accounts analyst Company Reporting.

Auditors issue "qualifications" only when the scope of their examination is limited, perhaps by the lack of important documentation; or the auditors disagree with a treatment or disclosure in the accounts of a company. Company Reporting analysed 325 companies, mainly in the FTSE-100 and mid-250 range. It found that the issue of qualified reports has been on the increase since 2001, indicating in particular emerging "rifts" between companies and their auditors concerning accounting treatments.

In 2004, one in 40 companies in the sample had their accounts qualified, compared with less than one in 100 three years ago. "The rise in qualifications can be attributed to two factors," Company Reporting commented. "Firstly, accounting standards have been tightened up over the last few years and practices that companies were able to get away with in the past are no longer acceptable. Secondly, in the aftermath of the recent world accounting scandals, auditors are under more scrutiny than ever before."

"Our suspicion is that auditors are less willing to toe the company line and, where any doubt exists, are more willing to issue a qualification" . . .

Source: The Herald, November 15, 2004.

In addition to providing a clear expression of opinion on the financial statements, the auditor should reinforce this by including confirmation that:

1. They comply with standards.
2. The audit process has included:

   - An examination of evidence relating to the amounts and disclosures in the various financial statements.
   - An assessment of any material estimates and judgements made by directors.
   - An assessment of whether the various accounting policies adopted are appropriate, consistent and adequately disclosed.
3. The audit was planned and executed so as to obtain reasonable assurances that the financial statements are free from material mis-statement.
4. The overall impact of the manner of presentation of the financial statements has been evaluated.

In practice:

Companies will be anxious to ensure that they receive an unqualified audit report, as anything less can often have serious consequences for both share price and market perceptions:

Flaws in controls take shine off Shell: Organisational overhaul threw reporting lines into disarray at the oil group, by Carola Hoyos and Adrian Michaels

The fact that three ratings agencies have downgraded Royal Dutch/Shell was a big blow for a company that saw its superior rating as one of its most prized accomplishments. But the reason

Moody's Investor Services gave for stripping the group of its triple A credit rating is arguably even more devastating. It pointed to this week's audit report, saying that it indicates "a range of reporting and oversight flaws inconsistent with a highly rated entity, and raises major questions about Royal Dutch/Shell's controls, reporting standards and corporate governance."

The report revealed the extent to which senior Shell management failed to disclose the true level of reserves at one of the world's biggest oil companies. How, despite an internal control system which should have picked up discrepancies, they kept the true picture out of the public arena for two years.

The root of the problem lies in the 1990s when Shell radically overhauled management and operations. These changes left controls confused and lines of reporting inadequate. In the mid-1990s, Shell was organised on geographical lines with semi-autonomous regions deciding on issues such as exploration expenditure. The changes meant that such decisions were now made by the global division rather than the region. But ridding Shell of its powerful fiefdoms – including Australia and Nigeria, where some of the biggest reserves misjudgments were made – was harder than expected. More importantly, at the time, those responsible for preparing Shell's accounts were not reporting to the chief financial officer. . .

Shell has begun to improve its lines of reporting, its financial controls and auditing functions. But the admission by former Shell employees and the auditors' report that Shell's internal controls were deficient is doubly important in the post-Enron era. . .

Source: Financial Times, April 22, 2004.

Operating and Financial Review (OFR)

The Cadbury Report was determined to ensure that shareholders received financial statements supplemented and supported "by a coherent narrative that combined to provide a balanced and understandable presentation of the company's performance". For this reason it emphasized the responsibility of the directors to allude to both negative as well as positive developments. However, it was also keen to ensure that these narratives did not adopt a purely historic perspective. The need for some assessment of the company's future prospects was identified as critical. These considerations combined to cause the committee to recommend that an Annual Report should include a report intended to address these issues.

The ASB was simultaneously devising a Statement of Best Practice that included just such a proposal. Issued in 1993, it proposed the inclusion of an OFR, although not on a mandatory basis. Such a review was envisaged as a forum in which the entity's past performance and future prospects as a whole might be discussed in a manner that would augment and not simply refer to the financial figures.

While government proposals requiring all UK quoted companies to prepare an OFR have been withdrawn, the OFR is likely to be produced by the bulk of large plcs. For those who do decide to include and OFR, its contents and structure will be governed by Reporting Standard 1 (RS1), issued by the ASB under its new legal powers to make standards for the OFR.

RS1 requires directors to prepare an OFR addressed to members, setting out their analysis of the business, with a forward-looking orientation in order to assist members to assess the strategies adopted by the entity and the potential of those strategies to succeed. The information disclosed in the OFR will also be of relevance to other stakeholders. The OFR should not, however, be seen as a replacement for other forms of reporting addressed to a wider stakeholder constituency.

The OFR should provide a balanced and comprehensive analysis, consistent with the size and complexity of the business, of:

- The development and performance of the business of the entity during the financial year
- The position of the entity at the end of the year
- The main trends and factors underlying the development, performance and position of the business of the entity during the financial year; and
- The main trends and factors which are likely to affect the entity's future development, performance and position.

The OFR is viewed, therefore, as a means of providing a range of information that allows readers, primarily shareholders, to assess the companies' strategies and their potential for success.

Disclosures outlined in RS 1 include the following:

- Analysis of performance and development
- Analysis of the position of the business
- Factors and trends underlying these
- Factors and trends affecting the future
- Description of business, objectives and strategies
- Resources available
- Risks and uncertainties faced, and
- Capital structure, treasury policies and liquidity.

Other information that should be included to the extent necessary would include information regarding:

- Employees
- Environmental matters
- Social and community issues
- Key relationships
- Returns to shareholders, and
- Appropriate key performance indicators (KPIs).

As the following extract (written while it was anticipated that the OFR would be mandatory) summarises, the OFR is viewed as a critical means of communication with users, particularly shareholders. It is intended to address their oft-repeated criticism that current narrative and financial disclosures do not allow a credible assessment of either current strategies or future prospects.

Investors Look Behind the Numbers

Robert Bruce Asks What This Means for Directors and Investors

Information that is more qualitative than quantitative has increasingly been included in annual reports and accounts in the UK over the past decade in an "operating and financial review"... The OFR has grown out of demand for companies to produce more qualitative information. American companies have had to provide management discussion and analysis information since 1968; the UK followed, with a voluntary "statement of best practice" drawn up by the Accounting Standards Board, in 1993. The growing number of people wanting to make use of corporate data were finding intangible items more valuable than traditional accounting information. Facts about customer satisfaction or benchmarking to competitors' performance, for example, were seen as better indicators of how a particular company was faring.

Sixty per cent of UK companies already produce OFRs, says Nigel Sleigh-Johnson, head of financial reporting at the Institute of Chartered Accountants in England & Wales... "The objective is to assist investors to assess the strategies adopted and the potential for those strategies to succeed," says the ASB. This has always been contentious. The idea that companies will provide enough information to allow such judgments when times are difficult is seen by many as far-fetched. To be useful, as one commentator put it recently, J.Sainsbury, the UK supermarket giant, would have had to issue an OFR 10 years ago that said: "Our years of arrogance as number one supermarket in the country have so alienated our suppliers that they are actively working with Tesco to topple us."

Source: *Financial Times*, March 31, 2005.

The OFR can, therefore, have a significant effect on the disclosures made by companies. In particular, narrative disclosures that relate to strategy and forward-looking factors are becoming a common element of most Annual Reports. These represent a substantive and significant advance in disclosure culture and, as intended, allow investors to better understand the risks inherent in their investments. While the government has decided not to proceed with the mandatory OFR, best practice, coupled with the requirements of RS 1, may ensure significantly improved disclosure in various areas. EU initiatives in this area will also be important.

Historical Summaries

Although not required under statute or any regulation, it has been the practice for many years for companies to provide historical summaries as part of their Annual Reports.

These summaries are essentially tabular or graphical presentations of significant financial performance measures over a period of a few, normally 5, years. Their main function is to provide sufficient information to users to enable them to interpret current data over a longer time frame than would otherwise be provided by the Annual Report. Their main usefulness, therefore, is that they allow trends to be established, a critical factor in any considered evaluation of a company.

In practice:

The Tesco historical summaries are shown on pages 64 and 65 of the Annual Report under the heading 'Five Year Record.' Some of these figures will be particularly useful in identifying trends when seeking to interpret the company's performance. This issue is covered in various chapters that follow.

Use of Graphs and Pictorial Representations

Graphs and pictorial representations are an obvious element of most Annual Reports. In fact, most companies employ these presentation techniques to a considerable extent. Curiously, however, the use of these is almost entirely unregulated. One consequence is that companies will commonly employ graphs that present data in a manner that materially misrepresents the underlying data. In fact, some research has suggested that the incidence of such misleading graphs may be extremely high, with deliberate manipulation being attempted by a considerable percentage of public companies.

Summary

The Annual Report is one of the most important documents produced by a company. Indeed, it represents the primary means of communication between a company and its stakeholders. Its format means that it supplements the financial statements with narrative comment and information that is important in enabling users to arrive at informed conclusions and decisions with regard to the company.

Because it is such an important document it is subject to considerable control and regulation. This applies not only to the financial statements, but also to the narrative elements, such as the Directors' Report, Auditor's Report and, now, the OFR, which are viewed as integral parts of the reporting package.

Indeed, increasingly the attention of users is being directed to the narrative sections for important supplementary information as well as insights into future prospects, investment plans and corporate strategy. These points will be explored in more detail in Chapters 14 and 18.

Review Questions

Question 1
Explain why the narrative sections of Annual Reports have assumed such importance in recent years.

Question 2
List the principal narrative elements of an Annual Report and for each indicate the component parts and the user group that would be most interested.

Question 3
Only some of the narrative elements of an Annual Report are subject to legislative control with regard to content. Is this appropriate or should each element of the Annual Report be subject to regulation?

Question 4
To what extent have the various additional disclosure requirements resulting from recent legislation and standards succeeded in remedying the "information deficiency" identified by many users?

Question 5
Consider the implications for auditors of increasing disclosure and reporting requirements.

Question 6
"The OFR means a significant amount of additional information is now made available to readers of an Annual Report. The main importance of the OFR is that it encourages management to not only disclose information but also to comment upon it and give opinions as to its significance". Explain how the OFR, where presented, significantly increases the information available to users regarding future prospects for a company.

Question 7
To what extent do financial analysts allow their analysis to be informed by the information contained in the narrative portion of Annual Reports?

Question 8
Explain how requirements in relation to narrative disclosures are likely to develop. For instance is it likely that there will be even greater disclosure requirements placed on companies? As a result is it possible that there might be resistance on the part of companies concerned at both the cost and the disclosure of sensitive information to competitors?

Case Studies

Case 1

Professor Prem Sikka has been one of the most insightful observers of corporate reporting practices over the last two decades. Here, in an article written when it was assumed that government proposals for the mandatory OFR would proceed, he takes a critical view of the OFR and the claims made for it. Having read it, consider the points raised and how champions of the "new" OFR might view them. In addition, consider his critique of the role of corporations in modern society in the context of what was covered in the earlier chapters of this text.

Revelation, Chapter One, by Prem Sikka

Corporations shape our lives from cradle to grave by providing goods, services, jobs and ideologies. They control our savings, pensions and investments. They can boost or destroy whole communities by closing mines, offices and factories, opening call centres, superstores and fast food outlets of the low-wage, shelf-stacking economy, or transferring whatever is movable to shed labour and increase profits.

Millions of people have directly experienced the cold-hand of corporate power through pension mis-selling and endowment mortgage scandals. Credit card companies, banks, phone companies and utilities have established new ways of making a quick buck. Corporate boardrooms, rather than Mother Nature, are producing new diseases, such as smoking related cancers, thalidomide, BSE and variant Creutzfeldt-Jakob disease.

Companies finance political parties, presidential campaigns and think-tanks to shape the domestic and foreign policies of governments. Yet people have little say in their affairs. There is an urgent need to bring corporations under public control, enhance stakeholder rights and change the way they are governed. But that is not on the government's agenda. Instead of deep reforms, the government is asking companies to publish some soft information in the shape of an operating and financial review – OFR – not too dissimilar to the US requirement for a management's discussion and analysis of financial condition and results of operations.

The OFR would require quoted companies to publish forward looking non-financial information about their strategy, prospects and opportunities to enable shareholders to make assessments of risks, earnings, dividends and performance. The OFR assumes that the primary goal of companies is to maximise profits rather than engaging in activities which are beneficial to all stakeholders.

The advent of OFR may be welcomed by supporters of corporate social responsibility, but there are a number of problems. The focus on quoted companies means that many large businesses exercising social power would be exempt. Examples include companies such as Northern & Shell, Portland Investment, Portland Enterprises and RHF Productions, which through control of national newspapers shape public choices and even elections of governments; privately owned utilities, which can charge excessive prices and cut off supplies to the vulnerable sections of our communities. Airlines, such as Virgin Atlantic, are major polluters but would be exempt from the OFR requirements.

Audit failures at Enron, WorldCom, Barings, Transtec, Maxwell and Parmalat have resulted in real losses to many stakeholders, but major auditing firms are exempt from the OFR. Britain is estimated to be losing up to £111bn each year in tax avoidance schemes, many designed and implemented by major accounting firms, but they would be exempt from OFR. Just to put this in perspective, the global income of PricewaterhouseCoopers, Ernst & Young, Deloitte, and KPMG is $55bn, which is greater than the gross domestic product of oil-rich Nigeria, or Kuwait. Yet they would not be required to explain their activities.

The OFR assumes that what is good for shareholders is also good for other stakeholders and society at large. This is highly problematical. Shareholders in tobacco companies benefit from the sale of cigarettes, but many smokers pick up lung diseases and society picks up the health and social costs. Many companies achieved record sales of animal feedstuff and paid record dividends, but consumers collected the mad cow disease. The same story can be told about pensions, endowment mortgage and other failures. Of course, directors could be forced to consider the interests of other stakeholders and wider society, but the OFR proposals are not accompanied by any enforceable director obligations to stakeholders. To publish any information, companies need to focus upon key performance indicators. However, the Companies Acts will not specify the indicators. Instead, the government expects the Accounting Standards Board (ASB), in collaboration with business and other parties, to develop the appropriate indicators and methodologies for reporting key information. The business-funded ASB has involved the TUC and some NGOs in the identification of these. Such processes may create impressions of pluralism but they cannot develop hard-edged policies, as they do not give stakeholders any enforceable rights. The key performance indicators will effectively be the residue of negotiations and bargaining amongst unrepresentative elites, with governments rubber-stamping or legitimising their lawmaking powers.

UK history shows that change often had to be imposed in the teeth of opposition from the entrenched business elite. Think of the minimum wage, health and safety and sex discrimination laws, even the need for the companies to publish the profit and loss account, balance sheet, audit report, turnover figure and fees paid to auditors for non-audit work. Yet, in the case of the OFR, the teeth of parliament are being drawn. Regulatory control is slipping away from parliament and any notion of representative government to a network of elite, unrepresentative and unaccountable private actors. Parliament will not have any real opportunity for vetoing the standards developed by the ASB. What is parliament for?

In an environment of voluntarism, many companies will continue to produce statements, proclaiming "core values of honesty, integrity and respect for people". Yet that may not be the whole story. Christian Aid has drawn attention to the anti-social activities of Shell in Nigeria. The company's annual corporate social responsibility reports stayed silent. Recent media attention has focused upon bribery and clandestine operations of BAE to secure defence contracts, while its annual reports are silent on such matters. The financial reports of NewsCorp and Virgin Atlantic are silent on the tax avoidance schemes operated by the companies.

Many UK companies massage their financial reports by using tax havens and concocting transactions which have no commercial substance and whose sole purpose is to avoid taxes. These practices have created new political risks for the companies and their shareholders, as evidenced by the Russian government's lawsuits against Yukos to recover past taxes, and the US government lawsuits against Enron and WorldCom and their advisers for devising questionable tax avoidance schemes. Yet no company provides the required information to enable anyone to assess these risks.

No major company publishes details of its "transfer pricing" policies. These are the policies which enable multinationals to price and transfer goods and services throughout their global operations; a crucial device for tax avoidance, flight of capital and worldwide laundering of profits. Through such techniques, WorldCom managed to avoid taxes on $20bn of its income. More recently, fingers have been pointed at major multinational drug and car companies.

The corporate mammoths are unlikely to volunteer any meaningful information about tax dodges, transfer pricing, use of tax havens, deaths and diseases caused by their products unless parliament lays down firm enforceable requirements for the OFR. The possibilities of that are slim. In such a climate, companies are more likely to publish self-congratulatory statements rather than hard data which would enable stakeholders to question corporate power and operations. Overall, the sentiments behind the OFR are probably right, but it is unlikely to deliver the promised accountability and responsible capitalism.

Prem Sikka is professor of accountancy at Essex University.

Source: *The Guardian*, November 8, 2004.

Case 2

The following article reports on the "ValueReporting Framework" devised by PwC. Access the complete ValueReporting Framework report on the PwC website, and use this to assist in identifying the critical components of a "good" Annual Report.

A Good Account of Yourself

What makes a good annual report? If you can answer this question, your business is more likely to enjoy investor loyalty and receive analyst 'buy' recommendations. Clue: it has got a lot more to do with how you explain your success and strategy than cool design, by Sarah Perrin

If you've ever had to judge an annual report quickly, you've probably learned to appreciate quality. Deloitte partner Isobel Sharp has done her time on such judging panels and says the winners are those that best describe their business. "A good report sets out very clearly what its segments are and gives information about the markets in which it is reporting," she explains. "I want you to tell me about your competitors, your relative market position, your order book. I want you to tell me about the people and the key players. Then the whole report has to tie together." Too often, Sharp says, the highlights page doesn't exactly correspond to the segmental analysis, or to the chief executive's report.

Presentation also matters. "It has to be visually interesting, but that doesn't mean just including pictures of employees smiling at you," Sharp says. "There should be charts and graphs that give the message clearly, rather than lots of text. You also need a decent size font and should avoid using shiny paper."

Producing a good annual report means taking the needs of readers into account. "We have done research among both equity and bond analysts," says David Phillips, ValueReporting partner at PricewaterhouseCoopers. "Their plea is that companies make sure the basic information is given to them. For example, the people trying to analyse companies from the bond market perspective really want to know what the proper cash flows of the business are, what all the borrowings of the business are (in one place), and when those borrowings are being repaid on a year-by-year basis. On the equity side, again they have some basic requirements. They really want to know how growth is being achieved and whether it is organic or via acquisition; they want to know the return on investment."

PwC has developed a reporting model – the ValueReporting Framework – which aims to deliver a complete picture of a company. The model consists of four blocks which build on each other. The first is the market overview, which sets out the external operating environment. The second reporting block – the company's strategy, its goals and objectives – naturally follows on. The way that the company delivers its strategy is then covered by the third block, which PwC calls "value-creating activities". These include activities related to recruitment and retention, innovation, brands, the supply chain, and environmental, social and ethical issues. Finally, the fourth reporting block – financial performance – builds on all that has gone before, explaining the outcome of the company's strategy, activities and market environment.

"Most investors would say that the market space in which the company operates and its strategy are the two most important elements of information," says Phillips. "For example, if a company has a dominant position in the marketplace, and the market is growing very quickly, you don't have to be Einstein to work out what the opportunities for that company to succeed are likely to be."

Throughout the report, companies need to tell a coherent story, Phillips says. The financial information should be supported by other information that helps readers put it in context, such as relevant key performance indicators. These might include customer satisfaction indices, measures of innovation or employee retention figures. Data enabling the company to be compared against its peers is also particularly useful.

One company that has developed a powerful reputation for the quality of its annual reports is Geest, which has won ProShare's award for the best annual report by a non FTSE-100 company for the past five years. Asked what makes a good annual report, Michelle Doughty, chief executive of ProShare, said: "Helpful descriptions of the company's business, its objectives and strategy, and the industry and markets within which it operates.'' Key dependencies, relationships and risks should be identified. ''The report should give a comprehensive picture of the company's financial performance, likely future performance and trends,'' Doughty said. ''Clear style, ease of use and effective design are also important.''

Paula Cooper, Geest's group communications manager, says work on the annual report begins about six or seven months before publication. ''We try to give a balanced picture of our business – the upside and the downside. The market reports have been important for us and our investors. We put in a lot of information to say this is why you should still be investing in Geest. It's still a growth story. We give all the reasons why we think this is the case. On the other hand, we also spell out the risks to the business very clearly. You can't spin it so it's all a bed of roses, because business isn't like that.'' . . .

Source: *Financial Director*, July 2004.

FINANCIAL STATEMENTS [6]

When you have completed this chapter you will understand:

- The complex structures typical of many large business combinations.

- How these structures impact upon the nature and content of the Annual Report.

- The formatting regulations relating to financial statements included in an Annual Report, for instance the IFRS requirements set out in IAS 1.

- The accounting principles and disclosure requirements relating to the various elements of financial statements.

- Some of the current issues surrounding financial reporting, specifically those relating to IFRS.

(a)   (b)

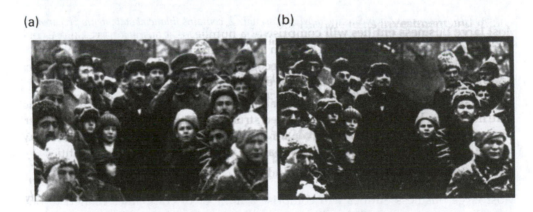

Figure 6.1 (a) Lenin and Trotsky celebrate the second anniversary of the Russian Revolution in the Red Square. (b) Lenin celebrates, but Trotsky has been airbrushed. Source: David King, *The Commissar Vanishes*, 1997.

Introduction

Financial statements, and in particular balance sheets, are often compared to photographs – they attempt to capture company performance in a snapshot. However, in the same way that ordinary photographs can be manipulated, so too can financial statements. Just as political circumstances in 1920s Russia made it expedient for Stalin to attempt to erase Trotsky from public memory, it is often tempting for companies to seek to construct their accounts in such a way as to communicate a particular message.

For this reason there are extensive and rigorous regulations relating to the presentation of financial information in an Annual Report. In particular, the ways in which the balance sheet and income statement are to be presented are heavily controlled, allowing only limited scope for variability within strict formats.

This chapter deals with the rules covering the disclosure of financial information. This involves identifying the accounting regulations and disclosure rules relating to items normally included in financial statements and in the accompanying notes. The provisions relating to the balance sheet are dealt with first, followed by those relating to the income statement, statement of changes in equity and the cash flow statement. While the requirements outlined are quite extensive, they are intended to be indicative and not exhaustive.

Before this, however, the chapter looks at the implications for companies of the fact that most large business entities are actually business combinations, i.e., they are comprised of a parent company and several others in some form of relationship with that parent.

In practice:

The IFRS Restatement, which is included in Appendix 2, contains financial statements prepared using IFRS. This should be referred to throughout for examples of how the IFRS provisions referred to in this chapter are applied. Reference should also be made throughout to the financial statements in the Tesco plc 2005 Annual Report in Appendix 1. A particular advantage of having access to both is that it will be possible to gain an appreciation of the impact of IFRS on financial statements. In fact, the impact is mixed: in some case, the impact is substantial; in others, negligible.

Corporate Structure

Most large business entities will comprise a number of companies related to one overall parent company. This will have an effect on the information to be included in an Annual Report because accounting recognizes such a business combination (or group) as a separate entity for reporting purposes.

The nature of these inter-company relationships can be varied and complex and there may often be a deliberately ill-defined structure in place. This will be dealt with in more detail in Chapter 11. However, for the purposes of this chapter it is necessary to have some idea of the relationships that can exist between corporate entities.

The nature of these relationships include:

- Parent/wholly-owned subsidiary, where one company owns another entity (subsidiary) entirely.

- Parent/partly owned subsidiary, where one company controls another, but does not own it entirely. That portion of the subsidiary owned by entities other than the parent company is called the "minority interest".

- Investor/associate company, where one company has a substantial participating interest (normally 20% or more) in another company.

- Investor/investee, where one company simply makes an investment in another, usually for the short term.

In a situation in which this parent company is called P, a group structure might comprise any combination of the following permutations (Figure 6.2).

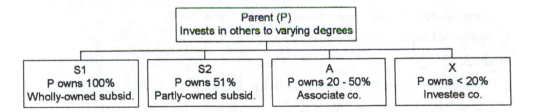

Figure 6.2   A group structure.

The Annual Report filed for P must recognize the fact that P has these relationships with other companies. This is usually satisfied by preparing an additional set of accounts – called group (or consolidated) accounts. The procedure for preparing group accounts will be covered in more detail in Chapter 11, but can be summarized as follows:

- P has one or more wholly-owned subsidiaries: combine results of these companies entirely with those of P.

- P has one or more partly-owned subsidiaries: combine results of these companies entirely with those of P, but reflect the claims of other interests by indicating these under the heading "minority interest" in both the balance sheet and the income statement, respectively.

- P has one or more associate companies: recognize the claim of P to a share of the total profits made by these associates proportionate to P's investment and indicate the total value of the investment in the balance sheet as a proportion of the net assets of the associates.

- P has one or more investees: simply include these as short-term investments in the balance sheet and record any resulting income in the income statement.

Financial Statements

While a substantial part of an Annual Report will be made up of the narrative elements and reports, the financial statements and notes still constitute its core. Where the reporting entity is a group these will include:

By statute:

1. Balance sheet of the parent company as an individual company.

2. Income statement of the parent company as an individual company. (Under S.230(3) CA85 this may be omitted if the parent company balance sheet discloses the parent company's profit for the year.)

3. Consolidated balance sheet for group as a whole.

4. Consolidated income statement for the group as a whole.

5. Additional explanatory notes.

By IFRS:

1. Cash flow statement for parent and group (IAS 7).

2. Statement of Changes in Equity (IAS 1)

The principal IFRS dealing with these at a general level is IAS 1, *Presentation of Financial Statements*. This standard prescribes the basis for presentation of general-purpose financial statements. It also sets out the overall framework and guidelines for their structure as well as the minimum requirements for disclosure.

The IAS adopts a number of overall principles:

- **Fair presentation**: Financial statements are required to "present fairly" the financial position, performance and cash flows of the entity. The implications of the change from the "true and fair requirement" was discussed in the previous chapter.

- **Compliance with IFRS**: the entity must provide an explicit and unreserved statement to the effect that the financial statements are in compliance with IFRS. In almost all circumstances there is a presumption that a fair presentation is achieved by compliance with applicable IFRS (para. 13). Additional disclosure or use of notes to the accounts does not rectify inappropriate accounting policies.

- **Offsetting**: assets and liabilities and income and expenses should not be offset (netted-off) against one another unless required or permitted by IFRS.

- **Comparative information**: this should be disclosed for the previous period for all amounts disclosed in the financial statements. In cases where there have been reclassifications of items in the current year, then the equivalent figures for the previous period should reflect this.

- **Materiality and aggregation**: each material class of similar items should be presented separately (unless immaterial).

- **Accounting concepts**: basic accounting concepts such as going concern, accruals and consistency (see Chapter 4) are also explicitly accepted.

Under IAS 1, a complete set of financial statements comprises the following (para. 8):

1. Balance sheet

2. Income statement

3. Statement of changes in equity showing either:

    i) all changes in equity; or
    ii) changes in equity other than those arising from transactions with equity holders acting in their capacity as equity holders

4. Cash flow statement; and

5. Notes, comprising a summary of significant accounting policies and other explanatory notes.

The remainder of this chapter deals, in turn, with the formats, accounting principles and disclosure requirements appropriate to each of these. For the more important elements of these primary financial statements, general accounting principles and disclosure requirements are outlined. However, these are not intended to be either exhaustive or comprehensive, as this text is not primarily concerned with detailed accounting and disclosure provisions.[1] Nevertheless, the chapter is somewhat more specific in its contents than others and it is important not to become so consumed by the detail that the overall picture, and the fair presentation requirement, are overlooked.

---

[1] For more detailed information on presentation and disclosure issues see http://www.iasplus.com/fs/2005checklist.pdf This is an excellent website and provides one of the most complete and up-to-date resource bases relating to IFRS.

1. Balance Sheet

Because IAS 1 does not prescribe a format, merely a list of items that must be disclosed, it does not cause any significant conflict with the formats set out in CA85. However, other considerations, partly related to the influence of US regulators and markets on information flows, may incline plcs to adopt the US approach of listing assets and liabilities in order of liquidity.

Overall Presentation

A critical feature of IAS 1 is the requirement that every reporting entity should sub-divide assets and liabilities between current and non-current. These should then be presented as separate classifications on the face of the balance sheet (unless, as is the case for certain financial institutions, a presentation based on other liquidity considerations would be more appropriate).

A net asset presentation (assets minus liabilities) is allowed. The traditional approach used in the UK and elsewhere (fixed assets + current assets − short term payables = long-term debt plus equity) is also acceptable.

The distinction between current and non-current is critical, therefore, and the criteria need to be rigorously applied:

Current/non-current Assets

Essentially, an asset will be classified as current when it satisfies any of the following criteria:

a) it is expected to be realized in, or is intended for sale or consumption in, the entity's normal operating cycle; or

b) it is held primarily for the purpose of being traded; or

c) it is expected to be realized within twelve months after the balance sheet date; or

d) it is cash or a cash equivalent (as defined in IAS 7, *Cash Flow Statements*), unless it is restricted from being exchanged or used to settle a liability for at least twelve months after the balance sheet date.

All other assets are to be classified as non-current. IAS 1 uses the term "non-current" to include tangible, intangible and financial assets of a long-term nature.

Current/non-current Liabilities

A liability will be classified as current when it satisfies any of the following criteria:

a) it is expected to be settled in the entity's normal operating cycle; or

b) it is held primarily for the purpose of being traded; or

c) it is due to be settled within twelve months after the balance sheet date; or

d) the entity does not have an unconditional right to defer settlement of the liability for at least twelve months after the balance sheet date.

All other liabilities are to be classified as non-current.

Minimum disclosure requirements

At a minimum the following should be presented on the face of a balance sheet (IAS 1, para. 68):

(a) property, plant and equipment;

(b) investment property;

(c) intangible assets;

(d) financial assets (excluding amounts shown under (e), (h) and (i));

(e) investments accounted for using the equity method;

(f) biological assets;

(g) inventories;

(h) trade and other receivables;

(i) cash and cash equivalents;

(j) trade and other payables;

(k) provisions;

(l) financial liabilities (excluding amounts shown under (j) and (k));

(m) liabilities and assets for current tax, as defined in IAS 12, *Income Taxes*;

(n) deferred tax liabilities and deferred tax assets, as defined in IAS 12;

(o) minority interest, presented within equity; and

(p) issued capital and reserves attributable to equity holders of the parent.

The face of the balance sheet should also include line items that present the following amounts:

a) the total of assets classified as held for sale and assets included in disposal groups classified as held for sale in accordance with IFRS 5, *Non-current Assets Held for Sale and Discontinued Operations*; and

b) liabilities included in disposal groups classified as held for sale in accordance with IFRS 5.

As a general principle, additional line items may also be needed to present fairly the entity's financial position. (para. 69)

Reflecting these disclosure principles, IAS 1 provides the following illustrative balance sheet:

XYZ Group – Balance Sheet as at 31 December 20-2	20-2 £000's	20-1 £000's
ASSETS		
Non-current assets		
Property, plant and equipment	X	X
Goodwill	X	X
Other intangible assets	X	X
Investments in associates	X	X
Available-for-resale investments	X	X
	X	X
Current assets		
Inventories	X	X
Trade receivables	X	X
Other current assets	X	X
Cash and cash equivalents	X	X
	X	X
Total assets	X	X
EQUITY AND LIABILITIES		
Equity attributable to equity holders of parent		
Share capital	X	X
Other reserves	X	X
Retained earnings	X	X
	X	X
Minority interest	X	X
Total equity	X	X
Non-current liabilities		
Long-term borrowings	X	X
Deferred tax	X	X
Long-term provisions	X	X
	X	X
Current liabilities		
Trade and other payables	X	X
Short-term borrowings	X	X
Current portion of long-term borrowings	X	X
Current tax payable	X	X
Short-term provisions	X	X
	X	X
Total liabilities	X	X
Total equity and liabilities	X	X

In practice

Note that Tesco, like most UK plcs, has decided to adopt the more traditional structure. Thus, while disclosing the line items shown above, Tesco's IFRS Restatement balance sheet shows Equity in the bottom section and all other items in the upper section. The almost complete continuity between this format and that adopted previously can be confirmed by viewing the balance sheet presentation shown under UK GAAP in the 2005 Annual Report.

The accounting principles and disclosure requirements relating to the balance sheet headings and sub-sections required under IAS 1 are now outlined in more detail. [Note: Disclosures under these sub-headings are quite extensive and beyond the scope of this text. Refer to, for instance, the IASplus website mentioned earlier for fuller details. Only the first section, that dealing with Property, plant and Equipment, covers the requirements in any depth.]

(a) Property, Plant and Equipment

Property, plant and equipment are defined (IAS 16, *Property, plant and equipment*) as "tangible assets that are held by an entity for use in the production or supply of goods and services, for rental to others, or for administrative purposes, and are expected to be used during more than one period". These types of asset will usually constitute a substantial portion of the total assets of any business and, as such, are likely to have a major impact on operations.

Key issues relating to these items are the timing of their recognition in accounts, the amounts at which they should be carried in the accounts and the related depreciation (or impairment) charges.

Essentially, an item of property, etc., should only be recognized a) when it is probable that future economic benefits will flow to the entity from it; and b) the cost or revalued amount is measured reliably. At its most basic, cost comprises purchase price and any directly attributable costs relating to bringing the asset to the location and working condition necessary to operate in the manner intended by management. These costs might include site preparation, delivery costs and professional fees. In some instances interest costs can be capitalized (IAS 23, *Borrowing Costs*). The same criteria apply to self-constructed assets.

An entity should adopt either the cost model or the revaluation model and apply that policy consistently to the entire class of property, plant and equipment. Under the cost model these assets should be carried at cost less any accumulated depreciation and impairment losses to date. Under the revaluation model these assets should be carried at fair value at the date of revaluation, less any subsequent accumulated depreciation and impairment losses. The fair value of property is usually taken to be its market value as established by professionally qualified valuers. Revaluations should take place regularly and under controlled circumstances: for instance, property values that are prone to volatile movements should be revalued annually. Less volatile assets in this class might be revalued every three or five years. It is also permissible for revaluations to take place on a rolling basis. When an item is revalued, the entire class must be revalued. A 'class' is a grouping of assets of a similar nature such as motor vehicles, furniture, etc. Any revaluation increase should be recognized directly in equity except to the extent that it reverses a revaluation decrease of the same asset previously recognized as an expense, in which case it should be recognized in the income statement. A decrease should also be recognized in equity until the carrying amount reaches its depreciated historical cost, and thereafter in the income statement.

The basic principle in relation to depreciation is that the depreciable amount should be allocated on a systematic basis over an asset's useful life. The method adopted (straight line, reducing balance, etc.) should reflect the pattern in which the asset's future economic benefits are expected to be consumed. Thus a fleet of cars would usually be depreciated using the reducing balance method, reflecting the more significant loss in value in earlier years of useful life. Each part of an item of property, plant and equipment with a significant cost in relation to total cost should be depreciated separately.

IAS 36, *Impairment of Assets*, is intended to prescribe the procedures an entity should apply to ensure that its assets are carried at no more than their recoverable amount (that is, the higher of net selling price and value in use). Essentially, in circumstances where an asset's carrying value in the books of an entity, i.e. its book value (NBV), is above its recoverable amount, it is said to be impaired. Such an impairment loss must be recognized immediately.

An entity should assess at each balance sheet date whether or not there are indications of impairment losses. Some indicators of these might include: a significant decline in market value; significant and adverse changes in the technological or economic environments; evidence of obsolescence; or plans to discontinue or restructure parts of the business.

General Disclosures:

The financial statements should disclose, (usually by way of notes) for each class of property, plant and equipment:

a) The measurement bases used for determining the gross carrying amount

b) The depreciation methods used

c) The useful lives or the depreciation rates used

d) The gross carrying amount and the accumulated depreciation (aggregated with accumulated impairment losses) at the beginning and end of the period

e) A reconciliation of the carrying amount at the beginning and end of the period showing:

- Additions
- Assets classified as held for sale or included in a disposal group classified as held for sale in accordance with IFRS 5 *Non-current Assets Held for Sale and Discontinued Operations* and other disposals
- Acquisitions through business combinations
- Increases or decreases during the period resulting from revaluations under paragraphs 31, 39 and 40 of IAS 16, *Property, plant and equipment*, and from impairment losses recognized or reversed directly in equity under IAS, 36 *Impairment of Assets*
- Impairment losses recognized in profit or loss in accordance with IAS 36
- Impairment losses reversed in profit or loss in accordance with IAS 36
- Depreciation
- The net exchange differences arising on the translation of the financial statements from the functional currency into a different presentation currency, including the translation of a foreign operation into the presentation currency of the reporting entity; (see Chapter 12) and
- Other changes.

The financial statements must also disclose:

- The existence and amounts of restrictions on title, and property, plant and equipment pledged as security for liabilities
- The amount of expenditures recognized in the carrying amount of an item of property, plant and equipment in the course of its construction
- The amount of contractual commitments for the acquisition of property, plant and equipment; and
- If it is not disclosed separately on the face of the income statement, the amount of compensation from third parties for items of property, plant and equipment that were impaired, lost or given up that is included in profit or loss.

An entity must disclose the nature and effect of any change in an accounting estimate relating to property, plant and equipment that has an effect in the current period or is expected to have an effect in subsequent periods, in accordance with IAS 8, *Accounting Policies, Changes in Accounting Estimates and Errors*.

If items of property, plant and equipment are stated at revalued amounts, the following must be disclosed:

- The effective date of the revaluation
- Whether an independent valuer was involved
- The methods and significant assumptions applied in estimating the items' fair values

- The extent to which the items' fair values were determined directly by reference to observable prices in an active market or recent market transactions on arm's length terms or were estimated using other valuation techniques

- For each revalued class of property, plant and equipment, the carrying amount that would have been recognized had the assets been carried under the cost model; and

- The revaluation surplus, indicating the change for the period and any restrictions on the distribution of the balance to shareholders.

Entities are also encouraged (but not required) to disclose the following amounts:

a) The carrying amount of temporarily idle property, plant and equipment

b) The gross carrying amount of any fully depreciated property, plant and equipment that is still in use

c) The carrying amount of property, plant and equipment retired from active use and not classified as held for sale in accordance with IFRS 5 *Non-current Assets Held for Sale and Discontinued Operations*; and

d) When the cost model is used, the fair value of property, plant and equipment when this is materially different from the carrying amount.

In practice

The IFRS Restatement is not required to include detailed notes relating to fixed assets. However, note 13 in the Tesco 2005 Annual Report gives some indication of the level of detail to be provided.

(b) Investment Property

IAS 40, *Investment Property*, defines Investment Property as "land or buildings held to earn rentals or for capital appreciation or both". It allows an entity to choose either the fair value or cost model. Whichever is chosen must be applied to all of the entity's investment properties:

- Fair value model: under this option the property is measured at fair value and any movements in fair value are recognized in the income statement.

- Cost model: property is carried at cost less any depreciation and impairment losses. The fair value of the property must also be disclosed.

Specific disclosures that must be made include: the method by which fair value is determined; the criteria used to classify whether property is investment or not; the amounts recognized in the income statement.

In practice:

300% increase in IFRS profit

Measuring its investment property at fair value will increase profit by 300% at French real estate company Unibail. The company explains that 95% by value of its property portfolio is considered to be investment property. Following a reclassification, it measures the property at market value whereas previously it was carried at depreciated historical cost.

The result is that an increase in fair value of €597m (£408m) is recorded through the income statement with a further boost arising from depreciation charges reducing from €156m to €5m.

Source: Accountancy, May 2005.

(c) Intangible Assets

Intangible assets are increasingly being recognized as critical sources of value. As such, their accounting treatment and disclosure, which have traditionally been somewhat opaque, are assuming increasing importance. IAS 38, *Intangible Assets*, defines intangible assets as "an identifiable non-monetary asset without physical substance". Examples include, but are not limited to, goodwill, market knowledge, software, intellectual capital, patents, copyrights, brands, customer lists, customer or supplier relationships, market share, customer loyalty, import quotas and fishing licences.

To be capitalized (i.e. included as an asset in the balance sheet) they must satisfy the following criteria:

- **Identifiability**: the asset must be separable, that is capable of being separated or divided from the entity and sold, or arise from contractual or other legal rights.
- **Control**: an entity controls an intangible asset if it has the right to obtain future economic benefits from it and restrict the access of others to these benefits. In circumstances where it is protected by copyright then market knowledge could qualify under this heading. It would be more difficult, however, to show that skilled staff or customer relationships satisfied this criterion.

Where an intangible asset is acquired, for instance as part of the acquisition of another company, then it is usually possible to identify and value (using fair value principles) goodwill and other separable intangible assets.

Considerable difficulties arise, however, in relation to internally generated intangibles. These are of increasing economic importance, particularly in high-tech, knowledge-based sectors where, for instance, most of the corporate value may consist of intellectual capital. On the basis that it is not normally either separately identifiable, controlled by the entity, or reliably measurable, such internally generated intangibles should not be recognized as an asset.

However, driven in part by commercial imperatives, regulators have shown a more nuanced approach to dealing with some forms of internally generated intangible assets. Essentially, if an internally generated intangible asset can be identified as being in the development phase with, amongst other factors, a demonstrable feasibility, attributable development expenditure and a likely completion, then it can be capitalized. Examples include the costs of developing new production processes, systems and services. However, internally generated brands, publishing titles, or customer lists cannot be capitalized, on the grounds that they cannot be distinguished from the cost of developing the business as a whole.

For the purpose of accounting subsequent to initial acquisition, intangible assets should be classified as:

- **Indefinite life**: there is no foreseeable limit to the period over which the asset is expected to generate cash flows for the entity, or,
- **Finite life**: there will only be a limited period of benefit to the entity.

Generally the cost of an intangible asset with a finite life is amortized (depreciated) over that life. If the asset has a quoted market price in an active market, a revaluation model is permitted, under which the asset is carried at revalued amount, i.e. fair value less subsequent amortization. Intangible assets with indefinite useful lives are not amortized, but must be tested for impairment at each reporting date. If the recoverable amount is lower than the carrying amount, an impairment loss is recognized.

(d) Financial Assets

All financial assets are recognized on the balance sheet under IFRS. They are initially measured at cost, which is the fair value of the consideration given plus transaction costs (IAS 39, *Financial Instruments: Recognition and Measurement* para. 66).

Most financial assets, subsequent to initial recognition, are remeasured to fair value at each balance sheet date. There are two classes of assets that are carried at amortized cost subject to a test for impairment. These are originated loans and held-to-maturity investments. There is also an exception to the fair value measurement rules for financial assets that cannot be reliably measured. It is expected to be rare that an entity cannot reliably measure all of its financial assets (IAS, 39 para. 69).

(e) Investments Accounted for Using the Equity Method

These are explained and discussed in detail in Chapter 12.

(f) Biological Assets

These are to be disclosed for security as well as health and safety reasons that are outside the scope of this text.

(g) Inventories

The use of the term "inventories" rather than the more traditional term "stocks" reflects both the existing influence of US accounting terms and a determination on the part of global standard setters to institute a common vocabulary as part of a broader convergence agenda (see Chapter 15).

Inventory will usually comprise one of the most valuable resources of a company and consequently its incorporation, disclosure and valuation receive considerable attention in statute and accounting standards. Under IAS 2, *Inventories*, it should be shown in the balance sheet at the lower of cost and net realizable value. Net realizable value is defined as "anticipated selling price less completion, sales, marketing and distribution costs". Surprisingly, determining "cost" can often be more problematic. Except for businesses that simply purchase goods and then sell them on, questions as to what actually comprises cost will arise. For instance, for manufacturing firms it will often be difficult to determine how much overhead should be attributed to stock. This is also the case where raw materials are processed and at the end of the year remain unfinished. Long-term contracts, where costs cannot always be matched to particular accounting periods, will also pose problems.

In response to these situations, various valuation methods have been developed. Thus, techniques such as First In First Out (FIFO), Last In First Out (LIFO), Weighted Average and other methods may be used to determine cost, subject to the overriding consideration that the basis adopted must be one which, in the opinion of the directors, is appropriate to the company. LIFO, however, is not permitted under accounting standards. (These valuation methods are discussed in more detail in Chapter 8.)

CA85 (as amended) requires stock to be disclosed under the following sub-headings where appropriate:

1. Raw materials and consumables

2. Work-in-progress

3. Finished goods and goods for resale

4. Payments on account for items not yet received

IAS 2 requires the following disclosures:

- Accounting policies adopted in measuring inventories, including any cost formulae used

- Total carrying amount sub-divided into appropriate classifications

- Carrying amounts at fair value less costs to date

- The amount expended during the period

- The amount of any write-down of inventories

- Carrying amount of any inventories pledged as security for liabilities.

Long-term contracts: many large entities, particularly those engaged in industries such as construction, must deal with the added inventory-related complications created by long-term contracts. For instance, they pose problems in terms of calculating the amount of profit to be taken, and the value of any closing inventory, because costs and profits cannot always be neatly attributed to arbitrary accounting periods.

It would be unacceptable to force entities to wait until completion before incorporating some element of profit on such contracts. Consequently, IAS 11, *Construction Contracts*, allows companies engaged in such long-term contracts to include revenue and profit from partly completed projects in their income statement while the project is in progress. This is provided that the outcome can be determined prior to completion and reasonable prudence is exercised. The normal apportionment basis is "percentage of completion" and will involve some subsidiary inventory valuations.

(h) Trade and Other Receivables

Almost without exception, entities carry some type of receivables on the face of the balance sheet. Ordinary operations give rise to trade receivables; receivables due from customers under construction contracts; and financial instruments with positive fair values and short-term loans for non-bank entities. Prepayments are to be distinguished from trade and other receivables in that a prepayment balance will not result in receipt of cash. An entity would usually present these items within trade and other receivables on the face of the balance sheet.

Most receivables and loans fall within the definition of financial assets and are subject to the recognition and measurement rules that apply to those assets.

(i) Cash and Cash Equivalents

Most entities will hold cash. IAS 7, *Cash Flow Statements*, defines cash equivalents as "short-term, highly liquid investments which are readily convertible into known amounts of cash and which are subject to an insignificant risk of changes in value". Thus, it would not include time deposits where there are restrictions on the right to withdraw funds at notice. Such items would be shown as investments.

(j) Trade and Other Payables

Trade and other payables are current liabilities for which the amount to be settled is usually known rather than uncertain. Entities, almost without exception, carry some type of trade and other payables on their balance sheet. Items generally included in trade and other payables are: trade payables; amounts payable under statutory obligations such as social security obligations and payroll taxes; and guarantees of certain value and financial instruments with negative fair values.

These items are presented within the "Trade and other payables" line item on the face of the balance sheet.

Most trade and other payables fall within the definition of financial liabilities and are subject to the recognition and measurement rules that apply to those liabilities.

CA(85) also imposes some specific disclosure requirements in relation to such items.

(k) Provisions

Provisions can be defined as "amounts provided in relation to which there is some element of uncertainty, either in regard to amount or timing". A common example is deferred taxation, which is discussed in more detail in Chapter 12. In recent years some companies have also begun to make provision for future liabilities deriving from the environmental impact of their activities.

Historically, provisions have provided one of the most potent means of manipulating accounting figures. Typically, a business would create a provision and, instead of reversing this provision when the anticipated event or loss failed to materialize, would use it as a fund against which subsequent costs could be written off.

IAS 37, *Provisions, Contingent Liabilities and Contingent Assets*, has effectively countered this practice by providing that a provision will only be recognized when:

- An entity has a legal or constructive obligation.
- It is probable that an outflow of resources will be required to settle the obligation; and
- A reliable estimate can be made of the amount of the obligation, as a result of past events.

Because of the nature of provisions, estimates are usually involved. IAS 37 provides that the amount recognized will be the "best estimate of settlement amount at balance sheet date". It also requires a review of such provisions at each subsequent balance sheet date.

In relation to any class of provision, the following disclosure requirements apply:

- The net book value at the start and end of the period.
- Details of additional provisions made during the period.
- A brief outline of the nature of the obligation and expected timing of any outflows.
- An indication of the uncertainties surrounding the timing or the amount involved.

Contingent liabilities: Provisions and contingencies have much in common. However, contingent liabilities are less certain to result in a transfer of economic benefits and it is not possible to arrive at reliable estimates of potential liability. In other words, they fail to satisfy the three recognition criteria set out above in respect of provisions.

A common example is losses that might occur as a result of a legal action against the company. Other examples include financial exposure deriving from guarantees and warranties given.

IAS 37 provides that an enterprise should not recognize a contingent liability. Instead, it should be disclosed by way of note. The following disclosures should be made in respect of such a contingent liability:

- An estimate of the likely financial effect
- An indication of the uncertainties relating to the amount or timing of the outflow; and
- An assessment of the likelihood of any reimbursement.

(l) Financial Liabilities (excluding amounts shown under (j) and (k)

The emergence of derivatives and other financial instruments (see Chapter 9) in recent years poses significant challenges for accounting. Incorporating options, futures and a variety of derivative types, and embracing a range of trading strategies such as hedging, they bring complexities that raise a variety of recognition and measurement issues. At one and the same time they promise hugely significant financial benefits, particularly for those operating in the financial services sector, while simultaneously exposing those involved to significant risk.

IAS 32, *Financial Instruments: Disclosure and Presentation*, is specifically intended to assist users in understanding the significance of on-balance and off-balance financial instruments to an entity's financial position. This revolves, to a large extent, around an issuer's initial classification of a financial instrument as being either a liability or an equity instrument.

IAS 32 requires that this classification depend on the substance, and not the legal form of the instrument. Thus, an instrument is a financial liability if the issuer may be obligated to deliver cash or another financial asset in the future, or if the holder has the right to demand cash or another financial asset. An example is mandatory redeemable preferred shares (see later) which may be given the legal form of equity, but which are, in substance, a form of liability. Where these instruments are employed for hedging purposes, risk management and hedging policies (including accounting policies) must be disclosed. Likewise fair values of all financial instruments must be disclosed along with information about any exposure to interest or credit risks.

IAS 39, *Financial Instruments: Recognition and Measurement*, also deals with financial instruments, but is more concerned with recognition and measurement issues. For reasons that will be explained in later chapters, IAS 39 has proven to be one of the most controversial standards issued in recent years. However, in terms of its impact upon the balance sheets of companies its provisions are relatively straightforward. Essentially, all financial assets and liabilities, including underlying and embedded derivatives, must be recognized on the balance sheet. Such financial instruments are to be initially measured at fair value on date of acquisition or issuance. In most instances this equates to cost. (The technical and operational aspects of these instruments are discussed in more detail in Chapter 9.)

For the purpose of measuring a financial asset or liability subsequent to initial recognition, IAS 39 sub-divides them into four categories:

1. Loans and receivables not held for trading.

2. Held-to-maturity (HTM) investments such as debt securities.

3. Financial assets and liabilities measured at fair value – this will always include derivatives unless designated as hedging instruments.

4. Available-for-sale (AFS) financial assets and liabilities – this category contains all other instruments.

Subsequent to initial recognition, all financial assets in categories 1 and 2 are carried at amortized cost subject to an impairment test; all in category 3 are carried at fair value with changes recognized in the income statement; all AFSs are measured at fair value with changes recognized against equity in the balance sheet (or at cost if fair value cannot be determined.) In the case of liabilities most are measured at original recorded amount less repayments and amortization.

Many firms will employ financial instruments as a means of "hedging" against future risks, i.e. they might buy or sell instruments in order to fix the price of an underlying contract. Hedge accounting, which recognizes the offsetting impact of changes in fair value of both the hedging instrument and the hedged item in the same period income statement, is allowed, provided that the hedging relationship is defined, measurable and effective. For instance, in the case of what is called a "fair value hedge", where an entity is securing itself by means of hedging against changes in fair value of a recognized asset or liability, any gain or loss arising on remeasuring the hedging instrument and the hedged item should be recognized in the income statement.

(m) Liabilities and Assets for Current Tax

IAS 12, *Income taxes*, prescribes the accounting treatment and disclosures relating to taxes (including taxable profits). Current tax liabilities (or assets) for present or prior periods should be recognized immediately as a liability. Tax assets and liabilities should be distinguished from other balance sheet assets and liabilities and a distinction should be made between current and non-current items.

(n) Deferred Tax Liabilities and Deferred Tax Assets

IAS 12, *Income taxes*, also deals with Deferred Tax. This is discussed in more detail in Chapter 12.

(o) Minority Interest

This term is explained and covered in detail in Chapter 11.

(p) Issued Capital and Reserves

The amount of share capital that any company can issue is called its authorized share capital and is indicated in the Memorandum of Association. This amount must be shown either on the face of the balance sheet or by way of note. However, it is an information item only and is not included in calculations.

The issued share capital figure, which is the portion of the authorized share capital actually issued, appears on the face of the balance sheet and is included in calculations. A note to this item will normally include reference to the following:

- **Allotted**: i.e., the company has decided who is to receive shares from those who applied.

- **Called-up**: i.e., the company has asked for those who have been allotted shares to pay the amount due.

- **Fully paid**: i.e., the amounts called-up have been paid. In the event of liquidation, shareholders would be required to pay any amounts unpaid.

Shares can have a number of values:

- **Nominal value** of a share is the original value assigned to a share when a company is formed. It is also called **par value**. In the UK shares cannot legally be issued at a price below this value, i.e., at a discount. Most shares will have a nominal value of £1. Other common values are 50p, 25p and £5. It is used as a basis upon which the amount to be distributed as dividends may be computed and expressed. This value will usually be disclosed on the balance sheet, for example: "£1 Ordinary Shares".

- **Issue price** of a share is the amount at which a share is made available to those who may wish to purchase. For example, a company may have £1 Ordinary Shares that it makes available to the public at a price of £1.15. In these circumstances the nominal value is £1 and the issue price is £1.15. The difference between these two values is known as **Share Premium**. Statute requires that the Share Premium element of any share issue be shown separately from the nominal value element in the balance sheet.

- **Market value** is the price that a share can command on the open market. If the company is a public limited company then this will be the current market price. If it is a private company, then it is the amount which a family member, friend or investor would be willing to pay.

Reserves arise from a variety of sources and can form a substantial part of the funding profile of a company. In the UK there are strict rules as to the classification of reserves and the uses to which they can be put.

Reserves are sub-divided into two types:

1. **Distributable**: These are reserves that can be used as a source for the payment of, for example, dividends. The principal reserve of this type is "Retained Earnings", sometimes called "Revenue Reserve". This reserve results principally from the accumulation of profits.

2. **Undistributable**: These are reserves that cannot normally be distributed:

   - **Share Premium Account**: as illustrated above, when shares are issued at a price higher than their nominal value an amount equivalent to this excess must be transferred to a Share Premium account and disclosed separately. Once such an account is created it is legally treated as part of share capital. This account can, however, be used to finance a bonus issue (see Chapter 9) or can have preliminary formation expenses or share issue costs charged against it.
   - **Revaluation Reserve**: when assets are revalued in the balance sheet an amount equal to any increase in value of the asset should be credited (or debited in the event of a decrease) to such a reserve.
   - **Capital Redemption Reserve**: where a firm redeems its own shares using its distributable reserves then it must transfer to a Capital Redemption Reserve an amount equal to the amount by which the company's issued share capital has been diminished. This is in order to maintain the company's share capital and non-distributable reserves level. Where such redemption is financed by the proceeds of a new issue of shares then such a transfer is not necessary.
   - **Reserves that cannot be distributed under the company's Memorandum of Association**: these are specific reserves which the company's own rules preclude it from distributing.

Under the provisions of IAS 1, every entity should disclose the following, either on the face of the balance sheet or in the notes:

a) For each class of share capital:

   - The number of shares authorized
   - The number of shares issued and fully paid, and issued but not fully paid
   - Par value per share, or that the shares have no par value
   - A reconciliation of the number of shares outstanding (effectively, issued) at the beginning and at the end of the period
   - The rights, preferences and restrictions attaching to that class, including restrictions on the distribution of dividends and the repayment of capital
   - Shares in the entity held by the entity itself or by subsidiaries or associates
   - Shares reserved for issue under options and contracts for the sale of shares, including the terms and amounts; and

b) A description of the nature and purpose of each reserve within equity.

2. Income Statement

IAS 1 identifies certain minimum headings to be presented on the face of the income statement as well as guidance for the identification of certain line items. Significantly, there is no particular format or order of presentation specified.

At a minimum, IAS 1 requires that the following should be disclosed on the face of the Income Statement:

- Revenue
- Finance costs
- Share of profit or loss of associates and joint ventures (see Chapter 11)
- Pre tax gain or loss recognized on the disposal of assets or settlements of liabilities attributable to discontinued operations
- Tax expense
- Profit or loss

The following two items must also be disclosed on the face of the Income Statement as allocations of profit:

- Minority interest (see Chapter 11)
- Profit or loss attributable to equity holders of the parent.

Additional items should be presented when such presentation is relevant to providing a full understanding of the entity's financial performance. However, extraordinary items are no longer permitted to be disclosed in the statement or notes.

Where they are material, the amount and nature of income and expense should be disclosed separately. Examples of items that would normally be considered material include discontinued operations, inventory write-downs, restructurings and disposals of plant.

Expenses can be analysed either by nature (raw materials, staff costs, etc.) or by function (cost of sales, administration, selling expenses, etc.). This can be done either on the face of the Income Statement or by way of the notes. If an entity categorizes by function then it must also provide information on the nature of expenses, including depreciation, amortization and employee benefit.

The entity must also disclose either on the face of the Income Statement or by way of note (or via the Statement of Changes in Equity), the amount of dividends recognized as distributions to equity holders during the period as well as the related amount per share. In addition, by way of note, the entity must disclose the amount of dividends proposed or declared before the financial statements were authorized for issue, but not recognized as a distribution to equity holders during the period, as well as the related amount per share.

IAS 1 provides the following two templates, illustrating how the income statement might be presented according to the two expense classification options:

XYZ Group Income Statement for year ended 31 December *(Illustrating classification of expenses by function)*	20-2	20-1
	£000's	£000's
Revenue	X	X
Cost of Sales	(X)	(X)
Gross Profit	X	X
Other Income	X	X
Distribution Costs	(X)	(X)
Administration expenses	(X)	(X)
Other expenses	(X)	(X)
Finance costs	(X)	(X)
Share of profit of associates	X	X
Profit before tax	X	X
Income tax expense	(X)	(X)
Profit for the period	X	X
Attributable to:		
Equity holders of the parent	X	X
Minority Interest	X	X
	X	X

XYZ Group Income Statement for year ended 31 December *(Illustrating classification of expenses by nature)*	20-2	20-1
	£000's	£000's
Revenue	X	X
Other Income	X	X
Changes in inventories of finished goods and work-in-progress	(X)	(X)
Work performed by the entity and capitalized	X	X
Raw material and consumables used	(X)	(X)
Employee benefits expense	(X)	(X)
Depreciation and amortization expense	(X)	(X)
Impairment of property, plant and equipment	(X)	(X)
Other expenses	(X)	(X)
Finance costs	(X)	(X)
Share of profit of associates	X	X
Profit before tax	X	X
Income tax expense	(X)	(X)
Profit for the period	X	X
Attributable to:		
Equity holders of the parent	X	X
Minority Interest	X	X
	X	X

IFRS 5, *Discontinuing Operations*, provides that the results of discontinued operations are to be shown on the face of the income statement. This will usually involve parallel disclosures under many of the headings listed above.

Comprehensive Income

Problems of definition with some elements of "income", lack of consistency in how entities apply and present their income statements, as well as an awareness on the part of regulators that there are underlying conceptual problems with how and where some items are recorded, has prompted the IASB to embark on a project to examine how income is reported. In the US the introduction of SFAS 130, *Reporting Comprehensive Income*, has lead to the use of the notion of "comprehensive income" and the disclosure of a range of "income" items. Initial proposals suggest a matrix structure that would highlight not only income and expenditure from different functional areas, but also the type of gain or loss, as well as details of remeasurements, for instance, those relating to property revaluations or inventory write-downs.

Whatever the outcome, the IASB initiative suggests both a determination to ensure more focused and informative disclosures in relation to income, as well as a willingness to follow the lead of FASB where appropriate.

3. Statement of Changes in Equity

IAS 1 requires that every entity provide a Statement of Changes in Equity. This effectively replaces the Statement of Total Recognized Gains and Losses. Its purpose is to track and disclose events and transactions that have impacted upon equity. This is often necessary because a number of gains and losses are either permitted or required to be dealt with through reserves, and this statement ensures that they are disclosed.

The statement must show:

- Profit or loss for the period
- Every item of income and expense (and gain or loss) that is recognized directly in equity
- For each component of equity, the effects of changes in accounting policies or fundamental errors (in accordance with IAS 8, *Accounting Policies, Changes in Accounting Estimates, and Errors*.)

Either within this statement, or separately in the notes, the entity must also disclose:

- Capital transactions with owners
- The balance of accumulated profits at the beginning and end of the period, together with movements for the period in question

- A reconciliation between the carrying amount of each class of equity, share premium and reserve at the beginning and end of the period, disclosing each movement.

As the pro-forma outline below demonstrates, this statement can often be quite detailed and entail a number of complex reconciliations:

XYZ Group Statement of changes in Equity for the year ended 31 December 20-2
Attributable to equity holders of the parent

	Share capital	Other reserves	Translation reserve	Retained earnings	Total	Minority interest	Total equity
Balance at 31 December 20-1	X	X	X	X	X	X	X
Accounting policy changes				(X)	(X)	(X)	(X)
Balance at 31 December 20-1	X	X	X	X	X	X	X
Gain on property revaluation		X			X	X	X
Available-for-sale investments:							
Gains/(losses) taken to equity		(X)			(X)		(X)
Transferred to profit or loss		(X)			(X)	(X)	(X)
Cash flow hedges:							
Gains/(losses) taken to equity		X			X	X	X
Transferred to profit or loss		(X)			(X)	(X)	(X)
Exchange differences			(X)		(X)	(X)	(X)
Tax on items taken to equity		(X)	X		(X)	(X)	(X)
Net income recognized in equity		X	(X)		X	X	X
Profit for the year				X	X	X	X
Total recognized income & expense		X	(X)	X	X	X	X
Dividends				(X)	(X)	(X)	(X)
Issue of Share Capital	X				X		X
Equity share options issued		X			X		X
Balance at 31 December 20-2	X	X	(X)	X	X	X	X

4. Cash Flow Statements

IAS 7, *Cash Flow Statements*, requires an entity to provide users with a mechanism for assessing its ability to generate cash and cash equivalents (short-term, liquid and convertible investments) and the needs of the entity to utilize those cash flows. This requirement is satisfied by the presentation of a Cash Flow Statement prepared in accordance with IAS 7. This focus on the cash activity of an enterprise reflects the critical role cash plays in commercial life (see Chapter 8) and the unique insights that the "cash life" of an entity provides.

A cash flow statement must contain details of cash flows under the following headings:

- **Operating activities**: the principal revenue-producing activities, such as trading, and other activities that are not investing or financing activities. IAS 7 allows the use of the indirect or direct methods when calculating operating cash flows. The indirect method simply reconciles profit from operations to cash flow generated; the direct method identifies the actual constituent elements of cash flow – receipts from customers, payments to suppliers and employees, etc. Both methods lead to the same figure, but the direct method may result in additional operational information being disclosed.

- **Investing activities**: this discloses cash flows relating to a variety of investing activities. Cash flows relating to the following should be disclosed under this heading: acquisition and disposal of long-term assets and other investments; total consideration relating to acquisitions and disposals; dividends and interest received may be listed here or under either operating or financing activities. In any case, dividends and interest received or paid are to be disclosed separately and not offset.

- **Financing activities**: those that result in changes in the size and composition of equity and borrowings. Examples include cash proceeds from share, debenture and loan issues and cash repayments of loans.

The figure shown at the end of the cash flow statement is the cash increase or decrease for the year resulting from movements in cash and cash equivalents. This should reconcile to the difference between the relevant opening and closing balances shown on the Balance Sheet.

IAS 7 provides for the following type of presentation:

Cash flow statement for year ended 31 December	20-2 £000's	20-1 £000's
Cash flows from operating activities:		
Net Profit before Tax	X	X
Adjustments for:		
Depreciation	X	X
Investment Income	(X)	(X)
Interest Expense	X	X
Operating profit before working capital changes	X	X
Increase/decrease in trade and other receivables	(X)	(X)
Increase/decrease in inventories	X	X
Increase/decrease in trade payables	(X)	(X)
Cash generated from operations	X	X
Interest paid*	(X)	(X)
Income taxes paid	(X)	(X)
Cash flow before extraordinary items	X	X
Proceeds from earthquake disaster settlement	X	X
Net cash from operating activities:	X	X

Cash flows from investing activities:

Acquisition of subsidiary net of cash acquired (note a)	(X)	(X)
Purchase of property, plant and equipment	(X)	(X)
Proceeds from sale of equipment	X	X
Interest received*	X	X
Dividends received*	X	X
Net cash used in investing activities:	(X)	(X)

Cash flows from financing activities:

Proceeds from issuance of share capital	X	X
Proceeds from long-term borrowings	X	X
Payment of finance lease liabilities	(X)	(X)
Dividends paid**	(X)	(X)
Net cash used in financing activities:	(X)	(X)
Net increase in cash and cash equivalents	X	X
Cash and cash equivalents at the beginning of the year	X	X
Cash and cash equivalents at the end of the year	X	X

* Interest and dividends received can be classified under either investing or operating cash flow. Interest paid can be classified as operating or investing cash flow.

** Dividends paid can be presented under financing or operating cash flows.

Additional information may be supplied by means of note.

5. Notes to the Financial Statements

Notes to the accounts form an integral part of the reporting process. They should present information about the basis of preparation of the financial statements and the specific policies adopted. In effect, they provide additional information in an orderly and systematic manner, with each note cross-referenced to the appropriate element of the primary statements. They are intended as a means of presenting information required by IFRS not actually included on the face of one of the primary financial statements. They should also, where appropriate, provide detailed analysis in narrative form of items shown on the face of the primary statements as well as supplementary information encouraged by IFRS and other disclosures necessary to provide a fair presentation.

The notes, as a minimum, should disclose the significant accounting policies adopted by the entity. These will normally be found in a separate section of the Annual Report headed "Accounting Policies". The accounting policies section should, under IAS 8, *Accounting Policies, Changes in Accounting Estimates, and Errors*, include a description of the various measurement bases adopted in preparing the financial statements. This section should also provide details of any judgements that management has made in the process of applying those accounting policies that most significantly impact the amounts at which items are shown. Similar disclosures should also be provided in relation to estimates or judgements relating to the future.

Prior Period Adjustments

In many cases an entity will need to make adjustments to prior periods arising from the correction of fundamental errors. These do not include normal recurring adjustments or corrections of accounting estimates made in prior periods. IAS 8, *Accounting Policies, Changes in Accounting Estimates, and Errors*, provides that all such errors should be corrected by restating comparative prior period amounts and appropriate disclosure should be made, usually by way of note.

Segment Reporting

Most businesses operate several classes of business or operate in several geographical areas, with different rates of profitability, different opportunities for growth and different degrees of risk. It is normally impossible for a user of the financial statements to appreciate this unless the financial statements provide some segmental analysis of the information they contain.

IAS 14, *Segment Reporting*, is intended, therefore, to ensure that the segment information reported by an entity is disclosed on a consistent basis, year by year. These disclosures are intended to facilitate more informed judgements about the business as a whole.

IAS 14 requires every entity to identify its reportable segments. One basis of segmentation is primary, that is, segments based on business and geographical considerations. The other is secondary, where the entity uses its own organizational structure or internal lines of reporting, to identify reporting segments. In any case, a reportable segment exists where:

- Revenue of the segment is 10% or more of total revenue, or
- Segment profit or loss is 10% or more of the combined result of all segments, or
- Segment assets are 10% or more of total assets of all segments.

Sufficient segments need to be reported so that at least 75% of total consolidated revenue is included.

Post-Balance Sheet Events

The Annual Report is issued several months after the financial year-end. In the interim, it is possible that circumstances could have changed for the company, or information that clarifies the position of the company at the balance sheet date may have come to light. IAS 10, *Events after the balance sheet date*, recognizes these possibilities and provides guidance for companies in dealing with them.

Its approach is to divide such events into two types:

- **Adjusting events**: these are post balance sheet events that "provide additional evidence of conditions existing at the balance sheet date". Such events, for example, the confirmation of the amount of a bad debt where the amount had been uncertain at the balance sheet date, should be recorded for the period under review, but need only be disclosed if material.

- **Non-adjusting events**: these are post balance sheet events that concern conditions that did not exist at the balance sheet date. An example would be an acquisition or disposal by the company. It is not relevant to the period under review but is significant because it may affect future prospects. Where material, the nature of the event should be disclosed along with an estimate of the likely financial effect where this can be quantified.

One significant change that this IAS recognizes is in relation to proposed dividends. Normally, dividends, particularly final dividends, will only be proposed or declared after the balance sheet date. In these circumstances they do not meet the criteria of a liability under IAS 37, *Provisions, Contingent Liabilities and Contingent Assets*. These should now be identified as contingent liabilities and disclosed by means of a note, rather than being accrued in the accounts of the period under review.

Summary

The impact of both statute and accounting standards on the presentation of financial information in the Annual Report is considerable, particularly in terms of the level of disclosure now required in respect of a growing range of items. This merely confirms the general thrust of financial information presentation in recent decades: the emphasis has been more and more on disclosure as a means of satisfying user requirements.

The impact of IFRS will be significant in increasing the quantity and nature of information disclosed.

The disclosure requirements given in this chapter have been detailed and quite specific. In later chapters further disclosure requirements and accounting regulations relevant to particular areas, such as groups, taxation, foreign currency and pensions, will be outlined.

Review Questions

Question 1
In terms of group structure, describe the types of relationships that it is possible for one company to have with another.

Question 2
List the primary financial statements that appear in Annual Reports. Comment on whether and how they complement one another.

Question 3
List the principal constituent parts of the balance sheet.

Question 4
Explain why the disclosures now required in relation to intangibles have become so significant.

Question 5
List the principal constituent parts of the income statement.

Question 6
Explain the thinking behind the introduction of the statement of changes in equity.

Question 7
Identify the additional information disclosed by a cash flow statement. Explain why this information might be of use to potential investors in deciding whether or not to invest in the shares of a reporting entity.

Question 8
"No amount of legislation or regulation will overcome the fact that most financial statements are essentially propaganda documents bearing little relation to the underlying commercial reality of business". Discuss.

Case Studies

Case 1

The following article summarizes some of the more significant effects of IFRS. Consider whether you agree with the author, that the introduction of IFRS will "aid investors to allocate capital to companies with the best chance of securing good returns".

In Search of Needles in a Data Haystack

Jane Fuller Examines Some of the Knock-on Effects Emerging from the Spread of International Financial Reporting Standards

International financial reporting standards, spreading across Europe and elsewhere, may not be quite as detailed as US standards, but they have enough bulk to prompt the question of whether we will be able to see the wood for the trees. One way of looking at it is that the spread of IFRS marks a territorial gain for some clear trends in financial reporting.

The first is fair value accounting, which switches valuations from historic cost towards market values. Where inadequate markets prevent the application of fair value, its companion, "value in use", pops up, using methods that rely on discounted cashflow forecasts. There are two crucial points about this trend. The first is the forward-looking nature of the information and the second is that management's view of value is being subjected to external tests.

This supports the aim put forward in the framework – that accounts should help users make economic decisions. Notably, they should aid investors to allocate capital to companies with the best chance of securing good returns. Critics say this mars accounts as a record of the directors' stewardship of shareholders' assets. It is not hard, however, to regard changes in market values of those assets during the period as relevant to the assessment of that stewardship.

Whatever the relevance of current values, this does not mean users of accounts want this information muddled with trading performance; or that they attach the same importance to unrealized "paper" gains as they do to a cash sale. And if paper profits threaten to prompt tax authorities to send out real cash bills, the crunching of gears between IFRS and the regulatory uses of accounts becomes particularly uncomfortable.

The second important trend is the attack on manipulated or smoothed earnings. This includes forcing companies to: recognize share options as staff costs; treat lumpy restructuring charges as just another business expense, booked as incurred; and cease squirreling away surpluses into reserves that will offset future losses.

IAS 39, the controversial standard on financial instruments, can be seen in this context. Hedge accounting has preserved the black-box approach to risk management: investors are expected to take on trust that assets and liabilities are either well matched or well hedged. The standard often requires the unpicking of a netting off exercise, and proof that hedges really do reduce exposures in the way management says they do.

If hedges are not effective, a company is more risky than it appeared and earnings will be more volatile. Fannie Mae, the US provider of mortgage finance, flouted FAS 133, father of IAS 39, by saying hedges were effective when they were not. The standard has changed the view of the business from one that was simple, with smooth earnings and stable finances, to one that is none of these.

These early standards on financial instruments are over-complicated and clumsy, but they do pose serious questions about both risk controls and earnings management. If they discourage the use of hedges for cosmetic purposes then that is welcome.

The third important trend is balance sheet reform. Traditional measures of net assets often neglect valuable parts of a business, particularly in knowledge-based companies. Hence the move to leave acquired goodwill on the balance sheet at the purchase price. This should even satisfy fans of historic cost: you continue to see what was paid for an acquisition. Other disclosures will help users judge whether an adequate return is being made.

But the growing demand for certain intangible assets to be separated from goodwill and amortized over their useful life muddies the picture. It will still be a chore to assemble the information needed to calculate return on investment. The elephant in the room remains internally generated goodwill. IFRS nods in the elephant's direction by decreeing that some development costs be capitalized. But there is a long way to go before such things as human capital are captured. Without this, measurements of intangibles will, to some extent, ring hollow. They ignore the intellectual input that will determine how much profit is made from, say, a patent or a customer relationship.

Other attempts to make the balance sheet more realistic have led to more crunching of gears. Investors do need to know what interests a company has in other entities, such as pension funds and special purpose vehicles containing securitized assets. This explains the tighter tests of where control lies and whether all risks/rewards have been transferred.

Where previously "ring-fenced" vehicles bounce back on to the balance sheet, ratios such as return on equity and gearing will be called into question. The rating agencies will take a look, so will bank lenders. The existence of the interest that has recrossed the fence is unlikely to be news to them. But sometimes covenants will be altered; and if a group's level of responsibility for liabilities, such as pensions, is greater than thought, this will threaten credit ratings. For equity investors, the impact of any newly consolidated deficits on distributable reserves will raise questions about dividend payments.

These knock-on effects, some unintended, are a more important challenge than the overdone worry about volatile numbers leading to share-price volatility. Where new disclosures present a more accurate reflection of underlying – and volatile – economic reality, that is welcome. Where they record changes in market values with no cash impact, the information is useful, but of a lower order.

In only two scenarios should IFRS trigger lasting damage to the market's view of a company. The first is where, as with Adecco, the employment services group, it fails to come up with a timely explanation, suggesting inadequate internal controls and weak leadership. The second is where a company turns out to have been much more risky than thought, as with Fannie Mae. The share price noise that will surround the minor outbreaks of confusion should not worry anybody.

Source: *Financial Times*, February 24, 2005.

SECTION III

Analysis

Financial Information Analysis is an art. It is a highly subjective exercise where the experience and intuition of the user are critical factors. However, it is also a skill. It can be facilitated and assisted by learning various techniques that have been developed by those seeking to understand financial information.

Building on the previous section which dealt with the information content of an Annual Report, this section of the text identifies techniques and approaches that have been developed by accountants, investors, financial analysts and others to help in identifying and extracting significant information from accounting statements.[1]

This section begins with a macro-discussion of the various techniques that have been developed by accountants and analysts, concentrating, in particular, on the Fundamental Analysis and Technical Analysis approaches.

Adopting the Fundamental Analysis approach as its preferred methodology, the text then identifies and illustrates the techniques developed under this approach for dealing with specific financial issues such as Activity, Liquidity, Financing, Profitability and Return on Investment.

This section deals primarily with techniques. However, there are reminders throughout that these are only a means to an end and not an end in themselves. The goal of the analysis of financial information is to facilitate a robust, informed and contextual interpretation leading to sound decision-making.

This can only be achieved by allowing the results derived from mathematical techniques to be properly contextualized and related to both the wider commercial context and the firm-specific environment. The text will return to this point in Section V when the various techniques discussed in this section are brought together to illustrate their proper use.

---

[1] Readers should refer throughout to the Tesco 2005 Annual Report included in Appendix 1. Reflecting the change to IFRS, Appendix 2 includes the Tesco IFRS Restatement for 2005. This presents the financial information in the format required under IFRS. As such it allows a comparison between the two schemes. It also allows a parallel analysis of a second set of financial information. This is further supplemented by the inclusion on the text website of an analysis of the Tesco Annual Report for 2006 and any subsequent years.

FUNDAMENTAL ANALYSIS [7]

When you have completed this chapter you will understand:

- The different approaches that have been developed to facilitate the extraction of information from financial statements.

- The nature and role of both fundamental analysis and technical analysis.

- That this text, while respecting the insights that technical analysis can bring, adopts the fundamental analysis paradigm.

- The usefulness, but also the limitations, of ratios as a means of analysis.

- The importance of context and trends in properly applying these techniques.

Chance Encounter with Lion Leads to Key Discovery

Buying into documentary media group was only natural after being bowled over by impact of wildlife shows screened on high definition TV set. Diary of a Private Investor, by James Bartholomew

On a trip to Miami, my wife and I were strolling along the waterfront when we came across a Discovery Channel shop. Many people will have seen this cable and satellite channel which shows nature programmes but I did not know it had shops as well. It was full of things connected with science – particularly toys and gadgets. But suddenly I noticed something I had never seen before: a high definition television. It was, of course, showing Discovery Channel programmes. But not like we have ever seen them before. The African savannah looked so real it was as if it were outside your window. The prowling lion looked as if you could touch it – or it could eat you. The effect was dramatically more realistic than any other moving image I have ever seen. It was not just better, it was wonderful. And nature programmes are ideal for showing off its quality.

More recently I stayed the weekend with a fund manager and took the opportunity to ask what shares he and his staff were excited about at the moment. One of them turned out to be Discovery Holding Company. This owns the Discovery Channel and plenty of other channels, too: TLC, Animal Planet, The Travel Channel, Discovery Health Channel and nine other emerging networks in the US. It reaches over a billion subscribers around the world. The shares only came on to the market in July, after they were "spun off" by another group, Liberty Media.

The price had fallen from around $16.20, soon after the launch, to $14.00. This was probably because some Liberty Media shareholders who had been issued with Discovery shares were not interested in holding them. They had therefore been selling and depressed the price. But, on a fundamental analysis, the shares were good value. What was more, the shares were beginning to recover. It seemed like a good technical situation of artificially-prompted selling appearing to have come to an end. I did not wait to do my own financial analysis. In situations like this, waiting can mean missing out. I rang up my broker the following Monday and bought a stake straightaway at $14.70 a share. It has turned out well so far. The rally has kept going in the two weeks since then, they have reached $15.32.

Afterwards I thought I ought to look at some of the numbers. On the kind of simple analysis I usually do, the shares don't look cheap at all. One of the more optimistic brokers has forecast earnings per share of 54 cents next year, which puts the shares on a 2006 price to earnings (p/e) [see Chapter 10] ratio of 28.4 – rather high by British standards. My friend's staff, some of whom were visiting, looked at me with kindly, amused expressions. Do I still use p/e ratios? How quaint! But it is hard for a private investor to devote enough time to do detailed balance sheet, profit and cash analyses.

The other tip mentioned by my friend is more obscure but is more obviously attractive. Next Media is a Hong Kong company that has successfully built up a newspaper business based on its publication, Apple Daily. The company has since gone on to create a publication in Taiwan, too – the Taiwan Apple Daily. The fund manager argued that the stock market had got the company wrong, valuing it as though it only had the Hong Kong business. That was because the Taiwan business has been making losses. But that was a short-term thing. The initial stages of creating a paper necessarily involve taking losses while creating the newspaper and building up its circulation. This investment should – if all goes well – be followed in due course by profits. His faith in the company's skill is encouraged by its track record of success and his regard for the chief executive.

I liked the "story". The main thing in successful investment is seeing the true value of a company when the market doesn't – but will in due course. I bought a few straightaway at HK$3.45. The price has since firmed to HK$3.50. When I finally got around to looking at a few figures, I found that different brokers had very different ideas about Next Media's future. They forecast earnings per share for the year to next March at 16 cents or 31 cents, depending on which you prefer to believe. So the ratio of prospective earnings to the current share price is anywhere between 20.4 and 10.5. Say the truth lies in between and the prospective p/e ratio is 15. That would not be expensive, if my friend's confidence turns out to be justified.

It is good to get some new investment ideas. I must spend more weekends in the country.

Source: *Daily Telegraph*, September 3, 2005.

Introduction

As previous chapters have highlighted, the Annual Report contains a mass of financial information. The user of this information is confronted, therefore, with a huge volume of data, both quantitative and qualitative, out of which he or she must make some sense. The problem of having to deal with such a mass of data is compounded by the fact that information of this nature is relatively meaningless of itself. That is, it is presented in a manner that rarely contextualizes it. In other words, unless the information is given some context it is not possible to assess its significance either in whole or in part.

In order to deal with these twin problems of mass of data and lack of contextualization, a number of approaches have been developed by accountants, analysts and others. These can broadly be classified into two categories:

1. Fundamental Analysis, which identifies and analyses business, economic and financial fundamentals relevant to the business.

2. Technical Analysis, which seeks to predict future share movements on the basis of patterns identified in historical share prices.

These are simply alternative ways of looking at information relating to a company and its shares. As the following extract explains, they approach this information from different perspectives.

What is the Difference Between Technical Analysis and Fundamental Analysis?

There are basically two schools of thought when we talk about market analysis: technical analysis and fundamental analysis. Let us start with fundamental analysis.

Fundamental analysis is the study of the fundamentals of the market. "Great," you say, "What are fundamentals?" Fundamentals are all things that affect the supply and demand of the underlying commodity. For example, if you were analysing the price of wheat and you thought that the price of wheat was going to go up because there is a drought in the mid-western US, then you would be basing your analysis of the wheat market on fundamentals.

Technical analysis, on the other hand, is the study of the market based on a chart of its price data... If you were to look at the chart of the price of wheat over time and saw that the price of wheat is the lowest it has been in 20 years, then you are said to be using technical analysis. You do not need to know anything about the underlying commodity to be a technical analyst and that is one of the advantages of being a technical analyst.

If you wanted to study the fundamentals of Coffee, then you would want to know everything about coffee: how it is grown, what the planting cycles are, who the big buyers of coffee are, what are their plans in the future and how would that affect the demand for coffee and so on. The problem in researching coffee is that it takes a very long time to find out this information and then even more time to examine and interpret it. Technical analysts claim that all of the fundamentals, or things that affect the price of a commodity, are shown on the price chart anyway.

Source: *http://www.learninvesting/courses/commodity105.htm.*

There are, therefore, significant differences in the perspectives adopted by these two approaches. Nevertheless, while the following sections highlight these, it is important to remember that there are also similarities, for instance, in the emphasis on trends.

Fundamental Analysis

Fundamental analysis describes the process of identifying the fundamental drivers of company performance and value and of applying techniques to extract, summarize and contextualize these. It involves attempting to understand the range of macro and micro contexts within which a company operates. Thus, a user adopting this approach will seek to gain information about the industry in general, the company's place within that industry, the macro-economic climate, inflation rates, recent wage disputes and any other pertinent information. In all of this financial data will be a key data set. However, it will not be considered in a vacuum: any insights that the financial data yield will be informed by the full range of information available.

The measurement techniques embraced by this approach, all of which will be dealt with over the course of this section of the text, are outlined in the following extract, which is also useful in identifying at a very general level how a fundamental analyst might approach the task.

Fundamentals Apply in Analysing Stocks: Doing the Math

Stock-picking is the primary job in managing most portfolios and the toolkit for this chore is called fundamental analysis. As the name implies, it involves getting down to basics. The approach is similar for both stocks and bonds. Fundamental questions deal with the actual or expected profitability of the issuer. Can it earn enough to sustain regular dividend payments or continue the flow of interest payments on bonds? And if the issuer is a company, can it expand its market position so that stockholders can share in the growth? As a general rule, there are two components to this line of inquiry: an analysis of different groups of issuers, and then an assessment of the best performers in the best group.

An analysis of sectors depends partly on broad economic trends. For example, resource stocks usually lead the market when the economy is coming out of recession. But part of this exercise involves looking at whether the resource sector is growing and how it is changing. For example, what is the impact on mining companies of a trend in the auto industry to replace galvanized metal with plastic? Are the mines finding new customers as demand from the old ones declines? If prospects for the sector look promising, the job then is to compare the players in that field. This rating often involves looking for the lowest-cost producers, but investors also need to consider their own time horizons.

A company can be a low-cost producer by cutting back on research and development, a strategy that can give a quick boost to profits in the short term but ultimately put the company at a competitive disadvantage.

Here are some things to watch for.

- Revenue, profit and cash flow: Are these rising with no serious breaks in the pattern?
- Profit margin: Is the company getting a reasonable return on its revenue and invested capital?
- Interest, asset and dividend coverage: Is the earnings flow strong enough to ensure that interest and dividends can be paid with no strain and is the asset base big enough in relation to the current debt load?
- Debt-to-equity ratio: Is the size of the ownership stake big enough to provide a proper balance against bonds and bank debt? (Acceptable standards for the debt-to-equity ratio will vary from industry to industry.)
- Product innovation: Is the company keeping up with its peers in research or, better still, is it out in front?
- Quality of management: Is there depth on the bench in the key areas of operations, marketing and finance?

Source: *Financial Post,* November 16, 1999.

There are two principal fundamental analysis techniques employed by proponents of this approach:

- Common-size statements
- Ratios (and percentages).

It is important to remember, however, that these are merely techniques. They facilitate the contextualization of firm-specific data and the comparison of the financial performance or position represented by that mathematical representation. They enable the informed user to interpret the firm's performance or position but only when placed in the context of, say, other firms, previous performance, budgets, or industry averages.

For instance, consider the following information extracted from the income statement of X plc:

Revenue: £11 million

Of itself this discloses very little information. It is impossible, for example, to determine whether or not this represents an increase or decrease over the previous year's performance. If it is discovered that Revenue for the previous year was £10 million, then the user can begin to contextualize the information and to appreciate that Revenue this year represented a 10% increase on the previous year. In other words, as financial information is made relative to other information its significance gradually emerges.

It can be argued, therefore, that financial data and their various representations, for example ratios, only acquire their real significance when placed in an appropriate context. This "appropriate context" will depend on the purposes for which the information is being analysed, but can range from industry averages to previous year's results, to market expectations.

Furthermore, the significance ascribed to financial data may vary depending on the context in which it is placed. For example, the superficially "good" performance of X plc in improving its Revenue by 10% is placed in a different light if it transpires that its nearest competitor managed to increase Revenue by 60%. One of the attributes of sound financial analysis, therefore, is placing the information being analysed into appropriate contexts.

The ascription of value judgments such as "good", "poor", etc., to financial measures raises other issues. While ratios and other techniques reduce financial information to standard formats that facilitate comparison, individuals with their own sets of values, expectations and outlook carry out this comparison. In other words, their interpretation is not conducted in a value-free manner. What is "acceptable" to one will be "unacceptable" to another. It is important for each user of financial information to be aware, therefore, of his or her perspectives, prejudices and paradigms. This is not necessarily with a view to eradicating them, but with the intention of informing the interpretative process and enabling the user to appreciate that interpretations are neither value-free nor infallible.

Common-Size Statements

One problem when attempting to assess a firm's performance over time is that firm size is in a constant state of flux. This makes inter-period comparison very difficult. Similar difficulties confront users attempting to compare performance between firms.

Common-size statements, by means of which financial data for a number of accounting periods, or for different firms, can be expressed as a percentage or ratio of a relevant base figure, remove some of these difficulties.

The following example illustrates the use of four successive common-size income statements in which sales are taken as the base figure (100%) and all other amounts for the same year are expressed as a percentage of this base (Table 7.1).

Table 7.1. The use of four successive common-size income statements in which sales are taken as the base figure (100%) and all other amounts for the same year are expressed as a percentage of this base

£(000s)					Common size percentage			
1	2	3	4	Years	1	2	3	4
500	600	700	800	Sales	100	100	100	100
125	180	210	240	Cost of sales	25	30	30	30
100	90	112	136	Selling expenses	20	15	16	17
50	66	84	104	Admin. expenses	10	11	12	13
225	264	294	320	Operating profit	45	44	42	40
10	12	14	40	Interest	2	2	2	5
215	252	280	280	Profit before tax	43	42	40	35
75	96	98	96	Corporation tax	15	16	14	12
140	156	182	184	Profit after tax	28	26	26	23
40	48	56	80	Dividends	8	8	8	10
100	108	126	104	Retained profits	20	18	18	13

As Table 7.1 illustrates, there are several advantages to this approach:

- It makes it possible to relate each item to a common base, in this case Revenue for the year.
- Relative changes over time can be easily identified. For instance, while the absolute figures show that Operating profit is increasing, as a percentage of Revenue it has decreased.
- It provides users with a mechanism by which the financial and economic trends and characteristics of individual firms and whole industries may be discerned.
- It is easily graphed, thus increasing its usefulness in determining trends.

While this example demonstrates how the common-size technique can be employed in relation to one firm over a period of time, the common-size statement facilitates various other comparative approaches:

- **Cross-sectional**: the scaling effect of common size statements means that firms of different size can be reduced to a common comparative base. This allows comparison of firms of different size within the same industry or sector. One of the problems with this, however, is that this very process may disguise the fact that size difference, and the economies of scale that result, may actually be the explanatory variable.
- **Segmental**: some differences between firms may derive from the fact that, while operating in the same industry, different segments may predominate within different firms. This can often be resolved by reference to the segmental analysis that will be provided in the Annual Report.

- **Time-based**: perhaps their greatest usefulness is as a means of comparing firm performance over a number of years. Thus, as in the example above, common-size statements can be prepared for a period of, say, 4 years, and the firm's performance can be observed over that period in either a firm or industry context. Graphs constructed using such data from common-size statements are a particularly useful way of highlighting such trends.

Used with caution, common-size statements can prove very useful in facilitating the analysis and interpretation of financial performance and position.

Ratios

The most important fundamental analysis technique is "ratio analysis". Ratios (or percentages) allow the reduction of financial data to a manner that facilitates comparison, and ultimately the interpretation of the significance of that financial data. Thus, they enable comparison between firms of different size and also over extended time periods.

Although there are many different ratios, often with variations in the way in which they are framed, traditionally ratio analysis is considered under five categories, reflecting five different aspects of the risk/return relationship. These areas relate to:

1. **Activity**: the efficiency with which management manage the firm's assets (see Chapter 8).
2. **Liquidity**: the ability of a firm to meet its short-term cash obligations (see Chapter 8).
3. **Financing**: the long-term financing structure (see Chapter 9).
4. **Profitability**: profits relative to revenue and investment (see Chapter 10).
5. **Investment**: returns enjoyed by investors, particularly equity investors (see Chapter 10).

Examples of ratios under each category are shown in Table 7.2.

Qualities of Ratios

The obvious attraction of ratios is that they reduce complex financial data to a form that allows for the easier understanding of that data. Thus, loss of detail is offset by simplicity. However, the ease with which ratios have traditionally been assumed to facilitate comparison and analysis needs to be considered in the light of some of the fundamental conceptual problems inherent in their use:

- **Accounting numbers and policies**: this text has already highlighted some of the weaknesses inherent in accounting practice, for example the often subjective nature of many accounting policy choices. Reducing the accounting data to another

Table 7.2. Examples of ratios

Category	Quantifies	Examples
Activity	Efficiency	Inventory receivables/payables days
		Asset turnover
Liquidity	Ability to satisfy debts	Current ratio
		Quick ratio
Financing	Financial structure	Gearing
		Debt/equity ratio
Profitability	Operating performance	Return on capital employed
		Gross profit rate
		Net profit rate
Investment	Return to owners	Earnings per share
		Price/earnings ratio
		Dividend yield
		Dividend cover

form of expression does not eliminate these problems, in fact it perpetuates them.

- **Economies of scale**: one of the primary functions of ratio analysis is the removal of size as a factor in inter-firm comparison. However, this can obscure the fact that size may itself be an explanatory variable, in other words that size, by virtue, for example, of economies of scale, may actually explain some of the differences being investigated.

- **Industry benchmarks and norms**: the proper use of ratios requires their comparison with industry norms and other measures. However, for a variety of reasons there may be no benchmark against which firm-specific measures may be reasonably compared.

- **Timing factors**: the imposition of arbitrary accounting periods can often have a somewhat distorting effect on measures of financial performance and position. For example, the closing inventory figures of a large retail entity that adopts a financial year-end date of January 31 – since this is a time of low inventory – holding point in the wake of New Year sales – will not accurately reflect the firm's normal inventory-holding activity.

- **Creative accounting**: creative accounting practices can also distort ratios since they manipulate the underlying accounting numbers. Some of the more prevalent forms of creative accounting are discussed in some detail in Chapter 13.

- **Statistical issues**: by their very nature ratios raise a number of computational issues which must be considered:

  - **Negative numbers**: the incidence of such numbers can be problematical and this will be compounded where both numerator and denominator are negative.
  - **Small numbers**: the potential for distortion where small numbers are involved, particularly when dividing by a small number, are considerable.

- **Distributional characteristics**: the use of comparative bases and industry averages implies certain assumptions about the probability distributions of the population. These may not always be sustainable.
- **Relationship between numerator and denominator**: for ease of comparison it is usually assumed that the relationship between numerator and denominator is linear. However, this may not always be the case, for example where economies or diseconomies of scale exist.

Fundamental Analysis and the Use of Ratios

In spite of these difficulties, ratio analysis remains one of the most common techniques used by financial analysts and others. It is important to remember, however, that it is but one step in the process. Far more important than the calculation of ratios is their incorporation into the decision-making process.

This can best be illustrated by understanding the reduction of financial information to summary statistical form as but one element in a five-step process:

1. **Observation**: this involves being aware of the financial data to be interpreted. For example, it might simply mean identifying that the Annual Report forms the principal source of information available.

2. **Calculation**: this involves the reduction of the financial information to a common base such as ratios or percentages.

3. **Analysis**: this involves placing the figures calculated at step 2 into some form of context, such as previous year figures, budgeted expectations or industry averages. At a very basic level this allows a simplistic evaluation of performance. For example, it may be possible after comparing current year ratios with previous year ratios to say there has been an "improvement" or "disimprovement" in performance.

4. **Interpretation**: this involves placing the results in a context that will highlight their real significance as far as the company is concerned. For example, ratios calculated at step 2 may relate to profitability. Analysis at step 3 may disclose that profitability has decreased when compared to previous year results. Stage 4 requires that the significance of this development be explored. It may, for example, lead to questions about the strategic plans of the company or its long-term viability.

5. **Decision-making**: this is the final step in the process and represents the ultimate goal of the financial information analysis process.

In practice:

The application of fundamental analysis to a company, in this case Cisco Systems, is illustrated in the following extract, which demonstrates how ratios enable comparison with competitors, in the process facilitating effective decision-making:

Fundamental Analysis

... A fundamentalist will compare the earnings growth rate as well as sales growth rates. Negative numbers are obviously viewed negatively. However, even positive numbers are scrutinized as a positive correlation between the earnings growth and sales growth is desirable. Earning increases on flat sales are not as impressive as earnings increases on increased sales.

Debt is another parameter fundamentalists will examine. If a company is growing, but increasing its debt, the fundamentalist will be leery. The business may by putting all of its profits into an interest payment, rather than building up book value. Companies that have no debt and have increasing sales and earnings are most attractive.

Another parameter is the capitalization of the company. Capitalization is merely the price per share of the stock multiplied by the number of shares outstanding (in issue). A fundamentalist would be impressed by large capitalization as it takes more earnings and profits to make the percentages positive. A company with large capitalization with sales and earnings increasing together and no debt would be a dream stock for the fundamentalist, particularly if it happened to be selling below book value. Although such qualities would be rare, the fundamentalist sifts carefully through the financial pages.

A fundamental analysis of a security such as Cisco Systems, which was featured in the July Supplemental issue of the Women's Street Journal, might read like the following: Cisco Systems, ticker symbol CSCO, trades on the Nasdaq with 4194.4 million shares outstanding with a $251,664 million capitalization. CSCO boasts 0% debt. Sales in the last four quarters have increased an average of 27% with sales increasing at 42%. Although the lag in earnings increases is a tad negative, the 5-year earnings growth rate is a healthy 43% and the company has a particularly large market capitalization for such a high growth rate.

The earnings performance of Cisco Systems outperforms its major competitors: MMC Network, Emulex Corp, Brocade Communication Systems Inc. and Performance Technologies, by a comfortable margin...

Source: Women's Street Journal. http://www.womensstreetjournal.com/members/ fundamental.htm.

Technical Analysis

Technical analysis is based on the idea that share price can be determined by identifying trading patterns which tend to repeat in cycles. Unlike fundamental analysis, therefore, it does not seek to analyse macro-economic, industrial and firm-specific fundamentals. Instead, it focuses on patterns and trends disclosed by historic share price movements.

Being a market-centred measure, this approach has much in common with the EMH perspective outlined in Chapter 3, particularly in ascribing to the market the ability to best capture "value". It owes its origins to the work of Charles Henry Dow, the originator, with Edward Jones, of the Dow Jones Industrial Average Index. Dow first articulated his theories in the *Wall Street Journal* in the 1890s. His ideas stemmed form his observations of the closing prices of shares and the conclusion that it was possible to construct a representative stock average that would act as a barometer for the market as a whole.

Technical analysis is sometimes called "charting" for the simple reason that most of the information content of this technique is reduced to the form of charts. Thus, there will be charts for markets, exchanges, commodities, industries and individual company stocks. Figure 7.1, with comments added by the analyst, gives an example of the conclusions that a technical analyst might draw from such a presentation, in this case with regard to the Nasdaq index as a whole.

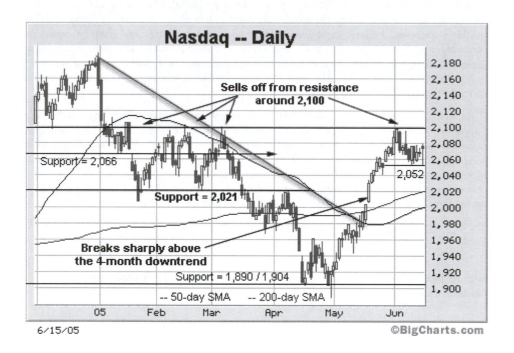

6/15/05   ©BigCharts.com

Figure 7.1   Technical analysis. Source: BigCharts.com

In practice:

The following two extracts outline in more detail how the technical analysis approach works:

Know your J. Lo if you want to top the charts, by Jim Stanton

If you think a candlestick is just an ornament, MACD is shorthand for a popular burger chain, and head and shoulders is a shampoo, then perhaps you're not as savvy a stock market player as you

could be. There's no doubt that as increasing numbers of people have exposed their hard-earned cash to the vagaries of equities in recent years, lessons – often painful and costly – have been learned.

To any investor or share trader, one of the most important things is timing: the holy grail being to buy at the bottom and sell at the top. We've all read headlines such as "Crash wipes £50 billion off stock market." But while the headline reflects a fall in value of the shares, it doesn't tell the whole story. That's because for every person losing money on the markets, there's someone making it – and that someone is possibly using what professional equity traders call "technical analysis".

The idea uses historical information on price patterns and volume, presented in chart form, to help predict the future activity of a share, index or commodity, such as oil. Technical analysis is a jargon-lover's dream. Advocates spend hours poring over charts trying to find pennants, flags, head and shoulders, wide-ranging days, breakouts and continuation patterns – and the J.Lo. They'll use "indicators" such as MACD to get a handle on moving price averages and other pointers such as trendlines or "relative strength" to determine entry or exit strategies...

... Jordan Kotick, global head of technical analysis at Barclays Capital and president of industry group, the Market Technicians Association (MTA), agrees that interest in technical analysis has mushroomed in recent years. "Hedge funds are competing against each other... they're very aggressive and to do that, you need to use the charts." The advent of widespread use of the internet has given amateur investors access to the type of trading data that was previously only affordable by the professionals. And with the FTSE-100 at three-year highs and a flood of expected flotations, including PartyGaming, Hovis-maker RHM and Land of Leather, interest is again building in the stock market. Mr Kotick believes that following the dotcom collapse "people realized that timing really does make a difference."

... The premise with share prices suggests that prices are determined by the expectations of the people already in the market and those contemplating getting into it – essentially the struggle for supremacy between buyer and seller. The price a share stands at, therefore, reflects the hopes, knowledge, fears and expectations of the people who either own or are thinking of owning the share. That theory was encapsulated by Garfield Drew, a well regarded chart technician who made his name in the 1940s. He said: "Stocks never sell for what they're worth but for what people think they are worth." One wonders what he'd have to say about the dotcom boom and its crazy share valuations.

Technical Analysis is loaded with terms and jargon. Here are a few of them and their meanings:

- J.Lo – a slang term referring to a rounding bottom in a stock's price pattern, which can indicate a positive market reversal.
- Candlestick – a price chart that shows the high, low, open, and close for a stock each day.
- Head and shoulders – a chart pattern which rises to a peak then falls before rising again above the first peak then declining again. After the second fall it rises again, but not as high as the second peak. The first and third peaks are shoulders, and the second peak forms the head.

- *Relative Strength Index – a comparator of the days when a share finishes up in price against when it finishes lower.*
- *Moving Average – a line which plots the price of a share or commodity over a specific period of time.*
- *MACD – an indicator showing the relationship between two moving averages of prices which shows whether a stock is on an upward or downward trend.*
- *Bollinger Band – a band plotting two standard deviations away from a simple moving average.*

Source: Evening News, July 6, 2005.

Picking a winner

Still another way of evaluating stocks is technical analysis, which largely ignores the fundamental details of a company's sales and profits. Instead, the technical analyst may chart past trends in the movement of the firm's stock price and in trading volumes to time the next significant move up or down in the shares. From these charts, the analyst expects to be able to spot heavy demand, indicating an upward trend in the stock, or sudden supply, suggesting a downward trend.

Here is an example of how technical analysis works. It is assumed that the news of a favourable development related to a firm tends to spread from group to group in waves. First one group of people will buy the stock, and its price will go up on heavy volume. Then there will be a quiet period and the stock will sell off. After a while, a new group of people will hear the news and buy the stock, and again it will go up on heavy volume.

When technical analysts spot this pattern on a chart, they are alerted to the buying, and probably will favour the stock.

Source: National Post, December 2, 2002.

Technical analysis is, therefore, a widely used technique. It has a solid track record and is heavily influenced by market based theory and research. In the hands of experienced analysts it produces potent and profitable insights into share movements and patterns.

Fundamental or Technical Analysis?

The Fundamental and Technical Analysis approaches not only focus on different information sources, but approach "information" *per se* from essentially different perspectives. Ostensibly, therefore, they would appear to be at odds. Increasingly, however, the complementary nature of these two techniques is being appreciated. Indeed, experienced traders are incorporating both approaches into their strategies for identifying which securities to trade and when to do so. As the following "In practice" extract illustrates, the strengths of Fundamental Analysis are best employed in identifying which shares to buy or sell, while Technical Analysis is often critical in identifying when to do so:

In practice:

Charting course in market action

The saying that a picture is worth a thousand words could describe what the technical analysts believe, reports James Dunn. Technical analysis (or charting) is the study of share price and volume action through the use of charts (graphs), for the purpose of predicting future market action. The theory behind charting is that a share price chart reveals not only the historical record of movement, but patterns of behaviour it might suggest for the future. What technical analysts are looking for are patterns of buying or selling pressure on the chart: once they have identified the pattern, they believe they know where the share price is headed – that the chart gives them, in effect, clear signals of when to buy and sell.

The basic concepts of technical analysis are:

- *__The trendline__: which is the direction of the price.*
- *__Support levels__: the troughs in a share price graph. These are areas where a fall in a share price has tended to stabilize and recover, because buying pressure has become stronger than selling pressure. Multiple support levels are called "bottoms" and may indicate that a rebound in the stock is imminent.*
- *__Resistance levels__: the peaks in the graph. These are areas where a price rise has tended to falter and fall away, because more investors felt the price would fall. Multiple resistance levels are called "tops" and may indicate the stock price is about to fall.*
- *__The moving average (MA)__: a calculation that smoothes out price action to show the underlying trend. The MA is drawn on the same chart as the price, and curves under and over the price line. Traders use the MA as a signal: when the price closes above the MA, it's a "buy" signal; when the price moves below the MA, it's a "sell".*

As an approach to share market investment, technical analysis differs greatly from fundamental analysis, which is the study of numerical and statistical data of companies – including revenue, profit, costs, dividends, assets and liabilities – derived from the annual and interim (half-year) company reports. Both approaches have their adherents; some investors like to use both. It's common to hear the saying "fundamental analysis tells you what to buy; technical analysis tells you when to buy it".

David Rogers, technical analyst at broking firm Tolhurst Noall, is such an advocate of using the two approaches: "Not everything is clear using technical analysis, and technical analysis can only predict a portion of the movements in the market. Valuations are also important to stocks: if a stock is too far away from its valuation, it is generally not going to be sustainable." Rogers says he uses fundamental analysis as an aid to "go looking for a technical story on a stock", but at the same time, technical analysis may tell him when to buy. . .

Charles Browne, president of the Australian Technical Analysts Association, says the technical/fundamental "debate" depends on an investor's time frame. "Fundamental analysis is not much use to a short-term trader, who is really looking for inflection (turning) points, and price and volume action will give him those," Browne says. But he argues that if a longer-term investor sees a broker recommending a certain stock, it is a simple matter to look at the chart and if it is neutral to rising, "you've got a second opinion". Browne stresses that technical analysis will not "do the work" for an investor. "Unfortunately that's the myth," Browne says.

Source: The Australian, June 28, 2005

To some extent, the tendency is for both techniques to be used in this complementary fashion, with the unique perspectives provided by each being employed. From an information perspective, however, it is obvious that there are significant differences in emphasis. While technical analysis will be concerned with patterns of trading, Fundamental Analysis will draw on a variety of sources ranging from economic, political and social data to financial accounting information.

Because this text is concerned with dealing with these larger contextual issues, (as well as *what* shares to buy and sell, as distinct from *when* to do so) and also because Technical Analysis can be subjected to some of the same criticisms as EMH, Fundamental Analysis is favoured throughout this text.

In practice:

Many well-known investors, for instance, Warren Buffet and Peter Lynch, employ Fundamental Analysis. The following websites provide useful information on their strategies and approaches:

www.valueline.com

www.advfn.com

Summary

Fundamental analysis and technical analysis describe two different approaches to information. While technical analysis focuses on patterns in market-based data such as historic movements in share price, fundamental analysis turns its attention to fundamentals impacting on a company such as financial performance.

To this end fundamental analysis has identified various techniques and methods which assist in this process. The most potent of these is ratio analysis. Properly understood, ratio analysis forms one part of a five-step process that sees informed decision-making as its goal.

The five elements of this process are:

1. Observation
2. Calculation
3. Analysis
4. Interpretation
5. Decision-making.

Techniques such as ratio analysis must be applied with caution and the results interpreted in an appropriate context. Indeed, on occasion, their contribution to the decision-making process may be quite limited, providing nothing more than an initial screening mechanism that identifies factors to be analysed by other means.

Properly used, however, they have proven to be potent and insightful means of extracting meaningful information from financial statements. Reducing often-complex financial data to summary statistical form, they provide a means of contextualizing firm or industry-specific information and of identifying trends. The comparative exercise that they enable is often the key to any considered evaluation of an entity.

Review Questions

Question 1
Identify the principal differences between fundamental analysis and technical analysis.

Question 2
Explain the use of common-size statements as a means of identifying trends within a company and of facilitating inter-firm comparison.

Question 3
"It can be argued that financial data and their various representations, for example ratios, only acquire their real significance when placed in an appropriate context". Explain what is meant by this statement.

Question 4
Explain what each of the following terms mean and list examples of ratios under each:
- Activity
- Liquidity
- Financing
- Profitability
- Investment

Question 5
List some of the qualities of ratios and identify some features of ratios that require that they be treated with caution.

Question 6
List the five-stages involved in a healthy decision-making process based on accounting data. Identify the role of fundamental analysis in this process.

Question 7
Identify at least three features of technical analysis that make it a unique approach to data analysis.

Question 8
What were the main features of the theories of Charles Henry Dow that have so strongly influenced modern technical analysis?

Question 9
Explain why using both Fundamental Analysis and Technical Analysis could yield benefits for investors.

Case Studies

Case 1

The following article explores how fundamental analysis has been employed by one particular exponent "to make abnormal returns". In the light of the information gathered from this chapter and also from Chapter 3 (which considered the theoretical aspects of this possibility) analyse and discuss the conclusions reached by the researchers, that "Careful analysis of published financial statements can indeed help an analyst or investor identify mispriced stocks – even in large companies".

Financial Statement Analysis Not Futile

US Retired Professor Abraham Briloff's Independent Studies Underline the Fact, by The Hooi Ling

Given the large number of companies, coupled with the time pressure on the analysts to come out with reports quickly, do presentations, and talk to clients, it means that most analysts have little time to pore over all the information disclosed by the companies, especially that provided in the numerous footnotes to the financial statements in the companies' annual reports. On top of that, a certain expertise is needed to interpret the numbers disclosed by companies. In an ideal world, the user of financial statements could only focus on the bottom lines of financial reporting, i.e. net income and stockholders' equity. But the financial reporting system is not perfect. Economic events and accounting entries do not correspond precisely – they diverge across the dimensions of timing, recognition and measurement. Financial analysis is further complicated by variations in accounting treatment among companies.

There are rules and conventions on how companies should prepare their financial statements, so as to make it easier for users to compare the financial numbers across companies or industries. But because each company, each business and each industry are different, managers are given enough flexibility – within the confines of the rules – to make certain assumptions and appropriate judgments with the aim of portraying the underlying economic reality of their respective companies. The accounting discretion granted to managers is potentially valuable, because it allows them to reflect inside information in reported financial statements. However, since investors view profits as a measure of managers' performance, some managers may find it an incentive to use their accounting discretion to 'manage' reported profits by making aggressive assumptions.

Against this backdrop, it would not be surprising if someone who knows how to read financial statements and realize the implications of the various accounting practices were able to spot a mispriced stock ahead of the market and profit from it. But for many of the retail investors who may not be too familiar with what to look out for in a financial statement, they will have to depend on the analysis of an independent 'analyst' – someone who is not beholden to the companies to write only good reports.

But in the US, there is one person who is as close to being independent as anyone can claim to be when it comes to financial analysis. Abraham Briloff, a retired professor of accounting and author of several books, is well-known for more than four decades of insightful analysis and criticism of accounting practices of various companies. His articles, published in Barron's, are based almost exclusively on publicly available information, for example, information found in annual reports.

Focus on Statements

Briloff focuses primarily on financial statements and does not usually address a company's products, the economy, interest rates, or other variables that many analysts frequently incorporate. In a study published last year, two US university professors, Desai and Jain, wanted to find out the long-term performance of companies highlighted by Briloff and to ascertain if, indeed, one can make abnormal returns purely by doing financial statement analysis.

Prior studies have shown that companies criticized by Prof Briloff experienced significant abnormal return of -8.6 per cent on average on the first day after the article came out, with no reversal of that trend for the subsequent 30 days. Profs Desai and Jain extended the study of the stocks' performance to three years after the articles were published. Their motivations for doing that were two-fold. Firstly, in the wake of the market's negative reaction following Prof Briloff's analysis, several companies responded that his criticism was without merit, that the market's initial negative reaction was excessive, and that a reversal would occur in the long run.

One company, Waste Management, and its auditors Arthur Andersen vigorously defended their accounting practices and audit, saying that the company had properly applied the accounting rules and that 'sophisticated investors will have understood the academic and inconsequential nature of the issues raised' by Prof Briloff. The authors wanted to examine the validity of such claims.

Secondly, only the long run allows a full understanding of the magnitude, speed and permanence of the market's adjustments to information contained in Prof Briloff's financial statement analyses. Between 1968 and 1998, Briloff criticized 48 companies in 31 articles. Profs Desai and Jain found that, on average, these companies had outperformed companies with similar characteristics by some 45 percentage points (pps) in the 25 to 13 months before his writing the articles. And the cumulative outperformance was 28 pps 12 to two months before the publication of the articles. Profs Desai and Jain examined the accounting ratios of the companies during that period and found no clear fundamental reasons for the outperformance. They conjectured that the lack of fundamental reasons accompanied by the stock price run-up might have triggered Briloff to take a close look at these companies.

So how did these companies perform one, two and three years after Prof Briloff's scathing criticisms of their accounting practices? Well, on average, they lagged by a significant 12 pps, 17 pps and 23 pps compared with the average performance of control portfolios with similar characteristics. 'Overall, the results show that the valuation effect of Briloff's articles is not restricted to the time period immediately surrounding the day of the publication,' Profs Desai and Jain wrote. 'The market continues to adjust to the information at least for one year and possibly two years after publication of the articles.'

But this is not to suggest that Prof Briloff was the cause of this downward effect on the stock prices. 'His articles seem to have triggered a re-evaluation by the market, and his analysis apparently helped move prices towards the fundamentals. If Briloff had not written, someone or something else would in time have brought about a revaluation of these stocks. Without Briloff, however, it would have apparently taken longer for the information to be impounded in the prices,' they said. Meanwhile, in terms of operating performance, these companies' return on assets also trailed their industry peers one, two and three years after Prof Briloff's articles.

Profs Desai and Jain also compared the performance of stocks criticized by Briloff with those given a 'sell' recommendation by analysts. On average, stocks which analysts advised their clients to sell, underperformed their peers by between 5 and 8 after one year. So the impact of Prof Briloff's criticism on stock prices is much stronger than that of a typical 'sell' recommendation. It is even more impressive that the companies Prof Briloff criticized are mostly big companies. And while the stocks picked on by Prof Briloff had an average neutral rating from analysts before, the consensus rating turned slightly bearish after his articles were out. Profs Desai and Jain's results indicate that Briloff was better able to foresee the coming performance decline than the market, on average.

Varying Impact

Although his articles covered topics usually discussed in most accounting books, the authors found Prof Briloff has a particular interest in finding out if the company is making an effort to overstate its financial results through aggressive accounting. Profs Desai and Jain noted that the varying degrees of impact of Briloff's articles and those of analysts' recommendations may stem from three differences. First, Prof Briloff is staunchly independent. So the chance of leakage prior to publication is small. Second, he is an excellent analyst. Third, he only publishes an article when he is highly confident of his analyses. The study thus shed light on the importance of accounting and financial analysis in valuation.

'Careful analysis of published financial statements can indeed help an analyst or investor identify mispriced stocks – even in large companies,' Profs Desai and Jain concluded.

The writer is a CFA charterholder.

Source: *The Business Times*, May 14, 2005.

Case 2

The following article adopts an imaginative, storytelling approach to a putative share-trading scenario. In the process, it provides some interesting comparisons and insights. Identify and discuss the key issues raised and explain how to deal with the questions raised in relation to Symantec's shares.

Analyse, My Dear Watson, by Siva Nara and Priya Raghavan Racy

"Grandpa, how is your search for a vacation home in Florida going on?" seven-month-old Crick asked of his scientist-grandfather, Dr Watson. Dr Watson proudly looked at the super-baby he had produced through years of DNA mutations. He said, "I picked a great one after doing a lot of research, carefully considered the reasons, convinced myself that it is a great buy; like buying a stock based on fundamental analysis." The baby wiped his drool and volleyed back, "I would just buy it because many people who bought this must have done all the research; I would also check with the Florida real estate index and find that the prices are going up. Thus, you can invest in a property expecting it to go up, like buying stocks using technical analysis." Dr Watson laughed, "I disagree. Before I altered your genes and spliced them in the lab, I did years of study on your dad and mom. Checking their health, their DNA structure and so on. Why did I do it? To ensure that you live a long and healthy life"

Similarly, if you want to invest in a company, the first step is to analyse if the company is producing consistent earnings and if it is free from debt, to avoid debacles such as Enrons and WorldComs. I am a 'fundamentalist', I check for the financial stability of a company before investing. I would then check if the price is right, because a fundamentalist would never invest in a company that is overpriced. "I believe in investing in a company that I am likely to hold for the long term. Being a patient and prudent investor, I would have picked up some of the best companies such as American Express, Pfizer, Bed Bath and Beyond and CDW Corporation. As a fundamentalist I don't believe in buying and selling shares on the fly. I am willing to wait till the stock goes up."

"I would do the reverse. Not wait for a long time," said baby Crick. "Even in procreation, I simply followed the gene-altering pattern adopted by research scientists like you and created a new baby. That is successful too, though she is a little annoying. "I am a technical analyst, I don't look at the financial health of a company. Instead I believe that history repeats itself."

Ron, Crick's father, was amused. "So which approach would work the best?" Baby Crick spoke at length: "Grandpa, being a fundamentalist would not have invested in, say, Google. He would be sceptical about the company as the earnings are purely based on advertisement and the company has no other revenue stream. However, I, being a technical analyst, would have learnt that if so many investors are investing in the company, there should be a reason behind it. I would, therefore, jump in when the share price goes up. Imagine, what an opportunity a fundamentalist would have missed! "During September 2004, when Google was rising from a mere $85, inching slowly towards $100 and rising to $150, a technical analyst would be simply learning that when so many investors are buying, there should be a reason. Thus, I would have invested in Google and now the price of

Google has gone beyond $300. A technical analyst would have made more than 100% by investing in Google."

Dr Watson said, "My dear grandson! We all know that to reproduce, a cell must copy and transmit its genetic information (DNA) to all of its progeny. To do so, DNA replicates. But sometimes, copying errors happen because of unpredictable environmental factors, such as sunlight or cigarette smoke. Similarly, when you consider technical analysis, even though patterns repeat, a company might fall short, because of, say, poor financial health, which you do not measure while doing technical analysis. For example, Jamdat Mobile, the maker of cell phone games, fell from $29 to $22 in just one day and that is a loss of 25 per cent. As a fundamentalist, I wouldn't have invested in this company at $29, as I avoid investing in higher price."

Grabbing a spoon of cereal, Crick said, "There might be DNA mutations or copying errors, but aren't scientists trying to work on minimising the DNA copying errors. The same way, a technical analyst can buy stocks at the right price following the patterns and studying the charts. Let me prove this. What would you do when a financially healthy company like Symantec's (the maker of Norton anti-virus) stock price falls from $24 to $23 to $22.50, as it happened last week?" "Simple," Dr Watson replied: "I would have bought as and when it kept dropping, because I believe that if the price of a good stock falls down, then it is a great buy." "Aha," the baby let out an angelic laughter. "No doubt it is a great buy. But think of it this way. Using technical analysis and following the history of patterns of Symantec Corp, and studying their charts, I would have learnt that it would fall down to $21.50 and not below. Thus, a technical analyst, would wait till the prices of shares drops to $21.50 and then buy the shares."

Ron laughed, "Can't believe you are applying genetic research theories to stock picking." Dr Watson said, "The biggest advantage for me, a fundamental analyst, is that I invest only in sound companies and thus, over the long term I make very good profit. I do admit that learning to analyse the fundamentals of a company requires the effort to master the different methodologies involved in evaluating the fair value of the company. I buy when the prices of the shares go below the fair value." "True," said Crick, "I must admit that even though technical analysis is simple, one has to be careful as misinterpretation may lead to wrong judgment." Ron said: "Who makes more money in the stock market? A fundamentalist or a technical analyst?" Baby Crick answered, "I agree that a fundamental analyst makes a good return over a longer time. Technical analysts invest only when they know that the prices are going to go up, and thus lose the advantage of initial growth. By combining fundamental and technical analyses, an investor can profit well and also make much more returns than anyone." Dr Watson turned to his son and said: "Ron, can you find out why Microsoft shares have never gone up beyond $30 for almost the past two years and never below $24?" Ron cuddled his baby and said, "Sure. I will use both fundamental and technical analyses; or to put in your language, adopt the 'double helix' solution!"

Source: *Business Line*, August 21, 2005.

Case 3

Referring to the Tesco plc Annual Report 2005, and to recent share price data for the company, explain how a technical analyst and a fundamental analyst might each approach the task of determining whether or not to invest in the company's shares.

ACTIVITY AND LIQUIDITY [8]

When you have completed this chapter you will understand:

- That activity (efficiency) and liquidity are related concepts.
- The importance of working capital management.
- How to calculate ratios that assist in determining the activity and liquidity levels of a business.
- The difficulties posed by inventory and its valuation.
- That cash is the lifeblood of a business and must be managed closely.

Timber! The Felling of Cedar

The financial collapse of software group Cedar in the autumn of 2001 was spectacular by any standards. Barely 12 months earlier, the company was worth almost £1bn and appeared to be on the verge of cracking the US market after acquiring American IT consultancy Enterprise Solutions Group. Then, in January 2002, after a series of profit warnings, it was bought for just £4.2m by venture capital firm Alchemy after warning investors that, in the absence of a takeover, bankruptcy seemed inevitable.

The short-term causes of Cedar's collapse centred on poor control over sales invoicing and trade debtors, coupled with a cavalier approach to revenue recognition. The company's auditors, KPMG, who were brought in to replace Arthur Andersen, discovered that in the financial year to 31 March 2002 there was a total breakdown of financial controls at the company. Little information was available, for example, on crucial matters such as sales invoicing and payroll expenses.

Some of these problems would have been impossible to spot from outside the company. But there had long been signs that trouble was brewing at Cedar. One worry was the company's long – and lengthening – sales cycle. In 2000, average debtor (receivables') days – the length of time it takes a company to collect payment for its sales – already stood at an alarming 130 days. This lurched even higher to 140 days in 2001, thanks to the ESG takeover. As a general rule, anything more than 100 debtor days is an indication that a company is providing long-term credit and that revenue recognition could be an issue.

The level of accrued income on Cedar's balance sheet was also consistently troubling. This is income a company expects to receive – and which has been put through the profit and loss account – but which the company has no right yet to invoice. At its March 2000 year-end, Cedar's accrued income stood at a staggering £18.5m. That amounted to 51 per cent of total sales. This alarming performance was reflected in the company's Achilles heel: a consistent failure to turn operating profits into cash.

In any one year, it is not particularly worrying if a company's operating cash flows and operating profits diverge dramatically. But there must be question marks over a company that reported operating profits totalling £10.94m during the three years from 1998–2000, while generating a cash outflow of £2.5m over the same period. A prolonged mismatch between profits and cash generation is usually a harbinger of trouble...

Source: *Investors Chronicle*, November 14, 2003.

Introduction

"Cash is King!" In recent years, particularly as suspicion of accounting numbers has grown, and as trading difficulties have afflicted many firms, this has become the cry of businesses and investors. Increasingly, as outlined in Chapter 6 when discussing cash flow statements, various stakeholders have sought a clearer explanation of the cash-life of the business.

As suggested in the opening account, there should, for example, be a traceable relationship between profitability and liquidity (the availability of cash to pay debts): the expectation is that a business will be able to generate sufficient cash from its trading activity to meet debts arising directly from that activity. In other words, the usual business dynamic would see a business generating cash from the sale of goods which could then be used to meet any indebtedness relating to the purchase of those goods. This is not always a linear relationship, however, and it will usually take an understanding of "working capital" and its constituent parts, before appreciating how liquidity and cash in general can be managed.

As the following extract highlights, working capital management, particularly in the manner in which it impacts the cash flow profile, is a vital and often unappreciated aspect of business life.

Cash Management: High Cost of Idle Capital, by Jenny Luesby

If working capital were to be renamed "waiting capital", perhaps a revolution of comprehension and corrective action might follow. Instead, companies large and small raise valuable finance only to lock it up in boxes in warehouses, unpaid invoices and stockpiled raw materials. The result is a worldwide excess of idle working capital. In the UK, REL Consultancy estimates that companies are holding 28 per cent – €100bn – too much working capital. Across Europe, the same international consultancy puts the cost of such excesses at €65bn in profits foregone...

... For many advisers there is simply no divide between managing cash well and managing well. "Companies need to be thinking about cash in everything they do and in every strategic decision they take," says Shaun O'Callaghan, restructuring partner at KPMG.

Slow moving product lines keep cash locked up for longer than fast sellers. Products made to order rather than held in stock tie up fewer resources. Well-organised supply chains that see raw materials delivered just as they are needed save on storage space, reduce risk and cut working capital.

Companies that think about cash first are organised differently from those that concentrate on sales and profits. They are also far more resilient when activity slows. "When companies are run for profits, stock levels that are fine when sales are steady or growing can quickly gallop out of control in the face of a downturn," says Bob Ward, of PwC.

This is why cash managers need finance directors who see and care where the money is located. Left alone to perfect their cashflow forecasts, treasuries are far removed from the signs of change on the ground. They can only model future cashflow on the past and secondary signals. The finance director must act as bridge between the operations and the cash management, which requires clear sight of both. For all the tools on offer, the rule of cash begins when companies can see where everything is located.

The ultimate test is as simple as this: any company that does not know how long things have been in the warehouse is being poorly managed.

Source: *Financial Times*, February 24, 2003.

In practice:

Proper and efficient management of working capital, i.e., receivables (debtors), payables (creditors) and inventory (stock), will lead to the availability of cash when needed in a profitable business. According to the following report, this could increase average profit levels by as much as 10%. Not surprisingly, companies characterised by poor management in this area will often see much of their cash tied up unnecessarily.

Poor cash management hits profits, by Jonathan Moules

Leading UK companies have £62bn (€100b) of cash unnecessarily tied up in working capital as a result of poor cash management, according to a report by REL Consultancy Group. The survey found that inefficiencies in the cash management policies of the UK's 285 largest companies was costing them as much as £4bn in net profits annually.

The British companies reduced their working capital – a measure of how much cash is tied up in payables, receivables and inventory – by 4 per cent in the last year, a bigger reduction than in all the Euro zone countries except Italy.

By tying up these resources unnecessarily, companies deny themselves opportunities to use their cash more effectively for investments or acquisitions. Improvements in cash collection, shorter customer payment terms and inventory and supply-chain management initiatives would typically raise the net profit of the companies surveyed by as much as 10.1 per cent, according to REL. It also calculated that such action could cut total net debt by 38 per cent and improve the return on capital employed by as much as 12.3 per cent.

REL, which specialises in working capital improvement, estimates that the top 1,000 companies across Europe have €480bn (£328bn) tied up in excess working capital. The largest Italian companies cut their excess working capital by 7 per cent in the last year to €32bn, while their French counterparts achieved a 3 per cent reduction to €98bn. German companies were the least successful in the major European economies, cutting their excess working capital by 2 per cent to €121bn. The UK has historically operated with lower levels of working capital than other European countries.

Source: Financial Times, August 29, 2005.

The remainder of this chapter illustrates the calculation of various ratios. The financial statements in the Tesco 2005 Annual Report in Appendix 1 are based on UK GAAP. However, future Annual Reports will be based on IFRS. Appendix 2 contains the 2005 financial statements restated in their IFRS form. Ratio analysis of both sets of figures is supplied in this and the following two chapters. This means that the text allows comparison between the results under the two systems. In fact, there are almost no material differences.

IFRS will also introduce new terminology. For instance, 'creditors due within one year' will now become 'current liabilities,' 'debtors' will be 'receivables,' 'creditors' will be 'payables,' and 'stock' will be 'inventory.' To avoid confusion, the new IFRS terms are employed throughout.

Activity

In order for a business to function efficiently there must be funds available to pay debts. This requires that working capital (usually, receivables, inventory and payables) be managed properly. Activity (or efficiency) ratios quantify the trading activity of the business in a way that recognizes that there is a direct relationship between that activity and the availability of adequate cash resources on an ongoing basis. For instance, they recognize that credit sales recorded in the income statement are directly related to receivables shown in the balance sheet.

Any examination of liquidity and efficiency, therefore, requires an understanding of the elements of working capital.

Receivables (Debtors)

Receivables are claims to future inflows of cash. The most common such claim is trade receivables, which is the amount of money owing to the business in respect of credit sales. Other claims would include prepayments or amounts still owed to the business in respect of fixed assets sold. Since the claims relate to future inflows the question of valuation arises. However, because the collection period is usually short-term this does not normally pose problems, and discounting is rarely employed.

A more pressing issue is the fact that a debt may be defaulted upon and go unpaid. Consequently, companies are required to make provision for doubtful debts. The figure for receivables should, therefore, be shown net of any such provisions.

Trade Receivables (Debtors)

Trade receivables will usually be the most substantial component of this section.

In attempting to quantify the financial position of the business it will be important that users of financial information be able to reduce the accounting numbers to a form that enables comparison. One approach commonly used in relation to receivables is to produce an "age profile" of amounts owed to the business at a particular moment in time. This simply involves classifying debts into various sub-sections based on the length of time each debt is outstanding, e.g., less than 30 days, 30–60 days and 60 days or more. The business can take then action appropriate to the length of time the debts are unpaid.

This type of classification can be usefully supplemented by ratios. The ratio most commonly employed for receivables is Receivables' Days.

Receivables (or Debtors) Days

This ratio measures the length of time it takes trade receivables to pay. Since receivables are a direct consequence of credit sales a useful way of quantifying them will be as the fraction that receivables at the end of a period represent of the total credit sales for a year. This can then be expressed in terms of days by multiplying the resulting fraction by 365.

The formula is:[1]

$$\frac{\text{Closing Trade Receivables}}{\text{Revenue}} \times 365$$

In practice:

The figure for Tesco based on its accounts for the year ended February 26, 2005 is nil (see note 16 to the accounts) because it does not have any trade receivables as its sales are entirely for cash. Items indicated as 'Other Debtors' or 'Other Receivables' in this note do not include trade-related items.

The IFRS Restatement shows that the same applies to IFRS figures as there are no trade receivables.

Receivables Days is a measure of the length of time being taken by a company's customers to pay their debts. Time such as this, when resources are tied up, represent a cost to a business since it is effectively giving free credit to its customers out of its own resources. Obviously, it must fund this cost itself, for example by undertaking an overdraft. It is in a company's best interests, therefore, to keep Receivables Days period to a minimum.

When interpreting the Receivables Days ratio a number of points need to be borne in mind:

1. It is usually not possible to determine the level of credit sales from the Annual Report, as there is no requirement on firms to distinguish between cash and credit transactions. Ironically, it will be easiest to calculate this ratio for those entities that have either all credit sales, such as large contractors, or those with almost no credit sales such as supermarket chains. However, the bulk of firms operate a mix of cash and credit sales and this means that informed estimates as to the credit sales levels may be required.

2. Revenue must be stated VAT exclusive. Trade receivables, however, will be VAT inclusive since the individual receivables are liable to pay the full VAT inclusive debt. This poses problems in terms of the compatibility of a formula which comprises elements that are based on different valuations.

3. Seasonal factors may need to be taken into account when interpreting the result. For instance, a year-end receivables figure where business is seasonal may not be representative.

---

[1] This formula obviously indicates the Receivables days figure represented by year-end Receivables. The numerator can also be the average level of Receivables during the year ((Opening Receivables + Closing Receivables)/2). The resulting figure gives the average Receivables days over the course of the year in question.

4. Most large businesses will have developed fairly advanced credit control systems using age profiles, normally expressed in terms of less than 30, 60, 90 days, etc., to control and target outstanding debts. This will provide useful additional information in analyzing the Receivables Days figure.

5. Where companies have a small number of receivables there is considerable potential for distortion if even one of these changes its payment habits.

6. Other possible explanations of changes from levels of previous years include:

   - Sales volume may have expanded or contracted materially towards the end of the year.
   - Some receivables should more properly be classified as bad or doubtful debts.
   - The company operates an instalment payment method.
   - The sales mix may have changed to include more or less cash or credit sales.
   - The company operates a factoring arrangement.[2]

In practice:

The following three extracts highlight a widespread 'late payment culture' as well as different challenges faced by businesses that relate directly to their capacity to generate cash from Receivables. Note in particular the reference to 'Overtrading' a common problem in the third extract:

No improvement in plc bill paying

There has been no improvement in the time it takes leading companies to pay their bills for the last four years, according to a new survey. The average time a plc takes to pay its bills is 46 days, says the Federation of Small Businesses (FSB) in its latest private sector payment performance league tables.

Retailer Next has the best payment record of FTSE 100 companies, with an average payment period of two days. BAA (11 days) and BT Group (18 days) are also strong performers. Enterprise Inns has improved from 60 days in 2002 to 29 days in 2003/4, while Reuters has improved from 32 days to 18 days over the same period. Cable and Wireless, at 70 days, is among the poorest performers.

But most worryingly, says the FSB, fewer companies are reporting on their payment practices. Government regulations require all plcs and their large subsidiaries to state in their annual reports the average length of time it takes them to pay their bills. But this year's tables contain the payment information for only 2,706 companies compared to 3,243 in 2002 and 4,001 in 2001 – a 66% fall over two years.

Source: Accountancy International, May 2004.

---

[2] Factoring and invoice discounting are techniques used by businesses to raise funds on the strength of their Receivables. Essentially, a company transfers legal ownership of its Receivables to a factoring or discounting agency in return for a cash payment. It is effectively selling a current asset to a credit control agency. The cash payment may be refundable, in which case it is said to be "with-recourse".

Late payment culture creates domino effect: small companies are hit hardest when customers persistently fail to pay up, by Nicholas Neveling

Last week, two AIM companies, Avionic Services and Interior Services Group, warned the market that payment and contract delays would hurt their financial position. Interior Services told shareholders that it had not been paid for two projects carried out last year and had been forced to resort to adjudication to receive payment. Avionic, meanwhile, said its financial position had deteriorated 'significantly' because certain contracts and prospective orders had 'slipped' into the next financial year. These were not the types of announcements that would make front-page headlines, but served as a reminder of the damage that late payment can do to a business.

News of the problems encountered by these companies emerged as credit manager Intrum Justitia warned that small companies faced the greatest risks from the UK's late payment culture, where 1.6% of income was lost because of late payment. In its European Payment Index report, Intrum Justitia found that average payment in the UK was 17.4 days late. The credit manager said such delays caused a 'vicious circle', as companies awaiting payment did not have the cash flows available to pay their suppliers. It also said margin squeeze and inadequate bank financing were the other causes of late payment. 'The vicious circle of payment delay is continuing its negative effect on UK businesses. It is companies at the end of the supply chain that suffer the most,' said Shaun Purrington, commercial business unit director at Intrum Justitia UK. 'There is a distinction between companies that go out of business because they are badly run and those that close shop when they run out of cash because of late payment.'

Vivian Bairstow, corporate recovery partner at Begbies Traynor, said it was 'almost inevitable' that a company would go bust if it was continually blighted by late payment. 'Businesses can only succeed if they have funds, and if those funds are with customers who are paying late, then companies are going to go bust,' Bairstow said. The report said that, despite the risks posed by late payment, business support for creating a 'punctual payer' benchmark was tepid. Only 26% of the companies surveyed across Europe supported such a yardstick, with the rest either not interested or indifferent.

Source: Accountancy Age, June 30, 2005.

What if the money runs out?

Overtrading is when new business absorbs working capital faster than its customers pay their invoices. If the money runs out, an ostensibly successful company can be left unable to take on new work. At worst, the business could fail. If a company suspects it is overtrading, it should take immediate action to maintain positive cash flow. This means speeding up the time it takes to collect payment from customers and arranging for an additional cash injection to cover the shortfall in working capital.

Tell-tale signs of overtrading 1) Have your profit margins dropped over the past 12 months? 2) Has there been a large rise in the number of companies you are invoicing? 3) Does any one company represent more than 25 per cent of your outstanding invoices? 4) Are your customers taking longer to pay than 12 months ago? 5) Are you struggling each month to meet your fixed overheads? 6) Would your bank turn down your request for a larger overdraft? 7) Have you increased your workforce to help meet new orders? 8) Is your turnover increasing while your profit stays the same, or falls? 9) Have you purchased new plant or equipment recently? 10) Has there been a sharp rise in your variable costs (labour, material)? Remember: "Cash is king – profit is a matter of interpretation." If this is a concern to you, a good accountant and business adviser will be able to offer various solutions.

Source: Evening Post, November 18, 2004.

Inventory (Stock)

To be classified as inventory an item should be intended for resale or should be used or consumed in the course of production of goods for resale, for instance, raw materials. Inventory will usually comprise a substantial part of every company's current assets. Consequently the control of inventory will typically form a large part of management's responsibilities.

As outlined in Chapter 6, inventory consumed and closing inventory must be valued at the lower of cost and net realizable value. For many firms the identification and valuation of inventory will not be difficult. For instance trading firms, which simply purchase goods and then resell them, will have little problem in identifying closing inventory and determining its historic cost or net realizable value where appropriate.

Apart from valuing closing inventory, the question also arises as to the value at which it should be issued from stores to the factory floor or the consumer. This apparently simple task can often prove quite complex. For example, if materials were purchased exactly as needed or used, the cost of raw materials consumed could be fairly easily determined. However, in practice materials are purchased in large quantities at different times and prices, and issued to production in small amounts. This can make it extremely difficult to trace the cost of raw materials consumed.

It is because of difficulties such as these that a number of techniques have been developed to assist in valuing inventory. These are known as "perpetual inventory systems" because they are methods of recording the receipt and issue of individual items of inventory as they occur in terms of quantity and value.

The most widely used of these methods are:

- **First In, First Out (FIFO)**: this system prices each issue at the price paid for the material first taken into inventory for which there are quantities still remaining.

- **Last In, First Out (LIFO)**: this system prices each issue at the price paid for the material last taken into inventory for which there are quantities still remaining.

- **Weighted average**: pricing is based on the mix of materials in inventory and the prices at which they were acquired.

- **Standard cost**: pricing involves assigning predetermined values/prices to units.

[For a comprehensive example of the effects of these different valuation methods see the website for this text.]

Most large organizations such as Tesco will have complex, computer-based stock control systems that will determine and activate economic order quantities, economic order times and reconcile the cost/benefit implications of various stock-holding permutations.

Inventory (Stock) Days

This measures the length of time items are held in inventory before being sold. It recognizes the relationship between the total amounts of an item consumed during the year, i.e., cost of sales, and the amount of that item held at the end of the year. In businesses where there are finished goods, work-in-progress and raw materials, it will make more sense to calculate figures for each category than to calculate one composite figure.

The formula is:[3]

$$\frac{\text{Closing Inventory}}{\text{Cost of Sales}} \times 365$$

In practice:

Referring to notes 3 and 15 to the accounts in the Annual Report in Appendix 1, the figure for Tesco is:

$$\frac{1,306}{31,271} \times 365 = 15.2 \; days$$

The IFRS figure is almost exactly the same. See page 5 of the IFRS restatement where Cost of Sales is slightly adjusted. The figures under IFRS are: (1,306/31,310) × 365 = 15.2 days.

Alternatively, inventory levels can be assessed in relation to Revenue, in which case this is substituted for Cost of Sales in the formula above.

The figure for Tesco is:

$$\frac{1,306}{33,974} \times 365 = 14.0 \; days$$

The IFRS figure is exactly the same. For the constituent figures see IFRS Restatement page 5.

---

[3] As was the case with Receivables, the numerator can also be the average inventory over the course of the year, i.e., ((Opening Inventory + Closing Inventory)/2), in which case what is being identified is the inventory days figure relevant to the financial year as a whole.

Businesses will want to ensure that the Inventory Days period is kept as low as possible since a longer inventory holding period means extra warehousing and security costs. More critically, it also means additional amounts of cash tied up in inventory. However, this will need to be balanced against the need to have inventory available as necessary.

When interpreting this ratio a number of considerations need to be borne in mind:

1. The constituent parts of the ratios used may need to be investigated, and allowance may need to be made for VAT.
2. Seasonal factors must be taken into account when interpreting the result. For instance a year-end inventory figure where the business is seasonal may give an unrepresentative result.
3. Where companies trade in a small number of high value items there is considerable potential for distortion where even one item is unsold.
4. Comparative bases, such as industry averages, must be sensitive to product mix.
5. The following considerations may also need to be taken into account:

   - Sales volume may have increased or decreased materially towards the end of the year.
   - The company may have found it necessary to carry more inventory due to changes in customer profile, market changes or new product lines.
   - Because of changes in price, total values may have changed without any change in the underlying inventory volumes.
   - Purchasing policy may have changed in the light of discounts for bulk purchases.
   - There may be high levels of deteriorated or obsolescent items.
   - The company may have introduced a policy designed to move goods through more quickly.

Inventory Turnover

This formula (also known as Stockturn) is a variation on Inventory Days, employing the same figures to compute its result, although in a different arrangement. It yields a measure of the number of times that the company has converted its inventory into sales. The higher the factor, the quicker inventory is moving through. As with Inventory Days, either revenue or cost of sales can be used as the basis of the calculation.

The formula is:

$$\frac{\text{Cost of Sales (or Revenue)}}{\text{Closing Stock}}$$

In practice:

Using Cost of Sales as the numerator, the figure for Tesco is:

$$\frac{31,271}{1,306} = 23.9 \text{ times}$$

The IFRS figure is: $(31,310/1,306) = 23.9$ times.

These figures indicate that inventory turnover is very high, although not untypical for the retail sector.

In practice:

The critical importance of well-managed inventory levels is illustrated by the following example of a company that identified Stockturn as a crucial item to be monitored if it was to benefit fully from a large contract. Notice too the reference to trends:

. . .Stock cycles differ from industry to industry. These differences relate to variety in manufacturing processes or, in the case of retailers like Kingfisher, to the types of goods they sell. Obviously, food retailers have faster stockturn (lower stock days) than retailers – like Kingfisher – that sell durable goods.

What matters most is the trend in the ratio rather than its absolute level. Companies in broadly similar businesses should be measured against the ratios achieved by the most efficient company in the industry to see how they stack up.

A problem of interpretation that crops up in the case of Kingfisher is common to all multi-format retailers. A stockturn figure for a retail group operating more than one type of outlet – pharmacy chains and DIY superstores, for example – may not reveal much about the company's overall efficiency. Slow or declining inventory turnover in one area may be offset by fast or improving stockturn in another, making it difficult to pinpoint potential problem areas.

Remember too that inventory days (or stockturn) are of no help in assessing a business that does not normally have inventory as part of its day-to-day business. Software or intellectual property licensing companies, bookmakers and casinos are just some of the businesses where it is of little use.

Source: Financial Times, May 11, 2001.

Operating Cycle

The operating cycle is the time between purchase of inventory and the eventual realization of cash from the sale of that item. It represents the length of time that an average good takes to move through the various elements of the trading process before yielding cash. It can be calculated using the Receivables days and Inventory days figures.

The formula is:

Inventory days + Receivables Days

If, for example, the Inventory Days period was 60 days after which goods were sold on credit, and the subsequent Receivables Days period was 45 days, then the operating cycle would amount to 105 days.

In practice:

The figure for Tesco is:

15.2 + 0 = 15.2 days

The IFRS figure is exactly the same.

Payables

Payables are claims against future inflows of cash. The most common such claim is trade payables (creditors), which is the amount of money owed by the business to those from whom it has bought goods on credit. Other claims would include amounts due for taxation, accruals or other items unpaid. Typically amounts payable such as these are divided between those due to be paid within the next twelve months ("current liabilities" or "creditors amounts due within one year") and amounts due after more than one year.

Trade Payables (or Creditors)

This is the amount due to providers of goods and services. It is a significant means of finance for most businesses since, while unpaid, it effectively equates to a loan from suppliers. It also represents a relatively cheap source of funds, particularly where payment is within the allowed credit period and penalties are avoided. In fact, even where penalties are incurred it represents a relatively cheap source of funds. Consequently, many firms will exploit its potential to the full.

Payables (Creditors) Days

Trade Payables result from credit purchases of goods or services, and the Payables Days ratio provides a measure of the time taken by a firm to pay suppliers for those goods or services. The proper figure against which to gauge trade creditors therefore, is credit purchases. However, this will not usually be available. One commonly used approximation is cost of sales. Alternatively, revenue may be taken as the denominator.

The formula is:[4]

$$\frac{\text{Closing Trade Payables}}{\text{Cost of Sales}} \times 365$$

In practice:

Referring to notes 3 and 18 to the accounts, the figure for Tesco is:

$$\frac{2{,}819}{31{,}271} \times 365 = 32.9 \text{ days}$$

The IFRS figures will yield almost exactly the same result: $(2{,}819/31{,}310) \times 365 = 32.9 days$. (The IFRS adjustment of £417m referred to on page 7 of the IFRS Restatement under 'Trade and other payables' relates to a reversal of the dividend provision required under IFRS and, so, does not affect the figure for Trade Payables.)

Payables Days is a measure of the length of time being taken by a company to pay its customers. This period represents a period in which its suppliers are effectively giving the company free finance. Consequently, the company will want to extend this period where possible, although without compromising other considerations such as its payment reputation and legal requirements.

In practice:

No laughing matter

...A recent Lloyds TSB commercial finance survey has revealed that although there are few justifiable reasons for late payment, the excuses businesses dream up stretch the imagination, not to mention the patience, of many in the business community.

---

[4] As was the case for Receivables days and Inventory days, the numerator can be changed to Average Payables ((Opening Payables + Closing Payables)/2) to give the average number of days credit taken by the company during the period in question. If the information is available, the Cost of Sales figure could be adjusted for changes in inventory levels and other items included, such as, depreciation in order to more closely approximate to goods purchased on credit during the year.

> 'The boss has died and the cheque book was in the suit we buried him in,' and 'I've just been diagnosed with agoraphobia – I can't go out to post the cheque,' were two of the excuses recorded by the survey.
>
> 'While you can't deny the inventiveness of the excuses, the problem of late payment is itself no laughing matter,' says Nick Goulding, FPB chief Executive. 'Many businesses are pushed close to the wire financially while chasing debt and it has long been recognized as a significant barrier to growth.'
>
> A recent survey on www.fpb.co.uk revealed that 63.6% of businesses that voted said late payment had adversely affected their business. . .
>
> Source: Accountancy, June 2004.

When interpreting this ratio a number of points need to be borne in mind:

1. It is often difficult to determine the level of credit purchases from the Annual Report.
2. Potential VAT complications may need to be considered.
3. Seasonal factors must be taken into account. For instance, a year-end Trade Payables figure where the business is seasonal may yield an unrepresentative result.
4. The following may also need to be considered:

   - Purchases volume may have increased or decreased materially towards the end of the year.
   - The company may have deliberately withheld payment of certain accounts.
   - In order to avail of discounts, the company may have made earlier than usual payments.

Asset Turnover

Thus far this chapter has looked at activity measures in the context of the efficiency with which working capital is managed. However, management efficiency should also be assessed in relation to overall asset management.

This is normally gauged by measuring asset turnover. This is a measure of the relationship between net assets employed in generating business and the revenue that this yields. The figure for net assets employed can vary, depending on whether particular items are taken into account or not. For the purposes of this exercise, the Net Assets figure taken is that shown on the face of the balance sheet. The ratio is, therefore:

$$\frac{\text{Revenue}}{\text{Net Assets}}$$

> ### In practice:
>
> *For Tesco the figure is:*
>
> $$\frac{33,974}{9,057} = 3.8\ times$$
>
> *The IFRS Restatement Consolidated Balance Sheet shows Net Assets of £8,657 after various IFRS adjustments. The resulting figure is not materially different:* $(33,974/8,657) = 3.9\ times.$
>
> *This means that for the year in question the net assets employed by Tesco yielded almost four times their balance sheet value. Only when compared against industry averages or other comparative bases can the significance of this be assessed.*

An alternative measure of Asset Turnover changes the denominator to include all fixed assets. Yet another variation uses fixed assets adjusted for net current assets (liabilities) as a measure of net assets. In this case the formula is:

$$\frac{\text{Revenue}}{\text{Total assets less net current liabilities}}$$

> ### In practice:
>
> *For Tesco the figure is:*
>
> $$\frac{33,974}{14,338} = 2.4\ times$$
>
> *[The significance of this approach will be revisited in Chapter 10]*

Activity Measures Overall

Activity measures are, therefore, useful techniques for quantifying the relationship between trading activity and the related trade receivables, inventory and trade payables figures shown in the balance sheet. Indeed, it is as much for the fact that they highlight this interrelationship as for any results they yield, that it is important to understand and apply them. They also allow the efficiency with which the overall asset portfolio is managed to be assessed.

However, activity ratios can only be fully appreciated when considered in the context of liquidity and the ratios that have been developed to quantify this.

Liquidity

Liquidity relates to the capacity of a business to pay its short-term debts as they become due. Therefore, the focus is on the relationship between current assets and current liabilities (creditors due within 1 year), since these measure short-term sources of cash and short-term calls on that cash.

Current Ratio

The ratio most commonly used to assess liquidity is the Current Ratio, which is a simple assessment of the relationship between the two primary elements of liquidity.

The formula is:

Current Assets: Current Liabilities

or

$$\frac{\text{Current Assets}}{\text{Current Liabilities}} \times 100\%$$

In practice:

The figure for Tesco is:

$$\frac{3,457}{6,072} \times 100\% = 57\% \text{ (or, in terms of a ratio: 0.57:1)}$$

The IFRS calculation yields exactly the same result: 3,224/5,660 = 57%

Traditional approaches to interpreting this ratio have tended to emphasize ratios such as 2:1 or 1.5:1 as prudent. However, more recently, the emphasis has moved away from these simplistic evaluations to considerations such as the age of receivables, the imminence of liabilities, and seasonal factors. These, and any relevant points raised earlier when discussing Receivables Days, Inventory Days and Payables Days, should all be taken into account when attempting to interpret the significance of the result yielded.

Quick Ratio

Because the focus is on the ability to pay debts in the short term, it is sometimes appropriate to exclude inventory from the equation on the grounds that this will often take a considerable time to translate into cash, particularly where inventory includes raw materials or is initially sold on credit. This results in the Quick ratio (or Acid Test).

The formula is:

Current Assets − Closing Inventory: Current Liabilities

or

$$\frac{\text{Current Assets} - \text{Inventory}}{\text{Current Liabilities}} \times 100\%$$

In practice:

The figure for Tesco is:
$$\frac{3,457 - 1,306}{6,072} \times 100\% = 35\% \text{ (or, in terms of a ratio: 0.35:1)}$$

The IFRS calculation yields almost exactly the same result: (3,224 − 1,306)/5,660 = 34%. In the case of Tesco, however, this calculation may not be hugely relevant, as its Inventory Days period is quite low and it does not sell on credit.

As is the case with the Current Ratio, it is not appropriate to think in terms of a "normal" Quick Ratio. The point is that there should be evidence of proper and efficient management. This can usually only be assessed in the light of appropriate benchmarks, such as industry averages.

Cash Flow Ratios

While the Current and Quick ratios are useful measures of liquidity, analysis of information included in the Cash Flow Statement, particularly Net Cash Flow from Operating Activity, can often provide important additional insights into the liquidity position.

This focus helps to emphasize the importance of cash in relation to both its generation and efficient use. As the following extract highlights, it must always be central to management's planning and to any analysis:

Cash Machine – by Iveystone

There really is nothing like running your own business to teach you the importance of cash flow and cash management. One develops a keen awareness of payables, receivables and capital investments as each pay-day rolls around (and tax payment day and mortgage payment day, etc.). Cash flow becomes more important than almost anything else, because sometimes just a few hundred or a few thousand dollars a few days earlier can spell the difference between being in business and being out of business.

And when the business achieves a cash flow positive position and outlook, then the business can really be called a success, because its the excess cash that can be used to pay off the debt, provide a return to the shareholders, make acquisitions, but most importantly, not to have to worry about having enough cash for payroll and payroll taxes. Anyone who has started a business or run a business knows what I mean.

Having said that then, the real measure of an investments success, in my humble opinion, is not earnings per share (although important), not market share, not marketing, not new products, not even quality management. But a combination of those things that is measured first, second and third as the ability and potential to generate cash. Period. Give me current cash flow and I am happy. Give me current recurring cash flow and I am ecstatic. Give me current recurring cash flow that is already big and is still growing, and I am in heaven.

Source: *The Motley Fool, http://search.fool.com/community/.*

Quality of Profits

In order for a business to survive or to avoid having to constantly raise funds from non-trading sources, it must generate cash from its trading activity. The Quality of Profits ratio provides a critical measure of its ability to do this since it relates the Net (or Operating) Income, calculated according to accruals principles, to the actual cash flow generated from trading activity. The figure for Net Cash Flow from Operating Activity will be available from the cash flow statement.

The ratio is:

$$\frac{\text{Net Cash Flow from Operating Activity}}{\text{Operating Profit}}$$

In practice:

Using the information supplied in the cash flow statement and in note 32, the figure for Tesco is:
$$\frac{3,004}{1,949} = 1.5:1$$

As per page 6 of the IFRS Restatement, there is no impact of IFRS on reported cash flows. Small differences in the calculation of Operating Profit are highlighted on page 19, but are not material.

This is a very healthy result, and indicates that Tesco's profits yield positive cash flows.

Quality of Profits is increasingly being recognized as a critical measure of the "cash health" of a business since it measures the fundamental link between the basic activity of a business and the cash generated by that activity. For that reason it needs to be closely monitored and managed.

In practice:

Contractors count the cash

... for contractors, profit has often been seen as a notional figure. When to take profit on a five- or 10-year contract is a matter of judgment. Often a contractor will not know whether a profit has been made until the end of the contract. Investors who get confused by that approach can take the easier option and look for the cash. Cash is the killer for contracting companies. A company showing profit year after year without cash will raise eyebrows. "Conservative accounting" has become the slogan of those contracting companies that want to prove their prudence. In the past month, three of the smaller contractors have shown three different ways of treating cash.

At its half-year results, Kier – the housebuilder and contractor – showed a near-doubling of pre-tax profit as well as a strong cash position. The cash generation of the company, whose other activities include rail, private finance initiatives, support services, property and mining, has long been impressive. It has earned Kier an enviable reputation in the City as a company with a clear-eyed focus on deliverables. Even with the departure of Colin Busby, its long-standing and respected chairman, the company has not suffered. In the past month, its shares have risen from 848 1/2p to 896 1/2p.

Rok Property Solutions, the contracting and regional building company, reported a 30 per cent rise in annual turnover and announced plans to expand its building arm from 27 branches to between 75 and 100 in the next three to five years. The company's management are ambitious and make no secret of it. But they are not above admitting some slight failings. Although profit increased over the year, cash generation was not so healthy. The company pointed out, quite correctly, that the year-end cash position of any company is only a snapshot, and Rok had just invested a chunk of that cash in a big development. Nonetheless, the company's finance director admitted it "could do better" in terms of cash generation. Rok's shares rose 60p to 534p in the past month.

In contrast, Mowlem had an altogether tougher time. After profit warnings and stating that "accounting issues" would hit performance, the company produced a pre-tax loss of £15.3m. The new chief executive said getting a better correlation between profit and cash would be a priority. Its shares fell 2 1/2p to 199 3/4p over the month.

Source: Financial Times, March 30, 2005.

Free Cash Flow (FCF)

A number of businesses and CEOs have begun to talk about Free Cash Flow as an important measure of corporate health. While there is no agreed definition, it is generally accepted to be cash available to the company after all other commitments have been satisfied.

It is usually computed as Profits before Tax plus depreciation, on the basis that the latter has been deducted in calculating profit, but does not involve any cash movement. Further additions or subtractions might then be made for cash inflows or outflows deriving from, for example, disposal of assets.

As a concept FCF is not unrelated to quality of profits in that it attempts to relate activity levels to cash flow.

Cash Flow Adequacy (or Cash Cover)

This is an important measure of the capacity of funds generated by trading to cover payments such as creditors, dividends and short-term debt without having to seek recourse to other sources of funds.

The ratio is:

$$\frac{\text{Net Cash Flow from Operating Activity}}{\text{Current Liabilities}}$$

In practice:

The figure for Tesco is:

$$\frac{3,004}{6,072} = 0.49:1$$

The IFRS equivalent is $3,004/5,660 = 0.53:1$. *The difference derives, in the main, from a change under IFRS in the manner in which dividends are to be treated.*

This is an important complement to the Current and Quick Ratios since it demonstrates whether or not the business needs to generate funds from non-trading sources in order to cover short-term payments. It can also be made specific to one or more individual elements of Current Liabilities by inserting this figure as the denominator.

Cash Cycle

The operating cycle was defined earlier as the number of days it takes to sell goods and subsequently collect the cash. It can be calculated as Inventory Days + Receivables Days. To the extent that a business uses credit itself, however, for instance by purchasing these goods on credit, the cash life of the business is imported.

This result is the "Cash Cycle", which is a measure of the length of time that a company has to finance its trading activity from other sources.

This measure is particularly useful in expressing the relationship between inventory, receivables and payables, effectively crystallizing it into one figure. The ambition of every business will be to reduce both the Operating Cycle and the Cash Cycle to as low a figure as possible or indeed, like Tesco, to generate a negative figure.

It can be computed as follows:

Receivables Days + Inventory Days − Payables Days

In practice:

The figure for Tesco is:

$0 + 15.2 - 32.9 = -17.7$

The IFRS figure is exactly the same. It indicates that Tesco is a net beneficiary in the cash cycle. If this is extrapolated and related to the cash benefit enjoyed by the group as a whole, then the potential savings are very significant.

A variation of this formula excludes inventory days from the calculation.

A positive result indicates that the company must pay for the item before it receives payment. Many businesses will find themselves in this position, as goods will normally have to be paid for before payment is received from customers. This is especially the case where sales are made on credit.

A negative result, on the other hand, indicates that the company is receiving cash from customers before having to pay its own suppliers from whom, presumably, it will have purchased on credit. In other words, such companies are essentially receiving funding from their suppliers since they are receiving cash before having to pay it out.

In practice:

As the following extract highlights, large retailing operations such as Tesco, which buy on credit but sell predominantly for cash, can leverage this virtuous circle to considerable advantage:

Cash benefit: how big supermarkets fund expansion by using suppliers as bankers, by John Plender, Martin Simons and Henry Tricks

. . . Sales at Tesco – £34bn ($59bn, €50bn) in its latest reported financial year, of which £27.1bn came in the UK – have been growing much faster than the UK economy. So, too, at Asda, where last year's sales were £14.3bn. At the same time, the amounts owed by the two retailers to their trade creditors have increased at a far faster rate than either sales or stock. At Tesco the five-year

increase in payments owed to creditors was £2.2bn, compared with a £0.7bn increase in stocks, leaving £1.5bn to finance the business. At Asda trade creditors were up £0.7bn while stocks rose by £0.2bn, yielding a net cash benefit of £0.5bn over the period.

Working capital in a conventional business is the amount required to finance stock and debtors after deducting the credit made available by suppliers. But food retailing is different, in that stock is turned into cash at the check-out counters long before suppliers have to be paid. Debtors are relatively insignificant and creditors exceed stock by a considerable margin. So there is a negative working capital requirement. Trade credit can end up providing finance for investment in fixed assets.

The result is a virtuous circle that has permitted £2bn to be released to help finance a combined £12bn of capital investment in Tesco and Asda over the past five years. For every £1bn of extra sales, these retailers have attracted roughly £100m of extra creditor finance – with Tesco, much larger than the Wal-Mart subsidiary, demonstrating how much size pays.

In effect, suppliers have acted as surrogate bankers to the two groups on a remarkable scale, contributing growing amounts of finance in a period when cash flow from depreciation covered only one-third of the combined investment outlay. This has reduced Tesco's and Asda's need for bank finance and support from the capital markets (or in Asda's case, its US parent) while mitigating balance-sheet strain. . .

Source: Financial Times, December 7, 2005.

The determination of the Cash Cycle is important for a number of reasons:

- It enables a company to establish whether, on average, it receives cash from customers in advance, or must source funds to pay suppliers.

- If it requires to source funds on an ongoing basis, then it can quantify the amounts required and the means by which they can be raised. Associated costs, for example interest charges, can be estimated by applying appropriate rates.

- In circumstances where it generates funds prior to payment of suppliers it must initiate an active fund management strategy to ensure efficient use and application of these funds.

- It brings together in one number the results of a variety of company strategies designed to deal with cash management.

Summary

A firm's working capital must be carefully managed. This is because it relates directly to its capacity to generate cash, the lifeblood of any business. Consequently, it requires particular attention when analyzing a firm's position and performance, yielding, as it does, insight into the performance of the business under a number of related headings, as well as providing tangible measures of management efficiency.

The inter-relationship that exists between these ratios is an important consideration. This is best illustrated in the manner in which the Cash Cycle is constructed from the Receivable Day, Inventory Days and Payables Days figures. When interpreting the results of these ratios, this inter-connectivity must be kept in mind if their usefulness is to be fully exploited.

Review Questions

Question 1
Cash has been described as "the lifeblood of business". Explain whether this statement can be justified.

Question 2
Explain the importance of working-capital and the different aspects of corporate financial performance and position that can be highlighted from its proper analysis and interpretation.

Question 3
Distinguish between liquidity and activity measures, and explain how each targets different aspects of corporate activity.

Question 4
Identify the particular elements of management efficiency captured by the following:
• Receivables days
• Inventory days
• Payables days

Question 5
Comment on the advisability of arguing that there are "normal" results for the Current and Quick Ratios.

Question 6
Identify the specific aspects of cash-related activity that the following assess:
• Quality of Profits
• Cash Flow Adequacy

Question 7
Explain the significance and usefulness of the Cash and Operating Cycles and how they add a useful additional perspective when assessing company performance and management efficiency.

Question 8
Taking the relevant activity and liquidity ratios for Tesco plc from the chapter, discuss what is revealed by these figures and whether they provide sufficient information to allow any meaningful conclusions to be drawn regarding Tesco plc's performance and financial position.

Question 9
Identify any additional information that would be necessary in order to properly assess Tesco's performance under the headings of liquidity and activity.

Case Studies

Case 1

The ratios for Tesco 2005 have been given throughout this chapter under the various headings covered. Go to the company website, access the 2006 Annual Report, and compute the equivalent ratios for that year. These can be checked against the report for that year available on the website for this text.

Case 2

The following article concludes that while "excess cash is good for tactics ... it is bad for strategy..." In the light of the arguments made and the examples provided, consider how sustainable this view is.

A Surplus of Cash Invariably Leads to a Shortage of Sense, by Simon London

It is more than 30 years since Gulf Oil tried to buy Ringling Brothers Circus, but investors still get twitchy when companies hoard large amounts of cash. History shows that most chief executives put in charge of a company with billions in the bank are compelled to act like Coco the Clown.

There is plenty to be twitchy about. These days it is not only big oil companies that are generating more cash than they can invest with a straight face. The cost-cutting, outsourcing and restructuring of the last few years means that market leaders in most sectors are enjoying tremendous operational gearing: relatively modest revenue growth translates into substantial increases in earnings and, all things being equal, free cash flow.

At the last count, more than a third of the companies in the Standard & Poor's 500 index of US stocks had net cash on their balance sheets. The combined cash hoard: $650bn (£377bn), up from $329bn five years ago. The richest of them all is Microsoft, the world's largest software company, which has $40bn in the bank even after paying out $33bn last year to shareholders as a special dividend.

The good news is that really comical attempts at diversification are these days rarely a problem. Gulf Oil's proposed move from hydrocarbons into lion-taming was probably the high point (or, more accurately, the low point) of the fashion for conglomerate strategies. Today's managers have been educated to believe in focus. But they are no less vulnerable to cash-induced madness than their forebears – it is just that their madness is expressed in different ways.

Recall, if it is not too painful, the cash-fuelled acquisition binge that turned General Electric Company, once the pride of the UK electronics industry, into the listing hulk that is Marconi. A quick scan of the financial pages reveals the telltale signs of cash again burning holes in trouser pockets. Would Porsche have acquired a substantial stake in Volkswagen unless it had a few billion euros stashed in the corporate glove compartment?

Cash breeds not only slapstick action but also tragicomic inaction. General Motors might have been forced to produce cars people actually wanted to drive had it not been sitting atop a $29bn (as of 2003, now down to $19bn) cash pile. Sun Microsystems might have been forced to concede that its technology strategy was a dud had its coffers not been filled to overflowing during the bubble years.

To be fair, there are some legitimate reasons for companies to keep what looks like surplus cash in the bank. Managers operating in feast-or-famine industries can argue that a fat balance sheet helps them to survive lean years. Yes, carrying around the extra weight is inefficient. But it is less inefficient than teetering on the edge of bankruptcy during every downturn.

Then there are industries where success depends on persuading customers to make long-term commitments to products. In these circumstances, a rock-solid balance sheet is an invaluable marketing tool, without which customers and business partners will be reluctant to make "co-investments" required to train employees or develop complementary products. Curiously, this was always Sun's main justification for maintaining a cash pile – which goes to show that surplus cash can be useful and harmful simultaneously.

Big bucks can also be an important weapon for companies engaged in "wars of attrition" – long-term struggles where the enormous costs are justified by the potential for a winner-takes-all outcome. Thus Microsoft's extreme cash riches might be justified because it allows the company to pitch its Xbox games console against Sony's PlayStation in an epic struggle for dominance of the world's living rooms.

The snag is that companies that can afford to fight wars of attrition tend to see everything in those terms. Thus Microsoft in the 1990s won what it thought was a war of attrition against Netscape for control of the internet browser market, only to find competition re-emerging in recent years in the form of Firefox, a browser developed by the open-source software community. The winner may not take all, after all.

A wider problem, notes Preston McAfee, professor of business, economics and management at the California Institute of Technology, is that cash-rich companies tend to rush to invest in new markets when it might be more sensible to hang back. "The strategic value of delay is widely underappreciated," he says.

John Roberts, professor of economics and management at Stanford Graduate School of Business, is sceptical of the idea that keeping cash on hand "just in case" ever makes sense from a strategic perspective.

"Excess cash is good for tactics," he says. "But it is bad for strategy on all kinds of dimensions."

Poster boy for this hair-shirted philosophy is BP's John Browne, who has committed the company to returning every last dollar of surplus cash flow to investors. BP will this year return roughly $20bn through its share buy-back programme as well as paying a hefty dividend.

Then again, as ever in management theory, every shining example yields a troublesome counter-example. Thus Toyota is not only the world's most profitable volume car manufacturer, one of the world's most respected companies and famed for its "lean" approach to business, it also has $30bn in the bank – and not a clown or a contortionist in sight. That's (show) business.

Source: *Financial Times*, November 30, 2005.

FINANCING

When you have completed this chapter you will understand that:

- Businesses must fund long-term requirements in a balanced and appropriate manner.
- There are a number of different sources of long-term funding.
- These can be classified into "Debt" and "Equity".
- There is significant interplay between long-term solvency and short-term liquidity issues.
- Ratios have been developed that enable the relationship between debt and equity to be captured.
- New forms of funding, such as derivatives, are constantly being devised, posing particular challenges for accounting regulators.

Box Clever in the Shadow World of Derivatives

Derivative Trading Can Reap Big Returns for the Experienced Player, by Allister Heath

Derivatives may have only recently made the headlines but they have been with us for at least 2,500 years. Like many of the other great inventions that underpin western civilisation, they were developed by the ancient Greeks. In his famous book, Politics, Aristotle tells the story of Thales, a poor philosopher from Miletus in Greece, who invented a 'financial device, which involves a principle of universal application' to prove to his critics that he could make some money if he wanted to.

Thales was convinced that his area of Greece was set for a bumper olive crop. He went to see all the oil press owners in the region and negotiated the purchase of what would now be called an option for the exclusive use of their facilities for the duration of the harvest period.

For a small fee he had the right but not the obligation to request that the presses be rented to him. The price for the option was low because the outcome of the oil harvest was uncertain and the olive-press owners were happy to be given the opportunity of hedging against the possibility of a poor yield, a situation where they would be getting little or no business at all.

'When the harvest came, and many presses were wanted all at once and of a sudden, he let them out at any rate that he pleased, and made a quantity of money. Thus he showed the world that philosophers can easily be rich if they like, but that their ambition is of another sort,' Aristotle recounts.

Today, options are only one of the many different types of financial derivatives designed or traded in all the leading financial centres. As their name suggests, financial derivatives are contracts that are based on or derived from some underlying asset (such as the use of an olive oil factory), reference rate (such as an interest rate), or index (such as the FTSE 100)...

Credit derivatives have emerged as the fastest growing segment of the overall derivatives market. These are used by banks to transfer some of the credit risk they take on when they lend money to borrowers; they are also used to create individualized credit-risk exposures for investors who wish to incur a predetermined amount of risk...

Derivatives are not merely the invention of armchair philosophers, they allow companies and investors to insure against risk. Risks can be isolated and sold to those who are willing to accept them at the least cost., while companies and investors can retain the risks they are most comfortable managing and transfer those they do not want to others.

Rather than making the economy more volatile, the increasing use of derivatives since the 1970s has helped inject some certainty in the global economy. While derivatives are occasionally misused, their growth should be welcomed.

Source: *The Business*, January 2004.

Introduction

Until relatively recently any discussion of financing would have been confined to a fairly straightforward description of equity and bank borrowings. A really adventurous treatment might have extended to include bonds. Now, however, given the rapid rate at which new financial instruments have evolved, derivatives, hedging and other exotic terminology will invariably feature.

One of the most important determinants of a company's capacity to develop is its funding structure. The liquidity and efficiency ratios covered in Chapter 8 concentrate on determining and quantifying a firm's capacity to satisfy its short-term funding requirements. However, it is also important for a company to be able to assess its capacity to satisfy its long-term commitments. Furthermore, it will be useful if a firm can quantify the source and nature of its long-term funding as this will enable a proper balance to be maintained between, for example, fixed-cost sources such as debentures, and variable-cost sources such as equity.

Likewise, the overall financial structure and stability of the company will be a critical consideration for existing and intending investors. Thus, potential equity investors will have considerable doubts about investing in a company that has high bank indebtedness because their claim on profits will be subordinated to the prior claim of these banks to be paid interest.

Sources of Finance

While it is true that there is a wide range of funding available, for convenience the various funding sources can usually be categorized as either "equity" or "debt". These classifications are useful in that they allow common characteristics of each to be identified.

Equity can be defined as "any issued share capital which has unlimited rights to participate in a distribution of either capital or profits". For practical purposes it is often assumed to mean Ordinary Share Capital together with any associated reserves such as Retained Profits.

Debt, on the other hand can be defined at its most basic as "amounts owed to outsiders". The use of the phrase "outsiders" is significant in that a distinction is being made between providers of debt and "insiders", i.e., equity providers.

Quantifying the relative importance of these sources of funding is important because it enables the implications of funding structure and financial risk to be more clearly understood. The real issue is the way in which a company funds its long-term activities, whether by debt or equity, as this will have implications for the company's cost of capital, cash flow and future funding requirements. For example, providers of equity do not normally expect a fixed return, while debt providers such as banks will often expect a pre-set return regardless of the level of profits. Since the existence of debt imposes definite obligations on a company, the higher the level of debt the higher the level of interest and repayments. This in turn will impact on the attractiveness of the company for equity investors, since the residual profits from which they draw their return will be correspondingly reduced.

In practice:

The following example illustrates the importance of quantifying the relative importance of different funding sources.

If a firm funded entirely by equity generates profits of £500,000 then this amount is available in full to the equity interest. If, however, the company were partly funded by debt, which had annual service costs of £300,000, then only £200,000 would be available to equity. The real implications

> *of this financial structure would become apparent if profits before interest and tax suddenly fell to £300,000. In those circumstances the debt providers could still be satisfied in full while the equity interest would receive nothing. The real risk-taker in a company is, therefore, the equity interest.*

A company's financial structure has implications, therefore, for the financial and strategic well-being of a company and its providers of finance. This chapter is concerned with explaining techniques such as ratios that can capture the critical features of this structure. First, however, it is necessary to explore in more depth the unique characteristics of equity and debt.

Equity

As explained in Chapters 1 and 6, equity funding derives initially from the issue of shares. The share capital of a company can comprise of a number of different types of share:

- **Ordinary Shares** are the most common type of share. The normal rights of ordinary shareholders are to vote at company meetings and to receive dividends. In some instances ordinary shares without voting rights or with varying rights to dividends may exist. Redeemable ordinary shares can be issued where a company already has some non-redeemable ordinary shares in issue. The term "equity" normally applies to ordinary shares.

- **Preference Shares** are less common. They entitle the owners to preferential treatment when dividends are being distributed, i.e., they are entitled to receive dividends before ordinary shareholders. Furthermore, the rate of dividends they receive is usually fixed so they attract a regular dividend every year. These characteristics make them very attractive to investors who may not be attracted to the risk inherent in ordinary shares. They also mean that preference shares exhibit many of the characteristics of debt rather from equity. In fact, in most calculations of the relative importance of equity and debt, preference shares are classified as debt. This is an important consideration when determining the funding profile of a firm and is consistent with the provisions of IAS 32. There are various sub-categories of preference shares.

    - **Cumulative**: in circumstances where the company does not pay preference dividends in one or more years, the payment is merely deferred in respect of such shares as any dividends in arrears accumulate.
    - **Redeemable**: the company can redeem such shares at a specified date.
    - **Convertible**: ownership of such shares confers the right to convert preference shares into ordinary shares at a pre-set rate.
    - **Participating**: such preference shares may receive additional dividends on top of the normal fixed preference dividends.

Rights Issues

The way in which companies raise funds by issuing shares was outlined in Chapter 1. It is normal for a company to seek to raise funds in this way at various times in its life. However, UKLA regulations impose some restrictions on companies' scope in this regard. For this reason companies often undertake rights issues.

These are offers of shares to existing shareholders in proportion to their existing shareholding. For instance, a company may offer to its existing shareholders the opportunity to purchase, at a slight discount to the market price, 1 extra share for every 5 currently held. The attraction for existing shareholders is that they are offered the shares at a discount to the market price. The financial advantage of the option is also a saleable item. The attraction for the company, apart from allowing it to circumvent some stock exchange restrictions, is that it allows its existing shareholder profile to be maintained. For companies that are satisfied with the balance and make-up of their existing investor base this may be an important consideration.

In practice:

The decision to undertake a rights issue is fraught with certain dangers and, as the following extract highlights, a rights issue may need to be interpreted with some caution by both existing shareholders and prospective investors:

Investors should be wary of a black hole

Rights Issues: Eric Uhlfelder looks at the advantages and pitfalls for both shareholders and companies from this form of capital generation

While 2003 was hailed as the year stocks finally remembered they could go up, the year will also be remembered as a time in which dozens of big, troubled corporations aggressively diluted their equity positions to help repair dismal balance sheets through rights issues. This form of secondary flotation is giving a growing number of existing investors the right to buy additional shares at a discount to the market price. The question too infrequently asked is whether they should.

Companies resort to rights issues for several reasons. Heavily indebted ones use them to de-leverage operations, especially when borrowing is no longer an option. For healthier companies, it's a cheap way to fund capital improvements and acquisitions. Driving earnings in such ways could offset share dilution brought about by the rights issue. A fundamental premise of this kind of offering is protection of existing shareholder interests. The discount enables stakeholders to sustain their existing positions or to immediately profit from selling the right like an option. Just as important, offering shares on the cheap ensures a company does raise a specified level of capital.

. . . In July 2002, Kingfisher announced a £2bn rights issue, the second largest in UK history. The one-for-one share offering, which gave existing investors the right to buy additional shares (an amount no greater than their existing holding) at a 50 per cent discount over the market price,

assured a successful issue. Because proceeds were raised to help finance a strategic acquisition, rather than to recapitalize a struggling operation, the 100 per cent dilution didn't seriously depress the share price. More than 95 per cent of existing shareholders subscribed to the issue. According to investment banking research firm Dealogic, the stock was up more than 37 per cent over the offer price just one month after the issue was completed in August 2002. And by the end of last month shares were up 55 per cent.

While rights issues have lately proved a boon for investors, there is a black hole when it comes to the discussion of whether shareholders should subscribe to an issue, sell the rights, or get out of the stock entirely before the offering and dilution begins. This is due in part to the lack of study on the impact of rights issues on share prices, as Richard Peterson, chief global market strategist at Thomson Financial, believes, as well as difficulty determining what the proceeds of some issues are to be used for. This lack of clarity is more important as more companies rely on this form of financing.

Source: Financial Times, February 14, 2004.

Bonus (Scrip) Issues

In circumstances where a company thinks that its share price is too high it may undertake a bonus issue. This involves giving shares for free to existing shareholders in proportion to their existing shareholding. There are no cash flow implications for the company and the process simply involves converting some of the company's reserves into share capital.

Reserves

The nature of reserves and the distinctions between distributable and undistributable reserves were outlined in Chapter 6.

Debt

Equity, in the form of share capital and reserves, represents one significant, and always-present, element of the funding profile of a company. The other significant, long-term source of finance for most companies is debt.

Debt is different from equity in that it does not give the provider any ownership rights. It can be short-term or long-term; fixed or variable cost; secured or unsecured; convertible (in which case the lender can convert the debt into equity in the company at a pre-set rate at some point in the future) or non-convertible.

In practice:

One of the principal effects of the introduction of IFRS has been to force companies to disclose sources of finance that were traditionally not disclosed on the face of the balance sheet. This Off-Balance Sheet Finance (OBSF) was often a significant element of many companies' funding profile but, for a variety of reasons, was not often visible to investors and other users of Annual Reports. As the following report highlights, IFRS has had a major impact on balance sheets in particular and, this in turn, has caused many companies to address the strategic and structural issues raised by their overall funding profile:

Debt rises up the agenda as IFRS brings balance sheets into focus

Some companies may suffer as the long-standing obsession with earnings may give way to a more rigorous scrutiny of assets and liabilities, writes Barney Jopson

Six months ago, when international accounting standards were yet to become a reality in the European Union, capital markets were filled with whispers that they could wipe out company profit or lift them by wild multiples. As the first figures emerged under International Financial Reporting Standards this year, investors and analysts therefore turned to income statements with an added sense of expectation. More often than not, they found little of consequence. Instead, the starkest and most consistent changes wrought by IFRS emerged on the balance sheet. "The impact of IFRS on earnings is more often negative rather than positive but we've seen winners as well as losers," says Peter Elwin, head of accounting and valuation research at Cazenove. "In terms of the balance sheet, however, I've not seen any companies that are showing higher net assets than before. In general, debt numbers are going up."

Dresdner Kleinwort Wasserstein calculates that net debt and other liabilities have risen by 16 per cent at 28 large EU companies. Compared to the effect of the new rules on revenue and earnings, the changes to debt are by far the biggest and have potentially far-reaching consequences. More debt can affect a company's ability to raise new funds, alter the perceptions and share prices of some businesses and prompt wholesale changes to the way companies are analysed. Reported liabilities are rising because IFRS make companies unearth accounting items that had been obscured and require greater precision in accounting for subsidiaries and financial instruments...

For analysts and investors, rising liabilities are throwing up more fundamental questions. At a glance, the new forms of disclosure behind the fresh numbers are welcome to the markets. "IFRS is giving a more realistic portrayal of company debt," says Mr Elwin. "Whilst we might not always take the precise reported figure straight to our valuations, we are definitely finding we have a clearer view of liabilities, which allows us to make judgments about what is economically significant."

Source: Financial Times, June 16, 2005.

Types of debt

There is a vast and ever-increasing array of debt funding available to companies. However, they can be broadly summarized as follows:

Bank Loans and Overdrafts

A bank loan is the simplest form of long-term debt. It commits the business to repaying both the interest and capital elements of the loan over a fixed period.

Debentures

These are quite similar to long-term, fixed interest bank loans. They are usually secured on a fixed charge, i.e., with a legal interest in specific assets of the business. They are long-term loans and the years during which they must be repaid are normally specified. Debentures can be issued to various holders or listed on the stock exchange, thus becoming negotiable instruments. They are usually subject to a debenture deed or trust document in which the often-complex legal arrangements surrounding the debenture are outlined.

Debenture Stock

This is a variant of a debenture and is a hybrid between equity and debt. It normally has all of the characteristics of a debenture but allows the bearer to take shares in the company at some future date instead of repayment of the debenture. However, until such an option is exercised, it will be classified as debt.

Leases

Leasing is a common means of acquiring fixed assets. Long-term obligations in relation to finance leases (see Chapter 12) will appear with long-term loans. Any amount due within 12 months will appear under "current liabilities".

Bonds

These are similar to debentures, are negotiable instruments and can be secured against a company's assets. Typically, a company will "issue" bonds on the Bond Market and investors, who then become bondholders, will acquire these. The rights and obligations of the various parties will be covered in a trust deed. This deed will usually impose some covenant restrictions on the company, requiring, for example, that the proportion of debt to equity never exceed a certain level, or that specified levels of profit be achieved.

> **In practice:**
>
> *In order to give themselves greater security, providers of finance will often impose restrictions on companies that limit their capacity to take on additional debt. These restrictions are often incorporated in legal "debt covenants" and are usually expressed in terms of certain ratio measurements. For instance, a bank might require a company to sign a covenant that states that "its gearing will not exceed 75%". In the event that this figure is breached the bank may call in the loan, increase interest rates, or impose such other penalties as the covenant specifies. [Gearing will be covered later in this chapter.]*

Bonds have become progressively more attractive to companies as they offer many of the advantages of both equity and debt, with the added attraction of an increasingly liquid and extensive bond market:

Benefit from Bonds

Don't Needlessly Limit your Finance Options. Derek Ross Considers how Corporate Bonds Can Provide a Useful Diversification of Funding Sources

With the substantial fall in equity prices since the end of 1999, there has been much greater interest in bond investment from both pension funds and retail investors. This is particularly the case in Europe; the euro was introduced in January of that year, and the liquidity in the bond market for euro denominated instruments has been notably increasing. For companies with large bank borrowings, say in excess of £100m equivalent, the bond market is an attractive option. There are a number of reasons why this is so.

Enhanced stability: Firstly, the banks can have a variable attitude towards corporate lending at various points in the economic cycle. This can lead to inconsistency in availability, pricing, covenants and so on. Companies that raise finance from their shareholders and banks alone are therefore limiting their investor base. Bond investors are a different group and widening the investor pool by diversifying funding sources will result in a more stable financial structure.

Tailored approach: The second reason why companies find the bond market attractive is that bond finance enables them to tailor the funds raised to their own requirements. That said, they must naturally also strike a balance with investor requirements if they are to achieve the lowest funding costs.

Key features: When raising finance there are four key, so-called liability features. However, because of the sophistication in the financial markets, particularly in the use of swaps, it is not necessary for the bond issue to match the requirements of investors and the borrower in respect of all of the features. Two features which must be matched are the source of funding, namely the investor base, and the ultimate maturity of the debt. Two features that can be independently managed, however, are the currency in which the finance is raised, and the matter of whether it is fixed or variable, or indeed a mixture. If the currency required is sterling but the best price can be obtained by issuing the bond in euros, then the bond will be issued in euros; a separate currency swap with a different counterparty, whereby the company receives euros and pays sterling on the maturity date, will produce the most appropriate financing. Similarly, bond investors will often require a fixed interest coupon, but the company may wish to pay interest at variable rates. If the cheapest spread over the risk-free rate is obtainable by issuing fixed, a separate interest rate swap will be entered into whereby the company receives fixed and pays variable interest to another counterparty.

Less onerous covenants: A third advantage of tapping into the bond market is that Eurobonds in particular are much more straightforward in terms of financial covenants. Most bank loans for all but the bluest of blue chips will have a range of covenants that the company must be careful to monitor continuously. Such covenants as do exist in bond documentation are generally much less onerous; bond investors are normally attracted by the company's credit quality rather than the tightness of covenants.

Credit ratings: Companies must manage the process of obtaining a rating. Historically, particularly in the European markets, only the best-known companies could attract investors. Name recognition was the most important factor. However, the best-known names do not necessarily imply the best quality credit and there have been some high-profile failures of well-known companies. The market has become much more sophisticated over the years. Now, although a household name remains a considerable advantage, a credit rating is normally required.

Derek A Ross is the partner responsible for treasury and financial markets at Deloitte.

Source: *Accountancy*, April 2004.

In practice:

Gunners need on-pitch success to pay off bond: Arsenal is refinancing its ground with a £200m bond issue

The link between financial security and performance on the pitch has become even more important than normal for Arsenal after the announcement that it would be refinancing its new 60,000 capacity stadium at Ashburton Grove. The refinancing has been secured against future ticket sales, which will make it essential for the club to succeed on the field to maintain robust attendance at matches. Arsenal is refinancing its stadium with a £200m bond issue, accompanied by a £60m loan note, in order to retire bank loans that funded the construction of the new ground. The bond issue will be managed by Royal Bank of Scotland and Barclays.

Harvey Hoogakker, assistant director of debt advisory services at Ernst & Young, said securing a bond against ticket receivables was a common practice in the UK and Europe, but warned that it was important for any club doing so to succeed and keep fans coming through the turnstiles. 'Lazio, Real Madrid, Leeds United and Leicester City have all used this type of asset-backed bond. It is not an unusual practice, but if a club does not perform well and attendances drop, it will battle to repay debts,' Hoogakker said.

The bond issue will provide Arsenal with more flexibility in how it manages its debt, providing the FA Cup holders with a longer time to repay arrears. Bank loans typically have a life of three to five years, but bond issues can last in excess of 10 years, which reduces the pressure to make repayments. Hoogakker said bank loans were usually used as a 'bridge' to bond issues, which typically take longer to put in place.

Source: Accountancy Age, September 8, 2005.

Hybrid Debt

As the name suggests, this form of debt has the characteristics of both debt and equity. For example, hybrid debt pays interest at fixed intervals to those who hold it, but at the same time it carries some of the characteristics of equity. On occasion, these features allow this form of debt to be classified as equity by ratings agencies – even while appearing as debt on the balance sheet – making it possible for some companies to raise funds without facing a credit rating downgrade.

In practice:

Hybrid debt gains another convert: Thomson to take dip in revitalized asset class, writes Ivar Simensen

Thomson will today price its debut hybrid bond issue, underlining the growing popularity of the asset class in Europe. But as the new asset class is finding its feet, there remains great uncertainty about where the bonds should be priced. The French media technology company is set to issue €500m of hybrid bonds in the sixth issue since the market sprang to life this summer, taking the total amount raised to €4.75bn.

The hybrid bond gets its name from combining features of both bonds and shares. It pays creditors interest at fixed intervals like a bond but also carries some equity characteristics, such as a perpetual maturity and the opportunity to defer coupon payments. These features give the bond a high equity treatment by credit agencies, allowing companies to raise capital without putting its rating at risk. The bonds can also be treated as debt for accounting purposes...

Source: Financial Times, September 16, 2005.

Securitization

This is an increasingly common funding technique by which claims on future cash flows are packaged by businesses into "securities" that are then sold to investors. (See Case 3 at end of this chapter where more detail is provided on the nature and functioning of this type of debt.)

Derivatives and Other New Financial Instruments

While there are different types of derivative, they are essentially a contract between two parties, which specify one or more future cash flows the size of which are not fixed in advance. They are so-called because they derive their value from other underlying items. These could be shares, other types of debt, assets, bonds or currencies typically tied to the future value of some index such as the S&P 500, FTSE 100, or gold price.

There are four principal types of derivative contract:

- **Forwards**: these are an agreement between two parties to buy or sell a certain quantity of an asset at a predetermined price at an agreed date in the future

- **Options**: these give a right, but no obligation, to buy ('call option') or sell ('put option')

- **Swaps**: are the most complicated form of derivative. They are often used to allow companies to fix the value of the underlying asset or liability in circumstances where a business is dealing in foreign currency. Typically, investors borrow in one currency while simultaneously investing in a different currency. This allows the investor to benefit from interest rate differences while hedging against currency fluctuations

- **Futures**: are like a forward contract, but they are based on standardized assets and delivery dates and are traded on exchanges.

In practice:

Between 2000 and 2003 the value of UK equities traded remained fairly constant at some £7.5 billion per day. Meanwhile, the number of FTSE 100 index futures contracts traded on the Euronext.Liffe exchange in London rose from 49,605 a day to 79,110 (equivalent in money terms to about £3.2 billion).

Some of the accounting and disclosure provisions relating to these financial instruments were outlined in Chapter 6. Prior to IFRS, the most glaring omission from the accounts of many European companies was that they made almost no reference to derivatives. To have valued these at their original cost – the preference of many in the banking industry – would have been absurd because of the exposures involved, especially once underlying indices have moved. IAS 32, *Financial Instruments: Disclosure and Presentation*, and IAS 39, *Financial Instruments: Recognition and*

Measurement, require that derivatives and other financial instruments be placed on the balance sheet at fair value – the price a buyer would be willing to pay for them on the market. Resulting changes in valuation should be shown in the income statement, unless the derivatives meet very stringent criteria on hedge effectiveness. These provisions will lead to more transparent accounts, but they will also hugely increase volatility. As a result they have encountered considerable political opposition. (See Case 1 for more detail on the political aspects of this saga.)

Derivatives are essentially means by which entities, such as banks, reduce or cover their exposure to future risks. However, because of their somewhat obtuse nature, and the explosive growth in the use of credit derivative products in particular, they have raised concerns amongst regulators.

What's All the Fuss About?

Risk Spreaders or Time Bombs? Michael Goddard Looks at the Good and Bad Sides of Derivatives

What are derivatives? Essentially, these instruments call for money to change hands at some future date, with the amount to be determined by one or more reference items, such as interest rates, stock prices, or currency values. If, for example, you are either long or short a FTSE 100 futures contract, you are a party to a very simple derivatives transaction – with your gain or loss derived from movements in the index. Derivative contracts are of varying duration (running sometimes to 20 or more years), and their value is often tied to several variables. Unless derivatives contracts are collateralized or guaranteed, their ultimate value also depends on the credit-worthiness of the counterparties to them. In the meantime, though, before a contract is settled, the counterparties record profits and losses – often huge in amount – in their current earnings statements, without so much as a penny changing hands.

The range of derivatives contracts is limited only by the imagination of man (or as Warren Buffett, the billionaire investor and chairman of Berkshire Hathaway, once said, sometimes madmen). At Enron, for example, newsprint and broadband derivatives, due to be settled many years in the future, were put on the books. Many people argue that derivatives reduce systemic problems, in that participants who cannot bear certain risks are able to transfer them to stronger hands. These people believe that derivatives act to stabilize the economy and facilitate trade and solve problems for individual participants.

$128 Trillion Market

The derivatives market has boomed from its beginnings in the late 1980s to become a $128 trillion (£71 trillion) market, according to figures from the Bank for International Settlements. It is one particular type of contract – the fast growing credit derivatives products – which has created most concern. These transfer credit risks from one party to another and can include complex financial instruments where lower quality loans are bundled up as higher quality investments. The market is estimated at $2,000 trillion globally. Credit derivatives appear to spread risk through the financial system. But there have been concerns that these products have been mis-sold by banks to other financial institutions, such as insurers, which do not understand the risks. A second anxiety is that some banks may also hold a disproportionate share of the risks. JP Morgan, Deutsche Bank and Salomon Smith Barney, part of Citigroup, are the leading banks in derivatives, although all major global banks, including Barclays, HSBC and UBS, have a significant presence.

Last year, the Bank for International Settlements warned that disclosure on credit derivatives was too 'patchy' and drew attention to the fact that just 13 banks controlled 80% of the market. In recent years there have been several separate disasters with derivatives that have involved losses of more than a billion US dollars – including the $1.4bn loss on Japanese equity index financial futures that brought down Barings. In 1998, the leveraged and derivatives-heavy activities of a single hedge fund, Long-term Capital Management (LTCM), caused the Federal Reserve such severe anxieties that it hastily orchestrated a rescue. In a later congressional testimony, Fed officials acknowledged that, had they not intervened, the outstanding trades of LTCM – a firm unknown to the general public and employing only a few hundred people – could well have posed a threat to the stability of American markets. The Fed acted because its leaders were fearful of what might have happened to other financial institutions had the LTCM domino toppled. And this affair, though it paralysed many parts of the fixed-income markets for weeks, was far from a worst-case scenario...

Out of Control?

The derivatives business continues to expand unchecked. Central banks and governments have so far found no effective way to control, or even monitor, the risks posed by these contracts. Even experienced investors and analysts encounter major problems in analysing the financial condition of companies that are heavily involved with derivatives contracts. Warren Buffett says that when he has finished reading the long footnotes detailing the derivatives activities of major banks, the only thing he understands is that he does not understand how much risk the institution is running.

Derivatives generate reported earnings that are often wildly overstated. This is because today's earnings are based on estimates whose inaccuracy may not be exposed for many years. Of course, both internal and outside auditors review the numbers, but that is no easy job. Each contract has a plus or minus value derived from one or more reference items, including some of mind-boggling complexity. Expert auditors could easily and honestly have widely varying opinions. The valuation problem is far from academic. In recent years derivatives trades have facilitated some huge-scale frauds...

Michael Goddard is a chartered accountant and retired finance director.

Source: *Accountancy*, May 2004.

The essential characteristic of derivatives is, therefore, that the parties are entering into a contract designed to either quantify and/or reduce exposure to risk. One issue for accounting relates to the fact that the commercial reality of any such transaction is intimately tied to the existence of an underlying asset or liability, and it is this that must be tracked, often only with great difficulty. In addition, and often of greater potential significance, the underlying contracts may expose those involved to huge unquantifiable risks at some point in the future. Meanwhile, parties to derivative contracts are booking substantial and often uncertain profits.

The complexities relating to derivatives and other financial instruments as critical sources of funding have been heightened by the concurrent emergence of a hedge fund industry that relies heavily on such instruments and on hedging strategies.

In practice:

Over the hedge: money slushing into hedge funds, poor returns and a trend towards long-only funds are beginning to look like a witch's brew of misfortune, by Richard Willsher

There are about 8,000 hedge funds worldwide managing in excess of $1 trillion (£555bn) worth of assets. This is before adding in the leveraging raised on the back of core holdings.

The soaring growth in the sector is set to continue, according to LJH Hedge View, an industry newsletter published by Florida-based LJH Global Investments LLC, which projects that hedge fund assets could reach $4 trillion (£2.22 trillion) by 2010.

Source: Financial Director, February 1, 2005.

This sheer scale of these funds and the relatively unregulated nature of the industry have prompted recent calls for increased regulation and disclosure.

In practice:

See the OFR and Note 21 in the Tesco 2005 Annual Report for some details on Tesco's use of derivatives and other financial instruments. See also the IFRS Restatement pp. 8–9.

Ratios

The financial structure of a business is an important consideration is assessing the financial health of any entity. This is particularly so where the long-term viability of a business is being assessed. It will be important for both existing and potential equity and debt investors to quantify the relative importance of each source. A number of ratios have been developed which highlight different elements of the debt/equity relationship.

As indicated already, it may not only be difficult to classify a type of funding (for instance, whether equity or debt), but the focus of the user may itself influence the classification.

For example, consider a situation in which a company enjoys the sources of funding shown in the table.

Ordinary share capital	£1,000,000
Preference share capital	£900,000
Revenue reserves	£2,000,000
Fixed cost 5-year bank loan	£100,000
Variable cost 1-year overdraft	£300,000
Current Liabilities	£200,000

It would be possible to construct ratios that assess the nature of the funding structure of the company in a variety of ways, each reflecting different characteristics of the relevant sources and the priorities of the users.

For instance, rather than a straightforward subdivision quantifying the relationship between debt and equity, management might want to quantify the ratio of short-term funding to long-term funding. This would give the following result:

$£300,000 + £200,000 : £1,000,000 + £900,000 + £2,000,000 + £100,000$

$= £500,000 : £4,000,000 \text{ (or } 1 : 8)$

Alternatively, if the user is a potential investor, he or she might be more concerned with the relationship between fixed-cost and variable cost sources, as this would enable an assessment of the likely security of dividends. In this case, since the potential investor would also have a long-term perspective, it would be usual to exclude Current Liabilities. (Although the "Variable cost 1 year overdraft" remains in the calculation on the grounds that such a facility is usually recurring, a similar argument could be made for its removal.) This would result in the following configuration:

$£900,000 + £100,000 : £1,000,000 + £2,000,000 + £300,000$

$= £1,000,000 : £3,300,000 \text{ (or } 1 : 3.3)$

Alternatively, a bank manager might want to assess the ratio of funds supplied to the company by the bank in which case an entirely different arrangement of these sources would be required. The point is that the ratios employed are flexible and should be configured in a way that respects the actual question being asked of the financial data.

Gearing Ratio

The most commonly used measure is the Gearing ratio, which quantifies the relationship between debt and equity at its most basic. The Gearing (or Debt/Equity) ratio can be expressed in a number of ways.

The approach most commonly employed simply quantifies the relationship between Debt (Loans, Debentures, Bonds and Preference Shares) and Equity. The higher the proportion of debt, then the more vulnerable the company is perceived to be since there is a high and fixed call on its profits before equity interests can be satisfied. A company with a relatively high level of debt would be termed "highly-geared" or "highly-leveraged".

The formula is:

$$\frac{\text{Debt}}{\text{Equity}} \times 100\%$$

In practice:

Using information from note 20 in the Annual Report, the figure for Tesco, based on Gross Debt (including amounts due within twelve months), is:

$$\frac{4,988}{9,057} \times 100\% = 55\%$$

(The numerator used here is the Gross Debt figure shown in note 20. Alternatively, the Net Debt figure shown in the same note – £3,842 – might be used. This is the figure that Tesco uses in its own presentations of gearing. Note 19 provides another alternative: £4,511, which is the Gross Debt figure less amounts shown in note 20 as due to be repaid within twelve months (471 + 6). Minority Interest, which is immaterial in size, is included as part of Equity.)

Based on information on page 21 of the IFRS restatement, the IFRS equivalent figure for Gross Debt (including amounts due within twelve months) is £ 4,567 + £ 482. Therefore the IFRS equivalent ratio is 5,049/8,657 = 58%. [Note: Tesco has availed of the option to delay applying IAS 32 and 39 until 2006.]

There are, therefore, a number of variations for this basic gearing calculation, and for comparison purposes it is necessary to determine the actual numerators and denominators used.

A commonly used variation of this Debt/Equity ratio simply expresses the Debt figure as a function of the total funding profile i.e., Debt + Equity.

The formula is:

$$\frac{\text{Debt}}{\text{Debt} + \text{Equity}} \times 100\%$$

In practice:

Based on the explanations provided above, the figure for Tesco is:

$$\frac{4,988}{4,988 + 9,057} \times 100\% = 35.5\%$$

The IFRS figure is: $5,049/(5,049 + 8,657) = 36.8\%$.

This confirms Tesco as a moderately geared firm with only slightly over one-third of its total funding requirement provided by non-equity sources.

Because they measure such an important element of corporate finance (and because many firms will find that they have little room in which to manoeuvre because of limits on borrowing imposed by debt covenants) these are critical measures that every company will want to present in as positive a light as possible. In outlining future strategy, therefore, it is important for CEOs to indicate the likely impact on measures such as gearing.

In practice:

IFRS hammers housebuilder, by Nicholas Neveling

George Wimpey's net assets have fallen by £107.7m, after the FTSE250 homebuilder restated its 2004 accounts to comply with international financial reporting standards.

George Wimpey said the fall in assets from £1.3bn would increase gearing from 36.8% to 39.1%.

The main cause of the drop was due to new accounting for pensions, which required the company to take the deficit of its defined-benefit scheme onto the balance sheet.

Speaking to Accountancy Age, George Wimpey's group finance director Andrew Carr-Locke said the increase in the gearing ratio was not of concern and would have no impact on the group's banking arrangements.

'The increase in gearing is not significant, but like other companies we have maintained our banking arrangements on existing UK GAAP to avoid uncertainty,' Carr-Locke said.

Source: Accountancy Age, June 23, 2005.

Debt to Total Assets ratio

Another ratio that relates to the financial structure of a company is the Debt to Total Assets ratio. This measures the percentage of total assets funded by debt. (On occasion, this ratio uses Net Assets as the denominator.)

The formula is:

$$\frac{\text{Total Debt}}{\text{Total Assets}} \times 100\%$$

In practice:

The figure for Tesco is:

$$\frac{4,988}{16,953 + 3,457} \times 100\% = 24.4\%$$

The IFRS figure is almost exactly the same: 5,049/(16,927 + 3,224) = 25%

In other words, only a small percentage – a quarter – of the total asset base of the company is funded by ongoing debt.

Weighted Average Cost of Capital (WACC)

As the term implies, WACC is a measure of the cost to the firm of its various sources of funding, computed in a way that respects the mix and relative importance of each type. In other words, it is an attempt to quantify the cost to the company of the funding mix that it employs. This will be different for different companies and industries and provides a useful basis for inter-company comparison.

It is usually computed by calculating the cost of each individual source and then weighting these according to their relative importance. The cost of each individual source can be determined using future projections or past experience. The former would be appropriate when assessing different funding possibilities for future investments, the latter when assessing the cost implications of gearing.

For example, assume that X plc is funded 75% by debt and 25% by equity (it is a 'high-geared' company) and that the cost of each source is 10% and 20%, respectively.

The WACC for X plc is:

$$(10\% \times 0.75) + (20\% \times 0.25) = 12.5\%$$

At its most simplistic it is possible to say that X plc requires a return on any investments it makes of at least 12.5% if it employs this funding structure. For the purposes of this discussion on financing it is sufficient to consider WACC as a useful, single-figure measure of the cost implications of a company's funding structure.

In practice:

The following extract explains how Malcolm Wyman, CFO of SABMillers, adopts a WACC approach to investment appraisal:

SABMiller was quick to expand out of South Africa when it was able, quick to get into China, and also, as it turns out, quick to adopt a financial methodology that would help it create value for shareholders, evaluate investment opportunities and reward senior managers. The group took on board the principles of Economic Value Added, or EVA [see Chapter 17]. The methodology puts the weighted-average cost of capital (WACC) at the heart of the company's investment criteria. The WACC for the group is 8.75%, but Wyman uses a "project-based" cost of capital rather than one number across the board. What that means is that for investment opportunities in some parts of Africa, for example – "which is a little bit more volatile and risky" – the hurdle rate could be in the "upper teens", whereas in the US it would be 7% or below.

Source: Financial Director, September 5, 2005.

Interest Cover

Financial ratios examine an entity's capital structure, and, as a result, its ability to satisfy debt obligations. Another, more immediate, measure of this is the Interest Cover ratio. This quantifies the capacity of the firm to meet interest payments due out of Operating Profits (or, on occasion, Profit before Interest and Tax).

The formula is:

$$\frac{\text{Operating Profit}}{\text{Interest expense}}$$

In practice:

The Operating Profits figure used is £1,949. It would also be acceptable to include Share of Operating Profit of Joint Ventures and Associates of £130m. Based on note 8, the interest payable figure is £269m. The figure shown on the face of the income statement (£170m) is after deducting income received by Tesco from its own investments. In order to get a truer picture of Tesco's interest obligations, most analysts' calculations are based on the actual interest paid of £269m. (It would also not be uncommon to adjust for "Interest Capitalized of £63m.) Based on these figures, the result for Tesco is:

$$\frac{1,949}{269} = 7.2 \, times$$

The IFRS equivalent information is available from page 5 of the IFRS Restatement. The figure used for Operating Profit above (£1,949m) is obtained by adjusting the Operating Profit of £2,002m shown there for Profit on disposal of fixed assets (£53m) – a non-operating income. The IFRS equivalent, therefore, is £1,909m (1,958−49). The interest paid figure of £234m is lower than that used above because of the adjustments to finance costs deriving from the change in accounting treatment under IFRS s – see IFRS Restatement, page 19. Using these numbers the IFRS equivalent is: $(1,909/234) = 8.1$ times. This is materially different and can be explained by the impact that IFRS has on the calculation of the figure to be included for interest paid.

This ratio quantifies the relationship between loan interest obligations and operating profit. It provides a measure of the confidence with which a lender may expect interest payments to be met. And, as with all ratios, whether this is an "acceptable" ratio or not will depend upon the comparative base against which it is considered.

In practice:

UBS: Measuring Leverage, by LEX

For humans, leverage is simply the balancing item between what they desire and what they can afford. Companies are more systematic, trading off a lower tax bill against higher risk to optimise their cost of capital. Yet when it comes to measuring leverage, no consensus exists. Which methodology is best?

Starting with the proportion of the capital base funded by debt seems sensible. Traditionalists compare net debt to book capital employed. The global strategists at UBS put this at 21 per cent currently, down from 28 per cent in 2000. The contemporary equivalent compares net debt to market-based enterprise value: globally, this is 15 per cent versus 14 per cent in 2000. These conflicting ratios point to a problem. Book values can be arbitrary – companies silly enough to base debt covenants on them have been hit by new accounting rules. But so can Evs [Economic Values]: in 2000, France Telecom looked under geared measured by net debt/EV.

The best alternative may still be interest cover, classically defined as underlying operating profit divided by net interest. This captures both the interest rate paid and, using depreciation as a proxy, maintenance reinvestment. Cover has improved from a low of 6.5 in 2001 to 12 today.

Source: Financial Times, September 19, 2005.

Interrelationship Between Activity, Liquidity, Gearing and Cash Flow

It is important when assessing the financial stability of a business to remember that it is the business as a whole that is being assessed, not just its component parts.

For example, focusing solely on the liquidity of a business to the exclusion of other considerations, would ignore the fact that this is only one element in the complex and interrelated financial mix which every business must manage. To concentrate on the gearing structure of a business to the exclusion of other factors would be similarly misguided.

What is required is a holistic perspective that recognizes not only the interplay between liquidity, gearing, activity and other measures, but also the need for a balanced portfolio of short, medium and long-term funding sources.

One consequence of a failure to maintain such a balance is "overtrading". As indicated in the previous chapter, this occurs where a business expands rapidly, but without due care being paid to the ways in which this expansion is financed. Eventually this translates into cash flow problems; usually when cash flow from trading activity is unable to sustain the repayments due on large and ill-advised loans.

The resulting mismatch can often lead to even profitable businesses being forced into retrenchment or liquidation. Such companies are often the target of corporate "carpetbaggers" – speculators who specialize in identifying profitable, but unwisely structured, companies that can be quickly turned around and resold.

In practice:

The following account of the trials of Jarvis plc – incorporating reference to working capital, cost cutting, debt restructuring, rights issues and debt-for-equity swap – emphasizes the need to adopt a holistic approach when analyzing a company's operational activity and its funding profile:

Jarvis shares fall as its debts pile up

Fears over the future of Jarvis reared up again yesterday when the ill-fated services group revealed that it had been forced to borrow a further £17m and would have to pay back more interest. Shares in the private finance initiative (PFI) player fell 30% at one point as the chief executive, Alan Lovell, admitted that Jarvis had "working capital issues" but declined to give details. A hefty rights issue or a debt-for-equity swap are under consideration as Jarvis struggles with a £280m debt mountain, which will rise by up to £3m as a result of yesterday's move.

Mr Lovell insisted that a deal with major lenders for more cash should be seen as positive, even though it involved a change in the finance arrangements. "These agreements are positive steps which demonstrate the ongoing support of our lending group," he said in a formal stock market statement, adding that the main cost-cutting was completed. But the fact that the firm needed more money to help with working capital and a wider restructuring only served to unnerve investors used to unwanted surprises.

At the end of January, Mr Lovell celebrated the signing of binding documentation with Royal Bank of Scotland, Barclays and others to extend debt facilities for 12 months. It had also sold its stake in Tube Lines, one of the companies running parts of the London Underground, to its partner Amey for £147m. Jarvis has handed some of its stalled hospital and schools PFI projects to third parties and set its sights on prospering as a much smaller road and rail services company to be based in York rather than London. That switch has already meant the departure of its finance director, Alistair Rae, and its public relations boss, Jonathan Haslam, a former spin-doctor for the then Conservative leader John Major.

Mike Foster, an analyst with KBC Peel Hunt, said: "Clearly the shares are likely to open lower but the important point is the ongoing support of the banks and the robust cost-cutting allied to healthy operating profits in the continuing divisions looking forward." Michael Donnelly, of

Bridgewell Securities, was less forgiving. "Is Jarvis going to be a recovery story? Is it worth the risk? Probably not," he bluntly told Reuters.

Jarvis is in a £50m-a year cost-cutting exercise and KBC is forecasting a "good possibility" that the firm will be able to record ebita [earnings before interest tax and amortisation] profits of £30m for the year to March 2007. Before then there must be another major refinancing and this could come as early as the next three to four months. "One thing we would probably contemplate is a heavy rights issue and I've talked previously about a new strategic investor ... picking up some part of the equity and some of our existing shareholders expressed some interest," said Mr Lovell, who joined in October. He added that a debt-for-equity swap would be considered if banks were underwriting a proportion of it.

Source: *The Guardian, March 30, 2005.*

Summary

There is a large and growing range of funding options available to modern businesses, including a range of new financial instruments, such as derivatives. However, for convenience these can be classified as either "equity" or "debt". The key is that businesses must ensure a balanced portfolio.

It will be important for every company to be able to calculate and express its dependence on each of these sources. This is done by means of ratios that quantify the relative weightings of debt and equity in a way that allows a company to assess its risk profile in comparison to other companies.

Such an assessment is one important ingredient in interpreting the position and performance of a business. It allows insights to be gleaned not only into the financial structure of the business, but into the relative power and influence of the providers of debt and equity. This in turn allows a more nuanced appreciation of related corporate governance issues since much of the "balance-of-power" manoeuvring that goes on in companies can be traced to clashes between these two vested interests.

Review Questions

Question 1
"When raising finance, it is imperative that the funding being considered should be appropriate in terms of both time-scale and structure. One would not attempt to fund a new factory with an overdraft". Explain the funding implications of this statement.

Question 2
Distinguish between "Equity" and "Debt" and explain why this distinction is necessary.

Question 3
What particular issues are raised by preference shares when considering whether they should be classified as "Equity" of "Debt".

Question 4
Identify and distinguish between the various types of preference share that a company can issue. Consider the particular challenges posed by "Redeemable Preference Shares" for a company's future funding requirements.

Question 5
Why is there such a range of preference shares available? Identify investors for whom each type might hold attractions.

Question 6
Derivatives have emerged in recent years as a complex form of financing. Identify the unique characteristics of this type of funding and explain some of the accounting-specific issues that they raise.

Question 7
Explain the regulatory challenges, if any, that are posed by the proliferation of hedge funds.

Question 8
Identify the unique characteristics of bonds as a form of funding and explain why they have become established as an alternative to bank funding for companies.

Question 9
Assess the usefulness of gearing as a measure of risk.

Question 10
Explain the importance of understanding the interrelationship between Activity, Liquidity, Gearing and Cashflow issues when interpreting a company's financial position and performance.

Case Studies

Case 1

The ratios for Tesco 2005 have been given throughout this chapter under the various headings covered. Go to the company website, access the 2006 Annual Report, and compute the equivalent ratios for that year. These can be checked against the report for that year available on the website for this text.

Case 2

The IASB and the EU Commission have been embroiled in conflict over IAS 39, *Financial Instruments: Recognition and Measurement*. Essentially, IFRS would require both increased disclosure of financial instruments and fair value measurement of risks and underlying assets and liabilities. The financial services industry in Europe, and in particular banks, are resisting this strenuously. The following article outlines some of the issues involved. Consider the extent to which political input of the type described should be allowed to impact accounting standards.

Under Scrutiny

Spats with the EU have put the IASB's Standard-setting Processes in the Limelight, by Liz Fisher

The world's attention will be focused on the International Accounting Standards Board during the coming months, as the psychologically important year of 2005 unravels. Whether they are prepared or not (and the available evidence suggests that many are not), listed companies in the European Union will have to prepare their financial statements under International Financial Reporting Standards from this point onwards. Many people, as a result, are suddenly waking up for the first time to the activities of the IASB.

In the public eye: The board and its umbrella body, the IASC Foundation, are no doubt conscious that their discussions and decisions will be examined with increasing interest from now on. If the press coverage of recent months is any indication, it should not expect an easy ride. In the relatively dry environment of accounting standard setting, colourful spats such as the recent disagreements between the European Commission and the IASB over the financial instruments standard IAS 39 make, unfortunately, an eye-catching headline.

Whatever the feelings behind the scenes, the board itself, under chairman Sir David Tweedie, gives the strong impression that it is business as usual, in spite of increasing tension between the EC and the standard-setter. The 2005 deadline imposed by the EC for the implementation of IFRS in Europe looked, a few years ago, like a tough target to meet but the IASB has been largely successful.

True, its 'stable platform' of standards – a window during which the core standards would not be amended – has wobbled on occasion but with one notable exception, the major requirements have been met on time.

The trouble with IAS 39: The disagreements with the EC over IAS 39 have undoubtedly scarred the IASB and the standard-setting process. The EC's decision to issue its own version of the standard with the more controversial elements carved out, has created confusion among users. US analyst Pat McConnell told the Standards Advisory Council recently that her clients had told her that the episode had seriously damaged the credibility of the standard, with many users unsure whether the full version was any better than the EC's version.

Even so, IASB member Bob Garnett told the same meeting that larger banks in Europe were likely to adopt the full version of the standard, since any using the carved-out version may be treated with scepticism by investors.

While moves go on behind the scenes to improve relations between the EC and the IASB, in public the impression remains that the EC would like to have more control over the standard-setting process. In January, Charles McCreevy, the EU internal market commissioner, told the Financial Times that the standard-setting process was 'very complicated' and was not purely a technical exercise. The question of the IASB's accountability would have to be addressed, he said.

The IASB took an additional blow in December when the independent European Financial Reporting Advisory Group (EFRAG) failed to endorse an IFRIC interpretation on emission rights. The issue was complicated by the fact that EFRAG members felt that IFRIC had come to the correct conclusions when interpreting the requirements of existing standards but were concerned about the volatility that would be caused by those requirements. In other words, EFRAG disagreed with the existing accounting requirements in standards that had already been endorsed by the EC.

EFRAG is due to discuss its concerns with the IASB before formally releasing its advice and it remains to be seen what the implications will be if it refuses to endorse the interpretation.

Source: *Accountancy*, March 2005.

Case 3

Securitization as a means of generating funding was mentioned briefly earlier in this chapter. The following article provides more detail on securitization, as well as outlining some of the accounting issues that it raises, including off-balance sheet financing. Consider the implications of the sentiment with which the article concludes, i.e. that "Financing methods that are flattered by international standards today may appear in a very different light tomorrow". Are there other areas of accounting practice to which this view might apply?

Instruments Struggle with Stricter Rules

The New Accounting Standards are Forcing Companies to Reassess their Use of Convertible Bonds and Securitisation, writes Barney Jopson

In early 2002, and to much self-generated fanfare, the French marketing services group Publicis sold €690m of convertible bonds in an offering billed as an "unprecedented success". In early 2005, and to a different kind of fanfare, the French group had a change of heart and said it wanted to scrap the lot. Investors were given an enticing offer to redeem the convertibles years before their 2018 maturity so Publicis could replace them with €750m (£520m) of plain-vanilla bonds.

The about-turn, a dramatic example of how companies can flit between financial instruments, was triggered in part by the advent of international accounting standards in the European Union. The new rules force companies to change the way they account for convertibles – bonds that investors can exchange for the issuer's shares – and are making companies reconsider their merits.

The new standards also put a different complexion on securitization, a technique by which claims on future cash flows are packaged into securities for sale to investors. Together the changes affect a key area of corporate policy: how companies raise money in the capital markets. The trend belies the notion that accounting standards do not influence corporate behaviour.

With convertibles, the rethink stems from an accounting technique that increases the charges they produce in the income statement. In the past, convertibles have been accounted for as straight bonds. But international standards, which encourage precision to the point of pedantry, demand that companies split the debt and equity components. A convertible valued at €100 should appear as €80 of liabilities together with a share option worth €20.

It sounds reasonable, but it creates a problem for companies. The €100 they have to pay back to investors is now greater than the €80 on their balance sheet and that difference has to be written off gradually every year. Nothing changes in reality, because the write-off is a non-cash charge, but cosmetically things look worse. Publicis says: "We were not happy to have our interest charges rise going forward."

In the Netherlands, Numico, a baby-food maker, has stood by its convertibles, but had to warn investors this month that the additional charge would have cut 21 per cent from its 2004 net income of €145m. Analysts say the favourable accounting treatment of convertibles was one reason for their popularity. And although issuance is slowing as corporate Europe cuts debt, the end of that advantage is likely to be a further blow to the market.

Publicis, however, has emphasised a higher motive for switching to straight bonds: simplicity. "We had received criticism about the clarity of our balance sheet and the clarity of earnings per share," said Publicis, "and we thought there might be a discount on the share price associated with that." Here lies one of the unintended consequences of international accounting standards. By requiring financial structures to be shown in all their mind-bending complexity – causing headaches for preparers and readers of accounts – the standards encourage the use of more comprehensible alternatives. ''There is a price for complexity now,'' says Adrian Marsh, group treasurer at AstraZeneca, the Anglo-Swedish pharmaceuticals group. ''You have to get people to understand all the accounting implications. Ultimately, you will still do what is in your best economic interests, but you have to be clear about why.''

In the case of securitization, too, the demand for clarity makes it more difficult for companies to get the accounting result they want. For many, the main purpose of securitization is raising finance – from trade receivables, mortgages or any other asset – which is often cheaper than issuing bonds or equity. But it also allows assets to be shifted off-balance sheet because companies are giving away some of the risks and rewards they carry. That can give balance sheets an alluring slimness.

But international accounting standards are undoing the hard work. Stricter rules demand companies demonstrate a more definitive transfer of risk and rewards – and, as many fail to do so, assets and the associated liabilities are coming hurtling back into the accounts. Telecom Italia has seen €700m of debt swept back and Lafarge, the French building materials group, has been compelled to reabsorb €183m of debt linked to its receivables. Other companies are scrambling to restructure securitizations so they stay off-balance sheet. ''They are reasonable rules, but they make life more difficult,'' says Gilles Saint Marc, a securitization lawyer with Gide Loyrette Nouel in Paris. ''The negative impact of these vehicles coming back on balance sheet is that it leads to a significant deterioration in financial ratios. That can have consequences, such as a downgrading of credit ratings or the termination of credit facilities.''

For European equity investors, supposedly the main beneficiaries of international accounting standards, the new approaches to securitization and convertibles are a mixed blessing. Less arcane financial wizardry and more realistic accounts should be welcomed. But they come at a price. In real terms, issuing straight bonds can turn out to be more expensive than convertibles. Ditching one set of securities for another costs money, as does restructuring securitization vehicles. The implications of not restructuring them can be even worse.

Perhaps all that could be taken as a one-off sacrifice for accounting harmonization? Sadly not. Despite the deceptive solidity of the accounting rule book, much of its contents remain fluid. Financing methods that are flattered by international standards today may appear in a very different light tomorrow.

Source: *Financial Times*, March 24, 2005.

PROFITABILITY AND RETURN ON INVESTMENT

When you have completed this chapter you will understand:

- The importance of profits to a business.
- The usefulness of the various profitability ratios that have been developed.
- That return on investment ratios have been developed that enable investors to assess their return.
- The importance, and limitations, of earnings per share (EPS) as a measure of performance.
- The nature and role of dividends.
- The increasing importance of share buybacks
- The need to consider profitability and return on investment ratios in an overall context.

Investors Look for Action on Cash as Top Footsie Groups Prepare to Reveal all

Nine Companies Unveil Results Tomorrow. But How They Plan to Use Their Spare Money is Key, reports Henry Tricks

Those who work in the City will set their alarm clocks especially early tomorrow. That is because at 7am, trading screens will light up with the annual results of nine companies whose combined market capitalisation of £100bn accounts for almost 10 per cent of the FTSE 100. After an earnings season that has, so far, been surprisingly positive, the busiest reporting day in the calendar might be reason to head to work with a spring in the step – all but one of the companies is expected to announce strong earnings increases.

But this week, the spectre of higher interest rates will lead to close scrutiny of the outlook for Royal Bank of Scotland, the largest company to report on Thursday, which is exposed to interest rate rises in the US and UK. Higher interest rates also erode the relative attraction of high-yielding equities, such as utilities, which investors have gorged upon recently. That fuels a debate that has been running through the markets this year – should companies return spare cash to shareholders or invest it in profitable growth opportunities? Analysts say such a conundrum will resurface on Thursday in discussions about Centrica, the energy company, and Hanson, part of the fast-consolidating building materials sector. Other FTSE 100 companies to issue annual results that day are BAE Systems, the defence and aerospace company, Legal & General, the insurer, Hilton, the hotel group, Rentokil Initial and Capita, the support services companies, and Alliance UniChem, the chemical group.

After paying down debt in the wake of the dotcom boom, many of these companies have healthy balance sheets and one of the key issues will be how they plan to use their spare cash. Akber Khan, strategist at Deutsche Bank, says: "The question over the next few weeks is, are people going to start rewarding companies who are investing in growth, or do people still want the safety of those who are aggressively returning cash to shareholders?"

...Two companies that analysts say enjoy solid growth prospects as well as throwing off cash report on Thursday – Centrica and Hanson. Elaine Bucknell, utilities analyst at Brewin Dolphin, says Centrica's pay-out ratio is increasing while growth rates are in double digits. Hanson, meanwhile, is at the heart of an industry that is in the throes of consolidation at racy multiples following Cemex's takeover of RMC, and Holcim's of Aggregate Industries. Though asbestos liabilities are a potential poison pill against an unwanted takeover, some analysts believe Hanson will have to increase in size through a large acquisition to ward off interest from potential predators, such as Lafarge. Darren Shaw, construction analyst at Dresdner Kleinwort Wasserstein, says Hanson has the cash either to make acquisitions or fill shareholders' pockets. "People want cash back or they want deals," he says. "The worst thing is for them to do nothing. People want to see action."

Source: *Financial Times*, February 23, 2005.

Introduction

Earnings... surplus cash... and what to do with it!! Return it to investors by means of dividends and share buybacks or use it to finance acquisitions? These are just some of the issues facing companies that manage their resources well.

Providers of funds invest in a company with a view to earning a return on that investment. This return can come in many forms, for example, profits, interest, dividends or capital appreciation. Investors will, therefore, want to assess the performance of the company in this regard. This will require that they examine it under the following headings:

- Profitability
- Return on investment
- Payout policy: dividends and share buybacks.

Profitability

Measures of profitability will be important for a variety of users. (This is in spite of David Tweedie's comparison of profit with a haggis: "if you knew what was in it, you wouldn't touch it with a barge pole".) For example, shareholders will want to be reassured that the firm will be able to generate and sustain profits from which to distribute dividends. Banks and other lending institutions will also be interested in profitability since it will affect the company's liquidity, its capacity to finance debt and, ultimately, its ability to repay loans.

It is for this reason that a variety of measures and ratios have been developed.

Gross Profit Rate (Margin)

This is a significant ratio because it focuses on measuring that element of profit over which the firm has greatest control. This has much to do with pricing policy and interpretation of the results will need to be informed by sensitivity to the mix of activities within a company. For this reason it may be advisable to calculate rates for each segment of activity where possible. Industry averages will usually be available. The denominator most commonly used is Revenue. However, Cost of Sales would be equally valid and would yield a result called "Gross Mark-up".

The formula is:

$$\frac{\text{Gross profit}}{\text{Revenue}} \times 100\%$$

In Practice:

Based on additional information provided in note 3, the figure for Tesco is:

$$\frac{2,703}{33,974} \times 100\% = 7.9\%$$

The IFRS equivalent, based on figures provided on page 5 of the IFRS Restatement is $(2,664/33,974) \times 100\% = 7.84\%$.

Gross Profit Rate is an important measure of profitability for a number of reasons:

- It provides an easily understandable measure of the profitability of the main activity of the business.

- It relates the impact of direct costs, such as raw materials, to revenue

- It would be expected to remain relatively consistent over time.

- Industry averages provide a ready comparative base.

In practice:

P&G tackles rising cost of raw materials, by Jeremy Grant

Procter & Gamble yesterday delivered a 9 per cent rise in fourth-quarter earnings on booming global sales of Pampers nappies, Crest toothpaste and Tide detergent but the company's shares fell as gross margins were affected by rising raw material costs. The results showed that the largest US consumer goods company had managed to use price rises and higher sales to offset some, but not all, commodity and energy costs. Net income rose to $1.5bn (£850m), or 56 cents a share, from $1.37bn, or 50 cents, a year earlier. Sales grew by 10 per cent to $14bn in the quarter...

"Gross margin came in below expectations despite better pricing, as the difficult cost environment may be getting worse," he said. P&G's gross margins in the quarter slipped to 48.9 per cent from 50 per cent a year ago. P&G's shares were 1 per cent lower at $55 by midday in New York.

Source: Financial Times, August 2, 2005.

Operating Profit Rate (Margin)

Operating Profit rate is another important measure of business performance and provides a useful basis for comparing the company's performance with competitors or industry averages.

The formula is:

$$\frac{\text{Operating Profit}}{\text{Revenue}} \times 100\%$$

In practice:

Using the Operating Profit figures calculated in the previous chapter, the figure for Tesco is:

$$\frac{1{,}949}{33{,}974} \times 100\% = 5.7\%$$

The IFRS equivalent is (1,909/33,974) × 100% = 5.6%.

Note: Tesco's own calculation of Operating Margin is shown in note 2. It is essentially the same as calculated here, but uses Operating Profit of £2,064m, i.e., before goodwill amortisation and integration costs. The figures are: (2,064/33,974) × 100% = 6.1%.

Operating Profit rate, although important, is usually considered to be less informative than the gross profit rate because, given the range of expenses and other income that go into its calculation, it is much more difficult for the business to control. Nevertheless, declines in margin would suggest poor performance and should be of concern to shareholders, bankers and management.

Other profit figures

The structure of the income statement allows for the calculation of other 'profit' figures. For instance, one common measure is 'Profit before Interest and Taxation' (PBIT). This equals profits after including all income and costs, but before allowing for those with claims on profits and is something called 'net' profit. Those with claims include lenders (interest), government (taxation) and shareholders (dividends).

The formula is:

$$\frac{\text{Profit on activities before interest and taxation (PBIT)}}{\text{Revenue}} \times 100\%$$

In practice:

Based on information provided in the income statement for Tesco, the figures are:

$$\frac{2,132}{33,974} \times 100\% = 6.3\%$$

Based on the page 5 of the IFRS Restatement, the PBIT = £2,027(1,958 + 69). Therefore, the equivalent figure is (2,027/33,974) × 100% = 6%. The main reason for the difference is the reduced share of post-tax profits from joint ventures and associates allowed under IAS 28 and 31.

Another commonly used refinement of profit is 'Earnings before Interest, Taxation, Depreciation and Amortisation (EBITDA).' This figure is provided on page 5 of the Tesco IFRS restatement. (Because of the range of items excluded, EBITDA is sometimes dismissed as 'Earnings before the Bad Stuff'!)

In practice:

As the following explains, profit margin is a critical element in analyzing corporate performance. This is often more obvious in those industries where there are established benchmarks:

Nissan's profits hit by rising cost of raw materials, by David Ibison

Nissan Motor has reported its first full-year drop in operating profit margin in the six years since Carlos Ghosn took control of the company, underlining the impact that rising raw material prices are having on carmakers' profitability. The Japanese manufacturer yesterday reported record results for 2004, saying revenues rose by 15 per cent, net profit grew 1.7 per cent, sales 10.8 per cent and production increased 10.2 per cent. However, the operating profit margin dropped from 11.1 per cent to 10 per cent.

... Nissan's operating profit margin has risen from 1.4 per cent in 1999 to 11.1 per cent last year and, despite the drop to 10 per cent last year and an expected fall to 9.7 per cent in 2005, it remains one of the world's most profitable bulk carmakers.

Its performance also contrasts with its US rivals. Last week, General Motors reported a first quarter loss of $1.1bn (£570m), one of the worst in its history, and Ford Motor said earnings fell 38 per cent in the first quarter.

Source: Financial Times, April 26, 2005.

Return on Investment

While profit ratios quantify the relationship between profits and revenue, Return on Investment (RoI) ratios look at the link between profits and the investment required to generate them.

This will be an important measure for those who have supplied finance to a firm, whether in the form of equity or debt. Indeed, one of the characteristics of the RoI formula is that it can be used to measure the return on investment as a whole, or the return enjoyed by one particular element of the capital base. To achieve this it is critical that there be a direct relationship between the denominator (capital employed) and the numerator (i.e., earnings appropriate to the source(s) forming the denominator).

Return on Capital Employed (ROCE)

The most commonly employed RoI measure is Return on Capital Employed (ROCE). At its most basic ROCE measures return in terms of profit before interest and tax (PBIT) as a function of total capital employed.

The basic formula, using what Tesco identify as Capital Employed at the end of the balance sheet, is:

$$\frac{\text{PBIT}}{\text{Capital Employed}} \times 100\%$$

In practice:

On the basis of this approach, the result for Tesco is:

$$\frac{2,132}{9,057} \times 100\% = 23.5\%$$

The IFRS equivalent is: (2,027/8,657) × 100% = 23.4%

Typically, however, total capital employed is taken to mean total long term funding and does not necessarily correspond to the Total Capital Employed figure shown at the end of a balance sheet. In that case the formula would be:

$$\frac{\text{PBIT}}{\text{Long-term Debt} + \text{Equity}} \times 100\%$$

In practice:

Using figures for long-term debt (notes 19 and 20 – see also discussion of these points in Chapter 9) and equity, the figure for Tesco is:

$$\frac{2,132}{4,511 + 9,057} \times 100\% = 15.7\%$$

The IFRS equivalent is: (2,027/(4,567 + 8,657)) × 100% = 15.3%

While these calculations follow a standard adopted by most analysts, a number of alternative ROCE formulae exist. For instance, the denominator can also be the average for the year in question. Others would include all sources of funding, i.e., equity, current liabilities, non-current liabilities and provisions for liabilities in the calculation of Capital Employed. Others take an investment perspective and argue that Capital Employed should relate to the asset base of the entity.

Tesco itself presents a headline figure for ROCE of 11.5% (IFRS: 11.6%.) The manner in which this is calculated is explained in footnote 5 on page 65 of the Annual Report.

As long as the unique approaches that individual firms adopt are appreciated, ROCE can be useful for inter-firm comparison as it provides a good, albeit crude, assessment of the efficiency with which management in different firms use the funds entrusted to them.

In practice:
_____

The following account outlines both the application of the ROCE ratio to BOC and some reservations about its usefulness:

BOC still has what it takes to fuel investor interest, by Robert Cole

Return on capital employed (ROCE) is a good measure of corporate performance. Some say it is the crucial measure and since it tracks how much money is made on invested capital the fans have a point.

ROCE has its drawbacks, however. The first is that different companies have different capital requirements and this means it is hard to compare between enterprises. It is pretty difficult to draw meaningful conclusions from the ROCE numbers posted by companies in the same industrial sector, let alone businesses that are wholly dissimilar. Moreover, if the importance of ROCE is overblown it may lead managers to under-invest in businesses because that will flatter the result. A concentration on ROCE may also lead investors away from pledging cash to capital-intensive industries. And that is silly, and damaging to wider economic interests, because it suggests advertising agencies and lawyers are, de facto, better than bakers and boilermakers.

The return on capital employed by BOC, the industrial gases group, sits at 16 per cent. BOC is not the most capital-intensive business one could imagine but it requires more hardware than most. A string of well-publicized investments in recent years indicates that BOC has not stinted on its responsibility to keep its production facilities up to date and efficient. In this context BOC's 16 per cent ROCE is impressive, especially since the number has risen from 12 per cent over the past four years...

Source: The Times, February 2, 2005.

Relationship Between ROCE and Other Ratios

In the initial calculation of ROCE for Tesco plc above, capital employed as indicated by Tesco was used. However, it was also pointed out that it could also take an asset focus. For instance, sometimes ROCE is computed as:

$$\frac{\text{PBIT}}{\text{Net Assets Employed}}$$

Based on the balance sheet figure, the Net Assets Employed by Tesco amount to £9,057m.

From this it is possible to demonstrate that ROCE is actually the product of two other ratios: Net Profit Rate and Asset Turnover (which was covered in Chapter 8).

i.e.

ROCE = Net Profit Rate × Asset Turnover

i.e.

$$ROCE = \frac{PBIT}{Revenue} \times \frac{Revenue}{Net\ Assets\ Employed}$$

i.e.

$$ROCE = \frac{PBIT}{Net\ Assets\ Employed}$$

This can be demonstrated from the results calculated so far for Tesco:

$$ROCE = \frac{2,132}{33,974} \times \frac{33,974}{9,057} = \frac{2,132}{9,057} = 23.5\%$$

This is the same result as calculated for basic ROCE above.

The significance of this is that it allows the elements that together constitute ROCE to be isolated, enabling a more strategic targeting of particular aspects of company performance. If ROCE can be shown to be a product of net margin and the efficiency with which assets are managed, then obviously improvements in these will automatically lead to an improvement in the overall ROCE.

Return on Equity

The basic ROCE formula can be amended to take account of variations in the denominator. For instance, if what is being assessed is the return earned by equity, then the figure above the line will be the profit available to equity.

In these circumstances the formula will be:

$$\frac{Profit\ after\ interest,\ tax\ and\ preference\ dividends}{Equity\ (Ordinary\ Shareholders\ Funds)} \times 100\%$$

In practice:

The figure for Tesco is:

$$\frac{1,366}{9,006} \times 100\% = 15.2\%$$

(Note: Minority Interest is not included here as part of either the numerator or denominator. However, IFRS 3 requires that Minority Interest now be classified as Equity. In these circumstances it would be acceptable to include it in calculations of ROE. In any case, Minority Interest is not a material concern for Tesco.)

The IFRS equivalent, based on figures on pages 5 and 7, is: $(1,347/8,606) \times 100\% = 15.6\%$. The difference is due to the various IFRS adjustments to Retained Earnings indicated on page 21.

As with all other ratios, it will be important to identify a comparator constructed in a similar manner in order to appreciate the real significance of any ROE score.

In practice:

Deutsche bank cuts 6,400 jobs

Hundreds of City jobs at Deutsche Bank will be axed this year and the UK asset management business could be sold under a €1.2bn (£820m) cost-cutting plan to raise the bank's return on equity to 25% and propel it back up the global league, it emerged yesterday.

Josef Ackermann, chief executive, said in Frankfurt that 3,300 more jobs would go this year on top of the 1,900 in Germany announced in December. In addition, 1,200 would be "smart-sourced" from high-cost to low-cost locations such as eastern Europe and India, but also to cheaper cities in western Europe.

The bank refused to comment on reports that about 1,000 of the 6,400 redundancies would be in London but Mr Ackermann said 3,700 would be in back-office units and 2,700 in corporate and investment banking, and asset management, with the latter heavily based in the City.

The Swiss executive, who announced a 50% rise in pre-tax earnings last year to €4.1bn, has set his sights on achieving a 25% return on equity this year despite much investor scepticism. He said Deutsche made a return of 17% last year – or 19% before reorganization charges of €574m. It is now ranked only 23rd among global banks and 11th in Europe, where it was once the largest.

Source: The Guardian, February 4, 2005.

The following extract, particularly in referring to various macro economic and political issues, makes some interesting observations on the role of ROE and related considerations such as earnings quality:

Return on Equity, by Lex

According to Joseph Schumpeter, capitalism will eventually be destroyed by its own success, notably the rise of monopolistic giants. If consensus forecasts in the global equity markets are to be believed, the end must be drawing nigh. The world's listed companies are expected to generate a return on equity of 16 per cent in 2005.

At almost twice the cost of equity, this is inconsistent with both historic levels and healthy competition. Unless barriers to entry are high, excessive returns in any one sector attract new competitors. On an economy-wide basis, high returns induce fresh investment, generating overcapacity and deflation. In both instances, margins and returns should fall rapidly to more sustainable levels.

This need not happen if high returns on equity merely reflect inflated reported profits. There are signs that deteriorating earnings quality partly explains recent improvements in the US. But national income statistics – which tend to be more reliable, because they are based on tax accounts – also suggest that adjusted corporate profits relative to gross domestic product are approaching levels not seen since the 1920s. Meanwhile in Europe, estimated operating margins of 11 per cent this year are about 40 per cent above long-term averages.

The decline of organized labour has no doubt helped US Inc capture an increased share of national income. Similarly, European companies have benefited from improved bargaining power, with recent labour market reforms adding to pressure on unions. But none of this means that all the world's companies are now playing monopoly. Flexible labour markets make it harder for firms to collude in product markets – and easier for entrepreneurs to get started. Increased international competition also translates into pricing pressures. Globalization looks more like a gale of creative destruction than a bringer of monopoly power – just ask handset manufacturers, chipmakers or others fretting about Chinese competition.

All this suggests earnings growth is more likely to fall behind global economic growth than to outstrip it over the next few years. It also leaves investors who cheer on as companies outbid each other with unrealistic return targets looking short-sighted.

Source: *Financial Times*, February 28, 2005.

Earnings Per Share (EPS)

EPS is a widely used, if somewhat crude, measure of business performance. At its simplest it expresses earnings as a function of the total number of ordinary shares in issue. In accordance with IAS 33, *Earnings per Share*, EPS must be disclosed on the face of the income statement.

The formula is:

$$\frac{\text{Earnings (Profit)}}{\text{Weighted number of equity shares in issue}}$$

In spite of the fact that many regulators, investors and most analysts advise against placing too much dependence upon any single indicator of performance, companies and executives commonly advocate the use of EPS as a critical measure of company performance. In any case, it is the rate of growth in EPS, rather that the EPS *per se*, that is really critical.

IAS 33 requires that figures for basic and diluted earnings per share be presented on the face of the income statement in respect of each class of ordinary share that has a different right to share in the profit or loss of the period. The numerators and denominators of the calculations presented should also be disclosed and reconciled, respectively, to the net profit or loss for the period and weighted average number of shares used. It is acceptable for companies to disclose earnings per share figures computed according to other methodologies provided that they are not presented on the face of the income statement, they use the weighted average number of shares determined in accordance with IAS 33 and, where a net profit figure used is not a line item in the income statement, a reconciliation is provided between the figure used and a line item in the income statement.

In practice:

The EPS for Tesco, in its various forms, is provided at the end of the income statement. The manner in which it is calculated is explained in more detail in Note 11. Likewise the IFRS equivalent is provided at the end of the Restated IFRS income statement on page 5.

Basic EPS

Basic earnings per share is a measure of past performance, calculated by dividing the earnings attributable to ordinary shareholders by the weighted average number of ordinary shares outstanding during the period.

Under IAS 33 the weighted average number of ordinary shares outstanding during the period should reflect the fact that the amount of shareholders' capital may have changed during the period as a result of a larger or lesser number of shares being outstanding (i.e., in issue) at any time.

Diluted EPS

The inclusion of diluted EPS is a recognition of the fact that most companies now have share option schemes in operation for both executives and employees which, when vested and exercised could have a substantial diluting effect on the earnings per share. For the purpose of calculating diluted EPS, therefore, the net profit attributable to ordinary shareholders and the weighted average of shares outstanding should be adjusted for the potential dilutive effects of all such schemes.

In practice:

Companies 'are missing EPS forecasts'

In the third quarter of 2003, nearly 170 of companies in the S&P500 either exceeded or fell short of EPS estimates, says the poll by financial management consultancy Parson Consulting. It shows 17.5% of companies fell short, while 25.6% exceeded estimates by at least 10%. Financial services firms, such as banks and insurance companies, came closest to performing to forecasts, as 68% met expectations within 10 percentage points. However, materials, energy and utility companies register the most difficulty meeting analysts' forecasts, with 28.3% of them missing.

Source: Accountancy, February 11, 2004.

A word of caution is important in relation to EPS: it is the least suitable of all ratios for inter-firm comparison. This derives mainly from the fact that the capital bases of firms will differ dramatically, with the result that it is not possible to compare across entities. Thus, the simplicity of EPS is, in many senses, offset by its unsuitability for identifying any variations between firms. To overcome this, many analysts use EPS growth to compare across businesses and sectors.

In practice:

The following extract relating to Marks & Spencer highlights some of the problematic aspects of using EPS, as well as identifying a commonly used alternative, Total Shareholder Return (TSR), which is discussed later in this chapter:

Is M&S's board cavalier or just incompetent? By Robert Peston

The underpinning of the conventional way to value shares is what a company earns for each of its shares in issue, or its earnings per share (eps). As a theory, it's hard to fault: any investor would wish to know how much of a business's profit belongs in a notional sense to each unit of ownership. The problem is that, in practice, eps is a nebulous statistic. Take, as one example, the latest report and accounts of Marks & Spencer. There are six different numbers in its accounts, all purporting to be the eps for the year that ended on April 2, 2005. There's standard earnings per share, of 29.1p. Then there is diluted earnings per share, to take account of shares that are likely to be issued under share option schemes – which is a bit lower, at 28.9p. Also, there's "adjusted" eps, which adds back exceptional losses and takes away exceptional profits. It's an even smaller number: 21.9p. And there's a diluted version, which is 21.7p. Finally there is adjusted earnings from "continuing" operations (or those that haven't been sold or closed) which is 20.4p – and a diluted version of 20.2p.

So which tells us most about M&S's intrinsic profitability? Well, the biggest number, 29.1p, is the mandatory one under accounting rules. But it doesn't say much about the long-term earning power of M&S's existing assets. In fact the smaller numbers, adjusted earnings generated by the operations that M&S still owns, are a better indicator of core profit.

So far, so academic. However, there is a practical reason for stumbling around in this darkling accounting forest – which is that Marks & Spencer has just reinstated growth in eps as its primary measure of success. It has decided that targets for eps increases should determine rewards for senior executives in its new long-term incentive plan and its executive share option plan – which is a bold reform, as it goes against the grain of what most other companies have been doing and what M&S itself had been doing. The norm in most businesses is to judge success on the basis of the total return generated for shareholders – the change in the share price plus any dividends paid – compared with the total return generated by the company's main rivals and sometimes also by the stock market as a whole. The advantage of using relative total shareholder return, or TSR, is that it is an unambiguous number – dividends are paid in hard cash and a share price is an objective reality.

This is not to make the naive case that TSR cannot be manipulated. Unscrupulous execs can time the release of bullish news – or indeed concoct bullish news – for the perfect moment when a blip up in the share price lifts relative TSR from a smidgeon below the payout threshold to just above. Hey presto, a long-term incentive plan suddenly pays out a bundle. And there are other defects with relative TSR. A share price can move for reasons unconnected to the competence of the management. And it's a bit odd, perhaps, to reward managers for something they cannot control over more than the very short term, viz the share price.

That said, there are bigger defects in using eps as the be-all and end-all. For one thing, its calculation is opaque. It can be higher or lower depending on all sorts of subjective decisions made by a company about whether costs should be written off or capitalised, whether profits or losses are exceptional and should therefore be excluded from the relevant measure, and even whether a sale or a cost should be booked this year or next year. What's more, there's plenty of scope to indulge in financial engineering to pump up earnings per share – such as the simple device of borrowing cash to buy in shares that are on a relatively low rating (not necessarily a bad thing, but should it trigger rewards for directors)?. . .

Source: Sunday Telegraph, July 17, 2005.

Price/Earnings Ratio

While there are some difficulties in using EPS itself, it is a very important element in computing the Price/Earnings ratio, one of the most useful measures of company performance. The Price/Earnings (P/E) ratio measures the relationship between the earnings of a company and the stock market price. It is an indication of the market's view as to the future prospects of the company. This forward-looking aspect is critical.

The formula is:

$$\frac{\text{Market price per share}}{\text{EPS}}$$

In practice:

Using a closing share price of 308p on February 26, 2005 and the basic EPS calculation, the P/E ratio for Tesco is:

$$\frac{308p}{17.72p} = 17.4$$

The P/E ratio based on the diluted EPS for Tesco is:

$$\frac{308p}{17.50p} = 17.6$$

The respective IFRS equivalent figures, using the EPS calculations given on page 5 are: 308/17.48 = 17.6; and, 308/17.26 = 17.8.

The P/E ratio is a particularly important measure for investors and analysts. Essentially, the higher the P/E ratio the faster the market expects the company's EPS to grow. Therefore, a high P/E figure implies high investor confidence with regard to the future prospects of the company. Also since share price is influenced by, amongst other things, EPS and dividend levels, a company's dividend policy will usually impact upon its P/E ratio.

Industry and sector specific P/E ratios are widely available and provide a very useful comparative base.

Don't Bet Too Much on Long-term Predictions, by Graham Searjeant

Price-to-earnings ratios aim to measure how many times a company's earnings after tax you have to pay to acquire some of its shares in the market. Under American influence, the p/e ratio has become the most commonly used rating for comparing shares. The implication seems simple. The higher the p/e ratio, the faster the market expects profits to rise; the lower the p/e ratio, the more likely that profits will fall. Naturally, it is not as simple as that, even if you know which of many measures of earnings per share is in use...

When a company is expected to expand sales and profits strongly, it may well trade on a p/e ratio of 1.5 times or twice the current market average of about 17 as a way of valuing future above-average growth. Food retailers sell on an average p/e ratio of 26, though this owes something to recovery and takeover hopes. Healthcare rates 30 times earnings, property 33 and information technology 42. Top – end ratings for individual companies, which will be higher than the sector average, are looking many years ahead. At normal discount rates, profits up to 15 years in the future could be significant for valuation.

Experience suggests, however, that forecasts made so far in advance are liable to be inaccurate. At the end of the 1980s, Sainsbury still appeared to have better prospects than Tesco, life assurance companies seemed set to deliver low-risk, long-term growth indefinitely and British merchant banks were safe and solid. Apart from start-ups, most ratings need to be justified over a shorter period.

Goldman Sachs, the investment bank, has run an exercise projecting profits for European sectors up to 2009 and then comparing the implied 2009 p/e ratios. Goldman Sachs concludes that the most overvalued sectors at today's prices are probably cyclical industries such as paper, chemicals and transport, whose profits might even be turning down again by 2009. As so often, the massed flocks of fund managers have followed the fashion for fast-recovering cyclical stocks too far. High-priced sectors such as computer software and hardware and, less obviously, much of the drinks sector continue to look expensive. That might not be the case if profits were projected further on. But Goldman reckons that, at present prices, some would still have above-average ratings 15 years hence.

The cheapest sectors in 2009 are ones that look cheap today: banks and construction. Several other sectors are now unfashionable but are still likely to deliver rising profits. This makes the big telecoms and pharmaceuticals sectors, along with aerospace and biotechnology, look best value. The message, as ever, is to look beyond the headlines. Real investors buy shares rather than sectors. To verify growth we need to check that companies are investing enough to deliver the progress their ratings require without expanding so fast as to multiply the short-term risk. The p/e ratio is a stock market measure, not a rational score.

Source: *The Times*, February 26, 2005.

One useful derivative of the P/E ratio is the Price/Earnings Growth (PEG) ratio. This relates the P/E ratio to a prospective (estimated) future EPS figure. It is computed as:

$$\frac{\text{P/E ratio}}{\text{Prospective growth in EPS}}$$

(Prospective growth in EPS will be computed used various assumptions and projections.)

It is a useful measure in considering whether the share is underrated or overrated. For instance, where the P/E ratio is higher that the prospective growth in EPS (i.e., the PEG is over 1), it would usually indicate that a share price may be relatively high.

Payouts

Investors invest in companies for a variety of reasons. However, the usual motivation will be to earn a return.

A common measure of this return, as mentioned earlier, will be Total Shareholder Return (TSR). This assesses the overall return enjoyed by shareholders. Typically TSR measures the returns shareholders enjoy from a variety of sources: it is usually computed as the sum of any appreciation in share price plus dividends received.

This mixture of capital appreciation and cash dividends illustrates the variety of means by which returns may be achieved. Increasingly this mix is becoming an important consideration for companies in the management of their relationships with shareholders. Indeed, for many shareholders, particularly those who have invested in cash-rich companies, the question of the uses to which companies put surplus cash is increasingly important. However, in such circumstances there are competing interests, and long-term versus short-term benefits need to be considered:

Investors Divided Over Excess Cash, by Philip Stafford

Investors are becoming more and more polarized between those who want to see excess cash returned to shareholders and those who want to see it reinvested, according to a Merrill Lynch report. Merrill's August survey of fund managers found that 50 per cent said that companies were underinvesting in their businesses, while 53 per cent believed corporate balance sheets were under-leveraged.

Asked what they would like companies to do with excess cash, 38 per cent said they wanted to see increased capital spending – 42 per cent wanted cash returned to shareholders. In May, 49 per cent of respondents preferred share buybacks, compared with the 30 per cent who favoured increased capital spending.

"Return of cash still has the upper hand, but if capex [capital expenditure] were to start to dominate the agenda, it could mark the start of a new theme where investors focus on companies that are intent on growing their businesses again, rather than running them for cash," said David Bowers, chief global investment strategist at Merrill Lynch.

Source: *Financial Times*, August 17, 2005.

For businesses with a cash surplus the options range from using cash to fund further investment to returning cash, in one form or another, to shareholders. Essentially, the two principal means by which companies seek to return cash to shareholders are:

- Dividends
- Share buybacks.

Dividends

Dividends are distributions of profits to shareholders. They are usually paid in two instalments: interim and final, which together equal total dividend. Dividends are important to most shareholders. Indeed, in the case of "old economy" companies, they are critical in maintaining investor loyalty. They encourage investment on the part of those interested in an annual return on their investment as much as any capital appreciation of their shares.

In practice:

Dividends soar at three times rate of inflation

Three in four of Britain's 100 largest companies increased their dividends by more than the rate of inflation in 2004. This rate of increase was the fastest for seven years, with average growth of 11.4 per cent – more than three times the 3.5 per cent rate of inflation, according to Fidelity, the UK's biggest fund manager. The payouts from both Vodafone and BSkyB doubled last year, while Centrica, the gas group, and Yell, the phone directories company, increased their dividends by more than 60 per cent. Only five FTSE 100 companies cut their dividends. The worst reduction came from J Sainsbury, which cut its payout by 40 per cent.

Last year, dividends accounted for a third of the total return to FTSE100 investors. While the index rose by 7.5 per cent, dividend income took the total return to 11.3 per cent. John Stavis, the manager of Fidelity Income Plus, said the bumper year reflected the marked improvement in company balance sheets. He said that some of the surplus cash was being returned to investors in the form of increased dividends. "Investors have also become less tolerant of companies that waste cash on value-destroying acquisitions," he added.

Dividends allow investors to share in company profits, and are distributed every six or 12 months. They form a key component in the total return from shares.

Source: Sunday Telegraph, January 23, 2005.

Every firm will need to maintain a balance between payment of dividends and retention of cash for investment. This requires that funds at the disposal of management be used wisely so that cash reserves can be retained.

In determining dividend policy a firm will have to give attention to the following considerations:

- Previous dividend policy
- Competitors' policies
- Availability of distributable profits
- Availability of cash
- Other investment possibilities
- Market expectations.

In practice:

The continuing, and most likely increasing, importance of dividends is outlined in the following account:

Dividends set to double by 2010

Companies are expected to pay out at least half their earnings as dividends by 2010, according to a report by Eaton Vance, the Boston-based fund management group, as a result of increased investor pressure.

The group expects the average corporate dividend pay-out ratio to rise by nearly 60 per cent over the next four years. This ratio, which today stands at about 32 per cent, is far below historic norms. Since 1936, the dividend pay-out ratio has averaged 53.5 per cent, according to Standard & Poor's, the provider of investment research. Eaton Vance projects it will hit 50 per cent by 2010.

Judith Saryan, who manages Eaton Vance's utilities fund, said: "Companies are generating a lot of free cash flow and they've got to make a decision about what to do with it. Many are rethinking the dividend question because shareholders are demanding it."

In 1980, 469 companies in the S&P500 blue-chip index paid a dividend. That number reached a low of 351 in 2002. "Companies figured: 'Why pay a dividend when the stock is going up?'" says Howard Silverblatt, equity market analyst at S&P. At the peak of the stock market bubble, in March 2000, the dividend yield on the S&P500 dropped to a low point of 1.12 per cent, against a historical average of 3.92.

But the number of companies paying dividends for the first time, or increasing their dividend, has again begun to rise. This year, 306 companies, including Safeway, American Standard, Time Warner and, last week, Microsoft, have either started, restarted or raised dividend pay-outs, against 267 in 2004 and 236 in 2003, says S&P. The amount paid out is also increasing – 2004 was the best year for dividends since 1977, with the average dividend on the S&P500 rising by 15.3 per cent. The index yields 1.83 per cent today.

Source: Financial Times, December 20, 2005.

The importance of dividends is reflected in the variety of ratios developed to assess a firm's dividend policy. The following are three of the more useful measures. (Note: Changes in the accounting treatment of proposed dividends under IFRS noted earlier do not affect the calculations that follow.)

Dividend Yield

This quantifies the relationship between dividend per share and market value per share. It is a measure of the return enjoyed by shareholders. The formula is:

$$\frac{\text{Dividend per share}}{\text{Market price per share}} \times 100\%$$

In practice:

Based on information provided in note 10, the figure for Tesco is:
$$\frac{7.56}{308p} \times 100\% = 2.45\%$$

The dividend included is the total dividend, i.e., the interim dividend received plus the proposed final dividend. Thus, the entire benefit to the shareholder from dividends is incorporated.

In practice:

Europe is learning to profit from dividends. The UK pays out the most, but companies in other countries are recognizing the benefits for investors, by Deborah Hargreaves

Investors have begun to focus on dividends, as these provide a larger part of their total returns from equities in a low-inflation environment. Companies have also begun to give greater attention to payouts in the wake of the corporate governance scandals of the past few years. This month ARM Holdings, the UK chipmaker, said it would pay its first dividend. Sweden's SKF, the world's largest supplier of roller bearings, raised its dividend by 25 per cent and announced a new policy of paying out half of net profit over a business cycle. Banks such as BNP Paribas, ABN Amro and Deutsche have all recently increased their pay-outs.

While the UK is currently responsible for more than 40 per cent of all pay-outs in Europe, some strategists believe that more Euro zone companies are recognising the benefits of dividends as a way of rewarding investors.

In spite of the attraction of growth stocks for many fund managers, half of investors' total returns from 16 leading markets around the world have come from dividends since 1900, according to this year's study of long-term investment returns by three London Business School academics: Paul Marsh, Elroy Dimson and Mike Staunton.

A new analysis of European dividend stocks launched by Dresdner Kleinwort Wasserstein points out that since 1970, 70 per cent of total real returns from equities have come from dividends. It shows that outside the UK, the average contribution of dividend yield to total returns has been 62 per cent between 1950 and 2000. The exception has been Germany – where dividend yield contributed only 30 per cent to returns over this period, with capital growth outweighing income.

"The dividend yield is a much more stable way of planning long-run returns. By focusing on stocks with a dividend yield, investors become much less dependent on risky growth stocks," said Alex Stewart, strategist at Dresdner. . . Dresdner's top picks for dividend yield and future pay-out prospects include Repsol, the Spanish energy company, currently trading on a yield of 2.5 per cent with free cashflow to cover the dividend 3.3 times this year. Continental, the German tyre-maker, and Unilever, the consumer goods group, are also selected – they are on yields of 2 per cent and 3.4 per cent respectively. Dresdner also highlights Swisscom, the Swiss telecoms operator, and Eon, the German utility. These stocks would not necessarily be selected on the basis of yield alone. But Dresdner's analysis shows that the pay-outs are well covered by cashflow and that all the favoured companies have the ability to increase the dividend by 8–15 per cent over three years. . .

Source: Financial Times, February 9, 2004.

Dividend Cover

This provides a measure of the extent to which a company pays out its profits in the form of ordinary dividends and provides a measure of the scope that a company has to pay dividends. It expresses the dividend paid out as a function of the profit available to ordinary shareholders for this purpose. A high cover indicates that the company operates a conservative dividend policy and does not distribute a large portion of its profits to the equity interest.

The formula is:

$$\frac{\text{Profit after tax} - \text{Preference dividends}}{\text{Ordinary dividend}}$$

In practice:

Based on information from the income statement and note 10, the figure for Tesco is:

$$\frac{1,366}{587} = 2.3 \, times$$

Dividend Payout

This measures the portion of profit that is actually being distributed in the form of dividends. For young, fast-growing firms this would normally be low as the expectation is that profits would be ploughed back into the business rather than distributed as dividends. Industry averages enable inter-firm and industry comparison.

The formula is:

$$\frac{\text{Ordinary dividend}}{\text{Profit after tax} - \text{Preference dividends}} \times 100\%$$

In practice:

The figure for Tesco is:

$$\frac{587}{1,366} \times 100\% = 43\%$$

This is a relatively high figure. However, Tesco has traditionally paid a relatively high proportion of its profits in the form of dividends.

Share Buybacks

Increasingly, companies with cash surpluses are opting (or, in some cases, being forced by their shareholders) to engage in share buybacks as a means of returning cash. This essentially involves the company buying its shares in the open market and subsequently retiring them.

The net effect of such buybacks can bring benefits to both shareholders and companies. For instance, shareholders see an immediate return of cash. However it also means that the number of shares in circulation (the 'share count') is reduced. This, in turn, can often artificially improve ratio scores such as EPS where the result is impacted by a lower denominator. It can also have a positive effect on ROE, with the result that a marginal rise in share price can often follow:

Optimistic Companies at Odds with Nervous Shareholders, by Kevin Allison and Ivar Simensen

If the steep losses on global equities markets over the past two weeks are any guide, inflation fears and concerns about slowing earnings growth are leaving investors rattled. But at the same time, companies appear to be brimming with confidence. Corporate balance sheets are flush with cash, and instead of holding it for a rainy day, many companies seem to be giving it back to shareholders. "Corporate buying is just exploding," says Liz Ann Sonders, chief investment strategist at Charles Schwab. Ms Sonders said that US companies agreed to buy back a staggering $25bn in shares over the past week.

One interpretation of buy-backs is they are a way for a company to signal its shares are being judged unfairly. "It's a good sign that companies are confident that economic activity will continue to do well," says Peter Cardillo, chief strategist at SW Bach. "It sends a message they feel their stock is undervalued." In addition to the signals they send, buy-backs also tend to boost share prices in the short-term. "When a company does a buy-back of their shares, the return on equity goes up, so it's positive for stockholders," says Mr Cardillo. "Any time a company buys back shares I think it's a good sign..."

Source: *Financial Times*, April 22, 2005.

In practice:

Pubs group to pay cash surplus to investors, by Laura Smith

Enterprise Inns, Britain's largest pub group, is to pay an estimated £200m surplus cash to shareholders after announcing yesterday that its profits per pub had increased by more than 8% on the previous year. The company, which owns 8,650 individually run pubs across England, Scotland and Wales, intends to return the cash through increased dividends and a share buy-back programme.

Ted Tuppen, its chief executive, refused to confirm how much would be paid, but analysts believe it could be in the region of £200m, with the dividend expected to double from last year's 12p. Details will be revealed in the company's full-year results statement on November 22.

Source: The Guardian, September 24, 2005.

Summary

Those who provide equity or debt financing for a company do so with a view to earning a return on that investment. Consequently, investors will want to assess the performance of the company in order to gauge the success or otherwise of their investment. To this end a variety of ratios and other measures have been developed which allow various aspects of any return to be quantified and assessed.

As with all such ratios covered in this text the key to their proper use is not necessarily their correct mathematical construction, but an appreciation of what each actually assesses and the identification of a suitable comparative base against which results may be contextualized.

Nor should they be considered in isolation. There will usually, not surprisingly, be a relationship between return on investment and dividends or between profitability and ROCE. However, it will be the capacity to identify what the nature of this relationship is, to track any changes and to identify longer-term trends that will be the difference between an informed analysis and one that fails to grasp the bigger picture.

Review Questions

Question 1
"It is possible to survive several years of losses, but it is only possible for a business to run out of cash once". Taking this statement as a starting point, consider the relative importance of liquidity and profitability.

Question 2
Compare and contrast what is measured by the Gross Profit Rate and the Operating Profit Rate.

Question 3
Explain why it is important to measure Return on Capital Employed (ROCE) and distinguish between the interests of equity shareholders and other investors under this heading.

Question 4
Identify the reasons for the continued importance assigned to EPS and explain why it has been the subject of so much regulation.

Question 5
Explain the usefulness of alternatives to EPS such as Total Shareholder Return (TSR).

Question 6
Explain why some investors place such importance on dividends. Also, account for their relative unimportance to investors in so-called "new economy" businesses.

Question 7
Identify and discuss the various considerations that a board of directors must take into account in determining dividend policy.

Question 8
Distinguish between the different aspects of dividends that Dividend Yield, Dividend Cover and Dividend Payout attempt to quantify.

Question 9
Identify the key points made in the following extract relating to ICI. Explain why the price of the ICI shares rose.

"The dividend cut will save the group about £115 million a year and double its dividend cover to nearly three times, in line with the rest of the chemical industry. This year's dividend will be maintained at 32p. From 2002 the dividend will be equal to about a third of the group's profits. Some analysts said that the reduction in the 2001 pay-out had been expected and would help the company to fund future growth. "Reducing the dividend and investing in the business is exactly what investors want", said Martin Evans at Credit Lyonnais Securities. However, some US analysts said that the decision could disappoint US-based investors. ICI shares rose 10p to 427p".

Question 10
Explain the significance of the fact that companies are increasingly engaging in share buy-backs as a means of returning cash to shareholders.

Case Studies

Case 1

The ratios for Tesco 2005 have been given throughout this chapter under the various headings covered. Go to the company website, access the 2006 Annual Report, and compute the equivalent ratios for that year. These can be checked against the report for that year available on the website for this text.

Case 2

BT offers an interesting example of a company that has had to deal with many of the strategic and operational issues surrounding earnings and cash. The following extract outlines a number of the challenges it has faced and describes broadly how these have been dealt with. In addition to this extract, access the company's website as well as any other informed commentary with a view to identifying whether or not BT has used its cash well.

'New-wave' BT in Pay-out Boost, by Mark Odell

Shares Up 6% on News of £570m Pre-tax Profits; Evolving Business Marks Fifth Quarter of Growth

BT Group yesterday signalled higher pay-outs to shareholders as its management sought to underline the success of its strategy of transforming itself from a traditional telecommunications group into a global network IT services company. The group's shares rose strongly as investors reacted favourably to the prospect of cash windfalls from both a more aggressive dividend policy and larger share buy-back programmes. The shares closed 12 3/4p higher at 214p, a rise of over 6 per cent that made them the best performers in the FTSE100. The reaction came as the company unveiled fourth-quarter earnings at the top end of expectations with pre-tax profits of £570m, up from £423m a year earlier and equivalent to earnings per share of 4.9p (3.9p).

BT, Britain's dominant fixed-line operator, is refocusing in an attempt to wean itself off its traditional fixed-line business, where intense competition is driving prices down. The group continued to grow its top line with a fifth straight quarter of underlying revenue growth, as fourth-quarter revenues rose 2 per cent to £4.87bn. A 27 per cent increase in "new wave" turnover to £1.37bn, generated from areas such as corporate network services and broadband, and further boosted by acquisitions, helped offset a 9 per cent decline in turnover from the traditional business. New wave services now account for 28 per cent of total revenue. The full-year dividend is lifted 22 per cent to 10.4p, raising the pay-out ratio from 50 per cent to 57 per cent of underlying earnings. The group's dividend this year matches at least 60 per cent of underlying earnings, rising to two-thirds of earnings by 2007–08.

BT also signalled an early end to its debt reduction programme, as average net debt fell to £7.79bn. Mr Verwaayen said the group was "comfortable" with debt levels of about £8bn and would scrap the £7bn target set for the 2006–07 financial year.

Sir Christopher Bland, chairman, said any free cash after dividend payments would be available to fund the share buy-back programme followed by merger and acquisition activity. Matthew Bloxham, at Goldman Sachs, said: "Last year it was dividends, acquisitions then buy-backs, so there is slightly more emphasis on shareholder returns going forward."

Morgan Stanley calculated that the halt to the debt reduction programme would leave BT scope to increase its share buy-back programme from £250m to £500m a year for the next two years. The fourth-quarter performance helped BT achieve full-year pre-tax profits of £2.34bn, ahead of consensus forecasts, up from £1.95bn last year. Revenues rose to £18.6bn, from £18.5bn.

Source: *Financial Times*, May 20, 2005.

Case 3

Marks and Spencer is one of the companies most impacted by the rise of Tesco in the UK. In recent years the company's difficulties have been compounded by a number of governance and executive remuneration issues. The following extract points to some of these issues and describes attempts by the executives to institute various measures of performance. Investigate the claim made by M&S executives, that EPS is "the most appropriate measure of performance, particularly at this stage of the company's development". To what extent is this mere self-serving?

Desperate Measures at M & S

Clarity Needed Ahead of Annual Meeting

Three new executive pay plans have been proposed at Marks & Spencer, allowing lucky executives to quadruple their basic salaries if "stretching" performance targets are met. Shareholders will vote on the matter at the company's annual meeting on July 13.

One aspect that needs a little more clarity in advance is the fact that M&S is ditching the decidedly British measure of performance – total shareholder return, or share price gain plus dividends paid – and switching to the very American measure of earnings per share.

Apparently, according to the notice of the meeting sent out with last week's annual report, EPS is "the most appropriate measure of performance, particularly at this stage of the company's development. This is because it is the key measure of management performance taking account of growth in sales, cost reductions and margin improvements, all of which are necessary to drive the company's recovery and increase shareholder value''.

Putative raider Tina Green and her husband Philip might argue with that. They'd say getting the share price back above the 400p at which the Greens tabled their offer last year would present a much better target.

There are broader considerations, however. For a start, do we really want EPS to take over from TSR as the de facto measure of success in corporate Britain? It is possible to manipulate both figures – EPS is easy and can be done legally while TSR is difficult and carries a straightforward threat of jail.

In M&S's case, the company is already committed to buying plenty of its own shares, which enhances earnings, and there is also a sense that, after an ugly year, Stuart Rose and his colleagues have seen the worst in terms of profit erosion. These factors have already been priced in by the market but have yet to show through in raw EPS data...

Source: *The Guardian*, June 15, 2005.

Case 4

The following article takes a long-term view in assessing the importance of dividends. It also incorporates reference to many of the ratios identified in this chapter. It concludes that "ignoring dividends can be a very costly error". Assess this statement in the light of the data presented and any other relevant information.

Ignoring Dividends Can Prove a Costly Mistake, by Philip Coggan

Dividends do not matter. That is the confident view of some US investors. They see the low dividend yield on the equity market as irrelevant. Their case is simple. Until the Bush administration's recent reforms, the tax treatment of US dividends was disadvantageous. Companies accordingly preferred to retain their earnings for reinvestment, or to return cash to shareholders through the more tax-efficient mechanism of share buy-backs. All that has happened, say the bulls, is that the dividend payout ratio has fallen. But investors will be compensated for that decline by faster earnings growth over the long run, as those reinvested earnings are ploughed back into the business.

It is not an implausible idea. Indeed, some companies do regard dividend payments as an indication of defeat. Warren Buffett's Berkshire Hathaway has never paid a dividend, but the Sage of Omaha's company has prospered thanks to his ability to reinvest its cashflows. The problem, however, is that the benefits of earnings retention theory is not borne out by the historical data. This has been conclusively shown in a paper* by Robert Arnott and Clifford Asness.

The authors looked at the history of the payout ratio for US companies in the Standard & Poor's 500 index over the period 1950 to 2001. They found the opposite of what the bulls would expect; future earnings growth was positively correlated with the payout ratio. In other words, when the payout ratio was low, future earnings growth tended to be low as well; when the payout ratio was high, so was earnings growth. The easiest way to illustrate this is to divide the period into four. In the period with the lowest payout ratio, average real earnings growth over the subsequent 10 years was minus 0.7 per cent; when the payout ratio was high, subsequent 10-year real growth was 3.2 per cent.

The authors looked at other factors that might affect future earnings growth. The shape of the bond yield curve was one potential factor. When the yield curve is strongly upward sloping (when long-term interest rates are far higher than short-term rates) investors appear to be expecting faster economic (and thus corporate earnings) growth.

Another possible element is price/earnings ratios; when the p/e is high, investors must be expecting faster future earnings growth.

Third, earnings might revert to the mean. As earnings are more volatile than dividends, this would mean that when earnings were temporarily high the payout ratio would be low and vice versa.

Arnott and Asness found that all three factors had some relationship to future earnings growth but the relationship was nothing like as strong as the payout ratio. To test the robustness of their findings, they also looked at the period 1871 to 1950 and found a similar relationship between the payout ratio and future earnings growth. Furthermore, the recent growth in buy-backs did not seem to alter their findings.

Why should the payout ratio be such a good predictor? The authors have several suggestions. One possibility relates to management reluctance to cut dividends. A low payout ratio may thus signal lack of management confidence about the sustainability of earnings and a high payout ratio may signal the opposite. Alternatively, the explanation could lie in how managers use those reinvested earnings. Perhaps there are only so many attractive investment opportunities. When managers have little cash to spare they will spend it on the few good projects. When they have lots of money available they will fund more and more risky ideas; many of which will deliver disappointing returns. A related factor could be that too much cash simply burns a hole in the managers' pockets, leading them to "empire build", making disastrous acquisitions in unrelated areas.

These last two factors could clearly be seen at work in the 1990s. Telecommunications companies spent heavily on new projects, laying fibre optic cables and investing in third-generation mobile phones. Much of that cash now looks wasted. And merger and acquisition activity exploded in spite of all the academic evidence that most takeovers fail to add value to shareholders (and serve mainly to enrich investment bankers).

The payment of a dividend, however, imposes a discipline on the manager. Cash has to be found to keep shareholders happy. That may dissuade the board from pursuing excessively risky projects. For the shareholders, the dividend represents a tangible reward for their investment – a cash payment that "proves" the earnings power of the company in a way that audited profit numbers, with all their potential for manipulation, cannot.

What does this research tell us about future returns? Having dropped to a low of 0.3 in 2000, the payout ratio had edged up to 0.47 by the end of June, according to S&P. That is still a little below the long-term average, indicating that investors should expect below average real earnings growth over the next 10 years. The payout ratio is also dropping again (as earnings rise faster than dividends in the recovery) with S&P estimating its end-2003 level at about 0.37. The long-term earnings outlook is deteriorating again.

Markets are, however, trading on an above-average p/e, indicating that investors are anticipating a buoyant period for earnings growth. History, however, suggests that when the market is trading on a high p/e (and a low dividend yield) future returns are likely to be below average. That suggests investors have set themselves up for disappointment.

Ignoring dividends can be a very costly error. Earnings may look sparkling, but turn out to be just plain glass. A payout, like a diamond, is forever.

*Does Dividend Policy Foretell Earnings Growth? http://ssrn.com/ abstract= 295 974 or go to www.aqrcapital.com

Source: *Financial Times*, November 29, 2003.

SECTION IV

Issues

Most large companies will have to grapple with more complex accounting issues than those alluded to so far. This is not simply a function of their size, but also of their corporate structure, global focus and wider responsibilities.

Section IV addresses a number of the more common accounting-related issues that arise. These range from the accounting implications of group structures to the more prosaic aspects of accounting for foreign currency transactions.

The section begins with two rather technical chapters, one dealing with business combinations and the other with pensions, share options, leases, taxation and foreign currency transactions. It is important to work through the detail provided, as any interpretation will require more than a passing knowledge of these topics.

Three less technical chapters follow. The first deals with creative accounting and identifies past examples, regulatory responses and ongoing problems in this area.

Chapter 14 broadens the debate on governance, revisiting the whole notion of the company as a "corporate citizen" in the context of corporate social responsibility.

Finally, Chapter 15 places UK practice in its international context by considering accounting practice and governance regimes in Germany and France. It concludes with a review of the catalysts for international harmonization of accounting practice, together with an examination of the roles of IASB and FASB in this process.

BUSINESS COMBINATIONS [11]

When you have completed this chapter you will understand:

- The nature and structure of business combinations (groups).
- IFRS accounting principles and rules for accounting for business combinations.
- Political aspects of the standard setting process for business combinations
- How to account for investments in "associate companies".
- How to account for "joint ventures".
- Why related-party transactions must be disclosed.

Takeover Follies for Shareholders

Watching the all-too-predictable downfall of Carly Fiorina, who resigned as head of Hewlett-Packard last week, you could be forgiven for wondering whether the financial markets ever learn from their mistakes. As many, including this newspaper, warned at the time, her ill-thought-out $19bn (£10.3bn, €14.8bn) takeover of Compaq was always likely to fail: most major mergers and acquisitions (M&A) end in tears for the acquiring company and this one had grief written all over it. So why have American companies announced $140bn worth of transactions in the first five weeks of 2005, the biggest start for M&A since 2000?

The answer is that the remuneration and prestige of corporate executives tends to be tied to the size of the company they manage, so ego-driven CEOs will always be tempted to buy companies, regardless of results, a tendency that has cost shareholders dearly over the years. Almost $1 trillion in deals have taken place in the United States alone since the start of 2004; globally, the value of M&A transactions has hit $239.2bn in the first six weeks of the year. The biggest deals announced in 2005 include SBC's acquisition of AT&T, its former parent, for $14.7bn; MetLife's bid for Travelers, a life-insurance company, from Citigroup for

$11.5bn; and Procter & Gamble's $57bn purchase of consumer-goods company Gillette.

While this spate of deals is welcome news for bonus-hungry investment bankers, statistically, no more than one out of these three deals is likely to succeed. Yet still they are done. Shareholders need to make it clear to CEOs tired of the drudgery of organic growth and cost-cutting that only carefully-costed, value-enhancing deals are acceptable; the onus should be on management to prove they are not doing another HP-Compaq.

Study after study has showed that most takeovers usually only benefit the shareholders of the target company; those of the acquirer usually get a very raw deal. Bain, the global consultancy, believes only 28% of deals create shareholder value growth of more than 10% compared with peer companies. Within one or two years after a deal is announced, about 70% of big deals have failed to create any significant value. Almost 60% of takeovers create companies that underperform; 50% actually destroy shareholder value...

Despite its poor record, the resurgence in M&A activity should come as no surprise. Companies are flush with cash from bumper profits; many have spent the past few years making the most of loose financial conditions and low interest rates to transform their balance sheets... Defenders of this resurgence say it will all be different this time because companies are no longer paying insane premiums to market valuation. The real point is that if a share is massively over-valued, paying no more than its market price still makes no sense. P&G may be paying a premium of only 13% for Gillette but the latter's shares were trading at a prohibitive price to earnings (p/e) ratio of 28 times before the deal was announced. For it to generate value, P&G will have to obtain a return on its investment that is greater than could have been achieved through organic growth and greater than shareholders could have achieved had the money been returned to them.

Understandably, the M&A epidemic is starting to worry investors, who fear it could be coming at the expense of higher dividends: in its January poll of institutional investors, Merrill Lynch found that almost half of respondents want to see companies return extra cash to shareholders. This would make sense: not only do we know that takeovers usually fail, we are also know dividends are of critical importance in determining long-term returns on equity investments...

Source: *The Business*, February 13, 2005.

Introduction

Carly Fiorina was only doing what almost every other CEO of a large public company does: seeking to expand by acquisition. In fact, traditionally, mergers and acquisitions (M&A) have been important vehicles for corporate growth. Indeed, it can be argued that the governance culture and the presence of a vibrant stock market combine to encourage growth by acquisition rather than organic growth. The consequence of such M&A activity is that most large US and UK businesses are actually not individual companies, but complex webs of interrelated entities, with one identifiable 'parent' company. Such combinations are normally called 'groups' or 'business combinations'.

The importance of groups and the ways in which they can be structured or created was outlined in Chapter 6. This chapter will deal with the accounting implications of these business combinations, looking at acquisitions, mergers, associates and joint ventures.

Mergers and Acquisitions (M&A)

Companies grow by various means. One is organic growth, i.e., by developing business internally. While this will be a factor in the expansion of most entities, another will be growth by acquiring shares in, or merging with, other entities.

A merger (called a "pooling of interests" in the US) is essentially a coming together of companies to form a larger entity. Usually, but not always, these companies will be of similar size and none will be seen as aggressively acquiring the other.

An acquisition, on the other hand, usually involves one company actively, and often aggressively, acquiring shares in another with a view to obtaining sufficient shares to obtain control.

In the Anglo-American world the nature of corporate structure, together with the presence of a dominant capital market, ensure the enduring influence of mergers and acquisitions as means of growth.

In practice:

What's the big deal?

The great urge to merge is taking manager's attention away from the basics, writes Simon Caulkin.

Like it or not, companies increasingly inhabit a deal economy. Put baser motives like ego and self-aggrandisement to one side; impatience, competition for investor attention and the globalizing world economy are reasons why many chief executives these days feel compelled to pay as much attention to mergers, acquisitions and divestments as to products, services and customers.

With investors breathing down their necks, many CEOs find organic growth too snail-like to impress – particularly where turnarounds are concerned. Couple investors' shrinking attention span with the need to react quickly to changing conditions, add in ready access to global capital and the attractive targets (and hungry rivals) emerging in new economies such as India and China, and it's hardly surprising transactions are the newest field of strategic competition.

Last year, says a new report from Ernst & Young, corporate transactions totalled more than $1.5 trillion in deal value, $700m of that in Europe. No less than 88 per cent of European and 96 per *cent of US companies studied were planning a merger or acquisition in the next two years, and only slightly fewer had divestment projects in the pipeline. Transactions of all kinds, sums up the report, 'are an ever-increasing part of the way corporations do business, expand, and adapt to changing circumstances'.*

Source: The Observer, July 21, 2005.

The question of how to fund acquisitions is one of considerable strategic importance to both parties to a deal. As the following extract suggests, the nature of the funding may itself be a factor in the 'success' or otherwise of the venture:

Cash is King

How mega-mergers are financed does not often grab the headlines. Like checking the microphones at the Oscars, it is necessary, but unglamorous. Still, financing structures could affect value creation far more than is often acknowledged. Some studies suggest that deals paid for in cash, rather than stock, tend to generate better returns for investors in the acquiring company. A Citigroup study of US acquirers between 1990 and 2002, for example, found that cash-financed transactions outperformed the industry by 4.3 per cent in a two-year period; stock-financed deals, by contrast, underperformed by 5.2 per cent.

Why? One reason may be that cash-financed deals raise pressure on acquirers to extract the perceived value in a target. After all, interest payments focus the mind. Alternatively, stock financing may be not so much a cause as a marker of deals that are tricky to implement: mammoth acquisitions of publicly owned businesses, say, rather than manageable bolt-ons.

It is thus reassuring that cash leads as the preferred currency. Figures from JPMorgan Chase show that of $821bn US deals reviewed in 2004, 55 per cent were cash-financed, 23 per cent stock-based – and 22 per cent used a mix. If funding costs stay low this proportion could rise further, given that many companies are cash rich and have more relaxed attitudes towards credit ratings.

Intriguingly, many of the top 20 recent deals – worth $290bn, according to Thomson Financial – have been structured as a mix of cash and stock. Examples include Sprint/Nextel, Johnson & Johnson/Guidant and Kmart/Sears Roebuck. Indeed, more than half of recent deals, including Procter & Gamble/Gillette's buyback, are of this "mix and match" variety.

Unfortunately, cash does not guarantee a successful outcome. And investors should note another Citigroup finding: on average, the market's initial reaction is a good guide to whether the deal will dazzle, or disappoint, in the longer term.

Source: Financial Times, February 22, 2005.

Chapter 6 provided a broad outline of the nature of relationships within a business combination. This chapter now explores these in more detail, dealing with acquisitions and mergers in turn, before turning to the accounting rules governing them.

Acquisitions

Acquisitions are the most common means by which business combinations are created. Companies acquire shares in other companies for a variety of reasons. Some do so merely to make effective use of excess cash that is available in the short term. In such circumstances the intention is to hold these shares for a short period, and then divest of them in the hope that the return earned from dividends and any appreciation in value will be greater than would have been gained had the funds merely been left with a bank. Such an investment would be classified as 'available-for-resale investment' and shown in the balance sheet under that heading in the non-current asset section.

Another motivation for investing in a company's shares might be to control, or at least influence, the operation of that entity. In such circumstances the intention is to hold any shares acquired for at least the medium term and to attempt to actively shape the way in which that company develops. As indicated in Chapter 6, different levels of investment will result in various levels of influence and involvement. For instance, if H plc buys 100% of the share capital of S plc then it will have complete ownership of that company and total control of its operations.

Obviously, any stake that gives such control is not just different in degree but also in quality from an interest that is insufficient to give control. For instance, a company that owns 60% of S plc not only owns twice as much as a company that owns 30%, but is in a qualitatively different position in that it can control the operations of S plc because it holds a majority of the voting rights. The point here is that the question of who controls a firm is an important consideration. And this is reflected in accounting practice when accounting for such investments.

Definitions

Under IAS 27, *Consolidated and Separate Financial Statements*, a group exists where one enterprise (the parent) controls, either directly or indirectly, another enterprise (the subsidiary). A group consists, therefore, of a parent and one or more subsidiaries. With some few exceptions, where a group exists the parent company is required to prepare consolidated financial statements.

The critical issue, therefore, is determining the nature of the relationship between two entities. The key point is whether one controls another. IFRS 3, *Business Combinations*, defines control as "the power to govern the financial and operating policies of an entity or business so as to obtain benefits from its activities". Control is assumed when one entity owns more than 50% of the voting rights in another. This may be directly, i.e., by virtue of owning shares itself in the other, or indirectly, e.g., through another company that it controls.

Examples of Group Structures

The nature of relationships between companies can be very complex. However, the following diagram summarizes the more usual scenarios:

	A	B	C
	H plc	H plc	H plc
	↓	↓	↓
	100%	51%	25%
	↓	↓	↓
	S1 plc	S2 plc	S3 plc

A) This structure shows a situation in with a parent company (H plc) owns all of the share capital in another company (S1 plc). In these circumstances S1 can be described as a **wholly-owned subsidiary**.

B) This structure shows a situation in with a parent company (H plc) owns 51% of the share capital in another company (S2 plc). Since this is sufficient to give it control over S2 plc, S2 plc can be described as a **partly-owned subsidiary**. Entities or individuals known collectively as the "minority interest" own the remaining portion of S2 plc.

C) In this situation H plc does not own sufficient share capital in S3 plc to give it control. Thus S3 plc is not a subsidiary.

The following diagram presents a more complicated scenario in which S1, S2 and S3 themselves each have subsidiaries:

	A	B	C
	H plc	H plc	H plc
	↓	↓	↓
	100%	51%	25%
	↓	↓	↓
	S1 plc	S2 plc	S3 plc
	↓	↓	↓
	51%	51%	80%
	↓	↓	↓
	SS1 plc	SS2 plc	SS3 plc

The general rule is that a subsidiary of a company which is itself a subsidiary of another company is automatically a subsidiary of that latter company. Thus in examples (A) and (B), where S1 plc and S2 plc are subsidiaries of H plc, their own subsidiaries, SS1 plc and SS2 plc, automatically become subsidiaries (sometimes called "sub-subsidiaries") of H plc by virtue of the "chain of command" principle. SS3 plc is a subsidiary of S3 plc, but is not a subsidiary of H plc since S3 plc is not a subsidiary of H plc.

It is important to distinguish between control and interest. In the context of ownership, a company has an interest in another entity if it owns shares in that other entity. H plc, for instance, has a direct interest in S1, S2 and S3. It has an indirect interest in SS1, SS2 and SS3.

Significantly, SS2 is a subsidiary of H despite the fact that H's interest in SS2 is only 26%, (i.e., 51% of 51%). This is because the 51% interest in S2 is sufficient to give it control over S2's controlling interest in SS2. It is important to remember that the issue is control and H is in a position to control SS2 by virtue of its 51% shareholding in S2.

Even in circumstances where an entity does not control another by virtue of owning, directly or indirectly, 50% or more of the voting rights in another, it may still be possible to establish that a parent/subsidiary relationship exits. IFRS 3 provides that a business combination can exist where one of the entities acquires:

- Power over more than one-half of the voting rights of the other enterprise by virtue of an agreement with other investors

- Power to govern the financial and operating policies of the other enterprise under a statute or an agreement

- Power to appoint or remove the majority of the members of the board of directors or equivalent governing body of the other enterprise; or

- Power to cast the majority of votes at a meeting of the board of directors or equivalent governing body of the other enterprise.

In practice:

Leisure management group Kunick describes why it has accounted for Games Network as a subsidiary in its annual report and accounts for the year ended September 30, 1998. During the year Bell-Fruit Manufacturing and JPM International each acquired a one-third share in Games Network, which was set up to develop soft terminals.

Both the financial review and the notes to the accounts say that Games Network is considered to be a Kunick subsidiary, Kunick's effective holding arises from a direct shareholding of 33% and an indirect shareholding of 17% through its joint venture Precis. Kunick also holds the casting vote on the board thereby permitting control of the board of Games Network.

Source: Accountancy, March 1999.

Mergers

In an acquisition one company normally achieves control over another by acquiring shares in that company for cash. This has the effect of depleting the cash resources of the parent company and, consequently, of the group as a whole. The purchase accounting method, which will be explained later, reflects both this depletion in cash and the commercial reality of control.

However, there are circumstances in which two or more companies may come together and agree to form a combination for their mutual benefit. In these circumstances the arrangement might be accomplished by an agreement to create a new entity in which the shareholders in the existing companies receive shares. At the end of this process no resources will have left the new group. This is a called a merger or "pooling of interests".

Accounting for Business Combinations

Previously there were a variety of means by which business combinations could be accounted for. For instance, there were different accounting methods allowed depending on whether the 'business combination' derived from an acquisition or a merger. If the former, then a form of accounting called the purchase method was employed. If the latter, then a technique called merger accounting was used.

However, the advent of IAS 27 and IFRS 3 have significantly impacted how acquisitions and mergers are to be accounted for. Essentially, while mergers may actually occur, the accounting options are now limited to the purchase method. The merger (or "pooling of interests") approach is no longer acceptable. Once a business combination is established, therefore, the purchase method applies.

Purchase accounting is an accounting method that has been developed to reflect the essential nature of an acquisition, in particular, the fact that there is one dominant party and that the new combination has had its resources depleted by virtue of consideration being paid to the former shareholders of the new subsidiary.

The following points summarize the main features of the purchase method:

- The results of the acquired company are brought into the group accounts only from the date of acquisition.

- The identifiable assets and liabilities acquired (including identifiable intangibles) are included at fair value in the consolidated accounts.

- The fair value of the consideration given is allocated against its share of the fair value of the identifiable net assets in the subsidiary at the date of acquisition.

- Goodwill is not amortized, but is subject to an annual impairment test in accordance with IAS 36, *Impairment of Assets*.

Acquisitions, by Nick Rea

Far greater deal transparency and unpredictable results will arise from the new International Financial Reporting Standard 3 (IFRS 3) for *Business Combinations*, issued on 31 March 2004 by the IASB. This should be of interest as the new rules apply to all acquisitions in 2004, including deals (for UK institutions) that have already been completed. European institutions already applying IAS will need to comply from 1 April 2004.

The changes should transform the way companies plan and execute their acquisition strategies as there are major changes to the way transactions are recorded, evaluated and communicated. Understanding the implications of the new standards before making an acquisition, and specifically whether a deal will be earnings-enhancing or not will be critical as, in some cases, the acquisition may cause reduced earnings per share (EPS). The successful communication of the rationale for the deal, and the likely impact on earnings, will be vital for listed companies. This is clearly not just an issue for finance directors but for all senior management involved in acquisitions.

The major changes introduced by IFRS 3 are as follows:

- no more merger accounting – instead all business combinations are acquisitions
- more intangible assets will be identified and recognized on acquisition
- goodwill is not amortised but subject to an annual impairment test
- restructuring costs are charged to income
- contingent liabilities are recognized at fair value, and
- detailed disclosures about transactions and impairment testing are required.

Historically, in the majority of acquisitions, the excess purchase price over the fair value of the tangible fixed assets has all been allocated to goodwill rather than attributing value to acquired intangible assets. Under the new IFRS, when a deal is completed, the purchase price must first be allocated to all the acquired tangible and intangible assets before any excess is allocated to goodwill. The intangible assets such as brands, patents and even customer relationships, that were often part of 'goodwill', are now required to be identified separately, valued and carried on the balance sheet. This is part of the 'purchase price allocation' process and will lead to greater transparency over what companies have acquired and may throw up a few surprises on what the potential financial impact of the deal could be...

Under the IFRS, which closely follows US GAAP in this respect, goodwill and indefinite-lived intangible assets will no longer be amortised but reviewed for impairment at least annually. Any impairments will be taken to the profit and loss account which increases the risk of unwelcome surprises. As a result, poorly performing acquisitions will be highlighted sooner rather than later. In addition, the impairment tests themselves are not straightforward and present challenges (and opportunities) to allocate the acquired assets and liabilities to reduce the prospect of a future impairment for companies.

More rigorous evaluation of targets and structuring of deals will be required in order to withstand greater market scrutiny from now on. In addition, all acquisitions in 2004 will need to be recorded using the new rules and the acquisition process will need to become even more rigorous from planning to execution, with much greater emphasis on market communication. Companies will need to clarify to shareholders and analysts the impact of the new standards and, on future acquisitions, what they are buying and why. While mindful of the risks of disclosure of commercially sensitive information, institutions need to provide analysts and investors with a full understanding of the acquisition and its strategic rationale.

Nick Rea is director in the valuation & strategy practice at Pricewaterhouse-Coopers.

Source: *accounting & business*, May 2004.

The fact that intangible assets – such as customer relationships – must now be allotted an element of the consideration at fair value is significant not only in itself, but also for the fact that it recognizes the changed nature of the asset base of many modern businesses. It will lead to greater accountability as businesses are forced to both identify and manage a more transparent portfolio of assets.

Purchase Method

The following two sections deal with the construction of the consolidated balance sheet and income statement under the purchase method.

1. Consolidated Balance Sheet

Each company, whether parent or subsidiary, will prepare its own individual set of financial statements. At its most basic a consolidated balance sheet is constructed by amalgamating the individual balance sheets of the parent company and its subsidiaries and then eliminating any corresponding items.

Take the following example where S plc is the wholly owned subsidiary of P plc. P plc bought all of S plc's shares several years ago at par (nominal value). The individual balance sheets of the two companies are shown as follows:

P plc balance sheet as at December 31, 20X0		S plc balance sheet as at December 31, 20X0	
Tangible assets	200,000	Tangible assets	50,000
Investment in S plc	100,000[a]		
Net current assets	150,000	Net current assets	50,000
	450,000		100,000
Share capital	450,000	Share capital	100,000[a]

[a] Corresponding items that can be eliminated one against the other and neither will appear in the consolidating balance sheet.

The consolidated balance sheet is constructed simply by:

- Adding together the component parts of the individual balance sheets. For example the Net Current Asset figure in the consolidated balance sheet will be: £150,000 + £50,000 = £200,000.

- Eliminating any corresponding items. Investment in S plc shown in P's balance sheet and the Share Capital figure in S's balance sheet correspond not only in amount but also in nature since it was these shares in S that were actually acquired by virtue of P's investment. These amounts, therefore, can be eliminated one against the other and neither will appear in the consolidated balance sheet.

P plc Group consolidated balance sheet as at December 31, 20X0

Tangible assets (200,000 + 50,000)	250,000
Net current assets (150,000 + 50,000)	200,000
	450,000
Share capital (450,000 + nil)	450,000

Notice that the share capital figure for the parent company is unaffected. This will always appears in the Shareholders Funds section of the consolidated balance sheet.

Minority Interest

A parent does not need to acquire 100% of the equity of another in order to gain control. It will not be unusual, therefore, for some shares in subsidiaries to be owned by individuals or companies other than the parent. In these circumstances, the cancellation procedure is still applied, but will not lead to the complete cancellation of the share capital figure from the subsidiary company's books. This simply means that an amount will be left to be incorporated in the consolidated balance sheet. This is given the title "Minority Interest", reflecting the fact that entities outside the group own some of the share capital in one of the group subsidiaries.

This is explained by the following example, where P plc acquired 80% of the share capital of Y plc.

P plc balance sheet as at December 31, 20X0		Y plc balance sheet as at December 31, 20X0	
Tangible assets	120,000	Tangible assets	60,000
Investment in Y plc	80,000[a]		
Net current assets	200,000	Net current assets	40,000
	400,000		100,000
Share capital	400,000	Share capital	100,000[a]

[a] Corresponding items that can be eliminated one against the other and neither will appear in the consolidating balance sheet.

The principle of cancelling out corresponding items still applies. However, the amounts do not correspond exactly and so cancellation can only be partially achieved. Once the £80,000 "Investment in Y plc" has been cancelled against a similar amount from "Share Capital" in Y's balance sheet, £20,000 remains in the balance sheet of Y plc.

This element is known as "Minority Interest" and its interest is indicated in the consolidated balance sheet as part of the equity interest as follows:

P plc Group consolidated balance sheet as at December 31, 20X0	
Tangible assets (120,000 + 60,000)	180,000
Net current assets (200,000 + 40,000)	240,000
	420,000
Share capital	400,000
Minority interest	20,000
	420,000

The fundamental principles of constructing a consolidated balance sheet under the purchase method can be summarized as follows:

- The basic building blocks are the individual balance sheets of the parent and subsidiaries that comprise the group.

- Corresponding items are eliminated against one another to the extent possible.

- Any items remaining after this process are included in the consolidated balance sheet for the group, which is normally given the title of the parent company.

Goodwill

Since goodwill as an accounting issue arises most commonly in the context of an acquisition, i.e., where one entity is acquiring another, it is of particular relevance when dealing with consolidated accounts.

There are two issues:

- The accounting **treatment** of goodwill. Essentially, as outlined earlier, goodwill must be capitalized and subjected to impairment tests.

- Calculating the **amount** of goodwill. The share of shareholders funds acquired is taken as equivalent to the net assets acquired. Therefore the premium paid, i.e., goodwill, can be taken to be the difference between the cost of the investment and the share capital plus equivalent reserves acquired as a result. Alternatively, as discussed later, the fair values of the separable net assets can be set against the fair value of the consideration.

Take the following example where P plc acquired 75% of the share capital of Z plc at a cost of £100,000.

P plc balance sheet as at December 31, 20X0		Z plc balance sheet as at December 31, 20X0	
Tangible assets	100,000	Tangible assets	60,000
Investment in S plc	100,000		
Net current assets	200,000	Net current assets	40,000
	400,000		100,000
Share capital	300,000	Share capital	60,000
Reserves	100,000	Reserves	40,000
Shareholders funds	400,000	Shareholders funds	100,000

In this example P paid £100,000 to acquire a 75% share of Z, a company with a book value of only £100,000. Obviously, P has identified that the net assets of Z are worth more than their book value. Assuming book value to be the same as fair value (this is an important consideration and is discussed below), and that no other separately identifiable intangible assets are acquired, the premium paid can be calculated as follows:

Purchase consideration			£100,000
Acquired	75% share capital (£60,000 × 75%)	£45,000	
	75% reserves (£40,000 × 75%)	£30,000	£75,000
Goodwill			£25,000

Note that no goodwill should be assigned to the minority interest and, therefore, only the goodwill relating to the 75% holding of P plc would appear in the consolidated balance sheet. The Minority Interest amounts to £25,000, i.e., (£60,000 × 25%) + (£40,000 × 25%).

P plc Group consolidated balance sheet as at December 31, 20X0

Tangible assets (100,000 + 60,000)	160,000
Goodwill	25,000
Net current assets (200,000 + 40,000)	240,000
	425,000
Share capital	300,000
Reserves	100,000
Minority interest	25,000
	425,000

Fair Values

One of the problems historically associated with purchase accounting was the scope that it gave acquiring companies to manipulate the values of the assets taken over when acquiring another company. The temptation was to incorporate acquired assets at understated values such that subsequent depreciation charges would be lower, with a consequent favourable impact on profits in future years. A related issue was the overstatement of provisions for future losses or reorganization costs in relation to any newly acquired subsidiary. To the extent that such provisions were subsequently shown to be excessive they resulted in credits to the consolidated income statement, again allowing inflated profits in future years.

IFRS 3 tackles these issues specifically. Its aim is to ensure that when a business entity is acquired by another, all the assets and liabilities that existed in the acquired entity at the date of acquisition are recorded at fair values and that all changes to the acquired assets and liabilities that arise after control of the acquired entity has passed to the acquirer are reported as part of the post-acquisition financial performance of the acquiring group. This process requires the identification of fair values for the identifiable tangible and intangible assets and liabilities of the acquired entity as well as the consideration.

IFRS 3 defines fair value as 'the amount for which an asset could be exchanged or a liability settled between knowledgeable, willing parties in an arm's-length transaction.' It sets out rules for applying this principle to particular classes of assets and liabilities:

- **Tangible fixed assets**: fair value should be based, where possible, on market value, or, where this cannot be identified, at depreciated replacement cost;

- **Identifiable intangible assets**: fair value should, again, be based on market value, or, if no active market exists, on the best available estimate.

As the following example demonstrates, much of the scope for the manipulation of profits and reserves has now been eliminated.

P plc acquired 80% of the ordinary share capital of S plc on December 31, 20X0 for £800,000 cash. The net assets of S plc had a book value of £600,000 on that date.

The following information on the net assets of S plc is relevant:

- The factory included in net assets at a book value of £200,000 has recently been revalued at £300,000, but no entry has yet been made to incorporate this amount.

- The fair value, according to best estimates, of customer lists is £100,000.

- The fair value of closing inventory is reckoned to be £25,000 less than currently stated in the accounts.

- A decision to close one section of the company's operations has been made. The anticipated costs of this are £20,000 but no provision has yet been made.

The fair value of S plc's net assets at the date of acquisition will be:

Book value	£600,000
Revaluation of property	£100,000
Customer lists	£100,000
Revaluation of inventory	(£25,000)
Fair value of acquired assets	£775,000

The amount paid was goodwill was, therefore:

Fair value of consideration	£800,000
Net assets acquired	£620,000 (£775,000 × 80%)
Goodwill	£180,000

This figure for Goodwill will be capitalized and subjected to impairment tests. The other assets acquired, including customer lists, will be listed in the balance sheet.

2. Consolidated Income Statement

The basic principles outlined for the consolidated balance sheet also apply to the consolidated income statement. Thus, the elements of the consolidated income statement are constructed using the figures from the accounts of the individual companies comprising the group. And, once again, corresponding items such as inter-company transactions are eliminated.

Take the following example where the individual income statements of H plc and its 100% subsidiary, S plc, are provided. During the year in question S plc sold £80,000 of goods to H plc, all of which H plc had subsequently sold on to outside customers.

	H plc	S plc
Revenue	600,000	500,000
Cost of goods sold	300,000	320,000
Profit on activities before tax	300,000	180,000
Taxation	100,000	60,000
Profit after tax	200,000	120,000

The consolidated income statement, after eliminating the inter-company trading, would look like this:

	H plc
Revenue (600 + 500 − 80)	1,020,000
Cost of goods sold (300 + 320 − 80)	540,000
Profit on activities before tax	480,000
Taxation	160,000
Profit after tax	320,000

As is the case with the balance sheet, there are some specific items that may need to be adjusted for in the consolidated income statement. The more common of these are:

- Minority interest's share of profits
- Unrealized profits on stocks traded between companies in the same group

Minority Interest in Profits

The minority interest in a subsidiary will be entitled to a share of any of the profits made by that subsidiary. This will need to be calculated and disclosed on the face of the income statement, where it is shown after "Profit after Tax".

For instance, assume that the data above apply except that S plc is only an 80% subsidiary of H plc. The calculation of Profit after Tax will remain exactly the same. However, it will be necessary to indicate that 20% of the after-tax profits of the subsidiary ($£120,000 \times 20\% = £24,000$) belongs to the minority interest. This will be presented as follows:

	H plc
Turnover (600 + 500 − 80)	1,020,000
Cost of goods sold (300 + 320 − 80)	540,000
Profit on activities before tax	480,000
Taxation	160,000
Profit after tax	320,000
Attributable to:	
Equity holders of the parent company	296,000
Minority interest	24,000

Unrealized Profits on Inter-group Trading

In the example above where S plc sold goods worth £80,000 to its parent it was necessary to eliminate these from the consolidated Revenue and Cost of Goods figures, respectively. The important point was that none of these goods remained within the group, i.e., H plc had sold these goods to outside parties, thus realizing a cash benefit to the group as a whole. If there was no requirement that such inter-company trading be eliminated then the possibility would exist for a group to generate spurious sales/purchases between group companies with resultant inflated trading figures, yet no tangible benefits for the group as a whole.

This is not to suggest, however, that there are not legitimate transactions of this kind. Indeed, such symbiotic trading relationships often explain why one company acquires another in the first place. In the normal course of trading relationships between companies within a group, therefore, it is likely that there will be a network of trade dealings. Nevertheless, as far as the commercial reality is concerned, only when there is trading activity with entities outside of the group does any transaction occur which should be shown in the group accounts.

A complication arises, however, in circumstances where one company has supplied goods to another within the group but some of these goods remain in inventory at the end of the year. Since inter-company trading is usually conducted at a mark-up, the closing inventory figure in the company which has acquired these goods will include an unrealized profit figure, and consequently, an unrealized profit will be included in the group accounts. The amount of such "unrealized profits" must, therefore be removed from the consolidated accounts.

For instance, S plc sells goods costing £300 to its parent, H plc, for £400. However, all of these goods remained in the inventory of H plc at the end of the financial year. The sale, purchase and unrealized profit recorded in the individual company accounts of H plc and S plc will not be affected. However, because the group has not realized any change in its resources it will be necessary to eliminate the corresponding sale and purchase. It will also be necessary to adjust for the fact that the closing inventory figure of £400 includes an unrealized profit of £100. This will be achieved by adjusting the closing inventory figure to £300 in the consolidated accounts and removing profit from group reserves.

The Politics of IFRS 3

Thus far, this chapter has concentrated on the operational and computational aspects of accounting for groups and, in particular, on the practical accounting implications of IFRS 3. However, as with so much of IFRS, it is important to consider IFRS 3 in broader political and regulatory contexts.

IFRS 3 represents a significant development for both IASB and FASB as it is the first in what is expected to be a series of joint initiatives as part of a larger convergence project [see Chapter 15]. In other words, it is seen by both as a means of establishing a common set of accounting practices, while simultaneously exploring the possibility of a more harmonized global framework.

Reaction to IFRS 3 has, therefore, been informed by both the specifics of its requirements as well as the broader political implications. At a technical level there has been considerable opposition to various provisions. More fundamental criticisms have revolved around the political implications of such an ambitious project and, in particular, the theoretical and practical implications of the use of fair value:

IASB Should Think Again

Opinion is United Against the Proposed IFRS 3 on Acquisitions, writes Barney Jopson

The timing of accounting rule makers could not have been worse. Just as complaints about international financial reporting standards began to multiply, the International Accounting Standards Board offered up a perfect lightning rod to focus and magnify the ill will. It came in the form of IFRS 3, a proposed standard on mergers and acquisitions, which has the potential to steal from another clunky acronym – IAS 39 – the mantle of least-loved accounting standard. Since it was published in June, IFRS 3 has attracted criticism from a remarkable range of constituents: companies, analysts, investors, accountants, market regulators and – implicitly – European Union policymakers. Even for the IASB, which is well-accustomed to being buffeted by interest groups, the breadth of complaint gives it pause for thought.

It also does not bode well for attempts to narrow differences between IFRS and US standards. IFRS 3 – officially an exposure draft on "business combinations" – is the first standard produced jointly by the IASB and the US Financial Accounting Standards Board. Sir David Tweedie and Bob Herz, chairmen of the two boards, hailed it in early summer as evidence that they could work together effectively.

The vast majority of those with an interest in accounting support the principle of transatlantic – and indeed global – convergence, which promises to make accounts cheaper to prepare for companies and easier to read for investors. But the IASB and the FASB appear in danger of squandering some of that support by producing a standard that is not just "converged" but appears to be leaping ahead in a new direction. In the words of Goldman Sachs, the investment bank and leading M&A adviser, which responded to the boards' consultation on IFRS 3: "We have broad conceptual and practical concerns with the proposal and are not supportive of its issuance in its current form."

More than two years ago, IAS 39, the standard on other financial instruments, began to create an impression that the IASB was out of touch with reality and intent on pursuing its own pet vision of accounting. But under pressure from the EU, standard setters this year seemed to be changing their ways and making incremental progress in diluting some of those perceptions. One of two rules "carved out" of IAS 39 by the EU is even due to be reinstated after a compromise was reached.

IFRS 3, however, appears to have undone the good work and convinced the sceptics that their suspicions were right. The draft standard has attracted great interest because it can make or break business fortunes, and because accounting rules have a pivotal impact on post-transaction earnings per share, a key measure of deal success ... but the underlying message is that IFRS 3 represents a step toward a theoretical form of accounting where fair values are king – and one that is not needed now, or perhaps ever. "We believe these proposals will not enhance the quality and usefulness of the financial information provided to the primary users of (accounts)," says PwC, one of the big four accountants. The Hundred Group of UK finance directors said it was "fundamentally opposed" to them on conceptual grounds.

Sir David Tweedie, chairman of the IASB, was listening carefully at a roundtable discussion on IFRS 3 in London in November. He said he understood the desire for stability in accounting standards, but added: "We get conflicting advice. We are also asked to get rid of the reconciliation with the US, and that involves change and convergence." He noted that a new version of IFRS 3 would not come into effect until 2008 at the earliest anyway.

Contemplating their next steps, the boards could regroup and try to sell their ideas better, they could delay implementation further, or they could rewind the more radical shifts they have proposed. The most ominous warning, for the IASB at least, came in October from Charlie McCreevy, the EU commissioner responsible for accounting. Convergence was not an invitation to standard setters to try to advance the theoretical frontiers of accounting, he said. "I will not take on board any revolutionary new standards." Although one "carve out" is on course to be reinstated, his words indicated that the EU was not afraid to brandish the weapon again.

Source: *Financial Times*, December 8, 2005.

Apart from the specifics, what is most significant is the sheer number and range of those who see themselves as 'players' in this unfolding scenario. Far from being the concern of a few accounting technicians and regulators, the formulation of accounting standards is a political event with the potential to have significant economic and social consequences. The range and nature of the competing interest groups is merely a reflection of this. This topic is revisited in Chapter 15.

Associates and Joint Ventures

It is possible for companies to enter into relationships with other companies, which, while more formal than arms-length trading relationships, are not sufficiently substantial to rank with those discussed earlier in this chapter. For instance, a company might make a significant investment in another, but without gaining control.

Associates

An associate is defined by IAS 28, *Investments in Associates*, as "an entity over which the investor has a significant influence and which is neither a subsidiary nor a joint venture of the investor".

Significant influence is defined as "the power to participate in the financial and operational policy decisions of the investee, but is not control over these policies". An entity is deemed to be exercising significant influence if it has 20% or more of the voting power in another company, unless it can be specifically demonstrated that there is no such influence. IAS 28 also identifies the following as criteria that might help in determining associate status:

- Representation on the board of directors
- Participation in the policy-making process
- Material transactions between the investor and investee
- Interchange of managerial personnel; or
- Provision of essential technical information.

Equity Accounting

Where such a relationship is established then this must be reflected in the accounts of the investor. The accounting method developed to properly reflect the relationship between an investing entity and an associate is called "equity accounting". It has the following characteristics:

- The investment is reported in the group balance sheet in the non-current assets section
- Any goodwill arising is identified, but, because it is not separately recognized, it is grouped with other goodwill, which is then tested in its entirety for impairment under IAS 36
- The carrying amount of the investment is adjusted at the end of each period for the investor's share of the results of its investee adjusted for any impairment of goodwill, the investor's share of any relevant gains or losses, and any other changes in the investee's net assets including distributions to its owners, for example by dividend
- The investor's share of its investee's pre-tax results is recognized in its income statement
- The investor's cash flow statement includes the cash flows between the investor and its investee, for example, those relating to dividends and loans.

Joint Ventures

Companies can often join with other companies in order to manage one specific project or contract. This will often, but not always, lead to the creation of a separate entity. For many businesses, such as project management or construction entities, joint venture activity can form a substantial part of their activity.

For this reason the accounting treatment of joint ventures can often be significant. Under IAS 31, *Interests in Joint Ventures,* a joint venture is one in which "there is a contractual arrangement whereby two or more parties undertake an economic activity that is subject to joint control so that no single venturer is in a position to control the activity unilaterally".

The IAS identifies three broad types of joint venture:

- Jointly controlled operations: for instance, a collaboration such as the manufacture of an aircraft, where different parts are manufactured by different companies
- Jointly controlled assets: for instance, the use by a number of companies of a common gas pipeline
- Jointly controlled entities: a separate entity, with its own assets, liabilities, etc., is created in order to manage the venture.

Proportionate Consolidation or Equity Accounting

Accounting for joint ventures requires that each venturer or entity be able to identify the assets and liabilities committed to the venture as well as the results as they relate to the venturer. IAS 31 permits the equity method outlined above. However, it argues forcefully in favour of the proportionate consolidation method. Under this method every joint venturer's share of each of the assets, liabilities, income and expenses of the joint venture is combined, line-by-line, with similar line items in the joint venturer's own financial statements.

Related Party Transactions

A related party transaction is a transfer of resources or obligations between related parties, regardless of whether a price is charged. Related party relationships are a normal feature of commercial life. However, they are of such a nature that specific disclosure is appropriate, and IAS 24, *Related Party Disclosures*, is primarily concerned with ensuring that adequate disclosures are made.

A party is related to an entity if it:

- Controls, directly, or indirectly, or is controlled by or is under common control of that entity
- Has an interest in the entity that gives it significant influence over that entity
- Has joint control over that entity
- Is an associate (as defined by IAS 28)
- Is a joint venture (as defined by IAS 31)
- Is a member of the key management personnel of the entity or its parent
- Is a close member of the family of any individual referred to above
- Is an entity in which a controlling or joint controlling interest over voting power is owned; or
- Is a post employment benefit plan.

In such circumstances, it is important that the existence of these relationships and transactions be made public.

Disclosures

IAS 24 is concerned primarily with information being provided for users by means of additional disclosure. At a minimum, it requires the following to be disclosed:

- The nature of the relationship between parties
- The monetary amount involved
- The amount of outstanding balances
- Details of any guarantees provided or received
- Provisions for doubtful debts
- Bad debts written off; and
- Details of compensation of key management personnel.

Summary

Mergers and acquisitions are key vehicles for corporate growth. Consequently, an understanding of the accounting treatment of the business combinations that result will be critical when trying to analyze and interpret the financial performance and position of large corporate entities. Likewise, the incidence of associates and joint ventures has increased in recent years and played a significant role in generating growth and wealth increases in large companies.

The accounting treatment and disclosure requirements attaching to groups are extensive. To a degree they are also complex, and consolidated accounts can often seem daunting. However, it is essential not to lose sight of the fact that consolidated accounts are essentially nothing more than a combination of the individual accounts of the group's constituent companies.

In analyzing and interpreting group accounts it is important to be aware that at a strategic and operational level a group is often more than the sum of its individual parts. Economies of scale, symbiotic trading relationships and the possibilities offered by greater geographic reach must be factored into any consideration of a group's position, performance and prospects. This involves what has been consistently advocated throughout this text: informed and sensitive contextualization.

Review Questions

Question 1
Explain why merger and acquisition activity is so prevalent in the Anglo-American world.

Question 2
Identify the unique characteristics of an acquisition.

Question 3
Explain the significance of the concept of "control" in determining the existence of a business combination. Distinguish between "control" and "interest".

Question 4
Explain the significance of IFRS 3 in the context of global regulatory developments.

Question 5
Distinguish between the following:
- Wholly-owned subsidiaries
- Partly-owned subsidiaries

Question 6
Explain the main features of the purchase accounting method. Give examples of how it operates in practice.

Question 7
Explain how the purchase accounting method deals with each of the following and explain the rationale behind the accounting practice:
- Minority interest
- Goodwill
- Unrealized profits on inventory traded between companies in the same group

Question 8
Define the term "Fair Value" and explain why it is such an important concept in relation to business combinations.

Question 9
Explain the accounting treatment that applies to Joint Ventures and Associates. Why might the IASB favour the proportionate consolidation method, rather than the equity method, for Joint Ventures?

Question 10
Explain why related party transactions are subject to such detailed disclosure requirements and identify a number of the disclosures that IAS 24, *Related Party Disclosures*, requires.

Case Studies

Case 1

Using the Tesco 2005 Annual Report, identify the significant elements of the purchase method as applied in the group accounts. In addition, identify the manner in which the group has accounted for Joint Ventures and investigate how this has been reflected in the financial statements and notes.

Case 2

The following article identifies a number of potential M&A possibilities and identifies bid fever and liquidity as two principal catalysts. In the process, the author also identifies private equity as a key interest. Consider the role that bid fever and liquidity, as distinct from shareholder value, play in the M&A process.

Bid Frenzy Has Us in its Thrall, by Heather Connon

ITV, O2, Scottish Power, BOC, Pilkington – you name it, the old-bid favourites were being trotted out last week as merger mania hit the stock market in a big way. There was some justification for the excitement: Exel, for years one of the market's favourite bid targets, finally did seem to be attracting a suitor in Deutsche Post, suggesting that even the oldest of stories can eventually have a happy ending for investors.

There was plenty going on elsewhere too, as Saint Gobain finally posted its offer document for building products group BPB, Old Mutual put flesh on its proposed offer for Skandia – a formal offer is expected this week, as we say on page 4 – and Cadbury Schweppes put its soft drinks business up for sale, all adding to existing takeover moves around companies as varied as Rentokil and Amvescap.

Bid fever has been a key factor in allowing the market to shrug off worries, such as the impact of Hurricane Katrina on oil and petrol prices, and therefore on the broader US economy, as well as continued evidence of falling retail sales and a sluggish housing market. Last week alone the FTSE 100 was up about 2 per cent, despite the devastation on the US's Gulf Coast, and it has gained a healthy 18 per cent over the past year. So far, there is little sign of the merger-inspired boom expiring.

The key reason behind it is liquidity. Companies – and their investors – are flush with cash and looking for places to invest it. ABN Amro calculates that, for the top 300 European companies, debt as a percentage of total capital has been falling for three years and, at 37 per cent, is well below its long-term average. Borrowing costs are extremely low so, for many deals, the earnings enhancement offered from a takeover is more than enough to cover the increased borrowing costs.

For share deals, the increased investor confidence and lower volatility in the market means bidders can pounce without worrying that their own shares, or those of their target, will be hit by a market correction. And, while the stock market has had a good 30 months, it still does not look that expensive, making it easier for companies to justify deals to shareholders.

Private equity interest remains key – and it is odds on that Cadbury's soft drinks business will end up with one of them, given that its cash flow and brand profile are exactly what venture capital houses look for. And there is little sign of that disappearing: while they invested almost 25 per cent more in 2004 than 2003, and a similar increase is likely this year, they have also been raising large sums of new money, as well as selling off existing investments, so they still have significant firepower.

It is, of course, possible that the bid frenzy could evaporate if, say, there was a threat that the Bank of England could have to raise interest rates to stave off inflationary pressures, or soaring oil prices finally started to affect demand in the wider economy. Until that happens, however, investors should just enjoy the ride.

Source: *The Observer*, September 6, 2005.

Case 3

The manner in which goodwill is now treated under IFRS has been described in this chapter. The following article explains, amongst other things, how this will impact the results of Vodafone. In this context, consider the assertion of finance director Ken Hydon, that under IFRS "Employees and customers will now be able to see that we are a profitable company and not a loss making company. It is now more transparent".

New Accounting Rules Will Put Vodafone in the Black, by Richard Wray

Vodafone will lose its unwanted position as the producer of the biggest loss in British corporate history under new international accounting rules which allow it to stop arbitrarily writing off billions of pounds every year. The mobile phone giant yesterday talked analysts through the impact of International Financial Reporting Standards. While IFRS will mean lower headline earnings and slightly lower cash-flow this year, the major impact will be on the writing off of the tens of billions of pounds of goodwill the company amassed during its buying spree in the late 1990s.

Under the new rules, the company no longer has to write off goodwill – the difference between the price paid for an acquisition and the underlying value of the assets – over an arbitrary period. Instead it will carry out an "annual impairment review'', looking at the assets it bought and deciding whether they are worth less than they were – in which case it will take a specific one-off charge.

Over the six months to end September 2004, for instance, Vodafone reported revenues of £16.79bn and a pre-tax loss of £1.88bn under the old rules as it wrote off billions in goodwill. Under IFRS revenues would have been slightly less at £16.74bn because of changes to the way that the company accounts for certain overseas assets, but it would have made a profit of £4.5bn.

"Employees and customers will now be able to see that we are a profitable company and not a loss making company," said finance director Ken Hydon. "It is now more transparent." Vodafone has spent about £3m getting ready to implement the new accounting standard. It will provide an IFRS set of accounts for the year to end March 2005 alongside its traditional figures with the first IFRS-only accounts in the following financial year. While Mr Hydon welcomed the change as making it easier to compare companies across borders, he admitted that "while people get used to it, it will be slightly confusing". The new rules also alter the way companies deal with operations they do not wholly own.

Vodafone's Italian arm, for instance, will now be classed as a joint venture rather than a subsidiary. But the negative impact of this switch is alleviated somewhat as its joint ventures in South Africa, Poland, Fiji and Kenya will become subsidiaries.

Source: *The Guardian*, January 23, 2005.

Case 4

Please see the text website for computational questions relevant to this chapter.

PENSIONS, SHARE OPTIONS, LEASES, TAXATION AND FOREIGN CURRENCY

[12]

When you have completed this chapter you will understand:

- The basic IFRS treatment of pensions, share options, leases, taxation and foreign currency transactions.

- Some of the political issues surrounding their introduction.

- That the changes resulting from the introduction of IFRS have significantly impacted accounting practice in a wide variety of areas.

- That, in spite of increased regulation, considerable scope remains for estimates and creativity.

Fears Over New 'Fair Value' Accounts: 2005 Brings Big Changes to How Firms Report Results, by Nils Pratley

The big stock market story of 2005? It could be accounting – not a subject to set pulses racing under normal circumstances, but January 1 marked the start of a pan-European shake-up affecting 7,000 publicly listed companies. On the evidence to date, the International Financial Reporting Standard (IFRS) regime is likely to bring confusion and volatile share prices. Look, for example, what happened last month after Jonathan Pierce and Michael Lever, CSFB's highly rated banking analysts, suggested that Northern Rock's profits could be reduced by 10% under new rules relating to recognition of income. Northern Rock's shares fell almost 3% on the day and the bank was clearly annoyed. A week later the chief executive, Adam Applegarth, called the episode "a storm in a teacup" and said that the effect of IFRS on Northern Rock's profits would be "not a lot". Precise figures, he argued, were not yet possible: "Analysts can huff and puff, but we can't give them the information."

Huffing and puffing, though, is part of the game because IFRS is, in the view of accounting firm Ernst & Young, "the biggest change in financial reporting in a generation". Opportunistic hedge funds are known to be taking a keen interest, knowing that investors' instinct on seeing unexpectedly poor numbers will be to sell first and ask questions later. "As with any big change, it is likely to be chaotic," says Jeannot Blanchet, IFRS expert at investment bank Morgan Stanley. "Some companies will surprise us negatively, and others will utterly confuse us with numbers and metrics looking very different from historical ones. "Investors are likely to struggle for a while deciphering what is pure accounting noise versus new information relevant for valuation purposes."

Source: *The Guardian*, January 3, 2005.

Introduction

The introduction of IFRS has heralded "the biggest change in financial reporting in a generation". The consolidated accounts of large public companies have seen the significant impact of new accounting standards dealing with pensions, share options and a variety of other topics. The result has been a dramatically redrawn accounting landscape. Not surprisingly, this has not occurred easily or without resistance. Indeed, the entrenched opposition to some standards has revealed a depth of political self-interest and commercial antagonism that surprised many.

This chapter deals with IFRS relating to a number of areas that have, to a greater or lesser degree, generated some controversy. They have in common the fact that they involve either new accounting requirements (such as accounting for share options); have the potential to significantly affect accounting numbers and, in particular, balance sheet valuations (pensions and leases); or relate to some technical aspects of accounting practice (foreign currency and deferred taxation). While some technical detail is supplied, the emphasis is less on the specific requirements and more on the principles involved as well as the political contexts surrounding their introduction.

The specific areas covered are:

- Pensions
- Share Options
- Leases
- Taxation
- Foreign Currency transactions.

Pensions

From the perspective of employees, the pensions policy of a company will be hugely important. Meanwhile, from the perspective of a company, pension commitments are likely to constitute one of its most significant responsibilities. For these reasons the manner in which pensions are accounted for will be of interest to a variety of stakeholders.

There are two principal types of pension scheme:

- **Defined benefit**: such a scheme guarantees a pension related to the average or final pay of the employee. It is the more common of the two schemes in the UK. Because it depends on future salary levels it is not always possible to estimate whether the contributions to the pension scheme will be sufficient to meet the eventual cost.

- **Defined contribution**: the pension is determined by the level of contributions and is a more straightforward approach for the accounting and actuarial systems. Under this method the employer makes agreed contributions to a pension scheme and the benefits paid will depend upon the funds available from these contributions and any investment earnings thereon. There is, therefore, little of the estimations or actuarial interventions characteristic of the defined benefit scheme.

Accounting for pensions, and especially defined benefit schemes, raises two key considerations:

1. The amount to be charged annually to the income statement.
2. The amount at which the assets and liabilities in the pension fund should be measured.

IAS 19, *Employee Benefits*, prescribes the accounting and disclosure requirements in relation to pensions. (As the name implies, it also deals with a range of other employee benefits, such as sick leave, bonuses and non-monetary benefits.) Its fundamental principle is that the full cost of providing employee benefits should be recognized in the period in which the employee earns the benefit, rather than the period in which it is paid or payable. In the case of pensions, this means that treatment is dependent on a scheme's classification:

- Defined contribution plans: expenses are recognized in the period the contribution is payable.

- Defined benefit plan: a liability is recognized in the balance sheet equal to the net of:
  - The present value of the defined benefit obligation (i.e. the present value of expected future payments required to settle the obligation resulting from employee service in the current and prior periods);
  - Deferred actuarial gains and losses and deferred past service costs; and
  - The fair value of any plan assets at the balance sheet date.

The adoption of IAS 19 (like its ASB counterpart, FRS 17, *Retirement Benefits*) has had a significant impact on accounting for pensions. Essentially, the balance sheet approach means that IAS 19 prioritizes how the underlying assets and liabilities should be measured. The income statement charge then merely reflects the movement in balance sheet figures. Not surprisingly, the use of present values, fair values and other estimates has increased volatility in an area that already requires the incorporation of various actuarial estimates and macro-economic assumptions.

In practice:

Tesco shows big pension deficit: IFRS brings Tesco's pensions deficit onto the balance sheet, but overall effect is minimal, by Kevin Reed

Tesco has seen hundreds of millions of pounds wiped off the balance sheet due to the treatment of employee benefits under IFRS. In its 2004/05 restated figures, Net assets fell by £400m, mainly due to a £735m hit in accounting for its pension deficit. Despite this, the retailer's bottom line has been barely dented, with profit after tax for 2004/05 falling by £19m compared to UK GAAP. The retailer also suffered actuarial losses on its defined benefit scheme of £230m after applying the amended IAS19. . .

Source: Accountancy Age, May 25, 2005.

Compass issues a pensions warning, by Jenny Wiggins

Compass Group, the food service company, yesterday said its interim underlying profit fell 2.9 per cent to £328m as its UK division continued to struggle – and warned that international accounting standards would force it to recognise additional pension liabilities. The warning, coupled with the news that the company would pay a higher tax rate as a result of the UK government's move to clamp down on cross-border financing structures, disappointed investors. Shares in Compass, which has about a 5 per cent share of the £250bn global food service market, fell 5.6 per cent to 222 3/4p, their lowest level since October. Compass will recognise an additional £220m to £240m in pension liabilities as a result of moving to international financial reporting standards and has agreed to raise its contributions to its UK pension schemes by £10m to £15m a year from 2006 onwards. Its pension fund has a gross deficit of around £400m, which it is currently funding at the rate of £42m per year, according to Michael Bailey, Compass chief executive.

Source: Financial Times, May 19, 2005.

Pension black hole at BT

UK telecoms company BT estimates a reduction in net assets of £4.1bn following adoption of IAS 19, Employee benefits. BT discloses that it will adopt IFRS as the basis of accounting for the 2006 financial year and highlights that a subsequent adoption of IAS 19 will lead to recognition of the deficit of the defined benefit pension schemes on the balance sheet. The company estimates that this will increase operating profit by £123m and reduce net assets by £4.1bn. As a consequence net assets of £3.9bn under UK GAAP would turn into net liabilities of £0.2bn.

Since a revision of IAS 19 in 2004, a choice of accounting treatment exists for dealing with actuarial gains and losses, one of the principal sources of volatility.

1. **10% *corridor approach*:** where actual gains and losses are greater than the larger of 10% of the present value of the defined benefit obligation or 10% of the market value of the plan assets, then gains or losses should be recognized in the income statement

over the average remaining service lives of current employees. If they are below the 10% threshold then they can be part of the defined benefit liability for the year.

2. *Equity recognition approach*: this allows recognition of actuarial gains and losses immediately in equity. While this method avoids recognition of gains and losses in the income statement, it ensures greater balance sheet volatility.

IAS 19 has had the effect, therefore, of dramatically increasing balance sheet volatility, with the principal focus now on measuring and valuing the assets and liabilities underlying the pension scheme.

Share Options

Share (stock) options have become a common feature of the economic lives of large companies. For several decades companies have employed them as a means of rewarding executives and key employees. Critically, while ensuring a greater alignment between the long-term interests of the company and recipients, they did not lead to any expense being recorded in the income statement.

In practice:

Staff of Enterprise Inns, the FTSE 100 pub company, are celebrating an £11 million Christmas windfall after a three-year share option scheme reached maturity. About 180 Enterprise employees, from regional managers to office secretaries, have received a total of 1.7 million shares under an employee share option scheme that was launched in December 2002.

The shares, with an option price of 280p, were worth 925p at the scheme's maturity, equating to an average profit per employee of about £60,000. The scheme encompassed about 180 of the 250 staff employed by Enterprise at the time it was launched.

Source: The Times, December 26, 2005.

A typical share option scheme would have operated as follows:

Grant date (say, January 1, 20X1): the company and a director make an agreement that will entitle the director to receive an option in the future (say, December 31, 20X3), subject to, for example, achieving certain levels of profitability. This agreement will usually allow the director to buy the shares at some point in the future at their value on the grant date.

Vesting date (say, December 31, 20X3): if, over the course of the specified three-year period from the grant date (the **vesting period**) the director fulfils the requirements then he/she becomes entitled to the option;

Exercise date (say, December 31, 20X4): the director decides to exercise the option, that is, to acquire the shares under the terms of the option. Obviously, the director would only do this if there were an economic advantage, i.e. if the share price had increased since grant date, since he/she could now buy the specified number of shares at the price that applied four years previously.

Previously, regardless of what the director decided to do, there would have been no charge in the income statement. This flew in the face of accounting "theory" which strongly advocated their identification as a form of remuneration. This was essentially due to the influence of a powerful business lobby that argued against such a charge on commercial grounds.

More recently, as the role such payments played in various frauds has come to light, accounting regulators have sought to implement a change in accounting treatment that would see an income statement effect. However, in both the US and Europe, a strong business lobby backed by powerful political interests has sought to argue that expensing the costs involved would lower earnings and reduce share price, thus prejudicing access to capital and compromising international competitiveness. They cite the example of AOL Time Warner which reported profits of $700m in 2001 that would have been transformed into a loss of $1.7b had options been expensed. Proponents of this view also point to the fact that there are no cash outflow implications for granting companies, as well as to the difficulties of actually measuring any cost involved:

Politicians Fight US Share Options Reform, by Adrian Michaels

Among sweeping business reforms, US accounting standard setters said last year that all companies would have to record options as an expense from 2005. Nearly 500 public companies in the US have voluntarily made the switch, taking some large hits in their financial statements, and some, such as Microsoft, have radically redesigned their compensation structures.

However, a rearguard action has been building in Washington. This has been particularly strong among California politicians listening to the high-tech lobby in an election year. Technology companies argue that options are a crucial way to attract talent while the businesses are in start-up mode. Some politicians, including senior Democrats and Republicans in the House of Representatives, want to stop the formal accounting proposal from becoming law. They have criticized the Financial Accounting Standards Board, the standard-setter due to issue its plans more fully in the next month. Last week, a number of Silicon Valley lobbyists were in Washington to press their case. Reginald Reed, manager of software development at Cisco Systems, said in a House hearing: "If stock options are expensed, many companies will be forced to cut back on programmes that benefit rank-and-file employees."

People close to Richard Shelby, Republican chairman of the Senate banking committee, said the senator believed the FASB process should not be interfered with. His views are shared by Paul Sarbanes, highest-ranking Democrat on the committee. Washington analysts agree that, with Mr Shelby and Mr Sarbanes in the Senate still backing FASB, moves in the House are not likely to lead to changes in option reform. Senators are expected to take their cues from the banking committee.

Nonetheless, the scale of the backlash is acknowledged by people close to Mr Shelby, who said they would monitor the situation. Nancy Pelosi, the most senior Democrat in the House, who represents a California district, and Richard Baker, a highly-influential Republican on the financial services committee, co-sponsored a bill to limit option expensing. Their initiative would see the expensing only of those options granted to a company's top five executives.

Source: *Financial Times*, March 10, 2004.

While opposition remains, the mood has shifted in the wake of recent accounting scandals, particularly those such as Enron that have revealed grossly excessive stock option packages for executives. Those supporting the more conceptually acceptable accounting treatment that would see options expensed, have now secured a level of political support that has seen a range of new accounting standards introduced. These have at their core some mechanism for ensuring that the 'cost' element of such options now appears in the income statement.

While this has gone down in some corporate circles like a "rat sandwich" according to David Tweedie, the broad outlines of new regulations from both FASB (SFAS 123, *Share-Based Payment*) and IASB (IFRS 2, *Share-Based Payments*) require the application of various fair value related formulae (using option pricing models) to share values on the grant date. The resulting entry sees a charge to the income statement and a corresponding credit to the balance sheet over the vesting period.

The following simplified example outlines the basic mechanics:

X plc grants an option to an employee on January 1, 20X1 to buy 100,000 shares on December 31, 20X3 if certain profit targets are achieved. The share price on January 1, 20X1 is £5.

IFRS 2 requires that the estimated cost to X plc be charged to the income statement over the three-year vesting period. Obviously, this will require certain estimates and assumptions: using options pricing models it is estimated that the price is likely to increase to £5.50 over the next three years; and the company estimates that there is a 75% probability that the employee will meet profitability targets.

At the grant date the value of the option can be calculated as:

$$100,000 \times £0.50 \times .75 = £37,500$$

As the vesting period is three years, an annual charge would be shown in the income statement of £12,500 leading to a total corresponding balance sheet (provisions) impact of £37,500 by December 31, 20X3.

In practice:

No option on options: Peter Williams on the introduction of IFRS 2, which has faced much resistance

With world stock markets gently and cautiously nudging upwards towards levels last seen at the start of the decade, directors and employees may find their stock options becoming a more interesting topic of conversation. And, at the same time, options will be making a slightly less-welcome first-time appearance in many companies' reports and accounts.

One of the major changes in accounting and disclosure brought about by the IASB is the creation of an accounting standard on so-called share-based payment transactions.

The introduction of an accounting standard for share options has been fiercely resisted in some quarters, most notably hi-tech US companies. The US-based Employee Stock Option Coalition said that the way to provide investors with accurate and more meaningful information was through enhanced disclosures on a frequent basis, not through mandatory expensing that would 'mislead investors with bad numbers.'

Whether investors will be misled and whether the numbers are bad, investors are certainly going to see the impact of IFRS 2, Share-based Payments. According to a report released by British based actuarial firm Lane Clarke & Peacock, the requirement for companies to expense IFRS could hit profits of the UK's top 100 listed companies by more that £1b. This equates to a 2% drop in profits. And the figure is likely to rise as the charge under IFRS ramps in the first few years of its operations. Companies quoted on other stock markets will be equally affected...

But the overriding point is that companies will now insert a cost for shares or share options schemes. IASB won a significant victory over powerful lobbyists who argued that the cost was a nonsense because it never involves an outflow of cash from the company's coffers. In their opinion, if there was a cost it was an expense borne directly by the shareholders via the dilution of their stake, and that should not be reflected in the company's accounts.

But that argument seems to have been lost. Shareholders will be able to see what share option schemes are costing. IFRS 2 will have a significant impact on company profits and the way in which companies structure share plans. And, for that reason, you can expect to see more companies closing share option schemes in favour of the more transparent performance shares.

Peter Williams is a journalist and chartered accountant.

Source: accounting & business, October 2005.

Leases

The extraordinary increase in the incidence of leasing in recent decades, and the manner in which many leases went unrecorded in the balance sheet – they were effectively forms of off-balance sheet financing – have meant that accounting for leases has often been controversial. In particular, the decision of UK accounting regulators in the 1980s to adopt a policy that tracked the commercial substance of a lease, as distinct from its legal form, meant that business interests and those of regulators diverged strongly.

IAS 17, *Leases*, follows the lead given by UK regulators. It defines a lease as "an agreement whereby the lessor conveys to the lessee, in return for a payment or series of payments, the right to use an asset for an agreed period of time". A lease creates a set of rights and obligations that result directly from the use and enjoyment by the lessee of the leased asset. Such rights are, in effect, the rewards of ownership, whilst the obligations, especially the obligation to continue paying instalments over the period of the lease, constitute the risks of ownership. Thus, while legal title may not be transferred to the lessee, the commercial reality may well be that the rights and risks associated with ownership effectively do.

IAS 17 requires, therefore, that leases be treated in a manner that reflects the commercial reality, rather than the legal niceties that may inform any agreement. In other words, accounting principles require that issues relating to ownership and risk be considered in determining how to classify a lease. This has material consequences for their accounting treatment.

Following the UK model, IAS 17, distinguishes between two types of lease:

- **Operating leases**: these involve the lessee paying a rental for the hire of an asset for a period of time that is normally substantially less than its useful economic life. Under this type of lease the lessor retains most of the risks and rewards of ownership of the leased asset.

- **Finance leases**: these usually involve payment by a lessee to a lessor of the full cost of the asset as well as various finance charges. Under a finance lease the bulk of the risks and rewards associated with the ownership of the asset are usually transferred to the lessee. Even if title is not transferred, in circumstances where the lease term is for the major part of the economic life of the asset, a finance lease would be deemed to exist. This is also the case if, at the inception of a lease, the present value of the minimum lease payments, including any initial payment, amounted to substantially all of the fair value of the leased asset.

IAS 17 then specifies a different accounting treatment for each type of lease.

- **Operating leases**: these should be accounted for by the lessee merely including the instalment payments as an expense. In effect, in the lessee's accounts payments made under operating leases are simply expensed to the income statement and the balance sheet is unaffected. The lessor retains ownership of the asset.

- **Finance leases**: these should be accounted for as the purchase of the asset by the lessee, and as a sale by the lessor. The result is that an asset is shown on the lessee's balance sheet at the lower of the present value of the minimum lease payments and the fair value of the asset, while a corresponding liability is also recognized. At the inception of a finance lease, these amounts should equate. Depreciation is applied in a manner consistent with that applied to other owned assets. The finance lease payment is then apportioned between interest and reduction of liability using either an actuarial, sum-of-digits or straight-line method.

The accounting implications of this can best be illustrated by means of an example:

X plc can purchase a machine for £40,000 or lease it under the following terms:

- The period of the lease is 4 years from January 1, 20X1 with lease payments due at the end of each calendar year.

- The minimum lease payments will be £14,000 per annum, i.e., £56,000 in total.

- X plc must pay all maintenance, repair and insurance costs associated with the machine.

- Interest rate applicable is 15%.

X plc decides to lease. This requires that the company compute the present value of the minimum lease payments at the start of the lease. Discounting four annual payments of £14,000 commencing at the end of year 1 at a rate of 15% shows that the present value is £39,970 (i.e., $£14,000 \times 2.285$). Since this is substantially the same as the fair value of the asset, this qualifies as a finance lease. The lower of present value and fair value must be shown as an asset and as a corresponding liability from the outset.

The annual lease payment must now be subdivided into the capital repayment element and the financing portion. The total finance charge to be paid over the period of the lease will be £16,030 ($£56,000 - £39,970$). This must be allocated over the 4 years using one of a number of options. The actuarial method allocates the amount in proportion to the outstanding liability. Adopting this approach leads to the following computations:

Year Ending	Amount owed at start of year (£)	Finance charge 15% (£)	Sub-total (£)	Rental (£)	Amount owed at end of year (£)
20X1	39,970	5,995	45,965	14,000	31,965
20X2	31,965	4,795	36,760	14,000	22,760
20X3	22,760	3,414	26,174	14,000	12,174
20X4	12,174	1,826	14,000	14,000	nil

The finance element will be charged to the income statement every year. The balance sheet will show an asset of £39,970 (less depreciation in accordance with company policy), and a progressively declining liability as indicated in the right hand column.

Obviously, the way in which a lease is classified, whether as a finance or an operating lease, will be critical in determining levels of company debt. It will, for instance, directly impact upon performance measures such as profit and gearing.

Taxation

The importance of taxation and the manner in which it appears in financial statements has been alluded to already in Chapter 6. In this chapter the focus will be on some of the more detailed aspects of its calculation and presentation.

As they are separate legal entities, companies are liable to corporation tax in their own right under the Finance Act 1965, as modified by the Finance Act 1973. The emphasis, therefore, is on this tax, rather than PAYE and VAT, which derive not from a company's legal status, but from the specific trading or service activities that it undertakes.

Corporation Tax

The tax to which the corporate profits of UK resident companies are subject is known as Corporation Tax (CT). The system involves the application of a fixed rate of tax to the taxable profits (income and capital gains) of a company. Companies may also have income taxable abroad in which case they will also be liable to overseas tax.

For corporation tax purposes the financial year runs from April 1 to March 31. Corporation Tax rates are normally announced in the preceding budget. If a company's accounting year straddles two financial years, then the profits are subdivided on a time basis and subjected to the rate appropriate to each.

For instance, the Corporation Tax rate for 2005 (i.e., financial year April 1, 2005–31 March 2006) was 30%. The rate for 2004 was also 30%. A company with an accounting year ending December 31, 2005 and profits of £12 million would attract the following liability:

January–March 2005: (£12 million × 3/12) @ 30%	£900,000
April–December 2005: (£12 million × 9/12) @ 30%	£2,700,000
Tax liability	£3,600,000

Since 1999 companies with taxable profits in excess of £1.5m pay their corporation tax quarterly.

The UK operates what is known as an "imputation system" of taxation. This means that it recognizes that recipients of dividends from UK companies receive their money out of profits that have already been subjected to taxation, and therefore, imputes to them a credit in respect of such tax.

IAS 12, Income Taxes

IAS 12, *Income Taxes*, requires an enterprise to account for the taxation consequences of transactions in a manner similar to that applied to the underlying transactions themselves. In other words, entities must account for, and make disclosure in relation to, taxation in a manner that tracks the underlying transactions from which they derive.

IAS 12 requires that specific disclosures be made in the financial statements as follows:

- **Income Statement**: the tax expense relating to profit or loss from ordinary activities should be disclosed as a line item on the face of the income statement. The major components of this expense, such as current tax expense and adjustments recognized in the current period in respect of prior periods (such as under-provisions), should be disclosed separately.

- **Balance Sheet**: current tax due for current and prior periods should be recognized as a liability. Any net excess paid should be recognized as an asset.

Deferred Tax

In many continental European countries the accounting and tax codes are intimately related. If anything, tax codes take precedence. In fact, elements of accounting practice in countries like Germany can be shown to have been dictated by tax law.

In the UK, however, and in many other English-speaking countries, there has never been this type of relationship, with the result that tax and accounting principles often diverge. One of the consequences of this is that the "profit" disclosed by the financial statements may not be the same as that calculated under HM Customs and Revenue rules.

Consequently, although they will accept the financial statements as a starting point for their computations, HM Customs and Revenue will insist on making certain adjustments. For example, the financial accounts may contain a deduction in respect of entertainment expenses, but HM Customs and Revenue will refuse to recognise this and insist that it be added back to profit before applying the tax rate to determine tax liability.

These sources of difference between HM Customs and Revenue's approach and the accounting approach to the calculation of taxable profit can be grouped under two categories:

- **Permanent differences**: these are adjustments, such as that made in respect of entertainment expenses, which represent amendments that will never be reversed.

- **Timing differences**: these are differences that arise from the inclusion of items of income and expenditure in tax computations in periods different from those in which they are included in financial statements. Timing differences originate in one period and are capable of reversal in one or more subsequent periods, i.e., they do not result from differences of principle, but from the timing basis upon they are recognized by the accounting system and HM Customs and Revenue respectively. The most common example arises from the refusal of HM

Customs and Revenue to recognise depreciation as a deduction in calculating profits, insisting that its own equivalent – capital allowance – be substituted. Since the amount claimed under the capital allowances calculation will normally be different from that claimed under the depreciation calculation, the taxable profit (and hence the tax due) will be different from that incorporated in the financial accounts. Consequently, the CT liability indicated under "Current Tax Payable" may have to be amended, as it is possible that some element of the tax charge will be deferred. However, while the amounts under the respective headings may differ in any one year, over the life of an asset it would be expected that they would reconcile. That is, the source of difference is due solely to timing differences. Tax that has been temporarily deferred in this way is known as "Deferred Tax".

In practice:

Tax Corrector, by Lex

Accounting cynics quip that the only reliable guide to how much money a company really makes is the cash tax it pays. They may have a point. Enron, HealthSouth and World-Com together had tax charges in their profit & loss accounts, which are calculated off accounting profit, of $6.8bn over 1999 and 2000. Their Securities and Exchange Commission filings show the actual cash tax they paid was a mere 11 per cent of this – just $768m.

P&L tax and actual cash tax diverge for four likely reasons. First, timing differences. Second, P&L charges are estimates. Third, tax breaks from past losses or investments can often be offset against P&L tax costs. But fourth, and most interestingly, tax accounts are not the same as capital market accounts. They can treat key components of the P&L – depreciation, hedging and capital gains, for example – differently. Tax accounts are also prepared, and payment agreed, at the country subsidiary rather than group level.

Why might dodgy companies have low cash taxes? Often because of past losses: World-Com had accumulated a colossal $19.9bn of tax-deductible losses by 2002. But in the case of fraudulent companies, it may also be because the tax man's view of profitability is far less optimistic than that shown in capital market accounts. In the US this suspicion is borne out by national income accounts, which suggest that aggregate corporate profits in recent years, based on tax filings, have been lower than those reported to investors.

For big companies the gap is typically small. Over their last two reported years the 10 largest US companies paid $82bn of cash tax, or 79 per cent of their P&L charge. In the UK the ratio was 86 per cent. The outliers tend to be big and complex: General Electric (37 per cent), American International Group (55 per cent) and International Business Machines (52 per cent). All have legitimate explanations for this. Their shareholders should be delighted that the tax man is being short-changed. But, also, just a little curious.

Source: Financial Times, April 4, 2005.

IAS 12 originally accepted timing differences as the basis for calculating and accounting for deferred taxation. However, IAS 12 (revised) focuses instead on **temporary differences**, which are "differences between the tax base of an asset (or liability) and its carrying amount in the balance sheet". The tax base is the amount at which the asset (or liability) is carried for tax purposes. All timing differences are temporary differences. In addition, IAS 12 specifies the balance sheet liability method as the basis on which deferred taxation is to be calculated. This requires the recalculation of the amount of potential liability each year in the light of changing rates of tax, thus increasing or decreasing existing provisions.

The following basic example illustrates some of the mechanics involved in calculating deferred tax under IAS 12 (revised).

Y plc has plant that cost £300,000 with a carrying amount in the accounts of £200,000 after depreciation to date. Cumulative capital allowances to date amount to £180,000. The tax rate is 30%.

This translates into the following:

	Financial Accounts	Tax Statements
Cost	300	300
Depreciation/Capital Allowances	100	180
Carrying amount	200	120

In order to recover the carrying amount of £200,000, the company must earn taxable income of the same amount, but will only be allowed to deduct remaining capital allowances of £120,000. The temporary difference is equal to £80,000. As a result, the company will have to pay taxes of £24,000 (30% × £80,000) when it recovers the carrying amount of the asset. Therefore, Y plc must recognise a deferred tax liability of this amount in its accounts.

In practice:

As the following example illustrates, not all companies are happy with the accounting logic behind the deferred tax provisions of IAS 12:

Independent News and Media, which has reported an 80.6% rise in pre-tax profits to €140.7m (£95.2m) for the half-year ended 30 June 2005, has raised concerns about the treatment of deferred tax under IFRS. The media group said it had to make an 'illogical adjustment' under IFRS to its deferred tax liabilities, because the book value of certain assets exceeded their tax bases. It said: 'The group does not currently have a constructive or legal obligation for any tax liability associated with these assets and, therefore, the required deferred tax liability in this case is inconsistent with the accounting treatment for other provisions.'

Source: Accountancy Age, September 2005.

Foreign Currency

The globalization of commerce that has occurred steadily over the past number of decades has made it inevitable that most companies, particularly larger multi-national enterprises, will undertake foreign currency transactions.

The two most obvious means by which this will happen are:

- **Directly** by way of business transactions which are denominated in foreign currencies. In these circumstances these transactions will need to be translated into the "home" currency, i.e., the currency in which the company reports.

- **Indirectly** where foreign operations are executed through a foreign enterprise which maintains its accounting records in a currency other than that of the investing company. In these circumstances it will be necessary to translate the complete financial statements of the foreign enterprise into the "home" currency, i.e., the currency in which the investor company reports, in order to prepare consolidated financial statements for the group.

In practice:

A simple example illustrates some of the possible issues: X plc undertakes a transaction valued at $500,000 when the exchange rate was $1.20 = £1 which has to be incorporated into a balance sheet being prepared when the exchange rate has fluctuated to $1.30 = £1. It might be shown at either:

Rate applicable on transaction date = £416,667, or

Rate applicable on balance sheet date = £384,615

Obviously, therefore, the rate chosen can have a significant influence on the amount at which an item is included in the financial statements.

IAS 21, *The Effects of Changes in Foreign Exchange Rates*, covers the treatment of transactions involving foreign currency and identifies the manner in which foreign currency transactions should be recorded. For the purposes of identifying accounting treatment, IAS 21 distinguishes between an entity's functional and presentation currencies:

- **Functional currency**: this is the currency of the primary economic environment in which the entity operates. This would normally be the currency that mainly influences prices for goods and services. A company will need to decide whether its foreign operations, branches and subsidiaries are to have the same functional currency as itself; and

- **Presentation currency**: the currency a reporting entity uses for its financial statements.

In order to operationalize its provisions, IAS 21 also distinguishes between "monetary" and "non-monetary" items:

- Monetary items are balances, such as debtors, creditors, loans or dividends payable, owed by or to an entity that will be settled by cash

- Non-monetary items are other balances, such as fixed assets.

The basic rules on recording foreign currency transactions are:

1. Initial recognition: all transactions should be recorded using the exchange rate applying between the foreign currency and the functional currency on the transaction date.

2. At subsequent balance sheet dates:

   i. monetary balances should be translated using the closing rate on that date.
   ii. non-monetary items incorporated at historical cost must remain at their original rate, while those incorporated using fair value are translated at the rate applicable on the date fair value was determined.

3. Exchange differences arising on settlement of monetary items and on translation of monetary items at a rate other than that applying when initially recorded, should be recognized in net profit or loss (except for differences arising from monetary items that form part of the reporting entity's net investment in a foreign operation, which is shown separately under equity). See IAS 21 (paras 28–29).

For example, on April 30 X plc, a UK company, sold goods to a Russian customer for R50,000 when the rate of exchange was £1 = R10.

On the date of sale this should be recorded as:

| Dr | Debtors | £5000 |
| Cr | Sales | £5000 |

If at the financial year-end, June 30, this balance remained outstanding when the rate is £1 = R8, then the following entry would need to be made:

| Dr | Debtors | £1250 |
| Cr | Income Stmt | £1250 |

This would have the effect of showing the amount due as £6,250, the amount which X plc would receive in sterling were it to receive a draft for R50,000 on that date.

If the account is subsequently settled on July 11, by which time the rate has fluctuated again to £1 = R9, then the company would receive a draft for R50,000 which would yield £5,555. This would require the following entries to be made:

Dr	Cash	£5,555
Cr	Debtors	£5,555
Dr	Income Stmt	£695
Cr	Debtors	£695

The same approach would apply to other monetary assets such as loans and creditors.

In practice:

Rio Tinto and IFRS: Mining company Rio Tinto's earnings could swing by millions of dollars when it issues its first set of results under IFRS later this year

The company is only scheduled to release its full-year and half-year results for 2004 under IFRS in early May, but it is already clear that the new standards will influence the accounts significantly. Rio Tinto has operations in Africa, Europe, the Americas, Australasia and the Pacific rim and is exposed to fluctuations in exchange rates because of its geographic spread and the link between commodity prices and currency values.

New reporting standards will change how foreign-exchange gains on debt and derivatives are dealt with, which will have a significant impact on how the mining multinational manages the risk of foreign-exchange variations. Because of its global positioning and vulnerability to exchange rates Rio Tinto has financed its operations through US dollar debt and implemented numerous derivative contracts.

Rio Tinto's 2003 financial statements provide a glimpse of the massive swings IFRS can bring about. The company had always reported exchange gains or losses from US debt through its reserves. In 2003, reporting under US GAAP, Rio Tinto could only do this if the debt qualified as a hedge of US dollar assets. All other exchange gains had to be reflected in the profit and loss account. This saw a $1.01bn (£544m) pre-tax increase to earnings from exchange gains on US dollar debt that did not qualify for hedge accounting. After tax and minorities the addition to earnings was $623m...

Source: Accountancy Age, February 11, 2005.

Summary

This chapter has looked at the accounting regulations applying to several areas of accounting practice. The focus has, however, been as much on the broader issues such as political lobbying and international pressures for harmonization as on any presentation of detailed double entries. Both emphases are important when interpreting financial statements, as one requires macro-considerations to be taken into account while the other respects the fact that technical accuracy is also important.

In the process of discussing some of the catalysts for change in accounting practice in these areas this chapter has identified the broader "harmonization" agenda, particularly as espoused by the IASB, as a significant factor. This will be discussed in more detail in Chapter 15.

Review Questions

Question 1
IAS 19, *Employee Benefits,* is introducing increased volatility to the balance sheets of many companies. Explain how this is so and consider the view that this offsets any advantages championed by the IASB.

Question 2
"That IFRS 2, *Share-Based Payments,* is now in place is evidence of the decline of political factors in the regulatory process". Discuss.

Question 3
"Lease accounting provides one of the most fertile areas for creative accounting practices". Explain what is meant by this statement.

Question 4
Identify the principal features of the Corporation Tax code in the UK and explain the meaning of "imputation system".

Question 5
Explain why deferred tax arises and why it is significant in an accounting context.

Question 6
In the context of IAS 12, *Income Taxes*, distinguish between a timing difference, a permanent difference and a temporary difference, and give examples of each.

Question 7
IAS 21, *The Effects of Changes in Foreign Exchange Rates*, identifies a company's functional and presentation currencies. Outline what these are and the circumstances in which each applies.

Question 8
Explain the distinction between monetary and non-monetary items in the context of foreign exchange transactions and outline the significance of this distinction in the context of the application of the provisions of IAS 21.

Case Studies

Case 1

The following article discusses a number of the critical issues surrounding the debate about accounting for pensions. In particular, the author identifies the use of various estimates and assumptions as responsible for a significant degree of uncertainty and volatility. He observes, "If accounting is a grey area, then accounting mixed with actuarial practices becomes decidedly murky. Change the assumptions even by apparently a tiny amount and the balance sheets numbers can shift dramatically". Discuss the extent to which employing estimates and assumptions in this manner, undermines the credibility of IFRS. [Note: In terms of accounting for pensions, FRS 17, *Retirement Benefits*, is the ASB equivalent of IAS 19, *Employee Benefits,* and the two standards are similar in terms of overall principles.]

Transparency

Peter Williams Unpicks the Devil in the Detail of Pension Accounting

Paul Boyle, the first chief executive of the newly expanded UK Financial Reporting Council, recently gave a presentation at a pension conference to finance directors and treasurers entitled "Managing your pension liability". One section of the talk was called "The magic telescope" or, as Boyle put it, "How to make very big things appear very small".

The essence of this idea is that accounting for pensions is still more about sleight of hand than it is about honest presentations of the facts. As John Hawkins, the former head of finance and risk at Invensys and now a pension writer and consultant, puts it: "Essentially, the finance director can still work his magic on pension fund deficits. Especially if on the balance sheet he concentrates on mortality expectations and on discount rates. And, when it comes to the income, there is much that the FD can do on expected investment returns."

So is accounting for pensions the last great area for creative accounting? Well, maybe. But if that is the case then it is probably not the fault of the finance director or the standard setter. Indeed, the blame cannot be laid at any one door. The fact remains that pensions are complicated and, so, therefore is the accounting.

As Boyle said: "This is not about FRS 17, *Retirement Benefits*, or its international equivalent IAS 19, *Employee Benefits*; this is not about investment strategy. The drivers of pensions liabilities are salary increase, additional years of service, life expectancy improvements and discount rates."

For a subject, which by any stretch of the imagination cannot be accused of setting the pulse racing, pensions rarely seem to be out of the headlines. After a lengthy transition FRS 17 came into force in the middle of 2003. Around the time it was issued, the then UK Work and Pensions Secretary, Alistair Darling, summoned Sir David Tweedie, then chairman of the Accounting Standards Board (ASB), to express his view that the accounting standard was ruining the pension industry. It was a classic case of shooting the messenger. FRS 17 has helped a slowly dawning realization among politicians, corporates and would-be pensioners that the present systems of pension provisions are unsustainable. And many of us are in for a poverty-dominated old age.

But now, after having seen the deficits FRS 17 has produced, questions are being raised over how the numbers have been calculated. One of the major changes under FRS 17 is that pensions liabilities and assets are no longer confined to the footnotes of report and accounts, but now move to centre stage where any surplus or deficit immediately becomes an integral part of the balance sheet.

Such a material liability on the balance sheet has an impact on share price, dividend flexibility and loan covenants. The pension liability has become the new poison pill. Richard Farr, leader of the pension team at PricewaterhouseCoopers, says: "There is a lot of flexibility in FRS 17. What we are suggesting is greater disclosures." Farr worries that hostile bids are being blocked because the would-be takeover team cannot get the information they need to assess the pension issue properly. Quite a few deals have foundered on the premise that you may fancy the company but you won't take on the pension risk. Bob Scott, partner at actuarial outfit Lane Clark & Peacock (LCP), says: "Pension fund deficits continue to have a major impact on the way many FTSE 100 companies operate. Those companies with significant FRS 17 deficits on their balance sheets may well find themselves restricted in terms of the dividends they are able to pay to shareholders and the capital they can raise for refinancing. Pension deficits will also play a significant role in merger and acquisition activity and are already curtailing potential deals."

But what exactly is the risk? Probably no one really knows. Unique in the balance sheet, the pension liability (or asset) depends entirely on the use of actuarial assumptions. If accounting is a grey area, then accounting mixed with actuarial practices becomes decidedly murky. Change the assumptions even by apparently a tiny amount and the balance sheets numbers can shift dramatically. Consultants Pension Adviser Review recently published *FRS 17: The Finance Directors' Guide to Actuaries and their Assumptions*. Pension Adviser Review pointed out that the directors of the company are responsible for the accounts and the accounting policies – and, hence, the assumptions used in coming up with the pension numbers. However, any sensible board is going to take advice from professional actuaries on the sort of assumptions they should be making.

There are three key assumptions that finance directors and their boards need to consider and agree on before the numbers can be crunched and the pension deficit or surplus calculated.

- First, the amount of money the pension fund will have to pay out will depend partly on the salaries of employees. So what salary increases are they likely to get before they retire?
- Second, how long are pensioners (and dependant spouses) likely to live?

- Finally, defined benefits scheme liabilities are discounted at a rate that reflects the time value of money and the characteristic of the liability. FRS 17 says: "Such a rate should be assumed to be the current rate of return on a high quality corporate bond of equivalent currency and term to the scheme liabilities." Pension Adviser Review found that, in the fourth quarter of 2004, the assumed discount rate across all companies varied from a low of 4.85% to a high of 5.90%, a spread of 105 basis points. A spread of this magnitude represents a difference in pension liabilities of as much as 15% or more.

When the total deficit of pension assets to pension liabilities for S&P 500 companies amounted to $185bn and to FTSE 100 companies £58bn (figures from Mercer Human Resource Consulting) for the 31 December 2004, then you can see the odd percentage point here and there really matters.

One emerging point directors should note: companies should be wary of playing too fast and loose with changing assumptions. The sponsoring company directors and the trustees should be aware of falling foul of as yet untested anti-avoidance provisions under the newly-introduced Pensions Act 2004 which are designed to ensure sponsoring companies don't rip off the pension fund.

One accounting standard setter who declined to go on the record, but who had been heavily involved in drawing up FRS 17 and is still involved in standard setting, agrees the standard wasn't perfect. He told *accounting & business*: "There is a lot more information in FRS 17 than there was in SSAP 24 [the previous accounting standard]. There are various assumptions that companies have to make and that means that there are still some mysteries, but accounting for pensions is getting better."

It does seem that the disclosures around accounting for pensions will improve in the long run. Sir David Tweedie, now chairman of the International Accounting Standards Board (IASB), recognizes that IAS 19 is flawed and is due a makeover. When that will happen is not clear. Part of the problem is that the IASB is trying to march in step with the US Financial Accounting Standards Board (FASB). And, according to John Hawkins, the US accounting standard is a horrible cross between FRS 17 and SSAP 24.

It is clear that accounting for pensions is never going to be perfect. The figure in the balance sheet is a snapshot of obligations that will not actually kick in for decades. But Hawkins has some strong ideas on how to make the best of a difficult job. He would like to see the compulsory disclosure of the mortality tables used so it is clear how long companies think employees and pensioners will live. He also wants the actual rather than the expected return on investments put through the income statement. Finally, he wants pension liabilities to be discounted using a risk free rate rather than using a high grade bond rate.

Hawkins said: "The eminent economist, Jack Treynor, first explained why a risk free rate should be used over 30 years ago – he was right then and he is still right." Such moves will not make pension accounting crystal clear. Nothing will do that. But it could help to take away the sense of the black art.

Peter Williams is a journalist and a chartered accountant. He writes on accounting, financial reporting and auditing issues.

Source: *accounting & business*, October 2005.

Case 2

The following article claims to identify some changes in remuneration policy at several top firms resulting, in part, from "new accounting standards and pension rules". Discuss the extent to which changes in accounting rules have impacted remuneration policy and whether this is an acceptable response by companies.

Reviews Spark Fear of Jump in Top Pay, by Jill Treanor and Julia Finch

More than 200 companies listed on the stock market are conducting root and branch reviews of their top executives' pay, prompting concerns among investors that boardroom remuneration is spiralling higher. The unprecedented level of pay reviews is coming to light as companies publish their annual reports in which they must declare changes to remuneration policy. Some 210 of the companies listed in the All-Share index – about one in four – have hired pay consultants to consider whether their boardroom directors are adequately rewarded.

Companies such as BP, Shell, Barclays and Unilever, have all revealed they are planning to stop using share option schemes to link directors' pay to performance. Instead, they are setting up new schemes that use shares rather than options to provide the long-term bonus element of directors' incentive packages. Other companies, notably Aviva, are announcing new pay deals for their top executives which they admit will allow them to earn more than they do at present – provided they hit certain targets.

The impact that the revised pay plans will have on the overall level of directors' remuneration may not become apparent for three years or so because of the length of time on which the performance criteria is based. Damian Carnell of consultants Towers Perrin, which is believed to have more clients among the top 100 companies than any of its rivals, said it is a fact that executive pay moves up at a faster pace than average people's pay.

Many of the new schemes involve moving away from traditional share options – first introduced 20 years ago – to so-called share matching plans where executives are given free shares so long as performance targets are reached. Anita Skipper, of Morley Fund Managers, said: "It is very important to ensure performance targets are challenging because if they are not, you are literally giving away the shares."

The investment committee of the Association of British Insurers – whose members speak for about 25% of the shares listed in the London Stock Exchange – is known to be concerned about the number of reviews being conducted, and believes the end result is likely to be a ratcheting up of boardroom pay. It believes executives could be paid more for mundane performance if the new incentives are not linked to more taxing targets.

Peter Montagnon, head of investment affairs at the ABI, said pay reviews were not necessarily bad news as they meant greater consultation with shareholders. New accounting standards and pension rules, he added, were also partially responsible for many pay reviews.

But there was evidence the reviews are prompting an across-the-board rise in pay: "We are seeing a ratcheting-up. It is focusing on bonuses and variable pay, rather than fixed pay, which is good. But people are probably creating situations where more will be paid for the same performance."

Investors believe the upward pay spiral is being driven by remuneration consultants, whose objectivity may be compromised because they are paid by the companies whose top executives' salary packages they advise on. Mr Montagnon said: "There is a gut feeling of unease about what is happening. We should be looking at the role of remuneration consultants in driving the ratchet. "[We need to know] who do consultants work for? Is it the executives or the remuneration committee?"

Source: *The Guardian*, May 6, 2005.

CREATIVE ACCOUNTING

When you have completed this chapter you will understand:

- What is meant by the term "creative accounting".
- Some of the ways in which accountants, governments and regulators have attempted to deal with this phenomenon.
- That creative accounting practices persist.
- The role of ethics in countering a creative accounting culture.

Cooking the Books is as Easy as Ever, by Terry Smith

Ten Years Ago Terry Smith Caused a Storm by Exposing How Top Companies Inflate Their Profits. Little has Changed

IN THE words of Yogi Berra, the New York Yankee famous for his deceptively simple observations, "this is like deja vu all over again". A decade ago I wrote *Accounting for Growth*, the book about how companies used creative accounting to inflate profits and make their balance sheets look stronger. The result was that I was fired from my job as head of research at UBS and sued. Corporate executives who are willing to bend the rules of accounting are not shy about getting an analyst fired for exposing them... Here I am again, 10 years later, writing about creative accounting in the wake of the collapse of Enron and the related scares that have dragged down the share prices of companies tainted by association. One of them is Tyco, the American conglomerate forced to break itself up. Even the mighty GE, the world's largest company, has been affected: the whiff of complex financial statements and off-balance-sheet obligations has led to share-price panic.

What has happened is nothing new. The lessons about creative accounting have to be re-learnt in each new market cycle. Why? Partly because in each new cycle the stock market is staffed by young new fund managers and brokers who have never seen any of this before. And also because some of the old pros forget what they have learnt when they inhale the intoxicating fumes of a bull market.

The Enron scandal has its roots in the bull market of the 1990s. The market became obsessed with a search for growth companies. Why? Because there were so few of them. The 1990s was a period of disinflation, when companies lost much of their power to raise prices. The result was that profit growth was scarcer than it had been in the 1980s. And where it could be found, or manufactured, it became prized more highly. However, the notion that there are lots of big companies with massive growth potential just waiting to be found by shrewd investors is a myth. Research last year by Fortune magazine showed that of the top 150 American companies over the past 40 years, only three or four have been able to sustain earnings growth at an average of 15% a year for a 20-year period. But this does not stop many chief executives from claiming that they will double earnings within five years, equivalent to compound growth of 15% a year.

The chief executives have been telling investors what they said they wanted. And if there is one thing you can bet on, it is that what investors are willing to pay for, the market will give them. In some cases this was provided by the illusory growth of TMT (technology, media and telecoms) stocks, with the focus on internet "hit rates" and "eyeball metrics", with no growth in profits or cashflows at all. In other cases, managements faced with the need to generate earnings growth simply invented it by creative accounting.

The means by which this was delivered are nothing new. American investors are in shock because Enron, at its peak the seventh-largest American company, managed to get many of its liabilities off its balance sheet by using partnership structures that often involved its own directors. British companies were pulling similar strokes more than a decade ago with a technique quaintly known as the non-subsidiary subsidiary.

There is no really new way of cooking the books, and there never will be. Investors have been particularly shocked that the Enron scandal could occur when its accounts were prepared under US generally accepted accounting principles or US GAAP. This is reckoned to be the best accounting regime in the world in that it requires the greatest disclosure by companies and is prescriptive, meaning that it allows little leeway to companies in the preparation of accounts. But the fact is that once you have any set of rigid accounting rules, accountants will find a way round them.

The job of accounting regulators worldwide is a bit like painting the Forth Bridge. As soon as you have finished, you need to start again. So what should investors be wary of now? There are some simple tell-tale warning signs or, as Yogi Berra also said, "you can observe a lot just by watchin'..."

Source: *Sunday Times*, February 3, 2002.

Introduction

The collapse of Enron was a cathartic event in the history of accounting. Although there have been larger frauds, the heady mix of greed, political favouritism and accounting chicanery has meant that, for many, it stands as a witness to regulatory, professional and commercial failure. Indeed, some commentators speak and write about "pre-Enron" and "post-Enron" in an attempt to signify the impact the collapse has had on accounting practice and regulation. While time will undoubtedly reveal a more complex story, the creative role played by accountants in facilitating what happened at Enron, points to the key role assigned to accounting information in modern economies.

The circumstances outlined in the opening article provide a timely reminder of the nature and extent of the problems that these practices have posed for both accounting and society as a whole. Long understood by accountants and regulators as a key factor in undermining the credibility of financial reports, efforts have been ongoing for many years to limit the scope of companies to "cook the books". From the South Sea Bubble collapse in the early 18th century to the financial manipulation surrounding the collapse of Maxwell Communications Corporation in the early 1990s, the need for tighter control of accounting practices has been obvious.

Indeed, events such as the collapse of the Maxwell empire and a spate of similar scandals in the late 1980s were critical catalysts in bringing about the establishment of the Accounting Standards Board (ASB) in the UK. "There were only three things wrong with company accounts in the 1980s", Sir David Tweedie has observed, "the profit and loss account, the balance sheet and the statement of sources and applications of funds (the predecessor of the cash flow statement)". In other words, everything was wrong with the basic financial statements upon which investors were relying for a "true and fair view" of company performance and financial position.

The sense of urgency communicated by Tweedie was well warranted. By the late 1980s accounting and auditing regimes were under fire from all quarters in the wake of a series of financial scandals that implicated them as principal actors in a failed system. More recent frauds and accounting-related corporate collapses have merely perpetuated the perception that creative accounting is a cultural issue that accounting regulators have done little to eradicate.

Creative Accounting

Creative accounting has been defined in a number of ways, ranging from "outright fraud" to "the imaginative use of accounting numbers". However, it has probably been best defined as "the use and abuse of accounting techniques and principles to achieve financial results which, intentionally, do not provide a true and fair view".

This is a preferable definition for a number of reasons:

- It emphasizes the fact that it is an intentional act with a particular goal in mind.
- While recognizing that accounting practices and techniques can be manipulated, it resists the temptation to reduce creative accounting to the manipulation of practices and techniques alone.

- Instead, it extends the definition to embrace the more fundamental point that the problem lies in the fact that many accounting principles and concepts are flawed. The implication is that any resolution of the problem of creative accounting must address this reality. This helps to explain the significance which the IASB attaches to its "principles-based" standards and the joint conceptual framework project with FASB. Creative accounting can only be countered by developing a coherent conceptual framework from which an integrated set of practices emerges. Concentration on principles rather than specifics helps to engender a culture more concerned with the application of the spirit, than the letter, of the law. This in turn greatly reduces the incidence of certain creative accounting practices.

- By considering creative accounting within the context of "true and fair" (or "fair presentation") it provides a measure against which creative accounting practices can be gauged.

- By extending the definition to embrace both "use and abuse" it recognizes that much of what is called creative accounting is actually passive manipulation or "creative compliance". In other words, a mentality exists in which it is seen as legitimate to exploit loopholes or the silence of a standard on a particular issue. Again, such practices will only be countered by developing a reporting culture in which compliance with the spirit, rather than the letter, of the law is championed.

In practice:

The following extract provides a slightly different, but not inconsistent, definition of creative accounting. Whatever the actual definition, the important point is the objective: to create "an altered impression of a firm's business performance":

The Financial Numbers Game

The Enron Corp collapse has forced various quarters to take a closer look at their accounting practices and strategies. Enron is not the first, and surely not the last, to take the road of massaging its financial books. But the enormity of the event served as a wake-up call to corporate leaders and regulators. A newly-released book, The Financial Numbers Game: Detecting Creative Accounting Practices, could not have made a better entry. The book discusses actual Enron-like cases. Judging from its well-illustrated content, there must have been plenty of them. In a nutshell, it's a help book for those who need to wade through the end work of accountants and related parties. It attempts to show readers of financial statements how to avoid being misled by financial results that have been altered with creative accounting practices.

Creativity may be the cutting edge of a fashion designer. But in the hands of an accountant, the word takes on a different meaning. Here, the authors describe it as 'steps used to play the financial numbers game, including the aggressive choice and application of accounting principles, both within and beyond the boundaries of generally accepted accounting principles, and fraudulent financial reporting. Also included are steps taken toward earnings management and income smoothing.' The impact of this 'game' can be chilling. Enron, perhaps, can be dropped into the worst-case-scenario basket. In the case of the US energy giant, its shareholders saw the company's stock price crashing from strong double digit numbers to a couple of cents. And it happened almost overnight upon revelation that the firm had over-stated its profits for a number of years. The author cites other corporate manipulations that have happened in the past. In 1998, US-based Sybase's shares dropped an additional 20% when the company reported improper practices at the Japanese subsidiary, which included booking revenue for purported sales that were accompanied by side letters allowing customers to return software later without penalty. In the same year, Sunbeam Corp slashed its reported earnings for 1997 by 65% due to premature booking of revenue.

Be it Enron or Sunbeam, the financial game has a singular ultimate objective – creating an altered impression of a firm's business performance.

Source: Investor Digest, April 16, 2002.

In spite of attempts by regulators, governments, professional bodies and others, creative accounting as a practice has persisted. It has however, begun to take different forms, thus emphasizing the capacity of those engaging in it to devise new and ever more fanciful schemes.

Earnings Management

Creative accounting is probably most commonly employed in circumstances where companies are seeking to produce profits figures that conform to market expectations. Known as 'earnings management' - that is, the use of accounting techniques to present corporate performance in a favourable light that does not properly reflect the underlying commercial reality – this practice is often driven by a determination to ensure that analysts' expectations are met.

Markets Grow Wary About Earnings Guidance, Reports John Authers

The rules of Wall Street's earnings game have changed. And if chief executives in the US have anything to do with it, they will change much more. During the bull market of the late 1990's, the practice of earnings 'guidance' from companies, and the setting of expectations by Wall Street analysts, had a predictable pattern. Analysts would set their forecasts and slowly reduce them over time, as the company guided them lower. Then the company would beat those expectations, generating positive publicity and a rise in the share price on the day they announced.

> That pattern has now broken down. At the turn of the decade, companies suddenly started drastically under-performing expectations, in the middle of accounting scandals and at the end of the Internet boom...
>
> Earnings 'management' – using the leeway offered by accruals accounting to ensure that earnings came in ahead of expectations – is believed to have contributed to the accounting scandals. According to Whitney Tilson, a hedge fund manager who also serves as a company director: "What led to virtually every accounting scandal I know of is when companies guide on precise numbers and know they can be punished severely if they don't meet those numbers. There are a million ways to manage earnings plus or minus a few pennies a share."...
>
> Source: *Financial Times, December 12, 2005.*

A culture exists, therefore, in which earnings management, analysts' expectations and accounting scandals are linked. In this context, whatever the motivation, whether to satisfy market expectations, ensure large bonuses for management or simply deflect criticism, earnings management now constitutes a significant feature of the lives of many corporate entities. Arthur Levitt, former chairman of the Securities and Exchange Commission, has described it as a "grey area where the accounting is being perverted; where managers are cutting corners; and where earnings reports reflect the desires of management rather than the underlying financial performance of the company." As recent frauds and various SEC and FRRP investigations have shown, the short-termism that results can often significantly compromise the long-term viability of entities.

The range of techniques employed – ranging from legitimate use of accounting techniques to outright fraud – is extensive. Examples include:

- 'Big-bath' accounting: overstating one-off restructuring changes in order to give a hidden reserve for future exploitation in smoothing profits;

- 'Cookie-jar reserves': creating reserves, to be used in future loss-making periods, by over-providing for future warranty costs or sales returns in profitable periods;

- Recognising revenues in advance: incorporating an item as revenue before appropriate (see later in this chapter);

- Deferring necessary expenditure in order to improve short-term results, thus damaging the medium to long-term viability of an enterprise.

In practice:

Aggressive earnings management warning

The introduction of International Financial Reporting Standards (IFRS) could increase the risk of aggressive earnings management, according to research commissioned by the ICAEW's Audit

& Assurance Faculty. John Collier, a past secretary general of the Institute, conducted the qualitative research, which involved a series of one-to-one interviews with finance directors, audit committee chairmen of large listed companies, senior auditors, investment analysts and senior business journalists. All agreed that the threat of aggressive earnings management is still present and that constant vigilance by those concerned with integrity in financial reporting is needed.

In addition to the introduction of IFRS, a change in the economic climate, such as the threat of recession, was also identified as a key factor increasing the risk of aggressive earnings management in future. Interviewees' suggestions for minimising this risk included wider investor communications programmes, increased monitoring of the link between executive rewards and financial performance and raising awareness of the vulnerability of corporate reporting arising from the introduction of IFRS. Interviewees also emphasised the need for standard-setters and legislators to consider quality, as opposed to quantity, in published corporate information.

Source: Accountancy, November 2004.

The critical issue is the extent to which market and analysts' expectations (as well as a determination on the part of management to secure bonuses) have insinuated themselves into the process as significant drivers of corporate culture and reporting policies. Meeting or exceeding market expectations has, in many cases, become a paramount consideration, particularly since the consequences of missing analysts' forecasts can be so detrimental to the company's share price.

In practice:

Figure massaging poses threat despite Enron

UK companies continue to be tempted to present their performance in a more favourable light by massaging the figures, says a report from the Institute of Chartered Accountants. A survey of audit partners, finance directors and audit committee directors found that aggressive earnings management is a regular occurrence, despite efforts by regulators to eradicate the problem in the wake of the Enron scandal. The survey concluded: "The threat of aggressive earnings management will always be with us."

One audit committee chairman told the institute: "Aggressive earnings management is always there but someone has to look in the rear view mirror to see evidence of it. It is rarely evident at the time. Some people get away with it."

The survey identified two principal motives for companies to massage their numbers: the need to exceed market expectations and the fact that management remuneration is closely related to results. One auditor said: "Pay is one of the top influences – it is human nature that it should be." The report concluded that the incidence of aggressive earnings management has decreased in the past few years, thanks to new regulations covering audit committee practice and accountancy supervision. It said, however, that bad habits could return. John Collier, the report's author and a former partner with Price Waterhouse, now PricewaterhouseCoopers, said: "Aggressive earnings management may well increase when the post-Enron reporting climate changes or if recession returns. Memories can be short and business failures often go in cycles."

Source: eFinancialNews.com, November 7, 2004

Examples

Creative accounting is best explored, explained and understood using examples. The following section outlines some of the more common techniques used, many of which prove fertile ground because of the subjective nature of so much accounting practice:

Off-Balance Sheet Financing

Off-balance sheet finance describes a process by which certain funding sources and/or associated assets are effectively kept off the balance sheet. The intention is usually to reduce the level of debt disclosed and thereby improve the gearing figure of the company.

In practice:

Enron employed Special Purpose Entities (SPEs) as a means of effectively removing billions of dollars of debt from its consolidated accounts:

Wheels within wheels

Like most oil companies, Enron created partnerships – with the assistance of banks, accounting firms, and law firms – for its projects, such as oil wells and pipelines. These partnerships – not Enron – borrowed money, purchased assets, and entered into contracts.

By using partnerships (or other legal entities, such as trusts or corporations), Enron could create non-recourse financing – meaning that the company could borrow for a project based solely on the assets of the partnership; investors in the partnership could not hold Enron responsible for debts.

So long as Enron controlled no more than 50% of the partnerships, accounting rules did not require that Enron consolidate the partnerships' assets and liabilities, any debts belonged to the partnerships, not to Enron, and they would appear only in a footnote to Enron's financial

> *statements. By keeping debt off its books, Enron would appear healthier, and the credit rating agencies would give it a higher rating.*
>
> Source: *The Guardian, February 14, 2003.*

The most successful attempts by accounting regulators to deal with off-balance sheet financing have focused on ensuring that firms record the commercial substance of transactions rather than their legal form. Thus, IAS 17, *Leases*, which requires that leases be accounted for on this basis, and the provisions of IAS 39, *Financial Instruments: Recognition and Measurement*, have sought to counter this practice by adopting this approach. Similarly, standards such as IFRS 3, *Business Combinations*, have sought to ensure that entities that are subsidiaries in all but the strictly legal sense (known as quasi-subsidiaries) are included in consolidated accounts.

Derivatives and Hedge Funds

Some of the difficulties posed by increasingly complex financial instruments have been outlined in Chapter 9. These range from fundamental recognition issues to basic measurement considerations. While valuation issues arise in relation to most assets and liabilities, those relating to, for example, derivatives involve far greater complexity. Quite apart from the fact that the underlying assets and liabilities are often difficult to determine, their values can swing dramatically from day-to-day. This problem is exacerbated when these derivatives are used for hedging purposes. The result is considerable scope for creativity in terms of both classification and valuation:

In practice:

Fannie did

For those outside the United States, it may be difficult to understand the significance of the Fannie Mae financial scandal. But the reality is that its problems really do matter – and not just in the US. Say it slowly to allow it to sink in. Fannie Mae owns or guarantees over $4,000bn of home mortgage debt in the US. And yes, that is billions – it is no misprint. Fannie Mae is the world's biggest financial institution outside of banking. So when Fannie Mae gets pneumonia, a lot of other people expect at least to get a bad dose of the flu.

The Securities and Exchange Commission has determined that Fannie Mae breached FAS 91 and FAS 133 from 2001 until the middle of last year, having used: 'Unique methodology to assess whether hedge accounting was appropriate,' said the SEC. As a result of the decision, Fannie

Mae must restate earnings and declare losses of around $9bn, arising from previously undeclared losses on derivatives. In doing so, Fannie Mae also goes into breach of its minimal capital requirement laid down by its regulator, the Office of Federal Housing Enterprise Oversight (Ofheo)...

Source: accounting & business, February 2005.

New financial instruments represent a unique challenge to accounting. This is a result of both the possibilities inherent in ever-more complex and imaginative financial instruments themselves, as well as the fact that regulators are continually seen to be playing "catch-up". While IAS 39 represents one attempt to deal with the challenges posed at both a conceptual and an operational level, the fact is that regulation offers only limited possibilities. The ongoing evolution of increasingly opaque financial instruments means that regulation alone is unlikely to yield immediate solutions.

Fair Values

Ironically, this latter point is not unrelated to the fact that some proposed "solutions" contain within themselves the potential for creative exploitation. Thus, the extended application of "fair value" to accounting numbers, while sustainable on a theoretical basis, also introduces greater potential for volatility and manipulation. This derives, in part, from the fact that estimates, subjective judgement and expert opinions are involved. This is not a new problem. Accounting has always required estimates, for instance in determining depreciation charges. However, the application of fair value to a range of assets and liabilities means that not just issues of complexity, but also of scale, must be considered:

The Ones That Get Away

Accounts are Increasingly More Art Than Science

...The scandals at Enron and WorldCom – as well as more recent accounting snafus at General Electric and a big scam at AIG – show that accounting numbers are malleable. And they are getting squishier as the use of estimates in company accounts increases. Whether this malleability is a problem is the subject of heated debate and carries with it important consequences. Reliable numbers mean that investors can make sound decisions. Bad ones lead not just to the inefficient allocation of capital but also to a loss of confidence in the markets and, when fraud is involved, to huge shareholder losses. A study by Glass Lewis, a research outfit, found that investors lost well over $900 billion in 30 big scams between 1997 and 2004.

Ever since accounting shifted from the simple tallying of cash in and cash out to "accrual accounting", where profits and expenses are booked when incurred, forward-looking estimates have played a critical role in measuring company profits. This role has grown as "knowledge-based" economies have begun to replace the old widget-making versions, and businesses have become more complex.

The biggest boost to estimation, however, has come from the gradual shift to "fair-value" accounting. Before, assets and liabilities were mostly carried at their historic, original cost; "fair value" is an attempt to show their current worth. Fair-value numbers are up-to-date and arguably more relevant than their static but verifiable precursors. But they also result in more volatile profits and a heavier reliance on estimates for the many items (bank loans, buildings) that may not have a ready market.

Standard-setters on both sides of the Atlantic have been urging this shift. In June America's Securities and Exchange Commission, in a long-awaited report commissioned by Congress after the Enron scandal, also endorsed fair-value accounting, which it thinks will simplify accounts and reduce firms' interest in structuring transactions to meet accounting goals.

Others are less sanguine. Even with the best will in the world, estimates can be wildly off the mark. And they are easy to manipulate. In a recent study, Daniel Bergstresser and Mihir Desai of Harvard Business School and Joshua Rauh of the University of Chicago's Graduate School of Business found ample evidence of tinkering. At delicate moments – before acquisitions and equity offerings and exercising stock options, for example – some bosses inflated the assumed rate of return on pension-fund assets, thus flattering profits.

Baruch Lev of New York University's Stern School of Business, and Siyi Li and Theodore Sougiannis, from the University of Illinois at Urbana-Champaign, harbour a deeper worry: that estimates, which are supposed to improve the relevance of financial information by giving managers a means to impart their forward-looking views (on how many customers might return their new cars, for instance), are not very useful at all. That is, they do not really help investors to predict a company's future earnings and cashflows.

The three analysed 3,500–4,500 companies a year from 1988 to 2002. They then tried to "predict" future performance (earnings or cashflow) with five models in which historic cashflows and estimates were used to different degrees. The trio found that cashflows predicted future performance robustly, but adding estimates to them was little help in predicting future performance, or in generating returns from portfolios based on these predictions. It was a "sobering result", they concluded.

Mr Lev blames this on the difficulty of making good estimates in a fast-changing, complex world as well as on a degree of earnings manipulation. "This is not to say we should toss the accounting system, which is overwhelmingly based on estimates, into the waste bin," he says, "but it does point to the urgent need to enhance the reliability of accounting estimates – especially given the move to fair value."

On this point, even proponents of fair value agree. The Financial Standards Accounting Board (FASB), America's standard-setter, is planning to release guidance on how to apply fair value later this year. It has devised a "hierarchy" of items according to how hard they are to value. At the top are items that have an observable price in a deep, liquid market (eg, listed corporate debt). In the middle are items where sophisticated valuation models are based on market inputs (eg, employee stock options). At the bottom are items where valuations are based wholly on management projections (eg, Enron's most esoteric financial instruments).

It is the lower end of the hierarchy that causes concern. "At this level, there is the risk that models can be used with prejudice," says David Bianco of UBS, a Swiss bank. Regulators, too, are worried. Research by the Federal Reserve shows that the fair value of bank loans can swing widely depending on inputs and methodology. Market values for lower-rated corporate bonds, one possible benchmark, can vary by as much as 2–5%, giving managers leeway to fiddle with numbers.

Source: *The Economist*, July 28, 2005.

Cash Flow Manipulation

Surprisingly, given the general belief that cash flow is effectively immune to "massaging", it has become obvious to some commentators that all is not what it seems, particularly in the way in which cashflow is presented. While what is happening in relation to presentation and calculation of cashflows amounts to little more than manipulation (as distinct from outright fraud), this is, nevertheless, a worrying development. This is especially the case since most users of accounts always took some consolation from the belief that the cashflow statement was sacrosanct.

In practice:

The penny drops but the numbers game continues, by Stephen Schurr

As sentiment in the US returns to levels reminiscent of the 1990s bull run, the question is whether accounting standards have markedly improved from the lax practices that defined that era. The accounting trickery of the 1990s stretched the already-pliable Generally Accepted Accounting Principles (GAAP) to breaking point. In a handful of instances, the numbers game crossed over into outright fraud.

While legislative change has reduced the risk of widespread accounting fraud, accounting experts say companies still play tricks – albeit legal ones – with their earnings. "The numbers game has migrated to the cashflow statement," said Charles Mulford, accounting professor at the Georgia Institute of Technology. This is an important development. Wall Street considers operating cashflow – the money a company generates as measured by revenue minus operating expenses – a better measure of financial strength than earnings as it is less vulnerable to manipulation.

While the increasing sleight-of-hand on cashflow reporting usually falls within the boundaries of GAAP, companies may give the impression that they are generating more cash than they are.

> *Manipulation of operating cashflow can be found, for example, in the manner in which companies account for acquisitions or loans, or by including increasing in-book overdrafts into operating cashflow...*
>
> Source: *Financial Times, February 27, 2004.*

Revenue Recognition

Without doubt one of the areas most prone to manipulation is revenue. This usually revolves around questions of "revenue recognition", i.e., whether or when to include revenue in the accounts. These possibilities are a function of the fact that companies have considerable discretion over when and how to book revenue and profits. Management also have the motivation to employ this leeway to satisfy market expectations. Enron, for instance, entered into a joint venture with Blockbuster Video and was able to record revenues from the venture in spite of the fact that the venture never actually got off the ground. Likewise, Global Crossing was able to enter into similar leasing arrangements with two large US customers, treating one as a source of immediate revenue and the other as a capital expense.

Specific techniques often employed to inflate or anticipate revenue include:

- Valuing turnover at full transaction value when only acting in the capacity of an agent: for instance, a travel agency should obviously only book as revenue the fee it charges customers. However, during the dot.com boom several on-line travel agencies booked the full value of any airline tickets sold as gross revenue in an attempt to inflate income.

- Booking revenue at the moment an order is placed.

- Booking revenues and profits immediately when the transaction will only be fulfilled over a longer term, for instance, in the case of long-term contracts.

The following article, presented in a Question and Answer format, identifies many of the critical issues relating to revenue recognition and earnings management:

Revenue Recognition: Know When a Sale is a Sale to Gain a Picture of a Company's Health, by Chris Nuttall

Accounting standards setters have been ranting about "revenue recognition". What are they on about? Quite simply, some of the biggest accounting scandals in the US and Europe have revolved round this issue. In accounting terms, it tries to answer the question: when is a sale a sale?

Why should that be so complicated? When I buy my groceries at the supermarket, a sale has taken place? Suppose you had the right to return, say, all of your canned goods within the next month at no penalty. How much did you buy? Increasingly, accounting experts say returnable goods should not be listed as full sales, particularly when customers are in the habit of returning a meaningful portion of purchases.

What difference does it make whether the supermarket records the sale in one month or the other? There are two good reasons. First, investors want to have a true and fair picture of the monthly demand for a company's goods. If customers have the right to return all unused goods without penalty, it might be misleading to claim the supermarket 'sold' them. Second, investors want to be able to make some forecasts about sales, and profits.

Hmmm ... Are you saying that some transactions that look like sales are really something else? Yes. Just looking at pure turnover can lead to too crude a measure of a company's health. The stated revenues may be part of recurring income or include only part of an announced sale.

Recurring income? It sure sounds like something I'd like to have. So do companies. Recurring income is the proceeds of sales that a company can count on. Let's say you sign a mobile phone contract for a full year with a minimum monthly tariff, and with a stiff penalty for cancellation that will hold you liable for the full year's basic tariff. Although the provider may record your income monthly – because that is how you would pay it – it is income the company can count on. The booking of a deal like that signifies customer commitment, commonly called the order book of future business that will occur over time.

Hang on. If the mobile phone company actually has me on the hook for a full year – no way I can wriggle out of paying – why can't it book the sale of a full year's contract in the month in which I bought it? Aha! Now you are catching on! You can see it is possible to argue for both forms of revenue recognition. The usual objective of the accounting policies is to match the customer commitment against the obligations of the company, in so doing matching the revenue against the costs the company will incur in satisfying those obligations over time. Another principle is companies must be conservative, and not anticipate revenue unless it is certain it will arrive.

Are there some companies or industries in which revenue recognition is a particularly sensitive issue? All companies and industries are affected by this issue. One area in which it has been scrutinized is in IT, as contracts can include current and future technology.

What do you mean? Can you give some examples? In the case of a company such as ARM, which reported full-year results last week, no revenues are recognized when contracts are signed for its chip designs – what you would think of as a sale. Up to 20 per cent are recognized when the intellectual property (IP) is delivered. The customer has the chance to test the technology, say during a six-month period and when it gives the 'okay', ARM will recognise another 50 per cent of the contract proceeds as a sale. The final 30 per cent is deferred until the provider of the IP is satisfied it faces no other obligations in the contract, such as fixing bugs.

Is revenue recognition a particularly acute problem for businesses that provide goods and services over a long time? Now you've really raised a topical question.

Last week, one of the leading providers of construction, maintenance and accommodation services, was forced to concede that income it said it could count on might not be all there.

Surely the need for companies to make sure there are no disputes about contracts before they book revenues is simply common sense? Why is there an issue in this case? It may not be obvious that a contract is disputed until some time after the revenues have been booked.

Is that why investors do not want companies to book revenues from long-term contracts until they are fully delivered? Precisely. Uncertain income is not really income. Is that all?

I guess I should only invest in companies that sell hard goods, cash on the barrel head, then? Not really! Any number of retailers have been unmasked after having inflated their sales figures by including the effects of bulk discount agreements. Suppliers encourage distributors to buy much more than they actually need – generally right before the end of an accounting period – and allow them to return unwanted goods, at no penalty, the next month. All sorts of sales incentives, such as volume discounts, are too often not subtracted from revenue figures, as they should be.

Just how widespread is the problem of company profits boosted through questionable revenue recognition practices? Very. More than half of accounting irregularities investigated deal with overstated revenues.

What are accounting standards setters doing to help investors? Accountancy bodies across the world refine their approach to revenue recognition.

Source: *Financial Times*, February 4, 2004.

IAS 18, *Revenue Recognition*, represents one attempt to deal with this practice. It requires that recognition and realization parameters be strictly applied before revenue is recognized. Like several other standards, however, it has been overtaken by commercial and technological developments and the imaginative application of its provisions.

Many creative opportunities exist beyond the few examples provided here. For instance, the possibilities revolving around accounting for pensions and stock options, particularly since so many subjective estimates and judgements are involved, have already been mentioned in Chapter 12. In fact, one common denominator in most of these is the fact that estimates, subjectivity and so-called "independent expert opinions" remain so central to the accounting process. The likelihood that accounting regulation, particularly regulatory paradigms that themselves draw so heavily on the need for estimates (e.g. fair values), will be the source of a solution to creative accounting, is highly improbable. This requires that other possibilities be considered.

Role of Ethics

One of the problems for the accounting profession and regulators is that the perpetrators of these practices are usually accountants. Ironically, therefore, in attempting to deal with these practices, accountants find themselves acting as both hunter and gamekeeper.

In this context the role of ethics in the training and professional lives of accountants and auditors has been assuming a greater importance. An increasing acknowledgement that deficiencies in accounting education, where ethical issues have traditionally been subordinated to technical ability, is slowly resulting in more emphasis being placed on such matters.

In practice:

Research by the UK's Institute of Business Ethics, based on FTSE 250 companies between 1997 and 2001, suggests that those with a well-established code of ethics or conduct were generally better at risk management, generated significant additional economic and market value, and had a more stable price-earnings ratio.

Source: accounting & business, May 2003.

Ethics describes that set of moral principles taken as a guide or reference point. Most humans adopt such a code in order to relate to the various environments within which they operate. These may range from the individual and personal to the corporate and professional. The problem with introducing an ethical perspective into the equation, however, is that it moves matters out of the technical and practical areas that constitute the "comfort zone" of most accountants, and into a less tangible domain.

Significantly, however, this is not an area unexplored by accountants. Indeed, accountants can take some solace from the fact that a substantial corpus of work relevant to the ethical nature of their work already exists. Furthermore, the professional contexts within which most accountants already operate come complete with ethical guidelines and boundaries.

For example, the various professional accounting bodies operate a system of partial self-regulation as part of which they promulgate systems of ethical guidelines within which members are expected to operate. These can cover standards of behaviour, relationships between members and clients, and acceptable practice in particular circumstances. These regulations are supported by a variety of codes, such as the Combined Code on corporate governance, and various statutes, as well as bodies such as the FRRP [see Chapter 1] which assist accountants in navigating the often-torrid waters that they find themselves in.

This raises other concerns, however, not least the fact that accountants too often and too easily take refuge in regulations – "they are more focused on solving problems than doing right". Ethical issues are perceived to be "distractions that need to be minimized, neatly packaged, and disposed of". Such sentiments betray a refusal on the part of many accountants to grapple with the real issues raised by creative accounting practices which are themselves merely symptoms of an attitude that views the end as justifying the means. As Arthur Levitt, former SEC Commissioner, has observed, "It is a basic cultural change we are asking for". The fundamental question is whether this can be fostered by regulation alone. In the increasingly flexible forms of social and commercial organisation that are developing, the answer, as the following important article argues, is probably "no":

The Bimoral Society

In Modern Business, Employers are Under Increasing Pressure to Balance Moral Obligation With Their Own Self-Interests

When we were first told that 'greed is good' in the 1980s, the idea seemed shocking. But like much else of the Thatcher-Reagan era it is now taken more or less for granted. The word 'greed' is still pejorative, but self-interest as a driving force is now socially legitimate to an extent unprecedented in history. Moreover, if corporate scandals are anything to go by, greed – good or bad – appears to be rampant. In response to these scandals, governments have done what they have always done and tightened the rules. Compared with a generation ago, financial, labour and product markets remain relatively deregulated, but business procedures and business reporting are regulated as never before. The assumption is that tighter rules mean better control, but what if the underlying problem is that rules no longer work?

For centuries, indeed for millennia, we have lived in a predominantly hierarchical culture, in which ethics have been all about our obligations to others, and ethical standards have been maintained through systems of rules and regulations, backed by hierarchical authority. Entrepreneurs have always sat slightly outside this culture, working by a different, market ethic of self-interest. But these values have traditionally been tolerated only within a carefully defined domain, and as business grew beyond individual enterprise the organizational form it adopted, the bureaucracy was precisely that of the hierarchy, with all its rules and obligations.

In recent decades, this traditional balance between hierarchical obligation and market self-interest has shifted significantly. The traditional moral authorities of church and state have lost much of their power and credibility. And while people seem, on the whole, to be no less moral than they used to be, the social force of morality and the rules through which that was expressed no longer carry the same weight. On the other hand the world of business and the economic thinking on which it relies have gained in power and influence, and the pursuit of self-interest has become increasingly respectable.

The result of all this is that we now live in a 'bimoral' society, in which we are in effect our own moral authorities. Moral obligation and self-interest are both legitimate, and the balance between them in any situation is a matter for negotiation. In business, this change has been reflected in a shift to new more flexible forms of organizing. As in society at large, the result has been a balance of markets and hierarchies rather than a shift to purely market structures. Most businesses retain strong elements of hierarchical structure. But the tightly defined 'offices' of classical bureaucracy have increasingly been replaced by networks and teams, organizational devices that fit properly into neither hierarchical nor market cultures, but create space for negotiation between them.

Old styles of command and control have given way to more personal leadership styles, designed to hold people's diverse self-interests together and bend them to a common purpose. Employees are encouraged to look after their own interests and make their own decisions, and are paid in ways that assume they'll do this. Whereas in the past they were expected to stick to the rules and conventions of a corporate culture, they are now strongly encouraged to break the rules, to challenge the conventions, and to find creative ways of doing things. Performance, not conduct, is what matters.

One consequence of this is that people are tempted to cut corners and take ethical risks – quite often to avoid performance risks, for which they are quickly punished. Another consequence is that self-interest, which is nurtured by the system, can easily transmute into (insatiable) greed. A third consequence is that, driven by the relentless push for performance, and surrounded by often conflicting calls on their attention, managers have no brain space left for ethical reflection.

Bureaucracies have often been criticized for disabling people's moral faculties by taking ethical decisions out of their hands, but flexible organizations simply crowd those faculties out. What is perhaps most striking about Enron and WorldCom is not the corruption but how so many people were too busy to notice that something was wrong. . .

John Hendry is professor of management and head of the University of Reading Business School. His most recent book, 'Between enterprise and ethics: business and management in a bimoral society', is published by Oxford University Press

Source: *Accountancy Age*, July 14, 2005.

In a context in which, as the author of this extract outlines, "performance, not conduct, is what matters", and personal ethics are increasingly seen as negotiable, the likelihood is that creative accounting is likely to be, at best, merely contained.

Whistleblowing

One initiative by governments and professions seeks to protect those who, for whatever reason, wish to disclose malpractice within businesses. Whistleblowing involves the disclosure of information relating to malpractice within business. The Public Interest Disclosure Act (1999) protects whistleblowers who disclose information that raises genuine issues of public concern from dismissal or victimization. In addition, companies are expected to have in place policies that provide employees with clear guidelines on the procedures to be followed if there are suspicions of malpractice:

Why It's Worth The Whistle

From the EU to the City Whistleblowers Continue to Make Their Mark. With the Combined Code Making it Easier for Staff to Raise Concerns, Financial Directors Must Have a Policy in Place, by Adam Griggs

The effects of corporate fraud can be devastating. I should know – I used to work for Arthur Andersen. With the criminal trials of Enron executives well underway in the US, the 'it could never happen in my organisation' mentality still prevails. Ironically, it's most common among those who complain about the 'red tape' of the revised combined code and the Sarbanes-Oxley Act, which came about as a result of this and other similar financial scandals...

Many people do not report their concerns because they 'just don't want to get involved'. They have families to feed and mortgages to pay, and will not come forward if they believe there is a chance that their personal circumstances will be adversely affected. The reassurance offered by the Public Interest Disclosure Act, which – within certain boundaries – protects employees who report their concerns, seems to be of little comfort to those finding themselves in difficult positions.

But there are some solid business reasons why whistleblowing makes commercial sense. Not only can it reduce losses through fraud and theft at the hands of employees, but it can also dissuade employees from feeling they have nowhere else to turn, and instead make damaging disclosures to the media and industry regulators.

Some public interest organizations insist that whistleblowing should not be an anonymous activity, and idealistically this is hard to contradict. The pragmatic view, however, must be that it is better to obtain information from an anonymous source than not to obtain it at all. This is the choice that organizations are faced with.

The most important feature of a whistleblowing procedure must, therefore, be that employees trust it. In that respect, the tone at the top of an organisation is critical to the effectiveness of a whistleblowing policy. In many boardrooms, the review of the policy will take place quickly and quietly and, with the compliance box ticked, whistleblowing will conveniently be forgotten.

There are a number of possible reasons for this: a belief that internal controls already in place make it impossible for employees to get away with fraud or malpractice; not really wanting to know what is going on behind the scenes;

not wanting to change the status quo; or a fear that something untoward will be uncovered, reflecting badly on management. Are any of these arguments justified? Even the strongest internal controls can be avoided if two or more collaborate, and not wanting to change the status quo is surely not the approach to business that leads to success. More worrying is the possibility that those organizations that refuse to demonstrate an acceptable level of openness have something to hide. The time will come when, regardless of the combined code or the Sarbanes-Oxley Act, investors will punish organizations that do not implement effective whistle-blowing procedures.

In almost all cases of corporate fraud or wrongdoing, someone other than the perpetrator knows what is going on before real damage is done. If you sit on or advise an audit committee, make sure that someone is you.

Adam Griggs is a former police officer, chartered accountant and director of The Hotline Limited.

Source: *Accountancy Age*, December 16, 2004.

In spite of various initiatives, both regulatory and ethical, the problem of creative accounting remains one rooted in the belief that it is not the perpetration of such practices that is the problem, but being caught. As the accounting scandals of recent years have demonstrated, while it will never be eradicated, unless it is addressed at a more fundamental ethical level, it will never be controlled. As Levitt remarks, what is required is change of culture.

Summary

Creative accounting can be defined as "the use and abuse of accounting techniques and principles to achieve financial statements which, intentionally, do not provide a true and fair view". Large financial frauds and scandals in recent years resulting from such practices prompted accounting regulators on both sides of the Atlantic to address the more obvious and common manifestations of creative accounting.

By a mixture of regulations aimed at specific abuses and more fundamental accounting and auditing standards that require the application of the spirit of the law rather than merely the letter, regulators have been successful in eradicating many of these practices.

The willingness of accountants and their professional bodies to deal properly and ethically with the challenges posed by practices such as creative accounting is open to question. This is particularly challenging in an environment in which ethics are increasingly viewed as negotiable.

The subject matter of the next chapter, Corporate Social Reporting, in which the role of the corporation as "corporate citizen" is considered, offers one area in which the *bona fides* of accountants on ethical issues might be tested.

Review Questions

Question 1
Define "creative accounting" and explain why it presents such a potent challenge to accounting regulators and users of accounting information.

Question 2
SEC commissioner Arthur Levitt argues that what is needed as "a basic cultural change". Explain what he means by this and why creative accounting practices may need to be addressed at such a fundamental level.

Question 3
Identify some of the more common examples of creative accounting used in the past and explain how recent accounting standards have attempted to deal with them.

Question 4
"Creative accounting is usually intended to support, or even increase, share price. Since this is in the interests of shareholders there is rarely any pressure from this group to eradicate such practices". Explain the implications of this, if true, and discuss whether there is pressure from shareholders to abandon creative accounting practices.

Question 5
Consider the extent to which it is realistic to expect ethical considerations to inform work practices.

Question 6
Discuss the extent to which, in an environment in which ethics are seen as negotiable, increased regulation can assist in eradicating creative accounting practice.

Question 7
What is the role of "whistle-blowers" in uncovering creative accounting practices? Should there be greater legal protection for those willing to act in this way?

Question 8
"Creative accounting has several positive features. It should not just be viewed as something to eradicate". Discuss.

Case Studies

Case 1

Many of the large corporate collapses of recent years have featured highly questionable creative accounting at their heart. The WorldCom collapse in particular displayed many creative accounting practices and raised a number of ethical issues and questions. Gather information and accounting data on this case and examine the nature and range of creative accounting practices employed.

Case 2

The following insightful article raises various philosophical issues in relation to what transpired at Enron. Consider the points made by the author and whether or not a form of 'ethno-accountancy' might assist in developing an understanding of the nature of the challenges involved.

A Philosophical Investigation Into Enron, by Donald McKenzie

When personal trust is impossible, modernity turns to "trust in numbers" (the title of an important book on these questions by Theodore Porter). Numbers are pervasive in finance and beyond: shareprices; price-earnings ratios (a key criterion for professional investors); bond ratings (which are not literally numbers, but have a quasi-numeric "hard fact" quality); school and hospital league tables; surgeons' success rates; university departments' Research Assessment scores. Trust in numbers, however, works only if those who produce the numbers can be trusted: it displaces, rather than solves, modernity's problem with trust.

Enron's production of numbers – the accountancy practices that generated its balance sheet – was not entirely covert. The existence of the special purpose entities was dutifully disclosed in footnotes to the accounts. True, those footnotes couldn't be said to give a full and transparent version of Enron's dealings with these entities. However, the readers of CFO (chief financial officer) magazine must have had a notion.

In 1998, as US wholesale electricity prices started to spike upwards, Enron used a special purpose entity to buy generating capacity close to New York City. Enron's CFO, Andrew Fastow, told the magazine: "We accessed $1.5 billion in capital but expanded the Enron balance sheet by only $65 million." The magazine seems to have approved, awarding Fastow its 1999 CFO Excellence Award for Capital Structure Management. CFO may not be on every news-stand, but it is surely on the reading list at Moody's, and in March 2000 the rating agency raised Enron a notch to Baa1.

Just how unusual were Enron's accountancy practices? Were they actually illegal? (Criminal charges have been brought against some Enron managers, and some cases have been settled by plea bargain, but at the time of writing no case against a senior figure has gone to court.)

Here we enter a murky world that almost no economists, and only a limited number of other social scientists, have sought to enter. Let's call it the world of "ethnoaccountancy". The term is analogous to "ethnobotany", which is the study of how cultures classify plants, and which sets aside the issue of whether these classifications are correct according to our modern botany. An ethnoaccountant, similarly, would study how people produce numbers, how they actually do their financial reckoning.

An ethnoaccountant couldn't just read the rule book, even though it exists in the form of GAAP, the Generally Accepted Accounting Principles of the Financial Accounting Standards Board. The ethnoaccountant has to be a Wittgensteinian. In the Philosophical Investigations, Wittgenstein pointed to the hidden complexity of the apparently simple notion of "following a rule". If we think of a rule as a set of words – written, for example, on the pages of GAAP – then following it seems to involve an act of interpretation of what the words "mean".

Interpretations, however, are contestable – especially if you have expensive lawyers and sophisticated accountants bent on finding an interpretation that will permit a valued client to do what he or she wishes. Of course, one can write rules for interpretation, but these rules themselves need to be interpreted: we are at the start of a potentially endless regress. If rules are simply verbal formulae, then, as Wittgenstein put it, "no course of action could be determined by a rule, because every course of action can be made out to accord with the rule."

All philosophers know Wittgenstein's discussion of following a rule. It seems as if the US Financial Accounting Standards Board does not, for it has progressed a long way into the interpretive regress: Fox reports that GAAP now comprises 100,000 pages of rules. At every stage of the regress, however, the Wittgensteinian analysis holds: even when expanded to 100,000 pages, what the rules of accounting "mean" can be contested.

Hence the need for ethnoaccountancy, for discovering how accountancy is actually done. Because there has been only a little of it, one can merely speculate as to what exactly would be found by an ethnoaccountant of the modern American corporation. It's certain that she would find a myriad of special purpose entities. Often their purpose is precisely to manage debt: to match it with a defined and predictable income stream in a way that will attract for the entities a higher rating from Moody's or Standard & Poor's. More generally, she would also find that the different ways in which rules can be applied can have major financial consequences. As Louis Lowenstein, a scholar straddling finance and law, put it in the Columbia Law Review in 1996:

"Accounting is not precise or scientific. It is an art, and a highly developed one... GAAP requires industry to use accrual basis accounting. Income is thus recognized when it is earned rather than when cash is received. The essence of the accrual basis is the matching of expenses with revenues, so as to produce a truer picture of a company's profitability. The rub is that accrual-basis accounting affords a great deal of flexibility and judgment in the timing of income and expense recognition.

Will American Airlines' new aeroplanes be serviceable for thirty years or should they be depreciated over just twenty? Should research and development expenses be charged to earnings as they are incurred, or should some portion be capitalised and charged only over time? And so on. There is no single, correct answer to such questions."

The ethnoaccountant might well find that timing is the key issue. It is, for example, greatly in managers' interests for share prices to be kept high at least until their share options can be exercised profitably – what happens in the more distant future may be of less concern.

More subtly, flexibility about when income and expenses are recognized on balance sheets permits what is known as "income smoothing": managing balance sheets in such a way that a corporation's profits rise smoothly and predictably (just beating the "forecasts" which investor relations departments have fed to Wall Street analysts), rather than fluctuating erratically.

One way of smoothing income is to have a "cookie jar", or a reserve of earnings that have not yet been declared on the balance sheet. A good moment to create or replenish a cookie jar is when a corporation takes a "big bath" or reports a large loss. The markets can be perfectly tolerant of an occasional large loss, so long as it seems to be one-off and can be explained satisfactorily, for example as the costs associated with doing things of which the market approves, like reducing employee numbers dramatically.

What better time to be very pessimistic in the way one values assets or provides for future liabilities? Such pessimistic reporting refills the cookie jar, because rising asset values or lower than expected liabilities then form the foundation for future reporting of profits.

It's easy to overstate the practical implications of Wittgenstein's "rule-scepticism". He was saying that words alone can't constrain us, not that nothing constrains us. Sometimes we just know (in ways we may not be able entirely to explain in words and can't really construe as acts of interpretation) that an action is right or wrong.

Intriguingly, while most of us would say that we can just see these things, Wittgenstein reversed the visual metaphor. He said we must ultimately follow a rule blindly. But however we choose to express the point, juries often have little difficulty convicting murderers, even though precisely how to distinguish between murder and legitimate or less culpable forms of killing is a matter of continuous legal and ethical debate.

There was certainly quite some unease among those who had an insider view of Enron's accounting practices. Had there not been, staff at its auditors, Arthur Andersen (one of the "big five" global accountancy firms before its spectacular Enron-induced collapse), would not have taken the fatal decision to shred Enron-related records when they learned that the corporation was being investigated by the Securities and Exchange Commission.

But unease is not the same as assertion of blatant illegality, especially when those with the most negative views were sidelined, as apparently happened to the most sceptical Andersen partner, Carl Bass. In February 1999, David Duncan, the partner in charge of its dealings with Enron, told the latter's audit committee that "Obviously, we are on board with all of these" – Enron's accountancy practices – "but many push limits and have a high 'others could have a different view' risk profile.'' He was warning the corporation that what it was doing had the potential to create a damaging dispute – not telling them they would end up in jail if they kept doing it.

Source: *The Guardian*, May 26, 2003.

Case 3

The following article, written from the perspective of one of the major professional bodies, makes a number of interesting observations in relation to ethical frameworks in general. Towards the end of the article the author makes the observation that ''Ultimately, the most powerful rationale for ethical behaviour in business is market forces''. Consider the extent to which this might form an effective and acceptable basis for ethical behaviour?

The Moral Maze, by Tony Bromell

Applying Ethics to Business Behaviour Isn't Easy, and Many Find Their Morals Slipping

Let us accept, for the moment, that being ethical in business is a good thing. How is it, then, that what seems like an easy objective is fraught with difficulties? Ethics underlie a great many actions, albeit classified in the business mind as financial, operational, people or systems issues. At its most basic, being ethical is doing the right thing according to society's values. By and large, most people want to do the right thing and, with a little help, recognise what that is when they see it.

But where does personal behaviour stop and business behaviour start? If a well-known businessperson commits a highly immoral, but legal, personal act is that bad business behaviour? Probably not, unless the personal behaviour has a direct bearing on the business. Of course, the magnitude of the behaviour may be such as to bring their credibility into doubt, or even bring disrepute to the business or profession – for example, at the extreme end of reasoning one could conclude 'x is a hypocrite, therefore all businessmen are evil'. The increasingly global nature of business, and the fact that it operates across societies, adds an interesting spin to the ethics debate. Bribery, for example, is considered totally unethical in our society, but seems to be the only way to do business in others.

Is imposing our values elsewhere unwarranted cultural imperialism, or a principled stance to help others escape corruption? If we are trying to positively help others, how do we ensure a common stance and prevent 'ethical' companies from being undermined by those less principled?

The law may have a role to play in some instances, as it already does with bribery of foreign public officials, though this needs to be on an international basis to be effective. For all these high-level issues, individuals in business most often find they are pressurised into being unethical because there will be adverse consequences if they aren't. These threats to ethical behaviour can take many forms, including: self-interest ('if I take this action we will make less profit and I will lose my bonus'); intimidation ('if you disclose that, you will be sacked'); and familiarity ('I should report that behaviour, but I don't want to get this person into trouble because they are a long-time friend'). Another possibility is that our intrepid businessperson gets unwittingly backed into a corner from which it is difficult to escape, honour intact. Perhaps the unethical position has been arrived at in a series of small steps, unnoticed until the cumulative effect becomes significant. Alternatively, public predictions of a certain outcome may have been made, the achievement of which turns out to be dependent on unethical actions.

So how do you prevent such a situation from arising? There are no magic solutions. The best protection would be to spot where the problems might be, minimise those where possible and face up to the others head on.

The ICAEW recently published guidance on ethical matters for members in business at www.icaew.co.uk/ethics. The guidance does not provide a unique solution to all ethical problems, because the dilemmas that arise are too disparate for a one-size-fits-all approach. But what it does do is recognise that accountants may face ethical dilemmas resulting from the responsibilities to their employer and the profession being in conflict. One solution it suggests is a 'do-it-yourself' ethical dilemma resolution framework, which helps to identify the problem by applying fundamental ethical principles – integrity, objectivity, competence, performance and courtesy – to business situations using a threats and safeguards framework. This seeks to raise the awareness of threats encountered when complying with the fundamental principles and guides you through analysis and case studies as to the nature of safeguards you might put in place to combat these threats.

But any amount of guidance that is followed by chartered accountants alone is not going to make business ethical. What we need is a concerted approach to increasing people's awareness of ethics and their importance, reducing the pressures to act unethically from all directions – a reporting/consultation mechanism that provides an escape route where pressures still exist and, if necessary gives protection to appropriate whistleblowing.

Some of these mechanisms already exist. For example, the combined code applying to UK-listed entities on a 'comply or explain' basis requires companies to have internal procedures for the reporting and investigation of 'possible improprieties'. It remains to be seen how this will work, but coupled with a genuine, positive tone at the top, it could prove a powerful weapon.

Another visible development is reporting of corporate behavioural aspects. Corporate social responsibility is, to a large extent, a separate issue from business ethics, focusing on an organisation outside of its own assets and liabilities as traditionally measured. However, CSR reporting and similar developments are indicative of a trend towards evaluating business performance on a variety of counts, not just purely numerical aspects such as earnings per share, free cash flow or operating profit before debits.

We might pause to ask why we should behave ethically in business at all, if it is so difficult? Ultimately, the most powerful rationale for ethical behaviour in business is market forces. Ethical behaviour does not directly earn money on a pounds-per-saintly-action basis, but the sum of individual ethical behaviour builds or destroys corporate reputation. Indeed in a few high-profile cases, one person's actions can achieve that. Similarly, if shareholders can see how individuals in a company behave (and thus by association, the company itself), they will start to vote with their pockets. Sooner or later, bad behaviour, while perhaps generating short-term super profits, will lead to long-term decline through public opprobrium or regulatory action – not an ideal long-term investment bet perhaps.

Doing good work quietly is the bedrock of ethical behaviour. However, a little transparency will do much to make the link between ethical behaviour and value to the business more obvious and thus make such behaviour more desirable – so long as it does not degenerate into a boilerplate 'form over substance' exercise.

Tony Bromell is head of accountancy markets and ethics at the ICAEW.

Source: *Accountancy Age*, February 1, 2005.

CORPORATE SOCIAL RESPONSIBILITY (CSR)

$$[14]$$

When you have completed this chapter you will understand:

- The factors that have led to the emergence of Corporate Social Responsibility (CSR) as an issue of corporate and social concern.
- The contribution and challenges that CSR presents to corporate reporting culture.
- That this new agenda poses difficulties and challenges for many companies.
- The meaning of the 'Triple Bottom Line'.
- The importance of theoretical perspectives such as stakeholder theory in advancing CSR.

Identikit Bureaucrats or Romantic Crusaders

Calls for Transparent and Serious Analysis of the Social and Environmental Impacts of Businesses have Resulted in Significant Successes. Steve Hilton Introduces Our Investigation Into How Far CSR has Come – and Cautions Against an Early Celebration

Considering their ostensible role as purveyors of the good news that big business cares about social and environmental progress and ethical behaviour, there's something almost comically depressing about most CSR reports. Perhaps it's the way that every "challenge" is dutifully "addressed". Or the impossibility, these days, of being a "stakeholder" without being dragooned into a carefully structured process of "engagement" by every passing corporation. Maybe it's the portrayal of social responsibility as a grimly Stakhanovite pursuit of targets, which always seem either to be "met", or "98.75% achieved". (And don't get me started on the oozing of "sustainability" from every pore.) Whatever it is, I can tell you in all honesty that as someone who is sent many of the social reports that are published, and (somewhat heroically, I would suggest) tries to read all those that are sent, I tend to emerge deflated and somewhat deadened from my encounters with these documents, reeling from the relentless uniformity and studied humility that characterizes the genre.

"But you've missed the point!", I can hear you cry. "CSR reports aren't supposed to be exhilarating page turners. They're the same type of thing as a company's annual report and accounts, and since when have they been a thrilling read? This is bookkeeping, not the Booker Prize." Well, up to a point. If social reports really were attempts to account for – literally account for – the social, environmental as well as economic impact and performance of businesses (the true "triple-bottom line" report) then we might accept (indeed welcome) a strong degree of standardization. But let's face it, we're nowhere near that stage.

Today's social reports can, at best, give readers a sense of a company's character: the way it behaves; the degree to which it's accountable; a snapshot of its impact on society. With some honourable exceptions, the characters that march across the corporate stage at the beginning of the twenty-first century look more like identikit bureaucrats than the romantic crusaders for a better world that their grandiose mission statements would have us believe.

Having said that, I suppose we should stop for a moment to applaud the fact that so many companies have committed to non-financial public reporting at all. It's stretching a point to say that social reporting is de rigeur for a big business today, but in the UK at least, we have, in the words of salterbaxter and Context, reached a "tipping point." These two CSR communications agencies produce a regular survey of social reports, and their latest published list (known in our office as "the bunny report" thanks to the presence of large numbers of rabbits throughout – an admirable if rather tortuous attempt to dramatize the authors' assertion that CSR reports are "breeding like rabbits") shows that 132 of the top 250 UK companies now report on one or more aspect of their impact on society...

And this leads on to the crucial question: is all this reporting actually making any difference? Or is it just, to borrow a well-worn but apt phrase, the "icing on the shit"?

I've always argued the case for social reporting on unashamedly free market grounds. Even the most swivel-eyed devotee of red-in-tooth-and-claw capitalism will accept that one of the critical factors underpinning the successful operation of the market economy is information. The better the quality of the information that buyers and sellers have, the better markets will work.

And there's absolutely no doubt that the production of a CSR report generates information that is beneficial both to a company's management and to those who want to see business making an ever-greater contribution to social and environmental progress. I have seen at first hand and on many occasions the effect of a social report in stimulating positive change within a company, and while it's easy to dismiss the production of social reports as pointless, politically-correct bureaucracy, the truth is very different.

> CSR reports play a crucial role in helping companies understand and tackle the risks to their business, and they can help identify creative ways to turn social and environmental needs into business opportunities. Given the tremendous and uplifting potential of social responsibility to make the world a better place, it's just a shame that so few CSR reports manage to capture the imagination.
>
> Steve Hilton is founding partner of Good Business, a CSR consultancy which helps produce social reports for a wide range of leading companies.
>
> Source: *The Guardian*, November 8, 2004.

Introduction

The view has long existed that companies exist primarily for the purpose of maximizing profits and, consequently, the wealth of their shareholders. Thus, while the responsibilities of companies to the broader community have been acknowledged, these have been understood to be adequately catered for under the legislative and contractual parameters within which companies operate. However, as the realities of corporate downsizing, takeovers, pollution and fraud have exposed the frailty of these controls as means of protecting the interests of employees, the local community and other interested parties, the role of the company in modern society has begun to be re-assessed.

As explained in Chapter 4, one of the consequences of this has been the emergence of an alternative view of the company as a "corporate citizen" with responsibilities towards, and answerable to, a broader community of "stakeholders". This would include employees, the local communities within which companies operate, and interest groups such as environmental agencies. One of the consequences of this, it is argued, is that companies should both act responsibly and report on this aspect of their activity. From this has emerged the notion of Corporate Social Responsibility (CSR) and its reporting.

CSR is less a set of techniques and more a mindset predicated upon notions of good corporate citizenship and transparency. It re-asserts the role of accounting in the broader context of accountability, seeking to devise and articulate a view of the company as an entity answerable to those whose resources it consumes, whether labour, environment or quality of life.

Thus, while the traditional accounting model champions the priorities of capital, i.e., wealth and profit, CSR seeks a broader frame of reference. It envisages both quantitative and qualitative measures of expression and attempts to capture the "true" cost of corporate activity to the local and global community. For instance, where the current accounting model does not allow for reporting on issues such as the risk of loss of employment or unethical business practices, CSR would deem it imperative that these be identified and reported on.

Some of the different perspectives on the nature and role of CSR in modern society are captured in the following article:

Defining the Value of Doing Good Business

In the Global Market Economy, the Role of a Company is About More than Maximising Profits Alone. Corporate Social Responsibility Means Doing Business with Integrity and Fairness – and it May Even Improve the Bottom Line by Thomas Donaldson

It is impossible for managers to sidestep corporate social responsibility (CSR). But while no manager can dismiss CSR, the broader and more pressing question is: "What does it mean?" CSR is one of the rare business topics whose very existence is regularly called into question. Yet almost no one denies that issues arising under its banner are important: the environment (including sustainability), obligations to employees, sourcing from developing countries, host country government relations, relationships with local communities, and regulating gifts and sensitive payments. Definitions of CSR range from broad ones that focus on large environmental and social problems, such as Aids, poverty, health and pollution, particularly in developing economies, to more specific ones that focus on doing business with integrity and transparency. The common denominator is that corporate activity should be motivated in part by a concern for the welfare of some non-owners, and by an underlying commitment to basic principles such as integrity, fairness and respect for persons.

The CSR Debate

It seems strange that anyone would allege that CSR is a bad thing but some intelligent critics do exactly that. The economist Milton Friedman famously argued that the only social responsibility of business is to maximize profit. To do anything else, the logic went, is to slide dangerously towards socialism. The incomparable strength of a free market is its ability to allocate resources efficiently, and misguided managers who struggle nobly to enhance social welfare forget their proper function in the market: to compete and win. Still worse, managers who pursue the dream of CSR are using other people's money. Investors give their hard-earned savings to managers in order to make more money. That is why they invest. So, managers who spend money to pursue CSR projects are "stealing" from their investors. In response, CSR defenders note that business organizations do not live in a vacuum; they owe their very existence to the societies they inhabit. Corporations are allowed status as a single agent in the eyes of the law as a fictional person (*persona ficta*), and are usually granted limited liability and unlimited longevity. What is more, they are granted access to society's labour pool and its storehouse of natural resources, two goods in which every member of society has a stake. Even Adam Smith, the father of capitalism, pointed out that the efficiency of the market rests partly on transparency, the absence of corruption and the avoidance of manipulation. At the same time, he did not believe that self-interested pursuit of profit was the right way to live. Benevolence,

Smith argued, is the highest virtue. In important ways, the battle over CSR is overblown.

On closer inspection it turns out to be largely about whether to endorse a "fat" or "skinny" interpretation of responsibility. Even critics of CSR quietly state exceptions to their more aggressive denials and usually end up embracing a slimmed-down version. For example, Mr Friedman readily acknowledges that the pursuit of profits does not excuse a manager from engaging in fraud or deception and, furthermore, corporations themselves are obliged to conform to the morality of the surrounding society. Mr Friedman and other conservative economists also frequently display moral concern; for example, when they observe managers abusing their responsibilities by gathering up lavish perks and compensation. Finally, critics of CSR willingly admit that free markets behave efficiently only in the context of an effective regulatory environment. Sadly, many developing countries lack this type of regime. Without effective legal and regulatory systems, corporations must assume heightened responsibilities. On the other side of the debate, even the most zealous defenders of CSR acknowledge that corporations have special and profound obligations to their investors. They also agree that corporate managers are not democratically elected, and that corporations should not adopt government-like social responsibilities. In short, as management thinker Peter Drucker once remarked: "Even if archangels inhabited corporate boardrooms instead of mere mortals, they would have to be concerned about profits."

Source: *Financial Times*, June 3, 2005.

As this article emphasizes, companies are motivated by a variety of factors. And while at one time these were often exclusively related to commercial factors, increasingly the view of the corporation as corporate citizen is influencing the manner in which they act. Nor are these two perspectives always, or even typically, at odds.

Because it is more a way of thinking than a set of accounting techniques, CSR will depend heavily upon a theoretical base for its legitimacy and development. While such a theoretical base has been only slowly forming, the emergence of stakeholder theory provides one useful avenue, allowing the competing interests of a more broadly based set of interested parties to be recognized. Within this paradigm it is possible, for instance, to identify the information requirements of groups not traditionally addressed, such as the local community and employees, and to formulate means by which the company can communicate with these groups through the Annual Report or by other means.

Essentially, CRS acknowledges the variety of ways in which companies interact with their environments. This in turn should impact the manner in which they deal with their employees, customers, suppliers and others. While key issues will vary across sectors, the following will all be relevant:

• Employment conditions

• Human rights

- Environmental impact
- Interaction with local communities
- Health effects of products.

Growing stakeholder expectations have meant that one of the responses of regulators to concerns in these areas has been an insistence on greater transparency and disclosure. Thus corporate reporting has grown significantly in recent years in response to the burgeoning CSR agenda. However, because this area is largely unregulated, the manner in which CSR is expressed varies from company to company. For instance, some companies such as BP, with Lord Browne at the helm, have been to the forefront of CSR, not only producing a range of dedicated environmental reports, but also ensuring that CSR issues are addressed in, and integrated into, the company's Annual Report. Other companies adopt a minimalist approach. In general, however, the thrust is towards greater transparency, a fact reflected in the best practice disclosures suggested for the OFR.

In practice:

The following article captures some of the reasons for the widespread scepticism that persists in many quarters in relation to CSR:

A worthwhile policy or simply propaganda?

Fortune magazine voted it "the most innovative company in America" six years running, it was consistently high in the lists of "best company to work for", it spent millions on literacy and community projects and was a pioneer of renewable, wind turbine technology.

It was, of course, Enron, now far better known for its corporate and financial mismanagement, its culture of secrecy and deceit, close ties to US politicians and alleged human rights abuses by subsidiaries in India.

This, then, is the big problem with corporate social responsibility (CSR). It has become big business for firms to invest in environmental, ethical, social and community projects. But behind the warm words and sentiments there is often a deep credibility gap.

And Enron's not the only one by any means. Closer to home, although undoubtedly not in the same league, Marks & Spencer is a well respected pioneer of CSR. Yet in the late 90s it was quite happy to dump UK suppliers in favour of cheaper overseas rivals. Now Stuart Rose is firmly in charge there are likely to be further cuts – even though the company insists on its website that "the importance of supplier relationships remains". It also abruptly shut down its French operations, leading to a storm of protest from workers.

Or take Shell. It suffered a series of public relations disasters in the mid-90s, notably the Brent Spar oil rig disposal fiasco and its association with human rights abuses in Nigeria. These debacles spurred it on to spend millions on rebranding, wooing environmentalists and human rights groups and investing in renewable energy. Yet, having done all that, it now finds a lot of its good work undone by the financial scandal of its under-reporting of oil reserves. "Shell

> *as a corporate entity has had a culture of seriously engaging with the issue of sustainability. The people running its programmes are skilled," concedes Mallen Baker, development director at Business in the Community. "I'd imagine a lot of those people are feeling rather let down by the actions of a few individuals."*
>
> *At the heart of the problem is the fact that CSR is very easy to do badly and quite a lot harder to do well. If, fundamentally, you are a bad employer, all you'll do by spending time and money producing CSR reports is create a culture of mistrust and cynicism among your employees...*
>
> *Source: The Guardian, July 17, 2004.*

Corporate Report

As with much else, the Corporate Report, a discussion paper commissioned by the Accounting Standards Steering Committee and published in 1975, and which took much of its inspiration from the Trueblood Committee in the US, played a seminal role in extending the business and accounting world's understanding of "accountability" and the expressions this might take.

It achieved this primarily by arguing that, as part of their "public accountability" function, economic entities of "significant size", (which it did not quantify), had a responsibility to report to a variety of users.

As a consequence the Report envisaged the publication of an Annual Report that not only provided financial information but was also sufficiently comprehensive that it sought to describe an organization's broader set of relationships and activities. While including basic financial statements such as the balance sheet and profit and loss account, it was envisaged that such a report would also include narrative elements and various descriptive statements.

In an attempt to address the information needs of a broader range of users, it suggested that several additional statements could be included in the Annual Report:

- **Statement of corporate objectives**: by challenging the corporate hierarchy to articulate its goals and objectives it was hoped to encourage the adoption of mission statements that would embrace a wider set of impulses, in the process recognizing the interests of stakeholders other than shareholders.

- **Value-added statement**: this was designed to highlight the various interest groups, for example employees, shareholders and government, who benefited from the wealth generated by a business. In the late 1970s these statements were widely produced. However, they have now disappeared almost entirely from UK Annual Reports. There was never a standard format for these statements. However, the following example illustrates how such a statement might highlight the link between wealth generated and those who benefited:

Value-added statement for X plc for the year ended December 31, 20X1

	£	£
Funds available		
Sales		8,000,000
Less: goods bought in		2,000,000
Value added		6,000,000
Applied as follows		
To employees as wages, pensions and other	1,500,000	
To government as taxes	1,000,000	
To providers of capital as dividends	3,000,000	
		5,500,000
Retained by company for capital investment		500,000

- **Employment report**: this was intended to provide information relating specifically to employees, such as details of gender ratios, training costs, health and safety and other matters.

- **Statement of foreign-currency transactions**: at a time when foreign trade was becoming a more significant element in corporate activity this was designed to highlight the financial implications of foreign currency activity.

- **Statement of monetary exchanges with government**: this was intended to indicate the level of financial interaction with government or government agencies. It was envisaged that it would embrace not only various taxation issues, but also grants and related matters.

- **Statement of future prospects**: while recognizing that there was resistance to such disclosure on the grounds of uncertainty as well as competitor sensitivities, it was felt that where it was intended to engage in activities that would impact upon employees or the local community that this should be disclosed. A typical example would have been the intention to construct a large new manufacturing facility in a particular community.

For a number of reasons, most significantly a change of government, coupled with resistance from business leaders to what were seen as onerous and extensive new disclosure requirements, the recommendations of the Corporate Report were never comprehensively implemented. It did, however, lay the foundation for discussion and research into the nature and role of CSR. And significantly, the current debate articulates many of these same objectives.

Triple Bottom Line

Throughout the 1980s the espousal of the primacy of the free market economy by Western governments, particularly in the US under Ronald Reagan and the UK under Margaret Thatcher, resulted in the subordination of concerns about social accounting issues. By the end of that decade, however, the contention that legislative protection was sufficient to protect the interests of stakeholders had been exposed as fallacious by a series of frauds, environmental disasters and huge employment losses resulting from financially-driven mergers and take-overs.

The result was a re-kindling of interest in CSR, which was seen to provide a framework within which this broader set of corporate responsibilities might be considered. The Turnbull Report, which requires boards to consider and assess risks from social, environmental and reputational sources, and to develop appropriate internal controls, has placed CSR firmly in the centre of the accountability agenda. In addition, a residue of the Corporate Report does persist in the form of Employee Reports and Value Added Statements that are still produced by a number of UK companies. The whole area of Human Resource accounting also offers scope for development, particularly as the role of intellectual capital as a source of corporate wealth increases.

Nevertheless, the adoption and assimilation of CSR as a significant element in the corporate reporting culture, while increasing, has been slow. There are a number of reasons for this:

- The attraction of the traditional accounting model

- The lack of a theoretical and conceptual base

- The resistance of some regulatory bodies on the basis of the perceived subjectivity and audit-unfriendliness of qualitative measures and reports.

However, in spite of considerable corporate reluctance, more recent years have seen a combination of political and regulatory pressures yield some significant results. These have been assisted in no small part by a number of high-profile cases of serious corporate misconduct. For instance, reports of the environmental degradation surrounding the activities of various oil companies in Africa as well as the use of child labour in Asia by sportswear companies focused attention on the unacceptable side of some commercial activity. Occurring at a time when regulators were already grappling with fraud-related corporate collapses, these acted as catalysts for a more transparent reporting culture. Supported by regulators, proponents argued that this should embrace both social and environmental reporting as well as more traditional accounting measures. This "triple bottom line" – measuring financial, social and environmental performance – underpinned by a focus on sustainability, has shaped much of the recent debate about the role and future of CSR.

In practice:

One of the champions of CSR in the UK has been BT. In the following extract from its Social and Environmental Report, which it issues along with its Annual Report, BT explains how it applies the triple bottom line concept:

Triple bottom line reporting

…This concept of 'triple bottom line' or 'sustainability reporting' has become a common feature of large companies. We believe it provides an invaluable holistic view of the company, making connections between aspects of performance previously evaluated separately and aiding our transition to a more joined-up approach to the management of social, environmental and economic issues. We also believe that companies have a responsibility to disclose the social and environmental performance information that their stakeholders – customers, employees, shareholders, suppliers and communities – need to make informed decisions. Our approach has been recognized by a number of external bodies and in the 2005 financial year we were joint winners of the ACCA award for the best web-based sustainability report.

The concept of triple bottom line reporting suggests that there are three separate and distinct bottom lines – each of equivalent standing.

We believe that, in the context of sustainable development, it's impossible to consider the economic dimension in isolation from the social or the environmental, and vice versa. We think the time has come for organizations to find new ways of reporting their total contribution to a more sustainable society in a way which fully includes the social, environmental and economic dimensions.

This is what we try to achieve in our Social and Environmental report.

As well as reporting on our performance, we also include 'Hot Topics' on some of our more controversial social impacts, such as extreme abuse of the Internet, offshoring and the implications for privacy in the digital networked economy. We have included these because readers want a qualitative insight into the way BT (and the industry generally) responds to its stakeholders. They want to see how we put our values into practice, and how our products and services can help contribute towards sustainable development.

Source: http://www.btplc.com/Societyandenvironment/Socialandenvironmentreport/

How to count the cost of being a good citizen

Despite the presence of champions such as BT, the Body Shop and BP, the response to CSR has been mixed. (The article from which this data is taken is reproduced in full in Case 3 at the end of this chapter and is worth reading in its entirety.)

…. Of course, the number of FTSE stocks disclosing meaningful environmental data in their annual report and accounts package remains worryingly low. Only 24pc of FTSE All Share index companies make any quantitative environmental disclosures of any kind and only 11pc link environmental issues to financial performance.

Absence of CSR disclosures in the annual report and accounts does not always imply absence of action. A survey of corporate reputation based on the question "what social responsibility initiatives has your company undertaken in the past two years" produced some interesting answers:

— 46pc of respondents claimed to have strengthened employee hiring policies to promote fairness and diversity

> — *41pc gave more money and time to the community and charities*
> — *37pc improved environmental practices*
> — *23pc imposed socially responsible criteria of codes of ethics on key suppliers.*
>
> *However, since only 22pc indicated that they had published a CSR or "triple bottom line" report, it seems fair to assume that many of these positive CSR initiatives remain unreported to, and therefore unrecognized by, the investment community.*
>
> *Source: Financial Times, October 21, 2004.*

With the acknowledgement of the rights of stakeholders other than investors, it has become increasingly difficult for business to sustain a reporting model predicated upon outdated modes of governance. The fact that accounting practice often merely reflects and perpetuates a corporate governance system dedicated to the rights of "owners" means that it too will be impacted by any changes in the culture of organizations. The likelihood is that changes in the corporate governance model induced by macro economic and social changes will force change on accounting and reporting practices.

One means by which many of the ambitions of those championing greater reporting of CSR issues may be achieved is the OFR. Although not compulsory, the possibility is that peer pressure amongst large plcs will ensure that it will contain disclosures on a number of items that are relevant to CSR (see Chapter 5).

As the following extract explains, however, while the possibilities offered by the OFR, triple bottom line reports, sustainability benchmarks and new media are considerable, CSR will be best championed in the broader contexts of governance, risk management and accountability. This will ensure that it is viewed in a more holistic manner; one that is more likely to impact corporate culture:

Good Practice Goes Far Beyond Box-Ticking

Today's Well-managed Company will have an Effective Board Plus a Culture that Ensures the Right Approach to Risk and Reputation Management, writes Alison Maitland

Many companies, notably in the US, continue to see governance purely in compliance terms, says Geoff Lye, director of SustainAbility, a long-established business consultancy on corporate responsibility. He argues that sticking to this narrow view could damage long-term shareholder value. Companies are vulnerable to an increasing range of risks, both legal and moral, as expectations of business increase. New areas of liability, including climate change and human rights, are emerging that would not have reached the radar screen of most companies a decade ago, he says in the report "The Changing Landscape of Liability".

The danger of relying on a purely compliance-led approach is illustrated by obesity, which has become at least partly a corporate responsibility issue. Food companies used to assume they had fulfilled their responsibilities if their products were manufactured, tested and labelled in accordance with relevant rules and regulations, says Mr Lye. "That model was smashed in the last five years – now they are scrabbling to reduce salt, fat and other ingredients."

According to SustainAbility, as yet only a small number of companies demonstrate in their reporting how they integrate social and environmental considerations into governance processes at board level. One company that is attempting to do this is MMO, the UK mobile operator. Each board member has the task of "championing" areas identified as key risks for the company. Peter Erskine, the chief executive, has responsibility for social, environmental and ethical risks.

These kinds of risk matter increasingly to investors, who are seeking not only more detailed but also more relevant information about companies. In a striking reflection of this trend, Bob Monks, the US corporate governance activist, has taken a stake in Trucost, a London-based environmental research agency, saying that green issues will soon have the same impact on share performance as corporate governance. "Shareholders who are more informed will make more money," he says.

Another illustration is the way that Standard & Poor's, the credit rating and investment research provider, assesses companies' relations with stakeholders such as employees, customers, suppliers and local communities as part of its corporate governance analysis. In Risks Opportunities, SustainAbility's latest research into non-financial reporting, George Dallas, managing director of S&P's governance practice, acknowledges that equity analysts often see such issues as a diversion from the main factors driving investment decisions.

In the UK, the policy committee of FTSE4Good, the ethical investment index, is examining how governance fits with corporate responsibility, with a view to introducing criteria on boards' role in promoting the latter.

Do indices and rankings make a difference? They are factors that mainstream investors would take into account, says Craig Mackenzie, head of investor responsibility at Insight Investment and chairman of the criteria committee of FTSE4Good. "If a company isn't in FTSE4Good, that's a crude indicator of its record on CSR. If it is in the Dow Jones SAM index, which is quite hard to get into, that's a positive sign. But investors still have to do due diligence." The bigger impact is on companies themselves, which use inclusion in these indices, or in rankings such as Business in the Community's corporate responsibility index, as a badge of approval to show to governments, regulators, employees and investors. The competition to be included in such rankings, and then to win a place at the top, is "quite powerful at driving change in companies", says Mr Mackenzie.

Source: *Financial Times*, December 14, 2004.

In Practice:

The consultancy firm SustainAbility has tracked changes in the CSR reporting practices of large UK companies for many years. Its findings also support the view that corporate governance developments may provide the context within which triple bottom line reporting will be more widely adopted:

CSR reporting and company performance: How closely are they correlated?

SustainAbility found that companies have made a "huge leap forward" in overall reporting quality, since publication of their "Trust Us" report in 2002, with "new highs in transparency and disclosure." Significantly, half of the top 100 in 2004 are newcomers, suggesting that leadership in corporate reporting is far from static, and that existing leaders will have to work hard to maintain position.

In contrast, the 2004 benchmark found that reports still fail to fully engage stakeholders, particularly financial analysts who continue to struggle to identify the data needed for their analyses of corporate performance.

The report also finds that "most companies still fail to identify material strategic and financial risks and opportunities associated with the economic, social and environmental impacts captured by the 'triple bottom line' agenda." SustainAbility suggests that corporate governance, board leadership and integrity are at the heart of the challenge facing business if corporate responsibility is to have real impact on business planning and decision making.

Source: The New Bottom Line, February 2005.

Sustainability and Environmental Accounting

The human impact on the environment, as measured by, for example, global warming, depletion of the ozone layer and pollution, has focused the minds of governments, regulators, business and ordinary individuals on the costs, both financial and environmental, of human activity. While industries belching out smoke and businesses engaging in environmentally damaging practices for short-term gain may well have been accepted as the inescapable consequences of progress a century ago, these are no longer tolerated.

Companies were previously able to "externalize" such costs, i.e., impose the burden of bearing such destruction or depletion on the local environment or community, or even customers, in the case of environmentally suspect products such as asbestos. However, they are now being forced to internalize such costs, i.e., to develop accounting procedures that see them incur the costs of their activities.

Prompted by initiatives such as the Pearce and Brundtland Reports, and to a lesser extent the Corporate Report, accountants began to consider ways in which the discipline might respond. One way in which this might be achieved, it was suggested, would be to develop accounting policies that required that the full cost of consuming environmental resources traditionally considered "free" would be absorbed, i.e., internalized. To this end a template has been developed that classifies resources into three categories, "charging" industry with a cost for consuming non-renewable resources. Predicated on the notion of sustainability, this approach classifies "capital" as follows:

1. Man-made capital, such as machines, roads, etc.

2. Renewable natural capital, i.e., items that are easily renewable such as most animals and plants.

3. Critical (non-renewable) natural capital, such as the ozone layer, non-renewable mineral deposits, tropical forests and rare flora and fauna. A business is considered unsustainable to the extent that it consumes these resources.

On the grounds that profit figures are misleading where they do not include a charge for the depletion of critical natural capital, those championing this approach argue that a charge should be incorporated when computing profit. Essentially, the environment is to be regarded as a resource held in trust for future generations, and sustainability, rather than financial profit, would be the true measure of corporate success.

For most companies this is a step too far. While willing to disclose amounts incurred to protect the environment from the effects of their activity, they resist proposals that would require that they indicate the cost to the global community of the depletion of non-renewable resources resulting from their activity.

Nevertheless, the implications for accounting are considerable. As the traditional arbiters of "cost", they might be expected to devise mechanisms by which "true" environmental costs would be recognized and measured, i.e., internalized, by business.

In practice:

This approach also challenges the role of accounting in advocating investment appraisal techniques, which, because of their use of high discount rates, incorporate an inherent bias towards short-termism. For example, the more common investment appraisal techniques favour less capital-intensive electricity generating facilities at the expense of those that avail of renewable resource approaches such as wind power, because the latter require heavy initial investment and only generate positive NPV cash flows over the long term.

Responding to these developments the accountancy bodies have taken some initiatives in this area. In 1990 the Association of Chartered Certified Accountants (ACCA) sponsored a major report, The Greening of Accountancy: the Profession after Pearce, written by Professor Rob Gray. And it has followed up this initial commitment with an annual award for Annual Reports indicating responsiveness to the "green" accounting agenda. In turn, many firms now produce "sustainability reports."

As part of this process the role of auditors has also been considered, with particular interest focusing on their capacity to report on the degree to which companies have complied with stated environmental policies as well as their role in carrying out environmental audits. This is consistent with a growing appreciation of their role as assessors of internal risk-control measures.

In practice:

Companies reap financial benefit from sustainability

The financial services sector is beginning to recoup millions of pounds back from reporting on sustainable issues. Documenting these issues allows companies to identify efficiencies which can save tens of millions of pounds a year.

Despite the costs involved in providing a sustainability report, including management time, advisers, internal systems, monitoring costs, engaging with shareholders and in some cases having the data assured by an independent auditor, companies are starting to recoup these costs and more.

Paul Monaghan, sustainable development manager at the Co-op Bank says: 'We have calculated ethical and ecological benefits of sustainability reporting to be in excess of £20m profit contribution to products and services.' British Telecom, in its 2003 sustainability report, points out: 'Our environmental programme, which includes energy efficiency and fuel savings, has saved BT more than £600m over ten years.'

Roger Adams, technical director at ACCA, believes that more financial institutions need to take this approach and look to the long-term gains of sustainability reporting. Only 24% of the FTSE All Share Index make any quantitative environmental disclosures of any kind and only 11% link environmental issues to financial performance. Adams believes this is because businesses rarely do anything unless they are obliged to by law or by weight of external opinion. Only 25% of UK investors rank CSR as important to them.

Source: Accountancy, November 2004.

While some progress has been made by the accounting profession in engaging with sustainability issues, successes have been limited. Nevertheless, the fact that environmental accounting has begun to appear on the accounting agenda is an achievement in itself. Indeed, as sustainability crystallizes as a political concern of global dimensions, the possibility is that it will require a more tangible response. For instance, as the accounting implications of emissions trading begin to be appreciated, there will be considerable scope for further integrating environmental accounting within an extended accounting model. It is an example of the extent to which accounting must increasingly engage with issues that previously would have been considered outside of its domain.

Summary

An increasing acceptance of the rights of a broader set of stakeholders, coupled with a growing awareness that corporate responsibilities extend to social and environment issues, challenges accounting both conceptually and practically. In particular, the notion of sustainable development and the consequent accounting and investment appraisal implications pose major challenges.

The traditional accounting model can only be extended to embrace this new agenda with some difficulty. And, despite valiant efforts by some individuals to force the pace on issues such as accounting for environmental costs, progress has been limited.

Nevertheless, the prognosis is good. The extent to which environmental reporting has succeeded in establishing its claims to a place in the accountability debate suggests that there is scope for other elements of the CSR agenda to be accommodated. The likelihood is, however, that this will only be achieved as governments and regulators respond to the more inclusive stakeholder and governance paradigms, and to the broader set of demands for good corporate citizenship that these both imply and facilitate.

Review Questions

Question 1
Identify and explain the various factors that have given rise to what is now commonly called CSR. Is this a fad or is it likely to influence corporate reporting into the long term?

Question 2
Explain the role played by the Corporate Report in identifying CSR as an area that was likely to have a considerable impact upon corporate reporting.

Question 3
What are the principal deficiencies in the traditional accounting model identified by those supporting CSR as a reporting paradigm?

Question 4
Investigate further and assess the significance for the nature and role of CSR of each of the following:

- Pearce Report
- Brundtland Report
- ACCA's Environmental Reporting Award
- Emissions trading

Question 5
In your opinion how does CSR relate to the whole question of the company as "corporate citizen"?

Question 6
Discuss the role that both stakeholder theory and broader governance and risk management issues could play in ensuring that CSR might be assimilated more fully into the financial reporting model.

Question 7
Account for the fact that environmental accounting has emerged as the one area within CSR capable of establishing a central role for itself in the reporting process.

Question 8
Explain what is meant by "sustainability" and why this is a central concern in CSR reporting.

Question 9
"The Turnbull Report may well be remembered as the report which finally established both environmental risks and social aspects of corporate life at the centre of the reporting and control agendas". Explain why the Turnbull Report could be seen in this light.

Case Studies

Case 1

Check the extent to which environmental and social issues are addressed in the Tesco plc 2005 Annual Report and any accompanying reports that the company issues. Identify whether the level of disclosure is adequate in view of the range of stakeholders attaching to such a large international enterprise.

Case 2

Access a copy of the most recent Annual Report and other supplementary CSR Reports for The Body Shop plc and compare the level of social, environmental and ethical reporting with that of Tesco.

Case 3

The following important article reports on a speech by Sir Adrian Cadbury, architect of many of the corporate governance reforms of recent years, that dealt with issues relating to CSR. In the process, it identifies a number of tangible results of focussing on corporate responsibility issues. It also seeks to determine whether there are any tangible economic motivators for companies to engage in CSR. Consider the arguments made and whether they are likely to influence those more sceptical of the whole CSR agenda in general.

How to Count the Cost of being a Good Citizen

Sir Adrian Cadbury Wants Business to Resist Corporate Responsibility Pressure Groups. Roger Adams Looks at the Implications

Businesses rarely do anything that has no obvious payback, unless they are obliged to by law or by weight of external opinion. Corporate Social Responsibility (CSR) appears to have become one such buzz-word to which top companies feel obliged to nod.

But is there a more positive, quantifiable economic reason for them to do so? I believe the evidence suggests there is. According to the British Standards Institute, CSR "is a mechanism for organisations to voluntarily integrate social and environmental concerns into their operations and their interaction with their stakeholders, which are over and above the organisation's legal responsibilities".

Voluntary integration brings with it an associated cost – management time, advisers, internal systems and monitoring costs are just the start. For the fully committed organization, CSR will also involve identifying and engaging with stakeholders (more management time used up there), responding to stakeholders' concerns, gathering data for public reporting; and, in an increasing number of cases, having that data assured by an independent third party.

For any commercial organization to embark on the CSR journey there must also be a set of benefits presumed to at least equal the costs. While most discussion of benefits centres on the largely intangible benefits of reputation and risk management, some organizations claim to have identified these benefits through more scientific means. Here are some examples: At the Co-operative Bank, Paul Monaghan, sustainable development manager at the bank, says: "We have calculated ethical and ecological benefits of sustainability reporting to be in excess of £20m profit contribution to products and services. Producing a sustainability report has enabled us to manage a whole host of ethically and environmentally motivated risks much more robustly." The sum of £20m is not small change even to a bank.

Baxter International, the American healthcare company, analyses its basic environmental compliance costs and other response programmes and compares them with the savings it derives from environmental initiatives. Last year Baxter reported savings of $69m (£38.5m) as compared with total environmental costs of $22m (£12.2m). Again, not chickenfeed. BT, in its 2003 sustainability report, pointed out that "our environmental programme, which includes energy efficiency and fuel savings, has saved BT more than £600m over ten years". BT also pointed out that its strong focus on social and environmental issues has been a crucial factor when it comes to bidding for new contracts – £900m in its 2004 financial year.

The ability to produce such direct evidence of CSR benefits may be of interest to some investors. There is likely to be more interest, however, in evidence that companies have integrated CSR activities across their strategies and operations.

The accountant Price Waterhouse Coopers and the investment bank Schroders conducted an experiment based on the accounts of the Danish company Coloplast, to find out how non-financial information can influence the future earnings potential of any given company – and thus the stock value. Two versions of the company's annual reports were prepared – one complete with non-financial (CSR type) information and one stripped of it. Each member of the investment team received one or other of the two versions and was asked to use its information to develop a forecast of revenue and earnings for the next two years and to provide a recommendation for the stock. They had two hours to complete their task, with no conferring. The results? The average revenue and earnings forecast by those with the full set of accounts were lower than those who had referred only to the financially based document. Despite the lower forecast, those with the complete information set were overwhelmingly in favour of buying the stock. This was in contrast to the other investors with the less complete information – almost 80pc of whom recommended selling the stock.

Of course, the number of FTSE stocks disclosing meaningful environmental data in their annual report and accounts package remains worryingly low. Only 24pc of FTSE All Share index companies make any quantitative environmental disclosures of any kind and only 11pc link environmental issues to financial performance.

Absence of CSR disclosures in the annual report and accounts does not always imply absence of action. A survey of corporate reputation based on the question "what social responsibility initiatives has your company undertaken in the past two years" produced some interesting answers:

— 46pc of respondents claimed to have strengthened employee hiring policies to promote fairness and diversity
— 41pc gave more money and time to the community and charities
— 37pc improved environmental practices
— 23pc imposed socially responsible criteria of codes of ethics on key suppliers.

However, since only 22pc indicated that they had published a CSR or "triple bottom line" report, it seems fair to assume that many of these positive CSR initiatives remain unreported to, and therefore unrecognized by, the investment community.

Attaching financial numbers to the direct costs and benefits of CSR initiatives is not difficult. Donations, in kind or in cash, can easily be costed, as can compliance costs attaching the environmental, health and safety or human resources.

One hazard of focusing on direct and reputational issues is that the wider issue of corporate sustainability can be overlooked. Some organizations have gone a step further than a direct cost and benefit focus and tried to compute the true costs of their indirect impacts on the environment.

The Natural Environment Resource Council, working with Forum for the Future, recently estimated that the cost of mitigating its impacts to air and water in 2003 would have amounted to about £2m (1.3pc of their total operating costs). For commercial organizations the mitigation costs are likely to be much higher. At the Anglian Water Group, for example, the same methodology produced a 2003 mitigation figure of £15.2m, representing some 3.5pc of other operating costs or 5.3pc of reported operating profits.

For capital-intensive manufacturing companies, power-generating companies and the extractive industries these ratios are likely to be much higher. These costs refer only to mitigating the costs of environmental impacts, not broader impacts on society, and will not be incurred in the absence of either government compulsion via law or through voluntary action on the company's part.

Attempting to assess the costs of indirect social impacts is a much more complex process. The US Government is currently staging a $280 billion lawsuit against the tobacco industry. How accurately this sum reflects the social costs incurred at state and federal level to address the consequences of smoking is anybody's guess.

Computing and disclosing sustainable levels of profits, however, is at an early stage and without a revolution in the way the market place looks at sustainable development issues, the most likely way forward is for social and environmental externals to be progressively and incrementally introduced into the financial bottom line via government action. We are already seeing the impact of carbon taxes on the profit-and-loss accounts of exposed companies and emissions trading will soon start to impact on balance sheets as companies begin to trade emissions surpluses and deficits as regular financial instruments.

UK company law is soon to be changed to give effect to a requirement that large listed companies should disclose information on social and environmental issues through their Operating and Financial Review (OFR) statements. These disclosures will be required when that information is likely, in the view of the directors, to be of "material" significance to business performance. At this stage it seems unlikely that any of the financially quantified data described above will find its way through into the OFR statements of large listed companies.

For CSR activities, as with environmental management issues, if you do not manage them then you cannot measure them. And if you do measure them try to measure both sides of the equation. If you take workplace health and safety issues seriously you will measure both the outlays and the returns. The same goes for initiatives to reduce waste and packaging, and for employee, supplier and customer satisfaction.

The Co-op Bank, BT and Baxter are not the only companies who have recognized that the benefits of CSR activities are neither one-offs nor of trivial size. They are just the companies that do it best.

Sir Adrian Cadbury, former chairman of Cadbury Schweppes and author of the pioneering report on corporate governance, was speaking at a conference organized by the Royal Society for the encouragement of arts, manufactures and commerce. Roger Adams is executive technical director at the Association of Chartered Certified Accountants.

Source: *Financial Times*, October 21, 2004.

Case 4

The following article outlines some of the practical benefits of CSR when integrated into a company's business culture. It also includes brief interviews with a number of academics and company executives. Consider the claim made by one academic, that "It is not what you do with your profits, it is how you make your profits", that is critical.

Profit with a Conscience

Corporate Social Responsibility is Not Only Essential, it Pays Off, by Gareth Chadwick

Corporate social responsibility (CSR) is nothing if not a mouthful. But the jargon disguises a very simple idea: that rather than being narrowly focused on the pursuit of profit at the expense of all else, businesses should behave responsibly in the course of their profit-making, taking into account their wider role and impact on society.

It is not a new idea. From philanthropic Victorian industrialists such as the Lever brothers, the Cadbury brothers and Titus Salt, to the Co-operative movement and recent innovators such as The Body Shop or Ben & Jerry's ice cream, businesses have tried to be forces for good in the community, not just exploiters of manpower.

Ben & Jerry's, for example, contracted the Greystone Bakery in Yonkers, New York, to bake its brownies, a firm that used its profits to house the homeless and train them as bakers.

But whether it is building links with community groups, treating staff fairly and ethically, implementing waste minimization policies or sourcing environmentally friendly suppliers, modern CSR, or CR (corporate responsibility) as it is often shortened to, has moved far beyond philanthropy.

Today, the case is focused on the practical, tangible benefits of businesses behaving in a more responsible way. ''Businesses are much more aware of the broader impact of what they do. They increasingly realise that it is a false economy not to consider the social aspect, including environmental issues. If you do ignore it, it will eventually come back and bite you and there are likely to be financial consequences in that,'' says Erik Bichard of the National Centre for Business and Sustainability.

Clearly, there is still a strong moral case for businesses to try to have a beneficial impact on society. But that has always been the situation and with one or two high profile exceptions, there has been very little to show for it.

But the business case has become harder to ignore. One issue is recruitment. An undergraduate survey in 2003 conducted across the world's 20 largest economies found that three in five undergraduates would choose to work for a company that could demonstrate its ethical values and positive impact on society, while in the UK 80 per cent said they were more likely to stay in their jobs if their employer adopted a responsible approach to the work-life balance.

A second benefit is in terms of the new ideas and innovation that a close connection with the community can engender. Businesses don't operate in isolation from the rest of society and a stronger link between the two facilitates a better understanding of the market, of who the customers are and how best to service their needs.

The third element is reputation and branding. Over 85 per cent of consumers have a more positive image of companies that are seen to be pursuing more responsible business practices and over half of European consumers say they are prepared to pay more for environmentally responsible products. It is a figure which is borne out by the rapid growth in the market for fair trade products. Sales of fair trade products grew by more than 50 per cent in the UK in 2004, with shoppers spending £140m on them.

CSR can also provide a competitive edge for smaller companies. As consumer choice increasingly takes ethical considerations into account, so larger organizations are exercising similar discretion when sourcing suppliers.

The CSR element can be a key differentiator. Businesses want to work with other businesses that reflect their own values and attitudes – and those of their customers. ''If as a business you are behaving in a way which doesn't accord with the way your customers thinks you should be behaving, it can withdraw your license to operate. Look at Andersen. It was tainted by the actions of its client Enron and disowned by the market. It never recovered,'' says Bichard.

CR merely for PR value doesn't work in the end: Nick Isles, associate director of The Work Foundation, formerly The Industrial Society, a not-for-dividend research and management consultancy.

"Corporate responsibility, or CR, is firmly entrenched in the business lexicon." No large or medium-size organization can afford to be without its CR policies. Many have CR directors and departments. For some of these organizations, CR is just a shield to fend off criticism of their poor business practices. For others, being CR is an integral element of their overall business strategy. These businesses are committed to strategies and practices that others may describe as CR, but which they themselves see more accurately as a means of securing high performance. It is in companies' long-term interests to be responsible to their workers, their supply chain, the environment in which they work and their customers.

"Long-term profitability and success requires long-term strategic vision. And companies have to understand that people have greater access to more information about what companies do and how they do that. CR merely for PR value doesn't work in the end. Just look at Enron's annual CR report the year before it went bust."

British companies take CSR seriously: Professor Jeremy Moon is director of the International Centre for Corporate Social Responsibility at Nottingham University Business School.

"CSR has had its up and downs. It was big in the USA in the late 1960s and early 1970s. It emerged in the UK in the early 1980s in the wake of riots, mass unemployment and social alienation, particularly in urban areas." But CSR is getting more institutionalized now, which suggests it will endure. There are business associations devoted to it. CSR guidance and reporting systems are built into general policies on accountability and governance. It is even increasingly an investment consideration.

A key phrase in understanding its development is: It is not what you do with your profits, it is how you make your profits, how you actually do business at a day-to-day level.

"British companies are among the leading international companies in CSR, whether it is signing up to relevant business associations, reporting their social responsibility or engaging in detailed stakeholder relations. Whatever the drivers may be, it is evidence that British companies take CSR seriously and feel it is important to demonstrate that, not just domestically, but internationally."

Integrating CR into the business is essential: Bruce Bendell is director of corporate responsibility at United Utilities plc.

"It may sound trite, but our main CR focus is on the business itself. Getting customer service right, getting our environmental approach right, using resources efficiently, treating our staff appropriately." I don't claim that we have got it absolutely right yet, but we try to integrate CR into the business. This is essential. If you treat CR as something else, a sideshow which is largely run by the marketing team, it never gets integrated and it will never become sustainable. And it fools nobody. "We have a partnership with the Prince's Trust, which encourages enterprise among young people. We work on projects with them, but the crucial glue in the relationship is that we encourage our staff to volunteer to be mentors on their programmes." If you look at it as a business driver, if you want to develop employees with leadership and teamwork skills, what better way of doing it? It teaches them more than a training course. "It might be hard to find a direct correlation between CR and business success. But if you look at the companies that take CR seriously they tend to be successful businesses. I don't think that is completely coincidental.''

Good to talk? We've found it's better to listen: Caroline Waters is director of people and policy at BT.

''Being socially responsible means treating your own employees responsibly. It is about sustainability. It's about the future and nature of business.'' Any successful business is about its people. By being a responsible business you're building trust-based relationships. It's a whole new kind of employment contract. A psychological contract with the individual which gives you huge voluntary contributions from them and really makes for a different kind of organization.

It makes basic business sense. Society – and that includes customers – is becoming more demanding and you have to respond to that. More and more people tell us that they make consumer decisions on the basis of whether they think a company behaves responsibly, and that includes its policy towards its employees and the role it takes in society. ''For a company that has had 'It's good to talk' as its strap line, what we've really found is it's better to listen. So we regularly engage with our people trying to understand what their needs are and how we can work in the broader society to help create that environment.''

Social enterprise takes CSR one step further: Jonathan Bland, chief executive of The Social Enterprise Coalition, the trade body for businesses that exist solely for a social purpose

''Social responsibility is an increasingly mainstream business issue. For example, there has been a big increase in FTSE-250 companies reporting on their activities to a far greater extent than they are legislatively required to do.'' Social enterprises take it one step further. The whole point of a social enterprise is to deliver social or environmental goals. They want to be profitable, but their purpose isn't to maximize shareholder value, it is to tackle some of the social and environmental challenges that face us. It's a totally different business model.

Social enterprise is about that triple bottom line, not just financial return, but social return and environmental return as well. But the enterprise bit is very important, too. It's about using a business model, not a traditional share-building model, but nonetheless a business model that has to operate in the market successfully and make profits. The profits are then re-invested into the business to do more good or to benefit a wider group of stakeholders than simply investors. ''You're in business solely for the benefit of that wider group of people.''

Source: *The Independent,* March 21, 2005.

When you have completed this chapter you will be understand:

- That accounting practice differs significantly between countries.
- Some of the principal features of the German and French accounting and governance systems.
- Why globalization has brought with it calls for greater harmonization of accounting practice.
- The role being played by the IASB in this process.

Have IFRSs Conquered the World?

It's Far from a Foregone Conclusion, argues Bob Parker

'Learning International Financial Reporting Standards (IFRSs) is a chore for us accountants in the UK but once we have mastered them, then not only do we know the rules of British accounting we also know the rules throughout the world.' How true is this? Have IFRSs really conquered the world?

Certainly they seem at first sight to have conquered the two parts of the world to which the UK has the greatest political attachment: the EU and the Commonwealth. From 1 January 2005 (or at the latest from 1 January 2007), the consolidated financial statements of listed companies within all 25 members of the EU are required to comply with all International Accounting Standards and IFRSs approved by the European Commission (EC). Leading members of the Commonwealth such as Australia, South Africa, New Zealand and Singapore all claim to have adopted international standards. Canada has pledged convergence by 2011.

Not the only game in town: But there is the great exception: the US is not giving up US GAAP. IFRSs are not the only game in town. The US Financial Accounting Standards Board is the best-funded in the world, and the Securities and Exchange

Commission (SEC) the strictest enforcer of accounting standards. Nevertheless, strenuous efforts are being made to bring IFRS and US GAAP closer together. There has been a 'race to the top' as international and US standard-setters have competed to produce standards acceptable to stock exchanges and government regulatory bodies. International standards have appealed to the EC not only because they are not US GAAP but also because they are not all that different from US GAAP.

However, within the EU, harmonization is not as great as it might appear to be. The UK is exceptional in its strong support of the concept of international standards. This should not surprise us. British accountants were active in the formation and development of the International Accounting Standards Committee from 1973 onwards. International standards have been much more influenced by UK accounting rules and practices than by continental European ones and thus the adjustment we have to make is much less.

Since IFRSs are mandatory within the EU only for the consolidated statements of listed companies, the great majority of German and French companies will not be applying international standards. In particular, the subsidiaries of German and French parent companies will be using local GAAP. Adjustments will of course be made during the consolidation process, but many local features (for example, the way depreciation is calculated) are likely to remain.

Casting doubts: One may also be permitted to have doubts about the extent to which IFRSs will be complied with in practice. For several years now several large companies in Germany and France have purported to be applying International Accounting Standards or US GAAP in their consolidated statements, but research has shown less than complete compliance and a tendency to pick and choose. The monitoring and enforcement of accounting standards is strongest in the US and the UK but noticeably weak in Germany. Germany has recently set up institutions based on both the US SEC and the UK Financial Reporting Review Panel. It remains to be seen how successful they will be.

Finally, there has been an understandable reluctance for national standard-setters and government authorities to accept international standards which they see as against their own interests, especially if major companies lobby against them. Commonwealth countries other than the UK are converging with international standards rather than adopting them. Close scrutiny of what is happening in Australia, for example, suggests convergence rather than adoption, with portions of standards omitted or amended.

So, have IFRSs conquered the world? Not quite, but the achievements of the IASC/B are surely greater than its founders in 1973 dared to hope.

Bob Parker is emeritus professor of accounting at the University of Exeter and co-author of Comparative International Accounting.

Source: *Accountancy*, November 2005.

Introduction

One of the principal themes of this text has been the way in which accounting practice and regulation have emerged and developed within definite socio-political contexts.

Accounting is an art, not a science, and is constantly mutating and responding to changing human and economic circumstances.

The opening account points to the continuing political pressures and economic imperatives dictating the nature and pace of developments in accounting practice and regulation. The emergence of the IASB as a rival to (and occasional ally of) FASB, the roles of the EU commission and the US government, calls for increased harmonization and convergence as globalization continues apace, as well as the fundamental tensions that exist between a principles and a rules-based approach to standard setting, all point to a range of possibilities for accounting over coming decades.

One of the reasons that it is necessary to view accounting in its international context is that over the course of recent decades a number of factors have conjoined to extend considerations about accounting practice beyond more obvious national, cultural and political boundaries. In the context of a pervasive globalization dynamic, one of the more important of these has been the huge growth in international trade and the cross-boundary Multi-National Enterprises (MNEs) that have evolved as a consequence. MNEs have a vested interest in promoting more uniform accounting practice and have been significant players in demanding greater harmonization across national boundaries.

Another critical catalyst has been the internationalization of money markets. In a global economy that is developing technology-supported international finance markets, national accounting regimes have come to be viewed as anachronistic hindrances. The advent of the Internet, which is no respecter of international boundaries, as well as a political vocabulary that has seen cold war rhetoric replaced by globalizing imperatives, have accelerated this process.

In these contexts, the previously regional aspirations of the larger accounting regulators such as IASB and FASB have morphed into ambitions that envisage the possibility of a global accounting regime.

European Accounting

Continental European civil-code countries share a particular accounting heritage, finding common origin in the Italian double-entry techniques disseminated throughout Europe in the Middle Ages. Unlike English-speaking common-law countries, however, for whom capital markets became significant sources of finance from the 18th century, European countries developed a system of small, family-based businesses where the need for extensive financial reporting was not as critical. Accounting practice and financial reporting in Europe did not develop in response to market demands, therefore, but to the less exacting requirements of a more focused group of owners. The fact that there was, as a consequence, a relatively underdeveloped accounting profession meant that there was no professional cadre in a position to articulate a preferred and coherent accounting practice. The result was that a rather legalistic perspective took hold in which tax and accounting law took precedence over the insights of an accounting-driven model.

This unique form of continental European accounting was further reinforced in the early 18th century by the extension throughout Europe of the Napoleonic Code which imposed uniform recording practices and pro-forma statements of account based on conservative valuations and creditor protection. Therefore, while national characteristics undoubtedly persisted, by the 19th century it was possible to identify an accounting culture in Western Europe that was developing a markedly different focus and expression from that emerging simultaneously in the Anglo-American world. This gulf widened over the course of the early part of the 20th century.

However, over recent decades, particularly under the influence of EU Directives, a degree of common practice has begun to emerge within Europe. For instance, the 4th and 7th EU Directives have ensured a high level of uniformity in terms of published financial statements. Likewise, the requirement that all listed companies within the EU produce consolidated accounts based on IFRS will ensure further convergence. Significantly, governance regimes have also begun to evolve in similar ways:

In practice:

As the following account relates, the governance cultures of many larger European countries, including the UK, have shown a remarkable degree of evolution and convergence in recent years:

Corporate Governance Evolving Fast in European Companies

Top European companies are improving their corporate governance at an impressive pace, according to recent analysis from Deminor, a Brussels-based research and ratings agency. In contrast with European scandals such as those at Parmalat and Ahold, the evolution in transparency, board and auditor independence and shareholder voting at FTSE Eurotop 300 companies during 2003 was very positive, said Jean-Nicholas Caprasse, author of the report. "Companies are keen on demonstrating their integrity, which is reflected in the steep rise in the publication of corporate ethics codes in Europe," said Mr Caprasse. In 2002 44 per cent of companies published their codes and in 2003 that figure had risen to 74 per cent.

More European companies than ever had installed audit, remuneration and nomination committees, he added. Deminor also disclosed the top three companies for governance performance in the nine largest European markets. Despite the recent furore over the appointment of Sir Ian Prosser as deputy chairman at J Sainsbury, the food retailer comes second in the UK for fulfilment of the rights and duties of shareholders.

Mr Caprasse said that institutional investors were also paying far greater attention to governance issues, with many using information from Deminor to monitor the risk in investments and more actively participating in shareholder voting. "There are a number of red flags we can raise on the downside of risk to aid investment decisions," he said. "Everyone is very wary of being caught in the next Parmalat." He added that many more large asset managers were voting more systematically and putting voting policies in place, especially on the continent.

Deminor expects that governance will continue to evolve through "comply or explain" style soft laws from country regulators, as happened in the UK after the review by Derek Higgs. The agency also said a further enhancement of shareholder participation in general meetings was likely to occur as institutional investors faced increasing pressure from regulators and some investment clients, particularly those clients from the UK and US.

The UK has recommendations on voting following a report from Paul Myners for the Shareholder Voting Working Group, while French and Spanish regulators require institutions to have a voting policy in place. Dutch regulators have gone the furthest and by 2005 will require asset managers to communicate each quarter how they have cast votes.

Deminor has provided corporate governance performance data and country ratings for the past three years. Information from: www. deminor-rating.com

Source: Financial Times, February 23, 2004.

Germany

The dominant role given to the principles of conservatism and prudent valuation in the German accounting system has made it markedly different in focus and emphasis from the Anglo-American model. The prominence of these two concepts is a function of both the country's economic history and the relative importance of law and accounting.

A notable feature of the German system is the subordination of accounting to the legal and taxation systems. Until recently accounting was essentially considered to be merely a sub-section of the law and to be capable of control solely by legal means. Thus, much of Germany's accounting culture and form of practice can be traced to the Napoleonic Code de Commerce that was subsequently extended in 1861 as the German Commercial Code.

This legalistic approach had the effect of placing the development of accounting practice and concepts in the hands of lawyers and officials. Their concerns were more with the application of rules than with the development of a coherent discipline such as that being attempted by the accounting profession in the UK and the US. Allied to an economic history in the first half of the 20th century that was characterized by regular bouts of economic depression and business collapse, this placed a strong emphasis on accounting as a means of assessing business liquidity and security. In this scheme of things issues such as valuation and repayment capacity became the principal concerns.

This automatically put an emphasis onto the balance sheet and the application of conservative and prudent valuation principles as a means of exercising some control over business. A consequence of this was an understanding of "income" as the difference between the "net asset" figures disclosed by successive balance sheets rather than as the difference between revenues and costs calculated by means of a profit and loss account.

The result of this perspective is a published "commercial balance sheet" – the *Handelsbilanz* – which is constructed according to strict and conservative valuation rules. It is intended to facilitate the calculation of a distributable income figure that can be distributed to the owners without compromising the capacity of the business to either satisfy its creditors or to continue as a going concern. One other consequence is the existence of often quite substantial hidden reserves regularly used to indulge in income smoothing.

The focus, therefore, has been on the production of accounting information that satisfies a limited range of users, principally owners. By extension, the primary emphasis has not been on making available information that facilitates an informed process of decision-making by a wider set of stakeholders.

Determination of tax liability is achieved by preparing a special balance sheet – the *Steuerbilanz* – which is constructed mainly in accordance with the principles applying to the *Handelsbilanz*. This principle is called the *Massgeblichkeitsprinzip*, which in effect means that recognition and measurement principles applied in constructing the commercial balance sheet must also be employed in constructing the tax balance sheet. Except for the large public companies that must use IFRS, there remains a considerable level of equivalence between both the commercial and tax balance sheets.

Corporate Governance in Germany

In contrast to the UK and US, a large "external" capital market such as the Stock Exchange does not dominate in Germany. This is because, traditionally, companies have sought funds from institutions such as banks, pension funds and other industry sources, rather than from the stock market. This explains, in part, the relatively small capitalization of the country's principal stock exchange in Frankfurt.

Thus, the ownership structure of German companies is not as disparate as in the UK or the US, and control of most companies can be traced to a relatively small number of institutions and individuals. The most common control structure is a "supervisory board" to which a management board reports. This body usually contains representatives of all of the significant investors as well as employees. This means that the company's primary reporting responsibilities can be fulfilled by "internal" disclosure to this board. As a consequence, the external reporting function is not as developed, important or thorough as in the Anglo-American world.

One of the consequences of the relatively stable governance system that has developed in Germany over the last 50 years has been that a focus on long-term planning has been possible. Another has been the concentration of ownership of much of the country's industrial base in a relatively small number of banks, pension funds and conglomerates. For example, banks such as Deutsche Bank have large shareholdings in many of Germany's companies. Likewise, "cross-ownership", where investment comes from other enterprises, often from within the same industry, is prevalent.

However, increasing exposure to international markets has highlighted a number of deficiencies in this system. For instance, the concentration of shareholding in such a small number of entities has led to charges of monopoly. In addition, larger German companies, such as Daimler-Benz, seeking major equity investment have found it necessary to list on foreign exchanges, particularly London and New York, in order to raise the necessary funding. This has caused both government and business leaders to acknowledge the limitations of the German corporate governance model.

Significantly, one of the principal constraints in ensuring the development of a modern accounting system remains the absence of a developed accounting profession in the sense that this is understood in the Anglo-American world. As a consequence of its governance model in which capital markets have traditionally played little or no part, external reporting has never been a strong feature of the German accounting landscape. This, coupled with the legalistic approach which the subordination of the accounting agenda to the legal and taxation agendas has fostered, has meant that the conditions within which a vibrant public accounting practice culture might emerge have not existed. Thus the two principal auditing and accounting professional bodies in Germany, the *Wirtschaftsprüferkammer* (WP) and the *Vereidigte Buchprüfer* (vBP) have neither the social nor the professional influence of their colleagues in the English-speaking world. Consequently, there is a lack of leadership in initiating change and much of the responsibility has devolved on state and federal governments and, increasingly, on the EU.

Recent Developments

Experiences such as the difficulties encountered by Daimler Benz when seeking to list on the New York Stock Exchange, coupled with a realization that its own capital market and corporate governance structures are limiting their capacity to operate efficiently in a global market, have forced both the business community and the government to reconsider many of the traditional elements of German commercial and accounting culture.

Like those in other EU countries, German listed companies have now adopted IFRS. This will have a significant impact on accounting, regulatory and governance cultures and result in a greater assimilation into international capital markets.

In terms of its governance culture and codes, Germany has also made considerable advances. For instance, it has recently adopted the Cromme Code of Corporate Governance. Indeed, as the following extract recounts, while retaining important aspects of its supervisory board structure, it has managed to develop a model that many consider more advanced than its Anglo-Saxon equivalent:

German Two-Tier Structure Seen as Role Model

It Contains Strengths and Weaknesses, But the New Corporate Governance in Germany Offers an Interesting Solution, by Ross Tieman

The introduction of a more comprehensive statutory corporate governance code a year ago, based on the work of a commission chaired by Gerhard Cromme, supervisory board chairman of engineering group ThyssenKrupp has reinforced perceptions that ethics and governance are issues German companies take very, very seriously. And with good reason. The pressure for a universal and enforceable new corporate governance code in Germany came not from legislators, not after the discovery of accounting fraud at US power group Enron, but from companies themselves, says Professor Lutter.

For half a century, German companies relied upon banks for their funding. During the past decade, however, German companies have been obliged increasingly to look to their shareholders for investment cash. Companies increasingly found that the absence of a single, comprehensive and easily-understood code of corporate governance caused doubt in the minds of foreign, and particularly British and American, fund managers whom they wanted to invest in their businesses. For although the German model has won some voluntary converts elsewhere – 10 per cent of French companies have two-tier board structures – the Anglo-Saxon single board continues to dominate worldwide, even in Spain and Italy.

But the clear – and now even clearer – separation of responsibility under German rules offers an interesting solution to the challenge of monitoring executive management. Traditionally, under the German system, the supervisory board was essentially responsible for electing the directors of the management board and deciding their remuneration. This system provided a theoretical barrier to the incestuous practice of chief executives hiring non-executive "yes-men" who would then pass executive remuneration on the nod. The management board chairman, meantime, and his fellow executive directors were responsible, not only for management and accounting policies, but for deciding the company's strategic direction. In practice, where the supervisory board was chaired by a controlling or dominant shareholder – as was often the case in family-based companies – the supervisory board could, of course, exert enormous influence over management if it desired.

The new corporate governance code, however, has formalized this hitherto unacknowledged power. It specifically adds to the supervisory board responsibilities the job of jointly overseeing the strategic direction of the company. One other feature should be kept in mind. Frequently, the supervisory board chairman of a German company is a former executive. This is the case with Mr Cromme, who used to be ThyssenKrupp's finance director, and with many more. Professor Lutter, who has examined practices in other countries, believes that with the additional strategic responsibilities given to the supervisory board, Germany now has a system that is as good as any, and better than many. "I would recommend it as a model," he says...

Source: *Financial Times*, February 23, 2003.

In practice:

While Germany has introduced new governance codes, the extent to which these are enforced in a civil-code environment is open to question:

Cromme Crumbles

The CFOs in Germany who have had their reservations about the country's governance code will be happy to learn that a new academic study offers compelling evidence that it's flawed. But that happiness might quickly fade if the recommendations by the study's authors to turn the self-regulatory Cromme Code into a codified law are followed through.

The three authors – Eric Nowak of the University of Lugano, Roland Rott of Frankfurt's Goethe University and Till Mahr of KPMG in Frankfurt – undertook their study to find out whether the capital markets reward companies for adherence to corporate governance codes, which in Germany's case include the 61 "comply-or-explain" requirements of the Cromme Code. Using data from over 300 companies in the Deutsche Börse's "Prime Standard" segment, they looked at how the market reacted in late 2002 when all listed companies in Germany had to publish first-time declarations about which parts of the code they were following. Nowak et al. found that those declarations had neither a short-term nor a long-term impact on stock price performance or relative market valuation. Another part of the research found that some companies didn't bother to explain, as recommended, why they are deviating from some or all of the code – yet they faced no sanctions from the market.

Studies in other countries have had similar results. For example, one paper published last year showed that in Spain, the market reaction to a firm's adoption of a governance code was generally positive, but only if it was accompanied by a major overhaul of the company's board structure.

The evidence of those studies has led Nowak to conclude that governance codes based on voluntary or mandatory disclosure are ineffective in civil law countries. The main reason: unlike in common law countries such as the UK, civil law countries haven't traditionally had high enforcement standards in investor protection.

With no official mechanism to monitor and enforce the code, German investors are left with a lot of "cheap talk," says Nowak. He predicts that the Cromme Code will have the same fate as two older German voluntary codes before it – involving insider trading and takeover practices – which were made law a few years after they were introduced. SPD politicians in Berlin seem to agree, and have stepped up discussions to turn the code into law.

That won't please corporate Germany much. A recent survey by Hamburg-based Psephos Institute of 885 senior managers found that 73% of respondents prefer self-regulation.

Source: CFO Europe, March 2005.

France

Not surprisingly, given their common European heritage, accounting practice in France shares many of the characteristics of the German system, most noticeably in the central role adopted by the state in its formulation and regulation. Increasingly, however, the profession and other interested parties are becoming proactive in articulating the need for change.

The most obvious expression of the centralizing role of the state is the *Plan Comptable General* (PCG). Ironically, given the unifying role of the Napoleonic code over 100 years previously, this has its origins in an initiative by the Vichy regime in the 1940s, undertaken in an attempt to harmonize accounting practice with the German code.

The most recent version of the code was produced in 1982 and incorporates or anticipates several of the key ideas incorporated in the relevant EU accounting instruments dating from that period, such as the Fourth and Seventh Directives.

The PCG, which is the responsibility of the *Conseil National de la Comptabilité*, adopts an essentially bureaucratic approach to the whole accounting function. In its current form it is produced as a book of over 400 pages with prescriptive rules determining the way in which specific items should be accounted for. It is presented in three parts:

Part 1: general rules, principles and terminology together with the account codes and entry classifications to be adopted.

Part 2: valuation and measurement rules together with financial statement formats.

Part 3: management accounting rules (this is not part of the regulatory system).

The PCG is supplemented by a legal framework that embraces various accounting-specific statutes and by the Commercial Code.

The effect of the PCG approach is to produce financial statements that are consistent not just between accounting periods, but across industries. These statements also incorporate concepts such as consistency, accruals and matching, going concern and historic cost.

In this relatively structured approach, the schematic nature of the recording process and the important role played by the state as regulator represent important similarities between the French and German systems.

However, there are also a number of important differences:

- The prominence given to tax law in Germany is not reflected in the French system. A strong tax code is in place, but the congruence expected in Germany between financial and tax accounts does not occur in France. Instead, while there are important rules regarding the availability of depreciation and the calculation of taxable profit which ensure a strong measure of compatibility, the accounting rules applicable under the PCG take precedence over tax law.

- There is scope within the French system for incorporating assets at values other than historic cost. Thus, replacement cost can be used to value certain assets in consolidated accounts.

Corporate Governance

As with Germany, French business has historically been dominated by small family-centred businesses. These have always been, and remain, significant engines of growth. This has significantly influenced the governance culture, for instance in ensuring that the stock exchange remains relatively unimportant.

However, probably the most unique characteristic of French corporate governance is the extent of state ownership of many enterprises in the country. Coupled with the influence of banks and the cross-ownership of shares by one company in another, this has the effect of limiting the range of investors and consequently the users of accounts. The result has been a financial reporting regime not unlike that in operation throughout much of Western Europe, in which demands for extensive external reporting have been muted.

Recent Developments

The influx of foreign MNEs, the fact that French companies are now experiencing the constraints of an underdeveloped domestic capital market and the impact of new technologies, have forced the government and other interested parties to address the question of accounting practice in a larger context.

Nor has France been immune to the same influences that have caused the UK to reconsider several aspects of its corporate governance culture. For instance, the consequences of operating in a global market, coupled with a stream of financial scandals involving several of its largest companies, have forced the French authorities to embark on a process similar to that undertaken in the Anglo-American world. Thus, the Vienot Report and, more recently, a commission headed by Daniel Bouton, chairman of Societe Generale, have made recommendations that will significantly strengthen the role of independent directors and impose greater levels of transparency upon companies and their boards.

As with most continental European countries, however, the greatest catalyst for change has been the adoption of IFRS. As in the case of Germany, this is already having a significant impact on French reporting and governance cultures, and is leading to greater integration with international capital markets and, as a consequence, access to a broader range and depth of funds.

In practice:

French call for common standards, by Peggy Hollinger

The French stock market regulator is calling for a common European standard on internal corporate controls, and as a first step has set up a working committee to develop more precise guidelines for French companies. The AMF, presenting its progress report on corporate governance in France, yesterday said it planned to approach the European Commission in a few months with the initial findings of its working committee. "Why draw up 25 standards for the 25 countries of the EU if we can create a single European reference?" said Michel Prada, president of the AMF.

Scandals such as Parmalat, the Italian dairy company that collapsed under €14bn ($18.5bn) of debt; Ahold, the Dutch retailer; and Royal Dutch/Shell's reserves debacle have given European corporate governance reforms fresh impetus. However, suggestions that wide-ranging European corporate governance standards should be imposed have sparked strong criticism from many countries. Jaap Winter, who heads the group of corporate law experts advising the EU on better standards, recently warned against pushing cross-border convergence too quickly. Yesterday, the AMF said the working committee would involve representatives from all market participants, accountants, companies and other interested parties. "First, we have a national need to clarify for French companies what they need to disclose," said Gerard Rameix, AMF director. "But I think the exercise is not sustainable only at a national level."

Since August 2003, French companies have had to report to shareholders on internal controls and the organisation and performance of their boards. Mr Rameix said the AMF report showed that French companies had made progress during 2004. However, there was much still to be done, he said, as many companies had interpreted the rules differently. "It has been a very important first step, but it is still a first step. Now we have to be more precise."

In its survey of 118 companies, the AMF found that two-thirds of companies and virtually all in the CAC 40 leading index, had independent directors on the board. Some 58 per cent of companies said they had remuneration committees but they failed to lay out the criteria by which variable performance was judged. On internal controls, the AMF said the absence of a common standard meant a wide divergence in what was disclosed. This could act as a hindrance in evaluating the relative effectiveness of a company's risk management, the AMF said. While more than 90 per cent of companies described in their reports the objectives and procedures of internal controls, only half set out their principal risks.

Source: Financial Times, January 13, 2005.

Globalization and the Accounting Agenda

For a variety of economic, social and historical reasons, by the mid-20th century the most powerful trading nations in the world were functioning under different accounting regimes. Thus the US and the UK were operating under an accounting scheme which could be broadly categorized as Anglo-American, while countries such as Germany, France and Italy operated under a loosely titled "Continental European" approach. Individual developing countries usually operated under some form of localized hybrid, while economic powers in the Far East, such as Japan, inclined to the US approach, albeit with some significant opt-outs that acted to protect its own industries. This was, however, increasingly at odds with the needs of a new international business phenomenon that paid little heed to national and cultural boundaries.

Over recent decades the role and power of MNEs and capital markets have increased. This, in turn, has led to greater international capital flows; the internationalization of capital markets; and increased funding by stock exchanges. One of the principal demands of MNEs was greater accounting compatibility across borders. Coupled with technological advances, this has been one important catalyst in setting the accounting agenda.

Harmonization and Convergence

One of the responses to this process of globalization has been an attempt by various professional and regulatory accounting bodies to push a "harmonization" policy. As distinct from standardization, which implies the application of exactly similar rules everywhere, harmonization is generally understood to mean "the reduction of reporting differences between countries". It is, therefore, sensitive to the fact that for historical and cultural reasons a complete uniformity of accounting practice is probably unrealistic, at least in the short to medium term.

The main arguments in favour of harmonization are that it would remove communication barriers, encourage cross-border trade, facilitate the creation of a more efficient capital market and, of particular interest to entities such as the EU, promote regional integration. It also offers the prize of convergence between IFRS and US accounting standards. This would allow market regulators in the US and EU to accept accounts from each other without undertaking the costly reconciliations currently required.

Critics counter that harmonization will not offer the advantages claimed, pointing out that it will impose extra costs on small and medium entities, while the only ones for whom the project is relevant are large MNEs. Others, critical of any project that further secures the role of the capital markets in the order of things, point out that there are far greater social, environmental and cultural issues at stake, particularly in developing countries, where a capital-markets driven agenda is simply unsuitable and unsustainable.

Accounting regulators have expressed no such reservations. In fact, over the course of recent decades they have consistently sought to engage with this process in a variety of initiatives. The success of the IASB in developing a set of standards that have been accepted by not only the EU, but also by a large number of developing countries, has considerably advanced the prospects of harmonization, indeed of convergence. In fact, it has so significantly revived this latter possibility that, in the process, it has provided a challenge to the erstwhile dominance of the FASB.

The considerable tensions that have accompanied the IASB's success in raising the possibility of greater convergence provide a reminder of the essentially political nature of the regulatory process. Thus, while broadly supportive of the IASB, internal EU tensions find expression in an instinctive reaction against what is perceived to be an attempt by the IASB to impose an essentially, Anglo-Saxon, UK-driven, accounting model. Meanwhile, US regulators fear a move away from their rule-based, prescriptive approach, to a more principles-centred scheme that allows for subjective application and interpretation.

As the following extract explains, some of the issues raised by this are fundamental in nature and the outcome will have enormous commercial and social consequences:

The Road Map

The Road Map to Global Convergence. With Backing from George W. Bush and the EU, Work on the True Harmonization of Standards can Start, writes Robert Bruce

In recent times the sound of a senior politician seeking to become involved in the process of setting financial reporting standards has led only to an increase in strife and misunderstandings. The intervention of Jacques Chirac, the French president, in the question of banking disclosure two years ago resulted in squabbling accountants deadlocked in meetings around the world trying to resolve a quirk of French banking practice. It did little to help bring about common global standards.

So accountants were worried when they heard George W. Bush, US president, intended to speak on the idea of harmonising international and US financial reporting standards. But his recent pronouncement took everyone by surprise. Recognising "the importance of US-EU co-operation for the well-being of our citizens and commercial relations", Mr Bush said this meant "promoting convergence of accounting standards as soon as possible". The EU issued a statement with identical wording.

This was the strongest political support so far for the "road map" that is taking shape and is hoped to produce true convergence of financial reporting by 2007. "From Brussels to Boston to Beijing", says Sir David Tweedie, chairman of the International Accounting Standards Board, "we all need to account the same way." The tide is moving in that direction. Israel is the latest country to allow the use of international financial reporting standards. That brings the tally to 96.

Even 10 years ago, and pre-Enron, it was unthinkable that anything but US GAAP, rules formulated by the US's Financial Accounting Standards Board, could be worthy of use as the foundation for a stock market listing in the US. Jim Leisenring, a member of the IASB from its foundation in 2001, had spent 20 years with the US FASB, latterly as director of international activities. "The change is absolutely extraordinary," he says. "In my 20 years on FASB we paid no attention to what was going on elsewhere. Now it is there, every day." The chief accountant at the US regulator, the Securities and Exchange Commission, Donald Nicolaisen, can now say that "elimination of the SEC's requirement that foreign private issuers reconcile financial statements prepared under IFRS to US GAAP" is the goal of the road map...

The task now is for the SEC and the European Commission to be aligned so that convergence can be achieved. Over the next year all listed companies in Europe will file accounts under international financial reporting standards for the first time. The SEC has strengthened its resources, in terms of technical understanding and people, and will in the early months of next year be examining the new accounts. It will look at them sector by sector and make cross-comparisons. The aim is to be in a position to report on the quality of information created under the new system with a view to removing the need to reconcile to US GAAP.

The other side of this arrangement will be what happens in Europe. Plenty of bodies exist that offer opinions on the state of financial reporting across Europe but there is no definitive oracle. This does not play well with the Americans. One prominent US standard-setter describes Europe as "a tower of Babel" on this issue. Indeed, speaking at a conference organized by the IASB two weeks ago Pierre Delsaux, acting director, internal market, at the EC, stressed the need for convergence, appropriate arrangements in Europe to bring this about, and effective enforcement. "Consultation and transparency need to be the key elements," he said. "All interested parties need to make their views known."

This will be tricky. Some European organizations are more involved in competing with one another than with producing definitive rulings. "The last thing we need," said one prominent banking accountant at the conference, "is the SEC and the EC competing against each other." But Mr Delsaux sought to damp such concerns, suggesting a forum group in Europe to sort out the issues. "There will be no new body," he says, "and we do not want to create a competing body with the IASB."

Last week's unveiling of a joint standard from the IASB and FASB on mergers and acquisitions was the first step on a road to convergence. But there are dangers ahead. Mr Delsaux puts his finger on the issue. "People say it is a political exercise. It is not. It is a technical exercise. But technical questions may become political."

Source: *Financial Times*, July 7, 2005.

In practice:

At the moment all companies trading on US exchanges must prepare a reconciliation with US GAAP if they use an alternative basis. The fact that the SEC is considering dropping this requirement for companies adopting IFRS is a significant achievement:

US Fillip for International Standards

The European Union has taken one step closer to the holy grail of equivalence between International Financial Reporting Standards (IFRS) and US GAAP. EU internal markets commissioner Charlie McCreevy announced on a trip to Washington DC that an agreement on a roadmap towards equivalence had been reached between the European Commission and the US Securities and Exchange Commission.

The roadmap sets out steps the SEC will take to eliminate the need for companies using IFRS to reconcile to US GAAP, possibly as soon as 2007, but no later than 2009. The agreement is something of a coup for the new commissioner on his first visit to the US since taking office in November last year. McCreevy said: 'Clearly there is much to do all round, but the bandwagon has now started.'

IASB chairman Sir David Tweedie told Accountancy he was delighted by the news and said the short-term convergence project with the US Financial Accounting Standard Board would be fast-tracked. 'It shows that FASB is really committed to IFRS. They're part of the family. The EC will be involved and hopefully we can get rid of this thing [reconciliation to US GAAP].' However, the SEC cautioned that achieving the final goal of equivalence would depend on a detailed analysis of the 'faithfulness and consistency of the application and interpretation of IFRS'.

Source: Accountancy, May 2005.

The success of the IASB in offering IFRS as an alternative to US GAAP is an extraordinary achievement. It is now possible to imagine a global GAAP within the next decade. And incredibly, the IASB has emerged as a viable alternative to FASB as guardian of such a regime. Whichever emerges supreme, however, it will be a victory for Anglo-American accounting regulation and philosophy. This is a significant factor. The fact that both IFRS and US GAAP are rooted in a markets-based, shareholder-centred accounting paradigm will have important consequences for political, governance and commercial developments over centuries to come.

Summary

For a variety of historical, cultural and economic reasons accounting practices differ across national and regional boundaries. Thus, even the accounting regimes in France and Germany, while similar in some respects, demonstrate considerable divergences. These in turn exhibit considerable differences from the principles and practices characteristic of the Anglo-American model.

As business becomes more global, abetted by technological innovation and an ascendant capital market economy, the need for accounting to respond appears self-evident. As a result, accounting regulators such as the IASB and FASB have attempted to advance a harmonization project that seeks to minimize differences between different national accounting codes.

The success of the IASB has, ironically, increased more quickly than anticipated, the prospect of a greater level of convergence, even standardization. This will only be resolved over the coming years in a process that will merely emphasize the essentially political nature of accounting regulation.

Review Questions

Question 1
Identify the main catalysts for change in international accounting practice and assess how these might impact differently on developed and developing countries.

Question 2
List some of the common characteristics, if any, of continental European accounting practice.

Question 3
Explain how accounting practice has developed in Germany to date and identify some of the principal characteristics of the German accounting system.

Question 4
"German accounting can be best described as conservative". Explain.

Question 5
Identify the principal characteristics of the corporate governance culture in Germany and explain how it differs from that operating in the UK.

Question 6
What is the role of the Plan Comptable General (PCG) in French accounting practice?

Question 7
Compare and contrast the accounting systems in Germany and France. Pay particular attention to identifying common features that distinguish them from the Anglo-American model.

Question 8
Distinguish between harmonization and standardization, and explain how recent developments in the EU and US may impact the prospects for convergence.

Question 9
Having developed a very prescriptive set of regulations FASB is, understandably, reluctant to surrender the initiative to the IASB, a body that it sees as too anxious to compromise on quality in order to reach consensus. Explain whether the US and its representatives can sustain this attitude towards the IASB in the face of a growing consensus on convergence.

Case Studies

Case 1

The following article is useful in providing a counter to the predominantly Anglo-Saxon perspective that this text has adopted. For instance, while broadly supportive of the UK-led corporate governance changes of recent years, it highlights evidence of opposition to a single Europe-wide code being imposed, particularly if seen to be too close to the Anglo-American model. In this context, discuss the extent to which a harmonized governance code for the EU might be beneficial.

Europe Adapts to Globalisation and Investor Unrest, by David Gow

Corporate governance reforms along British lines are being forced on companies throughout Europe by governments and investors to make them adapt to the growing international convergence of capital markets, accounting standards and ethical codes. It follows shareholder unrest at companies such as Deutsche Börse, Carrefour and the Swiss food group Nestlé, where almost two-fifths of shareholders voted against board proposals to give Peter Brabeck a dual mandate as chairman and chief executive.

Deutsche Börse, forced by rebel shareholders to abandon a bid for its London rival, will face a ferocious battle with the same investors at this month's annual meeting over their demands for the removal of up to 11 of its 14-strong supervisory board. It could buy some breathing space with its first quarter results released last night. Operating profits rose 18% to €177m (£120m) and it said it would pay €1.5bn to shareholders by May 2007 in an attempt to placate investors.

In France, Thierry Breton, the new finance minister, is drawing up legislation to enable shareholders to vote on directors' remuneration after the row over the reported €38m "golden parachute" for Daniel Bernard, chairman of retail group Carrefour. Stung by the response, including strikes by employees seeking a €50 a month pay rise, Bernard told Le Figaro his real package was worth three years' salary (€9.9m) if he kept out of the retail sector for four years plus a pension worth €7.5m over 25 years. Criticizing the proposed law as based on "a false polemic", he said: "A CEO is not someone who lives off the back of a firm but carries it on his back to bring it as far forward as possible."

The German government says it will press ahead with legislation to force companies to adhere to the voluntary Cromme code by publishing UK-style remuneration reports and has appointed a commission into reforms of the rules giving employee representatives half the seats on supervisory boards under 50-year-old "co-determination" laws.

In Belgium, home to the European commission which is promoting law changes to improve corporate governance, the government is being urged by business to endorse a voluntary code while MPs consider legal rules.

Maurice Lippens, president of the Belgian-Dutch Fortis Bank and author of the code, said it had drawn heavily on the City's combined code and the Swiss code of 2002 but had tried to go one better. Based on the same "comply and explain" principles behind the City code, the Belgian code takes account of the fact that 70 of its 80 listed companies are dominated by family shareholdings. Unlike Holland, where the Calvinistic culture has produced a legally binding code as strict as the US Sarbanes-Oxley act, the Belgian code gives greater self-regulating powers to directors and, above all, the chairman. Fortis is governed by both but primarily by the Lippens code.

Count Lippens told the Guardian: "We have been more open in letting directors take their own responsibilities." His code allows the chairman to lead the nomination process whereas in Britain, after the Higgs report, companies have a nominations committee of non-executive directors. Similarly, where Higgs proposes non-executives serve two three-year terms at most, Lippens argues that they should be allowed to stay for 12 years, and maybe longer.

He insisted that even the most stringent rules would not prevent scandals. "In the US we have just seen the scandal at insurer AIG and it was Sarb-Ox compliant. We will still have the WorldComs or Enrons or Parmalats or Aholds even when laws exist with codes on top." Count Lippens, one of Belgium's highest paid executives, earning €300,000 a month, said the EU should avoid imposing a single code on European companies.

"Harmonisation is a very Stalinistic concept ... In Belgium you should not own shares in the company if you sit on the board but it's different elsewhere. In Holland, where they told me they didn't like our one-tier board, companies like Shell and Unilever are adopting this system and giving up the two-tier system. People are moving with the flow."

Source: *The Guardian*, May 5, 2005.

Case 2

While this chapter has highlighted some of the advantages of harmonization, there are a number of critics who point out significant dangers. The following article identifies a number of these. Use the arguments the author makes to discuss the merits and demerits of this process.

Unharmonious Harmonisation

Harmonisation is a Euphemism for Control and Control Means Power, Always a Dangerous Drug, argues Emile Woolf

The International Accounting Standards Board (IASB) has recently published 13 revised international standards. Subject to European adoption they will be mandatory for UK companies from next year.

The debate on harmonization of accounting standards has focused on differences in individual standards rather than on the question of whether we should be doing it at all. This is because harmonization always sounds like a good thing. It has a soothing ring to it. The fact that in the political arena it breeds disharmony, always implies loss of home-grown individuality and has no history of ever, in any sphere, having worked successfully, does not deter its proponents. Witness decades of tax harmonization and the Common Agricultural Policy. Implementation by decree is easy. That doesn't mean it works.

Our accounting standards were devised and developed in the context of UK company law and commercial practice, in response to changing circumstances and perceived needs. The development and operation of counterparts in each EU member state could hardly be more different. It is not surprising that resulting reporting practices differ significantly.

Some years ago I was invited to Versailles to address the Anglo-French Accountants' Society on financial reporting under UK company law. A bi-lingual colleague, who had listened to the simultaneous French translation, congratulated me on my talk; the only problem, he said, was that the expert translators caused the Gallic half of the audience some puzzlement by rendering my many references to 'true and fair' as a requirement for accounts to meet the criterion of being 'fine and dandy'!

Inescapable compromise: Since the principal users to whom accounts preparers are first and foremost accountable are people and institutions in their own country, why serve up accounts distilled from a hotchpotch of distinct cultures and legal traditions, each wholly valid in its own territorial terms? Implicit in harmonization is compromise and something worthwhile is always lost. As long as overseas readers know whose GAAP applies they will not be misled.

The pundits miss the point by telling you that UK standards are so advanced that we have nothing to fear from the IASs. They will say, for example, that there are no significant differences between IAS 2 and our good old SSAP 9 on stocks and work-in-progress. Don't you believe it.

While IAS 2 scarcely addresses the measurement of long-term contracts in progress, SSAP 9 incorporates an appendix on this fraught issue that is a model of clear and concise expression. It sets out several examples of contracts in varying stages of completion and profitability, applying the standard's requirements to each in turn, covering measurement and disclosure in both profit and loss account and balance sheet.

This benchmark formulation for construction industry accounting over the past 25 years will next year lose its status to a poor shadow which, incidentally, gratuitously outlaws LIFO as a valuation option. LIFO arose to meet a need: it has traditionally shielded the accounts of commodity buyers from the distortions of external price fluctuations by charging goods to production at current prices, while allowing a low cost base-stock to be revalued periodically as necessary. It is an obviously practical method of inflation accounting. Yet IAS 2 says 'no'!

There are other examples. IAS 10 on post balance sheet events does not permit dividends declared, but awaiting shareholder approval, to be treated as liabilities, nor does it permit such dividends from subsidiaries to be treated as income in the accounts of parent companies. Does this reflect reality?

IAS 24 on related party disclosures, unlike FRS 8, allows no exemptions for 90%-owned subsidiaries even if the consolidated accounts which include those subsidiaries are publicly available. And IAS 17's convoluted gymnastics on lease classifications will drive you to buy the freehold just to save your sanity!

Shall I go on? Accounts prepared under regularly reviewed and updated SSAPs and FRSs have well served the UK users for whom they were systematically developed. As the old saying goes, if it ain't broke. But the bureaucratic urge is unquenchable and unstoppable. Harmonisation is a euphemism. Try 'control'. For control means power, always a dangerous drug.

Emile Woolf is head of Kingston Smith's forensic accounting service.

Source: *Accountancy*, February 2004.

SECTION V

Interpretation

The goal of this text is to equip readers with the skills and insights necessary to analyze and interpret financial information and reports, specifically that contained in an Annual Report. This has necessitated a review of the various contexts within which accounting information emerges; a consideration of the information content of financial reports; and an investigation of some of the more advanced provisions relating to accounting practice. A variety of techniques have also been introduced that underpin the Fundamental Analysis paradigm adopted by this book.

These themes are now brought together in one section, which applies the various techniques and perspectives covered thus far to Tesco plc.

The Annual Report 2005 as well as the IFRS Restatement for 2005 for this company are included in Appendices 1 and 2 at the rear of the text and should be referred to throughout. The fact that both are included gives the added advantage of being able to compare the results under UK GAAP and IFRS. In addition, the website for this text contains an equivalent analysis and report based on the Tesco 2006 Annual Report. This should also be accessed and read.

When you have completed this chapter you will be able to:

- Analyze, contextualize and interpret the performance and position of Tesco plc as disclosed by the Annual Report 2005.

- Draw on a variety of other sources to inform your analysis and interpretation.

- Produce a report to that effect.

Tesco: The Unstoppable Force? by Tony Grundy

On 13 April 2005 Tesco's reported profits broke the £2bn profit barrier. This was a first not only for Tesco, but also for any UK retailer. These results were as impressive as anything achieved in this sector previously – and certainly since M&S broke the £1bn profit barrier in the mid/late 1990s. What is even more remarkable is that this came at a time when many UK retailers were suffering tightening competitive market conditions – particularly M&S and Sainsbury's (see Accountancy, October 2004, p50, and April 2005, p66, respectively), Boots and WH Smith, which staged some profit recovery by April 2005, but which is still struggling.

Remarkably, the *Independent* on 13 April devoted its full front page to Tesco's achievements, namely: pre-tax profits of £2.03bn; a profits increase year-on-year of 20.5%; profits equivalent to £231,000 per hour; worldwide annual sales of £37bn; one in eight pounds spent in the UK spent at Tesco; 1,779 stores in the UK, 586 overseas (in 13 countries); 15m customers per week; 251,000 employees; market value of £24.7bn. Tesco's results over recent years prior to 2005 represent not only a phenomenal growth rate but also rapid growth without diluting profit.

Not always so good: But Tesco was not always in such a state of outstandingly high performance. Founded by Jack Cohen, Tesco's earlier positioning was very much at the budget end of the market, and in the 1960s/early 1970s got a reputation for 'Pile it high – sell it cheap'. I remember, as a student in 1972–75, when Tesco seemed to be incredibly cluttered, full of cheap offers on not-so-high quality products, while Sainsbury's offered much higher quality products, and a totally different shopping experience...

Regrouped: By 1995/96 Tesco had regrouped, and began its ambitious expansion path into, for example: non-food; financial services; new formats such as Metro, Express and the quasi-hypermarket Extras; international expansion. These were supported by efforts to strengthen its brand, its service and its people capability – and management processes. One example of the latter improvements in management processes was the use in 1997 of the Strategic Option Grid for prioritising new strategic projects.

Strategic speed: What was stunning in those days was Tesco's sheer speed, strategically. For example, I remember facilitating a workshop on home-shopping around that time. Within a matter of weeks the title 'Tesco Direct' appeared at my local superstore (this title had come up just weeks before). I was dumbfounded by the responsiveness. What took months, if not years to turn into reality at other companies, Tesco did in weeks.

'Speed as a source of competitive advantage' probably best encapsulates Tesco's strategy over 1995–2005. If you got points for strategic speeding, Tesco would have been banned for driving by 1998. Around 1996, with the acquisition of William Low in Scotland, Tesco had overtaken Sainsbury's and was now market leader. By 2005 Tesco was around twice the size of Sainsbury's, with an even greater multiple of profits. Challenged only by ASDA-WalMart in the UK and potentially nearing UK saturation, Tesco had set its sights on international expansion, especially in eastern Europe and the Far East...

Another, higher level way of looking as Tesco's strategy is to use what is now called the 'Optopus' for generating new strategic options. This tool highlights either possible dimensions or 'degrees of freedom' for developing strategy – for example, new market sectors, customer segments, or value creating activities (products or services) – and methods of value delivery. These eight dimensions are not necessarily eventually exclusive, but can be blended by a 'pick and mix' formula.

Particular strategies which Tesco deployed, for example, include:

- Customer segments – exploiting the increasing affluence in middle incomes.
- Value-creating activities – non-foods, financial services etc.
- Value delivery – the internet (and Tesco.com).
- Acquisitions – in the UK, Ireland and elsewhere.
- Alliances – in the Far East.
- Geographically – a presence in 13 countries.

So hopefully we have by now understood more about how Tesco's superior financial performance is based on establishing an aggressive but customer-led mindset which capitalises on scale, speed and on distinctive skills and exploiting these in carefully focused markets. Essentially the decisive factors which have differentiated Tesco from Sainsbury's over the period 1995–2005 have been of a 'softer' variety.

Dr Tony Grundy is senior lecturer in strategic management at Cranfield School of Management, and is also director of Cambridge Corporate Development.

Source: *Accountancy*, July 2005.

Introduction

One of the problems when studying financial information analysis in the traditional way is that the exercise can seem to consist of nothing more than the application of various techniques to masses of accounting data. This rather limited perspective is often reinforced by an approach that seems to present ratio calculation as an end in itself.

One of the key themes running through this text, however, has been the need to constantly contextualize accounting information, whether it is within relevant industries, governance cultures, past performance or other appropriate criteria. The point has been repeatedly made that accounting information only acquires its real significance when placed within a context that allows its full meaning to be properly explored.

And that will be the theme of this chapter; an interpretation of Tesco plc in a manner that brings together the various skills covered in previous chapters and yet is sensitive to the fact that the resulting ratios are only one step on the way to a more informed and holistic understanding of the company. The opening vignette provides one example of such a context, examining the company in a strategic context and identifying future possibilities.

Of necessity, this chapter is structured slightly differently from previous chapters. The focus is on producing a report on Tesco plc based on the Annual Report 2005 and the IFRS Restatement, which are provided in the appendices at the end of this text. The report also incorporates insights from a variety of other sources.

Report

The tenor and content of any such report will depend to a large extent on the audience being targeted. In this case the assumption is that the report is being prepared by a large stockbroking firm, whose primary audience will be existing or potential investors in Tesco plc. This means that the concerns addressed will be those of shareholders, whether current or future. In other words, the report adopts the perspective of a particular interest group. A report produced on behalf of a competitor, an environmental pressure group or a trade union would adopt an entirely different approach and might reach some radically different conclusions.

In practice:

For examples of other reports search the websites of stockbroking and investment firms. These will contain a variety of such reports and confirm that, while there are a number of standard items, there is no standard format.

The analyst's report that forms the core of the chapter is presented in a manner that separates computational detail from the body of the report. Thus, while ratios, percentages and trends are obviously central to the conclusions reached, their presentation has been relegated to supporting appendices. This is a standard approach and enables the report writer to concentrate on themes and argument without having to digress into the specifics of ratio construction. Meanwhile a graph is incorporated to demonstrate the usefulness of such visual techniques.

While there are no standard formats, it is possible to identify a number of sub-headings that might form the core of any analysis and interpretation. These would include:

- Background, including reference to macro-economic and industry contexts
- SWOT (Strengths, Weaknesses, Opportunities and Threats) analysis
- Financial analysis, showing ratios and interpretation under:
  - Activity and Liquidity
  - Financing
  - Profitability and Return on Investment
- Governance
- Strategic objectives
- Other relevant issues
- Conclusion: Buy/Sell/Hold recommendation
- Supporting appendices.

A report will normally begin with an introduction outlining the focus of the report and have an Executive Summary at the outset in which the main points of the report are summarized. It should also incorporate comparison with competitors and highlight trends, whether positive or negative.

There is no standard length for such a report. However, they should be readable and to the point. It is generally unusual to see a report, such as the one intended here, which is greater than 2,000 words in length. Where further detail or analysis is required, more detailed reports can be commissioned.

Report on Tesco plc 2005

Introduction

The following report is based on information provided in the Tesco plc Annual Report 2005, the IFRS Restatement, other information made available by the company during the year, as well as industry and peer group data. Reference should be made throughout to Appendix 1 where performance measures and ratios are summarised.

Executive Summary

Tesco plc continues to be the UK market leader in the food retail sector. It has established itself in a number of countries internationally and in various niche areas. All industry and firm-specific indicators suggest that it will sustain this position into the medium-term. At 308p its share price represents good value and the shares are now being accorded "moderate buy" status by this firm.

The following are the key observations made, and conclusions drawn, in the body of this report:

- *The company has established itself as a world player in the retail industry with worldwide sales of £34bn (excluding VAT);*
- *Pre-tax profits of £2.03b, represent a year on year increase of 20.5%;*
- *The company has a market value of £24.7bn (less than one-quarter that of Wal-Mart);*
- *Diluted EPS is 17.5p, an increase of 17.2% over the previous year;*
- *One in every three pounds spent on food in the UK is spent at a Tesco store;*
- *Turnover in Europe and South-East Asia now accounts for 20.5% of group turnover and 18% of group pre-tax profits. International profit levels were slightly below expectations;*
- *Tesco has a total of 2,334 stores worldwide;*
- *The company is the world's most successful and profitable online grocery retailer with £500m in annual sales and 110,000 UK orders every week;*
- *Non-food activity, including petrol, furniture and electrical goods, accounts for almost 1/6th of total revenue;*
- *Tesco Personal Finance, the 50% Joint Venture with Royal Bank of Scotland, has increased profits by 26.5% to £202m;*
- *The group has now established a presence in the telecoms market through Tesco.com in which sales grew by 24.1% to £719m and profits grew by 51.8% to £36m;*
- *The impact of IFRS saw net assets decline by £400m due principally to a negative £730m IFRS impact arising from application of IAS 19 to pensions. The group invested an additional £200m in pensions in 2005.*
- *The strategy of the company is well suited to current global macro- and micro-economic conditions.*
- *Funding exists for sustained development and growth by acquisition.*

Background

Over the course of the last two decades Tesco has transformed itself from an exponent of the "pile it high, sell it cheap" policy of its founder Jack Cohen, to a quality retailer specialising in out-of-town outlets with a reputation for quality and value. It is a policy which means that it can compete with peers that concentrate on price (for example, ASDA) and those that emphasise quality (such as J Sainsbury).

In 1994 Tesco overtook J Sainsbury as the market leader in the UK food retail market. It did this through a combination of aggressive and sustained price-cutting, the introduction of its Clubcard customer loyalty scheme, flexible store formats and innovative management practices. This position has been secured in recent years as the company has exploited its core competencies to develop the Tesco Personal Finance initiative, expand internationally and become a world leader in online grocery sales.

Tesco market capitalisation is now £24.7 billion and its market share of UK supermarket spending is 30.5% (ASDA, 16.7%). One part of group strategy is to build market share by cutting prices. This increases volume, which in turn enables discounted purchasing.

This is clearly consistent with the food policy of successive government's, which has been to ensure that food is made available as cheaply as possible. Along with other UK retailers, the group was recently cleared of price-fixing allegations in an Office of Fair Trading inquiry.

The company has 2,334 stores worldwide, with over 90% owned outright. The group currently employs in excess of 250,000 full-time equivalent individuals in thirteen countries, including the UK.

One of the group's strengths is a clear strategy implemented by an experienced management team headed by Sir Terry Leahy.

SWOT Analysis

Strengths:

- *The company is in a market leadership position in the UK.*
- *It has an unparalleled distribution system in terms of speed and efficiency.*
- *It has a committed and capable management team. The five key executives have an average age of 45 and a combined 121 years with the group;*
- *It has the strategy and resources to fulfil its ambition to become a global force.*
- *Surveys have shown the Tesco brand name to be the third most trusted in the UK, after Google and Nokia.*
- *The company is the world's most successful and profitable online grocery retailer.*
- *Its Loyalty Clubcard allows extensive data mining and focused marketing.*

Weaknesses:

- *Its principal market is highly competitive with little scope for organic growth.*
- *Opportunities for global expansion are limited and require heavy initial capital investment.*
- *The group is only the fifth largest global grocery retailer by sales.*
- *It is not yet big enough to compete with Wal-Mart or Carrefour, both of whom are about to embark on a round of international expansion.*
- *The Group has almost no presence in the US or Western Europe.*
- *Performance in some international markets, e.g., Poland, is weak.*
- *Security of supply chain cannot yet be guaranteed in some overseas markets.*

Opportunities:

- *Online grocery shopping business offers significant market leader possibilities.*
- *Liquidity difficulties of several UK and European competitors mean that some may become attractive takeover candidates for Tesco.*
- *Considerable possibilities offered by access to telecoms market through Tesco.com*
- *Several international locations offer possibility of increased market penetration.*
- *Share of non-food retail sector can grow significantly.*

Threats:

- *The company may itself become the target of an international buyer.*
- *There is a possibility of brand fatigue and reputational risks similar to those suffered by Wal-Mart in US where it has been accused of 'benign dictatorship.' Already there are planning difficulties and an incipient social backlash against Tesco's dominance in the high street.*
- *Much of its UK gains can be attributed to competitor weaknesses and there are signs that this is changing.*

- *Investments in some Asian economies may not yield returns for several years.*
- *The acquisition of UK competitor ASDA by US giant Wal-Mart has significantly increased price competition.*

Activity and Liquidity

A cash cycle of 17.7 days (2004: 15.9) testifies to the favourable cash flow enjoyed by the company. The absence of receivables, coupled with efficient inventory (inventory days = 15.2 days) and payables management (payables days = 32.9 days) ensures that the company enjoys a favourable cashflow from trading activities.

Much of the group's success in its Personal Finance initiative is built on this consistent and favourable cashflow profile.

The high-quality management practices implemented by the company in relation to its working capital mean this is likely to be sustained.

Low current ratios are not a problem in this industry as turnover rates are high. The Quality of Profits ratio of 1.5:1 (2004: 1.7:1) confirms that operating activity produces cash quickly and efficiently, even if there has been a recent, slight disimprovement.

Financing

The company has funded the bulk of its expansion through equity investment and cashflow from operating activity. Therefore, it is a low-geared company with a gearing ratio of 0.35:1. This is an improvement on the figure for 2004 (0.39:1).

As a consequence of its low gearing, the group has relatively low fixed interest charges and satisfies a large element of its funding by means of dividends. Interest cover of 7.2 times (2004: 6.4) confirms the healthy financing structure of the company and the fact that scope exists for additional external funding to be raised if necessary. The Group is rated A1 by Moody's and A + by Standard and Poor's.

The group owns 90% of its stores outright. In 2005 it invested £2.7bn, including acquisitions. This was financed through a mixture of profit growth, working capital improvements and property sale and leasebacks. The group expects to increase store space by 1.83m sq. ft in the coming year and also to continue overseas expansion. Continued internal efficiencies, the sale of some existing freehold's, and a share placing, will fund this.

The group's activity includes an actively managed and hedged derivatives portfolio.

Profitability and Return on Investment

A sustained policy of price-cutting has resulted in the industry margin declining over recent years. As a pioneer of the price-cutting strategy and with the advantage of its Clubcard customer loyalty scheme, and its Personal Finance facility, Tesco has been in a position to cut margins while increasing profitability by a combination of increased sales, greater efficiencies and increased economies.

Total shareholder return (TSR) over the eight-year period since 1997 has outperformed all competitors in the UK food-retailing sector by 50%.

As the graph illustrates, Underlying Profit Growth (see Annual Report p.64) has increased steadily for the last 5 years.

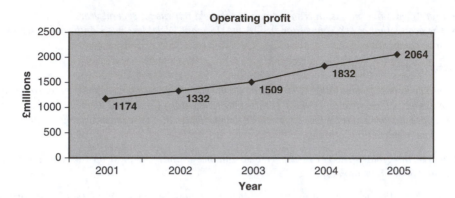

Gross Profit margins of 7.9% (2004: 7.8%) and Operating margins of 5.7% (2004: 5.6%) exceed those of all other major competitors. Allied to a low gearing which gives Tesco lower financing costs than many of its rivals, this has allowed return on investment to remain strong with an ROCE of 15.7% (2004: 14.7%).

EPS continues to show healthy growth, with a basic EPS of 17.72p (2004: 17.50p) and a P/E ratio of 17.4. Dividends have increased from 4.98p per share in 2001 to 7.56p in 2005. Dividend cover stands at a very secure 2.3 times (2004: 2.1 times).

Governance

Tesco has been a committed supporter of the combined code and has sought to implement its recommendations promptly and effectively. On a range of issues it has conformed to best practice and its compliance statement indicates almost complete compliance.

As part of its commitment to a broader range of stakeholders, the company has also begun to engage with the emerging CSR agenda and produces a number of separate reports. These can be accessed at http://www.tescocorporate.com/

Significantly, there are some signs that the company is encountering brand fatigue and there is a growing perception of excessive market dominance. This may suggest some reputational risks and it is important that the company addresses this immediately.

Future Strategy

Chief Executive Terry Leahy has outlined the following strategic objectives for the group:

- Investment will continue to focus on the four core areas of business: UK food; the growing market for non-food; developing retail services such as the Tesco bank; and international expansion.
- The group's international arm is set to become an increasingly important part of the business. This will require capital investment in existing and new stores as well as funding for acquisitions. China is to be the focus of particular attention in 2006 and 2007.
- Online grocery shopping via Tesco.com will consolidate the company's position as the leading global online food retailer. The group will invest in building its own supply chain to broaden the range of products, such as clothes, available online.

- *Tailoring products to local markets will continue. More stores are being modelled to suit local retailing conditions: these range from hypermarkets (Extras) to small convenience stores (Express) to forecourt garage outlets (Metros).*
- *Concerted efforts will be made to capture a larger element of the non-food market. Pricing strategy has been devised with the aim of undercutting competitors. The group will experiment with entirely non-food stores in 2006.*
- *Management have devised policies intended to ensure that the company stays in touch with customers so as not to repeat mistakes of some competitors.*
- *Double-digit annual earnings growth is anticipated.*

Recommendation

With forecast profits of £2.4 billion for 2006, and shares currently at 308p: Moderate BUY.

Appendix 1 Summary of Performance Measures

Summary of ratios used		
Item	2005	2004
Cash Cycle	17.7 days	15.9 days
Receivables days	0 days	0 days
Inventory days	15.2 days	15.4 days
Payables days	32.9 days	31.3 days
Quality of Profits	1.5:1	1.7:1
Gearing	35%	39%
Interest cover	7.2 times	6.4 times
Gross profit margin	7.9%	7.8%
Operating profit margin	5.7%	5.6%
EPS (Basic)	17.72	15.05
EPS (Diluted)	17.50	14.93
P/E ratio	17.40	16.83
ROCE	15.7%	14.7%
Dividends per share	7.56p	6.84p
Dividend cover	2.3 times	2.1 times

All of the company-specific ratios and performance measures alluded to in this report have been covered in the body of the text and the calculations underlying the results above can be accessed there. There are no material differences between the ratios calculated on UK GAAP and IFRS. Industry specific data can be accessed at www.igd.org.uk/, which is the site for the Institute of Grocery Distribution. Additional industry information is available at http://www.foodanddrinkeurope.com/ Performance data for competitors can be accessed at individual company websites. Competitors against which Tesco plc should be set include: Sainsbury, ASDA and Marks & Spencer.

Other Perspectives

The report above adopts the perspective of a firm of investment advisers preparing a briefing for its own clients. Its perspective is, therefore, shareholder specific.

However, a number of other stakeholders could also prepare reports. For instance, a more community-aware, environmental protection lobby group would have an entirely different agenda and focus.

The following points summarize the issues that such a group might focus on in their analysis of Tesco plc.

Tesco plc

- *The cheap food policy that the UK government has traditionally espoused has meant that health and safety issues have been subordinated to price. Thus, unlike several continental European countries, quality has often suffered at the expense of quantity. This is best illustrated by the various health scares in the meat industry where farmers operating under a regime that insists on ever-lower prices have been producing some products steadily declining in quality.*
- *Large-scale overseas investment in Eastern Europe and South-east Asia has seen the shopping culture of these areas affected by an influx of large bulk-buying entities. This brings much-needed employment, but often at a cost. The company has, however, committed itself to sourcing more of its products locally.*
- *The company has a good record in relation to health and safety of employees. It has introduced many local, national and global initiatives that have seen employees benefit from improved wage rates and conditions.*
- *A loose coalition called 'Breaking the Armlock' has sought to convince the public to back its call for fairer treatment of suppliers.*
- *The projected building programme of the group is of great concern. This will take place in both the UK and abroad. The likelihood that this will lead to the further use of the ubiquitous "Essex Barn" edifice is of particular concern.*
- *Overall, Tesco is an excellent company and a good employer, but has yet to make environmental issues central to its strategic outlook.*
- *There is a possibility of brand fatigue and reputational risks similar to those suffered by Wal-Mart in US where it has been accused of 'benign dictatorship.' Already there are planning difficulties and an incipient social backlash against Tesco's dominance in the high street.*

Summary

The main report produced here is, of necessity, limited in both its scope and its ambition. However, it does highlight what such a report might contain and indicates the general points that might be made.

The concerns of investors are dramatically different from those of other interest groups, as suggested by the additional report coming from the perspective of those more interested in corporate social responsibility and environmental reporting.

The key point to remember is that both the data available and the perspective of the user will influence every report. Regardless of this, the techniques and principles covered thus far in the text can be gathered together to present a useful insight into the business, with a view to facilitating the decision-making process.

Review Questions

Question 1
"The tenor and content of any report will depend to a large extent on the audience being targeted". Explain what this means and give examples of how user perspective will influence conclusions drawn from data.

Question 2
Explain why financial ratios should not be allowed to form the core of any report on a company.

Question 3
"Since analysts make their money by encouraging investors to buy shares, it is hardly surprising that the vast bulk of such reports conclude with BUY recommendations". Explain the role of analysts in encouraging investment, sometimes unwisely, by clients.

Question 4
"The executive summary is probably the most important section of an analyst's report". Explain why this might be so and give illustrations of the type of comments that might be found in that section.

Question 5
"Analyst's reports should be concise and to the point. There is no point in a rambling account of company performance and position. An analyst who cannot produce a report that presents a coherent analysis and recommendation in less than 2,000 words should be fired". Discuss.

Question 6
List the elements of the Tesco plc Annual Report that would be of most interest to a member of a local community concerned at the possibility that a new store might be built in her locality.

Question 7
List the principal ratios that should be included or referred to in any report that attempts to discuss the efficiency of management.

Question 8
Explain how the task of financial information analysis has been made easier by the availability of vast amounts of information on company websites. Identify some problems with depending exclusively on information from such sites when attempting an analysis of a company.

Question 9
Chapter 7 provided a five-point scheme to be adopted when undertaking financial information analysis. Consider the extent to which the process adopted for this report conforms to this outline.

Case Studies

Case 1

One of Tesco's main UK competitors is Marks & Spencer. It was also the first UK retailer before Tesco to generate profits in excess of £1 billion. For some years is has been undergoing a number of difficulties. Recently, however, there are signs that it has begun to recover. Using the article below as a starting point, consider some of the strategic initiatives that M&S might take to increase its market share in the UK.

M&S at The Crossroads

The Case of M&S is a Classic Story of Strategic Drift Followed by Ill-thought Through Turnaround Plans. Tony Grundy Analyses the Decline of a Giant in the Retail Sector

Marks & Spencer is a fascinating case of a company whose strategic and financial health has slipped, and this has been both caused and compounded by its internal management and culture. This case highlights how strategy and organisation are, in the long run, the key determinants of performance and shareholder value creation or destruction.

We begin our story in May 2004, when Philip Green pounced on M&S – seizing on a period of vulnerability and loss of confidence in the (then) board. M&S, flagship of the high street in the 1980s and 1990s, had lost its way – and its profits had slumped from over £1bn to less than half (even less after exceptional items). Although profits were back up to around £0.7bn by 2003, its 'turnaround' was faltering.

Before looking at this bid and M&S current dilemmas, we look backwards at M&S's evolution.

Building the brand: M&S's past success depended on a philosophy of value for money, quality and service. It had built an extremely strong brand which had an appeal to a high proportion of the 'middle market' in the UK who had high brand loyalty. M&S was very selective in having quality locations and relatively simple product ranges. But in the mid-1980s M&S began to lose ground to new competitors, such as Next, which targeted M&S and offered quality clothes with just that bit more fashion.

M&S's competitive advantage around the mid-1990s was then based on:

- M&S brand;
- value-for-money (as of 1994);
- very high market share in niche markets (e.g., luxury food and women's underwear);
- supplier linkages and innovation;

- systems; and
- sites.

M&S's traditional brand strength was supported by the M&S reputation for value for money and also its reputation for customer service (and its supporting culture). M&S's supplier linkages and product innovation were also its traditional sources of competitive advantage.

Between 1997 and 1999, a number of external market shifts (effectively external performance brakes) crystallised. Despite continued economic recovery, consumers became more discerning. Where they were asked to pay a premium, they appeared to want a brand and that brand was (at least in the young and middle-age groups) not M&S. Meanwhile, competition for upmarket foods increased significantly, for example, from Tesco's 'Finest' lines. M&S's international expansion (perhaps predictably) faltered, with a U-turn on investment in territories such as Germany. Last, new entrants to the UK retail market, such as Gap and Matalan, began to take more share of the younger market.

M&S then made some major changes to its strategy in the period 1998–2000 including its decision to partially abandon its dependency on its traditional brand, St Michael, and it also sourced increasingly from outside the UK, and began to accept credit cards. Following considerable boardroom acrimony, Sir Richard Greenbury had been replaced by a successful retailer, Luc Vandervelde, whose stated aim was to turn round M&S within two years. After this, M&S tried to enliven its underwear with joint ventures with Agent Provocateur appearing to push very aggressively into more adventurous and sensual markets. This again proved unsuccessful, and M&S's standalone lingerie shop pilot was halted. Second, M&S recruited George Davies (ex-Next) to form an alliance to create a new sub-brand, called Per Una.

Deeper water: By late 2000/early 2001, M&S appeared to be in ever deeper trouble. According to the Financial Times, Christmas trading had been even worse and, in the 16 weeks to January, group sales were down 3.1% (down 5.1% on a comparable store basis). Clothing, footwear and gifts were down 9.3%. Vandervelde was brought in 2001 and Roger Holmes was appointed CEO designate (having been headhunted from Kingfisher in January 2001).

M&S's underlying position had not improved by 2004, and there were a number of very major brakes on performance, each of which are ripe for further diagnosis. These include:

- service standards;
- dated store formats;
- lack of appeal to many under-30s;
- the alienation of traditional customer base (especially women's clothes);
- limited success of re-launch through designer clothes/store upgrades;
- slow time to market (new products) – an area now being worked on;
- low price, reasonable quality and new entrants;
- limited innovation in food; and
- lack of critical mass in new product areas (eg, mobile telephones).

And also internally:

- speed of internal change;

- employee morale;
- cost constraints; and
- supplier morale.

Press commentary began to become more and more critical, and by the first quarter of 2004 it was evident that sales were slipping. Vandervelde, chairman, was criticised for his involvement in other companies (he was now part time). Holmes, now CEO, came under more and more pressure as he battled to coordinate M&S's push against its competitors. Holmes had recruited a design guru, Vittorio Radice, from Selfridges to spearhead M&S's design improvements, but its first 'Lifestore' shop in Gateshead was well behind its sales targets. Each store was very expensive, so 'Lifestore' seemed to be an expensive flop. M&S's share price began to fall sharply, leaving it potentially exposed to a break-up bid.

In summary, by May this year:

- New innovations were only a patchy success, with new projects being costly and risky.
- Its appeal to its core womenswear markets appeared to be still fragile.
- Stores were often old-fashioned, lacked appeal, and were increasingly hard for a customer to understand.
- There were still gaps in M&S's management skills, leaving it vulnerable to the injection of top quality retailing skills from elsewhere.
- Its financial recovery was fragile, and the fall in its share price clearly left it exposed to a bid. Its shares had recovered to around 420p in late 2001, but by now had declined to around 270p. (In 1997 they had been worth a staggering 650p).

Philip Green's bid: And then, in May 2004, Philip Green, the retailing entrepreneur who had turned round BHS, and who had previously tried to acquire M&S in the early 2000s, bid for M&S. The bid occupied the press and media for many weeks. Its progression went like this:

- Green bid around 290p a share plus a 25% interest in a residual company, £8.3bn or around 350p a share.
- The existing CEO of M&S was removed and Stuart Rose, a seasoned retailer, was put in place, and M&S's chairman was removed.
- Rose began an aggressive fight back, removing management including design head Radice and others.
- On 17 June, Green increased his bid to 370p cash, a clear £8.4bn, asking M&S for more due diligence, which M&S refused to give him.
- In July, Green increased his offer to 400p, having re-used more finance, worth £9.1bn.

By July, the deal was on a knife-edge. Rose unveiled his strategy for:

- major cash reductions;
- the sale of M&S money;
- purchase of the Per Una brand;
- refund of £2bn-3bn to shareholders;
- closure of 'Lifestores' and some 'Simply Food' stores; and

• improvements to products/services and broadening M&S's appeal/customer base.

Green had stated that his offer was 'final', making it impossible to increase for six months – unless another bidder came forward. M&S's shareholders decided to back Rose, Standard Life being the decisive influence. Green then withdrew his offer, and M&S shares fell back to around 340p, or 60p less than Green's offer. This may not sound a lot, but it was actually around £1.3bn, which was quite a major psychological premium for having the perhaps more likeable, solid Rose in charge, rather than the aggressive, entrepreneurial Green.

Who won?: So where does this leave M&S, Rose and his board? Did Rose 'win', or has he only won the right to see what he can do with M&S, now it's still at a cross-roads? M&S, today, faces some massive challenges, which will take a tightrope-walker to navigate. So, the jury is still 'out' as to whether Rose has or hasn't 'won'. Might shareholders go to Green in 2005, begging him to have another go?

The case of M&S is a classic story of strategic drift then followed by ill-thought through turnaround plans, culminating with either disposal, or in effect (with Rose), a management buy-in. And even now, it is questionable whether shareholders have got best economic value out of M&S's strategy – should they have sold to an overpaying Mr Green? Or was he truly astute. Maybe we will know only in the course of time – but as of now, the jury is still very much out.

Tony Grundy is senior lecturer in strategic management at Cranfield University School of Management where he runs short courses on 'Breakthrough strategic thinking' and 'Strategic consulting skills'.
www.som.cranfield.ac.uk/som/executive/index.asp

Source: *Accountancy*, October 2004.

Case 2

Write a report on Tesco plc from the perspective of a trade union representative. Comment in particular on information that might be of interest to employees, but which is not included in the Annual Report 2005. Also, discuss the extent to which Tesco's claim on p.4 of the Annual Report that "Our people are our most important asset", is reflected in the Annual Report itself.

Case 3

Using the following article as a starting point and accessing additional information from the company's website and other sources as appropriate, prepare a report for Vodafone similar to that included in this chapter.

Reality Starts to Bite, by Paul Durman

For a small town like Newbury, the growth of Vodafone has been big news indeed. Newbury has a population of only 32,000; about 3,500 work at the mobile-phone giant's "global headquarters", a £120m development on the edge of the

Berkshire town. The building of the headquarters even rates a mention in the Wharf mosaic – a Bayeux tapestry-style tableau of local history set into the pavement in the town centre. Judging from this, the construction of the Vodafone HQ was the most exciting thing to happen in Newbury since the row over the bypass in the mid-1990s. Wags in the mobile-phone industry refer to the Vodafone campus as Planet Newbury – "the only place where it is still possible to believe that bigger is always better".

This is not a view widely shared by the company's shareholders, increasingly fed up with Vodafone's lacklustre share-price performance. The group's management, led by chief executive Arun Sarin, promises further growth and a bright future, but many investors remain unconvinced. With little in the way of returns to show for Vodafone's billions of pounds of investment, investors are losing confidence in the group's global strategy. Despite this, Sarin has continued the company's international spending spree, last year shelling out another £6.6 billion for assets in Romania, the Czech Republic, India, South Africa and Turkey.

Some shareholders would like Vodafone to rethink what it is doing. And the appointment of Sir John Bond as chairman from next July could present the perfect opportunity. Some critics want Vodafone to sell its struggling Japanese business; others want it to pull out of America. A third group believes the chief executive is the problem. "Bond will have a three-month window of opportunity when it will be possible to sack Sarin," said one analyst.

Vodafone began its global push in earnest in 1999 when, under the leadership of Sir Chris Gent, it bought AirTouch of America. Within a year, the company had combined its US assets with the mobile arm of Bell Atlantic to form Verizon Wireless, and acquired the German giant Mannesmann in a £101 billion takeover. Even as the telecoms bubble deflated, Vodafone carried on spending, buying into companies in France, Spain, Japan and elsewhere.

Today Vodafone is both financially strong and hugely profitable – it recently reported half-year operating profits of £4.5 billion. But shareholders have seen little reward from the enormous scale of the telecoms giant's operations. At 127p on Friday, the shares trade at less than a third of their peak in 2000. While much of this reflects the wider decline in telecoms valuations, Vodafone has continued to underperform the FTSE 100, even in the past two years. John Karidis, an analyst at Man Securities, has attempted to estimate the amount of value destruction since 1999, adjusting for the reduced value of the shares that were issued to acquire AirTouch, Mannesmann and others.

Vodafone issued £69.1 billion of shares to fund its expansion, and spent another £27.1 billion in cash. This includes the £13.3 billion it paid for "third-generation" mobile licences, and is net of disposal proceeds, principally from the sale of Orange to France Telecom. Karidis has conservatively valued Vodafone's original (UK) business at £5.4 billion, making a total shareholder "bet" of £101.6 billion. For this investment, shareholders have received dividends to date of £7.8 billion, and today hold shares worth £81.8 billion. In other words, the "bigger is better" strategy has destroyed £12 billion. Karidis said the value Vodafone had destroyed was arguably £5 billion more than this because the strong performance of its British business since 1999 could justify a much higher initial valuation.

Sarin has assured investors that Vodafone will reap the benefits of his One Vodafone project – pulling the numerous operations together to wring out savings and efficiencies. However, Karidis's analysis raises doubts about this as well. Vodafone has consistently lowered its operating and other direct costs since Sarin took over. Unfortunately, these gains have been overwhelmed by the increased amounts that the group is spending to acquire and retain customers – largely represented by the subsidies on expensive new handsets. Overall expenses are rising.

Charles Butterworth, Vodafone's investor-relations director, rejected Karidis's analysis, saying it was "arbitrary" to use today's share price to calculate the effects of its acquisitions. He said Vodafone should be judged against the weak performance of its rivals, and the full benefits of One Vodafone would not be seen until 2008.

The note from Karidis last week made two more telling observations. The first is that Vodafone's expansion strategy was supported by the majority of the existing board, which has changed little in the past seven years. Any director who called for a change of strategy – such as the sale of the Japanese business – would have to overturn his or her previous judgments.

Karidis also predicted increasing tensions between Vodafone and Verizon, its joint-venture partner in America. Verizon has just acquired MCI, another telecoms company with strong relationships with big business – the same customers most prized by Vodafone. In future, Verizon will have an increased interest in retaining corporate customers itself, rather than allowing them to deal with Verizon Wireless, where Vodafone would receive 45% of the benefit.

One hope among Vodafone's critics is that a breakdown in the relationship with Verizon could trigger the sale of the company's stake in Verizon Wireless. However, such a move would require Vodafone's board to start winding the clock back to 1999. Is Bond prepared to be the catalyst for such a reversal? Investors are keen to find out.

Source: *The Sunday Times*, January 15, 2006.

SECTION VI

Challenges and Opportunities

Section I of this text outlined some of the larger contextual issues that should inform any analysis of accounting information.

Section II then augmented this with specific information on the accounting and disclosure requirements governing Annual Reports.

Section III introduced a range of ratios and other fundamental analysis techniques that have been developed to facilitate the extraction of key items of information from financial statements. The point was made repeatedly that these techniques were merely a means to an end; that end being an informed decision-making process.

Section IV dealt with some advanced accounting matters and, in the process introduced related issues such as Corporate Social Responsibility and Creative Accounting, topics that must also be kept in mind when assessing the quality and dependability of any accounting information.

Section V brought these various themes together by applying them to Tesco plc.

Section VI, the final section, extends beyond the rather limited confines of the accounting world. Recognizing that the text has thus far adopted a financial information-focused view of the firm, Chapter 17 introduces a range of alternative approaches that have emerged in recent years as the limitations of the accounting-centred approach have become evident. Finally, Chapter 18 outlines the challenges and opportunities presented by evolving governance paradigms and the dynamics of the new economy.

When you have completed this chapter you will understand that:

- The Balanced Scorecard (BSC) challenges businesses to identify and measure areas typically not measured by the traditional financial model.

- Economic Value Added (EVA) is another approach that attempts to broaden the frame of reference.

- Multivariate analysis techniques have been developed to assist in predicting bankruptcy.

- Ideally, financial and non-financial measures should complement one another.

Companies Must Look Beyond Profit Margins

For companies such as the American Express, product and service innovation are key drivers of their competitive advantage. Measurement of performance in these areas is emphasised, as opposed to short-term profitability. The company's organisational scorecard encompasses not only financial metrics but also includes product quality, service response and "thinking out-of-the-box" which translate into corporate strategy and business plans that ultimately drive results. This framework of performance measurement and value creation is indoctrinated into its corporate culture.

Source: *Business Times*, December 15, 2005.

Introduction

Traditional financial measures, however complex and comprehensive, are simply incapable of allowing users to form a complete view of a firm's performance, strategic challenges and opportunities. Many companies realize that a more broadly constituted set of performance indicators is required. The Balanced Scorecard (BSC), Economic Value Added (EVA), and other business analysis techniques offer more holistic alternatives. However, these approaches do not seek to displace the traditional financial reporting and control model. Instead, they should be viewed as means by which financial measures can be augmented and informed. Nor are these non-financial measures complete in themselves.

Whichever method is adopted it is important to remember that, like financial indicators, these systems only provide information for decision-making purposes. Like ratios and other forms of information, they are merely means to an end and must be contextualized and interpreted properly.

Balanced Scorecard

Businesses must measure and control more than financial flows. Business success derives in the long-term from efficient and effective operational processes and cultures. Thus, financial measures on their own only provide a limited perspective. Attention has increasingly focused, therefore, on recognizing, measuring and managing non-financial elements of business activity.

Robert Kaplan and David Norton developed the Balanced Scorecard (BSC) in the early 1990s. The BSC broadens the frame of reference to incorporate four key aspects of performance. These are:

- Financial perspective

- Innovation and learning perspective

- Customer perspective

- Business process perspective

In relation to each of these aspects a business is encouraged to determine those measures that best capture and reflect operations deemed to be critical to future success.

Balanced Scorecards Indicate Whether a Firm has a Motivated, Prepared Workforce, by Penny Haw

The balanced-scorecard concept, which was developed more than 12 years ago by Prof Robert Kaplan of Harvard University and David Norton, an American management consultant, is widely used as a strategic management tool... Versions of the model are frequently introduced as one of the most effective ways of communicating the objectives, managing the response and measuring the results of incentive programmes in large and small organizations.

"We successfully use balanced scorecards as an integrated and holistic management and measurement framework for many of the performance improvement programmes we design for our clients," says Eleanor Muller, marketing director for Cape Town-based incentive and performance improvement company, the Achievement Awards Group. "The most effective balanced scorecard has a blend of measures that combine past performance with drivers for future performance in both big corporations and small businesses."

The balanced scorecard system is based on the fact that traditional financial accounting measures – such as sales growth, return on investment, operating expenses and cash flow – offer an incomplete and outdated picture of business performance.

This, observed Kaplan and Norton in 1992, could obstruct the creation of long-term business value. In response, they suggest that financial measures be supplemented – or balanced – with information that reflects customer satisfaction, internal business processes and the ability to learn and grow.

Kaplan and Norton's scorecard evaluates corporate performance from four perspectives:

- Financial: Are we meeting the expectations of our shareholders?
- Customer: Are we delighting (or at least satisfying) our customers?
- Internal process: Are we doing the right things and doing things right?; and
- Learning and growth: Are we prepared for the future?

The word "scorecard" refers to the quantified performance measures involved. "Balanced" indicates the system's balance between short- and long-term objectives, financial and non-financial measures, lagging and leading indicators, and internal and external perspectives.

At first glance, a balanced scorecard system helps managers see that financial measurements are necessary, but not sufficient. Importantly, it shows that traditional financial measures do not fully account for intangible assets, particularly knowledge-based assets.

Source: *Business Day*, January 17, 2005.

Kaplan and Norton outline how one company addressing its Customer and Learning Perspectives might use the BSC to develop the following sets of measures to track and control the goals it has set:

Customer perspective		Learning perspective	
Goals	Measures	Goals	Measures
New products	% sales from new products	Technology leadership	Time to develop products
Responsive supply	On-time delivery	Manufacturing learning	Process time to maturity
Preferred supplier	Ranking by key accounts	Product focus	%products = 80% of sales
Customer partnership	No. of co-operative efforts	Time to market	New product introductions

The significant point, of course, is that this process identifies key areas of strategic importance that the traditional financial measurement process will usually overlook.

The BSC offers a different and more comprehensive perspective of the business to which it is being applied. It forces management to recognize and incorporate strategic and human factors into its business planning and control models. It also provides a means by which intangible resources can be recognized and measured, usually in non-financial terms. In an economy in which intangible drivers of value such as intellectual capital and knowledge are emerging as the key sources of competitive advantage, this is a critical consideration.

As with any other technique, it has its limits. It must be sensitively applied and users must be aware of both its potential and its limitations. A cost/benefit analysis should normally precede any attempt to apply it and the template adopted should be sensitive to the unique value drivers of the firm. Finally, the way in which inter-firm comparison can be compromised by virtue of the uniqueness of each business's strategic and operational mix must be appreciated.

Economic Value Added[1]

Economic Value Added (EVA) is predicated on the notion that accounting profits adopt a very limited perspective when assessing performance. The economic understanding of profit on the other hand is informed as much by opportunity cost and the use of scarce resources as by any notion of "the excess of revenue over costs".

EVA is a performance measurement and analysis technique that focuses on economic profit as distinct from accounting profit. It stresses the importance of cash flow increments over and above the market-determined weighted average cost of capital (WACC). As Chapter 9 illustrated, WACC is the sum of the implied or required market returns of each component of a corporate capitalization, weighted by that component's share of the total capitalization. EVA is attempting, therefore, to incorporate a more economic notion of profit into the assessment criteria applied to business.

It is calculated as: Net Operating Profit after Tax and Weighted Average Cost of Capital (WACC).

For example, assuming a company has an Operating Profit after Tax of £10 million and a capital base of £100 million with a WACC of 8%, its economic profit under EVA would be: £10 million − £8 million (£100 × 8%) = £2 million. Further informed by cashflow information, this return would be compared with alternatives in order to see whether the money could be more profitably invested elsewhere.

As the following extract explains, EVA has been widely adopted and has as one of its primary effects the imposition of a stricter budgetary discipline on management.

---

[1] EVA is a copyright of Stern Stewart & Co.

Economic Value Analysis, by Dawne Shand

Remember Microeconomics 101? Maybe not. At any rate, the class would typically start with the professor striding slowly to the front of the room and announcing that "accounting profits are not economic profits." He would peer over his spectacles to see if any wide-eyed freshman had even a glimmer of the profundity of this statement, then he would sigh. No one gets it at first. Unfortunately, it's a tenet that often confuses many business and information technology managers as well.

Basic accounting practices define a profit as revenue minus costs. If you spent $10 million on a new plant and earned $10.5 million from the sales of the products it produced, you would claim an accounting profit of $500,000. But that same investment might have generated $11 million or more if it had been invested elsewhere. Suddenly, that $500,000 accounting profit doesn't look so compelling, especially to investors.

According to economic theory, capital eventually moves to the investment opportunities with the best returns because investors want to maximize their profits. An economic profit means that a business generates returns similar to an investment in the stock market. Getting decision-makers to think about economic profits as they evaluate new business opportunities is the purpose of using economic value added (EVA). Michael Contrada, executive vice president at Balanced Scorecard Collaborative Inc. in Lincoln, Mass., explains that "revenue minus costs doesn't tell you much about the cost of resources, such as equity and debt".

EVA says that assets used by a line of business have opportunity costs. Investments in one arena (such as distribution) detract from another (such as manufacturing) that may hold an opportunity for bigger returns. For example, London-based Diageo PLC, which owns United Distillers & Vintners Ltd., used EVA to gauge which of its liquor brands generated the best returns. The analysis determined that because of the time required for storage and care, aged Scotch didn't generate as much profit as vodka, which could be sold within weeks of being distilled. As a result of the EVA analysis, management at United Distillers began to emphasize vodka production and sales...

Source: *Computerworld*, October 30, 2000.

While EVA does take financial information as its starting point, it is normally classified as a non-financial measure on the basis that it forces management attentions onto economic profit. This requires that budgetary systems, strategic plans and investment appraisal techniques acknowledge more rigorous assessment criteria than are imposed by purely financial measures. The effect in many of those businesses in which it has been applied has been to identify those areas that are more profitable, thus ensuring than marginal funds are directed there. This in turn has positively impacted upon return on investment.

Multivariate Analysis and Corporate Failure Prediction

One area in which traditional financial measures and non-financial indicators have found common ground is that of company failure prediction. Considerable research has been carried out in this area in recent years and several studies have indicated that the models developed can be used with a certain degree of confidence.

The ability to predict corporate failure will be of particular importance to bankers and suppliers. Likewise, it will be of interest to auditors attempting to establish the degree to which a company can be considered a going concern. It will obviously also be critical for management and shareholders as a means of identifying corporate viability, or of assessing the stability of suppliers and customers.

There are several principal causes of insolvency and corporate failure:

- Failure to respond to market changes
- Overtrading
- High gearing in anticipation of growth that does not materialize.

Most corporate failure prediction models focus on the use of key ratios to highlight prospective difficulties such as these. They usually calculate a "score" for the company and then compare this with a "pass mark" which has been determined by previous study to be appropriate to entities operating in the business sector.

Altman's Z-Score

This was the original corporate failure prediction model and was developed in the late 1960s. It uses financial ratios as a means of predicting bankruptcy. The Z-score for a business is the product of a weighted average of five separate ratios. These weightings and ratios were derived from a major empirical study.

The formula is:

$$Z = 1.2X1 + 1.4X2 + 3.3X3 + 0.6X4 + 1.0X5$$

$$X1 = \frac{\text{Working Capital}}{\text{Total Assets}}$$

$$X2 = \frac{\text{Retained Earnings}}{\text{Total Assets}}$$

$$X3 = \frac{\text{Profit before interest and tax}}{\text{Total Assets}}$$

$$X4 = \frac{\text{Market capitalisation}}{\text{Book value of debts}}$$

$$X5 = \frac{\text{Revenue}}{\text{Total Assets}}$$

Companies that achieve a Z-score of >2.7 are considered to be going concerns, at least in the short- to medium-term. A score below 1.8 indicates potentially serious problems.

There have, however, been criticisms of the Z-score model on the following grounds:

- Lack of commonality of definition of similar items between companies
- Use of historic data
- Lack of conceptual base
- Lack of sensitivity to time-scale of failure.

Nevertheless Altman's Z-score approach (modified in several instances to take account of local conditions, for example, Taffler's model in the UK) is widely used by those wishing to assess the stability and solvency of companies.

Taffler's Model

Taffler's model for quoted UK companies, which is open to the same criticisms as Altman's Z-score, has also been widely employed. The formula is constructed in a similar manner to Altman's, with different weightings assigned to different components. As the following extract explains, however, these components are somewhat idiosyncratic:

'Z-scoring' Helps Separate the Junk from the Jewels, by Tony Jackson

At the root of Taffler's approach is the ''Z-score'', a form of credit analysis devised in the US in the 1960s. In bald terms, it looks at two groups of companies – those that have failed and those that haven't – and looks for the financial characteristics that most clearly differentiate between the two. So the more a company resembles the first group, the greater its risk of failure. That is obviously handy information for bankers and credit rating agencies. Taffler argues, though, that it can also work in the equity market: that in certain limited circumstances, his approach helps to predict share price movements...

So how does all this work? Taffler has decided, on the basis of trial and error, to use different models for broad sectors: industrial companies, retailers and so forth (he doesn't cover banks or insurers).

Take the industrial model as an example. This contains four ratios, measuring profitability, liquidity, financial risk and gearing. These are then weighted to give a total score for the company. All industrial companies are then ranked, and the company's risk rating shown relative to its peers...

Two essential points before we move on. First, the individual ratios Taffler uses are highly idiosyncratic. Profitability, for instance, is measured as pre-tax profit divided by average short-term liabilities (creditors, short-term debt and the like). Gearing is the ratio of total debt to total tangible assets rather than net debt to share-holders' funds. Never mind the reasons: Taffler argues simply that those particular ratios – and he has looked at hundreds – turn out the most statistically significant in practice. They are not, however, ratios that analysts generally look at. They are therefore not, to put it cynically, ratios that companies will generally aim to fudge.

This brings us to the second point. Taffler argues that his approach takes account of the interacting nature of a company's finances. Double-entry book-keeping dictates that if a company fudges one number, it shows up somewhere else. If you only look at a few ratios in isolation – and all analysts are guilty of that occasionally – you may miss the big picture.

To get an idea of how all this works in practice, go back to Marconi. By March 2000 – the peak of the technology bubble – the company had sold its safe old businesses and overpaid immensely for high-tech acquisitions in the US. At that point, its profitability was still high. But its balance sheet, as measured by liquidity, financial risk and gearing, was shot to pieces. So when profitability nose-dived, as it did the following year, the company had no strength left to weather the storm.

Balance sheet strength, of course, is in turn only part of the story. If a company's profits are declining – think of Marks & Spencer or J Sainsbury – that must ultimately be put right, or the company is doomed. But if it has financial strength in Taffler's terms, it has time to address the problem. Marconi had no time.

One further essential point. A weak score emphatically does not mean a company is going bust. No company, Taffler claims, has gone bust without previously dropping below the risk threshold. But plenty of companies have recovered.

All this suggests that Taffler's method is not a self-sufficient way of valuing companies. Nor does he claim it to be. Rather, it is a starting point for analysis. What he looks for is disjunctions: cases where the financial position has weakened but the share price has held up, or where the position has stabilised or improved but the share price is still on the floor...

There is plainly food for thought here. In future columns, I will look occasionally at companies this approach throws up. I will also submit some companies to the Taffler lens, to see if his findings agree with mine (in the case of Electrocomponents,

Argenti's Failure Model

This model was developed primarily through discussion with bankers, businessmen and investors, as well as a wide-ranging review of cases of failure. As a result it depends less upon financial information than an assessment of various aspects of a company's controls and systems.

The model requires that scores be assigned under the following headings:

		Score	Score
Defects (danger mark: 10)			
1. Management	Autocratic chief executive	8	
	Chief executive is also chairman	4	
	Unbalanced skill/experience on board	2	
	Passive board	2	
	Weak finance director	2	
	Lack of professional managers	1	
2. Accounting systems	Budgetary control	3	
	Cash flow plans	3	
	Costing systems	3	
3. Response to change	Products, processes, markets, etc.	15	
	Total possible		**43**
Mistakes (danger mark: 15)	Over-trading	15	
	Excessively high gearing	15	
	Impending project failure	15	
	Total possible		**45**
Symptoms	Deteriorating ratios or Z-scores	4	
	Signs of creative accounting	4	
	Decline in quality, morale, market share, etc.	3	
	Resignations	1	
	Total possible		**12**
	Overall total possible		**100**

The main rules of interpretation are:

- Total <25: company not in imminent danger
- Total >25: company may fail within 5 years
- Defects score >10: management likely to make potentially fatal mistake
- Mistakes score >15 (and Defects score <10): management somewhat risky

Like the Z-score, Argenti's model can be criticized on a number of grounds:

- The mix of indicators may be inappropriate
- The weighting given to indicators may be unsuitable
- Time factors may not be fully respected.

Application of Failure-Prediction Models

While these prediction models have been widely applied, some scepticism remains as to their efficacy. As with all ratio analysis, the interpretation of scores and results requires experience and sensitivity to the general economic environment as well as specific industry and national contexts. Nevertheless, properly used, these approaches have proven helpful in predicting corporate failure.

Summary

Alternative approaches have emerged in response to the rather limited perspective that traditional financial measures both adopt and encourage. An appreciation on the part of various stakeholders that such indicators would enrich the data flow for decision-makers and other users has resulted in their widespread use.

Significantly, such models are at their most useful when they are employed in tandem with financial measures. Indeed, those approaches, such as BSC, that recognize the potency of accounting information by including a financial perspective within the model offer more enriching insights into the role of financial information within the overall strategic vision of the business. The key is to ensure a balanced approach in devising any system for assessing a business, whether this is for the purposes of planning, decision-making, control or failure prediction.

Review Questions

Question 1
Explain why approaches that emphasise non-financial factors would be attractive to the management of many corporate entities.

Question 2
Identify some advantages and disadvantages of such approaches.

Question 3
"The starting point is understanding a company's value drivers, the factors that create stakeholder value. Once known, these factors determine which measures contribute to long-term success and, so, how to translate corporate objectives into measures that guide managers' actions". Explain what this statement means and how it would apply to a knowledge-intensive entity that views intellectual capital as its principal asset.

Question 4
Outline the key features of the Balanced Scorecard and list the four "perspectives" that it encourages. Suggest at least three measures that might be employed under each of these perspectives.

Question 5
Explain what Economic Value Added (EVA) means and how it operates.

Question 6
"EVA seeks to jog managers' memories by deducting from a firm's net operating profit a charge for the amount of capital it employs. If the result is positive, then the firm created value over the period in question; if the EVA is negative it was a 'value destroyer'. Providing a company knows how much capital its operating units use, it can work out their EVA too. For example, if a plc's share capital is $100 million and its cost of capital is 10%, its target rate of return will be $10 million. If it earns $50 million, then its EVA will be $40 million". Explain this statement and the budgetary implications for a plc.

Question 7
"There is nothing new in trying to predict corporate bankruptcy. Formal procedures using accounting ratios to distinguish between failing and surviving businesses have existed for almost 70 years. Like the alchemists of old who sought to turn base metals into gold, generations of researchers have tried to find a way to predict accurately which companies are on the road to bankruptcy". Explain the use of bankruptcy prediction models, specifically, the *Z*-Score and Argenti models. To what extent can these models be considered useful?

Case Studies

Case 1

One of Tesco's main competitors is Marks & Spencer. The following article considers M&S's performance and financial position in the context of both Taffler's model and the company's overall strategy. It also provides a variety of ratio scores. Critically consider the author's conclusion that "even if M&S is recovering, it is doing so from a weakened – and riskier – base".

Its Sales May be up, but M&S is Poor Value, by Tony Jackson

A couple of weeks ago, I did something I hadn't done for years. I popped into Marks & Spencer, looking for a sandwich, and ended up buying a jacket. A decade ago, that would have been routine; on some days in the office I was dressed by M&S from head to foot. But then, like a lot of other people, I gradually lost the habit. So why had I gone in this time? Mainly because I had heard good things in conversation with people in the trade. A designer with a rival retail chain said the M&S clothes were looking better. A small supplier to the company said its food sales were picking up.

All this would suggest that the recent revival at M&S, which has put 15 per cent on the share price in the past month, is real enough. But there are nagging questions of valuation. At 399.25p the shares are on a yield of 3.1 per cent and a multiple of 18 times earnings. The retail sector overall is on a yield of 3.8 per cent and a multiple of 13. Certainly, M&S is going through a better patch, which may prove sustainable. But isn't this overdoing it a bit?

Let us consider some numbers. When valuing retailers, the stock market can show a slightly narrow obsession with sales. It is certainly encouraging that M&S had underlying sales growth of 1 per cent last quarter – particularly since its old bugbear, Philip Green, saw Bhs's sales drop some 5 per cent in the past six months.

But margins count as well. It seems clear that M&S has been cutting its prices fairly aggressively. On my recent visit, I was slightly taken aback to see a pair of shoes at £15. And cutting margins is not something M&S can easily afford. It is sobering to reflect that since the peak year of 1998 M&S's UK sales have actually risen, by 5 per cent in total. But its UK operating profits have fallen by nearly a third. In 1998 the UK retailing margin was 13 per cent. Last year it was 8.6 per cent.

More basic again, to my mind, is the question of M&S's underlying financial health. Here, as I have done before in this column, I will call on the research of Professor Richard Taffler, now of Edinburgh University. His chart, as usual, shows three lines: the company's financial strength, the threshold below which it would be at risk of failure, and the share price.

The picture is one of apparent paradox. In the period 2001–02, when M&S's profits were at their nadir, its financial health was excellent. But over the past couple of years, while on the whole profits have been recovering, the company's financial health has declined sharply.

The Taffler method ranks retailers by four criteria: profitability, asset financing, gearing and working capital. The definitions are somewhat unusual. Profitability, for instance, is the ratio of pre-tax profits to average short-term liabilities; and on that measure there has been some deterioration recently. The sharpest decline, though, has come in gearing – defined as total debt to total capital employed – and working capital, here taken to include short-term debt.

The chief cause of this was last year's £2.3bn share buyback, undertaken as part of the company's defences against Philip Green.

I have talked before in this column about why I think buybacks are generally a bad thing, and I won't go over the ground again. Suffice it to say that if I owned shares in M&S I would want it to sell goods to the public on my behalf, not go to the bank for me; and if I wanted to sell the shares, I could do so in the market without the company's help.

The sad fact is that in its heyday, this company had a balance sheet as impregnable as Fort Knox. That legacy kept it financially healthy despite management bungles on the trading side. Now, as a result of financial engineering, its health has been compromised at a time when the trading outlook is still uncertain. I do not want to exaggerate here. On Taffler's calculations, M&S is now as financially strong as the average UK retailer, having been substantially stronger a couple of years ago. But then again, how strong is the average retailer at present?

The picture of balance sheet decline is borne out by more conventional measures. In the mid-1990s M&S had no debt. Its balance sheet gearing has been rising ever since, and last year shot up to 400 per cent, measured against shareholders' funds. That might be thought a technicality, given that shareholders' funds were massively reduced by the share buyback. Well, let us look instead at net debt in relation to the freehold property portfolio, which might be thought the best financial anchor against borrowings. Back in the peak year of 1998, net debt was £319m against freehold property worth £2.345bn – a ratio of 14 per cent. The position has been deteriorating ever since. Net debt is now £2.099bn, while the value of freehold property has fallen to £1.264bn, giving a ratio of 166 per cent. This leaves out of account small matters such as the pension fund deficit, one of the things that gave Philip Green pause for thought when he was looking at bidding for M&S. That still stands at about £470m, after a £400m cash injection the year before.

What about cash flow and the dividend? The picture here is slightly obscured by last year's disposal of the financial services business. But if we adjust for that, and for the fact that last year's capital expenditure was abnormally low, it looks to me that the dividend is covered by free cash flow slightly less than twice. Not too bad, but again – given that the shares are only on a market yield – not generous either.

In all this, you will notice, I have not expressed a view on whether M&S has indeed turned the corner. In today's turbulent retail environment, I take that to be effectively unknowable. And in any case, every reader will have his or her own view based on personal experience. My point is, though, that even if M&S is recovering, it is doing so from a weakened – and riskier – financial base. There is more to share valuation than like-for-like sales figures. I hope to be proved wrong, but I think the recent rise in the share price is a mistake.

Source: *Sunday Telegraph*, October 16, 2005.

Case 2

Assuming a WACC of 7% for Tesco, analyze the company's financial performance over recent years using the EVA approach.

Case 3

Referring to the Tesco plc Annual Report 2005, identify appropriate sets of measures to track and control the goals the company could set for itself under each of the following BSC headings:
- Financial perspective
- Innovation and learning perspective
- Customer perspective
- Business process perspective

Consider how the incorporation of these into the company's reporting and control regime might affect its self-assessment as well as its strategy formulation.

Case 4

Carry out the same exercise outlined in Case 3 above using the Tesco 2006 Annual Report.

When you have completed this chapter you will understand that:

- The evolution of governance paradigms will have a significant impact upon the focus and content of accounting information.

- That the social, economic and commercial consequences of the emergence of the new economy include changing wealth-creation dynamics that pose challenges for the traditional accounting model.

- New developments in technology and media bring a range of possibilities for accounting information and those who shape it.

What is the Purpose of Accounting

In the beginning there was earth, fire, wind and water. There was no accounting! Nowadays, among mankind's many inventions and creations we have accounting and accountants... Surely accounting must serve some useful purpose(s). But what is that purpose? And does accounting need to be done exclusively by accountants? Does it add value to organisations or is it simply a necessary evil which one day will be replaced by a single all-embracing software package?

Source: *The Evolving Role of the Financial Function*, by Ian Herbert, William Murphy and Richard Wilson, *accounting & business*, May 2004.

Introduction

A point made consistently throughout this text is that accounting is a social science. That is, it is not a set of unchangeable techniques, but rather a discipline that is responsive to the political, cultural and social environments in which it finds itself. In other words it can change and evolve. And just as the primary means of wealth creation has changed over time, so too accounting has managed to adapt to these challenges. For instance, over recent decades alone it has moved from a predominantly stewardship focus to one in which it is now a primary supplier of information for decision-making purposes.

This chapter begins with a look at some of the changes in the nature and governance profiles of firms that may impact on the role of financial information. It then identifies some of ways in which traditional reporting practices will be revolutionized by the innovative forms of delivery that new media and changing information economics allow.

The Nature and Governance of the Firm

A central, if unspoken, paradigm of most texts dealing with financial information is the supremacy and anticipated long-term hegemony of the Anglo-American capitalist model. However, political, social and technological changes are likely to dramatically impact existing governance models of the firm. For instance, a series of spectacular frauds that have impacted the investments and pensions of millions of ordinary investors, and that have seen society in general burdened with the cost of retrieving the situation, have called into question the efficacy of the current model. As the following extract highlights, this is causing some commentators to review the consequences of some key assumptions:

Why There's no Future in Shareholder Capitalism, by Donald Kalff

The time has arrived to take a fresh and agnostic look at the past, present and future performance of companies in the US and Europe that have embraced the American way of conducting business. Many believe in the virtues of this approach but their faith is misplaced. And, more importantly, attractive and highly competitive alternatives are not receiving the attention they deserve.

The defenders of the American Enterprise Model point to its stark and appealing features: the pursuit of shareholder value; a one-tier board; a strong CEO; the creation of independent divisions and business units that operate close to their markets; tight planning and control; performance evaluation based on financial (or at least quantifiable) targets; substantial monetary incentives; and managers who believe in competition and in winning with the widest possible margin. This model is emulated by virtually all large public companies in Europe and there seem to be no limits to its applicability. Outside its own realm, the model also sets standards for the organisational structure and culture of large sections of the public sector, such as utilities, public transport and healthcare.

The judgement that large American companies perform poorly is counter-intuitive but inescapable. At the top of the economic cycle in the late 1990s, profit per share – the favoured performance indicator of the top 500 companies in the US – remained stagnant, despite major share buy-back schemes financed with borrowed money. Moreover in retrospect, the profits reported in this period have to be corrected downwards to a very significant degree. Proper accounting of option schemes results in a 30% reduction in reported profits; the exclusion of profits from corporate pension funds accounts for a decrease of another 15%. On top of this, many companies among America's top 500 made insufficient contributions to their pension funds and failed to make provisions for a variety of long term obligations such as healthcare benefits for pensioners and deferred income of top managers. This should have decreased profits at the time by at least another 15%, bringing the total reduction to 60%. And it should be noted that this figure does not even include the financial impact of all the litigation and criminal investigations that originated in the 1990s. All in all, a very poor performance at a time of high economic growth spurred on by a technological revolution...

The damage caused by this corporate straitjacket can hardly be over-estimated. The bottom line is that, over the past five years, many US style companies, concentrating on "profit per share", have destroyed "shareholder value" in its original meaning of "economic value". They have done this in the name of their shareholders. This must be one of the great ironies of our time. All in all, there is ample reason to break away from the American Enterprise Model...

[The remainder of this article is to be found as part of Case 1 at the end of this chapter.]

Source: *accounting & business*, November/December, 2005.

At the same time as the deficiencies in the shareholder value paradigm are being exposed, the wealth creating dynamics of the new economy may provide the catalyst for a more democratized and inclusive corporate model. This may have at its core a greater appreciation of the ownership rights accruing to human capital. These developments could have profound social consequences and will only be worked out over coming decades.

Significantly, however, accounting does already possess a set of principles and practices which, albeit somewhat myopic, allows it to tackle some of the more obvious challenges of this revolution. For instance, it still produces and mediates much of the information used by management and investors for decision-making purposes. It also produces, via internal and external reports, a range of measures that allow corporate performance to be gauged and interpreted. Nevertheless, the challenges to the existing corporate model, particularly those posed by new economy paradigms, are profound.

Challenges of The New Economy

The dynamics of the new economy offer both great opportunities and significant threats to accounting at a variety of levels. Some relate to the fundamental challenges posed by the wealth creation, information economics and corporate governance dynamics of new economy firms. Others relate to specific aspects of accounting practice such as the way in which intellectual capital and other intangible assets should be recognized and measured.

This emphasis on knowledge as a key source of competitive advantage has led to a realization that the resource base of an entity comprises far more than its tangible assets. Indeed, the principal wealth-creating source in most non-traditional industries is now viewed as consisting of its intangible assets such as people competencies, relationships with customers and internal processes. These have come to be called the "Intellectual Capital" of a business.

However, traditionally, internally generated intangible assets such as this have been neither recognized nor measured by the accounting model. The reason for this is that accounting has traditionally focused its attentions on capturing and representing items that are tangible. Knowledge and people are outside the comprehension of this model. Thus, their largest "assets" go unrecognized in the balance sheets of most knowledge-intensive firms. As Bill Gates has remarked, "Our primary assets, which are our software and our software-development skills, do not show up on the balance sheet at all. This is probably not very enlightening from a pure accounting point of view".

Consequently, accounting's capacity to fulfil its function as supplier of relevant information has diminished as it has struggled to come to terms with items to which its limited conceptual framework can assign neither value nor tangible existence.

Recognizing that allowing this situation to persist would simply undermine the credibility of accounting, accountants and regulators have recently begun to suggest remedies. One is the presentation of a separate statement of intellectual capital. Another is the extension of the Operating and Financial Review (OFR) to incorporate narrative detail specific to internally generated intangibles. IAS 38, *Intangible Assets*, also offers a significant advance in recognizing and measuring some intangibles.

The extent to which people are coming to be seen as assets rather than costs suggests that one way in which issues such as intellectual capital might be accommodated would be by revisiting the whole concept of Human Resource Accounting. This would involve developing new templates and conceptual approaches that recognize employees as primary resources of a business with corresponding ownership rights.

This links to another related consequence of the dynamics of the knowledge economy – the changes being induced in corporate governance models. The existing corporate model strongly favours the providers of financial capital. However, in an environment in which the primary resource is seen as knowledge embedded in people, the existing model will be challenged to embrace a stakeholder approach that recognizes the claims of employees to a share of ownership since they provide the principal value-creating resource.

Nor is this likely to be satisfied by stock option schemes that are predicated upon notions of reward. A governance model that has traditionally linked ownership to provision of capital may be forced to recognize the consequences of this paradigm in an economy in which employees, not financial capitalists, provide the critical capital. It is also increasingly likely that employees will resist the attempts of financial capitalists to capture and establish ownership of knowledge by means of patents.

The nature of relationships internally will also be affected, with influence correlating more closely to knowledge and knowledge networks than to hierarchy.

Finally, the new economy emphasizes the importance of teams, knowledge flows, processes and collegiality as facilitators of value creation. This will require the development of internal management and accounting techniques that recognize and encourage these traits. It will also require reporting methodologies that distinguish between entities in which these traits are increasing and those in which they are diminishing. To achieve their purpose these techniques will need to recognize the often chaotic and intuitive process of creativity and ideas. This will require imagination and experimentation on the part of accountants, the traditional gatekeepers of internal management and reporting practices.

New Forms of Delivery

Quite apart from the accounting-specific issues that the wealth creation dynamics of the new economy raise, technology is itself a catalyst for change, challenging communicators to adapt in terms of content, access and speed of delivery. Commercial, technological and cost factors are combining to ensure that accounting reporting practices are not immune to the momentum towards real-time, widely disseminated, user-specific information that media such as the Internet facilitate.

In response, task forces in both the UK and the US are exploring the implications for accounting information dynamics of the technological revolution. Governments and regulators have already begun to take steps to ensure that web reporting is both facilitated and regulated. For instance, in the UK, the Companies Act (Electronic Communications) Order has removed legal obstacles to companies communicating in this manner with its shareholders in a number of specified areas; the IASB has released a draft that paves the way for more substantial online reporting; the ICAEW and ASB are engaged in similar exercises; and the Auditing Practices Board has published various bulletins that provide guidance for auditors in relation to electronic reporting.

Just as important as the use of new media to disseminate traditional reports, however, are the possibilities that the Internet and new approaches to reporting and disclosure might together enable. There is every possibility that the combined effect of electronic media, corporate governance changes that accommodate the rights of a range of stakeholders, and an insatiable appetite for information on the part of global capital markets, may lead to radical changes in the financial reporting culture.

eXtensible Business Reporting Language (XBRL)

Most large organizations have adopted the Internet as a means of communicating with their investors and other stakeholders. For instance, it is commonly used as a conduit for financial information, and it is usual to find a range of such information, from webcasts to complex data, being made available in electronic form.

Significantly, in most cases what is supplied is merely an electronic equivalent of the old paper-based information forms. However, with increasing demands being placed on the corporate financial reporting supply chain, there is an urgent need to change the format in which such information is both constructed and communicated. This has led to the development by a group of the world's leading accounting, technology and financial services "players" (including regulators, practitioners and government) of XBRL, an open specification standard language that will allow users to prepare, publish and exchange financial information. With XBRL, as the following account explains, information will be entered only once and the same information will be capable of being rendered as a printed financial statement, an HTML document for a website, a raw XML file, or a specialized report:

An End in Sight for Results Paper-Chase

This new language will allow financial information to be extracted in a variety of formats. A new computing standard offers to speed up and simplify company reporting at the click of a mouse. But so far too few people have heard of it, writes Jenny Hirschkorn.

If you have been keeping your ear close to the ground, you might have heard that the world of corporate reporting is set to undergo its most significant technological change since the arrival of the internet. As things stand, organisations have adopted the Net as a channel for communicating their financial data to investors and other interested parties with varying degrees of enthusiasm. You are likely to find anything from simple extracts from reports and accounts, to webcasts and complex supplementary information available in electronic form. But the reality is that for people looking to get to the heart of the information, as well as those concerned with preparing it, this is little, if any, improvement on the old paper documents that were the only medium available until a few years ago.

Recent research by Investor Relations magazine shows that most analysts still prefer to access information using hard copies rather than downloads. With ever-increasing demands on the corporate reporting supply chain, whether from regulators, banks, pressure groups or investors, there is an urgent need to eliminate the labour-intensive processes currently used to produce reports and consume their contents. "It's expensive, it's slow and it's error-prone," according to Mike Willis, deputy chief knowledge officer of PricewaterhouseCoopers' global assurance and business advisory practice.

Enter XBRL, or eXtensible Business Reporting Language. This electronic language will enable information to be tagged in such a way that it can be extracted at the click of a mouse. On the preparation side, it will eliminate the need to input manually, over and over, the same data into various reports.

XBRL was conceived through the efforts of more than 170 software, accounting, regulatory and finance organisations from around the world. According to the Institute of Chartered Accountants, users of accounts, from the smallest investor to the largest institution, stand to benefit from existing financial information being accessible in a more flexible fashion. John Court, who represents the institute on the UK XBRL steering committee, said: "Using the UK version of XBRL, companies will be able to publish their financial statements in a way that will allow information to be extracted in a variety of formats to meet the particular need of each user. "Investors, banks and regulatory bodies will then be able to reliably extract data in seconds," he said. Because of the differing regulations governing disclosure from country to country, each nation, or jurisdiction, needs its own XBRL community...

Among the still small number of early adopters are Microsoft, Morgan Stanley and Reuters which, in October 2001, became the first publicly-listed European company to release its financial results using the standard... With the backing of the International Accounting Standards Board and organisations such as the Inland Revenue, it is not so much a question of if XBRL is widely adopted, but when.

PricewaterhouseCoopers has collaborated with Nasdaq and Microsoft on a demonstration of XBRL that can be found at www.nasdaq.com/xbrl. See also www.xbrl.org

Source: *Daily Telegraph*, May 8, 2003.

Use of XBRL will equip users with a number of significant advantages. It will provide:

- Agreed terms by establishing uniform categories for financial data
- For the reliable extraction of specific, detailed information from the different forms of financial statements, thus removing the need for re-entering information
- A wide range of stakeholders with greater access to financial information on a continuous basis
- More powerful diagnosis of financial condition using real-time data; and
- Management with more meaningful information promptly.

XBRL will be capable of being used for financial statements, tax filings, regulatory filings, accounting and business reports, audit schedules and other forms of authoritative literature requiring standards-based input.

It will also provide a standards-based template that will assist firms currently experimenting with real-time access to accounting data for a variety of internal and external stakeholders. This, in fact, may be seen as one of the more significant developments: it is quite possible that accounting may move to the point where the notion of "reporting" evolves to mean, not the formal assembling of financial and non-financial information into an annual report, but the authorization of access to real-time data for a variety of stakeholders.

This, of course, also presents certain challenges for accountants. Traditionally, accountants' commercial and social power has derived from their capacity to act as the gatekeepers a key information resource. New forms of data collection, assimilation and communication that depend less on technical know-how and more on technology, will significantly undermine some of the supply lines that accountants understand and control. Nevertheless, the effect will be to further emphasize the role of accounting information, and those who understand it – whether accountants or others, such as risk managers – as key players in the decision-making culture of modern business.

Summary

The implications of the technological revolution, the dynamics of the new economy, and the changes these are inducing in the reporting and governance cultures of companies are already having a significant impact on accounting information and the means of its dissemination. The resulting democratization of the information dissemination process will in turn cause further moves in this direction.

The challenges for accounting are considerable. They extend from basic matters of practice to more fundamental issues such as the implications of "free" information available in real time, and the question of who will control it.

These issues are being responded to by a wide variety of professional bodies and regulators. However, it is likely to be some time before they are resolved. In fact, the notion of resolving such issues may itself have to surrender to the implicitly fluid and mutating nature of these new paradigms. The certainty with which accounting was once able to approach its world may no longer be sustainable.

Review Questions

Question 1
The traditional shareholder value paradigm has dominated the corporate agenda for many years. However, there are signs that it may now be threatened by newly evolving paradigms. Explain how this has happened and the extent to which it is vulnerable to being relegated in the broader economic context.

Question 2
Explain why the dynamics and nature of the new economy offer opportunities and pose threats to accounting's traditional role within the business world.

Question 3
What is meant by real-time access? Outline its implications for the financial reporting process in general and for accountants and auditors in particular.

Question 4
What does the term "Intellectual Capital" mean? Why is it such a crucial concept?

Question 5
Identify the critical challenges that the emergence of knowledge and intellectual capital as key wealth generators poses to accounting.

Question 6
"People represent the greatest resource of any business. Under any definition they must be considered an asset and accounted for as such". Explain what the implications of viewing people in this way would be for the accounting model.

Question 7
Describe some of the strategies being adopted by accountants in order to exploit the opportunities offered by new media for disseminating information.

Question 8
"Our notion of how corporations should be governed, and, in particular, the way in which 'knowledge-workers' will be accommodated, will be dramatically impacted by the democratizing influence of the Internet and the way in which employees are no longer viewed as costs, but as resources". Explain some of the ways in which accounting will be impacted by these developments.

Question 9
"A governance model that has traditionally linked ownership to provision of capital may be forced to recognise the consequences of this paradigm in an economy in which intellectual capital is provided by people who are not financial capitalists in the traditional sense. It is also likely that as part of this process the attempts of financial capitalists to capture and establish ownership of knowledge by means of patents or its physical expression in the form of recipes and manuals will be resisted by employees". Identify the principal arguments being made here and whether or not they are sustainable.

Case Studies

Case 1

The following article, the first part of which was used earlier in this chapter, discusses the extent to which the current American shareholder capitalism model is sustainable. It suggests that regulators and others should look instead at other models, such as operate, for example, in continental Europe. All in all it provides a powerful critique of the current business model and suggests that for a variety of reasons it will not survive.

In the light of the points made, consider the author's conclusion that "intelligent capitalism will drive out shareholder capitalism".

Why there's no Future in Shareholder Capitalism

Donald Kalff argues that intelligent capitalism will prevail, driving out the US business model

...This growth should partially be attributed to a totally unprecedented and, many would argue, irresponsible financial injection into the US economy. The combination of increased government spending, substantial tax reductions, the lowest interest rates in history and a feverish housing market all conspired to secure ongoing growth in consumer spending which, in turn, fuelled corporate profits.

Profits and profits-per-share also rose as a result of specific policies that flow from the basic characteristics of the American Enterprise Model.

Double digit growth of profit-per-share was increasingly seen as a stepping-stone to a higher stock price. Shareholder value (the net present value of future revenues and cost, including the cost of capital) was replaced by shareholder return on investment, the rise of the stock price per unit of time.

In combination with the short tenure of American CEOs and the strong link between their income and the performance of their company's stock, this resulted in a significant reduction in the repertoire of corporate policies. Only policies that would pay off within three to four years were worth pursuing. And, to make matters worse, each of these policies had serious flaws.

Companies that buy their own stock to support their share price sooner or later undermine their financial resilience. Poorly performing business units can be sold or dismantled to improve profits, but this is a one time gain. Friend and foe now agree that corporate acquisitions, generally aimed at cost cutting, destroy value for the shareholders of the acquiring company. Less well-known is that, in most instances, these cost savings are lower than projected, productivity and market share growth are reduced, and research and development expenditure and research output suffer. The outsourcing of corporate activities remains popular but, with each step, the risks increase. Flexibility in meeting changes in demand and specifications decreases, and the vulnerability of the supply, production and distribution chain increases. Staff reductions immediately add to profits, but each new round of lay-offs yields less and less and comes at a higher price in terms of the deterioration of the organisation's capacity to rebound, the destruction of imbedded knowledge and low morale of surviving staff.

To add insult to injury, interesting opportunities for increasing the economic value of a company, such as mergers, partnerships, international expansion and large investments were all too often ignored for the simple reason that profit-per-share would suffer during the tenure of the CEO.

Huge Damage

The damage caused by this corporate straitjacket can hardly be over-estimated. The bottom line is that, over the past five years, many US style companies, concentrating on "profit per share", have destroyed "shareholder value" in its original meaning of "economic value". They have done this in the name of their shareholders. This must be one of the great ironies of our time.

All in all, there is ample reason to break away from the American Enterprise Model.

The search is on for alternative enterprise models. And the place to look is Continental Europe. The key difference with the US is that only 25% of the capital requirements of Continental European companies are met by stock markets. This is in stark contrast to US companies that depend on stock markets for 75% of their capital requirements. As a result, most Continental companies escape the web of expectations spun by investment bankers, financial analysts, stockbrokers, strategy consultants and the financial media. Continental Europe harbours many small and large private companies, co- operatives and government-owned companies, each inclined to and capable of concentrating on value creation and producing excellent results.

There is also a need for the development of new models. Companies explicitly driven by the creation of economic value as a single objective provide clarity for all those whose interests are at stake. Companies that acknowledge that economic value is largely created by teams of middle managers and experts working inside and across corporate boundaries will do well. Those with managements that provide perspective, resources and protection for these teams will thrive.

The Rhineland or stakeholder model is no longer an alternative for the American Enterprise Model. Companies that pursue a multitude of objectives to satisfy customers, suppliers, shareholders and employees, each of them with their political supporters to increase their leverage, become, like their American counterparts, victims of short term interests.

The focus on economic value forces companies to take the interest of future customers into account. Cash flows five to 10 years from now contribute significantly to the economic value of the company. This stresses the need for continuity, continuity pre-supposes legitimacy and legitimacy implies the corporate imbedding in society. This is a far cry from the basically antagonistic stakeholder model, whereby vested interests first and foremost protect their inroads into the company.

Companies with a single objective that rely on the co-operation between increasingly specialised employees based on trust will outperform their competitors. Intelligent capitalism will drive out shareholder capitalism.

Donald Kalff MBA PhD, a former Shell manager and a former member of the KLM Executive Committee, is a writer, adviser and biotech entrepreneur. He is the author of An UnAmerican Business, due to be published by Kogan Page in November (and already available in the Netherlands, France and Germany).

Source: *accounting & business*, October/November, 2005.

Case 2

Finally, the text concludes with a return to the Fundamental Analysis approach adopted throughout. The following article outlines some of the strategies adopted by some of the most successful practitioners of this art, such as Warren Buffet and Peter Lynch. It also identifies where various useful web-based tools can be found. Having completed the text, use this account to consider the extent to which Fundamental Analysis provides a satisfactory and value-added approach to financial information analysis.

Put the US Gurus to the Test

Peter Temple examines the web-based tools that allow us to follow the methods of the great investors

Many investors rely on tips and hunches to pick stocks. But there are more scientific ways to comb the market for opportunities. One legitimate way is to mimic the ideas of successful investors and search for stocks that fit the criteria they have used. Many of these market gurus are based in the US, but that doesn't mean you can't apply their ideas here. Even taking just two at random can show how useful the technique is.

Take Peter Lynch, the highly successful manager of Fidelity's flagship Magellan fund during the 1980s. His ideas are as relevant today as they were when he piloted this fund to a stunning five times outperformance against the Standard & Poor's 500 index during his 13 years in charge.

Lynch's criteria for picking growth companies were relatively simple. He looked for companies that:

• Were increasing earnings at 20 per cent to 50 per cent a year.
• Had little or no debt.
• Had positive Peg ratio: a price/earnings ratio less than the company's earnings growth rate.

He also favoured smaller companies and made a point of getting to know the management.

One other factor governed his investing technique. He made a point of looking closely at stocks for which he or his family had positive personal experiences as consumers.

We can apply these criteria to the UK market using the Company REFs (www.companyrefs.com) subscriber service, which sifts company data, combined with the free stock-screening tool at the ADVFN financial portal (www.advfn.com). This is probably about the most comprehensive and flexible screen available online. The two systems combined turn up a list of 25 ungeared stocks for which recent earnings growth has been above 35 per cent and where the price-earnings growth factor (Peg) factor is 0.7 or less.

On closer examination, however, most have less consistent growth records than Lynch would probably want. Only stocks such as Aveva, Bloomsbury Publishing, Detica, James Halstead, Northern Recruitment and FW Thorpe make the grade on these stricter criteria. Readers should also remember that these are not automatic recommendations, but merely starting points for deeper investigation. Even here, few of these stocks have shown a completely flawless pattern of steady earnings increases. Others may have a great history behind them, but a less reliable future. In short, reasonably priced true growth stocks are as elusive as ever.

But there is always more than one way of selecting stocks that perform. Investors who slavishly follow one guru such as Warren Buffett might miss out on other opportunities that the more flexible investor can capture.

Going against the crowd can sometimes be profitable. David Dreman, who manages the Kemper High Return Equity Fund, has also produced a performance record that has beaten the S&P 500 by a significant margin. He focuses on stocks that are large and fundamentally sound, but out of favour. Dreman's contrarian criteria are decent earnings growth, good return on equity, low debt – and low ratios of price to earnings, to cashflow or to assets.

These are demanding yardsticks to satisfy. As with the Lynch screen we can plug them into the UK market to see what stocks emerge. Using a combination of the Company REFs service combined with the stock- screening tool at ADVFN turns up an interesting list.

The criteria used in this case were:

- Market value above £ 1,200m (roughly half the level needed to guarantee entry into the FTSE 100).
- Earnings growth averaging 12 per cent over the past three years.
- Net gearing of less than 20 per cent.
- A p/e ratio of less than 15.
- Ratios either of price to cashflow of less than 10, or price to book value of less than 1.

Four stocks emerge from the process. Only one, Vodafone, satisfies each criterion. The others, Man Group, Barratt Developments and Berkeley Group, satisfy all but the discount to assets criterion.

There is, of course nothing to stop any investor picking stocks with both screening systems. In fact that might be considered a sensible diversification. But this misses the underlying point which is that, whatever method you use, it is being systematic in stock picking that pays dividends.

Source: *Financial Times*, January 21, 2005.

REFERENCES

Alexander, D. and Nobes, C., *Financial Accounting: An International Introduction*, Pearson Education, Essex, 2001.

Bebbington, J., Gray, R. and Laughlin, R., *Financial Accounting: Practice and Principles*, 3rd ed., Thomson Learning, London, 2001.

Bernstein, P.L., *Against the Gods*, John Wiley & Sons Ltd., New York, 1996.

Blake, D., *Financial Market Analysis*, 2nd ed., John Wiley & Sons Ltd., Chichester, 2000.

Clarkson, M.B.E. (ed.), *The Corporation and its Stakeholders: Classic and Contemporary Readings*, UTP, Toronto, 1998.

Davies, M., Peterson, R., Wilson, A. and Davis, M., UK GAAP, Palgrove Macmillan, London, 1997.

Elliott, B., and Elliott, J., *Financial Accounting and Reporting*, 10th ed., Financial Times/Prentice Hall, 2006.

Ellis, J. and Williams, D., *Corporate Strategy and Financial Analysis*, Pitman Publishing, London, 1993.

Fraser, L., and Ormiston, A., *Understanding Financial Statements*, 7th ed., Pearson/Prentice Hall, New Jersey, 2004.

Gray, R., Owen, D. and Adams, C., *Accounting and Accountability: Changes and Challenges in Corporate Social and Environmental Reporting*, Prentice Hall, London, 1996.

Higgins, R.C., *Analysis for Financial Management*, 2nd ed., Irwin/McGraw Hill, Boston, 2001.

Higson, A., *Corporate Financial Reporting: Theory and Practice*, Sage, London, 2005

Holmes, G., Sugden, A. and Gee, P., *Interpreting Company Reports and Accounts*, 9th ed., London, Financial Times/Prentice Hall, 2004.

Horngren, C.T., Sundem, G.L., Elliott, J.A. and Philbrick, D.R., *Introduction to Financial Accounting*, Pearson/Prentice Hall, New Jersey, 2006.

Hutton, W., *The Stakeholding Society: Writings on Politics and Economics*, David Goldblatt (ed.), Polity, Cambridge, 1999.

King, D., *The Commissor Vanishes*, Metropolitan Books, London, 1997.

Koop, G., *Analysis of Financial Data*, John Wiley & Sons Ltd., Chichester, 2006.

Mathews, M.R. and Perera, M.H.B., *Accounting Theory and Development*, Chapman and Hall, London, 1991.

McBarnett, D. and Whelan, C., *Creative Accounting and the Cross-Eyed Javelin Thrower*, John Wiley & Sons Ltd., 1999.

Monks, R. and Minow, N., *Corporate Governance*, 2nd ed., Blackwell, Oxford, 2001.

Parker, R.H., *Understanding Company Financial Statements*, 5th ed., Penguin, London, 1999.

Pendlebury, M. and Groves, R., *Company Accounts: Analysis, Interpretation and Understanding*, 5th ed., ITP, London, 2001.

Rees, B., *Financial Analysis*, 2nd ed., Prentice Hall, London, 1995.

Robinson, T., Munter, P., and Grant J., *Financial Statement Analysis*, Pearson/Prentice Hall, New Jersey, 2004.

Romney, M. and Steinbert, P., *Accounting Information Systems*, 10th ed., Pearson/Prentice Hall, New Jersey, 2006.

Roslender, R., *Sociological Perspectives on Modern Accountancy*, Routledge, London, 1992.

Rutherford, B.A., *An Introduction to Modern Financial Reporting Theory*, Paul Chapman, London, 2000.

Soffer, L, and Soffer, R., *Financial Statement Analysis: A Valuation Analysis*, Prentice Hall, New Jersey, 2003.

Solomon, J and Solomon, A., *Corporate Governance and Accountability*, John Wiley & Sons Ltd., Chichester, 2004.

Sutton, T., *Corporate Financial Accounting and Reporting*, 2nd ed., Financial Times/Prentice Hall, London, 2004.

Thompson, J., and Martin, F., *Strategic Management: Awareness and Change*, 5th ed., Thomson, London, 2005.

Walton, P., Haller, A. and Raffournier, B., *International Accounting*, 2nd ed., Thomson, London, 2003.

Watts, R.L., Corporate Financial Statements: A Product of the Market and Political Process, *Australian Journal of Management*, 2, pp. 53–75, 1997.

Weston, J., Mitchell, M. and Mulherin, J., *Takeovers, Restructuring and Corporate Governance*, 4th ed., Pearson/Prentice Hall, New Jersey, 2004.

White, G.I., Sondhi, A.C. and Fried, D., *The Analysis and Use of Financial Statements*, 2nd ed., Wiley, New York, 1997.

APPENDIX 1

TESCO

ANNUAL REPORT AND FINANCIAL STATEMENTS 2005

CONTENTS

Tesco works hard to create value for customers to earn their lifetime loyalty.

We do this in each of the four parts of our strategy:

- Core UK
- International
- Non-food
- Retailing services

highlights

financials:

	Growth on 2004 53 weeks	Growth on 2004 52 weeks pro forma
Group sales	+10.5%	+12.4%
Underlying Group profit before tax[†]	+18.8%	+20.5%
Group profit before tax	+22.6%	+24.5%
Underlying diluted earnings per share[†]	+12.2%	
Diluted earnings per share	+17.2%	
Dividend per share	+10.5%	

	2005 52 weeks	2004 53 weeks	2004 52 weeks pro forma
Group sales (£m) (including value added tax)	37,070	33,557	32,989
Underlying Group profit before tax[†] (£m)	2,029	1,708	1,684
Group profit before tax (£m)	1,962	1,600	1,576
Underlying diluted earnings per share[†] (p)	18.30	16.31	
Diluted earnings per share (p)	17.50	14.93	
Dividend per share (p)	7.56	6.84	
Group enterprise value (£m) (market capitalisation plus net debt)	27,853	23,866	
Return on capital employed[#]	11.5%	10.4%	

[†]Excluding net profit/(loss) on disposal of fixed assets, integration costs and goodwill amortisation.

[#]2004 – restated as a result of UITF 38 and UITF 17 (revised), previously 10.5%. See note 1.

Operating and financial review

This operating and financial review analyses the performance of
the Tesco Group in the financial year ended 26 February 2005. It
also explains other aspects of the Group's results and operations,
including strategy and risk management.

SALES PERFORMANCE
£m

GROUP ■
UK ■

19,711 21,454 23,101 26,876 29,511

22,585 25,401 28,280 33,557 37,070

01 02 03 04 05

01 02 03 04 05
UK SALES GROWTH %

■ TOTAL
■ LIKE-FOR-LIKE
■ 53rd WEEK

8.4 8.8 7.7 14.2 16.3
4.7 6.0 4.0 6.7 9.0
             11.9

Group summary

	2005 52 wks £m	2004 53 wks £m	Change %
Group sales (including value added tax)	37,070	33,557	10.5
Underlying profit on ordinary activities before tax[†]	2,029	1,708	18.8
Profit on ordinary activities before taxation	1,962	1,600	22.6
Underlying diluted earnings per share (p)[†]	18.30	16.31	12.2
Diluted earnings per share (p)	17.50	14.93	17.2
Dividend per share (p)	7.56	6.84	10.5

UK performance

	2005 52 wks £m	2004 53 wks £m	Change %
Sales (including value added tax)	29,511	26,876	9.8
Underlying operating profit[†]	1,694	1,526	11.0
Operating margin[‡]	6.2%	6.2%	

Rest of Europe performance

	2005 52 wks £m	2004 53 wks £m	Change %
Sales (including value added tax)	4,349	3,834	13.4
Underlying operating profit[†]	218	184	18.5
Operating margin[‡]	5.7%	5.4%	

Asia performance

	2005 £m	2004 £m	Change %
Sales (including value added tax)	3,210	2,847	12.8
Underlying operating profit[†]	152	122	24.6
Operating margin[‡]	5.0%	4.6%	

[†] Excluding net profit/(loss) on disposal of fixed assets,
integration costs and goodwill amortisation.

[‡] Operating margin is calculated using sales excluding
value added tax.

Strategy The Group's four-part strategy –
to grow the core UK business, be as strong in
non-food as in food, develop retailing services
and become a successful international retailer,
was laid down in 1997 and it has been the
foundation of Tesco's success in recent years.
Our performance this year demonstrates this
very well. Our new growth businesses – in
international, in non-food and in retailing
services – have contributed as much profit
as the entire business was making in 1997.

We have continued to make strong progress
with all four parts of our strategy – by keeping
our focus on trying to improve what we do
for customers:

- making their shopping trip
  as easy as possible
- constantly seeking to reduce our
  prices to help them spend less
- offering the convenience of
  either large or small stores
- bringing simplicity and value
  to complicated markets.

Group performance Group sales, including VAT,
increased by 10.5% to £37.1bn (2004 – £33.6bn).
At constant exchange rates, sales grew by 11.5%.
Group underlying pre-tax profit increased by
18.8% to £2,029m (2004 – £1,708m).

UK Sales increased by 9.8% to £29.5bn. On a
52 week basis sales increased by 11.9%, with
like-for-like growth of 9.0% (including volume of
8.9%) and 2.9% from net new stores. Inflation of
0.1% was entirely driven by cost increases in our
petrol business. We saw deflation in our stores
as we invested in lower prices for customers.

Petrol had a significant impact on sales growth
in the year, with volumes growing exceptionally
strongly from the second quarter onwards, helped
by our efforts to keep fuel prices down during a
period of rising oil prices. Like-for-like sales growth
during the year, excluding petrol, was 7.5%.

During the second half, like-for-like sales increased by 9.5% including petrol and by 7.4%, excluding petrol.

UK underlying operating profit was 11.0% higher at £1,694m (2004 – £1,526m). The operating margin was maintained at 6.2%.

International Total international sales grew by 13.1% to £7.6bn and by 18.3% at constant exchange rates. International operations contributed £370m to underlying operating profit, up 20.9% on last year, with operating margins rising to 5.4% (2004 – 5.1%). At constant exchange rates, international profit grew by 26.5%.

In the **Rest of Europe**, sales rose by 13.4% to £4.3bn (2004 – £3.8bn). At constant exchange rates, sales grew by 15.7%. Underlying operating profit increased by 18.5% to £218m (2004 – £184m). In Asia, sales grew by 12.8% to £3.2bn (2004 – £2.8bn). At constant exchange rates, sales grew by 21.8%. Underlying operating profit increased by 24.6% to £152m (2004 – £122m).

Joint Ventures and Associates Our total share of profit (excluding goodwill amortisation) for the year was £135m compared to £99m last year. Tesco Personal Finance pre-tax profit post minority interest was £202m, of which our share was £101m, up 26.5% on last year.

Net interest payable was £170m (2004 – £223m), giving cover of 12.5 times (2004 – 8.2 times). Tax has been charged at an effective rate of 30.2% (2004 – 31.1%). Prior to accounting for the net profit on disposal of fixed assets, resulting mainly from the property joint venture with Topland announced in March 2004, as well as goodwill amortisation and integration costs, our underlying tax rate was 29.5% (2004 – 29.5%).

Underlying diluted earnings per share increased by 12.2% to 18.30p (2004 – 16.31p).

Cash Flow and Balance Sheet The Group generated net cash of £121m during the year, benefiting from a strong operating cash inflow of £3bn, after an additional £200m contribution to the Group pension scheme and the net proceeds of £646m from our property joint venture with Topland. Net debt reduced to £3.8bn at the year end, representing gearing of 43% (2004 – 51%).

After year end we generated around £350m from our most recent property joint venture with the Consensus Business Group.

Group capital expenditure during the year (excluding acquisitions but including the ten Safeway stores purchased from Morrisons) was £2.4bn (2004 – £2.3bn). We expect Group capital expenditure to be around £2.4bn this year. UK capital expenditure was £1.7bn (2004 – £1.5bn), including £835m on new stores and £288m on extensions and refits. Total international capital expenditure was £746m (2004 – £765m) comprising £282m in Asia and £464m in Europe.

Dividends The Board has proposed a final dividend of 5.27p per share (2004 – 4.77p). This represents an increase of 10.5%. Together with the interim dividend of 2.29p (2004 – 2.07p) already paid, this brings the full year dividend to 7.56p, also an increase of 10.5% on last year. The final dividend will be paid on 1 July 2005 to shareholders on the Register of Members at the close of business on 22 April 2005. Shareholders will continue to have the right to receive the dividend in the form of fully paid ordinary shares instead of cash. The first day of dealing in the new shares will be 1 July 2005.

Total Shareholder Return Total Shareholder Returns (TSR), which is measured as the percentage change in the share price, plus the dividend paid, has increased by 108.7% over the last five years, compared to the decrease in the FTSE 100 average of 6.2%. Over the last three years, Tesco TSR has been 34.5%, compared to the FTSE 100 average of 8.8%. In the last year, the return in Tesco was 25.1%, compared to the FTSE 100 average of 15.0%.

Return on Capital Employed (ROCE). At the time of our share placing in January 2004, we believed we could increase our 2002/03 financial year post tax ROCE of 10.2% by up to 200 basis points over five years based on then current plans. The excellent progress we have made in the year, combined with the effect of the Topland property funding initiative, means that post tax ROCE rose to 11.5%.

| | 01 | 02 | 03 | 04 | 05 |
Group: 1,944 / 2,027 / 2,134 / 2,285 / 2,417
UK: 1,206 / 1,276 / 1,228 / 1,520 / 1,671

CAPITAL EXPENDITURE
£m

GROUP ■
UK ■

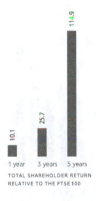

114.9 / 25.7 / 10.1

1 year   3 years   5 years

TOTAL SHAREHOLDER RETURN
RELATIVE TO THE FTSE 100

| 01 | 02 | 03 | 04 | 05 |
1,298 / 1,296 / 1,433 / 1,778 / 1,519

UK SALES AREA OPENED
000 sq ft

3

Operating and financial review continued

NUMBER OF INTERNATIONAL
HYPERMARKETS

INTERNATIONAL
UNDERLYING OPERATING
PROFIT
£m

TESCO PERSONAL FINANCE
PRE-TAX PROFIT POST
MINORITY INTEREST
£m

IFRS We are well advanced with our preparations for the adoption of International Financial Reporting Standards (IFRS) for our 2005/06 financial reporting. As communicated at our IFRS presentation in February 2005, the main changes to our profit and shareholders' funds will arise from accounting changes for share-based payments, goodwill, pensions, deferred tax, financial instruments and fixed assets. Details of the presentation can be found on our website www.tesco.com/corporate

In May 2005 we will issue 2004/05 financial information restated for IFRS. We estimate that the adoption of IFRS will have a small impact on 2004/05 statutory profit after tax (between zero and £30m). This impact excludes the effect of IAS 32 and IAS 39, where Tesco has elected to take a one year exemption on these standards, as allowed under IFRS.

Year End Convergence We announced in September 2004 that we had taken a decision to align our UK and International accounting periods, due to the increasing contribution our international businesses make to Group results. We will do this for the 2006 year end, which will be on 2 April 2006. Thereafter, the timetable will be as follows:

- Half year – last Sunday in September/first Sunday in October
- Year end – first Sunday in April
- 13 week quarters, with trading updates for Q1 and Q3 (Q3 to include Christmas trading period).

Employees With over 353,000 staff in 13 countries, and a further 14,000 retail employees working in our joint venture in China, we play an important role in creating employment, fostering skills and generating economic development. This year alone our UK workforce, already the largest in the UK private sector, grew by 14,000 and we also created 12,000 jobs in our international operations.

Our people are our most important asset. Looking after our people so that they can look after our customers is one of the core values of our business. We are committed to providing market-leading working conditions for our staff and we encourage our suppliers to do the same.

In the UK we offer staff an attractive benefits package, including wages that are amongst the highest in our industry, flexible hours and leave, profit sharing, subsidised meals, childcare vouchers and an award-winning pension scheme. Staff with more than 12 months' service receive 10% discount on their shopping at Tesco.

Shares in Success Almost a third of Tesco's shareholders – over 86,000 people – are members of staff. Our Shares in Success scheme this year gave £65m worth of shares to employees across the Group. In addition, our Save-as-You-Earn scheme, which gives employees the opportunity to buy shares at a 20% discount, resulted in a further £104m worth of shares being issued to staff during the year.

Pensions We are convinced our award-winning defined benefit pension scheme helps us to attract and retain the best staff. The UK scheme has nearly 137,000 members – nearly 60% of eligible staff. All eligible staff are encouraged to join the scheme as soon as they join Tesco. Approximately 1,200 staff join the scheme every month.

The last full actuarial valuation of the main Tesco PLC Pension Scheme was carried out as at 31 March 2002 and the next valuation will be performed as at 31 March 2005.

Ahead of the 2005 three-yearly full actuarial valuation of the scheme, which will be completed this autumn, the Group has paid an additional cash contribution into the scheme of £200m to strengthen significantly its funding position. We will review the level of contributions to the scheme when the actuarial valuation has been completed.

Details of the last full actuarial valuation can be seen in note 27(a). In line with accounting standards, a separate FRS 17 valuation has been performed as at the Group year end date. The FRS 17 disclosures can be found in note 27(b).

Training and Development We are committed to developing our people to bring out the best in everyone. Our staff have access to training programmes and a personal development plan, with six-monthly reviews, to ensure they have the right skills to do their job. This commitment is equally important in our international businesses, where we aim to build local workforce skills and promote from within.

Diversity We try to ensure that at all times and in every aspect of employment, including recruitment, training and development, everybody receives the same treatment, regardless of factors such as gender, age, colour, creed, race, ethnic origin, disability, marital status, religion or belief, trade union membership or sexual preference and orientation.

Core UK business UK sales grew by 11.9% in the year, on a 52 week basis, including a like-for-like increase of 9.0%. Over two million more customers are choosing to shop at Tesco today compared with a year ago, with most of the growth coming from our existing stores. Average spend per visit (excluding Express convenience stores) is also up – by over 2% – despite deflation in our stores, reflecting the success of our efforts to improve our inclusive offer on all fronts.

We have continued to invest in the things that matter for customers. For example:

- On-shelf availability has improved significantly during the year. Our measure of this, which is based on our in-store picking of Tesco.com orders, shows that availability improved by a full percentage point compared with last year.

- Self-service checkouts, which save time for customers, are now in over 100 stores, with over half a million shoppers now regularly using them.

- We have again strengthened our position as the UK's best value retailer by investing £230m in improving our price position through a series of price campaigns during the year. A further £67m of cuts were announced in early April 2005.

- The development of our Value brand continues and the range now extends to 2,200 products, including many non-food items. Our Finest range also continues to develop, with 400 new lines launched in the year, bringing the total to 2,300.

Tesco re-invests efficiency savings for the benefit of our customers. Our Step-Change programme has delivered savings this year of £270m, on top of almost £200m achieved last year.

We have made good progress with the development of our store formats. During the second half, we opened our 100th Extra hypermarket in the UK, having opened the first at Pitsea in only 1997. We anticipate being able to open up to 20 new Extras a year, mostly through extensions to existing superstores.

The new Extra stores at Dumfries, Stockport and Stafford, which opened in the year, were part of a programme of regeneration development partnerships, bringing jobs and modern retail standards to deprived urban areas. We have nine more such projects currently under development.

Across the country more customers have access to our Express convenience stores as we bring the Tesco offer and lower prices to new neighbourhoods. Over four million of our customers

walk to their local Tesco as a result of the growth of Express. We converted 202 T&S stores during the year, bringing the total number of Express stores to 546.

A further 26 T&S stores will be converted this year. Thereafter, the expansion of Express will be mainly through organic growth, with the One Stop fascia retained as a successful convenience format in over 500 smaller stores.

We have also completed the conversion to Express of the Adminstore stores in London (Cullens, Europa and Harts). On average, these stores have seen sales more than double and are nearly 20% above our forecasts.

A total of 1.5m sq ft of new sales area was opened during the year across all formats, of which 350,000 sq ft was in extensions to existing stores. This includes the ten former Safeway stores which we acquired last autumn – sales in these stores have almost doubled and are also nearly 20% above our forecasts.

Looking forward, we are aiming to maintain our rate of growth in selling area, from a combination of extensions and new stores.

We are planning a more normal year in terms of like-for-like sales growth and we are keeping an eye on costs, especially energy, with oil prices up 70% year on year, and the huge rise in business rates.

Non-food We have made further progress with our non-food offer. Sales growth, in the UK alone, was 17% during the year with total non-food sales increasing to £6.0bn (2004 – £5.1bn). Volume growth was even higher at 18%.

In all our large non-food categories we have seen strong growth. For example, our home entertainment sales grew by 20% and the stationery, news and magazines category by 26%. We saw particularly good performance from many of our seasonal non-food ranges up 27%.

Our clothing brands Cherokee and Florence + Fred have once again achieved significant growth, and remain the fastest expanding in the UK market in both value and volume. Clothing sales grew by 28% in the year. The fashion press has again regularly featured our products.

Retailing services Our efforts to try to bring simplicity and value to sometimes complicated markets are behind the success of our retailing services businesses.

In Telecoms, we now have a million customer accounts after only one full year of operation. We entered the broadband internet access market in August. We now have a very competitive offer in mobiles, domestic fixed line and internet access with considerable scope for future growth. The business, which is still in its start-up phase, made a small operating loss of £4m.

5

Operating and financial review continued

Tesco.com sales grew by 24.1% to £719m and profits increased by 51.8% to £36m. During the year, we added eDiets and Legal Store to the tesco.com offer, as well as a significant expansion in the non-food ranges available online.

Tesco Personal Finance (TPF) total profit has increased by 26.5% to £202m (2004 – £160m) of which our share is £101m. TPF is providing excellent returns in only its seventh year. £100m of surplus capital, representing 20% of the original investment in the joint venture, was returned to Tesco and Royal Bank of Scotland through a cash dividend. We now have almost five million customer accounts, an increase of 700,000 on last year.

International Our international operations have continued to make good progress, delivering strong profit growth and improving returns.

These businesses are well adapted to the needs of their local customers. They are run by strong local management teams who share Tesco Group expertise. In almost every country we are continuing to grow market share as we build our store networks and improve our like-for-like sales.

At constant exchange rates, sales increased by 18.3% in the year. At actual rates, sales grew by 13.1% to £7.6bn. Profit grew by 20.9% to £370m, with operating margins rising to 5.4% (2004 – 5.1%). At constant exchange rates, international profit grew by 26.5%.

International returns continue to rise. On a constant currency basis, cash return on investment (CROI) has increased to 11%, despite a high level of immature capital. CROI on like-for-like stores in our four largest international businesses – Thailand, Korea, Ireland and Hungary – where 60% of our international capital is invested, is running at over 15%. This demonstrates that our international model is not only delivering good growth but also developing good returns as we gain strong market positions, and our stores mature.

A total of 98 stores with 3.1m sq ft of selling area were opened during the year, including 47 hypermarkets. In addition we acquired 25 Fre'c stores in Japan, and since the end of the financial year we purchased 12 stores in Korea from Arum Mart. We plan to open 207 new stores, adding 5.4m sq ft of selling area.

In September, we successfully completed the acquisition of a 50% holding in Ting Hsin's Hymall business in China, extending our presence into Asia's largest market. Hymall now trades from 31 hypermarkets, and will open its first store in Beijing this summer as part of an enlarged new store development programme of 15 hypermarkets. Since the joint venture was established, Hymall's sales have grown strongly and the business made a small profit, of which our share, £1m, is included in our share of operating profit of Joint Ventures and Associates.

Our formats are rapidly being rolled out in our key international markets. With our large destination store networks now well-established and with first class supply chain infrastructure in place in many of our main markets, a growing part of our new space is coming through our smaller formats, such as compact hypermarkets and convenience stores. These serve the needs of customers in smaller catchments, as well as costing less to build.

At the end of the year, our international operations were trading from 585 stores, including 273 hypermarkets, with a total of 27.6m sq ft of selling space.

Rest of Europe Sales increased by 15.7% at constant exchange rates and by 13.4% at actual exchange rates. Profits grew by 18.5% at actual exchange rates and by 21.4% at constant exchange rates.

- In **Hungary**, we have grown our business in a more difficult economic and retail environment. We have strengthened our market leading position by lowering prices, expanding our store network and developing our infrastructure. We opened nine new stores in the year, adding 13% to our total space. In the current year, a further 14 stores with 688,000 sq ft of sales area are planned. In September, we opened our new 226,000 sq ft fresh food distribution centre at Gyál, which now accounts for over 95% of our volume.

- In **Poland**, the economic background is improving and signs of renewed consumer confidence, combined with an improving offer, have been reflected in strengthening like-for-like sales. We have invested significantly in cutting prices during the year. Our business is strong, we are growing market share and we remain well placed to benefit from a sustained economic upturn. The performance of the former HIT stores has been particularly pleasing. 95% of our volume now goes through our two new central distribution centres – our 400,000 sq ft ambient depot which opened in January 2004 and our new 160,000 sq ft fresh depot which opened in March 2005.

- In the **Republic of Ireland**, we have again traded well. Sales growth has benefited from strong like-for-like performance and an acceleration in the growth of our space. We opened seven new stores with 202,000 sq ft of new sales area, an increase of 11%. A further six new stores, with 108,000 sq ft of sales area, are planned for the following year. Our new formats, led by Ireland's first Extra at Clare Hall, Dublin, have all been very well received by customers.

- In recent months we have been meeting the more competitive market conditions in the **Czech Republic** with our largest ever programme of price reductions and promotions. This has involved substantial investment, paid for by higher sales and the benefits of improved buying and improved productivity. We have also accelerated our new store development, with three openings in the year, including one compact hypermarket, and a further eight openings planned this year, so that over two years we will have added 26% to our space. Profits grew by over 20% during the year.

- We have taken similar action in **Slovakia** where we have a strong market position. Customers quickly responded to our lower prices, with like-for-like sales showing an immediate improvement. Our new store programme is now supported by the growth of our compact hypermarket format. We now have five such stores, with five more planned. Our new fresh food central distribution depot at Beckov will open this summer.

- In **Turkey**, we have traded well, achieving good sales growth, improved margins and had a strong profit increase, whilst lowering prices and raising staff levels in our Kipa stores. Our first new store, a 55,000 sq ft hypermarket at Bodrum, will open in June 2005.

Asia Sales increased by 21.8% at constant exchange rates and by 12.8% at actual exchange rates. Profits rose by 24.6% at actual exchange rates and by 34.2% at constant exchange rates.

- Lotus has made further good progress in **Thailand**, delivering strong sales, profit and market share growth despite a slowing economy and some restriction on hypermarket opening hours. We now have 107 stores trading across four formats, including 46 Express stores and 12 Value stores. All the newer formats are performing well, giving us more opportunities to develop our national store network.

- In **Korea**, Homeplus has continued to make excellent progress, delivering increased sales, including solid like-for-like growth, profits and returns. During the year, we opened three new hypermarkets, and since year end, we opened our first 45,000 sq ft compact hypermarket in Namdaegu. We also introduced the Express convenience format and we now have seven stores trading. Following year end, we acquired 12 stores in Pusan, from Arum Mart. Our organic store development programme is accelerating, with a total of 31 stores, with 550,000 sq ft of space, planned for the current year.

- In **Taiwan**, our stores have made good progress in the year, delivering strong sales performance, increased market share and sharply reduced losses. We opened our fifth hypermarket, in Ching Hai, and in the current year our sixth in Hsin Tien.

- In **Malaysia**, we have seen strong sales growth and with five new stores under construction, including two hypermarkets, and more sites in the pipeline, we are making good progress towards building scale. We anticipate trading from 11 stores by the end of 2005. Our sixth hypermarket, with 107,000 sq ft of space, opened in Penang, in December.

- In **Japan**, C Two-Network completed its acquisition of 25 Fre'c stores in August. We are making good progress with the integration of the two businesses, combining Fre'c's expertise in fresh foods with C Two's excellent grocery operation to improve the overall offer for customers. The business now trades from 104 stores, with 15 new stores planned for 2005.

Corporate social responsibility As a responsible company, we work hard to bring real benefits to the communities we serve, the environment and the economy. Our commitment is embedded in the way we run our business.

Communities We are committed to making a difference to the communities around us in many different ways. For example, every year we adopt a Charity of the Year to support and in 2004 our staff and customers raised £3m for Help the Hospices. This year we will be supporting Age Concern.

Healthy Living Our customers tell us that they want us to make healthy living easier, so we are further improving the labelling of our products, increasing our Healthy Living own brand range to nearly 500 lines and reducing salt content in many of our products. We are trying to help keep the nation active and were the main sponsor of Cancer Research UK's Race for Life. Over 18,000 of our staff took part, raising over £20m for the charity. We are again sponsoring Race for Life and supporting a new event that will encourage men to take part for the first time. The Tesco Charity Trust adds 20% to money raised by our staff for charity.

Environment Our award winning store regeneration partnerships in deprived areas have now helped 2,000 long-term unemployed people back into work through our unique jobs and training guarantee. We completed three schemes this year, bringing the total to 12, and have another nine planned. To help protect our open spaces, we used brownfield (previously developed) land for over 96% of all new store developments.

Tsunami Support As our staff and customers would expect, we were one of the first companies to react to the tsunami tragedy in South East Asia. Within hours of the disaster, we made a donation to the British Red Cross. Our total donations are over £310,000 so far, from across the Group. A two day collection in our UK stores for the British Red Cross and our own in-store collections raised a total of £2.8m. As well as money, we provided lorry loads of food, water and shelter materials in Thailand, Malaysia and Sri Lanka.

Suppliers Tesco welcomed the findings of the recent review by the Office of Fair Trading (OFT) of the Supplier Code of Practice. After a lengthy independent audit of the workings of the code, the OFT announced in March that no breaches of the code had been found at Tesco and that consumers benefit from vigorous market competition on both quality

Operating and financial review continued

and price. Building on the constructive relationships we have with our suppliers, we recently conducted an anonymous supplier survey to understand what is good and where we can improve. The results were very positive, and although they show we are not perfect, the majority of our suppliers think we are professional, committed to our customers, fair and consistent.

Financial risks and treasury management The treasury function is mandated by the Board to manage the financial risks that arise in relation to underlying business needs. The Board establishes the function's policies and operating parameters, and routinely reviews its activities, which are also subject to regular audit. The function does not operate as a profit centre and the undertaking of speculative transactions is not permitted.

The main financial risks faced by the Group relate to the availability of funds to meet business needs, the risk of default by counterparties to financial transactions (credit risk), and fluctuations in interest and foreign exchange rates. These risks are managed as described below. The balance sheet positions at 26 February 2005 are representative of the positions throughout the year.

Funding and liquidity The Group finances its operations by a combination of retained profits, long- and medium-term debt capital market issues, commercial paper, bank borrowings and leases. The objective is to ensure continuity of funding. The policy is to smooth the debt maturity profile, to arrange funding ahead of requirements and to maintain sufficient undrawn committed bank facilities, and a strong credit rating so that maturing debt may be refinanced as it falls due.

The Group's long-term credit rating remained stable during the year. Tesco Group is rated A1 by Moody's and A+ by Standard and Poor's. New funding of £1,231m was arranged during the year, including a net £740m from property Joint Ventures, £368m from long-term bank debt and £123m from new medium-term notes. At the year end net debt was £3.8bn (2004 – £4.1bn) and the average debt maturity was eight years (2004 – nine years).

Interest rate risk management The objective is to limit our exposure to increases in interest rates while retaining the opportunity to benefit from interest rate reductions. Forward rate agreements, interest rate swaps, caps and collars are used to achieve the desired mix of fixed and floating rate debt. The policy is to fix or cap a minimum of 40% of actual and projected debt interest costs. At the year end, £2.6bn, 67% of net debt was in fixed rate form (2004 – £2.9bn, 71%) with a further £745m, 19% of net debt, collared or capped as detailed in note 21. Fixed rate debt includes £454m of funding linked to the Retail Price Index (2004 – £441m).

This debt reduces interest risk by diversifying our funding portfolio. The balance of our debt is in floating rate form.

The average rate of interest paid during the year was 5.4% excluding Joint Venture interest (2004 – 5.4%). A 1% movement in UK interest rates would change profit before tax by less than 1%.

Foreign currency risk management Our principal objective is to reduce the risk to short-term profits of exchange rate volatility. Transactional currency exposures that could significantly impact the profit and loss account are hedged, typically using forward purchases or sales of foreign currencies and currency options. At the year end forward foreign currency transactions equivalent to £479m were outstanding (2004 – £240m). See note 21.

We hedge the majority of our investment in our international subsidiaries via foreign exchange transactions in matching currencies. Our objective is to maintain a low cost of borrowing and hedge against material movements in our balance sheet value. During the year currency movements increased the net value of the Group's overseas assets by £19m (2004 – £157m decrease).

We translate overseas profits at average exchange rates which we do not currently seek to hedge.

Credit risk The objective is to reduce the risk of loss arising from default by parties to financial transactions. The risk is managed by spreading financial transactions across an approved list of counterparties of high credit quality. The Group's positions with these counterparties and their credit ratings are routinely monitored.

Tesco Personal Finance (TPF) TPF lending is predominantly to individuals through its credit card and unsecured personal loan products. TPF has also developed a significant insurance business, with motor insurance a major component. TPF risk is managed by observing and adopting industry best practices and drawing upon the expertise and systems of the Royal Bank of Scotland Group, including its subsidiary, Direct Line. All policies pertaining to risk within TPF are subject to the governance procedures of The Royal Bank of Scotland Group and ratified by the TPF Board, which has representation from both Tesco and The Royal Bank of Scotland Group. This has delivered a portfolio of products with strong asset quality. This asset quality is maintained through proactive risk management both at the time of acquisition and ongoing account maintenance.

8

Directors' report

During the year TPF changed its mechanism for hedging interest rate risk from the use of derivatives to cash instruments. This had the effect of increasing both the assets and liabilities in the TPF balance sheet by approximately £2bn as at the TPF year end of 31 December 2004.

The Tesco Group would support its 50% share of any further funding TPF may require to sustain liquidity ratios. However, we believe that provisions for bad debts and insurance losses (supported by the re-insurance of significant risks) are at prudent levels.

Insurance We have taken the decision to purchase Assets, Earnings and Combined Liability protection from the open insurance market at a 'catastrophe' level only. The risk not transferred to the insurance market is retained within the business up to various limits, with the balance self insured on a multinational basis by use of our captive insurance companies, Tesco Insurance Limited in Guernsey and Valiant Insurance Company Limited in the Republic of Ireland. Tesco Insurance Limited covers Assets and Earnings, while Valiant Insurance Company Limited covers Combined Liability.

Other information Additional financial and non-financial information, including press releases and year end presentations can be accessed on our website, www.tesco.com/corporate and in our Corporate Responsibility Review 2005.

The Directors present their annual report to shareholders on the affairs of the Group, together with the audited consolidated financial statements of the Group for the year ended 26 February 2005.

Principal activity and business review The principal activity of the Group is the operation of food stores and associated activities in the UK, Republic of Ireland, Hungary, Poland, Czech Republic, Slovakia, Turkey, Thailand, South Korea, Taiwan, Malaysia and Japan. During the year, we entered into a Joint Venture in China, through an investment of £145m in Hymall. A review of the business is contained in the Annual Review and Summary Financial Statement 2005 which is published separately and, together with this document, comprises the full Tesco PLC Annual Report and Financial Statements.

Group results Group sales including VAT rose by £3,513m to £37,070m, representing an increase of 10.5%. Group underlying profit on ordinary activities before taxation, net profit/(loss) on disposal of fixed assets, integration costs and goodwill amortisation was £2,029m, compared with £1,708m for the previous year, an increase of 18.8%. Including net profit on disposal of fixed assets, integration costs and goodwill amortisation, Group profit on ordinary activities before taxation was £1,962m. The amount allocated to the employee profit-sharing scheme this year was £65m, against £57m last year. After provision for tax of £593m, minority interests of £3m and dividends, paid and proposed, of £587m, profit retained for the financial year amounted to £779m.

Dividends The Directors recommend the payment of a final dividend of 5.27p per ordinary share, to be paid on 1 July 2005 to members on the Register at the close of business on 22 April 2005. Together with the interim dividend of 2.29p per ordinary share paid in November 2004, the total for the year will be 7.56p compared with 6.84p for the previous year, an increase of 10.5%.

Tangible fixed assets Capital expenditure amounted to £2,417m compared with £2,285m the previous year. In the Directors' opinion, the properties of the Group have a market value in excess of the book value of £13,175m included in these financial statements. In the year we received £646m from our new property Joint Venture with Topland.

Share capital The authorised and called-up share capital of the company, together with details of the shares allotted during the period, are shown in note 24 to the financial statements. Details of investments held in Tesco PLC are shown in note 25 in the financial statements.

Directors' report continued

Company's shareholders The company is not aware of any ordinary shareholders with interests of 3% or more.

Directors and their interests The names and biographical details of the present Directors are set out in the separately published Annual Review and Summary Financial Statement 2005.

Mrs K R Cook and Ms C McCall were appointed to the Board in the last twelve months and, as required by the Articles of Association, offer themselves for election. Mr R F Chase, Sir Terry Leahy, Mr T J R Mason and Mr D T Potts retire from the Board by rotation and, being eligible, offer themselves for re-election.

The interests of Directors and their immediate families in the shares of Tesco PLC, along with details of Directors' share options, are contained in the Directors' remuneration report set out on pages 511–25.

At no time during the year did any of the Directors have a material interest in any significant contract with the company or any of its subsidiaries.

A third party indemnity provision as defined in Section 309B(1) of the Companies Act 1985 is in force for the benefit of each of the Directors and the Company Secretary (who is also a Director of certain subsidiaries of the company) and remains in force in favour of Ms V Morali and Mr G F Pimlott who are retiring Non-executive Directors.

Employment policies The Group depends on the skills and commitment of its employees in order to achieve its objectives. Staff at every level are encouraged to make their fullest possible contribution to Tesco success.

A key business priority is to deliver an 'Every little helps' shopping experience for customers. Ongoing training programmes seek to ensure that employees understand the Group's customer service objectives and strive to achieve them.

The Group's selection, training, development and promotion policies ensure equal opportunities for all employees regardless of factors such as gender, marital status, race, age, sexual preference and orientation, colour, creed, ethnic origin, religion or belief, or disability. All decisions are based on merit.

Internal communications are designed to ensure that employees are well informed about the business of the Group. These include a UK staff magazine called 'one team' and the equivalents in our overseas businesses, videos and staff briefing sessions.

Staff opinions are frequently researched through surveys and store visits. We work to deliver 'Every little helps' for all our people across the Group.

Employees are encouraged to become involved in the financial performance of the Group through a variety of schemes, principally the Tesco employee profit-sharing scheme (Shares-in-Success), the savings-related share option scheme (Save-As-You-Earn) and the partnership share plan (Buy-As-You-Earn).

Political and charitable donations Cash donations to charities amounted to £4,576,210 (2004 – £3,953,582). Contributions to community projects including gifts in kind, staff time and management costs, amounted to £21,762,931 (2004 – £17,191,988).

There were no political donations (2004 – nil). During the year the Group made contributions of £40,929 (2004 – £44,713) in the form of sponsorship for political events: Labour Party – £9,250; Conservative Party – £5,132; Liberal Democrat Party – £5,350; Plaid Cymru – £1,000; Fianna Fáil – £1,340; Fine Gael – £1,667; Progressive Democrats – £2,190; Usdaw – £15,000. Contributions were made to trade unions in the Czech and Slovak Republics of £957 and £847, respectively.

Supplier payment policy Tesco PLC is a signatory to the CBI Code of Prompt Payment. Copies of the Code may be obtained from the CBI, Centre Point, 103 New Oxford Street, London WC1A 1DU. Payment terms and conditions are agreed with suppliers in advance.

Tesco PLC has no trade creditors in its balance sheet. The Group pays its creditors on a pay on time basis which varies according to the type of product and territory in which the suppliers operate.

Going concern The Directors consider that the Group and the company have adequate resources to remain in operation for the foreseeable future and have therefore continued to adopt the going concern basis in preparing the financial statements. As with all business forecasts, the Directors' statement cannot guarantee that the going concern basis will remain appropriate given the inherent uncertainty about future events.

Auditors A resolution to re-appoint PricewaterhouseCoopers LLP as auditors of the company and Group will be proposed at the Annual General Meeting.

Annual general meeting A separate circular accompanying the Annual Review and Summary Financial Statement 2005 explains the special business to be considered at the Annual General Meeting on 24 June 2005.

By Order of the Board
Ms Lucy Neville-Rolfe Company Secretary
11 April 2005

Tesco PLC
Registered Number: 445790

Corporate governance

Directors' report on corporate governance We are committed to the highest standards of corporate governance. We recognise that good governance helps the business to deliver our strategy and safeguard shareholders' long-term interests. We believe that the revised Combined Code provides a useful guide from which to review corporate governance within the Group. This statement describes the Board's approach to corporate governance.

Board composition and independence As at 26 February 2005, the Board of Tesco PLC comprised six Executive Directors and eight independent Non-executive Directors, and Mr D E Reid, the Non-executive Chairman. Mr D E Reid's appointment as Non-executive Chairman commenced on 2 April 2004 and was confirmed by shareholders at the AGM in June 2004. He has primary responsibility for running the Board. The Chief Executive, Sir Terry Leahy, has executive responsibilities for the operations, results and strategic development of the Group. Clear divisions of accountability and responsibility exist and operate effectively for these positions. Mr R F Chase became Deputy Chairman and Senior Independent Non-executive Director on 1 March 2004. The structure of the Board and the integrity of the individual Directors ensure that no one individual or group dominates the decision-making process.

Changes to the membership of the Board were announced last year as part of an ongoing process to ensure that the balance of the Board reflects the evolving needs of the business. Mrs K R Cook joined as a Non-executive Director on 1 October 2004. Ms V Morali retired from the Board on 26 February 2005. Ms C McCall joined the Board on 1 March 2005. The process for nomination and appointment is set out in the Nominations Committee report on page 506.

The Board requires all Non-executive Directors to be independent in their judgement. In our view, all Non-executive Directors meet this requirement. Mr G F Pimlott has served as a Non-executive Director at Tesco for 12 years and retires from the Board in May 2005. He has, again, provided excellent independent advice and challenge throughout the year in his capacity as a Non-executive Director. During the year he resigned from the Audit Committee, Nominations Committee and Remuneration Committee.

Board responsibilities The Board meets nine times a year and annually devotes two days to a conference with senior executives on performance and longer-term planning giving consideration both to the opportunities and risks of future strategy. The Board has set out clearly the Schedule of Matters Reserved for the Board in order to ensure overall control of the Group's affairs. These include the approval of

financial statements, major acquisitions and disposals, authority levels for expenditure, treasury policies, risk management, Group governance policies and succession plans for senior executives.

All Directors have access to the services of the Company Secretary and may take independent professional advice at the company's expense in conducting their duties. We have reviewed and updated the insurance cover and indemnities provided for Directors and officers this year.

All new Directors receive an updated induction programme designed to develop their knowledge and understanding of the Group. On appointment the Director will liaise with the Company Secretary and Chairman to ensure their programme is appropriately tailored to their experience, background and particular areas of focus. It may include an overview of the business model, the Board processes, matters reserved for the Board, an introduction to Board Committees that the new appointee will serve on, briefings with senior management and site visits, at home and abroad. The need for Director training is regularly assessed by the Board.

Board processes The Board governs through clearly identified Board Committees to which we delegate powers. These are the Executive Committee, Audit Committee, Remuneration Committee and Nominations Committee. They are properly authorised under the constitution of the company to take decisions and act on behalf of the Board within the guidelines and delegations laid down by the Board. The Board is kept fully informed of the work of these committees. Any issues requiring resolution will be referred to the full Board. A summary of the operations of these committees is set out below. The three statutory committees (Audit, Remuneration and Nominations) are underpinned by the attendance of Non-executive Directors, who provide an independent insight to governance, and their Terms of Reference are available on the website www.tesco.com/corporate or at the AGM.

Executive Committee The Board delegates responsibility for determining and implementing the strategic plan, and for managing the Group, to the Executive Committee. This normally meets every week and its decisions are communicated throughout the Group, on a regular basis. The Executive Committee is chaired by the Chief Executive and comprises the Executive Directors and Ms L Neville-Rolfe, the Company Secretary. It has authority for decision making in all areas except those set out in the Schedule of Matters Reserved for Board Decision. The Executive Committee is responsible for implementing Group strategy and policy, for monitoring the performance of the business and reporting on these matters in full to the Board.

Corporate governance continued

The Executive Committee has also set up further operational groups or boards aimed at seeing through the key elements of the strategic plan, managing the UK and international operations, Joint Ventures, property acquisitions, trading, finance, funding and people management. These groups are heavily populated with Executive Directors and senior management from relevant functions.

Nominations Committee In the light of assessment of Board capability, the Nominations Committee leads the process for Board appointments and the re-election and succession of Directors and the Chairman. The Committee is chaired by Mr D E Reid and its members during the year were Mr C L Allen, Mr R F Chase, Mr E M Davies, Dr H Einsmann, Mr K J Hydon and Sir Terry Leahy. Mrs K R Cook joined the Committee in October 2004 and Ms C McCall joined in March 2005. Where matters discussed relate to the Chairman, the Senior Independent Non-executive Director chairs the meeting.

In the last twelve months, two new independent Non-executive Directors were appointed to the Board. Prior to these appointments the Board agreed clear criteria against which to assess each of the candidates. External recruitment consultants were employed to advise and oversee the process. Both appointees underwent a rigorous nomination process before the Board agreed on their appointments.

Mrs K R Cook is a Managing Director and President at Goldman Sachs, Europe, and her appointment took effect from 1 October 2004. Mrs K R Cook has previously served for six years as a Non-executive Director at Dixons plc. She is a highly respected investment banker and brings with her considerable knowledge of the financial markets.

Ms C McCall joined the Board on 1 March 2005 and also has relevant experience of the retail industry having previously served as a Non-executive Director at New Look Group plc. Her strategic, brand marketing and media experience as Chief Executive of Guardian Newspapers Ltd will be an asset to the Board.

All new Directors are submitted for election by shareholders in their first year. All Directors have to submit themselves for re-election at least every three years if they wish to continue serving and are considered by the Board to be eligible.

Remuneration Committee The Remuneration Committee's role is to determine and recommend to the Board the remuneration policy for the Executive Directors. It monitors the level and structure of remuneration for senior management and seeks to ensure that the levels and structure of remuneration are designed to attract, retain and motivate the Executive Directors needed to run the company. Mr C L Allen chairs

the Committee which is composed entirely of independent Non-executive Directors. Committee members for the full year were Mr R F Chase and Dr H Einsmann. Mr E M Davies joined the Committee in October 2004 and Mr G F Pimlott resigned from the Committee during the year. The responsibilities of the Remuneration Committee, together with an explanation of how it applies the Directors' remuneration principles of the Combined Code are set out in the Directors' remuneration report on pages 511–25.

Audit Committee The Audit Committee's primary responsibilities are to review the financial statements; to review the internal control systems including risk management; to review the internal audit programme; to consider the appointment of the external auditors and their independence, and to review the Committee's own effectiveness. The annual schedule also includes a review of Protector Line, the company's 'whistle-blowing' procedure.

After the 2004 AGM, Mr G F Pimlott passed the Chairmanship of the Committee to Mr K J Hydon, who has recent and relevant financial experience. The other Committee members for the full financial year were Mr R F Chase and Mr E M Davies. Mrs K R Cook joined the Audit Committee on appointment to the Board in October and Ms V Morali resigned from the Committee on her retirement from the Board on 26 February 2005. The Committee consists entirely of independent Non-executive Directors. At the invitation of the Committee, the Finance Director, Head of Internal Audit and representatives of the external auditors normally attend meetings. The Committee meets with the external auditors without Executive Board members present at least once a year.

The Audit Committee's Terms of Reference are reviewed annually and represent current best practice. This year the Committee met five times. To facilitate the Committee's understanding of the Group's international affairs, a special meeting is held at an international location. The Committee has arranged an away-day for training and updating on audit specific matters. This training is for members of the Audit Committee and Executive and Non-executive Directors, with complementary sessions tailored to individual needs.

Board performance evaluation With the full support of the Board, the Chairman led a formal evaluation of the performance of the Board and its key committees. The process, which included interviews with each Director and the Company Secretary, was conducted by an external independent consultant. The review concluded that the Tesco Board is highly effective and that there have been significant improvements in the Board's culture, dynamics and administrative processes during the year.

Members attendance during the year ended 26 February 2005	Board meetings	Nominations Committee	Remuneration Committee	Audit Committee
No. of meetings held	9	1	5	5
Non-executive Directors				
Mr D E Reid (Chairman)	9	1	N/A	N/A
Mr C L Allen	8	1	5	N/A
Mr R F Chase (Senior Independent)	8	1	5	5
Mrs K R Cook[1]	2	1	N/A	2
Mr E M Davies[2]	6	1	3	4
Dr H Einsmann	9	1	4	N/A
Mr K J Hydon	8	1	N/A	5
Ms V Morali	7	N/A	N/A	3
Mr G F Pimlott	8	1	3	5
Executive Directors				
Sir Terry Leahy	9	1	N/A	N/A
Mr R Brasher	8	N/A	N/A	N/A
Mr P A Clarke	9	N/A	N/A	N/A
Mr A T Higginson	9	N/A	N/A	N/A
Mr T J R Mason	9	N/A	N/A	N/A
Mr D T Potts	8	N/A	N/A	N/A

Notes:

'N/A' indicates the Director is not a member of the Committee. Directors leave the meeting where matters relating to them are being discussed. It is expected that all Directors attend Board and Committee meetings unless they are prevented from doing so by prior commitments and all Directors attend the AGM.

1. Mrs K R Cook was appointed to the Board on 1 October 2004 and has attended all Board meetings and Audit Committees that have taken place since then.

2. Mr E M Davies joined the Remuneration Committee in October 2004.

The Chief Executive reviews the performance of each Executive Director. The Chairman reviews the performance of the Chief Executive and each Non-executive Director. During the year, the Chairman meets with the Non-executive Directors without the Executive Directors present. The Senior Independent Non-executive Director, Mr R F Chase, met with the Non-executive Directors in the absence of the Chairman, to assess the Chairman's effectiveness.

The Board scheduled nine meetings in this financial year and ad hoc meetings were convened to deal with urgent matters. The above table shows the attendance of Directors at regular Board meetings and of members at the Audit, Nominations and Remuneration Committees during the year.

Internal control and risk management The Board has overall responsibility for internal control, including risk management. We agree appropriate policies that will safeguard the achievement of the Group's objectives. Executive management is responsible for identifying, evaluating and managing financial and non-financial risks. It is the Executives' role to implement and maintain the control systems across the Group in accordance with the Board's policies and in line with best practice identified in the Turnbull Guidance.

Identifying risks The Board considers and approves the Key Risk Register and the mitigating actions. In addition, at the annual two-day Board conference, we also consider where future opportunities and risks lie, which helps shape our overall future corporate strategy. The key risks are a regular feature of the Board's agenda and further assurance on implementation comes from the reviews by management and internal audit, the Compliance Committee, the Corporate Responsibility Committee and the Finance Committee.

Internal controls and risk management From the Key Risk Register, we assess the impact and probability of each risk and the effectiveness of the mitigating controls. Methods for monitoring each specific risk are then agreed. Accountabilities for managing these operational risks are clearly assigned to line management. Risk assessments are carried out routinely by management throughout the UK and international businesses. Procedures exist to ensure that significant risks and control failures are escalated to senior management and the Board on a timely basis.

We have a five-year rolling business plan that focuses on delivering the Group's strategy. Each business unit and support function derives its objectives from the plan and these are cascaded to form individual objectives. The plan covers

Corporate governance continued

all the key trading and financial performance measures and targets to deliver the financial returns on the capital employed in the business.

On an annual basis these plans are combined with detailed budgets and also our balanced scorecard (which we call our Steering Wheel) which unites the Group's resources around our customers, people, operations and finance. This enables the business to be operated and monitored on a balanced basis with due regard to all stakeholders. In our fast moving business trading is tracked on a daily and weekly basis, financial performance is reviewed weekly and monthly and the Steering Wheel is reviewed quarterly. In addition, all major initiatives require business cases to be prepared, normally covering a minimum period of five years. Post-investment appraisals are also carried out.

We have a structured programme for internal communication of policies, procedures and performance. This provides employees with a clear definition of the Group's purpose and goals, accountabilities and the scope of permitted activities of companies, executive functions and individual staff. This ensures decision-making takes place at the correct level and that all our people understand what is expected of them and how we have performed.

Monitoring the controls The Board agrees clear processes for monitoring controls through the Statutory Committees: Audit Committee, Nominations Committee and Remuneration Committee. In addition, the Executive Committee monitors controls through three key committees: Compliance Committee, Corporate Responsibility Committee and Finance Committee. All of these provide assurance that the business is operating legally, ethically and within approved financial and operational policies. The Committee reports are circulated to the Board who hold a formal discussion on each at least once a year.

- **Audit Committee** The Audit Committee, described above, reports to the Board on its review of the effectiveness of the systems of internal control for the accounting year and the period to the date of approval of the financial statements. Overall, the Audit Committee seeks to ensure that the whole management process provides adequate control over major risks to the Group. This is achieved through consideration of regular reports from internal and external audit, alongside discussions with senior managers. It should be understood that such systems are designed to provide reasonable, but not absolute, assurance against material mis-statement or loss.

- **Internal and External Audit** The internal audit department is fully independent of business operations and has a Group-wide mandate. It operates on a risk-based methodology so ensuring that the Group's key risks receive appropriate regular examination. The head of internal audit also attends all Audit Committee meetings.

PricewaterhouseCoopers LLP, the company's external auditors, contribute a further independent perspective on certain aspects of the internal financial control system arising from their work, and report accordingly.

The engagement and independence of external auditors is considered annually by the Audit Committee before they recommend their selection to the Board. The Committee has satisfied itself that PricewaterhouseCoopers LLP are independent and there are adequate controls in place to safeguard their objectivity. Such measures include the requirement to rotate audit partners every five years. We have a non-audit services policy which sets out criteria for employing external auditors and identifies areas where it is inappropriate for PricewaterhouseCoopers LLP to work. Non-audit services work carried out by PricewaterhouseCoopers LLP is predominantly transaction work and corporate tax services. PricewaterhouseCoopers LLP also follow their own ethical guidelines and continually review their audit team to ensure their independence is not compromised.

- **Finance Committee** Membership includes Non-executive Directors with relevant financial expertise, Executive Directors and members of senior management. The Committee usually meets twice a year. Its role is to review and agree the Finance plan on an annual basis; to review reports of the Treasury policies; and to review and approve Treasury limits and delegations.

- **Compliance Committee** Membership of the Committee includes two Executive Directors, the Company Secretary and members of senior management. It normally meets four times a year. The Board delegates its responsibilities for compliance with all necessary laws and regulations to the Compliance Committee. This Committee has established a schedule for the regular review of the Group's operational activities and legal exposure to ensure compliance with accepted practices and policies.

- **Corporate Responsibility Committee** The Committee is chaired by the Company Secretary and membership is made up of senior managers from across the business. It meets at least four times a year to support, develop and monitor policies on social, ethical and environmental issues. It reviews threats and opportunities for the Group. Key Performance Indicators (KPIs) for key areas of corporate responsibility are tracked through the 'Responsible and safe' segment of our

Steering Wheel. In addition to the Board discussion of the work of the Committee that takes place at least annually, the Chair of the Committee reports regularly to the Executive Committee on corporate responsibility matters.

Other specialist functions, notably the Corporate and Legal Affairs department and the Trading Law and Technical department provide assurance and advice on health and safety, legal compliance and social, ethical and environmental matters. These functions report their findings on a regular basis to the relevant committees and escalate matters as appropriate. Subsidiary businesses also maintain key risk registers and confirm their compliance with Group policies annually. These statements confirm that the Board's governance policies have been adopted in practice and in spirit. For certain joint ventures, the Board places reliance upon the systems of internal control operating within our partners' infrastructure and the obligations upon partners' Boards relating to the effectiveness of their own systems.

Non-financial risks We manage a broad range of financial and non-financial risks, including social, ethical and environmental responsibilities. The construction of the Key Risk Register takes into account all these matters. The risk management policies, procedures and monitoring methods described in this report apply equally to corporate responsibility activities.

In addition, in accordance with ABI guidelines on social responsibility, the Group has dedicated specific time and resource to this area. In our view, there are appropriate controls in place to manage both financial and non-financial risks.

- Customer focus is fundamental to delivering the overall strategy and is key to the way risk is managed. Business practices centre on serving the customer and in meeting those challenges the Group recognises its responsibility to deliver safe, quality products at the right price.

- We recognise that our people may have to face ethical dilemmas in the normal course of business and our guidance to them stems from the Tesco Values. The Values set out the standards that the Board wish to uphold in how we treat our people. These are supported by Codes of Ethics and govern the relationships between the Group and employees, suppliers and contractors. The Compliance Committee regularly monitors adherence to these codes. We are a founder member of the Ethical Trading Initiative and a signatory to the UK Government's Supplier Code of Practice.

- Excellent health and safety standards are a high priority. We are committed to providing a safe shopping and working environment for customers, staff and contractors. The company has established policies, procedures and training to identify and minimise the risks inherent in a retail and distribution business. The Group has established, over many years, a comprehensive due diligence process supported by technical and product development standards and procedures. This assurance covers staff training, and providing guidance for, and auditing of, suppliers to ensure they supply quality products in a safe and ethical way.

- The Group has conducted a comprehensive risk analysis of products, suppliers and factories upon which the audit programme is based. Auditing is carried out on both a routine and unannounced basis. Supply chain risks can include, for example, a failure of standards relating to product safety, quality, labour standards and animal welfare. Technical, due diligence and crisis management procedures are regularly reviewed in the light of the latest scientific research and expert opinion, to ensure that these risks are managed effectively. In-house experts are used as well as external advisors to look for and analyse emerging issues so that appropriate action can be taken.

We recognise that some investors and other stakeholders take a specific interest in how companies are managing non-financial risks. We report further detail on our approach, policies and KPIs in this area in our Annual Corporate Responsibility (CR) Review and on our website, www.tesco.com/corporate

Relations with stakeholders We recognise the importance of understanding stakeholder views and the need to balance their opinions in order to achieve a sustainable business model. Customers need to be able to trust our business and they will only trust us if we do the right thing by all our stakeholders. Our programme of engaging with stakeholders, including customers, staff, suppliers, investors, non-governmental organisations and others, is set out in more detail in the CR Review and on our website. We carry out external research to help us understand how well we are communicating with these groups.

We are committed to maintaining a good dialogue with shareholders through proactively organising meetings and presentations, as well as responding to a wide range of enquiries. We want to understand shareholder views on a range of issues from strategy to corporate governance, and we recognise the importance of communicating appropriately any significant company developments. This shareholder communication is mainly co-ordinated by the Investor Relations department. During the year, the Group met with 75 of the leading shareholders, representing over 42% of the issued shares of the company. Inevitably institutional shareholders may be in more regular contact with the Group than others, but care is exercised to ensure that any price-sensitive information is

Corporate governance continued

released to all shareholders, institutional and private, at the same time in accordance with the Financial Services Authority requirements. The Board is kept informed of the views of shareholders either through direct meetings or through updates from the Investor Relations department.

Since appointment, the Chairman has conducted a number of meetings with major shareholders independently from the Executive team. Shareholders have also been offered the opportunity to meet with the Senior Independent Non-executive Director, although none have requested a meeting. We regard the Annual General Meeting as an opportunity to communicate directly with all shareholders. The whole Board attends the meeting and is available to answer questions from shareholders present. All resolutions will be voted on a poll so that the views of shareholders are reflected proportionately.

Every shareholder may choose to receive a full Annual Report and Financial Statements or the Annual Review and Summary Financial Statement. At the half year, all shareholders receive an Interim Report. These reports, together with publicly-made trading statements, are available on the Group's website, www.tesco.com/corporate

Pension funds The Tesco PLC Pension Scheme is a defined benefit scheme with nearly 137,000 members and about 14,000 pensioners. Note 27 in the Report and Financial Statements sets out the Group's pension arrangements in detail.

During the year ended 26 February 2005, the Trustee board comprised nine directors including three nominated by the members. Mr V Benjamin retired as the Chairman of the Trustees and was replaced by Mr R S Ager. Management of the assets is delegated to a number of independent fund managers. These fund managers have discretion to invest in shares of Tesco PLC providing they do not exceed the proportion of the shares in the total market. Details of pension commitments are set out in note 27 to the financial statements on pages 552–4.

Compliance In April 2004, Mr D E Reid, previously an Executive Director and Deputy Chairman (having resigned in December 2003), re-joined the Board as Non-executive Chairman following a rigorous nomination process that began in 2001 and culminating in over 93% of shareholders voting in favour of his appointment at the AGM in June 2004.

Subject to the above paragraph, Tesco complied in all respects with the Revised Combined Code on Corporate Governance throughout the year ended 26 February 2005.

Directors' remuneration report For the year ended 26 February 2005

Remuneration Committee

The Remuneration Committee (the 'Committee') is governed by formal Terms of Reference, which were reviewed and updated by the Board this year.

Composition of the Committee

The Committee is now composed entirely of independent Non-executive Directors. The members of the Committee are Mr C L Allen (Chairman of the Committee), Mr E M Davies (appointed to the Committee in October 2004), Dr H Einsmann, and Mr R F Chase. During the year Mr G F Pimlott resigned from the Committee, prior to retiring from the Board. No member of the Remuneration Committee has any personal financial interest in the matters being decided, other than as a shareholder, and no day-to-day involvement in running the business of Tesco.

Ms L Neville-Rolfe is Secretary to the Committee and attends meetings. Mr D E Reid, Non-executive Chairman, and Sir Terry Leahy, Chief Executive of the Group, both attend the meetings at the invitation of the Committee except when their own remuneration is being discussed. The Committee is supported by Mrs C M Chapman, Personnel Director of Tesco Stores Ltd and has continued to use the services of Deloitte & Touche LLP as an external, independent advisor. Deloitte & Touche LLP also provided advisory services in respect of corporate tax planning, share schemes, pensions and international taxation to the Group during the year. Members' attendance at committee meetings is listed in the Directors' Corporate Governance report on page 507.

The role of the Committee

The Remuneration Committee's key objectives are to:

- determine and recommend to the Board the remuneration policy for the Chairman and Executive Directors;
- monitor the level and structure of remuneration for senior management, and

- ensure the level and structure of remuneration is designed to attract, retain, and motivate the Executive Directors needed to run the company.

Activities of the Committee:

The Committee normally meets four times a year and circulates minutes of its meetings to the Board. The rolling schedule for the Committee includes: a review of overall remuneration arrangements; an overview of best practice; Executive and Non-executive Directors' salary benchmarking; consideration of the relationship of reward between Executive Directors and senior managers; determining the level of awards and grants to be made under the Company's incentive plans; agreeing targets for next year; considering feedback from shareholders, and an annual review of its own effectiveness. In addition to the routine business this year, the Committee also started a review of pension provisions and share options in the light of recent legislative developments and accounting changes.

Executive Directors' remuneration policy We have a long-standing policy of rewarding achievement, talent and experience. We also seek to provide incentives for delivering high growth and high returns for shareholders. The Committee believes that a significant proportion of total remuneration should be performance-related and at risk of forfeiture. In addition, performance-related reward should be delivered largely in shares to closely align the interests of shareholders and all Executive Directors. In determining the balance between the fixed and variable elements of the Executive Directors' remuneration packages, the Committee has regard to policy and also market practice. Our policy is for performance related elements to form a major part of the total remuneration opportunity for all Executive Directors. The table below shows the current balance of fixed and performance related elements, for levels of performance, on target and above target.

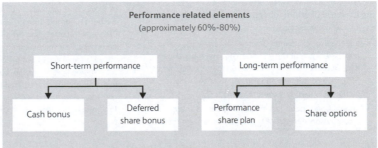

17

Directors' remuneration report continued

In our last Annual Report and Financial Statements, we explained that the Remuneration Committee had conducted a review of executive remuneration arrangements. Following extensive consultation with shareholders and their representative organisations we introduced a number of important changes. The revised remuneration strategy for Executive Directors and other key executives is clearly tailored to emphasise the delivery of strong year-on-year earnings growth as well as sustained performance in the longer term including an element of compulsory deferred shares. This ensures continued emphasis on strong annual performance combined with long-term executive share ownership, with a better link between the incentives received and shareholder value delivered. We remain committed to the focus on driving strong financial performance and will actively monitor the level of reward and performance emphasis to retain the close links to the business strategy and the appropriate market positioning.

Tesco operates in a highly competitive retail environment. Business success depends on the talents of the key team, but outstanding business performance comes from teamwork. Building and retaining that team at senior levels within Tesco is vital to success, particularly with a world-class executive team and high churn in executives in our marketplace. The Committee also ensures that the remuneration relationship between the Executive Directors and senior executives of the company below this level is appropriate. In particular, any exceptional remuneration arrangements for senior executives are advised to the Committee.

Total remuneration

The total remuneration levels of Executive Directors are reviewed annually by the Committee. The Committee considers external independent remuneration surveys to ensure it has proper regard to competitive market practice. We are conscious of the risks involved in paying unjustified amounts and therefore monitor carefully the basic salary and total remuneration that each Director receives.

The Board has reduced the number of Executive Directors whilst increasing the existing Executive Directors' levels of responsibility.

The Executive Directors' total remuneration package comprises the following elements:

- base salary determined by the responsibilities, skills and experience of the individual against a benchmark determined by reference to other large retailers, major FTSE 100 companies and certain major consumer companies operating internationally;
- annual bonus paid part in cash and part in shares with a compulsory deferral of the share element for three years;

- long-term performance share plan based on a stretching three-year Return On Capital Employed (ROCE) target. Shares must be held for a further 12 months after vesting;
- performance-related share option awards via the Share Option Scheme open to all senior managers;
- benefits (which comprise car benefits, disability and health insurance and staff discount);
- pension, and
- Executive Directors are also eligible to participate in the company's all-employee savings related share option scheme (SAYE), Shares in Success and Buy As You Earn scheme on the same terms as all other UK employees.

This year the Executive Directors received the maximum level of bonus reflecting the high level of business performance as described in the Operating and Financial Review.

Basic Pay

Basic pay must be appropriate to attract and retain talented individuals. It must reflect individual capability and any changes in responsibilities as the Group faces new opportunities and challenges both in the UK and internationally. The Committee takes into account pay conditions throughout the Group in deciding annual salary increases. The Committee seeks to set a level of pay that reflects changes in individual responsibility and market conditions. We seek to reflect salary levels at the top performing retailers and the leading FTSE companies in order to attract the best people and maintain excellent performance.

Annual Bonus and Deferred Annual Bonus

Tesco operates an annual bonus scheme simplified and updated last year and the targets and amount which can be earned are set each year in line with market practice. It is based on achievement of stretching earnings per share (EPS) targets, assessment of total shareholder returns (TSR) and specific corporate objectives. The Committee sets performance targets annually and confirms achievement of performance and awards to be made. Policy has been for Executive Directors to earn a bonus equivalent to up to 100% of salary paid in cash at the end of the year and a maximum of 75% of salary paid in shares with compulsory deferral for three years. The cash element is earned through achievement of previously agreed EPS growth targets and progress on specific corporate objectives. The share element has an additional measure, based on an assessment of comparative shareholder returns. Total shareholder return has been chosen as it is a clear indicator of the value created for shareholders. The Committee considers a comparator group comprising large international food retailers as the most appropriate basis for assessing relative performance. This comparator group includes Ahold, Carrefour, Metro, Morrisons, Safeway Inc. (US), Target (US) and Walmart.

Performance Share Plan

The Performance Share Plan (PSP) provides the opportunity to earn greater rewards for superior long-term performance. By assuring a focus on long-term business success and helping the Executive Directors to build up a shareholding in Tesco, the plan further aligns the interests of shareholders and Executive Directors.

Awards can be made up to 150% of salary. No award in the year exceeded 75% of salary. Awards will be made 'over' shares and will vest, according to the achievement of the ROCE targets. Awards will vest on a straight-line basis: 25% of the award will vest for baseline performance with the maximum award vesting for maximum performance. The vested shares must then be retained for a further 12 months. The Board set out objectives for profitable deployment of capital in a Placing Announcement of 13 January 2004. The 2004/05 award will vest based on the achievement of 11.5% (derived from profit before interest less tax) at the end of the three year performance period. This reflects the five-year objective of raising post tax ROCE by up to 200 basis points from the base point of 10.2% achieved in the financial year ended February 2003.

Share options

Share options with a value of up to 200% of salary are granted to the Executive Directors under the same conditions as for senior managers. The first 100% is subject to the achievement of EPS growth of at least RPI plus 9% over three years, with the balance vesting for achieving RPI plus 15% over three years. It is practice that the value of options granted to Executive Directors each year does not exceed 200% of salary other than in exceptional circumstances. There is no re-testing of performance.

Share options are an important part of the incentive framework for hundreds of senior managers within the Group. The Committee has considered fully the current accounting changes and concluded that share option plans remain in the best interests of shareholders.

Share ownership guidelines

Executive Directors are normally expected to build and maintain a shareholding with a value at least equal to their base salary. New appointees will typically be allowed around three years to establish this shareholding. Full participation in the Performance Share Plan is conditional upon this.

Summary of remuneration elements

All awards made to Executive Directors under the Annual Bonus, Performance Share Plan and all options granted under the Executive Share Option Scheme are subject to the satisfaction of performance conditions, which are explained above. If performance is unsatisfactory the cash bonus and long-term incentives will reduce accordingly. The Committee regularly reviews these performance conditions and considers that the proposed mix of performance conditions best supports the Group's business strategy and provides a set of comprehensive and robust measures of management's effort and success in creating shareholder value. A summary of the elements of the package is set out in the table below.

Part of remuneration	Performance measure	Purpose
Base salary	Individual contribution to the business success	To attract and retain talented people
Annual cash bonus	Earnings per share and specified corporate objectives	Motivates year on year earnings growth and delivery of business priorities
Annual deferred share element	Total shareholder return, Earnings per share and specified corporate objectives	Generates focus on medium-term targets and by incentivising share price and dividend growth ensures alignment with shareholder interests
Performance Share Plan	Return on capital employed over a three year period	Assures a focus on long-term business success
Share options	Earnings per share relative to retail price index with more stretching performance targets for the balance of awards over 100% of salary	Incentivises earnings growth and Executive Director shareholding

Directors' remuneration report continued

Other elements

- Shares In Success. Since March 2002 the Group has operated a UK profit sharing scheme (Shares in Success) for the benefit of employees, including Executive Directors. The scheme is available to employees with at least one year's service at the Group's year end and is recognised as a powerful incentive and retention tool for all employees. Shares in the company are allocated to participants in the scheme on a pro-rata basis to base salary earned, up to Inland Revenue approved limits (currently £3,000 per annum). The amount of profit allocated to the scheme is determined by the Board, taking account of company performance.

- Save as You Earn. Since 1981, the Group has operated an Inland Revenue approved savings-related share option scheme (SAYE) for the benefit of employees including Executive Directors. Under this scheme, employees save up to a limit of £250 on a four-weekly basis via a bank/building society with an option to buy shares in Tesco PLC at the end of a three- or five-year period at a discount of up to 20% of the market value. There are no performance conditions attached to SAYE options.

- Buy as You Earn. Since January 2002, the Group has operated the partnership shares element of an Inland Revenue approved share investment plan for the benefit of employees, including Executive Directors. Under this scheme, employees save up to a limit of £110 on a four-weekly basis, to buy shares at market value in Tesco PLC.

Pensions

Executive Directors are members of the Tesco PLC Pension Scheme which provides a pension of up to two-thirds of base salary on retirement, normally at the age of 60, dependent upon service. The scheme also provides for dependants' pensions and lump sums on death in service. The scheme is a defined benefit pension scheme, which is approved by the Inland Revenue. An internal working group has been established to understand the implications of Government proposals in relation to pensions and to advise the Remuneration Committee on future pension provisions and contributions. The Final Salary Scheme is now closed to new entrants but has been replaced by a different defined benefit pension scheme which accumulates each year and is based on career average earnings.

Further details of the pension benefits earned by the directors can be found on page 517.

Performance graph

The graph below highlights the Group's total shareholder return performance over the last five financial years, relative to the FTSE 100 index of companies.

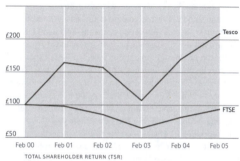

TOTAL SHAREHOLDER RETURN (TSR)
TSR is the notional return from a stock or index based on share price movements and declared dividends

In addition, there has been a very strong performance in TSR over the last one year, three years and five years against a comparator group of our major retail competitors in the UK, Europe and the US.

Service agreements

The Executive Directors all have service agreements, dated 14 June 2004, with entitlement to notice of 12 months by the company and 6 months notice by the Executive. Each agreement automatically terminates when the Director reaches the retirement age of 60.

If an Executive Director's employment is terminated (other than pursuant to the notice provisions in the service agreement or by reason of resignation or unacceptable performance or conduct) the company will pay, by way of liquidated damages, a sum calculated on the basis of basic salary and the average annual bonus paid for the last two years. No account will be taken of pension arrangements in these payments.

Termination payments will be subject to mitigation. This means that liquidated damages amounts will be paid in instalments to permit mitigation and earlier payment will be made based on long service in line with Tesco policy which respects and rewards loyalty. If the termination occurs within one year of retirement, the termination payment would be reduced accordingly.

The Committee has agreed that, in future, new appointments of Executive Directors will normally be on a notice period of 12 months. The Committee reserves the right to vary this period to 24 months for the initial period of appointment and for the notice period to then revert to 12 months. The service agreements are available for inspection at the AGM and Registered Office.

20

Outside appointments

Tesco recognises that its Executive Directors are likely to be invited to become Non-executive Directors of other companies. Such Non-executive duties can broaden experience and knowledge which can benefit Tesco. Subject to approval by the Board, Executive Directors are allowed to accept Non-executive appointments and retain the fees received, provided that these appointments are not likely to lead to conflicts of interest. Executive Directors' biographies can be found in the Annual Review and Summary Financial Statement, and fees retained for any Non-executive Directorships are set out below.

Director	Company in which Non-executive Directorship held	Fee retained by the Director in 2004/05 (£'s)
Mr A T Higginson	B Sky B	22,800
	C&J Clark	41,725
Mr T J R Mason	Capital Radio	32,000

Non-executive Directors

The remuneration of the Non-executive Directors is determined by the Board as a whole on the recommendation of the Chairman and the Executive Committee after considering external market research and individual contribution. The Remuneration Committee determines the Chairman's remuneration, having regard to packages awarded to Chairmen of other companies of a similar size, complexity and international reach.

Non-executive Directors have letters of appointment setting out their duties and the time commitment expected. These letters are available for inspection at the AGM and Registered Office. The Chairman meets with each Non-executive Director separately to review individual performance. All Non-executive Directors are subject to re-election by shareholders every three years at the Annual General Meeting and their appointment can be terminated by either party without notice. Non-executive Directors receive a basic fee of £50,000 plus a fee of £5,000 per Committee for membership of the Audit and Remuneration Committee. The chair of the Remuneration Committee and chair of the Audit Committee receive a further £3,000 for their additional responsibilities. Mr R F Chase, receives a total fee of £100,000 for his role as Senior Independent Non-executive Director and Deputy Chairman. Mr D E Reid, Non-executive Chairman receives an annual fee of £500,000 and has the benefit of the use of a company car.

Compliance

In carrying out its duties, the Committee gives full consideration to best practice. The Committee is constituted and operated throughout the period in accordance with the principles outlined in the Listing Rules of the Financial Services Authority derived from Schedule A and B of the Combined Code. The auditor's report set out on page 527, covers the disclosures referred to in this report that are specified for audit by the Financial Services Authority. This report also complies with disclosures required by the Directors' Remuneration Report Regulations 2002. Details of Directors' emoluments and interests, including executive and savings-related share options, are set out on pages 516 to 525.

Mr C L Allen
Chairman of the Remuneration Committee

Directors' remuneration report continued

Tables 1 to 7 are audited information.

Table 1 Directors' emoluments

| | Fixed emoluments | | Performance-related emoluments | | | | | |
	Salary £000	Benefits £000	Profit-sharing £000	Short-term Cash (new scheme) £000	Short-term Deferred Shares (new scheme) £000	Long-term (old scheme) £000	Total 2005 £000	Total 2004 £000
Executive Directors								
Sir Terry Leahy	1,036	67	3	1,030	773	285	3,194	2,977
Mr R S Ager (a)	21	9	–	–	–	–	30	1,634
Mr R Brasher (b)	415	9	3	541	300	–	1,268	–
Mr P A Clarke	588	65	3	594	446	95	1,791	1,657
Mr J Gildersleeve (a)	24	28	–	–	–	–	52	2,161
Mr A T Higginson	613	41	3	594	446	115	1,812	1,659
Mr T J R Mason	602	15	3	594	446	164	1,824	1,681
Mr D T Potts	580	39	3	594	446	130	1,792	1,661
Non-executive Directors								
Mr C L Allen	58	–	–	–	–	–	58	47
Mr R F Chase	100	–	–	–	–	–	100	49
Mrs K R Cook (c)	22	–	–	–	–	–	22	–
Mr E M Davies	57	–	–	–	–	–	57	28
Dr H Einsmann	55	–	–	–	–	–	55	44
Mr J A Gardiner (d)	38	–	–	–	–	–	38	431
Mr K J Hydon	58	–	–	–	–	–	58	1
Ms V Morali (e)	55	–	–	–	–	–	55	44
Mr G F Pimlott	73	–	–	–	–	–	73	72
Mr D E Reid (Chairman) (f)	467	72	–	–	–	–	539	2,724
	4,862	345	18	3,947	2,857	789	12,818	16,870

Benefits are made up of car benefits, disability and health insurance, staff discount and chauffeurs. The Long-term Bonus awarded on 28 July 2004 under the Performance Share Plan was awarded in the form of nil-cost options. Details of this award are shown in Table 6.

(a) Mr R S Ager and Mr J Gildersleeve retired from the Tesco Group on 15 March 2004. On their retirement Mr R S Ager and Mr J Gildersleeve were permitted to retain their company cars, which had a value of £58,745 and £95,566, respectively, for nil consideration.

(b) Mr R Brasher was appointed during the year. The figures in Table1 are calculated from Mr R Brasher's date of appointment. In 2001, as Non-food Director, Mr R Brasher was set challenging three-year targets to deliver a step change in the Group's clothing business. These performance targets ran from July 2001 to July 2004. Progress was above expectations so a performance-related payment was paid on 8 October 2004 following an internal audit confirmation of the performance against target. This was a contractual obligation that was agreed by the Remuneration Committee at the start of 2001, and is included within Performance-related emoluments - Short-term cash. In respect of the period from Mr R Brasher's appointment to the end of the three-year performance period, Mr R Brasher received £141,452.

(c) Mrs K R Cook was appointed during the year. The figures in Table 1 are calculated from the date of Mrs K R Cook's appointment.

(d) Mr J A Gardiner retired from the Board on 2 April 2004.

(e) Ms V Morali retired from the Board on 26 February 2005.

(f) Mr D E Reid was appointed a Non-executive Director on 2 April 2004, having retired as an Executive Director on 31 December 2003.

Table 2 Pension details of the Directors

	Age at 26 February 2005/ Years of company service	Total accrued pension at 26 February 2005(a) £000	Increase/ (decrease) in accrued pension during the year £000	Increase/ (decrease) in accrued pension during the year (net of inflation) £000	Transfer value of previous column at 26 February 2005 £000	Transfer value of total accrued pension at 28 Feb 2004 (old basis (b)) £000	Transfer value of total accrued pension at 28 Feb 2004 (new basis (b)) £000	Transfer value of total accrued pension at 26 February 2005 £000	Increase in transfer value less Directors' contributions £000
Sir Terry Leahy (c)	49/26	479	46	33	409	3,801	4,204	5,117	913
Mr R S Ager (d)	59/19	274	(13)	(14)	n/a	4,844	5,191	5,898	707
Mr R Brasher (e)	43/18	135	23	19	146	775	806	1,025	219
Mr P A Clarke	44/30	228	28	22	180	1,447	1,517	1,874	357
Mr J Gildersleeve (d)	60/40	405	1	–	n/a	7,273	7,717	8,537	820
Mr A T Higginson (f)	47/7	140	28	24	227	908	974	1,318	344
Mr T J R Mason	47/23	250	27	20	191	1,802	1,921	2,341	420
Mr D T Potts	47/32	253	31	24	227	1,833	1,965	2,425	460

(a) The accrued pension is that which would be paid annually on retirement at 60, based on service to 26 February 2005.

(b) The method used for calculating transfer values was revised during the year to bring it in line with latest actuarial professional guidance. Changes in financial conditions and improving mortality rates have meant that the previous basis for calculating transfer values, used since 1997, is not considered to produce suitable values. Transfer values at 28 February 2004 have been restated using the new method for comparative purposes.

(c) Sir Terry Leahy is entitled to retire at any age from 57 to 60 inclusive, with an immediate pension of two-thirds of base salary. Part of his pension may be provided on an unfunded basis within a separate unapproved arrangement.

(d) As disclosed in Table 1, Mr R S Ager and Mr J Gildersleeve both retired in March 2004. The total accrued pension shown is the pension immediately after retirement. Transfer values do not apply in retirement and the transfer values at 26 February 2005 have been calculated on a basis consistent with transfer values for non-retired directors.

(e) Mr R Brasher was appointed during the year. The increase in accrued pension shown is based on the increase since appointment. Similarly, the transfer value as at 28 February 2004 is based on the value of his pension as at the date of appointment to the Board.

(f) Part of Mr A T Higginson's benefits, in respect of pensionable earnings in excess of the earnings limit imposed by the Finance Act 1989, are provided on an unfunded basis within a separate unapproved arrangement.

All transfer values have been calculated in accordance with Actuarial Guidance Note GN11.

Directors' remuneration report continued

Table 3 Gains made on executive share options during the year

	Number of shares at exercise price (pence)							
	151.66	176.66	164.0	178.0	179.42	173.0	209.5	Sub-total
Sir Terry Leahy	120,660(j)	–	–	–	–	–	–	120,660
Mr R S Ager	299,904(c)	89,433(e)	26,831(e)	149,171(e)	–	36,994(e)	182,528(e)	784,861
Mr R Brasher	–	–	–	–	–	–	–	–
Mr P A Clarke	–	–	29,946(a)	146,991(a)	–	277,170(a)	–	454,107
Mr J Gildersleeve	504,999(g)	150,564(k)	56,100(k)	364,092(k)	–	73,988(k)	–	1,149,743
Mr A T Higginson	–	373,584(m)	63,415(m)	–	–	76,301(m)	–	513,300
Mr T J R Mason†	–	149,076(d)	63,415(d)	255,796(d)	–	87,861(d)	–	556,148
Mr D T Potts	–	–	38,756(f)	288,730(f)	–	199,827(f)	–	527,313
Mr D E Reid	–	–	90,245(i)	–	425,827(i)	117,920(i)	–	633,992
Date exercisable	07.10.2000	21.05.2001	30.09.2001	28.01.2002	21.09.2002	30.11.2002	20.04.2003	

		Number of shares at exercise price (pence)					Value realisable 2005 £000	Value realisable 2004 £000
	Sub-total b/f	205.0	247.0	259.0	197.5	Total		
Sir Terry Leahy	120,660	–	–	–	–	120,660	162	610
Mr R S Ager	784,861	390,243(h)	323,886(h)	321,236(h)	455,696(h)	2,275,922	1,567	–
Mr R Brasher	–	–	–	–	–	–	–	–
Mr P A Clarke	454,107	346,341(l)	–	–	–	800,448	707	–
Mr J Gildersleeve	1,149,743	517,073(k)	429,149(k)	425,483(k)	604,557(k)	3,126,005	2,840	142
Mr A T Higginson	513,300	419,512(m)	–	–	–	932,812	1,094	–
Mr T J R Mason†	556,148	419,512(n)	11,500(b)	–	–	987,160	895	209
Mr D T Potts	527,313	360,975(f)	–	–	–	888,288	846	–
Mr D E Reid	633,992	604,878(i)	502,024(i)	498,069(i)	707,848(i)	2,946,811	1,967	879
		26.06.2003	26.04.2004	15.04.2005	14.04.2006			

† Includes family interests

	Date of exercise	Market price at exercise (pence)
(a)	20.04.2004	256.5
(b)	25.05.2004	250.0
(c)	16.06.2004	260.0
(d)	12.08.2004	257.0
(e)	06.09.2004	270.0
(f)	21.09.2004	282.5
(g)	21.09.2004	282.0
(h)	21.09.2004	280.3
(i)	21.09.2004	280.0
(j)	30.09.2004	285.8
(k)	10.11.2004	295.0
(l)	16.11.2004	301.0
(m)	25.11.2004	305.5
(n)	09.12.2004	310.0

The value realisable from shares acquired on exercise is the difference between the market value at exercise and the exercise price of the option, although the shares may have been retained. The share price at 26 February 2005 was 308.5p. The share price during the 52 weeks to 26 February 2005 ranged from 241.0p to 323.25p.

Table 4 Executive share options held by Directors

Executive share option schemes (1984), (1994) and (1996)

	Date of grant	As at 28 Feb 2004	Options granted in year(b)	Options exercised in year	As at 26 Feb 2005	Exercise price (pence)	Date from which exercisable	Expiry date
Sir Terry Leahy	13.10.1995	248,256	–	–	248,256	104.0	13.10.1998	13.10.2005
	07.10.1997	120,660	–	120,660	–	151.7	07.10.2000	07.10.2004
	30.09.1998	126,832	–	–	126,832	164.0	30.09.2001	30.09.2008
	30.11.1999	228,901	–	–	228,901	173.0	30.11.2002	30.11.2009
	20.04.2000	17,673	–	–	17,673	209.5	20.04.2003	20.04.2010
	26.06.2000	780,487	–	–	780,487	205.0	26.06.2003	26.06.2010
	26.04.2001	647,773	–	–	647,773	247.0	26.04.2004	26.04.2011
	15.04.2002	642,471	–	–	642,471	259.0	15.04.2005	15.04.2012
	14.04.2003	939,747	–	–	939,747	197.5	14.04.2006	14.04.2013
	30.04.2004	–	766,041	–	766,041	253.3	30.04.2007	30.04.2014
Total		3,752,800	766,041	120,660	4,398,181			
Mr R Brasher	30.09.1998	14,088	–	–	14,088	164.0	30.09.2001	30.09.2008
	24.05.1999	120,220	–	–	120,220	179.4	24.05.2002	24.05.2009
	09.11.1999	22,039	–	–	22,039	184.0	09.11.2002	09.11.2009
	20.04.2000	189,546	–	–	189,546	209.5	20.04.2003	20.04.2010
	26.06.2000	106,613	–	–	106,613	205.0	26.06.2003	26.06.2010
	26.04.2001	101,215	–	–	101,215	247.0	26.04.2004	26.04.2011
	15.04.2002	100,386	–	–	100,386	259.0	15.04.2005	15.04.2012
	14.04.2003	151,900	–	–	151,900	197.5	14.04.2006	14.04.2013
	30.04.2004	–	296,150	–	296,150	253.3	30.04.2007	30.04.2014
Total		806,007	296,150	–	1,102,157			
Mr P A Clarke	30.09.1998	29,946	–	29,946	–	164.0	30.09.2001	30.09.2008
	28.01.1999	146,991	–	146,991	–	178.0	28.01.2002	28.01.2009
	30.11.1999	277,170	–	277,170	–	173.0	30.11.2002	30.11.2009
	20.04.2000	77,683	–	–	77,683	209.5	20.04.2003	20.04.2010
	26.06.2000	360,975	–	346,341	14,634	205.0	26.06.2003	26.06.2010
	26.04.2001	299,595	–	–	299,595	247.0	26.04.2004	26.04.2011
	15.04.2002	328,185	–	–	328,185	259.0	15.04.2005	15.04.2012
	14.04.2003	501,266	–	–	501,266	197.5	14.04.2006	14.04.2013
	30.04.2004	–	434,353	–	434,353	253.3	30.04.2007	30.04.2014
Total		2,021,811	434,353	800,448	1,655,716			
Mr A T Higginson	21.05.1998	373,584	–	373,584	–	176.7	21.05.2001	21.05.2008
	30.09.1998	63,415	–	63,415	–	164.0	30.09.2001	30.09.2008
	30.11.1999	76,301	–	76,301	–	173.0	30.11.2002	30.11.2009
	26.06.2000	419,512	–	419,512	–	205.0	26.06.2003	26.06.2010
	26.04.2001	348,178	–	–	348,178	247.0	26.04.2004	26.04.2011
	15.04.2002	358,301	–	–	358,301	259.0	15.04.2005	15.04.2012
	14.04.2003	523,544	–	–	523,544	197.5	14.04.2006	14.04.2013
	30.04.2004	–	434,353	–	434,353	253.3	30.04.2007	30.04.2014
Total		2,162,835	434,353	932,812	1,664,376			

25

Directors' remuneration report continued

Table 4 Executive share options held by Directors continued

Executive share option schemes (1984), (1994) and (1996)

	Date of grant	As at 28 Feb 2004	Options granted in year(b)	Options exercised in year	As at 26 Feb 2005	Exercise price (pence)	Date from which exercisable	Expiry date
Mr T J R Mason (a)	21.05.1998	149,076	–	149,076	–	176.7	21.05.2001	21.05.2008
	30.09.1998	63,415	–	63,415	–	164.0	30.09.2001	30.09.2008
	28.01.1999	255,796	–	255,796	–	178.0	28.01.2002	28.01.2009
	30.11.1999	87,861	–	87,861	–	173.0	30.11.2002	30.11.2009
	26.06.2000	419,512	–	419,512	–	205.0	26.06.2003	26.06.2010
	26.04.2001	359,678(a)	–	11,500	348,178	247.0	26.04.2004	26.04.2011
	15.04.2002	373,451(a)	–	–	358,301	259.0	15.04.2005	15.04.2012
	14.04.2003	540,494(a)	–	–	523,544	197.5	14.04.2006	14.04.2013
	30.04.2004	–	447,980	–	434,353	253.3	30.04.2007	30.04.2014
Total		2,249,283	447,980	987,160	1,664,376			
Mr D T Potts	30.09.1998	38,756	–	38,756	–	164.0	30.09.2001	30.09.2008
	28.01.1999	288,730	–	288,730	–	178.0	28.01.2002	28.01.2009
	30.11.1999	199,827	–	199,827	–	173.0	30.11.2002	30.11.2009
	26.06.2000	360,975	–	360,975	–	205.0	26.06.2003	26.06.2010
	26.04.2001	299,595	–	–	299,595	247.0	26.04.2004	26.04.2011
	15.04.2002	328,185	–	–	328,185	259.0	15.04.2005	15.04.2012
	14.04.2003	501,266	–	–	501,266	197.5	14.04.2006	14.04.2013
	30.04.2004	–	434,353	–	434,353	253.3	30.04.2007	30.04.2014
Total		2,017,334	434,353	888,288	1,563,399			

(a) Includes family interests. No options lapsed in the year except options over 45,727 shares granted to Mrs F Mason.

(b)These options are subject to performance conditions which are set out on page 19.

The market price at exercise is shown in Table 3.

Mr R S Ager and Mr J Gildersleeve no longer have any options under the Executive Share Option Schemes (1984), (1994) and (1996).

Mr R S Ager's and Mr J Gildersleeve's remaining options as at 28 February 2004 were exercised during the year.

Table 5 Save as you earn share options

Savings-related share option scheme (1981)

	Date of grant	As at 28 Feb 2004	Options granted in year	Options exercised in year(c)	Options lapsed in year	As at 26 Feb 2005	Exercise price (pence)	Value realisable 2005 £'000	Value realisable 2004 £'000
Sir Terry Leahy	28.10.1999	2,235	–	2,235	–	–	151.0	4	–
	26.10.2000	1,704	–	–	–	1,704	198.0	–	–
	08.11.2001	1,671	–	–	–	1,671	198.0	–	–
	08.11.2002	2,066	–	–	–	2,066	159.0	–	–
	06.11.2003	1,625	–	–	–	1,625	195.0	–	–
	04.11.2004	–	1,424	–	–	1,424	232.0	–	–
Total		9,301	1,424	2,235	–	8,490		4	–
Mr R S Ager (a)	28.10.1999	2,235	–	1,944	291	–	151.0	2	–
	26.10.2000	1,704	–	1,117	587	–	198.0	1	–
	08.11.2001	1,671	–	751	920	–	198.0	–	–
	06.11.2003	946	–	102	844	–	195.0	–	–
Total		6,556	–	3,914	2,642	–		3	5
Mr R Brasher	28.10.1999	2,235	–	2,235	–	–	151.0	4	–
	26.10.2000	1,704	–	–	–	1,704	198.0	–	–
	08.11.2001	1,671	–	–	–	1,671	198.0	–	–
	08.11.2002	2,066	–	–	–	2,066	159.0	–	–
	06.11.2003	1,625	–	–	–	1,625	195.0	–	–
	04.11.2004	–	1,424	–	–	1,424	232.0	–	–
Total		9,301	1,424	2,235	–	8,490		4	–

Table 5 Save as you earn share options continued
Savings-related share option scheme (1981)

	Date of grant	As at 28 Feb 2004	Options granted in year	Options exercised in year (c)	Options lapsed in year	As at 26 Feb 2005	Exercise price (pence)	Value realisable 2005 £'000	Value realisable 2004 £'000
Mr P A Clarke	28.10.1999	2,235	–	2,235	–	–	151.0	4	–
	26.10.2000	1,704	–	–	–	1,704	198.0	–	–
	08.11.2001	1,671	–	–	–	1,671	198.0	–	–
	08.11.2002	2,066	–	–	–	2,066	159.0	–	–
	06.11.2003	1,625	–	–	–	1,625	195.0	–	–
	04.11.2004	–	1,424	–	–	1,424	232.0	–	–
Total		9,301	1,424	2,235	–	8,490		4	2
Mr J Gildersleeve (a)	28.10.1999	2,235	–	1,944	291	–	151.0	2	–
	26.10.2000	1,704	–	1,117	587	–	198.0	1	–
	08.11.2002	1,188	–	511	677	–	159.0	–	–
Total		5,127	–	3,572	1,555	–		3	–
Mr A T Higginson	28.10.1999	2,235	–	2,235	–	–	151.0	4	–
	26.10.2000	1,704	–	–	–	1,704	198.0	–	–
	08.11.2001	1,671	–	–	–	1,671	198.0	–	–
	08.11.2002	2,066	–	–	–	2,066	159.0	–	–
	06.11.2003	1,625	–	–	–	1,625	195.0	–	–
	04.11.2004	–	1,424	–	–	1,424	232.0	–	–
Total		9,301	1,424	2,235	–	8,490		4	–
Mr T J R Mason (b)	28.10.1999	2,235	–	2,235	–	–	151.0	4	–
	26.10.2000	1,704	–	–	–	1,704	198.0	–	–
	08.11.2001	2,674(a)	–	–	1,671	1,003	198.0	–	–
	08.11.2002	4,132(a)	–	–	2,066	2,066	159.0	–	–
	06.11.2003	1,625	–	–	–	1,625	195.0	–	–
	04.11.2004	–	1,424	–	–	1,424	232.0	–	–
Total		12,370	1,424	2,235	3,737	7,822		4	–
Mr D T Potts	26.10.2000	1,704	–	–	–	1,704	198.0	–	–
	08.11.2001	1,671	–	–	–	1,671	198.0	–	–
	08.11.2002	2,066	–	–	–	2,066	159.0	–	–
	06.11.2003	1,625	–	–	–	1,625	195.0	–	–
	04.11.2004	–	1,424	–	–	1,424	232.0	–	–
Total		7,066	1,424	–	–	8,490		–	–
Mr D E Reid (a)	28.10.1999	2,235	–	1,869	366	–	151.0	2	–
	08.11.2001	959	–	698	261	–	198.0	–	–
	08.11.2002	2,066	–	447	1,619	–	159.0	–	–
Total		5,260	–	3,014	2,246	–		2	–

Save as you earn options are not subject to performance conditions since this scheme is an all employee share scheme.

(a) The market price at which Mr R S Ager and Mr J Gildersleeve exercised options was 261.25p. The market price at which Mr D E Reid exercised options was 260.5p.

(b) Includes family interests.

(c) Options were exercised on 2 February 2005 at a market price of 309.0p, except for Mr R S Ager, Mr J Gildersleeve and Mr D E Reid.

Directors' remuneration report continued

Table 6 Performance share plan share options
Performance Share Plan 2004

	Date of grant	As at 28 Feb 2004	Options granted (a)	Options exercised in year	As at 26 Feb 2005	Date from which exercisable	Expiry date
Sir Terry Leahy	28.07.2004	–	304,794	–	304,794	28.07.2008	28.07.2014
Mr R Brasher	28.07.2004	–	118,367	–	118,367	28.07.2008	28.07.2014
Mr P A Clarke	28.07.2004	–	175,774	–	175,774	28.07.2008	28.07.2014
Mr A T Higginson	28.07.2004	–	175,774	–	175,774	28.07.2008	28.07.2014
Mr T J R Mason	28.07.2004	–	175,774	–	175,774	28.07.2008	28.07.2014
Mr D T Potts	28.07.2004	–	175,774	–	175,774	28.07.2008	28.07.2014

(a) The options granted are nil-cost options. The share price on award was 253.45p. These options are subject to performance conditions set out on page 513. No options lapsed in the year under this scheme.

Table 7 Directors' interests in the long-term incentive plan

Name	Year of release	Award date	No of shares at 28 Feb 2004	Shares awarded during year	Shares released during year	No of shares at 26 Feb 2005	Value released £000	Date of release	MMP on release (pence)
Sir Terry Leahy	2005	11.05.98	79,525	12,166	91,691	–	286	10.02.05	312.45
	2005	08.05.00	181,792	27,812	209,604	–	655	10.02.05	312.45
	2005	11.04.01	149,712	4,043	–	153,755	–	11.04.05	–
	2005	09.04.03	523,938	14,149	–	538,087	–	09.04.05	–
	2006	16.04.99	96,193	14,717	–	110,910	–	16.04.06	–
	2006	11.04.01	117,891	18,034	–	135,925	–	11.04.06	–
	2006	10.04.02	230,677	6,230	–	236,907	–	10.04.06	–
	2006	04.05.04	–	442,170	–	442,170	–	04.05.06	–
	2007	08.05.00	91,747	14,036	–	105,783	–	08.05.07	–
	2007	10.04.02	348,671	53,345	–	402,016	–	10.04.07	–
	2007	09.04.03	329,887	8,909	–	338,796	–	09.04.07	–
	2008	04.05.04	–	294,780	–	294,780	–	04.05.08	–
Mr R S Ager(a)	2005	11.05.98	54,034	–	54,034	–	134	23.03.04	248.125
	2005	08.05.00	102,982	–	102,982	–	256	23.03.04	248.125
	2005	11.04.01	74,854	–	74,854	–	186	23.03.04	248.125
	2005	09.04.03	254,064	–	254,064	–	630	23.03.04	248.125
	2006	16.04.99	61,257	–	61,257	–	152	23.03.04	248.125
	2006	11.04.01	58,942	–	58,942	–	146	23.03.04	248.125
	2006	10.04.02	115,338	–	115,338	–	286	23.03.04	248.125
	2007	08.05.00	51,974	–	51,974	–	129	23.03.04	248.125
	2007	10.04.02	174,333	–	174,333	–	433	23.03.04	248.125
	2007	09.04.03	159,966	–	159,966	–	397	23.03.04	248.125

Date of award	11.05.98	16.04.99	08.05.00	11.04.01	08.05.01	10.04.02	07.05.02	09.04.03	14.05.03	04.05.04	27.05.04
Award price (pence)	186.66	168.83	174.00	259.25	247.50	248.00	261.50	197.25	202.88	248.75	249.88

Table 7 Directors' interests in the long-term incentive plan continued

Name	Year of release	Award date	No of shares at 28 Feb 2004	Shares awarded during year	Shares released during year	No of shares at 26 Feb 2005	Value released £000	Date of release	MMP on release (pence)
Mr R Brasher	2004	08.05.00	25,768	490	26,258	–	65	07.05.04	248.7
	2004	07.05.02	37,318	710	38,028	–	95	07.05.04	248.7
	2005	08.05.01	23,117	623	–	23,740	–	08.05.05	–
	2005	14.05.03	47,682	1,285	–	48,967	–	14.05.05	–
	2006	07.05.02	24,879	671	–	25,550	–	17.05.06	–
	2006	27.05.04	–	56,631	–	56,631	–	27.05.06	–
	2007	14.05.03	31,788	857	–	32,645	–	14.05.07	–
	2008	27.05.04	–	37,754	–	37,754	–	14.05.07	–
Mr P A Clarke	2005	11.05.98	23,714	3,627	27,341	–	85	10.02.05	312.45
	2005	08.05.00	66,528	10,176	76,701	–	240	10.02.05	312.45
	2005	11.04.01	69,241	1,869	–	71,110	–	11.04.05	–
	2005	09.04.03	279,469	7,547	–	287,016	–	09.04.05	–
	2006	10.04.02	117,834	3,181	–	121,015	–	10.04.06	–
	2006	04.05.04	–	250,714	–	250,714	–	04.05.06	–
	2007	08.05.00	37,712	5,769	–	43,481	–	08.05.07	–
	2007	10.04.02	178,107	27,247	–	205,354	–	10.04.04	–
	2007	09.04.03	175,962	4,752	–	180,714	–	09.04.07	–
	2008	04.05.04	–	167,143	–	167,143	–	04.05.08	–
Mr J Gildersleeve(a)	2005	11.05.98	69,080	–	69,080	–	171	23.03.04	248.125
	2005	08.05.00	137,222	–	137,222	–	340	23.03.04	248.125
	2005	11.04.01	99,185	–	99,185	–	246	23.03.04	248.125
	2005	09.04.03	337,058	–	337,058	–	836	23.03.04	248.125
	2006	16.04.99	79,822	–	79,822	–	198	23.03.04	248.125
	2006	11.04.01	78,101	–	78,101	–	194	23.03.04	248.125
	2006	10.04.02	152,767	–	152,767	–	379	23.03.04	248.125
	2007	08.05.00	69,254	–	69,254	–	172	23.03.04	248.125
	2007	10.04.02	230,909	–	230,909	–	573	23.03.04	248.125
	2007	09.04.03	212,222	–	212,222	–	527	23.03.04	248.125
Mr A T Higginson	2005	11.04.01	80,470	2,173	–	82,643	–	11.04.05	–
	2005	09.04.03	291,891	7,882	–	299,773	–	09.04.05	–
	2006	16.04.99	60,076	9,190	–	69,266	–	16.04.06	–
	2006	11.04.01	63,366	9,692	–	73,058	–	11.04.06	–
	2006	10.04.02	128,646	3,474	–	132,120	–	10.04.06	–
	2006	04.05.04	–	250,714	–	250,714	–	04.05.06	–
	2007	08.05.00	53,345	8,160	–	61,505	–	08.05.07	–
	2007	10.04.02	194,450	29,749	–	224,199	–	10.04.07	–
	2007	09.04.03	183,784	4,963	–	188,747	–	09.04.07	–
	2008	04.05.04	–	167,143	–	167,143	–	04.05.08	–

Directors' remuneration report continued

Table 7 Directors' interests in the long-term incentive plan continued

Name	Year of release	Award date	No of shares at 28 Feb 2004	Shares awarded during year	Shares released during year	No of shares at 26 Feb 2005	Value released £000	Date of release	MMP on release (pence)
Mr T J R Mason	2005	11.05.98	49,892	7,632	57,524	–	180	10.02.05	312.45
	2005	08.05.00	105,698	16,169	121,867	–	381	10.02.05	312.45
	2005	11.04.01	80,470	2,173	–	82,643	–	11.04.05	–
	2005	09.04.03	291,891	7,882	–	299,773	–	09.04.05	–
	2006	16.04.99	59,234	9,062	–	68,296	–	16.04.06	–
	2006	11.04.01	63,356	9,702	–	73,058	–	11.04.06	–
	2006	10.04.02	128,646	3,474	–	132,120	–	10.04.06	–
	2006	04.05.04	–	250,714	–	250,714	–	04.05.06	–
	2007	08.05.00	53,345	8,160	–	61,505	–	08.05.07	–
	2007	10.04.02	194,450	29,749	–	224,199	–	10.04.07	–
	2007	09.04.03	183,784	4,963	–	188,747	–	09.04.07	–
	2008	04.05.04	–	167,143	–	167,143	–	04.05.08	–
Mr D T Potts	2005	11.05.98	32,713	5,004	37,717	–	118	10.02.05	312.45
	2005	08.05.00	81,516	12,469	93,985	–	294	10.02.05	312.45
	2005	11.04.01	69,241	1,869	–	71,110	–	11.04.05	–
	2005	09.04.03	279,469	7,547	–	287,016	–	09.04.05	–
	2006	16.04.99	29,577	4,524	–	34,101	–	16.04.06	–
	2006	11.04.01	54,520	8,339	–	62,859	–	11.04.06	–
	2006	10.04.02	117,834	3,181	–	121,015	–	10.04.06	–
	2006	04.05.04	–	250,714	–	250,714	–	04.05.06	–
	2007	08.05.00	41,139	6,293	–	47,432	–	08.05.07	–
	2007	10.04.02	178,107	27,247	–	205,354	–	10.04.07	–
	2007	09.04.03	175,962	4,752	–	180,714	–	09.04.07	–
	2008	04.05.04	–	167,143	–	167,143	–	04.05.08	–

Long-term awards from 2001 are classed as four year cycles and Short-term awards from 2003 are classed as two year cycles as no election for enhancement is possible yet.

Long-term awards can be enhanced from the 4th year, extending the cycle to seven years. Short-term awards can be enhanced from the 2nd year, extending the cycle to five years.

(a) Mr R S Ager and Mr J Gildersleeve shares were all released on retirement.

Table 8 is unaudited information.

Table 8 Disclosable interests of the Directors, including family interests

	26 Feb 2005 or on retirement if earlier		28 Feb 2004 or on appointment if later	
	Ordinary shares (a)	Options to acquire ordinary shares (b)	Ordinary shares (a)	Options to acquire ordinary shares (b)
Executive Directors				
Sir Terry Leahy	5,754,819	4,711,465	4,915,893	3,762,101
Mr R S Ager	1,971,071	2,282,478	1,971,071	2,282,478
Mr R Brasher	282,264	1,229,014	205,278	815,308
Mr P A Clarke	1,428,082	1,839,980	983,778	2,031,112
Mr J Gildersleeve	1,829,760	3,131,132	1,829,760	3,131,132
Mr A T Higginson	1,573,861	1,848,640	1,160,023	2,172,136
Mr T J R Mason	1,756,775	1,847,972	1,519,084	2,261,653
Mr D T Potts	1,702,441	1,747,663	1,250,463	2,024,400
Non-Executive Directors				
Mr C L Allen	–	–	–	–
Mr R F Chase	50,396	–	50,000	–
Mrs K R Cook	–	–	–	–
Mr E M Davies	2,400	–	2,400	–
Dr H Einsmann	92,150	–	92,150	–
Mr J A Gardiner	618,464	–	669,111	–
Mr K J Hydon	30,093	–	30,093	–
Ms V Morali	–	–	–	–
Mr G F Pimlott	34,212	–	33,418	–
Mr D E Reid (Chairman)	193,014	–	189,682	2,952,071

(a) The ordinary shares include shares held as part of incentive plans shown in table 7. Between 26 February 2005 and 11 April 2005, 420 shares were purchased by Executive Directors as part of the Partnership Share Plan (BAYE) operated by the Group.

(b) Options to acquire ordinary shares shown above comprise options under the executive share option schemes and the savings-related share option scheme (1981).

Directors' responsibilities for the preparation of the financial statements

The Directors are required by the Companies Act 1985 to prepare financial statements for each financial year which give a true and fair view of the state of affairs of the company and the Group as at the end of the financial year and of the profit or loss of the Group for the financial year.

The Directors consider that in preparing the financial statements on pages 528 to 557 the company and Group have used appropriate accounting policies, consistently applied and supported by reasonable and prudent judgements and estimates, and that all accounting standards which they consider to be applicable have been followed.

The Directors have responsibility for ensuring that the company and Group keep accounting records which disclose, with reasonable accuracy at any time, the financial position of the company and Group and which enable them to ensure that the financial statements comply with the Companies Act 1985.

The Directors are responsible for the maintenance and integrity of the Annual Review and Summary Financial Statement and Annual Report and Financial Statements published on the Group's Corporate website. Legislation in the UK concerning the preparation and dissemination of financial statements may differ from legislation in other jurisdictions.

The Directors have general responsibility for taking such steps as are reasonably open to them to safeguard the assets of the Group and of the company and to prevent and detect fraud and other irregularities.

Independent auditors' report to the members of Tesco PLC

We have audited the financial statements which comprise the Group profit and loss account, the balance sheets, the cash flow statement, the statement of total recognised gains and losses and the related notes which have been prepared under the historical cost convention and the accounting policies set out in the statement of accounting policies. We have also audited the disclosures required by Part 3 of Schedule 7A to the Companies Act 1985 contained in the Directors' remuneration report ('the auditable part').

Respective responsibilities of directors and auditors
The Directors' responsibilities for preparing the annual report and the financial statements in accordance with applicable United Kingdom law and accounting standards are set out in the statement of Directors' responsibilities. The Directors are also responsible for preparing the Directors' remuneration report.

Our responsibility is to audit the financial statements and the auditable part of the Directors' remuneration report in accordance with relevant legal and regulatory requirements and United Kingdom Auditing Standards issued by the Auditing Practices Board. This report, including the opinion, has been prepared for and only for the company's members as a body in accordance with Section 235 of the Companies Act 1985 and for no other purpose. We do not, in giving this opinion, accept or assume responsibility for any other purpose or to any other person to whom this report is shown or in to whose hands it may come save where expressly agreed by our prior consent in writing.

We report to you our opinion as to whether the financial statements give a true and fair view and whether the financial statements and the auditable part of the Directors' remuneration report have been properly prepared in accordance with the Companies Act 1985. We also report to you if, in our opinion, the Directors' report is not consistent with the financial statements, if the company has not kept proper accounting records, if we have not received all the information and explanations we require for our audit, or if information specified by law regarding Directors' remuneration and transactions is not disclosed.

We read the other information contained in the annual report and consider the implications for our report if we become aware of any apparent misstatements or material inconsistencies with the financial statements. The other information comprises only the Directors' report, the unaudited part of the Directors' remuneration report, the Chairman's statement, the operating and financial review and the corporate governance statement.

We review whether the corporate governance statement reflects the company's compliance with the nine provisions of the 2003 FRC Combined Code specified for our review by the Listing Rules of the Financial Services Authority, and we report if it does not. We are not required to consider whether the Board's statements on internal control cover all risks and controls, or to form an opinion on the effectiveness of the company's or Group's corporate governance procedures or its risk and control procedures.

Basis of audit opinion We conducted our audit in accordance with auditing standards issued by the Auditing Practices Board. An audit includes examination, on a test basis, of evidence relevant to the amounts and disclosures in the financial statements and the auditable part of the Directors' remuneration report. It also includes an assessment of the significant estimates and judgements made by the Directors in the preparation of the financial statements, and of whether the accounting policies are appropriate to the company's circumstances, consistently applied and adequately disclosed.

We planned and performed our audit so as to obtain all the information and explanations which we considered necessary in order to provide us with sufficient evidence to give reasonable assurance that the financial statements and the auditable part of the Directors' remuneration report are free from material misstatement, whether caused by fraud or other irregularity or error. In forming our opinion we also evaluated the overall adequacy of the presentation of information in the financial statements.

Opinion In our opinion:

- the financial statements give a true and fair view of the state of affairs of the company and the Group at 26 February 2005 and of the profit and cash flows of the Group for the period then ended;

- the financial statements have been properly prepared in accordance with the Companies Act 1985; and

- those parts of the Directors' remuneration report required by Part 3 of Schedule 7A to the Companies Act 1985 have been properly prepared in accordance with the Companies Act 1985.

PricewaterhouseCoopers LLP
Chartered Accountants and Registered Auditors
London 11 April 2005

Group profit and loss account Year ended 26 February 2005

	note	Continuing operations 2005 £m	Acquisitions 2005 £m	2005 £m	2004 £m
Sales at net selling prices	2	37,001	69	37,070	33,557
Turnover including share of joint ventures		34,237	116	34,353	31,050
Less: share of joint ventures' turnover		(324)	(55)	(379)	(236)
Group turnover excluding value added tax	2/3	33,913	61	33,974	30,814
Operating expenses					
– Normal operating expenses		(31,785)	(60)	(31,845)	(28,925)
– Employee profit-sharing	4	(65)	–	(65)	(57)
– Integration costs		(46)	(7)	(53)	(45)
– Goodwill amortisation	12	(60)	(2)	(62)	(52)
Operating profit/(loss)	2/3	1,957	(8)	1,949	1,735
Share of operating profit/(loss) of joint ventures and associates		133	(3)	130	97
Net profit/(loss) on disposal of fixed assets		53	–	53	(9)
Profit/(loss) on ordinary activities before interest and taxation		2,143	(11)	2,132	1,823
Net interest payable	8			(170)	(223)
Profit on ordinary activities before taxation	5			1,962	1,600
Underlying profit before net profit/(loss) on disposal of fixed assets, integration costs and goodwill amortisation				2,029	1,708
Net profit/(loss) on disposal of fixed assets				53	(9)
Integration costs				(53)	(45)
Goodwill amortisation				(62)	(52)
Goodwill amortisation in joint ventures and associates				(5)	(2)
Tax on profit on ordinary activities	9			(593)	(498)
Profit on ordinary activities after taxation				1,369	1,102
Minority interests				(3)	(2)
Profit for the financial year				1,366	1,100
Dividends	10			(587)	(516)
Retained profit for the financial year	25			779	584
				Pence	Pence
Earnings per share	11			17.72	15.05
Adjusted for net profit/(loss) on disposal of fixed assets after taxation				(0.65)	0.11
Adjusted for integration costs after taxation				0.59	0.55
Adjusted for goodwill amortisation				0.87	0.74
Underlying earnings per share[†]	11			18.53	16.45
Diluted earnings per share	11			17.50	14.93
Adjusted for net profit/(loss) on disposal of fixed assets after taxation				(0.64)	0.11
Adjusted for integration costs after taxation				0.58	0.54
Adjusted for goodwill amortisation				0.86	0.73
Underlying diluted earnings per share[†]	11			18.30	16.31
Dividend per share	10			7.56	6.84
Dividend cover (times)				2.42	2.38

Accounting policies and notes forming part of these financial statements are on pages 532 to 557.

[†] Excluding net profit/(loss) on disposal of fixed assets, integration costs and goodwill amortisation.

Statement of total recognised gains and losses Year ended 26 February 2005

	Group		Company	
	2005 £m	2004 £m	2005 £m	2004 £m
Profit for the financial year	1,366	1,100	1,095	771
Gain/(loss) on foreign currency net investments	19	(157)	(71)	(2)
Tax effect of exchange adjustments offset in reserves	16	–	16	–
Total recognised gains and losses relating to the financial year	1,401	943	1,040	769
Prior year adjustment (note 1)	53			
Total recognised gains and losses since last annual report and financial statements	1,454			

Reconciliation of movements in shareholders' funds Year ended 26 February 2005

	Group[†]		Company	
	2005 £m	2004 restated £m	2005 £m	2004 £m
Profit for the financial year	1,366	1,100	1,095	771
Dividends	(587)	(516)	(587)	(516)
	779	584	508	255
Gain/(loss) on foreign currency net investments	19	(157)	(71)	(2)
Tax effect of exchange adjustment offset in reserves	16	–	16	–
Application of UITF 38	(29)	28	–	–
New share capital subscribed less expenses	130	844	146	869
Payment of dividends by shares in lieu of cash	93	158	93	158
Net addition to shareholders' funds	1,008	1,457	692	1,280
Opening shareholders' funds	7,998	6,541*	4,537	3,257
Closing shareholders' funds	9,006	7,998	5,229	4,537

Accounting policies and notes forming part of these financial statements are on pages 532 to 557.

* Originally £6,516m before prior year adjustment of £25m.

[†] Prior year comparatives have been restated due to UITF 38 and UITF 17 (revised) (note 1).

Balance sheets 26 February 2005

	note	2005 £m	£m	£m	Group 2004 restated† £m	Company 2005 £m	2004 £m
Fixed assets							
Intangible assets	12		1,044		965	–	–
Tangible assets	13		15,495		14,094	–	–
Investments	14		7		6	9,421	9,077
Investments in joint ventures	14						
Share of gross assets		4,280		2,006		–	–
Less: share of gross liabilities		(4,037)		(1,712)		–	–
Goodwill		145		15		–	–
			388		309	145	143
Investments in associates	14		19		21	–	–
			16,953		15,395	9,566	9,220
Current assets							
Stocks	15		1,309		1,199	–	–
Debtors	16		1,002		826	2,702	1,624
Investments	17		346		430	150	99
Cash at bank and in hand			800		670	–	–
			3,457		3,125	2,852	1,723
Creditors:							
falling due within one year	18		(6,072)		(5,516)	(3,152)	(2,456)
Net current liabilities			(2,615)		(2,391)	(300)	(733)
Total assets less current liabilities			14,338		13,004	9,266	8,487
Creditors:							
falling due after more than one year	19		(4,531)		(4,368)	(4,037)	(3,950)
Provisions for liabilities and charges	22		(750)		(593)	–	–
Net assets			9,057		8,043	5,229	4,537
Capital and reserves							
Called up share capital	24		389		384	389	384
Share premium account	25		3,704		3,470	3,704	3,470
Other reserves	25		40		40	–	–
Profit and loss account	25		4,873		4,104	1,136	683
Equity shareholders' funds			9,006		7,998	5,229	4,537
Minority interests			51		45	–	–
Total capital employed			9,057		8,043	5,229	4,537

Accounting policies and notes forming part of these financial statements are on page 532 to 557.

Terry Leahy
Andrew Higginson
Directors
Financial statements approved by the Board on 11 April 2005.

Group cash flow statement Year ended 26 February 2005

	note	2005 £m	2004 restated† £m
Net cash inflow from operating activities	32	3,004	2,942
Dividends from joint ventures and associates		135	60
Returns on investments and servicing of finance			
Interest received		83	41
Interest paid		(331)	(320)
Interest element of finance lease rental payments		(15)	(17)
Cash received on sale of financial instruments		–	235
Net cash outflow from returns on investments and servicing of finance		(263)	(61)
Taxation		(483)	(326)
Capital expenditure and financial investment			
Payments to acquire tangible fixed assets		(2,304)	(2,239)
Proceeds from sale of tangible fixed assets		856	62
Net increase in loans to joint ventures		(10)	–
Net cash outflow from capital expenditure and financial investment		(1,458)	(2,177)
Acquisitions and disposals			
Purchase of subsidiary undertakings		(84)	(269)
Net cash at bank and in hand acquired with subsidiaries		3	53
Proceeds from sale of subsidiary		16	–
Net cash at bank and in hand disposed with subsidiary		(11)	–
Invested in joint ventures		(146)	(48)
Invested in associates and other investments		(6)	(8)
Net cash outflow from acquisitions and disposals		(228)	(272)
Equity dividends paid		(448)	(303)
Cash inflow/(outflow) before management of liquid resources and financing		259	(137)
Management of liquid resources			
Decrease/(increase) in short-term deposits		97	(220)
Financing			
Ordinary shares issued for cash		146	868
Net purchase of own shares for share trusts		(143)	(51)
Net decrease in other loans		(18)	(180)
New finance leases		128	75
Capital element of finance leases repaid		(348)	(73)
Net cash (outflow)/inflow from financing		(235)	639
Increase in cash		121	282
Reconciliation of net cash flow to movement in net debt			
Increase in cash		121	282
Cash outflow from decrease in debt and lease financing		238	178
(Decrease)/increase in liquid resources		(97)	220
Loans and finance leases acquired with subsidiaries		(17)	(5)
Amortisation of 4% unsecured deep discount loan stock, RPI and LPI medium term notes		(19)	(20)
Other non-cash movements on loans		(14)	–
Other non-cash movements on finance leases		(16)	(2)
Foreign exchange differences		52	(6)
Decrease in net debt		248	647
Opening net debt	33	(4,090)	(4,737)
Closing net debt	33	(3,842)	(4,090)

Accounting policies and notes forming part of these financial statements are on pages 532 to 557.
† Restated due to UITF 38 (note 1).

Accounting policies

Basis of preparation of financial statements These financial statements have been prepared under the historical cost convention, in accordance with applicable accounting standards and the Companies Act 1985.

A summary of the more important Group accounting policies is set out below.

As in the prior year, the Group has continued to account for pensions and other post-employment benefits in accordance with SSAP 24 but has complied with the transitional disclosure requirements of FRS 17. These transitional disclosures are presented in note 27.

Basis of consolidation The Group financial statements consist of the financial statements of the parent company, its subsidiary undertakings and the Group's share of interests in joint ventures and associates. The accounts of the parent company's subsidiary undertakings are prepared to dates around 26 February 2005 apart from Tesco Global Aruhazak Rt., Tesco Polska Sp. z o.o., Tesco Stores ČR a.s., Tesco Stores SR a.s., Tesco Kipa A.Ş., Samsung Tesco Co. Limited, Tesco Malaysia Sdn Bhd, Tesco Taiwan Co. Limited, Ek-Chai Distribution System Co. Ltd and C Two-Network Co. Ltd which prepared accounts to 31 December 2004. In the opinion of the Directors, it is necessary for the above named subsidiaries to prepare accounts to a date earlier than the rest of the Group to enable the timely publication of the Group financial statements.

The Group's interests in joint ventures are accounted for using the gross equity method. The Group's interests in associates are accounted for using the equity method.

Turnover Turnover consists of sales through retail outlets and sales of development properties, excluding value added tax. Turnover is reported net of vouchers and on a commission-only basis for mobile phone airtime sales. Turnover is stated net of returns.

Stocks Stocks comprise goods held for resale and properties held for, or in the course of, development and are valued at the lower of cost and net realisable value. Stocks in stores are calculated at retail prices and reduced by appropriate margins to take into account factors such as obsolescence, seasonality and damage.

Money market deposits Money market deposits are stated at cost. All income from these investments is included in the profit and loss account as interest receivable and similar income.

Tangible fixed assets and depreciation Fixed assets are carried at cost and include amounts in respect of interest paid on funds specifically related to the financing of assets in the course of construction. Interest is capitalised on a gross basis.

Depreciation is provided on a straight-line basis over the anticipated useful economic lives of the assets.

The following rates were applied for the Group and are consistent with the prior year:

- Land premia paid in excess of the alternative use value – at 2.5% of cost.

- Freehold and leasehold buildings with greater than 40 years unexpired – at 2.5% of cost.

- Leasehold properties with less than 40 years unexpired – by equal annual instalments over the unexpired period of the lease.

- Plant, equipment, fixtures and fittings and motor vehicles – at rates varying from 10% to 33%.

Goodwill Goodwill arising on acquisitions is capitalised and amortised on a straight-line basis over its useful economic life, up to a maximum of 20 years.

Impairment of fixed assets and goodwill Fixed assets and goodwill are subject to review for impairment in accordance with FRS 11, 'Impairment of Fixed Assets and Goodwill'. Any impairment is recognised in the profit and loss account in the year in which it occurs.

Leasing Plant, equipment and fixtures and fittings which are the subject of finance leases are dealt with in the financial statements as tangible fixed assets and equivalent liabilities at what would otherwise have been the cost of outright purchase.

Rentals are apportioned between reductions of the respective liabilities and finance charges, the latter being calculated by reference to the rates of interest implicit in the leases. The finance charges are dealt with under interest payable in the profit and loss account.

Leased assets are depreciated in accordance with the depreciation accounting policy over the anticipated working lives of the assets, which generally correspond to the primary rental periods. The cost of operating leases in respect of land and buildings and other assets is expensed on a straight-line basis. Operating lease income consists of rentals from properties held for disposal or sub-tenant agreements and is recognised as earned.

Taxation The amount included in the profit and loss account is based on pre-tax reported income and is calculated at current local tax rates, taking into account timing differences and the likelihood of realisation of deferred tax assets and liabilities.

Deferred tax Deferred tax is recognised in respect of all timing differences that have originated but not reversed by the balance sheet date and which could give rise to an obligation to pay more or less taxation in the future. Deferred tax assets are recognised to the extent that they are regarded as recoverable. They are regarded as recoverable to the extent that, on the basis of all available evidence, it is regarded as more likely than not that there will be suitable taxable profits from which the future reversal of the underlying timing differences can be deducted. Deferred tax is measured on a non-discounted basis at the tax rates that are expected to apply in the periods in which timing differences reverse, based on tax rates and laws substantively enacted at the balance sheet date.

Pensions The expected cost of pensions in respect of the Group's defined benefit pension schemes is charged to the profit and loss account over the working lifetimes of employees in the schemes. Actuarial surpluses and deficits are spread over the expected remaining working lifetimes of employees. Note 27 in the financial statements provides further detail in respect of pension costs and commitments.

Post-retirement benefits other than pensions The cost of providing other post-retirement benefits, which comprise private healthcare, is charged to the profit and loss account so as to spread the cost over the service lives of relevant employees in accordance with the advice of qualified actuaries. Actuarial surpluses and deficits are spread over the expected remaining working lifetimes of relevant employees.

Foreign currencies Assets and liabilities in foreign currencies are translated into Sterling at the financial year end exchange rates. Profits and losses of overseas subsidiaries are translated into Sterling at average rates of exchange. Gains and losses arising on the translation of the net assets of overseas subsidiaries, less exchange differences arising on matched foreign currency borrowings, are taken to reserves and disclosed in the statement of total recognised gains and losses. Gains and losses on instruments used for hedging are recognised in the profit and loss account when the exposure that is being hedged is itself recognised.

Financial instruments Derivative instruments utilised by the Group are interest rate swaps, floors and caps, forward start interest rate swaps, cross currency swaps, forward rate agreements and forward exchange contracts and options. Termination payments made or received in respect of derivatives are spread over the life of the underlying exposure in cases where the underlying exposure continues to exist. Where the underlying exposure ceases to exist, any termination payments are taken to the profit and loss account.

Interest differentials on derivative instruments are recognised by adjusting net interest payable. Premia or discount on derivative instruments is amortised over the shorter of the life of the instrument or the underlying exposure.

Currency swap agreements are valued at closing rates of exchange. Forward exchange contracts are valued at discounted closing forward rates of exchange. Resulting gains or losses are offset against foreign exchange gains or losses on the related borrowings or, where the instrument is used to hedge a committed future transaction, are deferred until the transaction occurs or is extinguished.

Notes to the financial statements

Note 1 Prior period adjustment

The Group has implemented UITF 38 and UITF 17 (revised). Accounting for ESOP trusts under UITF 38 changes the presentation of an entity's own shares held. Shares held by ESOP trusts are now treated as a deduction in arriving at shareholders' funds, rather than a fixed asset investment. In addition, the net cash outflow from the purchase of shares by the share trusts has been reclassified within the cash flow statement from Capital expenditure and financial investment to Financing. Simultaneously with the issue of UITF 38, UITF 17 Employee Share Schemes was revised. As required by UITF 17 (revised) the Directors have reviewed the classification and basis of accounting for shares held within ESOP trusts. The net effect is an increase in net assets of £53m at 28 February 2004 (£25m at 22 February 2003).

Note 2 Segmental analysis of sales, turnover, profit and net assets

The Group's operations of retailing and associated activities and property development are carried out in the UK, Republic of Ireland, Hungary, Poland, Czech Republic, Slovakia, Turkey, Thailand, South Korea, Taiwan, Malaysia, Japan and China. The results for Asia and the rest of Europe, excluding the Republic of Ireland, are for the year ended 31 December 2004.

			2005				2004	
	Sales including VAT £m	Turnover excluding VAT £m	Operating profit £m	Net operating assets £m	Sales including VAT £m	Turnover excluding VAT £m	Operating profit £m	Net operating assets restated[†] £m
Continuing operations								
UK	29,511	27,146	1,694	9,243	26,876	24,760	1,526	9,038
Rest of Europe	4,349	3,818	218	2,139	3,834	3,385	184	1,861
Asia	3,210	3,010	152	1,517	2,847	2,669	122	1,234
	37,070	33,974	2,064		33,557	30,814	1,832	
Integration costs			(53)				(45)	
Goodwill amortisation			(62)				(52)	
Operating profit			1,949				1,735	
Share of operating profit from joint ventures and associates			130				97	
Net profit/(loss) on disposal of fixed assets			53				(9)	
Net interest payable			(170)				(223)	
Profit on ordinary activities before taxation			1,962				1,600	
Operating margin (prior to goodwill amortisation and integration costs)			6.1%				5.9%	
				12,899				12,133
Net debt (note 20)				(3,842)				(4,090)
Net assets				9,057				8,043

Inter-segmental turnover between the geographical areas of business is not material. Turnover is disclosed by origin. There is no material difference in turnover by destination.

The Group's share of turnover in the joint ventures, which is not included in the numbers above, is £379m (2004 – £236m).

[†] Prior year comparatives have been restated (see note 1).

Note 3 Analysis of operating profit

	2005 £m	2004 £m
Turnover excluding VAT	33,974	30,814
Cost of sales	(31,271)	(28,405)
Gross profit	2,703	2,409
Administrative expenses	(639)	(577)
Integration costs	(53)	(45)
Goodwill amortisation	(62)	(52)
Operating profit	1,949	1,735

Cost of sales includes distribution costs and store operating costs. Employee profit-sharing is included within administrative expenses.

Note 4 Employee profit-sharing

This represents the amount allocated to the trustees of the profit-sharing scheme and is based on the UK profit after interest, before net profit/(loss) on disposal of fixed assets and taxation.

Note 5 Profit on ordinary activities before taxation

	2005 £m	2004 £m
Profit on ordinary activities is stated after charging/(crediting) the following:		
Depreciation of tangible fixed assets:		
– owned assets	654	631
– under finance leases	79	69
Goodwill amortisation	67	54
Operating lease costs (a)	283	221
Operating lease income	(119)	(102)
Employment costs (note 6)	3,534	3,234

(a) Operating lease costs include £68m for hire of plant and machinery (2004 – £55m).

Amounts payable to auditors:

		2005 £m	2004 £m
Audit	– statutory audit (i)	1.7	1.2
	– other audit services	0.4	0.3
		2.1	1.5
Non-audit services	– Assurance	0.7	0.7
	– Tax services	1.1	0.5
	– Other services	0.2	0.1
		2.0	1.3

(i) Includes £0.1m (2004 – £0.1m) for the company.

Note 6 Employment costs

	2005 £m	2004 £m
Employment costs during the year		
Wages and salaries	3,089	2,891
Social security costs	217	183
Other pension costs (note 27)	228	160
	3,534	3,234

Number of persons employed

The average number of employees during the year was: UK 245,286 (2004 – 230,680), Rest of Europe 55,781 (2004 – 49,362), Asia 34,683 (2004 – 30,369) and the average number of full-time equivalents was: UK 163,006 (2004 – 152,408), Rest of Europe 47,204 (2004 – 42,399) and Asia 32,770 (2004 – 28,528).

Notes to the financial statements continued

Note 7 Directors' emoluments and interests

Details of Directors' emoluments and interests are given in the Directors' remuneration report on pages 511 to 525.

Note 8 Net interest payable

		2005		2004
	£m	£m	£m	£m
Interest receivable and similar income on money market investments and deposits		99		49
Less interest payable on:				
Short-term bank loans and overdrafts repayable within five years	(57)		(85)	
Long-term bank loans repayable after five years	(14)		–	
Finance charges payable on finance leases	(16)		(19)	
4% unsecured deep discount loan stock 2006 (a)	(11)		(11)	
0.7% 50bn JPY Medium Term Note (MTN) 2006	(2)		(2)	
6% 150m GBP MTN 2006	(9)		(9)	
7½% 325m GBP MTN 2007	(24)		(25)	
5¼% 500m EUR MTN 2008	(18)		(18)	
6% 250m GBP MTN 2008	(15)		(15)	
5⅛% 350m GBP MTN 2009	(18)		(18)	
4¾% 750m EUR MTN 2010	(25)		(26)	
6⅜% 150m GBP MTN 2010	(10)		(10)	
4% RPI GBP MTN 2016 (b)	(15)		(18)	
5½% 350m GBP MTN 2019	(19)		(20)	
3.322% LPI GBP MTN 2025 (c)	(14)		(15)	
6% 200m GBP MTN 2029	(12)		(12)	
5½% 200m GBP MTN 2033	(11)		(11)	
Other bonds	(8)		(6)	
Interest capitalised	63		62	
Share of interest of joint ventures and associates	(34)		(14)	
		(269)		(272)
		(170)		(223)

(a) Interest payable on the 4% unsecured deep discount loan stock 2006 includes £6m (2004 – £6m) of discount amortisation.
(b) Interest payable on the RPI GBP MTN 2016 includes £6m (2004 – £8m) of RPI related amortisation.
(c) Interest payable on the LPI GBP MTN 2025 includes £7m (2004 – £6m) of RPI related amortisation.

Note 9 Taxation

(a) Analysis of charge in year	2005 £m	2004 £m
Current tax:		
UK corporation tax at 30.0% (2004 – 30.0%)	426	433
Prior year items	(70)	(64)
Overseas taxation	56	33
Share of joint ventures and associates	30	27
	442	429
Deferred tax: (note 22)		
Origination and reversal of timing differences (i)	116	29
Prior year items	33	41
Share of joint ventures and associates	2	(1)
	151	69
Tax on profit on ordinary activities	593	498

(i) The total charge for the year of £116m includes £nil (2004 – £2m) debit to fixed assets.

Note 9 Taxation continued

(b) Factors affecting the tax charge for the year

The effective rate of corporation tax for the year of 22.5% (2004 – 26.8%) is lower than the standard rate of corporation tax in the UK of 30.0%. The differences are explained below:

	2005 %	2004 %
Standard rate of corporation tax	30.0	30.0
Effects of:		
Expenses not deductible for tax purposes (primarily goodwill amortisation and non-qualifying depreciation)	4.0	4.1
Capital allowances for the year in excess of depreciation on qualifying assets	(3.4)	(3.9)
Differences in overseas taxation rates	(0.8)	(0.9)
Timing of tax relief of share-based payments	(0.1)	1.4
Pension contributions	(3.1)	–
Prior year items	(3.5)	(4.0)
Other items	(0.6)	0.1
Effective rate of corporation tax for the year	22.5	26.8

(c) Factors that may affect future tax charges

The Group has not recognised deferred tax assets of £14m (2004 – £12m) in respect of certain tax losses which are available to carry forward and offset, should future taxable profits arise.

Note 10 Dividends

	2005 Pence/share	2004 Pence/share	2005 £m	2004 £m
Declared interim	2.29	2.07	177	151
Proposed final	5.27	4.77	410	365
	7.56	6.84	587	516

Note 11 Earnings per share and diluted earnings per share

Earnings per share and diluted earnings per share have been calculated in accordance with FRS 14, 'Earnings per Share', which requires that earnings should be based on the net profit attributable to ordinary shareholders. The calculation for earnings, including and excluding net profit/(loss) on disposal of fixed assets, integration costs and goodwill amortisation, is based on the profit for the financial year of £1,366m (2004 – £1,100m).

For the purposes of calculating earnings per share, the number of shares is the weighted average number of ordinary shares in issue during the year of 7,707 million (2004 – 7,307 million).

The calculation for diluted earnings per share uses the weighted average number of ordinary shares in issue adjusted by the effects of all dilutive potential ordinary shares. The dilution effect is calculated on the full exercise of all ordinary share options granted by the Group, including performance-based options which the Group considers to have been earned. The calculation compares the difference between the exercise price of exercisable ordinary share options, weighted for the period over which they were outstanding, with the average daily mid-market closing price over the period.

The alternative measure of earnings per share is provided because it reflects the Group's underlying trading performance excluding the effect of the profit/(loss) on disposal of fixed assets, integration costs and amortisation of goodwill.

	2005 million	2004 million
Weighted average number of dilutive share options	97	61
Weighted average number of shares in issue in the period	7,707	7,307
Total number of shares for calculating diluted earnings per share	7,804	7,368

Notes to the financial statements continued

Note 12 Intangible fixed assets

	Licence (a) £m	Goodwill (b) £m	Total £m
Cost			
At 28 February 2004	–	1,058	1,058
Currency translation	–	82	82
Additions at cost	2	70	72
Disposals	–	(5)	(5)
At 26 February 2005	2	1,205	1,207
Amortisation			
At 28 February 2004	–	93	93
Currency translation	–	8	8
Charge for the period	–	62	62
At 26 February 2005	–	163	163
Net carrying value			
At 26 February 2005	2	1,042	1,044
At 28 February 2004	–	965	965

(a) Licences are amortised over the life of the licence.

(b) Goodwill arising from investments in subsidiaries in the year has been capitalised and amortised over 20 years in accordance with the provisions of FRS 10, 'Goodwill and Intangible Assets'. 20 years is the period over which the Directors estimate that the values of the underlying businesses acquired are expected to exceed the value of the underlying assets.

Goodwill arising from investments in joint ventures and associates has been capitalised and amortised over 20 years in accordance with the provisions of FRS 9, 'Associates and Joint Ventures' and FRS 10, 'Goodwill and Intangible Assets' and is included in fixed asset investments (note 14).

Note 13 Tangible fixed assets

	Land and buildings £m	Plant, equipment, fixtures and fittings and motor vehicles £m	Total £m
Cost			
At 28 February 2004	13,718	4,479	18,197
Currency translation	359	87	446
Additions at cost (a)	1,689	728	2,417
	15,766	5,294	21,060
Acquisitions	45	1	46
Disposals	(841)	(436)	(1,277)
At 26 February 2005	14,970	4,859	19,829
Depreciation			
At 28 February 2004	1,709	2,394	4,103
Currency translation	17	34	51
Charge for the period	230	503	733
	1,956	2,931	4,887
Disposals	(161)	(392)	(553)
At 26 February 2005	1,795	2,539	4,334
Net book value (b) (c)			
At 26 February 2005	13,175	2,320	15,495
At 28 February 2004	12,009	2,085	14,094
Capital work in progress included above (d)			
At 26 February 2005	540	74	614
At 28 February 2004	353	100	453

Note 13 Tangible fixed assets continued

(a) Includes £63m in respect of interest capitalised, principally relating to land and building assets. The capitalisation rate used to determine the amount of finance costs capitalised during the period was 5.7%. Interest capitalised is deducted in determining taxable profit in the period in which it is incurred.

(b) Net book value includes capitalised interest at 26 February 2005 of £597m (2004 – £540m).

The cost of Land and buildings includes £16m (2004 – nil) in respect of assets held under finance leases. The related accumulated depreciation at the end of the year was £0.1m (2004 – nil).

The cost of Plant, equipment, fixtures and fittings and motor vehicles includes £397m (2004 – £842m) in respect of assets held under finance leases. The related accumulated depreciation at the end of the year was £358m (2004 – £572m).

(c) The net book value of land and buildings comprises:

	2005 £m	2004 £m
Freehold	12,070	11,023
Long leasehold – 50 years or more	552	501
Short leasehold – less than 50 years	553	485
At 26 February 2005	13,175	12,009

(d) Capital work in progress does not include land.

Note 14 Fixed asset investments

			Group				Company
	Joint ventures (b) £m	Associates (c) £m	Own shares £m	Other investments £m	Shares in Group undertakings £m	Loans to Group undertakings £m	Joint ventures £m
As previously reported	309	21	28	6	5,524	3,553	143
Restatement (i)	–	–	(28)	–	–	–	–
At 28 February 2004 (restated)	309	21	–	6	5,524	3,553	143
Additions (ii)	148	5	–	1	382	258	2
Effect of foreign exchange rate changes	(5)	(3)	–	–	–	–	–
Share of profit/(loss) of joint ventures and associates	72	(3)	–	–	–	–	–
Transfer to provisions (iii)	3	–	–	–	–	–	–
Goodwill amortisation	(4)	(1)	–	–	–	–	–
Income received from joint ventures and associates	(135)	–	–	–	–	–	–
Disposals	–	–	–	–	(9)	(287)	–
At 26 February 2005	388	19	–	7	5,897	3,524	145

(i) Restated in line with UITF 17 (revised) and UITF 38 (note 1). The Own shares held by the employee share ownership trust are now included within shareholders' funds (note 25).

(ii) Additions includes £140m of goodwill in respect of Joint ventures and £1m of goodwill in respect of Associates.

(iii) Transfer to provisions represents the Group's share of net liabilities within certain joint venture companies.

Notes to the financial statements continued

Note 14 Fixed asset investments continued

(a) The Group's principal operating subsidiary undertakings are:

	Business	Share of equity capital and voting rights	Country of incorporation
Tesco Stores Limited	Retail	100%	Registered in England
Tesco Property Holdings Limited	Property Investment	100%	Registered in England
Tesco Insurance Limited	Insurance	100%	Guernsey
Valiant Insurance Company Limited	Insurance	100%	Republic of Ireland
Tesco Distribution Limited	Distribution	100%	Registered in England
Tesco Card Services Limited	Card Handling Services	100%	Registered in England
T&S Stores Limited	Retail	100%	Registered in England
Tesco Ireland Limited	Retail	100%	Republic of Ireland
Tesco Global Aruhazak Rt.	Retail	99%	Hungary
Tesco Polska Sp. z o.o.	Retail	100%	Poland
Tesco Stores Č R a.s.	Retail	100%	Czech Republic
Tesco Stores SR a.s.	Retail	100%	Slovakia
Samsung Tesco Co. Limited	Retail	89%	South Korea
Ek-Chai Distribution System Co. Ltd	Retail	99%	Thailand
Tesco Taiwan Co. Limited	Retail	100%	Taiwan
Tesco Stores Malaysia Sdn Bhd	Retail	70%	Malaysia
Tesco Stores Hong Kong Limited	Purchasing	100%	Hong Kong
C Two-Network Co. Ltd	Retail	100%	Japan
Tesco Kipa A.Ş.	Retail	93%	Turkey

All principal operating subsidiary undertakings operate in their country of incorporation.

A full list of operating subsidiaries will be annexed to the next Annual Return, filed at Companies House.

(b) The Group's principal joint ventures are:

	Business	Share of issued ordinary share capital, loan capital and debt securities	Country of incorporation and principal country of operation
Shopping Centres Limited	Property Investment	50%	Registered in England
BLT Properties Limited	Property Investment	50%	Registered in England
Tesco BL Holdings Limited	Property Investment	50%	Registered in England
Tesco British Land Property Partnership	Property Investment	50%	Registered in England
Tesco Property Partnership ELP	Property Investment	50%	Registered in England
Tesco Personal Finance Group Limited	Personal Finance	50%	Registered in Scotland
Tesco Home Shopping Limited	Mail Order Retail	60%	Registered in England
Tesco Mobile Limited	Telecommunications	50%	Registered in England
dunnhumby Limited	Data Analysts	53%	Registered in England
Nutri Centres Limited	Complementary Medicines	50%	Registered in England
Hymall	Retail	50%	Republic of China
Taiwan Charn Yang Developments Limited	Property Investment	50%	Taiwan
Retail Property Company Limited	Property Investment	50%	Thailand
Tesco Card Services Limited	Personal Finance	50%	Thailand

The accounting period-ends of the joint ventures consolidated in these financial statements, range from 31 December 2004 to 26 February 2005.

Note 14 Fixed asset investments continued

The Group's share of the joint ventures, as at 26 February 2005, was as follows:

	Joint ventures in aggregate		Tesco Personal Finance	
	2005 £m	2004 £m	2005 £m	2004 £m
Fixed assets	717	348	8	6
Current assets	3,563	1,658	3,446	1,580
Creditors falling due within one year	(3,371)	(1,323)	(3,120)	(1,274)
Creditors falling due after more than one year	(666)	(389)	(103)	(103)
Net assets	243	294	231	209

There is no recourse to Group companies in respect of the borrowings of the joint ventures.

Tesco Personal Finance forms a substantial proportion of the gross assets and liabilities of the Group's joint ventures in aggregate. The following shows the Group's share of the results of Tesco Personal Finance:

	2005 £m	2004 £m
Other operating income	201	166
Profit before tax	101	80
Taxation	(30)	(24)
Profit after taxation	71	56

Hymall

The Group acquired a 50% share in Hymall on 1 September 2004. Of the £145m cost of investment, goodwill arising of £140m has been capitalised, and will be amortised over 20 years. The acquisition of the interest in Hymall comprised:

	£m
Group share of original book value of net assets	20
Fair value adjustments to achieve consistency of accounting policies	(15)
Fair value to the Group	5
Goodwill	140
Total cost	145

The principal fair value adjustments made to the net book values of the assets and liabilities of Hymall comprise: converting from cash accounting to accruals-based accounting; revaluation of stock; debtors and fixed assets; provision for onerous leases, and recognition of deferred tax assets.

(c) The Group's principal associate is:

	Business	Share of issued share capital, loan capital and debt securities	Country of incorporation and principal country of operation
GroceryWorks Holdings Inc.	Internet Retailer	39%	United States of America

The net assets and goodwill of associates are:

	2005 £m	2004 £m
Net assets	7	6
Goodwill	12	15
	19	21

Notes to the financial statements continued

Note 15 Stocks

	Group		Company	
	2005 £m	2004 £m	2005 £m	2004 £m
Goods held for resale	1,306	1,196	–	–
Development property	3	3	–	–
	1,309	1,199	–	–

Accumulated capitalised interest within development property at 26 February 2005 was £0.6m.

Note 16 Debtors

	Group		Company	
	2005 £m	2004 restated[†] £m	2005 £m	2004 £m
Amounts owed by Group undertakings	–	–	2,436	1,260
Amounts owed by undertakings in which Group companies have a participating interest	136	120	103	106
Other debtors	597	657	163	258
Prepayments and accrued income	48	37	–	–
Pension prepayment	221	12	–	–
	1,002	826	2,702	1,624

Of the amounts owed by undertakings in which Group companies have a participating interest, £126m (2004 – £109m) is due after more than one year. Included in Other debtors are amounts of £60m (2004 – £38m) due after more than one year. Included in Prepayments and accrued income is £2m (2004 – £1m) due after more than one year.

[†] Prior year comparatives have been restated (see note 1).

Note 17 Investments

	Group		Company	
	2005 £m	2004 £m	2005 £m	2004 £m
Money market deposits	346	430	150	99

Note 18 Creditors falling due within one year

	Group		Company	
	2005	2004 restated[†]	2005	2004
	£m	£m	£m	£m
Bank loans and overdrafts (a) (b) (c)	471	775	329	552
Trade creditors	2,819	2,434	–	–
Amounts owed to Group undertakings	–	–	1,957	1,189
Corporation tax	221	308	101	6
Other taxation and social security	221	190	2	3
Other creditors	1,229	1,040	331	323
Amounts payable to joint ventures and associates	29	10	–	–
Accruals and deferred income (d)	660	320	16	13
Finance leases (note 23) (e)	6	69	–	–
Dividends	416	370	416	370
	6,072	5,516	3,152	2,456

[†] Prior year comparatives have been restated (see note 1).

(a) Bank deposits in subsidiary undertakings of £119m (2004 – £217m) have been offset against borrowings in the parent company under a legal right of set-off.

(b) Floating rate liabilities bear interest at rates based on relevant national LIBOR equivalents. The weighted average rate of interest payable on these amounts at the year end is approximately 3.9%.

(c) Includes £9m of loans from joint ventures and associates.

(d) Accruals and deferred income includes £163m (2004 – £211m) attributable to realised gains on terminated interest rate swaps.

(e) Finance leases bear interest at a weighted average rate of approximately 5.7%.

Note 19 Creditors falling due after more than one year

	Group		Company	
	2005 £m	2004 £m	2005 £m	2004 £m
4% unsecured deep discount loan stock 2006 (a)	116	110	116	110
Finance leases (note 23)	25	166	–	–
6% 150m GBP Medium Term Note (MTN) 2006	150	150	150	150
0.7% 50bn JPY MTN 2006	285	285	285	285
7½% 325m GBP MTN 2007	325	325	325	325
6% 250m GBP MTN 2008	250	250	250	250
5¼% 500m EUR MTN 2008	345	345	345	345
5⅛% 350m GBP MTN 2009	350	350	350	350
6⅝% 150m GBP MTN 2010	150	150	150	150
4¾% 750m EUR MTN 2010	528	528	528	528
4% RPI GBP MTN 2016 (b)	226	220	226	220
5½% 350m GBP MTN 2019	350	350	350	350
3.322% LPI GBP MTN 2025 (c)	228	221	228	221
6% 200m GBP MTN 2029	200	200	200	200
5½% 200m GBP MTN 2033	200	200	200	200
Other MTNs (d)	334	266	334	266
Other loans (e)	449	230	–	–
	4,511	4,346	4,037	3,950
Other creditors	20	22	–	–
	4,531	4,368	4,037	3,950

All MTNs are redeemable at par value in the year stated, except as set out below:

(a) The 4% unsecured deep discount loan stock is redeemable at a par value of £125m in 2006.

(b) The 4% RPI MTN is redeemable at a par value of £226m, indexed for increases in the RPI over the life of the MTN, in 2016.

(c) The 3.322% LPI MTN is redeemable at a par value of £228m, indexed for increases in the RPI over the life of the MTN, in 2025. The maximum indexation of the principal in any one year is 5%, with a minimum of 0%.

(d) These MTNs are of various maturities and include foreign currency and sterling denominated notes swapped into floating rate sterling.

(e) Various amortising bank loans maturing in 2007, 2008 and 2022.

Notes to the financial statements continued

Note 20 Net debt

		Group		Company	
		2005 £m	2004 £m	2005 £m	2004 £m
Due within one year:	Bank and other loans	471	775	329	552
	Finance leases	6	69	–	–
Due within one to two years:	Bank and other loans	745	126	655	25
	Finance leases	9	69	–	–
Due within two to five years:	Bank and other loans	1,610	1,730	1,452	1,601
	Finance leases	1	94	–	–
Due otherwise than by instalments after five years:	Bank and other loans	1,930	2,324	1,930	2,324
Due wholly or in part by instalments after five years:	Bank and other loans	201	–	–	–
	Finance leases	15	3	–	–
Gross debt		4,988	5,190	4,366	4,502
Less: Cash at bank and in hand		800	670	–	–
Money market investments and deposits		346	430	150	99
Net debt		3,842	4,090	4,216	4,403

Note 21 Financial instruments

An explanation of the objectives and policies for holding and issuing financial instruments is set out in the Operating and Financial Review on pages 496 to 503. Other than where these items have been included in the currency risk disclosures, short-term debtors and creditors have been excluded from the following analysis.

Analysis of interest rate exposure and currency of financial liabilities

The interest rate exposure and currency profile of the financial liabilities of the Group as at 26 February 2005, after taking into account the effect of interest rate and currency swaps, were:

	2005			2004		
	Floating rate liabilities £m	Fixed rate liabilities £m	Total £m	Floating rate liabilities £m	Fixed rate liabilities £m	Total £m
Currency						
Sterling	–	2,203	2,203	360	2,702	3,062
Euro	577	24	601	508	23	531
Thai Baht	550	–	550	561	–	561
Czech Krona	335	139	474	317	77	394
Slovak Krona	13	31	44	70	6	76
Japanese Yen	23	141	164	54	99	153
Korean Won	654	–	654	272	–	272
Chinese Yuan	127	–	127	–	–	–
Other	149	22	171	141	–	141
Gross Liabilities	2,428	2,560	4,988	2,283	2,907	5,190

Note 21 Financial instruments continued

| | Fixed rate financial liabilities | | | |
| | | 2005 | | 2004 |
	Weighted average interest rate 26 Feb 2005 %	Weighted average time for which rate is fixed Years	Weighted average interest rate 28 Feb 2004 %	Weighted average time for which rate is fixed Years
Currency				
Sterling	5.7	7	5.3	6
Euro	5.4	1	5.4	1
Japanese Yen	1.3	5	1.0	5
Czech Krona	3.9	3	4.0	4
Slovak Krona	4.3	3	–	–
Malaysian Ringgit	7.9	12	–	–
Taiwanese Dollar	4.5	–	4.5	2
Weighted average	5.5	6	5.3	6

Floating rate liabilities bear interest at rates based on relevant national LIBOR equivalents. The interest rate profile of the Group has been further managed by the purchase of Euro interest rate collars with an aggregate notional principal of £145m (2004 – £135m). The average strike rate of the interest rate caps purchased is 6.76%, while the average strike rate of the interest rate floors sold is 2.98%. The average maturity of the collars is two and a half years. The current value of these contracts, if realised, is a loss of £1.7m (2004 – £2.6m).

Sterling interest rate caps with an aggregate notional principal of £600m were purchased during the year. The strike rate on these caps is 6% and the average maturity is five years. The current value of these contracts, if realised, is £3.5m.

Retail Price Index funding of £226m (2004 – £220m), maturing 2016, is outstanding and has been classified as fixed rate debt. The interest rate payable on this debt is 4% and the principal is linked to the Retail Price Index. Limited Price Index funding, of £228m (2004 – £221m), maturing 2025, is outstanding and has been classified as fixed rate debt. The interest rate payable on this debt is 3.322% and the principal is linked to the Retail Price Index. The maximum indexation of the principal in any one year is 5.0% and the minimum is 0.0%.

Analysis of interest rate exposure and currency profile of financial assets
The interest rate exposure and currency profile of the financial assets of the Group at 26 February 2005 were:

| | | | 2005 | | | | | 2004 |
	Cash at bank and in hand £m	Short-term deposits £m	Other £m	Total £m	Cash at bank and in hand £m	Short-term deposits £m	Other £m	Total £m
Sterling	411	231	104	746	517	161	112	790
Other currencies	389	115	4	508	153	269	4	426
Total financial assets	800	346	108	1,254	670	430	116	1,216

An investment in collateralised Deutsche Bank preference shares of £150m was held at 26 February 2005, paying fixed interest of 4.3%.

Other financial assets, in respect of amounts owed by undertakings in which the company has a participating interest, attracted a rate of interest of 5.7% (being LIBOR plus a margin). Surplus funds are invested in accordance with approved limits on security and liquidity and bear rates of interest based on relevant LIBOR equivalents. Cash at bank and in hand includes non-interest bearing cash and cash in transit.

Notes to the financial statements continued

Note 21 Financial instruments continued

Borrowing facilities

The Group has the following undrawn committed facilities available at 26 February 2005 in respect of which all conditions precedent had been met at that date:

	2005 £m	2004 £m
Expiring within one year	–	133
Expiring between one and two years	561	920
Expiring in more than two years	–	305
	561	1,358

All facilities incur commitment fees at market rates and would provide funding at floating rates.

Currency exposures

Within the Group, the principal differences on exchange arising, which are taken to the profit and loss account, relate to purchases made by Group companies in currencies other than their reporting currencies. After taking account of forward currency purchases used to hedge these transactions, there were no significant balances on these exposures at the year end. Also, rolling hedges of up to 18 months duration are maintained against the value of investments in, and long-term intercompany loans to, overseas subsidiaries and, to the extent permitted in SSAP 20, differences on exchange are taken to the statement of total recognised gains and losses.

Fair values of financial assets and financial liabilities

	2005		2004	
	Book value £m	Fair value £m	Book value £m	Fair value £m
Primary financial instruments held or issued to finance the Group's operations:				
Short-term borrowings	(477)	(475)	(844)	(852)
Long-term borrowings	(4,511)	(4,721)	(4,346)	(4,407)
Short-term deposits	346	346	430	430
Cash at bank and in hand	800	800	670	670
Derivative financial instruments held to manage the interest rate and currency profile:				
Interest rate swaps and similar instruments	–	(181)	–	(192)
Interest rate options	4	2	–	(3)
Forward foreign currency contracts	–	(15)	–	(13)
Currency options	2	(6)	–	–
	(3,836)	(4,250)	(4,090)	(4,367)

Other significant financial instruments outstanding at the year end are £479m (2004 – £240m) nominal value forward foreign exchange contracts hedging the cost of foreign currency denominated purchases. On a mark-to-market basis, these contracts show a loss of £15m (2004 – £13m loss). The fair values of interest rate swaps, forward foreign exchange contracts and long-term fixed rate debt have been determined by reference to prices available from the markets on which the instruments are traded. The fair values of all other items have been calculated by discounting expected future cash flows at prevailing interest rates.

Note 21 Financial instruments continued

Hedges

As explained in the Operating and Financial Review on pages 496 to 503, the Group hedges exposures to interest rate and currency risk. The table below shows the amount of such gains and losses which have been included in the profit and loss account for the year, and those gains and losses which are expected to be included in next year's or later profit and loss accounts.

All the gains and losses on the hedging instruments are expected to be matched by losses and gains on the hedged transactions or positions.

Unrecognised gains and losses on instruments used for hedging and those recognised in the year ended 26 February 2005 are as follows:

| | Unrecognised | | | Deferred | | |
	Gains £m	Losses £m	Total £m	Gains £m	Losses £m	Total £m
At 28 February 2004	6	(214)	(208)	211	–	211
Arising in previous years and recognised in the year ended 26 February 2005	(1)	44	43	(48)	–	(48)
Arising in the period to be recognised in future years	9	(44)	(35)	–	–	–
At 26 February 2005	14	(214)	(200)	163	–	163
Expected to be recognised in the period ending 2 April 2006	3	(41)	(38)	47	–	47

Note 22 Provisions for liabilities and charges

	Other provisions £m	Property provisions £m	Deferred taxation £m	Total £m
As previously reported	–	14	572	586
Prior year adjustment[†]	–	–	7	7
At 28 February 2004 (restated)	–	14	579	593
Currency translation	–	3	3	6
Additions	3	2	–	5
Amount (credited)/charged in the year	–	(3)	149	146
At 26 February 2005	3	16	731	750

Property provisions comprise future rents payable net of rents receivable on onerous and vacant property leases, provisions for terminal dilapidations and provisions for future rents above market value on unprofitable stores. The majority of the provision is expected to be utilised over the period to 2017. Other provisions represents the Group's share of net liabilities within certain joint venture companies.

| | Amount provided | |
	2005 £m	2004 restated[†] £m
Deferred taxation		
Excess capital allowances over depreciation	714	629
Other timing differences	20	(45)
Losses carried forward	(3)	(5)
	731	579

[†] Prior year comparatives have been restated (see note 1).

Notes to the financial statements continued

Note 23 Leasing commitments

Finance leases

	£m
The future minimum finance lease payments to which the Group was committed at 26 February 2005 and which have been guaranteed by Tesco PLC are:	
Gross rental obligations	60
Less: finance charges allocated to future periods	(29)
	31

	2005 £m	2004 £m
Net amounts payable are:		
Within one year	6	69
Between two and five years	10	163
After five years	15	3
	31	235

Operating leases

	Land and buildings		Other	
	2005 £m	2004 £m	2005 £m	2004 £m
As at 26 February 2005, the Group had lease agreements for which payments extend over a number of years. Annual commitments under operating leases expiring:				
Within one year	13	5	2	2
Between two and five years	16	21	30	28
After five years	210	144	12	9
	239	170	44	39

Note 24 Called up share capital

	Ordinary shares of 5p each	
	Number	£m
Authorised:		
At 28 February 2004	9,632,000,000	482
Authorised during the year	968,000,000	48
At 26 February 2005	10,600,000,000	530
Allotted, called up and fully paid:		
At 28 February 2004	7,680,158,055	384
Scrip dividend election	34,189,410	2
Share options	68,822,077	3
At 26 February 2005	7,783,169,542	389

During the financial year, 103 million shares were issued for an aggregate consideration of £239m, which comprised £93m for scrip dividend and £146m for share options.

Between 26 February 2005 and 11 April 2005, options on 1,110,348 ordinary shares and 2,198,903 ordinary shares have been exercised under the terms of the savings-related share option scheme (1981) and the executive share option schemes (1994 and 1996), respectively.

As at 26 February 2005, the Directors were authorised to purchase up to a maximum in aggregate of 768.4 million ordinary shares.

Note 25 Reserves

	Group		Company	
	2005	2004 restated[†]	2005	2004
	£m	£m	£m	£m
Share premium account				
At 28 February 2004	3,470	2,465	3,470	2,465
Premium on issue of shares less costs	143	851	143	851
Scrip dividend election	91	154	91	154
At 26 February 2005	3,704	3,470	3,704	3,470
Other reserves				
At 26 February 2005 and 28 February 2004	40	40	–	–
Profit and loss account				
As previously reported	4,051	3,649	683	430
Prior year adjustment[†]	24	53	–	–
As at 28 February 2004 (restated)	4,075	3,702	683	430
Gain/(loss) on foreign currency net investments	19	(157)	(71)	(2)
Tax effect of exchange adjustments offset in reserves	16	–	16	–
Issue of shares	(16)	(25)	–	–
Retained profit for the financial year	779	584	508	255
At 26 February 2005	4,873	4,104	1,136	683

[†] Prior year comparatives have been restated (see note 1).
Other reserves comprise a merger reserve arising on the acquisition of Hillards plc in 1987.

In accordance with section 230 of the Companies Act 1985 a profit and loss account for Tesco PLC, whose result for the year is shown above, has not been presented in these financial statements.

The cumulative goodwill written-off against the reserves of the Group as at 26 February 2005 amounted to £718m (2004 – £718m).

During the year, the qualifying employee share ownership trust (QUEST) subscribed for 10 million, 0.1% of called-up share capital at 26 February 2005 (2004 – 30 million, 0.4%), shares from the company. The amount of £16m (2004 – £25m) shown above represents contributions to the QUEST from subsidiary undertakings.

Included in the profit and loss account is an investment in own shares of £12m, which represents 5.89 million 5p ordinary shares in Tesco PLC (0.1% of called up share capital at 26 February 2005) with a weighted average value of £1.95 each. These shares are held by the QUEST in order to satisfy options under savings-related share option schemes which become exercisable over the next few years. The carrying value of £12m (market value £18m) represents the exercise amount receivable in respect of these shares subscribed for by the QUEST at market value. Funding is provided to the QUEST by Tesco Stores Limited, the company's principal operating subsidiary. The QUEST has waived its right to dividends on these shares.

The employee benefit trusts hold shares in Tesco PLC for the purpose of the various executive share incentive and profit share schemes. At 26 February 2005, the trusts held 70.88 million shares (2004 – 52.38 million), which cost £185m (2004 – £110m) and had a market value of £219m (2004 – £135m). In accordance with UITF 38, these shares have been treated as a deduction in arriving at shareholders' funds. The prior period figures have been restated accordingly.

Note 26 Share options

Company schemes
The company had the following share option schemes in operation during the year:

(i) The savings-related share option scheme (1981) permits the grant to employees of options in respect of ordinary shares linked to a building society/bank save-as-you-earn contract for a term of three or five years, with contributions from employees of an amount between £5 and £250 per four-weekly period. Options are capable of being exercised at the end of the three- or five-year period at a subscription price not less than 80% of the middle-market quotation of an ordinary share immediately prior to the date of grant.

Notes to the financial statements continued

Note 26 Share options continued

(ii) The Irish savings-related share option scheme (2000) permits the grant to Tesco Ireland employees of options in respect of ordinary shares linked to a building society/bank save-as-you-earn contract for a term of three or five years with contributions from employees of an amount between €12 and €320 per four-weekly period. Options are capable of being exercised at the end of the three- or five-year period at a subscription price not less than 75% of the middle-market quotation of an ordinary share immediately prior to the date of grant.

(iii) The executive share option scheme (1984) permitted the grant of options in respect of ordinary shares to selected executives. The scheme expired after ten years on 9 November 1994 and during the year all outstanding options under the scheme were exercised.

(iv) The executive share option scheme (1994) permitted the grant of options in respect of ordinary shares to selected executives. The scheme expired after ten years on 17 October 2004. Options were generally exercisable between three and ten years from the date of grant, at a subscription price not less than the average of the middle-market quotations of an ordinary share for the three dealing days immediately preceding the date of grant. The exercise of options will normally be conditional upon the achievement of a specified performance target related to the annual percentage growth in earnings per share over a three-year period. There were no discounted options granted under this scheme.

(v) The unapproved executive share option scheme (1996) was adopted on 7 June 1996. This scheme was introduced following legislative changes which limited the number of options which could be granted under the previous scheme. As with the previous scheme, the exercise of options will normally be conditional upon the achievement of a specified performance target related to the annual percentage growth in earnings per share over any three-year period. There will be no discounted options granted under this scheme.

(vi) The international executive share option scheme (1994) permitted the grant of options in respect of ordinary shares to selected non-UK executives on substantially the same basis as their UK counterparts. The scheme expired after ten years on 20 May 2004. Options were normally exercisable between three and ten years from their grant at a price of not less than the average of the middle-market quotations for the ordinary shares for the three dealing days immediately preceding their grant. The exercise of options will normally be conditional on the achievement of a specified performance target related to the annual percentage growth in earnings per share over a three-year period. There were no discounted options granted under this scheme.

(vii) The performance share plan (2004) was adopted on 4 July 2004. This scheme permits the grant of options in respect of ordinary shares to selected executives. Options are normally exercisable between four and ten years from the date of grant for nil consideration. The exercise of options will normally be conditional on the achievement of specified performance targets determined by the Remuneration Committee when the options are granted.

Tesco PLC has taken advantage of the exemptions applicable to Inland Revenue-approved SAYE share option schemes and equivalent overseas schemes under Urgent Issues Task Force Abstract 17 (revised 2003), 'Employee Share Schemes'. In schemes where options are granted at nil discount, there is no charge to the profit and loss account.

The company has granted outstanding options in connection with the six open schemes as follows:

Savings-related share option scheme (1981)

Date of grant	Number of executives and employees	Shares under option 26 Feb 2005	Subscription price (pence)
28 October 1999	1,489	1,912,412	151.0
26 October 2000	15,547	17,350,526	198.0
8 November 2001	20,591	21,123,441	198.0
8 November 2002	52,215	51,464,183	159.0
6 November 2003	58,332	46,066,547	195.0
4 November 2004	68,985	48,105,391	232.0

NOTE 26 Share options continued

Irish savings-related share option scheme (2000) Date of grant	Number of executives and employees	Shares under option 26 Feb 2005	Subscription price (pence)
2 June 2000	689	963,830	163.0
26 October 2000	210	244,695	198.0
8 November 2001	331	314,241	198.0
8 November 2002	963	982,303	159.0
6 November 2003	1,353	1,201,870	195.0
4 November 2004	1,471	1,188,164	232.0

Executive share option scheme (1994) Date of grant	Number of executives	Shares under option 26 Feb 2005	Subscription price (pence)
27 April 1995	2	210,102	90.3
13 October 1995	38	1,049,355	104.0
26 June 2000	628	5,235,061	205.0
26 April 2001	790	4,825,927	247.0
15 April 2002	546	2,992,196	259.0
14 April 2003	725	3,713,204	197.5
30 April 2004	501	3,264,848	253.3

Executive share option scheme (1996) Date of grant	Number of executives	Shares under option 26 Feb 2005	Subscription price (pence)
21 May 1998	260	4,116,743	176.7
30 September 1998	9	229,950	164.0
28 January 1999	337	5,108,019	178.0
24 May 1999	1	120,220	179.4
9 November 1999	10	273,412	184.0
30 November 1999	1	228,901	173.0
20 April 2000	15	770,836	209.5
26 June 2000	155	3,642,552	205.0
26 April 2001	802	10,395,207	247.0
15 April 2002	1,241	18,163,450	259.0
14 April 2003	1,454	29,085,597	197.5
30 April 2004	1,608	25,560,455	253.3

International executive share option scheme (1994) Date of grant	Number of executives	Shares under option 26 Feb 2005	Subscription price (pence)
21 May 1998	60	588,000	176.7
28 January 1999	104	1,094,500	178.0
24 May 1999	8	310,746	179.4
26 June 2000	231	2,400,709	205.0
26 April 2001	393	2,678,298	247.0
25 April 2002	544	3,919,010	259.0
14 April 2003	624	6,136,604	197.5
30 April 2004	796	5,897,635	253.3

Performance Share Plan (2004) – nil cost options Date of grant	Number of executives	Shares under option 26 Feb 2005	Subscription price (pence)
28 July 2004	6	1,126,257	Nil

Notes to the financial statements continued

Note 27 Pensions

The Group has continued to account for pensions and other post-employment benefits in accordance with SSAP 24 and the disclosures in note (a) below are those required by that standard. FRS 17, 'Retirement Benefits' was issued in November 2000, and the transitional disclosures required by that standard, to the extent they are not given in note (a), are set out in note (b). For the financial period ending April 2006 the Group will adopt International Accounting Standard 19.

The last full actuarial valuation of the main UK scheme was carried out as at 31 March 2002. The next full valuation will be performed as at 31 March 2005 and the results will not be known until the end of the financial period. An additional contribution of £200m was made in February 2005 to reduce the expected increase in the actuarial deficit since the last full valuation. Any decision as to the level of future contributions will be made once the results of the March 2005 valuation are known.

(a) Pension commitments
United Kingdom

The principal plan within the Group is the Tesco PLC Pension Scheme, which is a funded defined benefit pension scheme in the UK, the assets of which are held as a segregated fund and administered by trustees. The total profit and loss charge of UK schemes to the Group during the year was £218m (2004 – £152m). A SSAP 24 pension prepayment of £221m (2004 – £12m) is present in the Group balance sheet, which includes the additional contribution of £200m.

An independent actuary, using the projected unit method, carried out the latest actuarial assessment of the scheme at 31 March 2002. The assumptions that have the most significant effect on the results of the valuation are those relating to the rate of return on investments and the rate of increase in salaries and pensions.

The key assumptions made were a rate of return on investments of 6.75%, a rate of increase in salaries of 4% and a rate of increase in pensions of 2.6%.

At the date of the last actuarial valuation, the market value of the scheme's assets was £1,576m and the actuarial value of these assets represented 91% of the benefits that had accrued to members, after allowing for expected future increases in earnings and pensions in payment. The actuarial shortfall of £159m will be met via increased contributions over a period of ten years, being the expected average remaining service lifetime of employed members.

The T&S Stores Senior Executive Pension Scheme is a funded defined benefit scheme open to senior executives and certain other employees at the invitation of the company. An independent actuary, using the projected unit method, carried out the latest actuarial assessment of the scheme as at 6 April 2001. At that time, the market value of the scheme's assets was £5.8m and the actuarial value of these assets represented 110% of the benefits that had accrued to members, after allowing for expected future increases in earnings.

Overseas

The Group operates a number of schemes worldwide, which include defined benefit and defined contribution schemes. The contributions payable for non-UK schemes of £10m (2004 – £8m) have been fully expensed against profits in the current year. A funded defined benefit scheme operates in the Republic of Ireland. An independent actuary, using the projected unit method, carried out the latest actuarial assessment of the scheme as at 1 April 2004. At that time the market value of the scheme's assets was £62m and the actuarial value of these assets represented 99% of the benefits that had accrued to members, after allowing for expected future increases in earnings.

(b) FRS 17, 'Retirement Benefits'

The valuations used for FRS 17 have been based on the most recent actuarial valuations and updated by Watson Wyatt LLP to take account of the requirements of FRS 17 in order to assess the liabilities of the schemes at 26 February 2005. Schemes' assets are stated at their market values at 26 February 2005. Heissmann Consultants (Ireland) Limited have updated the most recent Republic of Ireland valuation. The liabilities relating to post-retirement healthcare benefits (note 28) have also been determined in accordance with FRS 17, and are incorporated in the following tables.

Note 27 Pensions continued

Major assumptions

The major assumptions, on a weighted average basis, used by the actuaries were as follows:

	2005 %	2004 %	2003 %
Rate of increase in pensionable salaries	3.9	3.8	3.6
Rate of increase in pensions in payment	2.6	2.5	2.3
Rate of increase in deferred pensions	2.6	2.5	2.3
Rate of increase in career average benefits	2.6	2.5	2.3
Discount rate	5.4	5.7	5.5
Price inflation	2.6	2.5	2.3

The assets in the schemes and the expected rates of return were:

	2005		2004		2003	
	Long-term rate of expected return %	Market value £m	Long-term rate of expected return %	Market value £m	Long-term rate of expected return %	Market value £m
Equities	8.2	1,908	8.1	1,399	8.6	945
Bonds	5.4	560	5.7	445	5.5	386
Property	6.8	183	6.9	92	7.1	88
Other	3.5	67	3.8	43	3.8	87
Total market value of assets		2,718		1,979		1,506
Present value of schemes' liabilities		(3,453)		(2,653)		(2,275)
Deficit in the schemes		(735)		(674)		(769)
Related deferred tax asset		218		202		229
Net pension liability		(517)		(472)		(540)

	2005 £m	2004 restated[†] £m
Group net assets		
Net assets prior to pension adjustments	9,006	7,998
FRS 17 pension liability	(517)	(472)
	8,489	7,526
SSAP 24 pension asset	(221)	(12)
Net assets after pension adjustments	8,268	7,514
Group reserves		
Profit and loss reserve prior to pension adjustments	4,873	4,104
FRS 17 pension liability	(517)	(472)
	4,356	3,632
SSAP 24 pension asset	(221)	(12)
Profit and loss reserve after pension adjustments	4,135	3,620

[†] Prior year comparatives have been restated (see note 1).

Notes to the financial statements continued

Note 27 Pensions continued

On full compliance with FRS 17, and on the basis of the assumptions noted above, the amounts that would have been charged to the consolidated profit and loss account and consolidated statement of total recognised gains and losses for the year ended 26 February 2005 are set out below:

	2005 £m	2004 £m
Analysis of the amount charged to operating profit		
Current service cost	272	201
Past service cost	–	–
Total operating charge	272	201
Analysis of the amount credited/(charged) to other finance income		
Expected return on pension schemes' assets	156	120
Interest on pension schemes' liabilities	(152)	(126)
Net return	4	(6)
Analysis of the amount recognised in the statement of total recognised gains and losses		
Actual return less expected return on pension schemes' assets	66	192
Experience gains and losses arising on the schemes' liabilities	(14)	(48)
Changes in assumptions underlying the present value of the schemes' liabilities	(282)	(4)
Total actuarial (loss)/gain recognised in the statement of total recognised gains and losses	(230)	140
Movement in deficit during the year		
Deficit in schemes at beginning of the year	(674)	(769)
Movement in year:		
Current service cost	(272)	(201)
Contributions (a)	437	162
Past service costs	–	–
Acquisition cost	–	–
Other finance income/(charge)	4	(6)
Actuarial (loss)/gain	(230)	140
Deficit in schemes at end of the year	(735)	(674)

(a) Total contributions of £437m in the current year include an additional contribution of £200m paid in February 2005.

History of experience gains and losses for the year to 26 February 2005	2005 £m	2004 £m	2003 £m
Difference between the expected and actual return on schemes' assets:			
Amount	66	192	(323)
Percentage of schemes' assets	2.4%	9.7%	(21.4%)
Experience gains and losses on schemes' liabilities:			
Amount	(14)	(48)	(53)
Percentage of schemes' liabilities	(0.4%)	(1.8%)	(2.3%)
Total actuarial (loss)/gain recognised in the statement of total recognised gains and losses:			
Amount	(230)	140	(569)
Percentage of schemes' liabilities	(6.7%)	5.3%	(25.0%)

Note 28 Post-retirement benefits other than pensions

The company operates a scheme offering post-retirement healthcare benefits. The cost of providing these benefits has been accounted for on a similar basis to that used for defined benefit pension schemes.

The liability as at 26 February 2005 of £7.4m, which was determined in accordance with the advice of qualified actuaries, is being spread forward over the service lives of relevant employees. £0.6m has been charged to the profit and loss account and £0.4m of benefits were paid. An accrual of £5.6m (2004 – £5.4m) is being carried in the balance sheet. It is expected that payments will be tax deductible, at the company's tax rate, when made.

Note 29 Capital commitments

At 26 February 2005 there were commitments for capital expenditure contracted for, but not provided, of £416m (2004 – £501m), principally relating to the store development programme.

Note 30 Contingent liabilities

The company has irrevocably guaranteed the liabilities as defined in section 5(c) of the Republic of Ireland (Amendment Act) 1986, of various subsidiary undertakings incorporated in the Republic of Ireland.

Tesco Personal Finance, in which the Group owns a 50% joint venture share, has commitments, described in its own financial statements as at 31 December 2004, of formal standby facilities, credit lines and other commitments to lend, totalling £5.2bn (2004 – £4.6bn). The amount is intended to provide an indication of the volume of business transacted and not of the underlying credit or other risks.

There are a number of contingent liabilities that arise in the normal course of business which if realised are not expected to result in a material liability to the Group.

Note 31 Related party transactions

During the year, there were no material transactions or amounts owed or owing with any of the Group's key management or members of their close family.

During the year the Group traded with its joint ventures: Shopping Centres Limited, BLT Properties Limited, Tesco BL Holdings Limited, Tesco British Land Property Partnership, Tesco Personal Finance Group Limited, Tesco Home Shopping Limited, dunnhumby Limited, Tesco Mobile Limited, Nutri Centres Limited, Taiwan Charn Yang Developments Limited, Retail Property Company Limited, Tesco Card Services Limited, Tesco Property Partnership ELP and Hymall. During the year the Group also traded with its five associates: Broadfields Management Limited, Clarepharm Limited, GroceryWorks Holdings Inc., Hussmann (Hungary) Kft and Greenergy Fuels Limited. The main transactions during the year were:

(i)   Equity funding of £3m (2004 – £20m) in joint ventures and £4m (2004 – £8m) in associates.

(ii) The Group made net loans to joint ventures of £10m. The Group repaid £1m (2004 – £1m) of loans from joint ventures.

(iii) The Group has balances due from joint ventures and associates of £136m (2004 – £120m) as at 26 February 2005. The Group has outstanding balances due to joint ventures and associates of £29m (2004 – £10m) as at 26 February 2005.

(iv) The Group made purchases of £456m (2004 – £72m) from joint ventures and associates.

(v)   The Group has charged joint ventures and associates an amount totalling £761m (2004 – £63m) during the year in respect of services, loan interest and assets transferred.

(vi) Tesco Stores Limited is a member of one or more partnerships to whom the provisions of the Partnerships and Unlimited Companies (Accounts) Regulations 1993 apply ('Regulations'). The accounts for those partnerships have been consolidated into these accounts pursuant to regulation 7 of the Regulations.

Notes to the financial statements continued

Note 32 Reconciliation of operating profit to net cash inflow from operating activities

	2005 £m	2004 £m
Operating profit	1,949	1,735
Depreciation and goodwill amortisation	795	752
Additional pension contribution	(200)	–
Increase in goods held for resale	(67)	(92)
Decrease in development property	–	15
(Increase)/decrease in debtors	(48)	17
Increase in trade creditors	337	261
Increase in other creditors	238	254
Decrease in working capital (a)	460	455
Net cash inflow from operating activities (b)	3,004	2,942

(a) The decrease in working capital includes the impact of translating foreign currency working capital movements at average exchange rates rather than year end exchange rates.

(b) The subsidiaries acquired during the year have not had a significant impact on Group operating cash flows.

Note 33 Analysis of changes in net debt

	At 28 Feb 2004 £m	Cash flow £m	Other non-cash changes £m	Acquisitions £m	Exchange movements £m	At 26 Feb 2005 £m
Cash at bank and in hand	670	121	–	–	9	800
Liquid resources (a)	430	(97)	–	–	13	346
Bank and other loans	(775)	348	(14)	(15)	(15)	(471)
Finance leases	(69)	63	–	–	–	(6)
Debt due within one year	(844)	411	(14)	(15)	(15)	(477)
Bank and other loans	(4,180)	(330)	(19)	(2)	45	(4,486)
Finance leases	(166)	157	(16)	–	–	(25)
Debt due after one year	(4,346)	(173)	(35)	(2)	45	(4,511)
	(4,090)	262	(49)	(17)	52	(3,842)

(a) Liquid resources comprises short-term deposits with banks and money-market investments which mature within 12 months of the date of inception.

62

Note 34 Acquisitions

The net assets and results of acquired businesses are included in the consolidated accounts from their respective dates of acquisition. The following table sets out the effect of the material acquisitions by the Group in the year to 26 February 2005 on the consolidated balance sheet. Acquisition accounting has been applied in all cases. The fair values currently established for all acquisitions made in the year to 26 February 2005 are provisional. Fair values will be reviewed based on additional information up to 2 April 2006. The Directors do not believe that any net adjustments resulting from such a review would have a material effect on the Group. The goodwill arising on these acquisitions has been capitalised and is being amortised over 20 years.

Adminstore

Adminstore was acquired on 17 April 2004 and included in the consolidated balance sheet at 26 February 2005. The purchase consideration was £56m. The net assets of Adminstore on acquisition and the provisional fair values were as follows:

	Book values of acquired business £m	Adjustments to align accounting policies £m	Revaluations £m	Fair values at date of acquisition £m
Fixed assets	3	–	1	4
Stock	3	–	–	3
Debtors	5	–	–	5
Cash	1	–	–	1
Creditors	(8)	–	–	(8)
Provisions for liabilities and charges	(1)	–	–	(1)
Net assets acquired	3	–	1	4

Consideration	
Cash	56
Goodwill	52

The principal fair value adjustment made to the net book values of the assets and liabilities of Adminstore was the revaluation of freehold property to market value, based on valuations obtained from independent experts.

For the year ended 27 September 2003, Adminstore reported an audited profit after tax of £1.3m, and for the period 28 September 2003 to 17 April 2004 audited operating profit before exceptional items of £0.7m and audited post-tax loss after exceptional items of £7.6m based on its then accounting policies.

Other acquisitions

During the year C Two-Network in Japan acquired Fre'c, which operates a small number of convenience stores in Japan, for cash consideration of £2m. Goodwill on the acquisition was £13m after taking account of Fre'c's liabilities at the time of acquisition.

The Group also acquired eDiets for cash consideration of £2m; there was £nil goodwill in respect of this acquisition. The company owns the licence to use the eDiets name in the UK and Republic of Ireland.

Five year record

Year ended February	2001	2002	2003	2004 53 weeks	2005
Financial statistics (£m)					
Group sales	22,585	25,401	28,280	33,557	37,070
Turnover excluding VAT					
UK	18,203	19,821	21,309	24,760	27,146
Rest of Europe	1,737	2,181	2,664	3,385	3,818
Asia	860	1,398	2,031	2,669	3,010
	20,800	23,400	26,004	30,814	33,974
Underlying operating profit [1]					
UK	1,100	1,213	1,297	1,526	1,694
Rest of Europe	70	90	141	184	218
Asia	4	29	71	122	152
	1,174	1,332	1,509	1,832	2,064
Operating margin [1]					
UK	6.0%	6.1%	6.1%	6.2%	6.2%
Rest of Europe	4.0%	4.1%	5.3%	5.4%	5.7%
Asia	0.5%	2.1%	3.5%	4.6%	5.0%
Total Group	5.6%	5.7%	5.8%	5.9%	6.1%
Share of operating profit before goodwill amortisation from joint ventures and associates	21	42	72	99	135
Net interest payable	(125)	(153)	(180)	(223)	(170)
Underlying pre-tax profit [2]	1,070	1,221	1,401	1,708	2,029
Integration costs	–	–	(4)	(45)	(53)
Goodwill amortisation	(8)	(10)	(23)	(54)	(67)
Net profit/(loss) on disposal of fixed assets	(8)	(10)	(13)	(9)	53
Profit on ordinary activities before taxation	1,054	1,201	1,361	1,600	1,962
Taxation	(333)	(371)	(415)	(498)	(593)
Minority interests	1	–	–	(2)	(3)
Profit for the financial year	722	830	946	1,100	1,366

Year ended February	2001	2002	2003	2004 53 weeks	2005
Group enterprise value (£m) [5]	21,590	21,290	16,896	23,866	27,853
Underlying diluted earnings per share [2]	10.66p	12.14p	13.98p	16.31p	18.30p
Underlying earnings per share [2]	10.87p	12.33p	14.10p	16.45p	18.53p
Dividend per share	4.98p	5.60p	6.20p	6.84p	7.56p
Return on shareholders' funds [4]	22.7%	23.2%	23.3%	23.6%	23.9%
Return on capital employed [5]	11.0%	10.8%	10.2%	10.4%	11.5%
Group statistics					
Number of stores [6]	907	979	2,291	2,318	2,334
Total sales area – 000 sq ft [6/7]	28,362	32,491	39,944	45,402	49,135
Full-time equivalent employees	152,210	171,794	188,182	223,335	242,980
UK retail statistics					
Number of stores	692	729	1,982	1,878	1,780
Total sales area – 000 sq ft [7]	17,965	18,822	21,829	23,291	24,207
Average store size (sales area – sq ft) [8]	27,636	28,576	29,455	30,890	31,677
Full-time equivalent employees [9]	113,998	121,272	133,051	152,408	163,006
UK retail productivity £					
Turnover per employee [10]	159,678	163,443	160,157	162,459	166,534
Profit per employee [10]	9,649	10,002	9,748	10,013	10,392
Wages per employee [10]	16,087	16,821	17,020	17,615	17,871
Weekly sales per sq ft [7/11]	21.75	22.43	21.86	22.48	23.89

1 Excludes integration costs and goodwill amortisation. Operating margin is based upon turnover exclusive of VAT.

2 Underlying profit, underlying earnings per share and underlying diluted earnings per share exclude net profit/(loss) on disposal of fixed assets, integration costs and goodwill amortisation.

3 Market capitalisation plus net debt.

4 Underlying profit divided by average shareholders' funds.

5 The numerator is profit before interest, less tax. The denominator is the calculated average of net intangibles plus net tangible fixed assets plus net investments in JVs and associates plus net working capital and long-term provisions. 2004 ROCE has been restated (previously 10.5%) to reflect the effect of UITF 17 and 38 (note 1).

6 In addition, there are 31 stores operated by our Hymall joint venture in China, which have 2,637,000 sq ft of sales area.

7 Store sizes exclude lobby and restaurant areas.

8 Average store size excludes Express and T&S stores.

9 Based on average number of full-time equivalent employees in the UK.

10 Based on turnover exclusive of VAT, underlying operating profit and total staff cost per full-time equivalent employee.

11 Based on weighted average sales area and sales excluding property development.

APPENDIX 2

IFRS RESTATEMENT

News release…

25 May 2005

Tesco releases IFRS accounts for 2004/05

As previously announced, Tesco today releases restated consolidated financial information for the 52 weeks ending 26 February 2005, applying International Financial Reporting Standards (IFRS).

The purpose of this release is to help investors and analysts understand the changes which will impact the company's reported accounts from the 2005/06 financial year as a result of the introduction of IFRS. These changes come into effect this year for all listed companies in the European Union and many other countries around the world.

The key headlines from the restated accounts are in line with the guidance given to investors and analysts at Tesco's IFRS seminar, held on 25 February 2005:

- No change to underlying business performance

- Small impact to reported 04/05 profit (profit after tax reduces by £19m*)

- No impact to group pre-tax cash flow

This full press release and accompanying financial information is available on the company's website, at www.tesco.com/corporateinfo

*This impact excludes the effect of IAS32 and IAS39 - Tesco has elected to take a one year exemption on these standards, as allowed under IFRS rules.

Contacts:

Investor Relations	Steve Webb	01992 644 800
Press	Jon Church	01992 646 606

Restatement of financial information for 2004/05 under International Financial Reporting Standards (IFRS)

Contents

Appendices

1. INTRODUCTION

Tesco PLC currently prepares its consolidated financial statements under UK Generally Accepted Accounting Principles (UK GAAP). Following regulation passed by the European Parliament in July 2002, we will be required to prepare our 2005/06 consolidated financial statements in accordance with International Financial Reporting Standards (IFRS) [1].

This change applies to all financial reporting for accounting periods beginning on or after 1 January 2005. The Group's first Annual report under IFRS will be for 2005/06 and first IFRS interim results for the 24 weeks to 13 August 2005.

The purpose of this document is to explain how Tesco's financial performance for the 52 week period ended 26 February 2005, and its financial position as at that date presented under IFRS differs to that reported under UK GAAP.

The financial information presented in this document is unaudited.

Summary of the effects of IFRS

Impact on 2004/05 profit

	£m
Share-based payments	(52)
Goodwill	61
Leasing	(4)
Pensions	(41)
JV and Associate presentation	(32)
Profit before tax	(68)
Tax	49
Profit after tax	(19)

Impact on net assets

	February 2005	February 2004
Net assets	£(400m)	£(305m)

Impact on cash flows

None of the adjustments arising from IFRS relate to cash, and therefore there is no impact on reported cash flows.

[1] References to IFRS in this document refer to the application of International Financial Reporting Standards (IFRS), International Accounting Standards (IAS) and interpretations issued by the International Accounting Standards Board (IASB) and its relevant committees.

2. RESTATED IFRS CONSOLIDATED FINANCIAL STATEMENTS

CONSOLIDATED INCOME STATEMENT
For the 52 weeks ended 26 February 2005

	2005 (under UK GAAP) £m	IFRS adjustments £m	2005 (restated for IFRS) £m
Revenue	33,974	-	33,974
Cost of Sales	(31,271)	(39)	(31,310)
Gross Profit	2,703	(39)	2,664
Administrative expenses	(754)	(1)	(755)
Profit on disposal of fixed assets	53	(4)	49
Operating profit	2,002	(44)	1,958
Share of post-tax profits from joint ventures and associates	130	(61)	69
Finance costs	(269)	35	(234)
Finance income	99	2	101
Profit before tax	1,962	(68)	1,894
Taxation	(593)	49	(544)
Profit for the period	1,369	(19)	1,350
Attributable to:			
Equity holders of the parent	1,366	(19)	1,347
Minority interests	3	-	3
	1,369	(19)	1,350

Earnings per share	Pence	Pence	Pence
Basic	17.72	(0.24)	17.48
Diluted	17.50	(0.24)	17.26

Non-GAAP measures			
	%	%	%
ROCE	11.5	0.1	11.6
	£m	£m	£m
EBITDA	2,932	(107)	2,825

CONSOLIDATED STATEMENT OF RECOGNISED INCOME AND EXPENSE
For the 52 weeks ended 26 February 2005

	UK GAAP 2005 £m	IFRS Adjustments £m	IFRS 2005 £m
Exchange differences on translation of foreign operations	19	(8)	11
Actuarial losses on defined benefit pension schemes	-	(230)	(230)
Tax on items taken directly to equity	16	76	92
Net expense recognised directly in equity	35	(162)	(127)
Profit for the financial period	1,369	(19)	1,350
Total recognised income and expense for the period	1,404	(181)	1,223
Attributable to:			
Equity holders of the parent	1,401	(181)	1,220
Minority Interests	3	-	3
	1,404	(181)	1,223

CASH FLOW RECONCILIATION
For the 52 weeks ended 26 February 2005

None of the adjustments arising from IFRS relate to cash, and therefore there is no impact on reported cash flows.

However, IAS 7 'cash flow statements' extends the definition of cash to 'cash and cash equivalents' which includes movements on short-term deposits. This results in a change in presentation of the cash flow information to include these cash equivalents.

	£m
Increase in cash as reported under UK GAAP	121
Movement on short-term deposits (cash-equivalents under IFRS)	(97)
Increase in cash and cash equivalents (per IFRS definition)	24
Cash and cash equivalents as at 29 February 2004	1,100
Effect of exchange rate fluctuations on cash and cash equivalents	22
Cash and cash equivalents as at 26 February 2005	1,146

CONSOLIDATED BALANCE SHEET
At 26 February 2005

	2005 (under UK GAAP) £m	Adjustments for IFRS £m	2005 (under IFRS) £m	2004 (under IFRS) £m
Non-current assets				
Property, plant and equipment	15,495	(1,046)	14,449	13,186
Investment property	-	637	637	539
Goodwill and intangible assets	1,044	364	1,408	1,221
Investments in joint ventures and associates	407	5	412	330
Other investments	7	-	7	6
Deferred tax assets	-	14	14	12
	16,953	(26)	16,927	15,294
Current assets				
Inventories	1,309	-	1,309	1,199
Trade and other receivables	1,002	(233)	769	811
Cash and cash equivalents	1,146	-	1,146	1,100
	3,457	(233)	3,224	3,110
Current liabilities				
Trade and other payables	(5,374)	417	(4,957)	(3,986)
Short-term borrowings	(477)	(5)	(482)	(847)
Current tax payable	(221)	-	(221)	(308)
	(6,072)	412	(5,660)	(5,141)
Net current liabilities	(2,615)	179	(2,436)	(2,031)
Non-current liabilities				
Long-term borrowings	(4,511)	(56)	(4,567)	(4,376)
Post-employment benefits	-	(735)	(735)	(674)
Deferred tax liabilities	(731)	232	(499)	(438)
Other liabilities	(20)	(1)	(21)	(25)
Provisions	(19)	7	(12)	(12)
	(5,281)	(553)	(5,834)	(5,525)
Net assets	9,057	(400)	8,657	7,738
Equity				
Share capital	389	-	389	384
Share premium account	3,704	-	3,704	3,470
Other reserves	40	-	40	40
Retained earnings	4,873	(400)	4,473	3,799
Equity attributable to equity holders of the parent	9,006	(400)	8,606	7,693
Minority interests	51	-	51	45
Total equity	9,057	(400)	8,657	7,738

5

3. BASIS OF PREPARATION

The financial information presented in this document has been prepared on the basis of all International Financial Reporting Standards (IFRS) and International Financial Reporting Interpretations Committee (IFRIC) interpretations that are expected to be applicable to 2005/06 financial reporting. These are subject to ongoing review and endorsement by the European Commission, or possible amendment by the IASB, and are therefore subject to possible change. Further standards or interpretations may also be issued that could be applicable for 2005/06. These potential changes could result in the need to change the basis of accounting or presentation of certain financial information from that presented in this document.

The Group may need to review some accounting treatments used for the purpose of this document as a result of emerging industry consensus on practical application of IFRS and further technical opinions. This could mean that the financial information in this document may require modification until the Group prepares its first complete set of IFRS financial statements for the 2005/06 financial year.

3.1. IFRS 1: First time adoption of International Financial Reporting Standards

The rules for first-time adoption of IFRS are set out in IFRS 1, which requires that the Group establishes its IFRS accounting policies for the 2005/06 reporting date and, in general, apply these retrospectively.

The standard allows a number of optional exemptions on transition to help companies simplify the move to IFRS. The exemptions selected by Tesco are set out below:

a) Business Combinations (IFRS 3)

The Group has elected to apply IFRS 3 prospectively from the date of transition to IFRS rather than to restate previous business combinations.

b) Employee Benefits (IAS 19) – Actuarial gains and losses on defined benefit pension schemes

The Group has chosen to recognise all cumulative actuarial gains and losses at the date of transition to IFRS. Going forward, we will apply the rules of the amendment to IAS 19 (issued in December 2004) which allows actuarial gains and losses to be recognised immediately in the Statement of Recognised Income and Expense. This approach is consistent with the treatment required by the UK standard FRS 17, the effect of which we have previously disclosed in our UK GAAP accounts.

c) Cumulative translation differences (IAS 21 – The effects of changes in foreign exchange rates)

According to IAS 21, cumulative foreign exchange movements on translation of foreign entities on consolidation should be disclosed separately within shareholders' funds. However, for simplicity, the Group has elected to reset the foreign currency translation reserve to zero as at 29 February 2004.

d) Financial Instruments (IAS 39 – Financial Instruments: Recognition and measurement and IAS 32 – Financial Instruments: Disclosure and presentation)

Tesco has opted to take advantage of the one-year exemption for implementation of the Financial Instruments standards. Therefore, for 2004/05 IFRS financial information, financial instruments continue to be accounted for and presented in accordance with UK

GAAP. For 2005/06 financial reporting, adjustments will be made as at 27 February 2005 to reflect the differences between UK GAAP and IAS 32/IAS 39.

3.2   Presentation of financial information

The layout of the primary financial statements has been amended in accordance with IAS 1 'Presentation of Financial Statements' from that presented under UK GAAP. This format and presentation may require modification as practice and industry consensus develops.

4. REVIEW OF MAIN CHANGES ARISING FROM ADOPTION OF IFRS

The following describes the most significant adjustments arising from transition to IFRS.

4.1 Share-based payments (IFRS 2)

a) Share Option Schemes

The main impact of IFRS 2 for Tesco is the expensing of employees' and directors' share options.

The expense is calculated with reference to the fair value of the award on the date of grant and is recognised over the vesting period of the scheme, adjusted to reflect actual and expected levels of vesting. We have used the Black-Scholes model to calculate the fair values of options on their grant date.

To ensure better comparability, Tesco will apply IFRS 2 retrospectively to all options granted but not fully vested as at 29 February 2004, rather than just to those granted after 7 November 2002. The fair values of awards granted prior to November 2002 were published on our website on 25 February 2005.

In 2004/05, application of IFRS 2 results in a pre-tax charge to the Income Statement of £48m; however, the pre-tax effect is offset by a deferred tax credit of £16m. Thus the net effect on post-tax profit for 2004/05 is £32m. Deferred tax is calculated on the basis of the difference between market price at the balance sheet date and the option exercise price. As a result the tax effect will not correlate to the charge. The excess of the deferred tax over the cumulative P&L charge at the tax rate is recognised in equity (in 2004/05 this amounted to a credit of £9m to retained earnings). The deferred tax asset recognised in February 2004 and February 2005 relating to the share option schemes is £25m and £49m respectively.

b) Share Bonus Schemes

Under UK GAAP we currently expense share bonus schemes to the P&L applying the rules of UITF 17. Whereas the UK GAAP P&L charge is based on the intrinsic value of the award, the IFRS 2 charge is based on the Fair Value. This results in an additional charge of £4m to the Income Statement in 2004/05.

As a result of IFRS, deferred tax assets recognised under UK GAAP relating to share bonus schemes have reduced by approximately £8m at both the 2004 and 2005 balance sheet dates.

4.2 Goodwill arising on Business Combinations (IFRS 3)

Under IFRS 3, goodwill is no longer amortised on a straight-line basis but instead is subject to annual impairment testing. Consequently, the goodwill balances were reviewed for impairment as at February 2004 and February 2005 and no further adjustments were identified.

In terms of adjustments to the income statement in 2004/05, the non-amortisation of goodwill results in an increase of pre-tax profit of £61m. There are no associated tax impacts.

In the February 2005 balance sheet, a foreign exchange gain of £2m has been recognised through reserves relating to the non-amortisation of goodwill; therefore, the total adjustment to net assets relating to goodwill amounts to £63m.

4.3 Recognition of dividends (IAS 10 - Post-balance sheet events)

Dividends declared after the balance sheet date will not be recognised as a liability as at that balance sheet date.

The final dividend of £365m declared in April 2004 relating to the 2003/04 financial year has been reversed in the opening balance sheet and charged to equity in the balance sheet as at 26 February 2005. Similarly, the final dividend accrued for the 2004/05 financial year of £410m has been reversed in the IFRS balance sheet as at 26 February 2005.

4.4 Leasing (IAS 17)

UK GAAP and IFRS accounting for leases are broadly similar except that IAS 17 requires the Group to consider property leases in their component parts (i.e. land and building elements separately).

Following a detailed review of our property lease portfolio, a small number of 'building' leases have been reclassified as finance leases and brought on balance sheet, based on the criteria of IAS 17. This has led to a relatively small increase in fixed assets, and a similar increase in finance lease creditors.

The following adjustments have been made at the opening balance sheet and as at 26 February 2005:

	29 February 2004 £m	26 February 2005 £m
Property, plant & equipment	29	49
Adjustment to net assets	(4)	(5)

The main impact on the income statement is that some UK GAAP operating lease expenses will be replaced with depreciation and financing charges for the building elements of the reclassified leases. Over the life of the lease, the total Income Statement charge will remain the same, but the timing of expenses will change, with more of the total expense recognised earlier in the lease term. The net pre-tax impact on the Income Statement is immaterial for the 52 weeks ended 26 February 2005.

In 2004/05 there is a one-off P&L adjustment of £4m, relating to the deferral of some profit from the sale and leaseback deal completed in April 2004, which instead will be recognised over the 25 year lease term.

4.5 Employee benefits (IAS 19)

Post-employment benefits

For UK GAAP reporting, we apply the measurement and recognition policies of SSAP 24 for pensions and other post-employment benefits, whilst providing detailed disclosures for the alternative measurement principles of FRS 17.

IAS 19 takes a similar approach to accounting for defined benefit schemes as FRS 17, 'Retirement Benefits', thus on transition, the deficit disclosed under FRS 17 has been recognised in the balance sheet. At the opening balance sheet, this has resulted in a pre-tax reduction in net assets of £676m which represents the sum of the deficit plus the reversal of a SSAP 24 debtor in the UK GAAP balance sheet as at February 04. An associated deferred tax asset of £199m has been recognised in respect of the pension deficit. Therefore the total adjustment to net assets is £477m.

Going forward, we have chosen to apply the amendment to IAS 19 which allows actuarial gains and losses to be recognised immediately in the Statement of Recognised Income and Expense i.e. the actuarial gains and losses will be taken directly to reserves.

The incremental pre-tax Income Statement charge for 2004/05 from the adoption of IAS 19, compared to SSAP 24, is an additional charge of £41m. This is split between the current service cost (increases operating costs by £45m) and the return on plan assets (increases finance income by £4m). The related tax effect of this is a £12m credit to the P&L. Therefore the 2004/05 after tax effect of the change to IAS 19 is a reduction in profit of £29m.

The actuarial loss on the scheme for 2004/05, recognised through reserves, is £230m, with an offsetting tax adjustment of £67m.

The February 2005 IAS 19 pension deficit is £735m, with an associated deferred tax asset of £279m.

4.6   Joint ventures (IAS 31) and associates (IAS 28)

Tesco has chosen the equity method of accounting for joint ventures (JVs) and associates, which is largely consistent with how they are accounted for in the UK GAAP accounts.

The adoption of IFRS will lead to a change in the presentation of the Group's share of the results of our JVs and Associates. Under UK GAAP, we currently include our share of JV and Associate operating profits before interest and tax and show our share of their interest and tax in the respective Group lines on the P&L. Under IFRS, JV and Associate profit is shown as a net figure i.e. post interest and tax. This will have the effect of reducing profit before tax, but will reduce the tax charge. Overall, there is no impact on the Group profit after tax as this is purely a presentational change.

4.7   Impairment of assets (IAS 36)

Under IAS 36, individual assets should be reviewed for impairment when there are any indicators of impairment. Where individual assets do not generate cash flows independently from one another, the impairment review should be carried out at the 'Cash-Generating Unit' (CGU) level, which represents the lowest level at which cash flows are independently generated. The IASB has determined that for retailers this is at the individual store level.

Following impairment reviews at the opening balance sheet date, we identified a small number of stores which in total required a provision for impairment of £142m. This has the effect of reducing the total fixed asset balance by approximately 1% as at 29 February 2004.

A similar review was performed for 2004/05 but no further stores required an impairment provision. However, due to movements in foreign exchange rates, the overall provision set against fixed assets has increased by £10m – this consolidation adjustment has been taken through reserves, with no impact on the 2004/05 Income Statement.

IAS 36 has the additional effect of reducing the deferred tax liability by £15m as at February 2004 and £17m as at February 2005 (the movement year-on-year relates to foreign exchange differences which have been taken to reserves). The deferred tax adjustments arise because the impairment reviews have reduced the net book values of certain assets qualifying for capital allowances, with no corresponding change in the tax base.

4.8   Intangible assets (IAS 38)

Under UK GAAP, we currently include licences and capitalised development costs within tangible fixed assets on the balance sheet. Under IAS 38, 'Intangible Assets', such items should be disclosed separately on the face of the balance sheet.

As a result, there is a reclassification of £256m in the opening balance sheet, and £306m in the balance sheet as at 26 February 2005, between property, plant and equipment and intangible assets. There is no impact on the Income Statement from this reclassification.

4.9   Investment Properties (IAS 40)

Under UK GAAP, we currently include all owned property assets within tangible fixed assets on the balance sheet. Under IAS 40, 'Investment Properties', we are required to split out any property which earns rental income or is held for capital appreciation.

As a result, there is a reclassification of £539m in the opening balance sheet and £637m in the balance sheet as at 26 February 2005 between property, plant and equipment and investment property. There is no impact on the Income Statement from this reclassification.

4.10   Deferred and current taxes (IAS 12, 'Income taxes')

Under UK GAAP, deferred tax is recognised in respect of all timing differences that have originated but not reversed by the balance sheet date and which could give rise to an obligation to pay more or less taxation in the future.

Deferred tax under IAS 12 'Income Taxes' is recognised in respect of all temporary differences at the balance sheet date between the tax bases of assets and liabilities and their carrying value for financial reporting purposes.

The change to a balance sheet liability method of providing for deferred tax leads to a number of adjustments, as follows:

	Feb 2004 Net Assets £m	2004/05 P&L £m	2004/05 Reserves £m	Feb 2005 Net Assets £m
Impact of IAS 12	(79)	(13)	(2)[*]	(94)
Tax effect of accounting changes	232	30	78	340
Net impact on tax balance/profit after tax	153	17	76	246
JV/Associate presentation change		32		
Total impact on tax (incl. JV presentation)		49		

* Foreign exchange loss on translation of foreign operations

The significant components of the balance sheet adjustments are the recognition of deferred tax assets on the pension deficit and share-based payments; less deferred tax provisions for potential future gains arising from rolled-over gains and for the potential future tax liabilities arising from fair value adjustments recorded for business combinations. Neither of these provisions were previously recognised under FRS 19.

4.11   Other adjustments

Other adjustments arise from the reclassification of money market deposits from current asset investments to cash and cash equivalents (as a result of the definition within IAS 7 'Cash Flow Statements'), and other minor presentation differences.

5. IFRS ACCOUNTING POLICIES

The following section provides a summary of Tesco's Group Accounting Policies under IFRS.

Basis of preparation

The financial statements have been prepared in accordance with International Financial Reporting Standards (IFRS) for the first time.

Basis of consolidation

The Group financial statements consist of the financial statements of the Company, entities controlled by the Company (its subsidiaries) and the Group's share of interests in joint ventures and associates.

Subsidiaries, associates and joint ventures

A subsidiary is an entity whose operating and financing policies are controlled, directly or indirectly, by Tesco PLC. The accounts of the parent Company's subsidiary undertakings are prepared to dates around the Group period end apart from Global T.H., Tesco Polska Sp. Z o.o., Tesco Stores CR a.s., Tesco Stores SR a.s., Tesco Kipa A.S., Samsung Tesco Co. Limited, Ex-Chai Distribution System Co. Ltd and C Two-Network Co. Ltd which are prepared to 31 December.

An associate is an undertaking, not being a subsidiary or joint venture, over which Tesco PLC has significant influence and can participate in the financial and operating policy decisions of the entity.

A joint venture is an entity in which Tesco holds an interest on a long-term basis and which is jointly controlled by Tesco and one or more other venturers under a contractual agreement.

Tesco's share of the results of joint ventures and associates is included in the Group income statement using the equity accounting basis. Investments in joint ventures and associates are carried in the Group balance sheet at cost plus post-acquisition changes in the Group's share of the net assets of the entity, less any impairment in value. The carrying values of investments in joint ventures and associates include acquired goodwill.

Use of assumptions and estimates

The preparation of the consolidated financial statements requires management to make judgements, estimates and assumptions that affect the application of policies and reported amounts of assets and liabilities, income and expenses. The estimates and associated assumptions are based on historical experience and various other factors that are believed to be reasonable under the circumstances, the results of which form the basis of making judgements about carrying values of assets and liabilities that are not readily apparent from other sources. Actual results may differ from these estimates.

The estimates and underlying assumptions are reviewed on an ongoing basis. Revisions to accounting estimates are recognised in the period in which the estimate is revised if the revision affects only that period, or in the period of the revision and future periods if the revision affects both current and future periods.

Revenue

Revenue consists of sales through retail outlets and sales of development properties. Revenue is recorded net of returns, vouchers and value-added taxes, when the significant risks and rewards of ownership have been transferred to the buyer. Commission income is recorded based on the terms of the contracts.

Property, plant and equipment

Property, plant and equipment assets are carried at cost less accumulated depreciation and any recognised impairment in value.

Depreciation is provided on a straight-line basis over the anticipated useful economic lives of the assets.

The following rates applied for the Group and are consistent with the prior year:

- Freehold and leasehold buildings with greater than 40 years unexpired – at 2.5% of cost
- Leasehold properties with less than 40 years unexpired are depreciated by equal annual instalments over the unexpired period of the lease.
- Plant, equipment, fixtures and fittings and motor vehicles – at rates varying from 10% to 33%.

All tangible fixed assets are reviewed for impairment in accordance with IAS 36, Impairment of Assets, when there are indications that the carrying value may not be recoverable.

Borrowing costs

Borrowing costs directly attributable to the acquisition or construction of qualifying assets are capitalised. Qualifying assets are those that necessarily take a substantial period of time to prepare for their intended use.

Investment property

Investment property is property held to earn rentals and/or for capital appreciation rather than for the purpose of Group operating activities. The cost model is applied to all investment property, using consistent depreciation policies to those described for owner-occupied property.

Leasing

Leases are classified as finance leases whenever the terms of the lease transfer substantially all the risks and rewards of ownership to the lessee. All other leases are classified as operating leases.

Assets held under finance leases are recognised as assets of the Group at their fair value or, if lower, at the present value of the minimum lease payments, each determined at the inception of the lease. The corresponding liability to the lessor is included in the balance sheet as a finance lease obligation. Lease payments are apportioned between finance charges and reduction of the lease obligations so as to achieve a constant rate of interest on the remaining balance of the liability.

Rentals payable and receivable under operating leases are charged to income on a straight-line basis over the term of the relevant lease.

Business Combinations and Goodwill

Goodwill arising on consolidation represents the excess of the cost of an acquisition over the fair value of the Group's share of the net assets of the acquired subsidiary, associate or joint venture at the date of acquisition.

At the acquisition date, goodwill acquired is recognised as an asset and is allocated to each of the cash-generating units expected to benefit from the combination's synergies. This goodwill is reviewed for impairment at least annually by assessing the recoverable amount of each cash-generating unit to which the goodwill relates. When the recoverable amount of the cash-generating unit is less than the carrying amount, an impairment loss is recognised.

Any impairment is recognised immediately in profit or loss and is not subsequently reversed.

Goodwill arising on the acquisition of joint ventures and associates is included within the carrying value of the investment.

Goodwill arising on acquisitions before 29 February 2004 (the date of transition to IFRS) has been retained at the previous UK GAAP amounts subject to being tested for impairment at that date.

Intangible assets

Acquired intangible assets, such as licences, are measured initially at cost and are amortised on a straight-line basis over their estimated useful lives.

Research and development costs

Research costs are expensed as incurred. Development expenditure incurred on an individual project is carried forward only if all the criteria set out in IAS 38 'Intangible Assets' are met.

Following the initial recognition of the development expenditure, the cost is amortised over the project's estimated useful life, usually at 14-25% of cost.

Inventories

Inventories comprise goods held for resale and properties held for, or in the course of, development and are valued at the lower of cost and net realisable value. Stocks are valued at retail prices and reduced by appropriate margins to take into account factors such as average cost, obsolescence, seasonality and damage.

Cash and cash equivalents

Cash and cash equivalents in the balance sheet comprise cash at bank and in hand and short-term deposits with an original maturity of three months or less.

Pensions

The Group accounts for pensions and other post-retirement benefits (principally private healthcare) under IAS19 'Employee Benefits'.

In respect of defined benefit plans, obligations are measured at discounted present value (using the projected unit credit method) whilst plan assets are recorded at fair value. The operating and financing costs of such plans are recognised separately in the Income Statement; service costs are spread systematically over the expected service lives of employees and financing costs are recognised in the periods in which they arise. Actuarial gains and losses are recognised immediately in the Statement of Recognised Income and Expense.

Payments to defined contribution schemes are recognised as an expense as they fall due.

Share-based payments

Employees (including directors) of the Group receive part of their remuneration in the form of share-based payment transactions, whereby employees render services in exchange for shares or rights over shares (equity-settled transactions).

The fair value of employee share option plans is calculated using the Black-Scholes model. In accordance with IFRS 2 'Share-based payments' the resulting cost is charged to the Income Statement over the vesting period of the options. The value of the charge is adjusted to reflect expected and actual levels of options vesting.

Income tax

The tax expense included in the Income Statement comprises current and deferred tax. Current tax is the expected tax payable on the taxable income for the year, using tax rates enacted or substantively enacted by the balance sheet date.

Tax is recognised in the Income Statement except to the extent that it relates to items recognised directly in equity, in which case it is recognised in equity.

Deferred tax is provided using the balance sheet liability method, providing for temporary differences between the carrying amounts of assets and liabilities for financial reporting purposes and the amounts used for taxation purposes.

Deferred tax is calculated at the tax rates that are expected to apply in the period when the liability is settled or the asset is realised. Deferred tax is charged or credited in the Income Statement, except when it relates to items charged or credited directly to equity, in which case deferred tax is also dealt with in equity.

Deferred tax liabilities are recognised for all taxable temporary differences and deferred tax assets are recognised to the extent that it is probable that taxable profits will be available against which deductible temporary differences can be utilised.

The carrying amount of deferred tax assets is reviewed at each balance sheet date and reduced to the extent that it is no longer probable that sufficient taxable profits will be available to allow all or part of the asset to be recovered.

Deferred tax assets and liabilities are offset against each other when they relate to income taxes levied by the same tax jurisdiction and when the group intends to settle its current tax assets and liabilities on a net basis.

Foreign currencies

Transactions in currencies other than Pounds Sterling are recorded at the exchange rates on the date of the transaction. At each balance sheet date, monetary assets and liabilities that are denominated in foreign currencies are retranslated at the rates prevailing on the balance sheet date. Gains and losses arising on retranslation are included in the net profit or loss for the period, except for exchange differences arising on non-monetary assets and liabilities where the changes in fair value are recognised directly in equity.

The financial statements of foreign subsidiaries are translated into Pounds Sterling according to the functional currency concept of IAS 21 'The Effects of Changes in Foreign Exchange Rates'. Since all consolidated companies operate as operationally independent entities, their respective local currency is the functional currency. Therefore, assets and liabilities of overseas subsidiaries in foreign currencies are translated at exchange rates prevailing at the date of the Group balance sheet; profits and losses are translated into

Sterling at average exchange rates for the relevant accounting periods. Exchange differences arising, if any, are classified as equity and transferred to the Group's translation reserve.

Financial instruments

The policy on financial instruments used in this document is consistent with UK GAAP as the Group has taken advantage of the exemption in IFRS 1 not to apply IAS 32 and IAS 39 to its 2004/05 figures. The accounting policies for IAS 32 and IAS 39 will be disclosed in the 2005/06 Interim Accounts.

APPENDIX 1: RECONCILIATION OF PROFIT
For the 52 weeks ended 26 February 2005

	Reported under UK GAAP £m	Share-based payments IFRS 2 £m	Business Combinations IFRS 3 £m	Leasing IAS 17 £m	Employee benefits IAS 19 £m	Presentation of JVs and Associates IAS 28/31 £m	Deferred tax IAS 12 £m	Total IFRS adjustments £m	Restated under IFRS £m
Revenue	33,974	-	-	-	-	-	-	-	33,974
Cost of Sales	(31,271)	-	-	1	(40)	-	-	(39)	(31,310)
Gross profit	2,703	-	-	1	(40)	-	-	(39)	2,664
Administrative expenses	(754)	(52)	56	-	(5)	-	-	(1)	(755)
Profit on disposal of fixed assets	53	-	-	(4)	-	-	-	(4)	49
Operating profit	2,002	(52)	56	(3)	(45)	-	-	(44)	1,958
Share of post-tax profits from joint ventures and associates	130	-	5	-	-	(66)	-	(61)	69
Finance costs	(269)	-	-	(1)	-	36	-	35	(234)
Finance income	99	-	-	-	4	(2)	-	2	101
Profit before tax	1,962	(52)	61	(4)	(41)	(32)	-	(68)	1,894
Income tax expense	(593)	16	-	2	12	32	(13)	49	(544)
Profit for the period	1,369	(36)	61	(2)	(29)	-	(13)	(19)	1,350

Reconciliation to underlying profit

	Reported under UK GAAP £m	Share-based payments IFRS 2 £m	Business Combinations IFRS 3 £m	Leasing IAS 17 £m	Employee benefits IAS 19 £m	Presentation of JVs and Associates IAS 28/31 £m	Deferred tax IAS 12 £m	Total IFRS adjustments £m	Restated under IFRS £m
Profit before tax	1,962	(52)	61	(4)	(41)	(32)	-	(68)	1,894
Net profit/ loss on disposal of fixed assets	(53)	-	-	4	-	-	-	4	(49)
Integration costs	53	-	-	-	-	-	-	-	53
Goodwill amortisation	67	-	(61)	-	-	-	-	(61)	6
Underlying profit	2,029	(52)	-	-	(41)	(32)	-	(125)	1,904

17

APPENDIX 2: RECONCILIATION OF EQUITY - As at 29 February 2004 (Opening balance sheet for IFRS)

	Reported under UK GAAP	Business Combinations IFRS 3	Pensions IAS 19	Dividends IAS 10	Investment property IAS 40	Intangible assets IAS 38	Leasing IAS 17	Share based payments IFRS 2	Impairment of fixed assets IAS 36	Deferred tax IAS 12	Other	Restated under IFRS
	£m	£m	£m	£m	£m	£m	£m	£m	£m	£m	£m	£m
Non-current assets												
Property, plant and equipment	14,094	-	-	-	(539)	(256)	29	-	(142)	-	-	13,186
Investment property	-	-	-	-	539	-	-	-	-	-	-	539
Goodwill and intangible assets	965	-	-	-	-	256	-	-	-	-	-	1,221
Investments in joint ventures and associates	330	-	-	-	-	-	-	-	-	-	-	330
Other investments	6	-	-	-	-	-	-	-	-	-	-	6
Deferred tax assets	-	-	-	-	-	-	-	-	-	-	12	12
	15,395	-	-	-	-	-	29	-	(142)	-	12	15,294
Current assets												
Inventories	1,199	-	-	-	-	-	-	-	-	-	-	1,199
Trade and other receivables	826	-	(12)	-	-	-	(3)	-	-	-	-	811
Investments	430	-	-	-	-	-	-	-	-	-	(430)	-
Cash and cash equivalents	670	-	-	-	-	-	-	-	-	-	430	1,100
	3,125	-	(12)	-	-	-	(3)	-	-	-	-	3,110
Current liabilities												
Trade and other payables	(4,364)	-	10	365	-	-	-	-	-	-	3	(3,986)
Short-term borrowings	(844)	-	-	-	-	-	(3)	-	-	-	-	(847)
Current tax payable	(308)	-	-	-	-	-	-	-	-	-	-	(308)
	(5,516)	-	10	365	-	-	(3)	-	-	-	3	(5,141)
Net current liabilities	(2,391)	-	(2)	365	-	-	(6)	-	-	-	3	(2,031)
Non-current liabilities												
Long-term borrowings	(4,346)	-	-	-	-	-	(30)	-	-	-	-	(4,376)
Post-employment benefits	-	-	(674)	-	-	-	-	-	-	-	-	(674)
Deferred tax liabilities	(579)	-	199	-	-	-	1	17	15	(79)	(12)	(438)
Other liabilities	(22)	-	-	-	-	-	-	-	-	-	(3)	(25)
	(4,947)	-	(475)	-	-	-	(29)	17	15	(79)	(15)	(5,513)
Provisions	(14)	-	-	-	-	-	2	-	-	-	-	(12)
Net Assets	8,043	-	(477)	365	-	-	(4)	17	(127)	(79)	-	7,738
Equity												
Share capital	384	-	-	-	-	-	-	-	-	-	-	384
Share premium account	3,470	-	-	-	-	-	-	-	-	-	-	3,470
Other reserves	40	-	-	-	-	-	-	-	-	-	-	40
Retained earnings	4,104	-	(477)	365	-	-	(4)	17	(127)	(79)	-	3,799
Total equity shareholders' funds	7,998	-	(477)	365	-	-	(4)	17	(127)	(79)	-	7,693
Minority Interests	45	-	-	-	-	-	-	-	-	-	-	45
Total equity	8,043	-	(477)	365	-	-	(4)	17	(127)	(79)	-	7,738

NB – The above UK GAAP numbers have been adjusted into IFRS format (in accordance with IAS 1)

APPENDIX 3: RECONCILIATION OF EQUITY - As at 26 February 2005

	Reported under UK GAAP £m	Business Combinations IFRS 3 £m	Pensions IAS 19 £m	Dividends IAS 10 £m	Investment property IAS 40 £m	Intangible assets IAS 38 £m	Leasing IAS 17 £m	Share based payments IFRS 2 £m	Impairment of fixed assets IAS 36 £m	Deferred tax IAS 12 £m	Other £m	Restated under IFRS £m
Non-current assets												
Property, plant and equipment	15,495	-	-	-	(637)	(306)	49	-	(152)	-	-	14,449
Investment property	-	-	-	-	637	-	-	-	-	-	-	637
Intangible assets	1,044	58	-	-	-	306	-	-	-	-	-	1,408
Investments in joint ventures and associates	407	5	-	-	-	-	-	-	-	-	-	412
Other investments	7	-	-	-	-	-	-	-	-	-	-	7
Deferred tax assets	-	-	-	-	-	-	-	-	-	-	14	14
	16,953	63	-	-	-	-	49	-	(152)	-	14	16,927
Current assets												
Inventories	1,309	-	-	-	-	-	-	-	-	-	-	1,309
Trade and other receivables	1,002	-	(230)	-	-	-	(3)	-	-	-	-	769
Investments	346	-	-	-	-	-	-	-	-	-	(346)	-
Cash and cash equivalents	800	-	-	-	-	-	-	-	-	-	346	1,146
	3,457	-	(230)	-	-	-	(3)	-	-	-	-	3,224
Current liabilities												
Trade and other payables	(5,374)	-	14	410	-	-	-	(8)	-	-	1	(4,957)
Short-term borrowings	(477)	-	-	-	-	-	(5)	-	-	-	-	(482)
Current tax payable	(221)	-	-	-	-	-	-	-	-	-	-	(221)
	(6,072)	-	14	410	-	-	(5)	(8)	-	-	1	(5,660)
Net current liabilities	(2,615)	-	(216)	410	-	-	(8)	(8)	-	-	1	(2,436)
Non-current liabilities												
Long-term borrowings	(4,511)	-	-	-	-	-	(56)	-	-	-	-	(4,567)
Post-employment benefits	-	-	(735)	-	-	-	-	-	-	-	-	(735)
Deferred tax liabilities	(731)	-	279	-	-	-	3	41	17	(94)	(14)	(499)
Other liabilities	(20)	-	-	-	-	-	-	-	-	-	(1)	(21)
	(5,262)	-	(456)	-	-	-	(53)	41	17	(94)	(15)	(5,822)
Provisions	(19)	-	-	-	-	-	7	-	-	-	-	(12)
Net Assets	9,057	63	(672)	410	-	-	(5)	33	(135)	(94)	-	8,657
Equity												
Share capital	389	-	-	-	-	-	-	-	-	-	-	389
Share premium account	3,704	-	-	-	-	-	-	-	-	-	-	3,704
Other reserves	40	-	-	-	-	-	-	-	-	-	-	40
Retained earnings	4,873	63	(672)	410	-	-	(5)	33	(135)	(94)	-	4,473
Total equity shareholders' funds	9,006	63	(672)	410	-	-	(5)	33	(135)	(94)	-	8,606
Minority Interests	51	-	-	-	-	-	-	-	-	-	-	51
Total equity	9,057	63	(672)	410	-	-	(5)	33	(135)	(94)	-	8,657

NB – The above UK GAAP numbers have been adjusted into IFRS format (in accordance with IAS 1)

INDEX